POLITICAL EPISTEMICS

CHICAGO STUDIES IN PRACTICES OF MEANING

Edited by Jean Comaroff, Andreas Glaeser, William Sewell, and Lisa Wedeen

Also in the series

Producing India: From Colonial Economy to National Space
by Manu Goswami

Parité! Sexual Equality and the Crisis of French Universalism
by Joan Wallach Scott

Logics of History: Social Theory and Social Transformation
by William H. Sewell Jr.

Inclusion: The Politics of Difference in Medical Research
by Steven Epstein

The Devil's Handwriting: Precoloniality and the German Colonial State in Qingdao, Samoa, and Southwest Africa
by George Steinmetz

Bewitching Development: Witchcraft and the Reinvention of Development in Neoliberal Kenya
by James Howard Smith

Bengal in Global Concept History: Culturalism in the Age of Capital
by Andrew Sartori

Peripheral Visions: Publics, Power, and Performance in Yemen
by Lisa Wedeen

Ethnicity, Inc.
by John L. and Jean Comaroff

Neoliberal Frontiers: An Ethnography of Sovereignty in West Africa
by Brenda Chalfin

POLITICAL EPISTEMICS

The Secret Police, the Opposition,
and the End of East German Socialism

Andreas Glaeser

THE UNIVERSITY OF CHICAGO PRESS   Chicago and London

ANDREAS GLAESER is associate professor of sociology at the University of Chicago. He is the author of *Divided in Unity: Identity, Germany, and the Berlin Police.*

The University of Chicago Press, Chicago 60637
The University of Chicago Press, Ltd., London
© 2011 by The University of Chicago
All rights reserved. Published 2011
Printed in the United States of America

20 19 18 17 16 15 14 13 12 11   1 2 3 4 5

ISBN-13: 978-0-226-29793-4 (cloth)
ISBN-13: 978-0-226-29794-1 (paper)
ISBN-10: 0-226-29793-4 (cloth)
ISBN-10: 0-226-29794-2 (paper)

Glaeser, Andreas.
    Political epistemics : the secret police, the opposition, and the end of East German socialism / Andreas Glaeser.
        p.   cm.
    Includes bibliographical references and index.
    ISBN-13: 978-0-226-29793-4 (cloth : alk. paper)
    ISBN-13: 978-0-226-29794-1 (pbk. : alk. paper)
    ISBN-10: 0-226-29793-4 (cloth : alk. paper)
    ISBN-10: 0-226-29794-2 (pbk. : alk. paper)   1. Socialism—Germany (East)   2. Germany (East). Ministerium für Staatssicherheit.
3. Germany (East)—Politics and government.   4. Socialism—Europe, Eastern.   I. Title.
    HX280.5.A6G53   2010
    320.53′150943109048—dc22
                                                        2010015801

For Fowzia

Contents

Illustrations

Abbreviations

For ease of reading I have kept current standard English abbreviations for the institutions discussed in this book (as, for example, in GDR) even though they are inconsistently oscillating between translation (e.g., CPSU) transliteration (e.g., KGB) and phonetic transcriptions (e.g., Cheka). Wherever there is no standard English usage I have retained the German abbreviations simply because I fear that the translation of acronyms can only add confusion in relation to the original language documents. Thus I keep Stasi rather than translating it into what might have been taken for an English equivalent such as Stasec (State Security) or I have kept SED rather than translating it into SUP for Socialist Unity Party, even though I do use the English long form. However, I have translated all Russian acronyms if there is no standard English form (e.g., CC for Central Committee) simply because the movement from Cyrillic to Roman script requires transliteration anyway, and because I do not make any references to untranslated Russian sources.

ADN — *Allgemeine deutsche Nachrichtendienst* (GDR newswire service)

BL — *Bezirksleitung der SED* (District Office of the SED)

BfS — *Bezirksverwaltung für Staatssicherheit* (district office for state security)

BStU — *Bundesbeauftragte für die Unterlagen der ehemaligen Staatssicherheit der DDR* (Federal officer for the documents of the former state security of the GDR)

Cheka — (All Russian) Extraordinary Commission (for Combatting Counterrevolution and Sabotage), originally VcheKa, name of the Soviet secret police until 1922, subsequently called GPU, OGPU, NKVD, MGB and KGB.

Comintern — Communist International, sometimes also called the Third International.

CPSU — Communist Party of the Soviet Union

CC	Central Committee of the CPSU or the SED
CDU	*Christlich Demokratische Union* (Christian Democratic Union) (West) Germany's conservative mass party in all states except Bavaria
CSCE	Conference for Security and Cooperation in Europe (also, Helsinki process)
CSU	*Christlich Soziale Union* (Christian Social Union) the Bavarian counterpart of the CDU
DDR	*Deutsche Demokratische Republik* (German Democratic Republic)
FDGB	*Freier deutscher Gewerkschaftsbund* (Free German Federation of Trade Unions)
FDJ	*Freie Deutsche Jugend* (Free German Youth), official socialist youth organization in the GDR
GDR	German Democratic Republic (translation of DDR)
Gestapo	*Geheime Staatspolizei* (secret state police of Nazi Germany)
IFM	*Initiative für Frieden und Menschenrechte* (Initiative for Peace and Human rights)
KGB	*Komitet Gosudarstvennoy Bezopasnosti* (Committee for State Security), the Soviet secret police, named thus since 1954
KPD	*Kommunistische Partei Deutschlands* (Communist Party of Germany)
MGB	(Ministry for State Security), name of the Soviet secret police between 1946 and 1954.
MfS	*Ministerium für Staatssicherheit* (Ministry for State Security) used to designate the whole apparatus as well as more specifically its ministerial level (as opposed to the district or county level)
NKFD	*Nationalkomitee freies Deutschland* (National Committee for a Free Germany), antifascist organization of German soldiers initiated and supported by the Soviet Union among German POWs in the SU
NKVD	(People's Commissariat for Internal Affairs), name of the Soviet secret police between 1934 and 1946
NÖSPL	*Neues ökonomisches System der Planung und Leitung* (new economic system of planning and steering)
M-L	*Marxismus-Leninismus* (Marxism-Leninism), standard abbreviation used throughout eastern Europe
NSdAP	*Nationalsozialistische deutsche Arbeiterpartei* (Nationalsozialist German Workersparty)
RIAS	*Radio in the American Sector* [of Berlin] (Radio im Amerikanischen Sektor)

SED   *Sozialistische Einheitspartei Deutschlands* (Socialist Unity Party of Germany), the Nazi party

SMAD   *Sovietische Militäradministration in Deutschland* (Soviet Military Administration in Germany)

SPD   *Sozialdemokratische Partei Deutschlands* (Socialdemocratic Party of Germany)

Stasi   *Staatssicherheit;* the popularly used acronym for MfS

UB   *Umweltbibliothek* ("Environmental Library")

VdN   *Verfolgte(r) des Naziregimes* ([person] persecuted by the Nazi regime)

ZK   *Zentralkomitee der SED* (Central Committee of the SED)

Preface

Two threads of argument entwine each other in this book. First, a theoretical strand offers sustained meditations on the dialectical relationship between the development of peoples' understandings of the social world as formed and transformed in everyday experiences and the rise and decline of political institutions created and recreated by their actions. More, it lays out in detail the dynamics through which this dialectic operates. Its particular claim is that processes of validation—that is, the interconnection of events certifying understandings across time—play a central role in these dynamics. Consequently, the book argues for a focus on processes of validation as an analytic angle from which the dynamics of institutions can be comprehended. Second, an historical strand of argument offers a reinterpretation of East German state socialism by analyzing it as an unacknowledged attempt to perform a revolutionary self-fulfilling prophecy. This perspective also enables an account of socialism's failure, which focuses on the GDR elites' failure to produce understandings of the everyday operations of socialism adequate to the maintenance of its institutions through timely reforms. I will speak in this sense of an epistemic explanation of the failure of socialism in contrast to the currently prevalent variants of economic and political systems accounts. My point is not that these are altogether wrong. They do provide valuable pieces for an answer to the puzzle of socialism's failure by guiding our attention to perverse incentive schemes and to institutional rigidities. Rather, I would like to argue that there is a dimension to socialism's demise that has so far not been properly addressed, that is, the generation and certification of knowledge about social life orienting the making and remaking of socialist institutions.

To see why knowledge is central it is helpful to remember that as an utterly modernist phenomenon, the very success of socialism was predicated on the promise of its superior reflexivity. Socialism claimed better insights into the social and economic conditions of our time that were supposed to afford reliable guidance for political action resulting in a humane social order. However, as socialism was economically and technologically falling ever more visibly behind its capitalist rival (something particularly obvious to East Germans), as socialism appeared ever less capable to manage its own affairs (palpable in persistent shortages and a crumbling infrastructure), the claims to superior insight lost their credibility at an accelerating pace during the 1980s. The unfulfilled promise to know better played a significant role in socialism's demise. Knowledge is important for my argument in yet another way. Individuals living within socialism—party functionaries included— were quite aware of the problems economic and political systems accounts of socialism's failure point to. Some of the very best analyses of systemic inadequacies were produced from within socialist officialdom—if in their mature version only at a distance from it.[1] And yet, typically, socialist officials could not do much with their locally produced insights. The institutional arrangements making up the party state systematically undercut both the deepening of locally produced knowledge and its systematic integration into an overarching analysis of socialism within a larger social world. Not that the party state did not possess a systematic understanding of itself. With what it called "Marxism-Leninism" it had a model of which it was only too sure, hastily condemning as puny, ungrateful, misguided, or even as inimical locally produced insights that questioned the central model. Accordingly, the issue at hand is to analyze how the party state failed to come to a genuinely *useful* understanding of itself at its center—one that would have enabled it to steer through its crisis more successfully. If we speak of reform failure in the context of socialism, therefore, we need to see it in light of socialism's political epistemics, the ways in which it produced and certified knowledge about itself. The move toward the epistemic in explanations of socialism's failure is, thus, not so much an attempt to direct our attention merely to a different area of social life as if the epistemic would be different from the economic or the political. Instead, I will undertake in this book a shift in perspective to the very principles underpinning the production and reproduction of social life. And there, I shall argue, the epistemic (in a wider discursive, emotive, and kinesthetic meaning) plays a central role. The account offered here is in this sense orthogonal to the two more established modes of explaining socialism's demise.

The shift in perspective to an analysis of processes of co-constitution between understandings and institutions entails changes in the general framework of how socialism is analyzed. The prevalent economic and po-

---

1. To name but the best known the list includes such illustrious contributions as (in order of the time of their original writing) Koestler 1968; Milosz 1990; Djilas 1983; Leonhard 1955; Havemann 1964; Voslensky 1984; Kołakowski 2008; Bahro 1977; Konrád and Szelenyi 1979; Kornai 1992; Henrich 1989.

litical accounts are typically couched in the ancient language of comparative systems analysis, methodically juxtaposing encompassing forms of social order. With respect to the Soviet world this has always meant explicitly or implicitly playing off a liberal-democratic market economy against a state-socialist planned economy. A variant of systems analysis has identified socialism with fascism under the rubric of totalitarianism while again juxtaposing this supposedly new form to liberal-democratic market economies. I see especially two problems with this analytic procedure. On the one hand, it compares highly idealized images of these forms that are often inadequate to understand people's experiences on the ground. The history and the ethnography of everyday life as it emerged with regard to socialism since the 1980s has shown this time and again.[2] On the other hand, explaining the troubles of one form has in this tradition little direct bearing on the analysis of the other. Worse, since the forms are typically imagined as mutually exclusive alternatives, problems identified in one are read all too often as validating the other. In extreme cases, the comparison leads to self-congratulatory explanations that attribute the failure of one form to the fact that it was in relevant aspects not like the other. In this sense socialism is said to have failed because it was not a liberal democracy, not a market economy.

The analysis I am undertaking in this book is, by contrast, self-consciously lodged at the level of institution-forming process dynamics. Even if the ones I will foreground in this study were more central or widespread in socialism, they still may be found to have a significant place in many other institutional arrangements, which rarely are the logical, internally coherent worlds that comparative systems perspectives have imagined them to be. Instead, social arrangements are better understood as more or less well-integrated thickets of processes, a number of which are typically shared between what comparativists have juxtaposed as distinct systems. In fact, the reason why I found socialism such a fascinating subject of inquiry is precisely that it brings to the fore, perhaps more clearly, certain process dynamics that are more widely shared among contemporary, highly complex and heterogeneous institutional arrangements. Connected to this shift of emphasis from forms to process dynamics constituting these arrangements is the hope that it will enable us to learn from the experience of socialism. I am indeed hope-

---

2. Following the pioneering work of ethnographers exploring everyday life still *during* socialism especially in the Balkans (Verdery 1983 and 2003; Kligman 1988 and 1998; Szelenyi 1988; Burawoy and Lukacs 1992; Lampland 1995; Creed 1998) the better access to archives after the fall of socialism has allowed historians to make enormous progress in recovering the experience of everyday life under socialism (e.g., Kotkin 1995; Fitzpatrick 1999; Merkel 1999; Markovits 1995 and 2005; Fulbrook 2005; Hellbeck 2006).

ful that this book will afford its readers a fair number of déjà vu experiences, which may enable them to recognize social dynamics in their environment in the mirror of socialism.

Eastern European socialisms are a particularly rewarding subject for the exploration of the dynamic interplay between understandings and institutions. For one, socialism is now a clearly circumscribed historical epoch with a beginning and an end. Both bookends are clearly marked by the introduction and the dissolution, respectively, of a characteristic set of institutions. These, moreover, were rationally planned and legitimated on the basis of a sophisticated ideology, thus directly foregrounding the link under investigation here. Contrary to Marx's theory of how social formations come about in a naturalistic process of continuous transformations, Eastern Europe's socialisms were thoroughly intentional projects. They proceeded on the basis of Soviet blueprints. And in this sense, they were the result of politics in its purest form. The German Democratic Republic (also known by its acronym GDR or, more popularly, as East Germany) recommends itself among its brethren, because its complete dissolution as a state has created a rather unique research situation characterized by open archives and the accessibility of former state employees.

Both the theoretical and the historical lines of argument emerged from the investigation of one particular social arena: the efforts of the secret police of the GDR, the Stasi, to control the peace and civil rights movements in East Berlin during the last decade of the country's existence. Spelling it out with such brevity may immediately raise the question, how one could aspire to make arguments as encompassing as the ones just set forth from such a limited domain of social interaction. No doubt, such a move involves a certain conceit, albeit, I hope, a productive one. In its defense I should point out that I did not start this project with an agenda quite as broadly scoped. Instead, I began research in 2001 with the question, how dictatorial political regimes draw and maintain the support of wider strata of the population. Modern states are highly complex institutional arrangements that cannot operate properly without such support. Furthermore, I was interested in how the exercise of dictatorial state power influences state agents' understandings of their own work within a larger political context. And what would be better as a research site for such questions, I thought, than to focus on those members of the Stasi who had actively participated in suppressing dissident activities. After all, the Stasi archives were at least in principle open, and the officers could potentially be interviewed. These more limited questions have not disappeared from this book, but they have become embedded in the wider framework just outlined, as I woke up to what appeared to me as the sociological potential of this particular research "site." It quickly dawned on me that what was at stake in both the efforts of the Stasi officers as they and the party state saw it and in the emerging opposition's efforts to create what they called a "parallel society" was nothing less than the understandings of socialism in its particular institutional form at a particular moment in time and the feedback of these understandings on socialism's institutional fabric. That question was only highlighted by socialism's demise, in which both the Stasi and the opposition played a much more passive role than one might have thought. Of course, the fact remains that I *am* deriving my argument from the investigation of one particular social arena, while generalizing it to GDR socialism as a whole and even with hopes of applicability to Eastern European socialisms more generally. My readings about the social life in other politicized domains of social life in the GDR (both primary and secondary) give me the confidence that this move has merit. This interpretation is further plausibilized by the highly centralized character of socialist governance that, tolerance for some local variations notwithstanding, asserted certain principles across domains of interaction (and the more politically relevant they were deemed to be the more so). Where the boundaries of the usefulness of my argument lie in the end can—given the detail knowledge required—only be ascertained in a wider discussion of comparisons that no scholar can produce alone.

Five Intertwined Empirical Perspectives on Understandings and Institutions

Throughout the research and writing process for this book, the historical and the theoretical lines of argument were developed together, moving constantly from one to the other. Thus theory became a method of fact finding and fact integration for the development of a historical narrative; narration in turn became the testing ground for theory, revealing gaps and overzealous reductions. This generative movement between theoretization and narration was further fueled by the fact that the social arena under consideration here, the Stasi's efforts to control the opposition in the GDR, could be seen as closely intertwining five different perspectives, each raising the question of understandings and institutions from a different angle and yet in complementary ways. These five perspectives lend structure to the book. From the first perspective (part I of the book), I inquire how the ruling party in East Germany thought about and set to work on developing and maintaining a socialist order. The first chapter spans a wide historical arch, wondering how the adherence to ideology (after all, largely an epiphenomenon for Marx) could come to be considered a, if not *the*, linchpin of the party state. I will show that anxious about the "unity and purity" of its ideology, the party aimed at engineering a monolithic intentionality that would bring about socialism in what can analytically only be understood as a self-fulfilling prophecy. Given this exalted role of ideology, this chapter also asks how the party determined the correct interpretation of Marxism-Leninism for a given historical situation. The second chapter follows suit by raising the question, how the party went about its proselytizing business. I will discuss both the positive (persuading) and the negative (restricting) side of this missionary effort. The first was instituted as a giant propaganda apparatus aiming to form socialist human beings. But what if these efforts failed to bear the fruit the state desired? I will show in this chapter that propaganda failure was one of the key domains of the secret police. I will emphasize that propaganda and secret police work were but two sides of the same coin.

The second perspective on the relationship between understandings and political institutions is provided by what one might want to call the epistemic careers of the Stasi officers. Chapter 5, the first in part III of the book, follows the officers on their path from childhood experiences to their employment by the Stasi to learn how their initial attunement to socialism came about. It also investigates how their understandings were shaped subsequently by different kinds of work experiences, marking different phases in the historical development of the GDR. By necessity this involves an inquiry into how particular historical events such as the building of the Wall in 1961 and the Warsaw Pact's smothering of the Prague Spring in 1968 has shaped their views of socialism and their role in it. Chapter 6 complements this picture by inquiring about the discursive culture of the Stasi with a particular emphasis on three questions. How did employees acquire authority in a state socialist bureaucracy? How did the networks of authorized others develop for Stasi officers in the course of time? And what could they talk about, with whom, in what terms about matters political?

The third perspective is provided by the development of the political understandings of peace and civil rights movement activists—the topic of part IV of the book. Chapter 7 traces their biographical trajectory from the emergence of government critical feelings and thoughts to their integration into a protest milieu. Chapter 8 continues this trajectory into the formation of a veritable—if small—parallel civil society from the foundation of politically active groups and countrywide networks of activists to the publication of nationally circulated samizdat. One emphasis of these two chapters lies, as in the case of the Stasi officers, in the *development* of political understandings as the result of a sequence of events. Another is the importance of emotions and the sensuous experience of moving bodies through concrete spaces for the development of political understandings. A perhaps surprising insight of these two chapters concerns the epistemic importance of intimate relationships. We shall see in these chapters, perhaps even more clearly than in the chapters on the Stasi officers, that spatial arrangements, the co-location of people and their interweaving through meeting spots can have profound epistemic consequences.

The fourth perspective is given by the very techniques the party state employed to induce men and women with government critical ideas to reverse their opinions or at least to abstain from further government critical action. What is interesting about these techniques is that they too were aimed at the formation of understandings of self and other. That does not mean that these techniques were in any way less violent. Systematic disinformation was used to disorient people and to destroy personal relationships. And yet, the success of these techniques was rather variable; and precisely this fact is theoretically interesting. It raises the question, under what conditions particular techniques of manipulating people's understandings work, or fail to work. This will also shed further light on the epistemic qualities of intimate relations.

The fifth and final perspective (conclusion) zeros in on the question, why the socialist project failed. Why did the call for reforms in the hot fall of 1989 not end like the Prague Spring in 1968, or the Hungarian uprising in 1956, or the East German protests of 1953, that is, in armed intervention on behalf of the existing order? Put differently, why did the secret police officers, who had sworn to defend socialism to the last drop of their blood, not even fire a single shot in its defense when its very existence came under threat? As the answer to the last question will be found in an increasing disorientation of party state functionaries caused by an accelerating discrepancy between lived experience and official party descriptions of life in the GDR, the central question becomes why the party state was unable to develop more successful action guiding understandings of itself in a wider social world.

The perspective that is most obviously missing is that of what one might want to call "common people," that is, GDR citizens who were neither seriously committed to socialism nor directly opposed to it. This seems problematic because in the fall of 1989 common people become important historical actors both in fueling a new refugee wave and in taking to the streets lending force to the groundswell of demonstrations. The reasons for this omission are mostly practical and therefore I do not want to make an attempt to justify it intellectually. Nevertheless, from all I know about my readings on everyday life in the GDR, the dynamics I am describing in this book about the development of understandings among Stasi officers and dissidents are those of common people too, albeit in different admixtures, differently distributed across time. Moreover, their action, and their performed understandings are present indirectly through the reactions of officers and dissidents. This is not ideal, but I think it is workable.

Hermeneutic Institutionalism

The details of the theoretical model as I will develop them in the introductory chapter as well as in the two chapters of part II of the book is the result of a careful comparison between these perspectives. And yet, the fundamental analytical framework of this study stands in a long tradition of hermeneutic social thought dating back to the eighteenth-century writings of Vico (1968; 1988) and Herder (1953; 2002). It found its way into the germinating social sciences in Germany via scholars such as Dilthey (1970), Weber (1980), and Simmel (1992), but also, mediated by Hegel, through the works of American pragmatists (e.g., Dewey 1925; 1997). Max Weber (1980) even qualified his own way of practicing sociology as "hermeneutic" (*verstehend*, literally: "understanding"). The hallmark of hermeneutic social thought is not only (as often foregrounded) the employment of interpretative techniques as a primary research method. Even more important is the prominence it affords to interpretation and communication as the central linchpin of human social life. Says Vico, this being a version of his famous "verum factum principle" (1968, 96), "the world of civil society has certainly been made by men, and that its principles are therefore to be found within the modifications of our own human mind." With "civil society" Vico means our social institutions. What he calls here "modifications of mind" is further analyzed by him as a thoroughly social and historical process of forming understandings about the world. If this is so, then understanding is also the method of choice to study processes of institution-formation because the ways in which we understand the social world is constitutive of the institutional arrangements in and through which we live. Our understandings shape our actions while our actions in concatenation with those of others call into being, maintain, and transform institutions. In practice this means, for example, that the ways in which we think, talk, feel, and habitually comport ourselves with respect to the law, the government, parties, elections, the mass media, nongovernmental organizations, constitutes them as the institutions that make up our political order. If this holds, then studying the transformation of understandings should be an apposite way of investigating the transformation of political institutions, including revolutions.

Given our currently prevalent social imaginaries, the links this framework establishes between understandings, actions, and institutions appear far too neat, however. We are only too well aware of the difficulties involved in changing established institutions even when their detrimental effects are well known and seemingly universally decried. We seem to understand what's wrong, and yet nothing happens. Alluding merely to power differentials in sorting out whose understandings do and whose do not matter is no solution here. Indeed, we find it obvious today that the institutional order in which we live conforms to nobody's understandings in particular. People who still believe in the powers of a social demiurge (and be it a secular one such as a class or a ruling elite), whose intentions we would only need to decipher to unravel the mysteries of society, would inevitably appear as naive conspiracy theorists. Instead, we tend to assume a bewildering plurality of competing understandings in operation. Worse, as we understand the world today this plurality is not only one among different people, but we imagine every single person to harbor a plurality of possibly contradictory understandings. Freud has taught us to be wary of the link between our manifest intentions and our actions. We largely accept his notion of the unconscious. In fact, we assume today that we are making sense of the world simultaneously through a plurality of means possibly yielding ambiguous or even contradictory understandings, some of which we are aware of while others operate silently in the background. And just to complicate this complex picture even further, already Vico and Herder pointed out that our understandings are as much the product of institutional arrangements as they are their source. Consequently, linear causal models will have to give way to some form of iterative, reflexive causation. And so the basic framework of hermeneutic social thought as laid out in the last paragraph seems to lose its marvelous coherence and simplicity as quickly as a pointillist painting viewed up close.

Perhaps not surprisingly, therefore, a great number of social scientists, and in particular those who label themselves (neo-)institutionalists of the one variety or the other, have for some time now abandoned the notion of understanding as a central focus of their analysis. Instead, many of them have looked to market models with the price mechanism as central decentralized arbiter, as a way to make sense of social orders that seem to emerge from chaotic individual actions.[3] And with this perspective they have adopted a rational choice framework as a universal and all-encompassing model of human behavior. Thus, they bypass the very notion of qualitatively differentiated, historically and culturally specific processes of understanding. This situation is not fundamentally altered by the many critics of the use of extreme neoclassical models.[4] Even though they take into account that choices may be constrained, and that rationality may be bounded, they still work with an optimizing choice model as their basis. Yet others have favored approaches relying on patterns of relationships to comprehend institutions.[5] And even though their emphasis on relationality is very fruitful

---

3. The literature is vast, especially among economists, economic historians, and political scientists. Paradigmatically, I should mention here as canonized ancestors Coase 1937 and Hayek (e.g., 1988) as well as among the currently most-noted practitioners: Chandler and Daems 1980; Nelson and Winter 1982; Williamson 1985; Elster 1989; North 1990; and Greif 2006.

4. Among them are neoinstitutionalists in political science, for example, March and Olsen (1989) and Steinmo, Thelen, and Longstreth (1992). The newer interest in heuristics (Gigerenzer 2000; Kahneman and Tversky 1982) and/or evolutionary psychology, for example by North (2005), simply substitutes one set of seemingly hard-wired psychological mechanisms with another.

5. The signal words here are *embeddedness* and *networks*. Notable exemplars are: Granovetter 1973, 1985; Bearman 1993; Burt 1995; and White 2003.

(and will be emulated in this study), practitioners in this line of work are more typically than not in the thrall of purely structural models as well as of formal modeling and thus an imaginary that sees human action as optimizing choice behavior. Where in this vast literature cognates of understanding play a role (as "beliefs," "norms," or "ideology"), they are typically treated as environmental conditions distributing rewards and punishments or as constraints on choice behavior. In other words, current mainstream (neo-) institutionalism has little space for *understandings* in the sense in which the hermeneutic tradition has used that term. I take this to be a fundamental shortcoming of the current literature on institutions. In the face of the admittedly serious challenges to the hermeneutic approach I have just outlined, most newer forms of institionalism have drained the baby with the bathwater as it were, practicing a social science that has shed what is quintessentially human about life in society. While acknowledging the problems I have just enumerated, I will make a case with this book for a renewed focus on understandings albeit on the basis of an updated model.

Political Epistemology

En route to such a model, I will return to fundamentals, asking the following questions: What is understanding; what does it do; and how does it operate? Are there different modes in which we understand, and if so, how do these interact? Clearly, we have to think again about the relationship between discourse and body. Then, how does understanding take shape in the course of time, how is it influenced by the successes and failures of our own actions, by our memory, our conversations with others, and thus with the different social networks within which we move? What would give us a handle on sorting understandings that matter from those that do not? We will in particular need a way to think through how the understandings of many people shape one another—for the ability to interweave myriad transactions into an encompassing whole is precisely the strength of the price mechanism. How does the process of understanding congeal into something more stable, a form transposable from one context to another, thus enabling learning. Consequently, also: How do such understandings as forms dissolve? Why and under what kinds of circumstances do they lose their operability? How does an understanding "shape" (or "inform," "structure," or perhaps even better, "orient") action, especially if we make room for the fact that we are working with a plurality of possibly contradictory, ambiguous, or insufficient understandings? Then, what is an institution, what does it have to do with actions and their concatenation across time, locations, and possibly large numbers of people? How do institutions stabilize? And turning the tables: How do these institutions possibly shape understandings, creating the possibility of feedback loops and self-reinforcing dynamics? What about power differentials both in the sense of whose understandings matter or who has the capacity to translate understandings into action? Finally, once a way to reason through this muddle is found in such a way that it could become a method for empirical research, the question still remains, which and whose understandings, which and whose actions, and which institutions can thus be linked?

I see in such questions, as they pertain to our understandings of the social and political world, the outlines of a field of inquiry that may be called political epistemology. Although both components forming this term are rather familiar, their conjunction is uncommon and therefore merits further comment. Unlike the classical philosophical discipline from which it borrows the latter half of its name, political epistemology does not inquire abstractly into the conditions for the possibility of objectively true knowledge. Instead, it investigates how, in an effort to orient themselves in the world, historically, socially, and culturally situated people actually form and interrogate what to them *appears* as valid understanding (Berger and Luckmann 1966). Framing the objective of political epistemology in this way instantaneously reveals its proximity to three principal directions in the social sciences: the various ancestral traditions in the sociology of knowledge ("Marxian" [e.g., 1958a], "Durkheimian" [e.g., 1995], "Mannheimian" [e.g., 1995]); the acronym branded post-Mertonian waves in the sociology of science (i.e., "SSK" [Bloor 1991; Collins 1992], "STS" [e.g., MacKenzie and Wajcman 1999], "ANT" [e.g., Latour 2005]); and Foucault's and Foucauldian "archaeologies" (Foucault 1972a) and "genealogies" of knowledge (e.g., Foucault 1995, 1978; also Hacking 1995). All three directions can be addressed as variants of "social epistemology" (in contradistinction to the philosophical discipline [Fuller 2002]). Political epistemology draws considerable inspiration from all three, and it is in fact a particular form of social epistemology addressing understandings of the social and political world. Thematically, therefore, it is closest to Mannheim and Foucault with their interest in political knowledges; methodologically, it is closest to the sociology of science with its focus on the ethnography and historical reconstruction of everyday interactions in specific kinds of contexts. Theoretically, it draws freely on all three with further inspiration from Marx, Weber, and Elias's "classical" institutionalism refracted by Meadian and Wittgensteinian pragmatism and speech act theory. Thus it develops a distinctive, process-oriented analytic focusing on the generation, maintenance, and transformation of peoples' understandings and their dialectical relations to political institutions. The main thrust of political epistemology is positive, that is, concerned with description and analysis of the real world. Yet this is undertaken at least with the hope that political epistemology would, like its philosophical namesake, offer normative insights into better ways to institute political knowledge-making.

The "political" in political epistemology indicates in the first instance simply the particular kind of object of knowledge formation. In other words, it indicates that the understandings investigated in this book are developed in relation to those processes, which are commonly designated as political. This includes the regulation of common affairs, especially the more or less contentious articulation of collective intentions and the division of labor in their execution. Put more narrowly, these are matters of governance and state-citizen relationships. However, social epistemologists have repeatedly pointed out that knowledge is political in a much more fundamental sense. If processes of generating and especially of stabilizing understandings always involve other people and institutions, they necessarily take place within webs of power relations. Conversely, understandings are political also because they are, acknowledged or not, constitutive of power-distributing institutions. Foucault (1978; 1980; 1995) has pointedly expressed the conjunction of both directions of influence in his popular "power/knowledge" formula. Yet, closer attention to the processes connecting power and knowledge quickly shows that this relationship is fraught with ironies (Glaeser 2003). Power and knowledge are neither solely the autonomous Socratic antipodes allowing knowledge to speak truth to power, nor are they simply Foucauldian bedfellows augmenting each other. As will became apparent through this study, power holders need to restrain their desire to manipulate the validation of knowledge that is the very source of their might. Their ability to demand and receive recognition of understandings as true knowledge and their possibilities to arrange for corroborating outcomes of situations testing understandings may quickly lead to a detachment between world and understandings. And, against their own instincts, knowledge producers need to become unscrupulous, and ready to act on the basis of always less than perfect concepts and methods, lest their desire to constantly refine and qualify knowledge suffocate any possibility to renew knowledge experientially.

To deal constructively with these ironies I propose, at the end of the introductory chapter, a concept of the political as a particular perspective on the social training its gaze on the nexus between actions and institutions, and of politics as intentional effort to form, maintain, or transform institutions of whatever kind, scale, or scope. Seen in this light, the formation of understandings of the social world for political purposes is common practice. We are all involved in politics, big or small. And its successful pursuit requires us to employ some understandings of the social world in which we live. One could define political epistemology, therefore, as the academic field studying the historically specific politics-oriented knowledge-making practices of people and their consequences.

A Sociology of Understanding

This book endeavors to make contributions to the field of political episte-mology on two different levels. On the one hand, it argues the fruitfulness of the field and its questions through a set of interrelated empirical case studies as I have outlined them further above. On the other, it develops a theoretical framework, a method to practice it. Picking up on the hermeneutic tradi-tion, the theory resulting from this exercise centers on the term *understand-ing* rather than *knowledge*, and it might therefore best be called a "sociology of understanding." Three reasons motivate this shift in terminology.

First, the term *understanding* signals an attempt to move beyond the nar-row confines of conscious thought. In the introductory chapter I will there-fore conceptualize understanding as a process of orientation that can take place simultaneously in a number of different modes. Each of these produces orientation in a different way. I will distinguish between discursive, emotive, and kinesthetic understandings. This differentiation of various modes of understanding helps us to investigate how they amplify or undermine one another in their orientational capacities, for example, when people feel the world in one way but think about it in another, or how our regular move-ments through a cityscape support or undermine our opinions.

Second, knowledge is very unlike an object. It cannot be stored away to be retrieved selfsame at a later moment in time. And in whatever way one endeavors to bound a "piece" of it, it never has an existence independent of other such "pieces." Instead, knowledge is much rather a knowing, an on-going process of orientation in the world. Even where knowledge pertains to particular facts, for example, that the German verb *verstehen* is typically rendered in English as "to understand," each time this knowledge is used for a project of translation it stands in a different context, bearing differ-ent associations. In ongoing practice the link between the English and the German word becomes ever more qualified, enriched with stories of good uses and bad. But this is to say that it is known differently. If this is so, then knowledge somehow carries with it the traces of its own historicity. More, to possess knowledge means to have the ability to reproduce it in the course of time. The history of its use is the condition for the possibility to remember it in the long run. In chapter 3 I will explore the reasons why this is so in ref-erence to Wittgenstein's private language argument. The grammatical form of "understanding" as a continuous and a gerund highlights these concerns with processual dynamics. It emphasizes the fact that knowledge is continu-ously made and remade through repeated use in successive encounters with the world, that is, in action and interaction.

The third reason for the terminological shift from knowledge to under-standing is an acute interest in the various degrees to which particular persons "own" or better "inhabit" particular understandings by corresponding to the certainty they carry. "Knowledge" in common parlance indicates in this sense a more specific degree of certainty and at least implied ownership. Yet, I am particularly interested in the movements between various degrees of certainty, for example, from "hunches" to "hypothesis" to "knowledge," or from implicit background assumption to "pangs of doubt" to "error." These shifts in the degrees of certainty have serious consequences for the readiness with which people act on the basis of particular understandings and therefore for the stability of the institutions. The erosion of the certainty among party and state functionaries that the GDR's political leadership knew what they were doing has much to do with the particular trajectory of the events of the fall of 1989.

Finally, the sociology of knowledge has never really made good of the full Vico-Herderian idea to explore the co-constitution between institutions and understandings. For it, knowledge has by and large remained something to be explained by linking it to "social factors." To be sure, there has been no shortage of critiques pointing to the problems with this unidirectional causal account. Most notably "cultural Marxists" (Althusser 1971; Williams 1977; Castoriadis 1987) have all pointed to the constitutive role of ideology. The attempted revival of the sociology of knowledge on the basis of a synthesis between phenomenology and pragmatism by Berger and Luckmann (1966) has even formulated a dialectical model based on the metabolistic imagery of "externalization" and "internalization." For the studies of scientific knowledge, Lynch (e.g., 1997) and Latour (1999) have offered fundamental criticisms of this objectivist framework. Accordingly, I will in the course of this study draw on these authors. And yet, the sociology of knowledge, its internal critics included, has been weak in specifying process dynamics through which this dialectic actually does its constituting work. The shift to the term understandings signals in this sense a return to the original promise inherent in the Vico-Herderian initiation of hermeneutic social thought.

Central to my account of what happens in remaking knowledge as well as in changing its degree of certainty and thus its ability to guide action are processes of validation. I will distinguish in the next chapter between a number of different forms of validation, which I will discuss in greater depth in chapter 3. Indeed, I will argue that by setting the stage for action, institutions feed back on understandings via validations. And thus we will have the process dynamics in hand to trace the dialectical relationship between understandings and other kinds of institutions. Even at the cost of sounding opaque at this early stage of the text, here is a full gyration of the dialectical screw: Understandings where certain shape actions that in concatenation with the reaction of others become institutions in repetition. In form of social relationships, and by shaping the likelihood that certain kinds of actions will fail or succeed, as well as by triggering or suppressing memories, institutions in turn create the environment in which understandings are validated positively or negatively. The understandings thus reproduced with an accrual or diminishment of certainty and possible changes of meaning will make renewed action more or less likely and possibly different. I will explore this dialectic in particular in the second part of chapter 4. That is also where I will investigate in detail the possibilities for this dialectic to descend into circularity and thus eventually producing understandings failing to provide us with meaningful traction for action.

The focus on validations also offers a number of other advantages. In particular it will allow us to comprehend why, especially in the realm of understandings about social life, we are frequently so beholden to the understandings of others. By investigating the difficulty to find simple practical corroborations for complex political understandings, it will become clear why it is hard for us to resist following crowds, and why we tend to regress with our opinions to some standard maintained within the networks of authority figures we respect. Conversely, paying attention to the ways in which the flow of validations is generated will also allow us to identify the conditions for resisting dominant opinion. These insights have clear implications for the kinds of institutions we should cultivate, and those we should be wary of, if we really care about a democratic, open society.

Political epistemology conducted in the mode of the sociology of understanding developed here will also allow me to integrate several different recent perspectives on the deeply cultural processes of state formation (Steinmetz 2002a): Foucault's interest in the historical emergence and transformation of ideologies and discourses of what governance is, what it is supposed to accomplish, and how it is to be conducted that is what he has called "governmentality" (1991); George Steinmetz's attention to the understandings of historically situated and career-bound bureaucrats about their work and their role in the formation of different German colonial regimes (2007), and the neo-Foucauldian (e.g., Said 1979; Scott 1998) and science studies concerns (Porter 1996; Carroll 2006) with states' technologies and practices of knowledge making. What helps in this respect is not only the focus of this study on the secret police officers who are as bureaucrats producers of knowledge, crafting and wielding knowledge machineries, while they are at the same time subject to the educational efforts of a proselytizing state. What allows this integration to succeed is precisely the focus of the theoretical framework of this book on understandings and their formation in different kinds of contexts through various forms of validation. More it is this theoretical framework that allows me to link these three strands of scholarship with recent studies on the transformation of theoretical knowledge into institutional arrangements that is on performativity (MacKenzie

2006; MacKenzie, Munesia, and Siu 2008), which is well understood, of course, but a contemporary strand of hermeneutic social analysis.

Political epistemology analyzes the development of understandings of all participants in a historical process with the help of the same analytic lens. It is as interested in people who in retrospect appear to have had it right as in those who seem to have erred.[6] After all, even if people in the latter group conceded *today* that they were wrong, they probably believed *then* that they were right. Consequently, the question is rather—for the present as much as for the past—how the various participants came to feel justified, and what precisely it was that might have led some of them to reconsider their understandings. This includes questions about why participants may have ignored signs that might have been identifiable as "early warnings." Right or wrong, as W. I. Thomas (1928, 572) has reminded us, actual understandings have consequence for actions and thus for the constitution of institutions, or, as he put it with much greater economy (hence known as the "Thomas theorem"): "If men define situations as real, they are real in their consequences."

The principle of analytical symmetry must extend into the domain of the moral. Consequently, I do not ask the question, how the Stasi officers may have become "victimizers" and the opposition members their "victims." Posing the question thus would be ahistorical, because, perverse cases notwithstanding, people who inflict suffering on others, the Stasi officers included, rarely perceive themselves as "victimizers." Instead, they typically feel that the suffering they have inflicted was fully justified either in the interest of preventing greater harm or as fair punishment. The question that political epistemology must pose is how all participants could come to their respective moral self-evaluations and other evaluations in their own terms, at their time. Accordingly, this study accounts for the ways in which Stasi officers became and remained socialist believers with the help of the same sociology of understanding by which it accounts for the path of the members of the peace and civil rights movement into the opposition. By recurring to the same principles it explains why both sides felt morally justified, even compelled, to do what they did. It will thus become clear what different understandings have to do with travel through different social, cultural, and experiential terrains. The question of who ended up on which side of the political conflict becomes, then, less an issue of character or of static demographic variables and more one of the contingent trajectories through institutional fabrics that are maintained and altered through these journeys.

---

6. Here I am building on the principle of "symmetry" characterizing the "strong programme" in the sociology of scientific knowledge (Bloor 1991, 7).

Acknowledgments

This book, eight years in the making, has greatly benefited from the help of many people, and accordingly I have incurred considerable debt to interview partners, archivists, colleagues, editors, and students. Without the patient and generous support of twenty-five officers of the former secret police of the German Democratic Republic this book would never have come into existence. I am very grateful for the interview time they have committed to this project. Two of these officers have not only dedicated more time than anybody else, but they have also been very helpful in facilitating my contacts with the other officers. They are Kurt Zeiseweis and Wolfgang Schmitt. I got to know these two thanks to Wolfgang Hartmann who introduced me to a monthly meeting of former officers interested in the history of the Stasi. While the large majority of my interview partners prefer to remain anonymous, these three can be named because they have taken a stance in public debates about the Stasi.

This book would have been just as impossible to write without the equally patient and generous support of twelve former activists of the East Berlin peace, civil rights, and environmental movements. Since all of them have played a public role in explaining their experiences during the late GDR, and since none of them requested to remain anonymous, they can be named. I am most grateful to Ulrike Poppe, Thomas Klein, Peter Grimm, Wolfgang Templin, Irena Kukutz, Wolfgang Rüddenklau, Martin Böltger, Beate Harembski, Ekkehard Maaß, Werner Fischer, Reinhold Weißhuhn, Christa Sengespeik-Roos, Gerd Poppe, Ruth Misselwitz, Hans-J. Misselwitz, and Carlo Jordan. Three former secret informants of the Stasi who were active in dissident circles were also willing to speak with me. I have learned a lot from these interviews and I am very grateful for their readiness to participate in this study.

Besides the interviews with former civil rights movement members and former Stasi officers, this book relies heavily on documentary evidence collected in archives and libraries. Especially for the foreign scholar whose time in Berlin is limited, there is no better source for the documents of the former secret police of East Germany than the Matthias Domaschk Archive in the Robert Havemann Society. At the same time this archive holds the most formidable collection of documents from Berlin dissident groups. I owe many thanks to Frank Ebert and Tom Sello for facilitating my work at this archive. Other important documents for this project came from the official federal Stasi document center, the archive of the Bundesbeauftragte für die Unterlagen der ehemaligen Staatsssicherheit der DDR (BStU). There I would like to thank Herrn Rothermud for facilitating my access to the Stasi documents, and Jens Gieseke from the department of education and research for useful consultations about the full-time employees of the Stasi. The Berlin branch of the German Federal Archives (Bundesarchiv Berlin), holding the collections on parties and mass organizations of the former GDR (SAPMO), always impressed me with its superb, prompt, and courteous service.

My colleagues at the University of Chicago were a wellspring of continuing inspiration, of encouragement and critique. I owe particular gratitude to Michael Silverstein and Andrew Abbott for mentoring me through my early career. Michael's initiative to jumpstart a faculty group for the study of communication in society also led to crucial and much appreciated funding of the fieldwork for this book by then provost Richard Saller. Andy Abbott, then chair of sociology, made a year's worth of fieldwork possible by allowing me to shift around teaching obligations. Apart from Michael and Andy, Susan Gal, Lisa Wedeen, Bill Sewell, John Lucy, Martin Riesebrodt, and Lis Clemens provided helpful commentary on chapter drafts of this book here at Chicago. Michael Geyer's advice was helpful in planning this project. I have repeatedly discussed parts of this work with graduate students in classes, in workshops, and during a special reading session of selected chapters. Many thanks to Paola Castano, István Adorjan, Dan Huebner, Beckett Sterner, Etienne Ollion, and Zoe Nyssa for their comments. Visiting scholar Hella Dietz provided inspiring feedback about the introduction. Doug Mitchell at the University of Chicago Press has been a cheerful, encouraging supporter of this project from its very beginning.

I am also grateful to have had a number of opportunities to present parts of this manuscript at other universities and conferences. The presentations at Cornell University, the University of Wisconsin–Madison, the University of Wisconsin–Milwaukee, Northwestern University, the University of Michigan, Yale University, and the University of Southern California helped me to advance and refine my thought. Thanks to everybody who has listened, queried, or commented on parts of this work on any of these occasions. The meetings of the American Sociological Association, the American Anthropological Association, the Social Science History Association, and the Council of European Studies also provided useful occasions to present parts of this book.

Dominic Boyer has had a persistent influence on the genesis and the final form of this manuscript. We have met many times over the years to discuss socialism, the GDR, and postunification Germany. Together we have organized a number of conference panels that gave rise to even further discussions. I am very grateful for these conversations, and even more grateful for a long, detailed, very helpful commentary on the entire manuscript. For the final revision of this manuscript the very encouraging words of Jeff Olick and the sympathetic yet critical eye of Nina Eliasoph and Alexei Yurchak were much appreciated. The German Marshall Fund of the United States—then still interested in funding research—provided much-needed funding for a leave of absence dedicated to writing. I am grateful to the Department of Sociology at the University of Chicago for a generous subsidy, which defrayed some of the printing cost for this book.

With nobody did I discuss the ideas underlying this book more thoroughly than with Fowzia Khan. She has also helped greatly in the final round to make this a more readable manuscript. To her I dedicate this book.

Note on translations: unless otherwise marked all translations from the German are mine.

Understandings, Politics, and Institutions

A VIEW FROM THE END

Social arrangements in decline often look farcical. They produce events that just a little while ago were literally inconceivable. They engender plots that are, judging by the received wisdom of their time and space, whimsical, indeed improbable in the dramatic sense of the word. Analytically such events are revealing. They confront the desperate assertion of an order as present, with its open rejection as passé; they feature the bold flotation of a presupposed future that is suddenly allowed to slip by as if it were already well established. Thus they also reveal clashes of political understandings in which the still presupposed commonplace is destabilized by views unthinkable only yesterday. Sitting at the crossroads between a past that is still there and a future that is little more than audacious anticipation, they perform the undoing of one social order while toying with another. I want to open this chapter by reporting just such an event from the fall of 1989 that has become emblematic for the decline and final disintegration of socialism in East Germany.

The punch line of the event as it is remembered is but a historical trifle. An octogenarian minister of secret police retorts criticism of his style of address to a moribund parliamentarian assembly with the words: *Ich liebe Euch doch alle!* (But I love you all!). That's it, or perhaps better: there is little more to it. And yet, this short phrase captured the public imagination. To many, these words spoken by this particular man in this particular context crystallized what socialism was, and as such it became a trope, a key to the memory of state socialism in the GDR. To understand how so little could do so much, some background is necessary. The protagonist is Erich Mielke, since 1957 head of the Ministry of State Security, the secret police, bureaucratically known under its official acronym MfS, and popularly referred to as the Stasi. A member of the politburo, a close confidant of the country's leader, Erich Honecker, a cabinet minister, and a four-star general, Mielke commanded an army of 91,000[1] full-time secret police employees and almost twice that many unofficial helpers of various categories.[2] With regard to his biography, Mielke was what an ideal GDR leader was supposed to be: of proletarian origin, *ein einfacher Arbeiterjunge* (a simple worker's kid), in his case from Berlin's poor Wedding district; and someone who appeared to have made the right decision when history called, someone with antifascist credentials acquired chiefly by participating in the Spanish Civil War.

The Background

During GDR times, nobody knew much about Stasi and its minister, not even the Stasi employees. The Stasi's size, its concrete range of tasks, its organizational structure, its methods were cautiously guarded state secrets. And yet, precisely because it was hiding, it was imagined to be everywhere. That, of course, meant different things to different people. Those in sympathy with the party were prone to see it as a necessary institution of national defense effectively protecting the GDR from its enemies. For many of them the Stasi was also an object of pride, mostly owing to its fabled foreign espionage prowess. Some even regarded it as an organization with more direct access to power and thus capable of circumventing regrettable bureaucratic stalemate. To the population not committed to socialism, the Stasi was mysterious and intimidating, something to stay clear of even as it became the butt of popular jokes targeting its supposed omniscience and power. For people with thoughts, interests, and desires deviating from the party's proscribed path, Stasi was a threat, the epitome of a powerful political machine ever ready to stamp out the very conditions for the possibility of their difference.

The scene for the event I want to report is the People's Chamber, the GDR's parliament that was integrated into the Palace of the Republic, the country's largest sociocultural center sporting several restaurants, bowling alleys, and a number of performance spaces that together made it the closest thing to a piazza in East Berlin's cityscape. It is important to remember that the People's Chamber was not what such an institution would be in a western parliamentarian democracy. It debated and finally promulgated the laws of the country. Yet, not only was law institutionalized in a different way (e.g., Dilcher 1994; Mollnau 1999), playing a different role in the political administrative make-up of socialist states, but these laws were drafted

---

1. All Stasi employment figures used throughout the book are, unless otherwise noted, from Gieseke 2000.

2. Throughout the book, all figures about secret informants (*Inoffizielle Mitarbeiter*) are, unless otherwise noted, from Müller-Enbergs 1995.

by the Apparat, the bureaucracy of the Central Committee (Uschner 1993; Modrow 1995). Once they arrived at the doorsteps of the People's Chamber they were already approved by the politburo, the most significant group of political decision makers in the country. Minor amendments were possible, but in principle the task of parliament was to acclaim them. Biannual meetings were sufficient for this work. The People's Chamber remained formally a multiparty assembly that included, besides the ruling Socialist Unity Party (SED), also a Christian, a liberal, a national, and a farmers' party in addition to representatives of the socialist mass organizations (youth, women, union, etc.). These parties and mass organizations were united and effectively controlled by the SED through the means of a "national front." Accordingly, elections were, as elsewhere in Eastern Europe, unitary list elections. Therefore, members of parliament without other higher party functions were, although carefully screened, rather removed from power, and as far as the non-SED members were concerned, even symbolically separated from it.

The time of the event is November 13, 1989. Since the preceding late summer months, tens of thousands of GDR citizens had fled westward through the newly opened Hungarian border or by spectacular occupations of West German embassies in Budapest, Prague, and Warsaw. That the GDR seemed to have nothing left to retain them was widely read as an indicator for the severity of the economic and political crisis of the country. The government's response to those fleeing had already produced one of the lines that began to galvanize the public imagination (and social memory afterward). In the prime newscast of the GDR, Die *Aktuelle Kamera*, a commentary of the state news agency (ADN) was read, declaring: "They [the refugees] have trampled all moral values locking themselves out of our society. Thus, no tears should be shed about them."[3]

The refugee crisis, the silence of government, and the widespread interest of the people in it provided a new, significant push for opposition groups in the GDR. So far they had operated only in limited circles. Now they saw a chance to reorganize themselves as open, countrywide citizen, discussion, and action platforms. The first one to get off the ground on September 10 was the Neue Forum ("New Forum") with a memorandum titled "Departure 89." As an absolute novelty in the GDR, it applied on September 19 for legalization that was, not unexpectedly, declined just a few days later. Nevertheless, soon others followed, some even with the open intention to establish themselves

---

3. *Aktuelle Kamera*, October 1, 1989. Krenz (1999, 74) suspects that this very line was formulated by Honecker himself. This is not implausible given what we know about the deep, micromanagerial interference of the party leadership, especially of Honecker and Herrmann, the politburo member in charge of the mass media (see Boyer 2003; 2005, 130–32).

as alternative political parties.[4] All of these new groupings were carried by a growing wave of public interest in political reform, which also found other forms of expression. On September 25, peace prayers in Leipzig's Nikolai Church led to a public demonstration with about a thousand participants. This was the birth hour of the famous "Monday demonstrations," which from now on were to convene weekly with ever-growing numbers of participants.

Just five weeks before Mielke's speech in the People's Chamber, the GDR had celebrated its fortieth anniversary with great pomp. Here another line was spoken that ended up sticking. In an address in the Palace of the Republic on the eve of the anniversary, the general secretary summarized the state of the party's project with an old labor movement ditty: "Socialism in its course can not be stopped by either donkey or horse."[5] At the same time, however, festivities took place amid increasingly voiced discontent among its population, which for the first time since 1953 burst across the country into a string of grassroots demonstrations. These provoked the party state into its most visible display of internally applied force since the building of the Berlin Wall in August 1961. Thousands of people were temporarily arrested. Subsequent reports of police abuse spread widely throughout the country. In consequence of what even the most loyal of party members perceived as complacent anniversary celebrations that significantly dampened hopes for reforms from within the party, the Monday demonstrations in the city of Leipzig had swelled to 70,000—and neither did the demonstrators use violence, nor did the party state try to dissolve it by force. Only three weeks before the Stasi minister's speech, Honecker, the GDR's leader since 1971,

4. Historical overviews over the citizen platforms emerging in the fall of 1989 are provided by Müller-Enbergs et al. 1991, Haufe and Bruckmeier 1993, Neubert 1998, Timmer 2000, Neubert and Eisenfeld 2001. A fascinating account in the Stasi documents tracing the emergence of this group is provided by Mitter and Wolle 1991.

5. Honecker had used the same slogan in a speech celebrating the first 32-bit chip manufactured in the GDR. On August 15, 1989, the ZK paper, *Neues Deutschland*, featured it on the title page. There is a photograph from 1959 that shows this slogan in a slightly different form on a billboard just across the border with West Berlin in the area of Potsdamer Platz. There, ox and donkey are replaced by the then mayor of Berlin (later chancellor of West Germany), Willy Brandt, and then American secretary of state, John Foster Dulles. The oldest historical records of the slogan seem to date back to 1886 when a socialist carpenter signed it into the visitors' book of a popular Berlin weekend hangout under the false name of Berlin's chief of police. It was popularized then through the ensuing forgery trial against him. Another famous line supposedly uttered in the same context is this one attributed to Gorbachev: "Those who come too late are punished by life" (*Wer zu spät kommt, den bestraft das Leben!*). In his memoirs Gorbachev claims to have used these words in a conversation with Honecker. On public record is only the following line uttered at Flughafen Schönefeld upon his arrival: "I think dangers are only waiting for those who do not react to life!" (*Aktuelle Kamera*, October 5, 1989) (*Die Zeit* no. 41, 1999, "Wer zu spät kommt, den bestraft das Leben' hat Gorbatschow gesagt. Stimmt's?").

had been deposed and replaced with his heir apparent. A little over one week prior to the event in question, East Berlin, a city of 1.6 million, had witnessed a demonstration for democratic renewal/socialism with a human face that attracted about half a million participants. Initiated by the Berlin theater companies, it featured a panoply of speakers ranging from civil rights activists Jens Reich and Marianne Birthler, who represented emerging new parties, over critical but essentially loyal artists such as Stefan Heym and Christa Wolf to more critical representatives of the GDR's political elites such as the former Stasi espionage chief Markus Wolf and stalwarts of the new younger party leadership represented by the Berlin district chief and politburo member Günter Schabowski. The latter two's voices, however, were drowned in catcalls. It was an ominous sign. Most significantly, however, a mere four days before the event I am about to narrate, the Berlin Wall had been opened in an attempt to stem the flood of refugees. In the intervening three days about 2 million GDR citizens[6] visited West Berlin or West Germany to get a firsthand glimpse of the consumption possibilities in "the other Germany."

Mielke's Speech

On this November 13, 1989, the People's Chamber assembled to vote for a new prime minister and a new speaker, to complement on the state side the previous changes at the head of the party's politburo.[7] Just before Mielke descended from the government bench to the speaker's podium the parliamentarians heard for the first time *officially* from the finance minister as well as from the head of the central planning commission about the extent of the GDR's foreign debt.[8] The reaction of the members to these revelations ranged from boundless amazement and disbelief to shocked sadness and muffled anger. Responding to prior written inquiries of parliamentar-

6. Number reported on Berliner Rundfunk, news, August 13, 1989.

7. Somewhat frustrated by the discrepancies between the two circulating transcriptions of Mielke's speech (besides the official records of the *Volkskammer* reprinted in relevant parts in Otto 2000, 699–700, there is a transcript originally published by *Frankfurter Rundschau* on November 16, 1989, which was reprinted later in *Deutschland Archiv*, vol. 23.1, 121ff.), I have obtained a copy of the telecast of the People's Chamber session including Mielke's speech made by GDR television and transcribed it myself. This tape was especially valuable as the cameramen were interspersing views of the speaker with glances across the assembly to capture the reaction of the audience. I was thus much better able to form an impression of the emotions of the speaker as well as those of the audience.

8. Although the Western media had always reported about the latest Federal Republic of Germany (FRG) credit to the GDR, it would have been hard for the members to assemble from such reports a complete picture, especially about the accumulated extent of the GDR's hard currency debt.

ians, Erich Mielke followed to deliver his first and only speech in the parliament to which he belonged since 1957 (i.e., as long as he was minister). No doubt exhausted from the preceding week's events, no doubt deeply worried that his life's work of building socialism in Germany was in grave danger, the eighty-one-year-old Mielke spoke extemporaneously—against well-established socialist practice and personal habit. I present this speech in some length, not only to contextualize the famous quote, but also because his speech offers an excellent overview over the Stasi's self-understanding and the means by which the party state GDR made sense of itself.

> Dear Delegates! I want to begin by clarifying the duties of our employees in the Ministry of State Security vis-à-vis the working people, vis-à-vis our people. We are sons and daughters of the working class, we come from all social strata . . . We represent the interests of the working people. This is our highest charge from the People's Chamber and we have always, we have always tried to fulfill it.[9]

To Mielke's subsequent assertion that the Stasi has an "extraordinarily high contact with the working people," the assembly responded with laughter, to which he replied, visibly surprised and slightly irritated:

> Yes we have the contact, we have that contact, you [intimate form][10] will see, you will see in a second why. I am not afraid of answering here without notes. That's democracy too. I have not worked out my speech before hand . . . We have had first the task, this was the most important thing, to uncover everything that was directed against peace. And we have supplied first-rate information about the development which has led us to where we stand now [the accomplishments of the GDR], comrades, not just for the GDR, but for the socialist camp as a whole. Second, and I say this only briefly, one of the most important tasks was the strengthening of our socialist economy . . . and many in the hall agree that we do excellent work in this regard. More

9. This sentence is interesting. The Stasi called itself the "sword and the shield of the party," and it took orders not from parliament, but from the party. The German original of the sentence is a bit more ambiguous with regard to the connections between charge and charging agency. Although this may reflect a momentary insight into rhetorical exigencies (taking parliament more seriously and treating it as independent), this appears hardly as the execution of some grand strategy, as the ensuing exchange amply illustrates.

10. Party members shared a stipulated intimacy regarding their commitment to an overarching goal in the face of which they were all equals, that is, "comrades." This was reflected in public by the use of the intimate, second person singular form of address. Accordingly, Mielke could be understood as implying that everybody present was sharing in that intimacy bestowed by a common goal, that for all practical purposes everybody assembled was a party member, or that conversely nonmembers did not matter. The reaction of the audience bears out this interpretation.

I need not say, I think. We have contributed extraordinarily, comrades, to the strengthening of our economy.

At this point Mielke had to face a heckler, who said:

Rising to order, I request that it be respected, not all members of this chamber are comrades, I request . . . [tumultuous noise in the background].

To that Mielke replied:

My apologies, this is only a . . . this is only natural love for humankind (*natürliche Menschenliebe*) . . . [applause] this is just a formality . . . [tumultuous protest] I love . . . [tumultuous protest] but I love all . . . [loud protest] all human beings . . . [loud laughter] well, but I love, but I commit myself to this.

Mielke then went on to explain that the Stasi, since its inception in 1950, continuously tried to address the problems of the GDR by operating as a kind of problem identification and information transmission system that informed the right people and frequently made suggestions for improvement. He especially mentioned problems with people fleeing the country, naming physicians and teachers as particularly important cases. He beseeched the audience to believe him that the Stasi did in fact report about all of these problems, adding that regrettably not all information provided found appropriate consideration. So he closed:

We have in this respect always seen what is important: maintenance of peace, the strengthening of the economy of the GDR, to see to it that the working people can communicate their troubles and problems.

Since then, in social memory, this speech has shrunk to the words *Ich liebe Euch doch alle!* (But I love you all!).[11] This phrase more than any other became a trope signifying the utter senility of the GDR leadership to some, its unbelievable aloofness to others, and its sheer cynicism to yet others. However, by the end of this book it will become clear, I hope, why it was probably none of these, as Mielke, not in the word sense alone but in that of the social arrangements that were GDR socialism, is likely to have meant what he said. For him as for the officers I interviewed, Stasi work was work for the party that was at the same time an expression of love for humanity even if the Stasi tried to uproot the most tender sprouting of extraparty civil society, even if it prepared

---

11. None of the more widely circulated transcripts report Mielke to have said "But I love you all!" Probably picked up for reasons of prosodic memorability these words got further popularized in the title of one of the first collections of Stasi documents published in 1990 (Mitter and Wolle 1990).

to imprison in times of war thousands of GDR citizens who were deemed unreliable and thus perceived as an acute security burden.

Mielke enacted in this speech particular understandings about the political institutions and organizations in the GDR, his personal role in it, and that of the bureaucracy and the party he represented. So did the ADN news commentary lambasting the refugees in early October, and Honecker in his unfazed, flat expression of confidence in the victory of socialism in his fortieth anniversary speech. Parliamentarians calling upon Mielke to justify the Stasi, or shouting or laughing at him during his speech, enacted what at least in this particular public location were absolutely *novel* understandings of the polity GDR. And so did the snowballing number of people taking the courage to participate in demonstrations first only in Leipzig and Berlin and then throughout the country (on the day of Mielke's speech alone, so estimated the police, a record 1 million). The refugees who took their two-stroke engine Trabbis across the Hungarian-Austrian border in late summer with nothing but what they had packed for their annual vacation at Lake Balaton had enacted their understandings of party, state, and country by seizing the first opportunity to flee. The people interpreting any of the events I just described, homing in on Mielke's words or Honecker's or the commentary on the evening news, ventured theirs.

Bill Sewell (2005, 127) argues that "events should be conceived of as sequences of occurrences that result in transformations of structures. Such sequences begin with a rupture of some kind—that is, a surprising break with routine practice. . . . But whatever the nature of the initial rupture, an occurrence only becomes a historical event, in the sense in which I use the term, when it touches off a chain of occurrences that durably transforms pervious structures and practices." What made the fall of 1989 "hot" in Eastern Europe, a "transformational event" in Sewell's sense, is precisely such a string of occurrences (or more basic events) building on each other in an amplifying manner to what Abbott (2001b, chap. 8) calls a "turning point." At the end stood the demise of an institutional order (or structure). Political epistemology, as I defined it in the preface, is a particular way of looking at such institutional transformations by focusing on processes of understanding. In all of the events building up to the dissolution of socialism, understandings were deployed in action or verbally or both. What was new or disruptive about these deployments was that understandings were, as in Mielke's speech, all of a sudden met with a challenge, an unexpected reaction or response. These had effects on the understandings themselves in the sense that some got weakened, others strengthened, background assumptions came to be problematized, new understandings emerged, old ones got transformed. And all of this had an effect on the reproduction of socialism as an institutional arrangement. In the remainder of the chapter I will enter a more theoretical mode of analysis, drawing on Mielke's speech as an example. What I will explore is, first, what I mean by understanding and by institutions as well as their interrelation. An important question in all of this will be how we can imagine these events to build onto each other, in what today is frequently called a "path-dependent manner" (Pierson 2004, 20ff.), both in maintaining and altering institutional arrangements.

TOWARD A SOCIOLOGY OF UNDERSTANDING

In the preface I defined political epistemology as a particular field of inquiry. As such it needs a suitable method of analysis. For the purposes of political epistemology it is important that a method is chosen that does not lead to a simple mapping between types of polities and types of knowledge making. That would lead us straight back to the comparison of forms that I argued should be avoided if we want to remain open to the possibility to learn from the socialist experience. Instead, it is important to find a method of inquiry allowing for a genuinely dynamic analysis of the interactions between institutions and understandings. What is equally important is to devise an analytical framework in which the relationship between power and understanding can actually by problematized. Now that I have talked about it so much, the obvious question to begin with is, "What is understanding?"

Understanding and Its Modes

We say "I understand," for example, when we want to emphasize that we got the meaning of a communication: when we feel we know what the world looks like from another's perspective; when we grasp the significance of an event, a person, or an object; when we begin to see through other persons' intentions and expectations; or when we finally know how to play a particular phrase on the piano. We say "now I understand!" when we just had an insight, when we tried to fit the pieces of a puzzle together (game, murder mystery, office intrigue . . .) and finally have come to see how everything hangs together. In all of these cases, understanding is achieved in a process of *orientation*; it emerges in the realization of what is what, and where located in relation to one another. This process is at once analytical and synthetic. It involves the *differentiation* of a totality into elements and simultaneously their qualitative *integration*. Orientation is principally indexical; it cannot be sought in the abstract but must be undertaken relative to specific goals, desires, intentions, interests, or pursuits, that is, from a particular point of view.[12] As some-

---

12. Even when understanding itself becomes the pursuit, or an entertaining parlor game, either previous endeavors of a similar kind (an ongoing practice, a tradition) or some form of simulation ("let us assume . . .") is needed to root and situate the process of understanding.

thing we do, understanding can also be seen as an interdependent two-level *ordering* of the world into a nonrelevant, blurry background and a *relevant* foreground thrown into sharp relief by specifying its configuration. In consequence, understandings necessarily stipulate a particular *form* in which the world *exists*. In sum: *Understanding is a process of orientation from within a particular pursuit in a specific context, which orders relevant aspects of the world by simultaneously differentiating and integrating it, thus stipulating a practical ontology.*[13] Understanding can be undertaken for its own sake, for the curiosity it satisfies, and for the pleasure it affords. Yet, the preponderant reason why we seek understanding is, as the hermeneutic tradition has argued time and again, that in the absence of instinctual determination we need it because it enables us to act (e.g., Herder 1953, 745ff.; Gehlen 1997, 32ff.).

In practice, understanding comes about in a number of different modes deeply intertwined with each other. Analytically, however, it is useful to distinguish them because they achieve their constitutive ordering in different ways, perhaps one could even say in different media offering—like oil, watercolor, or pastel for the painter, or compass, sextant, clock, and map for the navigator—characteristic possibilities and limitations with regard to how they enable processes of differentiation and integration. Technically speaking, each mode has its own way of producing understanding, its own poetics, which makes it relatively autonomous vis-à-vis the others. Each of our five senses, for example, differentiates and integrates the world in characteristic ways. And each sense can comment on the other in the production of a synthetic impression of an object. For instance, something that looks like snow but tastes sweet is in all likelihood rather powder sugar; somebody who speaks like a communist but wears a designer suit is in all likelihood a salon socialist (for a spy would not make so simple a mistake). The various symbolic media in which we think—images, the natural and the various formal

---

13. As I have indicated in the preface, the concept of understanding as I use it here stands in the tradition of hermeneutic social thought. Nevertheless, as stated here it bears resemblance with W. I. Thomas's notion of "the definition of a situation" (1923, 42). In conjunction with the "Thomas theorem" (1928, 572) it was coined and used with the same constitutive intentions as "understanding" in the older tradition. I will maintain the older language here not only because it has seniority rights, but also because Thomas's recourse to the verb "to define" introduces undesirable voluntaristic connotations. I also prefer the term understanding to "schema" as the latter term, much like "knowledge" (see the discussion on pp. xxii–xxiii), obscures the processual character, the becoming and necessary maintenance of what it purports to depict. The term "frame" was originally used by Goffmann (1974) in a very different sense. Its recent appropriation in the movement's literature (e.g., Snow et al. 1986) is problematic where it aims to do more than emphasize the instrumental character of deploying certain understandings. Using it as a synonym for "schema" or "understanding" brings into play a rather misleading metaphor.

languages—order the world according to different principles. Here, too, mutual qualification is important: a newspaper article that discursively strives to provide a "balanced" account of the relative merits and demerits of two electoral candidates can become partisan through the supplementary photographs; a difficult text can become more transparent through a graph, and so forth.

This wealth of possibilities notwithstanding, in what follows I will limit myself to only three modes, that is, discursive, emotive, and kinesthetic understandings. To see how they are different and yet conjointly constitutive of certain objects, consider the theory of history as a succession of epoch defining class conflicts. This discursive understanding may find an emotional counterpart in the actual hatred of people who are considered to be members of the opposing class and the loving solidarity for members of one's own class. Corresponding kinesthetic understandings may be embodied in certain patterns of movement through a cityscape, such that the territory of the class enemy is avoided wherever possible while one's bodily posture changes with home and enemy territory and the senses are exposed to some parts of the world rather than to others. Friend-foe distinctions are thus made simultaneously in three different dimensions.

The restriction to a distinction between discursive, emotive, and kinesthetic understandings owes itself, to some degree, to judgments of relevance for the historical context under investigation in this book. It will become apparent that the interaction between emotive and discursive understandings is important to appreciate the biographical trajectories of both communist functionaries and dissidents. Close attention to kinesthetic understandings is analytically also revealing in this particular case. In a city and a former nation-state divided by a wall severing family and friendship networks arbitrarily into an eastern and a western half restrictions on movement are important. In a country where activities in public spaces are tightly controlled, the freedom to go or not to go to certain places and to do or not to do certain things, the ability to see, hear, smell, taste, and touch certain things becomes one of the ultimate sources of value. However, this study's limitation to discursive, emotive, and kinesthetic understandings also owes itself to the data-gathering possibilities open to a historical ethnographer. Even where I wish I could have differentiated sensory modes of understanding more directly, as for example in experiences of imprisonment, I could not do so for lack of sufficiently detailed or sufficiently plentiful data. A differentiation into various kinds of symbolic media is not necessary, because the people I studied have used mostly different registers of German (rather than game theory, for example) to understand discursively the political world in which they lived. However, where necessary I will differentiate ordinary spoken German from the technical jargon of the party and that of the secret police. Since my primary access point to the past is discourse, even the identification of emotive and kinesthetic understandings poses methodological challenges that force me to consider them to a much lesser degree than I should have liked and would have been possible in a participant observation study.

What are, then, some of the fundamental differences between the poetics of discursive, emotive, and kinesthetic understandings? As a fully symbolic medium, *discourse* is more flexible than any other in making complex distinctions between a plentitude of elements, their qualitative characteristics, ways of existence, forms of connection, and so on. Precisely because they are so versatile in enabling the kinds of understandings we need for our everyday pursuits, natural languages often seem to blend with the world. Their limits come to the fore only in moments where we seem to "bump up against our languages," for example, when we become aware of lexical restrictions (compelling us to borrow from other languages, or to forge neologisms), suddenly bothersome conventions of language use (which we then might feel tempted to transgress), as well as limiting grammatical forms (which may urge us to think up noncanonical discourse or even to invent alternatives, for example, formal languages).

Michael Silverstein (e.g., 2004) has pointed out that the flexibility and versatility of discourse owes itself to the fact that it is perhaps better understood as a plurality of intersecting and interacting poetics that are projected onto a singular strand of discursive behavior. He places this insight into a longer linguistic tradition in which various authors have proposed to grasp this poetic complexity in different ways. Jakobson (e.g., 1960) has provided a much-cited approach in which he distinguishes six "functions" or levels of semiotic operations characterizing every linguistic utterance in varying degrees. He argues that besides communicating a particular content, utterances are arranged more or less artfully; that they open channels of communication while containing information about how to decode the message; that they communicate something about the emotive and cognitive state of the speaker while addressing the hearer in a particular way. More recently, much interest has been garnered by Bakhtin's (e.g., 1981) notions of the "dialogic" character of discourse, which he also describes as an immanent "heteroglossia" analyzable in terms of a simultaneity of different "voices" within one and the same text. The point of his analysis is to show that one and the same text often sets various, possibly even contradictory, perspectives in relationship to one another. It is the particular merit of linguistic anthropology to have explored the significance of the interactions of these multiple poetics for the dynamics of interaction and ultimately the macrocultural context (e.g., Silverstein 1993, 2004; Gal and Irvine 2000; Keane 2003).

A number of intellectual traditions have expounded on the ways in which symbols—and a fortiori discursive understandings—enable human beings to escape the strictures of the immediate context of action.[14] Their common denominator is that symbols allow human beings the (re-)presentation of the absent, both in terms of time and space. Symbols can translate the there and then into the here and now or conversely open the here and now to a there and then. Thus symbols do not only expand our spatial horizon beyond eyesight and earshot. They also span up temporality as we know it, with a past bleeding into the present constantly ready to leap ahead of itself into a future. In this way, symbols afford humans a world besides the world, a fifth dimension, if you like, in which they can play with ifs and ors, combinations and recombinations. Symbols and with it discourse afford human beings imagination, fantasy, counterfactuals, pure fiction. In the realm of discourse, the world can be differentiated and integrated in the lofty modality of the "as-if."

The poetics of *emotive understandings* cannot even be thematized as long as emotions are seen as erratic unsystematic eruptions. For rationalists, the very term emotive understanding is but a contradiction in terms.[15] Even though the sentimentalists, the romantics, and other critics of the Enlightenment had already emphasized "passion," "sentiment," or "affection" as a valuable source of orientation different and yet connected to reason, a real breakthrough came only with the work of Freud. In his wake it became commonplace that our actions are only poorly comprehended as oriented by discursive understandings alone. Instead he has shown how they are just as much guided by our (partially unconscious) wishes and fears, desires and aversions (2000e). What is more, our discursive understandings of the world, our very rationality along with our efforts to maintain ourselves and our social standing, all need to be sponsored by desires to become effective (2000f).[16] Thus, emotive understandings structure the world in the first instance into variously desirable and undesirable components that attain

14. Among them are, besides the already mentioned classics of hermeneutic social thought, American pragmatism (e.g., James 1956, 1975; Dewey 1997), early Soviet psychology and linguistics (esp. Vygotsky 1975, 1986; Volosinov 1973), the German philosophical anthropology of the 1920s and 1930s (e.g., Cassirer 1997; Gehlen 1997), and phenomenology (e.g., Schütz and Luckmann 1984, 1981).

15. In his ideal-typical scheme of action, even Weber (1980) still considers "affective" and "traditional" (i.e., habituated) action to hover at the margin of what can be called meaningful.

16. Freud has called our ordering of the world through desire the *pleasure principle*. He emphasized that we cannot live by desire alone, because we come to understand that following up on pleasure and displeasure may actually hurt us in the long run. He called *reality principle* the formation of meta-understandings allowing us to ponder whether or not we should follow our desires. Even though the latter may take shape in the form of discursive exhortations (internalized as a voice of authority) these, Freud makes clear, would remain ineffective if they were not themselves invested with desire.

their particular quality in the course of experience. According to Freud, desires and aversions orient action by directing it. But they do not do so in an unambiguous fashion; instead, they can quickly draw us into a maelstrom of different directions. The possibility of therapy shows that these configurations of desire can be rearranged not only in ordinary lived life but also by systematic efforts to work with them (2000b).

I understand emotions as the specific qualitative forms desire and aversion can take. The pioneering work of Silvan Tomkins (1962; 1963) on individual emotions ("shame," "fear," "anger," etc.) has yielded valuable insights about their poetics (Nathanson 1992). In comparison with discursive understanding, the poetics of emotion follows a much more limited, less differentiable, but also a much more immediate and thus forceful, way of understanding. Emotions differentiate between four classes of elements: feeling subjects, objects (which can literally be anything including things, fantasies, other people, self, thoughts, other feelings, activities, situations), emotive connectors (e.g., shame, love, hate, fear, curiosity, anger, frustration, nostalgia),[17] and finally triggers. They integrate these elements in the form of episodes such that the trigger gives rise to an emotive connection between subject and object, which becomes available to the subject in altered states of mind and body.[18] This ordering is oriented in two ways. Emotions, their strength and clarity, highlight the *relevance* of the object to the subject. And by virtue of the fact that emotions are experienced as pleasurable or displeasurable, they create powerful *motives* for the subject to seek more or less exposure to the object in the future. Emotions are immediately available to us through altered bodily states that make us present in our bodies and in the here and now. Even though there is still much controversy over what emotions are and how they work (and even whether they do constitute a unified set of phenomena (e.g., Griffith 1997), there is little disagreement today that emotions are key in signaling the relevance of various elements of the world to us (Frijda, Manstead, and Bern 2000; Reddy 2001). Thereby (acknowledged

---

17. The question of whether or not there are biologically encoded "basic emotions" (e.g., Tomkins 1962, 1963; Izard 1971; Ekman 1972) that can be usefully distinguished from culturally variant "higher" or "cognitive" emotions is mute for the purposes of this study (see Ekman and Davidson [1994] for a positive and Reddy [2001] and Griffith [1997] for a critical evaluation of this claim). All that matters here is the much less controversial proposition that emotions can provide orientations that are at least partially autonomous from discourse (for a support of this claim see especially Damasio 1994, 1999; and Ledoux 1996).

18. Often the object is the trigger, for example, when lovers see their beloved and embrace them in love. But this is not necessarily the case. Lovers might become awash in feelings of love for their beloved while being reminded of them through the gestures of a third person. Emotions also do not always have a specific object or trigger; sometimes objects and triggers become generalized (everything feels the same way), in which case we speak of moods.

or not), newer emotions research comes back to the older Freudian insight that emotions, that is, qualitatively differentiated desires and aversions, motivationally hook us to the world.

The poetic limits of modes of understanding are often the flipsides of their strengths. Emotions are always focused on the subject. I cannot feel (without intervening symbols) the relationship between two arbitrary objects, let us say two people, unless I identify with one of them. Otherwise I can only feel how their relationship affects me, from which I can then draw inferences in some symbolic medium about their relationship. In this sense (and only this sense) the adage that emotions are wholly subjective, that is, incapable of objective ways of looking at the world, is quite to the point. Although emotive understanding has in its unfolding its own temporality, and although it can acquire temporality in the sense that one particular emotional episode connects us to similar episodes in the past while also creating expectations about the future, such temporality can only be attained through symbolic mediation. The current fear of bears can only become a fear of future encounters with bears through symbolic intervention (minimally one needs the image of a bear). A fortiori, and perhaps even more importantly, emotions do not have a subjunctive mode, that is, they cannot be entertained hypothetically. They are there or they are not, and if they are not, they can only be represented symbolically. Feeling an emotion is, however, very different from symbolizing it.[19] Yet, often the process of representing emotions in discourse goes hand in hand with profound transformations of what we feel. As a first step this typically goes hand in hand with a shift in the object of the current emotive understanding away from the world to the represented emotion. In this sense we use words to entertain regrets about emotions past or hopes about better feelings. In effect, then, emotive understandings are firmly rooted in the present, much more so than discursive understandings whose mediation between here and there, then and now may also make us feel lost in the nowhere. The space of imagination, the fifth dimension of human life, can quickly turn into the limbo of neither here nor there, neither now nor then. These two characteristics of emotive understandings, their subject-centricity and embodied presentism, allow them to be especially effective indicators of relevance for the presence. Emotions, not discourse, make us feel alive.

The poetics of *kinesthetic understandings* arranges bodies or parts of bodies, most importantly our five senses, in time and space (Gehlen 1997, 175; Gebauer and Wulf 1992, chap. 2). Its differentiating principle is the play

---

19. Seen from this perspective, there is a gap left by the extant anthropology (e.g., Lutz 1988; Rosaldo 1980) and sociology of emotions (e.g., Hochschild 1989) by having focused much more on local discourses about emotions than on their actual feeling. Given the enormous methodological difficulties involved in studying the feeling of emotions this is, of course, not surprising.

of presences and absences, of a spatial "here, but not there," and a temporal "now, but not then" for a body or any of its parts. The integrating principle of kinesthetic understandings is the sequencing of the "now-heres," or
"chronotopes" (Bakhtin 1981), in front of an undifferentiated background of
relevant temporal and spatial extensions, of inaccessible now-theres, then-
theres, here-thens (which can be made visible through symbolic mediation).
There is an old saw that illustrates in a flash what I mean. It goes something
like this. "Playing the piano is totally simple: you just have to hit the right
keys, at the right moment, for the right duration with the correct fingers
and do this again and again." For the purposes of this study it is important
to see that kinesthetic understanding is not only manifest in the skills of
musicians, artisans, or sportswomen, it is for example also part of seating
arrangements at dinner tables, the walking patterns of tourists, shoppers, or
workers. What is particularly interesting about these larger scale sequences
is that they ground the body in a particular sensual perspective. They govern what is seen, heard, smelled, tasted, and touched. In other words, they
spatially and temporally structure experience. At the same time, contingent
events produce orderings of people and objects invested with particular understandings. They associate people and/or objects in complementary proximity; they also juxtapose people and/or objects becoming obstacles for each
other, triggering related emotive understandings. Thus the very kinesthetic
aspect of events can become a wellspring of new understandings, forming
the root of what Sewell (2005) has emphasized as the transformational character of events. Since bodily movements are part of almost every action, kinesthetic understandings play a significant role in the development of agency,
which becomes actually performing the differentiations and sequencing in
question. In the case of East Germans, the significance of kinesthetic understandings for a sense of agency was for many citizens dramatically highlighted by the fact that spatial mobility was limited not only by the Wall but
also by a number of other spatial regimes enforced through the allotment of
apartments, vacation spots, means and speed of travel, and the like.

These different poetics enable a number of interesting dynamic relationships or dialectics between discursive, emotive, and kinesthetic understandings. First, there is mutual commenting, which may be both amplifying and/
or differentiating. On the one hand the mutually amplifying coordination of
discourse, emotion, and bodily movement is central to any successful ritual;
it is the mutually supportive coordination of many layers of understanding
as an encompassing experience that lends it reproductive or transformative epistemic force. In chapter 1, I will show how such an alignment was
moralized as the ideal of the new socialist human being, and how state propaganda did in fact try to create it intentionally not only within designated

propaganda events but also as a general condition of socialist life. On the other hand, we all know that those who watch us take our postures, gestures, and emotional displays as qualifications of what we say. The simultaneous performance of different modes of understanding can reveal ambiguities or even contradictions that might take us by surprise if we could see them side by side. Now imagine a truly Shakespearean plot. What happens to the exemplary communist who talks, feels, and walks class warfare, if, perhaps at first unbeknownst to her, she falls in love with a bourgeois beauty? The question is, then, under what circumstances would the emotive understanding prevail or fail? Under what conditions would this love lead to the transformation of the kinesthetic and discursive understandings? What would the social arrangements have to look like for contradictory understandings to continue to coexist reasonably peacefully?

Second, changes in understandings sometimes begin in one modality to spread only later to others. Discourse can be both leader and trailer for kinesthetic and emotive understandings. To stay within the above example: class-hatred can be cultivated in response to the theory of history as class warfare. And yet, that theory may make sense precisely because one felt first uncomfortable encountering certain kinds of people in certain locations. Such lags in the ordering of the world produced by different modes of understanding will be significant in later chapters plotting the dynamics of political understandings among Stasi officers, opposition members, and secret informants.

Mielke again

Armed with this set of theoretical understandings about understandings, we can now orient ourselves in Mielke's speech by differentiating and integrating it according to the principles just discussed. I have already described the situation in which he speaks. The pursuit from within which Mielke performs his understandings is a justification of the Stasi in the face of two main lines of attack. There are party-internal critics who have voiced their concern that the secret police continued as a Stalinist holdout after the dictator's death, a "state within a state" that has been chiefly responsible for corrupting the good intentions of well-meaning communists. Their critique converges with that of a wider population not necessarily committed to socialism, which has come to see in the Stasi the agency that epitomizes the abuses of governmental power—as manifested most recently in the mass arrests and police brutality in the context of the fortieth anniversary celebrations. Mielke answers these criticisms with a speech that is, although short and anything but beautiful, a virtual enactment of the party's social

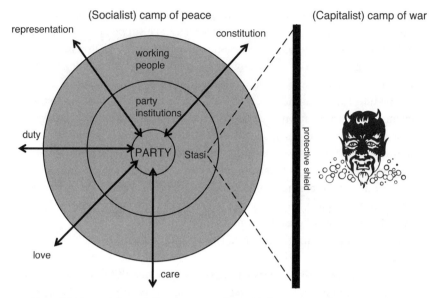

Figure 0.1. The socialist social imaginary according to Mielke

imaginary.[20] Mielke discursively differentiates his political world into a number of relevant players: There is a shifting "we"; there are the "employees in the Ministry of State Security," the "People's Chamber," the "working people," the "socialist camp" (also known as the "camp of peace") and, without naming it, the nonsocialist world (implicitly identified with the "camp of war"). At its core, this is a concentrically structured order in whose focal point rests the party, the root of the "we," the target of his actually performed and until quite recently normatively prescribed identification and self-location. From this center radiate party state organizations, such as the People's Chamber and the Stasi. Mielke frequently identifies both of these organizations through their link to the center. Members of both organizations are to him comrades in arms through and with the party for a shared goal. And thus to him anybody in this second circle can be naturally addressed in the informal second person.[21] The outer circle, finally, is made up of "the (working) people." This order specifies the fundamental claim of the socialist government to legitimacy as *of* the proletariat *through* the party *for* the proletariat *against* the capitalist exploiters.

20. The term imaginary is of Lacanian origin and was introduced into the social sciences by Castoriadis (1987). Recently Charles Taylor (2004) has renewed interest in it. What I mean by "social imaginary" is an integrated (but not necessarily coherent) set of discursive, emotive and kinesthetic understandings about social life. As such it is more encompassing than ideology.
21. In standard German, formal address calls for the use of the third person plural in connection with "Herr," "Frau," or title.

Mielke does not specify all the relationships between the various players directly. But given the indexical logic of the overall order, the unnamed ones can easily be inferred from his description of center-periphery relations. The notions of duty and care figure prominently in this respect. Mielke characterizes the relationship of the Stasi to the working people as a dedicated form of caregiving encompassing the maintenance of peace, the strengthening of the economy, the representation of interests, the lending of voice. The relationship of caring obtains an interesting note through the repeated use of the possessive in describing the center's ownership of the periphery: "our [i.e., the party's] employees in the Ministry . . ." and "our [i.e., the Stasi's] people."[22] In the other direction Mielke invokes the duty of the Stasi to provide "first-rate information" to the center here and elsewhere in the socialist world. By presenting the Stasi as a duty-bound caregiver, he indirectly presents an expectation of the party to behave likewise vis-à-vis the secret police. Feeling increasingly singled out and put on the spot, this is what his own officers expected him to demand when they watched him give this speech on television. Finally, using the standard socialist trope of the "sons and daughters of the working people," Mielke describes the center as generated by the periphery in such a way that the center can truthfully be seen as a part capable of representing the whole.

Mielke emotionally situates himself vis-à-vis this discursively constructed order. He presents his model of care and duty relations with solemnity; the possessives are saturated with pride. And so is his enumeration of the achievements of the Stasi. There is also exasperation in Mielke's voice, accessible to the observer through a number of ellipses carrying a sense of "you know already," "all of this is self-evident," "why do I need to tell you now." There seems to be some unacknowledged fear in his hyperbole of insisting on the contact with "the people," or when he repeatedly emphasizes that the Stasi has transmitted all the relevant information about the country's problems to the appropriate places. Yet, there also appears to be hope in Mielke, that reminding everybody of the common core assumptions has the power to hold together what seems to fall apart. What is remarkable in watching the speech is its emotional arch: he begins with solemn calm, and through the challenges he works himself into a desperate passion, to then finally vacate the podium disoriented by the lacking applause that just weeks ago would have been certain to come forth.

When Mielke describes the relationship between the Stasi and the work-

---

22. Interestingly, this combination of duty, care, and possession mirrors Prussian king Frederic the Great's "I am the first servant of my state," which is, as an article of faith in German nationalism (demonstrating superiority over Louis XIV's "L'état c'est moi"). Whether Mielke or anybody watching him then had associations of this kind is hard to tell.

ing people emphatically as one of "extraordinarily high contact," his speech becomes derailed for the first time. The intervention at this precise moment is, in keeping with the historical situation, at once surprising and predictable. On the one hand, Mielke's claim is no more than a much-repeated adage of the party—a credo central to its legitimacy. Had it been presented to the same assembly on January 13 of the same year, it would have passed without further comment; had it been made on September 13, careful observers might have noticed a number of raised eyebrows, furrowed foreheads, or pained smiles in the hall. On the other hand, making it now, on November 13, simply makes his performed understandings appear so inadequate to enough members of the audience that they laugh it off publicly. The reason is simple: the connection between the party-state, its organs, and the people has been at issue during the last four weeks of political turmoil. As Mielke is speaking 1 million people are gathering in several bigger cities throughout the country to participate in this day's Monday demonstrations, the biggest so far on record, to press for the continuation and deepening of political reforms. The slogan galvanizing these demonstrations is *Wir sind das Volk!* (We are the people!), indicating that the government claiming to represent the people has lost contact with it. Yet to Mielke this point of contact to the working people is central. He emphasizes this gesturally by putting his hand to his heart while he is responding to his critics.

When Mielke goes on to celebrate the successes of the Stasi in maintaining peace and strengthening the economy, when he presents these successes as commonly shared knowledge among comrades in the hub of his concentric socialist universe, he gets interrupted again. Interestingly the heckler does not attack Mielke's substantive claims, both of which have been challenged by the events of the preceding weeks as well as through the debates in the People's Chamber immediately preceding his speech. The very notion of the "maintenance of peace" obtained a different ring in wider circles of the population through the thousands of arrests and allegations of police abuse for which the Stasi was often thought to be responsible. As for the situation of the economy, the party leadership just had to undergo a sobering reconsideration of its actual state (cf. Schürer 1996; Krenz 1999), which led to the demise of Günter Mittag, the politburo member in charge of economic affairs who was, together with Mielke, one of Honecker's closest confidants. And in the barely four days in which the Wall has been open, 2 million of the GDR's nearly 17 million citizens, who in their majority scarcely harbored illusions about the economic situation in their country to begin with, have felt compelled to revise their comparative assessment of the standard of living in East Germany further downward. In view of this, the heckler's call to order insisting that not every member of the People's Chamber is a party member might sound rather harmless, because it does not seem to challenge

Mielke's claims about the Stasi's contributions to the GDR's economy, which is once again presented as an achievement. And yet, the heckler's intervention is *in potentia* already a full-blown attack on the very core of Mielke's understandings, because it denies the taken-for-granted unity of the center, the *communitas* between the heckler and Mielke, between the SED and the block parties, and by extension between the People's Chamber and the Stasi, and in the last instance between the party and the people. Even if these consequences might not have been fully discursively articulable by the heckler, he certainly began to make this break in his emotive understandings, which come most clearly to the fore in the fact that he is obviously vexed by Mielke's speech and what it implies about him.

The understandings inherent in Mielke's retort to the heckler can perhaps best be described as those of a "loving but misunderstood father" who intertwines two lines of defense. The first addresses what to him appears as the correction of the facts underlying the, in his eyes, unjust withdrawal of affection by the heckler who is treated like an errant son. Mielke argues that the differentiation insisted upon by the heckler is in fact merely a nominal one. No doubt, until quite recently this was true. The other parties represented in the People's Chamber were completely assimilated into the national front dominated by the ruling SED.[23] That fact is even documented in practice during the very same session of the People's Chamber. When time comes to elect a new prime minister (*Vorsitzender des Ministerrates*), everything goes ahead according to the old script: The SED nominated a candidate of its own (Hans Modrow, the Dresden party chief who has the reputation to be a reformer), and the chamber votes in his favor—if not entirely unanimously this time, for *one* member votes against him.[24] The outcome of this election was therefore preordained in the old sense. And yet, the fact that Mielke's insinuation leads to tumultuous protest indicates that the heckler's understanding of a real difference between the parties is in fact more widely shared in the house. The unity at the hub of a concentric model of socialism shows cracks in performance. And it is noteworthy that there was a second election this day. The house needed a new speaker. This election became

---

23. This does not mean that the block parties were not, in the early years of the GDR, kept separate precisely because this distinction could be taken as a real distinction by outside observers. But then the ideology of the party also still assumed that there were de facto different classes in the GDR needing their own representation even if in alliance with the party of the proletariat. However, later it was assumed that the GDR had established the basic structures of socialism that entailed that there were no longer any real class differences. Hence, there was no need for representational differentiation.

24. This made for an awkward moment as the video recording of the session shows. The parliamentarians voted by open hand sign. Once the newly elected speaker announced the result, everybody turned around to find out who had voted no.

contrary to custom a fully competitive process with alternative candidates, second rounds, and all. The outcome of that election was contingent, opening new vistas of possibilities.[25] The People's Chamber session as a whole shows understandings on the move.

It is Mielke's second line of defense, however, that makes his last public act as a GDR leader appear farcical in the eyes of so many observers. He fleshes out his political understandings by adding a further relational dimension to his concentric model of socialism. He insists that addressing the parliamentarians as comrades is an expression of "natural love for humankind" (*natürliche Menschenliebe*). And for that he earns applause from some quarters. Obviously, that too struck a chord with some members of the assembly, not least, perhaps, because it was an antidivisional move. The next two times Mielke gears up to continue with his speech by invoking his love, he is answered with uproar, which may still be mostly the echo of the reaction to his argument that the distinction between comrades and members of other parties is merely formal in nature. When he adds, increasing volume, pitch, and emphasis, "all human beings," many in the hall burst into laughter. Mielke's understanding is thus branded as an absurdity, and right into his face by men and women who just weeks ago would have fallen head over heels to assure him of their solidarity. And all Mielke knows to do in this moment is to repeat the same understanding and connect it with a public declaration of commitment in an effort to authenticate it. But then he catches himself; with an apology accompanied by humorous gestures, he tries to stitch together what has so obviously come apart.

Forms of Validation

Mielke's speech, and in particular his exchange with the audience, shows an interesting contrasting deployment of political understandings, some discursive and some emotional, some kinesthetic. This exchange is notable because it catches a moment when several people's understandings, which were not too long ago still aligned with one another, begin to show clear signs of differentiation. The commonplaces of yesterday, the array of taken-for-granted assumptions about the world, become challenged. Mielke's claims about the Stasi's successes, his declaration of love for humankind, appear absurd—but only relative to some newer understandings that for some reason seem more adequate to the current historical moment. From the perspective of those

---

25. It would be quite interesting to find out what led the members of the house to proceed during different parts of the session according to different procedural logics mixing old ritual with the entirely unheard of. Alas, living far away from archives and participants, I had no opportunity to pursue it "on the side."

whose understandings become rapidly transformed, some parliamentarians included, Mielke appears stuck. And thus, yesterday's powerful man who instilled respect and fear in many becomes an object of ridicule. Of course, the contrast between the old and the new is fully indexical, for all of the members of parliament together seemed stuck, too, in the eyes of those whose understandings moved still faster. This includes the wider population who never quite saw the world as the party did and many of whom had already visited West Berlin. In fact, this very People's Chamber debate confirmed for many outside observers that the system was incapable of truly reforming itself. The near unanimous vote for the new prime minister was commonly cited as proof for this assessment. Given this glimpse into a process of transformation the question appears, how could we possibly account for such a movement in understanding? How could we begin to think about the influence of an event such as this People's Chamber debate on the understandings of those who participated in it or followed in it in the media?

The embodied participation in an event, its perception through the senses, the feelings it triggers, and the attempt to interpret discursively what is going on may suggest differentiations and/or integrations other than the ones brought into the event. In Marshall Sahlins' (e.g., 1987, 145) felicitous expression, they are put at "risk." Whatever the individual member of parliament or GDR citizen may have thought or felt about Mielke before the televised November 13 session of the People's Chamber, their very witnessing of Mielke heckled, laughed at, and sent from the podium without even as much as a final applause, their experience that these occurrences were no longer marked and reacted to as unwanted "incidences" (e.g., by immediately reprimanding hecklers, interrupting proceedings, or at least their broadcasting) may have suggested to people new understandings of the man Mielke (e.g., as "ridiculous" rather than "powerful") and the organization he represented (e.g., as "no longer in control" rather than "omnipresent"). Although events may suggest a restructuring of understandings in progress, these suggestions do not necessarily crowd out previous understandings. Instead, the process of transformation is typically more gradual; neither are older understandings given up right away, nor are newer differentiations and integrations transpiring from events accepted instantaneously.

The best way to think about such transformations is to see understandings as having two basic dimensions. Besides the ordering dimension saying something about the world (the dimension I have discussed so far), there is an ownership dimension indicating how "reliable," "useful," or "certain" this ordering appears to us. This distinction about degrees and quality of ownership is reflected by lexical differentiations we feel compelled to make regarding our discursive understandings. In present-day standard English, for example, people may choose carefully between the phrases "I understand that," "I suspect that," "I believe that," or "I know that." While "understanding" implies little more than grasping the significance of the ordering at hand (possibly uttered with sympathy for why one may end up ordering the world thus), "knowing" conveys trust that the ordering is indeed "true" in conjunction with the belief that this could be demonstrated in some acceptable way. These discursive differentiations are also used as metaphors to designate degrees of certainty in emotive or kinesthetic understandings. Accordingly, we speak of "uncertain," "lukewarm," or "strong" feelings as well as of a "wavering," "steady," or "sure" hand in accomplishing a kinesthetic task. In other words, if people thought before that "Stasi is the most powerful organization in the country" their witnessing of the People's Chamber session has certainly raised doubts.

Thinking in terms of various degrees and/or kinds of certainty directs our attention to understandings that do not have this characteristic, that is, understandings we think are "misguided," "misplaced," "inappropriate," "implausible," "merely hypothetical," or even plain "false." What we need to differentiate, then, are *actual* understandings, that is, those we do in fact hold in some way, using them to orient our actions and merely *possible* understandings, that is, those we do not enact because their orientational benefits are suspect. What we need to comprehend, then, is how our understandings do become actualized with various kinds and degrees of certainty (cf. Swidler 2001). The theoretical framework to answer this question is the cornerstone of chapters 3 and 4, but I will provide a brief summary of it here.

My central argument is that understandings come to be actualized or deactualized (if you like inhabited) through processes of *validation*. Analytically I distinguish three different kinds of engagements with the world producing three distinct forms of events with validating effects that de facto produce various kinds and degrees of ownership in understandings. There are, first, our interactions with other human beings in which we check their understandings against ours. Not everybody's approval or disapproval, belief, knowledge, or sense of reality matters to us. Instead, we make a number of distinctions about whom we are taking seriously in what way and in which context. This is to say that we are enmeshed in highly differentiated networks of authority relations with other human beings whose performance of their own understanding or direct verbal validation of ours we endow with validating force.[26] I call this form of validation *recognition*. Take Erich Mielke's speech before the People's Chamber again. His discursively and emotionally relevant understanding that Stasi had a close relationship with the people

---

26. That these networks can not simply be taken as determining "structure," but must be understood as processes in various degrees of institutionalization will become apparent below and especially in chapter 4.

was laughed away by some members who thus ventured to recognize it negatively. The fact that Mielke reacted to the laughter in a defensive way shows that he accepted the laughing parliamentarians as authorities, or at least that he feared that others might take them as such.

Second, there is the experience of the relative success and failure of our actions that are always structured by more or less explicit understandings of the world. Understandings become validated because they are seen retrospectively as useful guides to achieve what we wanted to accomplish. In other words, the "as if " implicit in understanding appears to be "true." Understanding and world seem to melt into each other. Conversely, if we fail we may account for this failure by pointing to misunderstandings we think now might have led us astray. Moreover, we often undertake little tests that we invest with validating power. Scientific experiments are tests of this sort as much as trials of courage, or probes of the limits of friendship or love. I call this form of validation *direct corroboration*. Through the course of events in the People's Chamber, Mielke's implicit understanding about the distribution of roles between him and the parliamentarians was negatively corroborated. The effect was quite visible in his discombobulation. When we draw conclusions from an event on whose unfolding we had no significant influence (say a historical event) for the validity of our understandings, *indirect corroboration* occurs. During his speech he argued that economic success and the maintenance of peace during the past forty years positively corroborated the work of the Stasi and ipso facto the understandings on and through which it proceeded. The kind of corroboration at stake here is indirect. One of the central problems of political understandings is that the most interesting ones can only be corroborated indirectly.

Finally, there is a "holding up" of particular understandings against what else we believe, know, or take for real against our desires as well as against our values. Understandings are rendered more credible by showing consistency with our existing knowledge, by answering to our desires, and by being compatible with our values; in cases where they are inconsistent, unanswerable, or incompatible, credibility is lost. I call this complex of validations *resonance*. The parliamentarians' new understanding that it is their right or even their role to call upon Mielke to defend the Stasi is sure to have resonated negatively with the departing minister. In his world, the general secretary had such authority, and so did the politburo, but the People's Chamber? Conversely, Mielke's attempt to invoke the unity of all present by invoking the old socialist order resonated negatively with the members who were laughing, heckling, or questioning him.

In sum, then, we come to inhabit our understandings through the encounter with others whose authoritative judgment recognizes ours; through the interactions with people and the material world in which success gives us confidence in our ways of ordering the world; and finally by checking understandings against our established knowledge, our values, feelings, desires, and skills.[27] Here is a very simple example to illustrate the differences characterizing these three forms. You believe that $2 \times 3 = 6$. Yet, you have some remaining doubt about your ability to multiply correctly. Asking your best friend, whom you respect as a math wiz, whether you are right is asking for recognition of your understanding. Translating the equation into action by putting twice three marbles into a bowl and counting them out one by one is a way to corroborate it directly. Remembering finally that multiplying a number by two is like adding that number to itself while being absolutely certain about your adding capabilities you perform the operation $3 + 3 = 6$ thus validating your belief qua resonance.

Meta-Understandings

From the historical and ethnographic records about how people produce knowledge about the world, it is clear that recognition, corroboration, and resonance can be thought of, felt about, and handled in astonishingly different ways. Performing an ordeal or a chicken oracle (e.g., Evans-Pritchard 1937) is a very different form of judicially accepted corroboration than a mental status exam or a DNA test, for example. The three forces can also be combined and distributed quite differently over different kinds of knowledge-producing practices in the same society. Present-day academic philosophers or mathematicians do not value direct corroboration very much; they do not try to validate their arguments by translating them into a domain of action that is markedly different from the manipulation of symbols. Instead, they highly value consistency, which is a particular form of resonance.[28] People who identify themselves as "experimental scientists" claim to have the inverse inclinations. Action outside of the realm of the manipulation of symbols is afforded primacy, which does not deny the fact that the systematic translation of what happens in this realm into symbols is not key to their enterprise. Even though the modern natural sciences may agree about the importance of corroboration, the ways in which it is produced

27. It bears mentioning here that although resonances and corroborations are crucially dependent on ongoing communicative interactions and thus recognitions, the former two are not reducible to the latter. I will elaborate this issue in chapter 3.

28. What philosophers and mathematicians do is an active, systematic production of resonances in the process of writing out (or merely thinking through step by step) an argument or a proof. This said, even philosophers and mathematicians cultivate understandings of what it means to practice their craft. Since these meta-philosophical and meta-mathematical ideas (e.g., of how to proceed in a proof) can be put to the test in practice, they can become corroborated.

and interpreted and the ways in which it interacts with the production of resonances are very different, for example in high-energy physics and in molecular biology (Knorr-Cetina 1999). Finally, the very same natural scientist who hails corroboration in producing knowledge about the world of matter can have very different ideas about how relevant political knowledge ought to be produced. We will get to know in Robert Havemann just such a man. He was not only a GDR science celebrity but also a Stalinist and later became the pivot of the GDR opposition in the 1970s and early 1980s.

What is needed, then, is a concept to capture *the ways in which we think, talk, feel, and do validity*, a concept addressing the fact that we have understandings about how appropriate understandings are made, actualized, and lost. A similar kind of reflexivity has been addressed in linguistics and in linguistic anthropology. The term that has won acceptance, denoting ideas about how language works, what about it matters, and how it ought to be properly deployed, is *linguistic ideology* (Silverstein 1979, 1993; Gal 1993; Gal and Irvine 2000).[29] Wherever discursive understandings explicitly address the making of all three forms of understanding, I will therefore speak in analogy of "epistemic ideologies."[30] However, the processes of generating, maintaining, changing, and distributing understandings are also regulated by practices, they are inscribed kinesthetically. The proverbial ostrich who is burying its head in the sand, or the popular imagery of the "three wise monkeys" (seeing no evil, hearing no evil, speaking no evil) remind us that the cultivation of particular understandings is contingent on bodily attunement. Many of these practices are by their very nature not explicit, not even consciously available. Finally, we often have acute feelings about our understandings, feelings that are not just spontaneous and momentary, but are also regularly attached to the process of crafting and validating them. The actualization of some understandings may be thought to entail happiness, while that of others may be understood to devastate. Advances in the certification of some understandings may be subject to pride, while the mere encounter with others may be seen as contaminating and shameful. While we fear the attainment of some understandings, we ardently desire others. Indeed, we may be afflicted with some kind of general dread at the loss of some understanding (Nietzsche's "horror vacui"), even if we may also feel

---

29. The idea that we should all spell the same word in the same way, even though our system of literation is far from unambiguous and in spite of the fact that we might, due to dialectal or idiosyncratic variations pronounce it differently, is such a linguistic ideology; and so is the romantic notion that languages express the soul of a people or the idea that language is a neutral medium fit to transport any information without shaping it.

30. The notion has proved fertile. Likewise in analogy—if closer to the original, Keane (2003) speaks of "semiotic ideologies," Hull (2003) of "graphic ideologies."

the better once certain understandings become deactualized (e.g., stigmata). Because emotions feel good or bad, because they carry what psychologists call a "hedonic tone," they can become motives to get, hold onto, change, or forget understandings, which translates into a motive to look for or avoid validation. These epistemic feelings, therefore, govern the way we come to understand the world with more or less certainty at least as much as our epistemic practices and ideologies. Therefore, where I speak more generally about understandings, organizing processes of understanding and validation, I shall speak of meta-understandings.

Meta-understandings are not necessarily a special class of understandings immediately recognizable as such. They may simply be other "substantive" understandings that organize the constitution of others. To illustrate what I mean I want to return once more to Mielke's speech. Parliaments everywhere play a role in the validation and invalidation of political understandings. Where taken seriously, deliberation is an effort to take stock of and develop recognitions, corroborations, and resonances of particular understandings; the rituals of debate lead to majority recognition; investigative committees are supposed to corroborate certain facts. In an important sense, then, differential validation is what parliament is about. Particular parliamentarian procedures are in this sense epistemic practices because they have considerable influence on how understandings come to be validated; a particular theory of parliamentarianism operates in this sense as an epistemic ideology by supplying parliamentarians and those who judge them with ideas about what members ought to do, thus helping to shape their behavior. The session of the People's Chamber in which Mielke gave his speech is a wonderful example for a transition from one set of meta-understandings to another. The parliament as an acclamatory organ, that is, a body that asserts that there is massive recognition for particular understandings, cautiously began to transmogrify itself into an investigative one. Instead of working predominantly with recognitions, it ventured, if still rather timidly, into the business of producing corroborations.

TOWARD A HERMENEUTIC INSTITUTIONALISM

The major empirical argument of this book is that socialism in the GDR failed primarily because the party state had instituted highly problematic ways of generating and validating understandings about itself in the world. Put differently, the party state failed for its political epistemics. This overarching argument follows two sublines. First, I argue that GDR socialism failed because it was institutionalized in such a way that the state was unable to produce understandings adequate for what I will call at the end of this chapter *self-politics*, that is, the management of the conditions of its own institutional reproduction. Empirically, I will make this argument especially in chapter 9 where I will show how and why the party state was unable to understand and therefore unable to even create the conditions for the possibility to deal successfully with the phenomenon of political dissidence. I will demonstrate that the understandings produced by the state were inadequate in the sense that the actions based on them actually exacerbated the very problem the state aspired to control. In effect, the party state was institutionalized in such a way that it could not come to a realistic understanding of the consequences of its own actions. That this is by no means only true for socialism makes it an interesting case to learn from. Second, I argue, GDR socialism failed because the administrative and political elites of the country lost confidence in the political understandings they helped to produce and propagate. Especially in the concluding chapter I will show how their confidence, especially in the party's leadership to address key problems of the country, came to be eroded during the late 1980s.

Framing the main argument of this book in terms of the failure of institutional self-maintenance and subsequent disintegration based on inadequate and weakening understandings of a particular kind presupposes that I explain more clearly what I mean by institutions and how understandings play into processes of institutionalization and deinstitutionalization. This is what I will begin to do in the following two subsections. A fuller treatment of the dialectics between institutions and understandings will follow in chapter 4.

Weaving Action-Reaction Effect Flows into Institutions

The ontological centerpiece of the sociological imaginary is the idea that the social world is not only human made, but also that it exists exclusively in the *process* of making and remaking it through our actions. Hence, social phenomena never gain an existence apart from our living bodies and minds. Even the material objects we mobilize or produce have a social reality only to the degree that they continue to play a role in the ongoing actions of people. Due to their existence in actions, which are physically grounded in human bodies, social phenomena are always local and temporally specific, even if, as I shall argue below, this is typically a distributed specificity. This specificity in the *here* and *now* is the first ontological characteristic of the social (three more are to follow further below). The question that thus occurs is how we can *imagine* the process of making and remaking the social world to yield interesting insights into *how* social life takes a particular form at a particular time. And since we have no choice but to participate in these processes, this imagination should also provide clues about how we could participate in them such that we enable ourselves to lead a life we deem worth living.

Social processes

At the roots of social processes lie the fundamental need, capacity, and effort of human beings to affect and be affected by others. Simmel tries to capture this phenomenon of interpersonal effect flows as "interaction" (*Wechselwirkung*) (Simmel 1992, chap. 1); his paradigmatic case is exchange (Simmel 1989). This formulation was not only influential (e.g., setting the discursive frame for the Chicago school as well as for symbolic interactionism), but also very productive, leading to many important insights culminating in Mead's (1934) theory of self-construction, Goffman's brilliant oeuvre on self-presentation and self-management in public places (1955; 1959), Schütz and Luckmann's (1984) account of intersubjectivity, and Garfinkel's (1967) dazzling pieces on reality construction. Yet, there is nothing about the social flow of effect that limits it to mutuality or reciprocity. Effects can flow from one person's action to be picked up by another without there being any reverse flow. In fact, the actions can be spatiotemporally separated, and actor and reactor need not—and very often and in highly complex societies typically do not—know each other. What makes this possible are sociotechnical means of projectively articulating actions across space and time through mediating communication, transportation, and storage. Techniques of projective articulation do not only enable one person to influence faraway others, they even empower the dead to have a continuing impact on the living. All that matters to spark the flow of social process is that someone reacts, picks up, or attunes to the actions of another. For this reason, and even though the expression is cumbersome, it is better to talk about *interlinked or interwoven action-reaction effect flows*[31] rather than interaction. The latter is merely a special case of the former where the interlinking is produced by spatiotemporal copresence and mutual attunement. In the sense that there is no action that is not also a reaction to antecedent actions that have taken place at other times in other places, *social phenomena are always translocal and transtemporal.*[32] This *there* and *then* spans up the second ontological dimension of the social. And thus one can say, only seemingly paradoxically, that the social is always here and there as well as now and then. Elsewhere (Glaeser 2005), I have called *consequent processualism* the imagination of the social in terms of a dense thicket of processes analyzable

---

31. Minimally the effect is the reaction. However, most importantly for this book, action-reaction sequences have, as I will show especially in chapter 4, effects on the validity of understandings, including understandings of self (identity) and of relationships.

32. This also means that whether we would want to call something an action or a reaction is merely a matter of perspective. It is an action if we look forward and it is a reaction if we look backward. Also calling something a reaction by no means implies that it is not creative.

in terms of interconnected, often projectively articulated action-reaction effect flows.

Over the last century and a half a long list of authors has contributed significant pieces to the refinement of this imagination. I can only highlight a few central contributions here. With his fundamental distinction between "social action" (any orientation toward others), "intended meaning," and "unintended consequences," Max Weber (e.g., 1980) enriches our comprehension of social processes in two ways. He follows the hermeneutic tradition in arguing that although we need to understand *why* people act the way they do because actions form institutions, social processes cannot be comprehended satisfactorily by recourse to motives (intentions, meanings, affects, habits) alone, because all actions face the possibility of principally unforeseeable reactions that are not only outside of the actors' control, but also may or may not be in line with their intentions (1988b). Yet, these unintended reactions are, where regularized, constitutive of the institutional order as much as intentional, affective, or habitual actions. Therefore, according to Weber only a simultaneous attention to the principles of action *and* the principles underpinning the interlacing of their effects can lead to satisfying accounts of institutions.

Speech act theory (Austin 1962) radicalizes the Weberian focus on the openness of reactions to the indeterminacy of the act. The central point is that a string of verbal behavior cannot only be seen as made up of different kinds of acts, but also that these become more clearly bounded particular acts only in the "uptake" of others, that is, in their reactions to it. Take the question of what Erich Mielke has done in his speech by addressing the assembly as "comrades," for example. He may have had no particular intention in mind with the use of this locution since it had become a habitualized form of address for party members in party dominated contexts. However, I have shown that in his speech Mielke presented a concentric model of the party state involving certain stipulations of solidarity and order for which the use of "comrade" as an address was not only a symbol but also an invitation to concur. Invitation and answer together helped to recreate the party. The member rising to order clearly understood Mielke to have in fact *appealed* to him to agree with this stipulation of order not only through his wider discourse but also through his form of address. Until quite recently, this member of the Peoples' Chamber might not even have perceived the form of address as an appeal while still answering it in a customary way, but now he does at least emotively understand that he should no longer heed the call to concur with the stipulation of traditional order. A beginning is made for unwinding the party as a socialist vanguard institution (something the heckler may or may not have intended). In response, Mielke then offers an interpretation of what he has done as an act of universal human love—an interpretation and thus determination of his action that came to be welcomed by some with applause while being brusquely rejected in laughter by others. Thus challenged, Mielke accepts that he has merely made "a mistake in etiquette" in calling everybody "comrade," putatively in order to save his larger point: the validity of the socialist order itself and the role of the secret police in it. In fact, the answer to the question, what has Mielke *done* by addressing the members of the People's Chamber summarily as "comrades," fluctuated in the exchange. The question, what has he done with his universal declaration of love, is still lingering—as the continuing efforts to interpret it here and elsewhere demonstrate. The reason why action is only determined in reaction is that behavior becomes a particular action only once its (discursive, emotive or kinesthetic . . .) intersubjective meaning is established.

Austin participates with his analysis of speech acts in the twentieth-century recovery and further development of the much older insight of the hermeneutic tradition that to speak is in fact not just to describe the world, but also to intervene in the flow of social processes and with it in the making and remaking of its institutions.[33] Austin calls the act of triggering a social effect in speaking a *performative*. His next move is to show that the reaction of others inevitably influences how we would have to describe behavior as a particular kind of act. Action thus understood is not choice, a solipsistic, individual accomplishment. Therefore, unlike the motives giving rise to them, what actions are is never quite determinable as long as they keep triggering reactions that make them into something, and potentially always into something new regardless of their motives. Even if formulating the indeterminacy of action explicitly may sound strange because it violates fundamental presuppositions of modern individualism, it is a thoroughly familiar phenomenon. The indeterminacy of action is the very stuff of our comedies, our satires, our tragedies.[34]

33. For a long time, however, this insight was taken to pertain only to what was thought to be a particular mode of speaking, namely rhetoric. Much like the poetic, which too was thought to pertain to only particular modes of linguistic utterances (Jakobson 1960), the rhetorical came to be understood as an aspect of almost all verbal utterances (as an address to others for the production of an effect) only from about the mid-twentieth century onward (Perelman and Olbrechts-Tyteca 1969; Burke 1969; Billig 1996).

34. In fact, the everyday use of "intention" and "act" is fully consistent with this view. The reprimand "look what you have done" would make little sense otherwise. It highlights the importance of consequences in the designation of the act that may radically deviate from an actor's intentions. Incidentally, this is also the reason why historians have traditionally been wary to interpret events within a still open process instead favoring the interpretation of events between two epochal bookends. The idea is precisely to wait for a moment in which some major strands of processual flows takes a new direction, which is incidentally the case when institutional

Institutions

This said, life in society does not all appear to us as an open flow that keeps running as long as there are reactions to actions. There are social phenomena that at first glace share a resemblance with stable, solid, seemingly unalterable things, namely *institutions* (e.g., Hughes 1936, 180). They are aspects of social life made and remade in action-reaction effect flows in such a manner that they are seemingly self-same across time.[35] Almost all aspects of social life can become institutionalized: behavior can congeal into habits; thoughts can crystallize into logics or mentalities; contacts can solidify into ongoing social relations; feelings can develop into emotive schemata or transferences; moods can extend into character; injunctions and goals can form into norms and values, dialogues can sediment as selves; and momentary expectations can gel as hopes or even develop into eschatologies. Typically, institutions are bundled into clusters, or better perhaps, thickets that we then call by other names. Among the more prominent ones are groups, organizations, ideologies, parties, states, or even cultures. These institutional clusters are interconnected with one another by sharing in particular elemental institutions, and even more basically by being maintained at least partially by actions located simultaneously in several action-reaction effect chains. For example, the oath of allegiance to the party performed by a Stasi officer does not only contribute to the maintenance of party and Stasi as organizations but also to the maintenance of oaths as cultural form, the language used, and the identities of the participants.

The misleading impression of institutions as objective, unalterable things derives not only from their stability relative to a faster-changing social environment, but also from the fact that it is hard for us to observe a causal connection between our actions and any particular institution. This is so because the process of making and remaking institutions is distributed over minimally two, but typically over many more, sometimes millions of human beings whose actions become interconnected through complex, projectively articulated effect flows. If we endeavor to change institutions, we are therefore faced with a collective action problem the extent of which is dependent on the scope and temporal structure of the tapestry of action-reaction effect flows maintaining institutional self-semblance. This issue is compounded by the fact that except for those institutional thickets we call organizations,

---

orders consolidate or disintegrate relatively rapidly. See Bearman, Moody, and Faris's (1999) interesting network-theoretic attempt to solve this problem of historical bookends.

35. I say "seemingly" because an institution existing in flow only cannot strictly be identical to itself; it is merely self-similar. Institutions, as long as they last, are stable only as continuous metaphoric invocations of themselves.

institutions have no orchestrating center. Instead, they come about as articulations of a multiplicity of intentions, deep motivations, as well as of systematically recurring unintended consequences.[36] The more radically decentralized they are the more difficult it is to change them deliberately. The making and remaking of institutions can therefore only imperfectly be described as a process of *production*—the term favored by Marx (and the Marxist tradition), or *construction*—the expression that has won widespread currency not only among the (neo-)Kantians but also in poststructuralist writing. Both of these terms are far too closely aligned with ideas of rational planning, the product of which is known in advance. Elias's (1976) concept of "sociogenesis" avoids these pitfalls. However, it places more of an emphasis on historical emergence than current reproduction. For this reason I prefer the term *formation*. It is wide enough to subsume intention and unintended consequences, it does not presume a pregiven telos, it can accommodate several crosscutting processes, and it allows for an existence that is wholly wrapped up in the processes of making it (as, for example, in the flight formation of geese).

Since we cannot usually make or break institutions at will, and since our actions produce unintended consequences, the social world faces us as an objective reality. This does not only happen to us where the institution in question is clearly maintained in other people's action-reaction effect flows, but also where we are actively implicated in the process of forming it. Marx (1958a, 33) has captured this experience succinctly: "this ossification of social activity, this consolidation of our own product into an objective force which has power over us, outgrows our control, thwarts our expectations, [and] obliterates our calculations." In fact, we are often oblivious to the fact that we too are part of the action-reaction flows forming institutions that appear to us as wholly other. The reasons for this oblivion have been paradigmatically explored by Marx (e.g., 1958a; 1962b, chap. 1; cf. Postone 1996). The most important one is the complexity of the chains of action-reaction flows that are shot through with projective articulations. This complexity has two main effects. On the one hand it prevents us from tracing the consequences of our own participation. Marx has exemplified this point with the division of labor that keeps us from seeing how the various stages of the production process dovetail to make a final product. On the other hand, Marx argues,

---

36. If the reader is reminded here of Latour's (1999; 2005) actor-network theory (ANT), this is no accident. ANT can very usefully be read as an account of a particular kind of institution formation, namely organization. As a general theory of institutions, however, it is too much focused on intentions, side-tracking unintentional consequences that (as Weber has argued, for example, in his *Protestant Ethic*) often adds as much if not more to stabilizing institutions. For a general theory of institutions, Latour's ANT focuses too much on one organizing center.

the complexity of the effect flow also creates different interests among the various participants in the process of institutionalization. With the different parts people play in the formation and in the utilization of institutions, they begin to occupy different social positions. This has serious consequences for people's understandings and ultimately their subjectivities. It is this double effect—the intractability of the impact of one's own actions in combination with an increasing physical, cultural, and psychological separation from other human beings ossifying into positionalities—that makes up what the young Marx has called alienation.

The older Marx intertwines the same two consequences of distributed institution formation—opaqueness and social estrangement—in his concept of "commodity fetishism," which he defines as the misrecognition of the qualities of goods as inherent in their materiality rather than as the results of the combined effort of many hands (1962b, 86). Marx's analysis can be generalized to a *fetishism of institutions* whose characteristics (e.g., their durability) is taken to inhere in them rather than in their continuous formation in the actions and reactions of diverse sets of people. Given that institutions are formed by webs of regularized action-reaction effect flows, one can immediately see that the flipside of the fetishism of institutions is given by a *fetishization of actors* as autonomous beings, disregarding their formation within a thicket of institutional arrangements of which they are but a part. What we have, then, appears as the third ontological dimension of the social, its simultaneously "subjective" and "objective" character (often referred in reference to Giddens [1984] as "duality"). Alienation as Marx understood it grows in the gap between the polar ends of this third ontological dimension; fetishization naturalizes it.

What is at issue here is the particular qualitative relationship between individuals and social others. The antidote to an alienated subject-object relationship has often been seen in a different relationality, one where the other is a partner with whom one can negotiate. There is a relationality that is dialogic, not just monologic, to borrow Bakhtin's (1984) concept pair. In other words, the other cannot only appear as an objective "it" to the thinking, feeling, acting "I" but also as a "you" (Buber 1995). What characterizes the dialogic for both Buber and Bakhtin is mutuality, the empathetic treatment of the other as a fellow subject, open to being transformed by the dialogic partner. Since there is a plural subjectivity in form of a "we," and since the other can also appear as a dialogic plural "you" as well as a monologic "they," description of the third ontological dimension becomes more complex than stated above. We have to analyze it along a number of constitutive subrelationships, all of which can be monologic or dialogic. We have to look at least how "I" and "we" relate to singular and plural others, as well as to the ways in which collective subjects relate to individual ones.

Against the claims of nationalism or fascism to create at least an unalienated "we" (if against an alien "they"), Marx and his followers have argued that monologicity (objectification) is in fact a constitutive feature of capitalism (Lukács 1923). Only a communist world-encompassing thoroughly dialogic society will overcome alienation. In the experiential world of actually existing socialisms we will also see how the subjective "Is" and "wes" could vanish in staunchly demanded and actually performed self-objectification toward objective "mes" and "thems." This does not mean that the "Is" and "wes" disappeared entirely. But it does mean that they had to find acceptable niches or go underground.

The social's ontological characteristics are these, then: it is at the same time spatially and temporally local and translocal (i.e. here-there, now-then), relationally monologic (I/we-it/they), dialogic (I/we-you) or even completely objectified (me/them-it/they) and finally it is *in actu* and *in posse* (is-might). Understandings play a constituting role for these ontological dimensions of the social. The time and space transcending characteristics of the social are made possible through understandings as much as through relationships and technology (e.g., through millenarian or progress expectations, space related notions of belonging, or emotions such as *Fernweh* ("longing for distant places"). The same holds for relationality (e.g., with ideas of what friendship or love mean, or practices creating networks of "weak-ties"). The *in actu–in posse* dimension of the social is unthinkable without the subjunctivity enabled by symbolic differentiations and integrations. In other words, understandings give these four ontological dimensions a particular, historically specific content.

Understandings and Institutions

The Socialist Unity Party of the GDR was an institution, or better, a complex of institutions. And unlike what I said about institutions more generally, it endeavored to make itself the center of the even wider institutional fabric of socialism, that is, almost all of public social life in the former GDR. The party existed in the regularized actions and reaction of its members as members, as well as the actions and reactions of outsiders toward members as members. Every time members addressed each other as "comrades," went together to a party meeting or a propaganda event, volunteered for extra shifts at their workplaces or "subotniks" in their apartment complexes, every time they dutifully read the party papers or watched the evening news on television as "theirs," every time they hung up a portrait of the general secretary, every time they swallowed their "subjectivist inclinations" in adjusting their speech, thought, or conduct to the "lines" mandated by they party, they maintained the party as an institution. Every time outsiders offered admiration of or disdain for the party, triggering an identifying response of the member with the party, the party as institution was reproduced in a particular shape or form.

The actions and reactions forming the institutional fabric of the party state were predicated on a host of different understandings. There were distinctions between members and nonmembers; codes of conduct; a socialist ethic; ideas of short-term goals and long-term missions; understandings about the legitimate divisions of labor within the party; incentive structures and their justification; forms of discourse; forms of inquiry; objects of admiration and love; objects of disdain and hatred; gestures; oratorical forms of listening and speaking; celebrative forms of marching, chanting, shouting, and being silent—just to mention a few. The packaging of these discursive, emotive, kinesthetic, and sensory understandings into ideologies, practices, and rituals was constitutive of the party—through their enactment. Mielke's speech in the People's Chamber is a moment when the old action-reaction effect chains are broken. The episode shows how not only the national front under the leadership of the SED but also ultimately the SED itself began to crumble as a particular thicket of institutions. The reason why they began to crumble is that certain understandings seem to have lost actuality while others were taking their place. The question that thus emerges is how discursive, emotive, and kinesthetic understandings *do* become constitutive of institutions. Since institutions are regularized social processes based in interwoven action-reaction effect flows, one can disaggregate this problem into two steps by asking first how understandings shape action-reaction effect flows to wonder then how they contribute to their stabilization.

Understanding as moments in action-reaction effect flows

It is useful to differentiate at least four different moments in which understandings shape the concatenation of actions and reactions into processes (with something of a division of labor between the different modes): together they *orient, direct, coordinate, explain, and legitimate or justify* action. Seeing them as moments does not imply that they follow each other in any particular temporal order. Instead, they build a complex of dialectical entanglements in which each moment presupposes and constitutes the others in a temporal flow.

The first moment, *orientation*, is wrapped up with the very notion of understanding as I developed it in the preceding pages. Discursive, emotive, and kinesthetic understandings differentiate and integrate the world, thus orienting us vis-à-vis a natural and/or social environment. In other words, understandings tell us what is what, they indicate in which way phenomena exist, how these are related with one another, and how they matter to us. This orientation in the world includes a conscious or unconscious interpretation of the past and possible future actions of others. In short, understandings sort out *what we are reacting to and why we are acting at all*; they are the interface through which we interpret and engage with the world, they tie our actions as reactions to various kinds of contexts. Mielke had to figure out before and while giving his speech what he was responding to, what the event in which he acted was about both in terms of the unusual call to appear before the People's Chamber, in terms of the ever more dramatic events unfolding in the fall of 1989, and certainly in his mind in terms of history, that is, the class warfare between the socialist and the capitalist world. His performance indicates that he interpreted the situation as if it was a somewhat quirky and yet in all relevant respects standard socialist event. He seems to have assumed that the party continued to be in full control of what was going on in the People's Chamber, and that the party itself would follow more or less tried standard procedures.

Second, understandings provide a notion of *what to do*, that is, *how* to react to the situation that is already understood to some degree. They supply discursive, emotive, and kinesthetic templates to *direct* action. They give us a sense where we might be able to intervene successfully in the proceedings of the world to shape them in accordance with our interests and values, that is, in accordance with other understandings. Mielke reacted to his orientation within the historical situation with a standard speech reiterating the party's old social imaginary. Mielke's speech departs in this respect considerably from those of other high-ranking party members speaking on November 13, 1989, in the People's Chamber. They tried to respond to the perception of crisis in novel ways by revealing facts, for example about the GDR's hard currency debt, or by offering thoughts that deviated in content and form significantly from existing practice. Like Honecker during the anniversary celebrations, Mielke seems to have thought that business as usual, that yet another reiteration of the old fundamentals, was an apt means to preserve a system that should not and need not be changed. Moments one (orientation) and two (direction) together cover what Weber (1980) had in mind with his notion of a meaning guided "social action," which Geertz (1974, 95) felicitously interpreted with his notion of culture as "model *of* [the world]" and "model *for* [action]." Together they form the basis for what is commonly called agency, that is, human beings' capability to act.

Third, John Searle (1992) picks up an older Rousseauian theme in arguing that symbols are essential for coordinating actions in forming an institution. In his model, the process of institutionalization requires that something, or more often someone, is treated in a particular way by several people at the same time. His favorite example is money. A particular piece of paper becomes money only through the pattern printed on it. It is precisely this mark that allows it to be used as a medium of exchange because it indicates to all parties involved how to treat it. The same applies to police officers whose uniform or badge facilitates the coordination of action with and toward them.[37] In general, seals, stamps, or insignia, but also forms of behavior, registers of speech, and paraphernalia play this coordinating role. Althusser (1971) has earlier described the same phenomenon as "hailing" people into a particular role through the deployment of a particular sign instantaneously legible as a call for a particular kind of behavior. It bears noticing (especially since Althusser does not make much of it), that hailing is only possible to the degree that people already have orienting and directing understandings telling them what the coordinating symbol is and what it requires them to do. This connection has been explored by linguistic anthropologists, notably Michael Silverstein (e.g., 2004), who have shown us how the denotational deployment of signs in context mobilizes cultural knowledge which facilitates the emergence of formed action-reaction effect sequences. Mielke's speech, his conjuration of the socialist order, his appeal to acknowledge it, can be read as an attempt to hail the assembly into its traditional role. He failed because the underlying orienting and directing understandings had become questionable. Of course, when ultimately the new prime minister was elected the procedure succeeded in hailing everybody but one into their old roles.

Fourth, Berger and Luckmann (1966) argue that the transgenerational perpetuation of institutions is unthinkable without understandings that *explain, justify, or legitimate* them. The "new institutionalists" in sociology (e.g., Meyer and Rowan 1977; DiMaggio and Powell 1983) have made the related point that legitimation facilitates or even drives the replication of institutional orders in the present that can lead to the emergence of institutional isomorphism. What both approaches overlook is that justification is not just a natural "given"; it is not something people demand out of inborn curiosity or similarly anchored democratic sensibility. Many institutional arrangements are mimetically acquired within and across generations without the need of explicit explanation or justification. Linguistic phenomena are an all-pervasive case in point. However, in situations where institutional orders become defetishized, when people become aware again that they are anything but natural, which often happens when alternative arrangements become thinkable and for some actors desirable, that justification and

---

37. Where the images of people who publicly carry institutions come to be known, formal marking is no longer necessary; the face becomes the coordinating symbol. Today's rulers are for this very reason much less dependent on the symbolism of office than their counterparts before the "time of mechanical reproduction" (Walter Benjamin). Precisely because the use of these coordinating symbols is a semiotic game, it is open to abuse by impostors while generating the possibility for real and fictional comedies (and tragedies) of error.

legitimation becomes important.[38] This can happen not only where conflict emerges, for example, over the unequal distribution of advantages created by an institutional order, but also in situations of an ongoing competition between different social orders, as in the Cold War. The point of the hot fall of 1989 and the November 13 meeting of the People's Chamber was the acknowledgment that the GDR had reached a point of crisis that the old institutional arrangements had not only produced but also had failed to even recognize, thus preventing the timely generation of possible solutions. In this context, Mielke's efforts to justify the Stasi with the help of the established formulas of the Honecker years failed already at the level of his own subordinates who watched him with bewilderment in front of their television sets; it failed at the level of a good number of his fellow deputies; and it certainly fell through with the wider public.

As important as understandings are in directing the flow of effect in social processes, it has to be remembered that they do not determine it completely. There are several reasons why this is so. On the one hand, there are situations in which understandings are not fine-grained or evaluative enough to orient and direct action. On the other hand, people often operate with a plurality of understandings across several modes that may yield equally plausible, possibly even contradictory orderings of the world. What helps in such cases of under- and overdetermination is not just the will to complement, discard, or hierarchize understandings, that is, a set of meta-understandings (Frankfurt 1988; Bieri 2001), but the gift of whim that brings an element of arbitrariness into action-reaction effect flows.[39] Beyond all understanding, action presupposes material resources as well as time. Both the economies and the ultimately irreducible complementarity between both with regard to action have busied political thinkers at least since Aristotle. Following them, contemporary social scientists have tried to understand processes of institutionalization exclusively from a resource perspective. They have overlooked,

---

38. In this context it is more than odd that one of the most sustained efforts of recent times to theorize the practice of justification and locate its importance in social life, Boltanski and Thévenot's *On Justification* (2006), excludes situations of conflict from explicit consideration. In consequence, this book refuses to engage with the literature on rhetoric (Perelman and Olbrechts-Tyteca 1969; Burke 1969; Billig 1996), overlooking what especially Burke makes clear, that unity needs to be constructed only where chasms are already perceived as existing. What the book offers is an in-depth exploration of a handful of possible modes of justification, which they derive from what they consider as genre-setting philosophical texts.

39. Whim is a true blessing in as far as it helps us out of situations in which we cannot produce decisive understanding. It does not only help us to avoid the fate of Buridan's ass, who worried himself to starvation over two equally big stacks of hay, but by putting understanding at risk, action allows for the transformation of understanding through the play of further validation to overcome stalemate and to further creativity.

however, that neither material resources nor time are useful without understandings. They can do no more than generally enable action. Thus they determine the social world only *in posse*, but not *in actu*. Only understandings give the flow of actions and reactions and thus institutions a particular direction, a qualitatively recognizable shape. In other words, any account of social processes has to take material resources and time into account in their relationship to available or formable understandings (Glaeser 2005).

Finally, it is important to remember that in order to form common institutions, the understandings of the individuals acting and reacting do by no means have to be the same. Nobody has made this point more clearly than Bruno Latour with his actor-network theory (1999; 2005).

Understandings as institutions: Agency

If understanding undergirds the flow of effects between actions and reactions, its stabilization offers a clue to comprehend the regularization and thus institutionalization of social processes. The central questions are then: How is understanding transformed into *an* understanding; how does the continuous become a noun; or how do the processes of differentiating, integrating, orienting, directing, coordinating, justifying, explaining gel into a thinglike state? Put differently: how do understandings become institutionalized?[40] An answer to these questions is important, because the

---

40. Unfortunately, the traditional sociology of knowledge in its Marxian, Durkheimian, and neo-Marxian instantiations offers only a very limited, ultimately unsatisfying answer to this question. To see why this is so it is best to quickly restate their respective approach. Mannheim's (1995) definition of the sociology of knowledge as centrally concerned with the relationship between being and thinking (*Seinsverbundenheit des Denkens*) is useful for this purpose because it provides a simple tool to map the differences between the classical approaches. One only has to compare what each means by being, thinking, and the relationship between the two. For Marx (1958a), being means the struggle between two antagonistic classes, members of which, each in their own way, characteristically misunderstand their situation. Thinking is for Marx first and foremost ideology, that is, the dominant class's systematic misunderstanding of society, which it is able to spread to the rest of society thanks to its power position. The nexus between the two is provided by Marx through commodity exchange, and especially the commodification of labor, which reproduces antagonistic class relations and ideology. For Durkheim (1995), being is life in a complementarily, that is, harmoniously organized society. Thought is for him collective consciousness structured by the categories of mind, such as space, time, class, etc. Unfortunately, Durkheim has never endeavored to think through the relationship between them beyond the mere statement of formal homologies. For Mannheim, finally, being is a particular existential problematic tied to a specific, enduring situation in social life stimulating particular kinds of thought—in the political case, ideologies or utopias. People sharing this problematic attempt to contribute to its solution. For all three authors, the institutional character of thought is not developed beyond the conditions of being, which supposedly give rise to it. In other words, the development of our capabilities to act requires the institutionalization of understanding.[41] The differentiations and integrations inherent in any sequence of behavior need to be abstracted into a handier, memorable, and hence mobile form that can be deployed across contexts. Alfred Schütz (1981; 1984) and his students Thomas Luckmann and Peter Berger (1966) were following Simmel (1992) in describing such a process as typification. Psychoanalysts (e.g. Freud 2000c; Chodorow 1999) have described similar processes for emotive understandings in a number of different ways (e.g., neurosis, transferences, etc.). And in the very same vein, the abstracted transportability of kinesthetic understandings has been described variously as skill or more technically, for example, as "hexis" (Bourdieu 1977) or "arts of doing" (Certeau 1984). The three forms of validation accomplish this work by selecting and lifting off a bounded set of differentiations and integrations from an endless flow of doing and happening. Validations convert the processes of understand*ing* into thinglike understanding*s*; their repetition converts a processual flow into a more context-independent form. And it is thus that fixated understandings can contribute to steadying action-reaction sequences across time to reproduce institutions in a seemingly identical manner.[42]

---

stability of social conditions is theorized to give rise to the stability of thought patterns. For several reasons this is problematic. First, the social constellations and existential problematics that prompt the emergence of a particular understanding are not necessarily the ones that maintain it as an institution throughout its existence. In other words, the action-reaction chains underpinning the institutional maintenance of a particular understanding may change in the course of time. This points to the second, more significant problem in all three classical accounts of the institutionalization of knowledge. Brilliant insights notwithstanding, their analyses of the processes by which people come to inhabit or move out of understandings in everyday life remain rudimentary. In fact, more often than not the attestation of homologies substitutes for the analysis of process. We are left with dazzling claims that there is a link between the commodity form and enlightenment thought (Marx 1958a; Lukács 1968; Sohn-Rethel 1970) or between the physical layout of a village and the category of space (Durkheim 1995) without as much as even the means to think through *how* the two are connected in practice. This is precisely where I hope to improve matters by attending to processes of validation. For it is my claim that understandings become actualized and thus institutionalized in particular ways through the interplay of historically specific processes of recognition, corroboration, and resonance.

41. In general, the argument developed in this section is strongly influenced by the philosophical anthropology of the 1930s and 1940s (Gehlen 1997; Cassirer 1997), which in their turn build on the hermeneutic tradition.

42. It should be noted here that the movement from understanding to an understanding, that is, the institutionalization of a more stable form of understanding, does not pose itself to a rational choice or related "heuristics and biases" theorist. The reason is simply that the optimizing calculus is, in these traditions, assumed to be hard-wired into our brain. Accordingly, they analyze the stability of institutions in terms of incentive structures and their transformation.

These institutionalized understandings provide, on the one hand, enormous versatility to human existence. They enable learning and cultivation from situation to situation and from person to person, which adds a quantum leap to human beings' ability to act. On the other hand, however, lifting off differentiations and integrations from the flow of life, abstracting them into schematic, memorable form, sets in motion an inevitable process of reification. The more consistently and regularly validated understandings become, that is, the more they are formed into institutions, the more certain and thus actionable they are, but also the more thing- and eventually fetish-like they become. Thus the constitution of agency in the process of increasing validation can be thought of as framed by two boundary zones. The first demarcates the transition from possible to actual understandings. There, understandings gain or loose actionability (see figure 4.3 on p. 213). Where this boundary lies is very context sensitive, as even the simplest examples demonstrate. What kind of validation would one need before one would accuse a particular person of a specific immoral or criminal behavior? How is that different depending on whether one airs it in front of intimate friends, a reporter's microphone, or a court of law? The other boundary zone, equally determined by meta-understandings, sets off a degree and kind of certainty that no longer admits any doubts. Beyond it, the play of validating forces is so continuous, so decisive that understandings become naturalized and essentialized. This is the domain of unquestioned background assumptions; it is the territory of the phenomenologists' "natural perspective" (*natürliche Einstellung*) and Wittgenstein's "background." The uncontested nature of these understandings begins to remove them first from critical reflection and then from consciousness altogether. Behavior flowing from these understandings is quasi-automatic.

The more actions are based on background understandings, the more efficient they are: things can get done fast, without much deliberation; actions and understandings are for all practical purposes fused; the coordination with others who share in the same background can proceed with a minimal degree of communication. In extension of Durkheim (1997) one could say the *conscience collective* is at the same time *action collective*. This seems desirable for situations in which fast, coordinated reaction is necessary. It is the ideal to which military commando units and secret service organizations aspire. Whether background understandings remain effective (as opposed to efficient) in practice, however, in the sense that they are good guides of the world and for action, depends entirely on the degree to which the domains of activity validating these understandings are actually integrated with the domains of activity in which these understandings are deployed. If they begin to drift apart, for example in situations of fast social change, there looms the danger that understandings that feel entirely certain and justified become increasingly misleading. As we will see, such disintegration happens easily in contexts that privilege recognition at the expense of direct corroboration either because this mode of validation is preferred according to the meta-understandings in question, or because direct corroboration is very complex or simply unpractical. Just consider for a moment how ordinary citizens would want to directly corroborate their government's claims about another government's intentions. In such disjunctures between the space of validation on the one hand and the field of action on the other lies one of the roots of catastrophic failures of understandings. The fate of socialism is a case in point.

The stability of institutional arrangements

From what I have said so far it should be clear that although the actualization of understanding is necessary for the stabilization of action-reaction effect flows, and thus of all institutions, understandings are *not* the ultimate ground on which other institutions rest. In matters social there is no such thing as an ultimate ground. This is so because understandings rest in turn on validations, which rest on meta-understandings and institutionally conditioned possibilities to occur. This may at first look like a game of infinite deferment, and in a sense it is. A better way to think of the relationship of these processes is to see them as dialectically co-constituting each other, which also means that they stabilize and/or destabilize each other. However, they do so at different rates creating the appearance of "structures" in front of a faster changing background. What is or is not in this sense "structural" can not be assumed but must be adjudicated empirically (Sewell 2005, 151; Silverstein 2004, 622; Abbott 2001b, 259). And as before, textile metaphors suggest themselves to capture the particular kind of stability institutional arrangements display. Institutionalized processes may be seen as various kinds of threads interwoven into a fabric. Even though certain threads may be more important than others, there is typically no single thread that literally weaves everything together. Rather, the stability of the whole is provided by the mutual support of a number of these threads supporting one another. This metaphor can help to grasp a peculiar characteristic of institutional dynamics. On the one hand, they are rather resilient. While some threads may run out in the course of time, they can be replaced by others. Organizations, for example, can accommodate fluctuations of members and changes in rules. On the other hand, the weakening of a number of parallel threads can lead quickly to catastrophic failure. What is needed, then, is an analysis of how the mutual buttressing of processes works. Because as I just argued, understandings give action-reaction effect dynamics their qualitative shape, the dialectics of validation will shed a particularly interesting light on processes of institutionalization and deinstitutionalization. Yet this has to wait until chapter 4.

THE POLITICAL

An analytical definition of politics immediately follows from consequent processualism, that is, the imagination of the social world as a complex of interconnected processes of people-entangling flows of actions and reactions that—where regularized—form institutions. The political is best grasped as a particular take on social life; it is a way of looking at actions in view of their role in forming institutions, no matter whether only judging or planning them. In this sense we commonly speak of a "political person" as someone who cannot but look at actions from the perspective of their consequences for institutional arrangements. Conversely and equally commonly, someone may reproach others for being apolitical because they fail to regard the effects of what they do for institutional arrangements. "Politicization" is accordingly a process that reflexively tries to bring into view the fact that particular kinds of actions do form institutions that may or may not be deemed desirable. It is hated by some precisely because it involves a certain loss of innocence. Politics is more than a point of view, however. It is the deliberate *effort* to effect, maintain, or alter particular institutions. Politics is therefore a metapractice, a practice about practices.[43] Although a large number of actions have consequences for the existence of particular institutions, which may justify an analyst to call them political in their objective effects, only a small number of them qualify as politics from the subjective perspective of the actor, because most institution-forming action effects materialize only as unintended consequences. Simply conflating the political and the social is tantamount to conflating intentions with consequences, planning with the unpredictable concatenation of action-reaction-effect flows. As socialism has shown, as a peculiar form of (mis-)understanding society, this conflation can lead to the fantastical attribution of intentions (more on this in chapter 9). And as I will show in chapter 1, a politics failing to understand its own limits, that is the limits of intentionality within a particular institutional matrix, is in danger of drifting into idealism (in the philosophical sense).[44]

43. The formulation I am using here is indebted to one of Foucault's definitions of governmentality as "conduct of conduct" (1991; Gordon 1991). And the beginning of the discursive understanding of action as political in this sense comes about precisely in the historical context Foucault describes with the other meaning of the term *governmentality*, the emergence of the state/ruler's self-understanding as actively shaping the conditions of its own self-reproduction in managing territory and population development. For historically illuminating case studies see Scott 1998 and Carroll 2006.

44. The distinction between the political and the social, which follows from consequent processualism, is very much in line with the historical development of first the philosophical and then the social scientific imaginaries of what it means for humans to live together with other humans. As evinced by the great contract theoretical tradition from Hobbes to Rousseau, during the

This said, the definition of politics as *deliberate effort to shape institutions* leaves its domain consciously wide. In the sense of the definition, there are, for example, family politics dividing labor between husband and wife (e.g., Hochschild 1989); there are politics of language establishing the predominance of particular codes for creating patterns of inclusion or exclusion in use (e.g., Gal 1979, 1993; Gal and Irvine 2000); there are politics of religion establishing the boundary between different creeds and rituals (Riesebrodt 2007); there are politics of economic behavior aiming to make people into consumers (e.g., de Grazia 2005); and there are intensifying politics of scientific knowledge (Collins and Pinch, 1993, 1999; Stehr 2003; Rose 2007). There is even a politics of nature, because to an ever-increasing extent, the natural environment in which we live has become an institution that can only be maintained in a particular form through widely scoped interconnected flows of actions and reactions (Diamond 2005).

Political Organizations

Politics itself is subject to institutionalization. In fact, as especially Lenin (1961h) and Weber (1980) have argued, in order to be effective in a complex mass society, politics must be organized. In the simplest case, particular individuals' politics can become institutionalized if others help them to regu-

---

Enlightenment these imaginaries were thoroughly political. Togetherness was conceived in terms of a rational construct, as the effect of joint action to create institutions, that is, politics. However, during the baroque a second tradition breaks way beginning to conceive order in togetherness no longer as the consequence of reasoned intentions, but as the unintended consequence of actions that were undertaken for reasons that have nothing to do with the emergent order, which may in fact be its polar opposite. Mandeville with his *Fable of the Bees* is among the first authors we still read today to articulate such a radical departure from contractarian thinking. His thought, prefiguring Adam Smith's "invisible hand," leads to the market-tradition in thinking through the concatenation of unintended consequences. The other is the hermeneutic tradition that can be thought of as starting with Vico. Both start in self-conscious opposition to the prevailing contractarian thought of their time. In this shift of emphasis lies the origin of the thoroughly modern notion of the "social," which as Peter Wagner shows (2000), pertained at first to that unruly sphere between the private household (which the paterfamilias could imagine as following his whim) and the state (the conception of which was still based on the fiction of a sovereign actor). The sphere in between does include the market, which as Smith most famously argued, follows in the generation of order nobody's intentions in particular. Since then we have something of a tug-of-war between the social and the political, which Dominic Boyer (2005) has so aptly described in reference to German intellectuals as a dialectic between "spirit and system." The social is the unintentional; the political is the intentional.

larize their efforts to shape institutions.[45] Once the institutional character of a person's efforts is understood, it can be abstracted from any particular individual as a role, which might eventually find other incumbents. That entails that the support likewise becomes abstracted in the form of roles. Assemblies of such roles working in some coherent fashion at the realization of particular kinds of institution-forming effects are organizations; they operate as self-conscious, political institutions. The promise of organizations is that they are much better suited to overcome a number of fundamental problems involved in doing politics than individuals. In particular, they allow for the pooling and redistribution of skills, material resources, and time; they can be used as conduits to projectively articulate actions and reactions; and they can help to disseminate and stabilize understandings by forming an established network of authority. More generally speaking, they can ease the collective action problem involved in all politics by getting a significant number and/or significantly located people to maintain or alter their reactions to the actions of others.

Seen from this perspective, marketing companies aiming to sustain specific forms of consumer behavior or even consumer subjectivities, as well as churches hoping to establish a certain form of piety, can be as much understood as political organizations, as citizen initiatives, and the White House. Seen from the perspective of the sociology of understanding, politics is objectively what social organization is about. This is, however, not necessarily how organizations present themselves. Their politics may in fact be hidden, if not necessarily for political reasons, then certainly with political consequences by a language suffused with institutional fetishism. Yet, no matter whether their "goals," "objectives," or "missions" are "profits," "security," or "education," they are merely names for particular regularized interwoven action-reaction effect flows. And trying to give those a particular enduring form is an activity aiming at institution formation and thus an act of politics.

What distinguishes organizations from institutions is self-reflexivity. In other words, at least some people who participate in their formation know—not necessarily in language used here—that they are institutions that need to be actively maintained. This insight leads them to engage in self-politics on behalf of the organization. Self-reflexivity in this sense is an immense opportunity in that it allows organizations to identify and fight threats to their own institutional upkeep. Yet, especially for political organizations, this is a fateful moment as self-politics (on behalf of self-maintenance) and

---

45. What exactly the role of others in this context is, that is, the reasons why it is often difficult for people to institutionalize their own behavior, I will discuss in chapter 3 in reference to Wittgenstein's late philosophy.

politics (on behalf of a target institution) begin to compete for attention. Because political organizations typically operate at a much smaller scale than the institutions they have targeted, self-politics is usually also much easier to do, providing extra incentives to engage in it rather than in efforts to accomplish the more elusive external political goals an organization is pursuing.

Since so much of social life is about institutionalization, a further institutional layer has emerged to regulate the political in the wider sense in which I have so far used the term. What is at issue here is the regulation of peoples' rights and duties to participate in or withdraw from any kind of processes of institution formation. This regulation of politics is constitutional politics. Since constitutional politics has to be organized if it is to be effective, it must be self-reflexive, including the regulation of peoples' rights and duties to participate in this process of regulating regulation, of participating in the politics of politics. Historically, states have emerged as sets of political organizations to engage in constitutional politics at the most general level. However, states are not the only sets of organizations engaged in it. In principle, any voluntary association does to the degree that it distributes rights and duties, encourages or discourages its members to involve themselves in some kind of institution-forming processes but not in others; and so do many "traditional" types of organizations such as churches and families. Not surprisingly, the boundaries between different domains of constitutional politics have become one of the major objects of contention between various schools of political philosophy, their embodiment in fighting ideologies, and of course day-to-day politics itself.

Falling in line with the need of organizations to engage in self-politics, states are at least as much concerned with the participation of their citizens and that of foreign states in their own reproduction as they are in external political projects or constitutional politics. In fact, their very position has allowed them to become the most powerful institution building, maintaining, and destroying set of organizations around, challenged in capabilities only by very large private corporations. Needless to say, the state has used these very capabilities for purposes of self-politics. That in turn has given constitutional politics a different flavor: the rights and duties to participate in or withdraw from processes of institution formation have become increasingly focused on the institutions of the state. Small surprise, then, that the state as a set of political organizations has become a thoroughly ambiguous phenomenon. For good reasons, it is the object of as much hope as of fear. This is why politics in a narrow sense has emerged as state-centered politics; it is the state's effort to shape institutions, and other peoples' and institutions' efforts to shape the state.

Main Forms of Politics

Consequent processualism also provides a simple analytical framework to study the means of doing politics. This will be useful when I discuss the politics of the party state to institutionalize socialism in the following two chapters, as well as in chapter 8 when I will discuss the ways in which dissidents empowered themselves to engage in politics, and in chapter 9 when I provide an overview of how the Stasi in particular tried to disempower them. Following the logic of consequent processualism, politics can intervene at the level of general enablement as well as at the four principal moments of process, that is, understanding, action, projective articulation, and reaction. This yields an ideal-typical schema. With the exception of the last type, each can come in more or less dialogic or monologic varieties, depending on how politicians address others to become involved in the setting and execution of politics.

There is first a *politics of general enablement or disablement*, which is the very basis of any form of constitutional politics. Instead of aiming at the foundation, maintenance, or change of particular institutions, one may want to enable or disable a person, a group, or whole categories of persons from participating in processes of institution formation more generally. Enablement means to provide people with material resources, time, and perhaps some secondary, enabling set of institutions that allow for the development of understandings and social networks. Disablement can analogously proceed by attempting to prevent people from developing or maintaining more stable understandings—for example, by means of terror, psychological and social destabilization, or by the creation of some kind of information overload. Moreover, it can work by depriving people of material resources in form of income, shelter, or health, thus creating a cobweb of time-consuming and thus freedom-extinguishing "necessities." Finally, it can work at least selectively by absorbing people into the reproduction of particular institutions (e.g., through overwork and through completely organized leisure time), thus preventing people from participating in other kinds of activities.

Intervening at the moment of action, there is, second, a *politics as policy* whereby actors spell out and often communicate to others the conditions for their own participation in forming particular kinds of institutions.[46] Policies are explicit understandings, not necessarily put in practice but certainly credibly realizable in performance about what kinds of actions one does or does not want to engage in under what specific circumstances. Of course, ef-

---

46. Policies are relatively simple devices because to some degree it is easier to self-regulate than to influence others in a persistent way. However, in chapter 3, I will have more to say about the limits of self-regulation.

fective policies presuppose adequate understandings about how processes of institutionalization actually proceed. One has to know something about how the mere communication or actual performance of one's own actions, either directly or as signs, influences the formation of the targeted institution.

Then, there is a *politics of (projective) articulation/disarticulation* that aims to intervene at the moment of effect flows in action-reaction chains. Most simply speaking, one can either try to stimulate or prevent certain kinds of face-to-face interactions. Since more broadly scoped institutions all depend on projective articulations across time and space one may wish to block such flows by disarticulating, that is, isolating, actions from potential reactions. Managing or preventing the circulation and storage/maintenance/ residence of all forms of understandings, goods, and people in the form of secrecy, censorship, customs, permits, licenses, passports, and such are all political means in this sense. Conversely, one may want to create articulations where there were none before. Any form of publication may do this (be it by a public relations agent or a whistle-blower trying to trigger a scandal). Put more generally, the politics of articulation rests on easing, managing, or preventing the access to communication, transportation, or storage/ maintenance/residence.

Next, one can try to induce others to undertake (or refrain from undertaking) targeted actions that according to one's own understandings about action-reaction effect flows are constitutive of institutions. Short of violent force, all ways to do so have to take into account targeted actor's understandings, which the politician has to come to know and engage with. There are two principle approaches to this *politics of induction*. On the one hand, one can take the basic understandings of others as fixed—either because one believes that they are part of human nature that is by definition unalterable (as rational choice theorists do), or because one believes one does not have the institutional means to influence them. In this case one has to work with the existing understandings, for example, by providing positive or negative *incentives*. This style of politics typically aims to utilize existing understandings about desirable goods or undesirable states by rewarding target actions or by punishing deviations from them. This is the politics of sin taxes, tax holidays, performance bonuses, but also of medals, prizes and other honors. Much political rhetoric also works with existing understandings by making appeals to identities, moral, aesthetic, or logical norms. On the other hand, one might want to pursue an *educational approach*, which aims at reshaping the understandings of target actors. This can be done by either teaching them directly and/or by helping to actualize those of their understandings, which promise to increase the likelihood that the target performance will in fact occur. In other words, educational politicians must try to become authorities. They do their work by selectively recognizing certain understandings; they try to make visible how certain events indirectly corroborate desired understanding; and they try to make sure that target understandings will resonate with people.

Finally, there is *politics by brute force*. Unfortunately, as the global success of large-scale theft, murder, and genocide shows, force is an inefficient means of politics only where the ongoing willing and knowing cooperation of the subdued is needed. Where it is, however, brute force typically gives way to other forms of politics. Yet, even they usually face a dilemma. Wanting changes in institutions, all politics has to change how targeted people act and react to one another in a sustained way. To achieve this, politicians have to relate to people. Since dialogic relating implies the openness of politicians to change their goal, it is the great temptation of politics to relate to people in an objectifying way, both to honor the goal's presumed dignity as well as in the interest of efficiency. Where politics' goals are not universally shared by the targeted people, objectification may trigger resistance, however small, that can ultimately thwart goal attainment. The degree to which politics is monologic or dialogic may therefore have consequences for its success. How much this matters and in what way reactions to politicians' initiatives will form depends entirely on the way that people understand these initiatives in the first place, as Nina Eliasoph has shown (1998).

Power

This has consequences for the concept of *power*. It should no longer be seen as what politics is primarily about (Weber 1980, 822), but much more its precondition, that is, the ability to engage successfully in politics. Central to power is the ability to make reactions follow actions in a predictable way, which necessarily includes means of projective articulation, or what Michael Mann (1984) has called "infrastructural power." More, however, since we cannot build, maintain, or transform institutions on our own, power is the ability to maneuver not only within, but most notably with the help of existing institutional arrangements and thus always with the assistance of others, to achieve a political goal. This is where what often is called "soft power" comes in (Lukes 1974). Seen in this way, power is the ability to play given sets of institutions for the sake of influencing some of them. Needless to say, depending on the institution targeted for creation, maintenance, or change, and the situation in which this is supposed to be done, power requires rather different kinds of understandings, theories, emotive dispositions, and skills that can be more or less suitable for a particular situation.

Every form of politics, every effort at politicization, is contingent on understandings orienting, directing, coordinating, explaining, and legitimating actions. From the perspective of consequent processualism they *should* pertain to understandings about the processes forming the target institution. This should include ideas about the understandings of the various participants located in the fabrics of action-reaction effect flows that constitute the institution targeted by politics. The social imaginary of people who want to shape the fabric of institutions in and through which they live need not follow this ideal-typical sociological construct. To analyze the success and failure of politics, it is indispensable to study *how* politicians imagine the social world, how they understand its operations, and how they therefore understand their possibilities for intervention. Of course, and contrary to simplistic understandings of Foucauldian power/knowledge dynamics, these understandings can be misleading. They can actually undermine power rather than further it. Consequent processualism provides at least a critical framework to begin with an analysis of the suitability of particular understandings for politics.

It is not uncommon that human beings understand their world in such a way that they see, at least for themselves, no possibilities for effective intervention. This is the case, for example, wherever people believe that the social world is determined by transcendental powers, no matter whether they be called by the name of some personal god or some abstract principle such as history. Dominic Boyer (2005, 10–13) calls this "negative dialectical knowledge."[47] If it prevails, politics in the sense presented here (in extreme cases even the political as a way to think) ceases to exist. The very condition for the possibility of politics is the defetishization of institutions by comprehending them as susceptible to human influence. What this enables is what Boyer terms "positive dialectical knowledge." I call understandings orienting politics *political understandings*. They enable institutional creation or transformation. The process of their imagination, negotiation, testing, certification, their formation into institutions, can then properly be called a political epistemics. In spite of its lofty name it takes its home in the humble quarters of poor families and street gangs as much as in the hallowed halls of governments, universities, think tanks, and corporate headquarters.

Political understandings may carry the promise of a social world more to the liking of the politician. Historically speaking, the appeal of political philosophy and later also of ideology and the social sciences lay precisely in

---

47. With his notion "dialectical knowledge," Dominic Boyer (2005, 10) uses a concept related to what I call *political understanding* albeit with the more specific sense of "knowledges of social dynamics, relations and forms that center on perceived ontological tensions between the temporality of potentiality and actuality and between the spatiality of interiority and exteriority." He traces the oscillation between a positive, agency-affirming form of such knowledges and a negative agency-denying one through the contexts of their emergence in over two hundred years of German history.

their potential to defetishize institutional orders and thus to enable politics. This does not mean that they were right. Political understandings as ideologies can become fetishized themselves—and socialism is the prime example. This has led to the paradoxical phenomenon of an ultimately enslaving politics of liberation. To develop a few useful tools to think through this problem more generally by way of an intensive engagement with GDR socialism as an exemplar is the hope of this book.

At the end of this section an important reminder is in place. Many institutions are not the consequence of politics, and most, if not all, are not the consequence of politics alone. This has important consequences for the possibilities and limits of political knowledge. Being capable of developing appropriate political knowledge is no guarantee for the ability to engage in successful politics and self-politics. Institutions with a larger base may always exceed the very possibility of politics. Nevertheless, for politics to be as effective as it can be, adequate political knowledge is a precondition (the possibility of lucky ignorance notwithstanding).

CONCLUSIONS

Stated in the shortest and most general possible way, my argument so far has been that the particular dynamic of institutions needs to be analyzed in reference to understandings and the ways in which they are stabilized or destabilized. A fortiori this is true for political institutions and organizations. The rationale behind this argument follows a genetic account of the formation of institutions. I argued that they are formed in action-reaction effect flows that are, although generally enabled by material resources and time, moved in a particular direction only by understandings that orient, direct, coordinate, and explain or legitimize particular actions, thereby linking them as reactions to past or expected future actions. Understandings contribute significantly to the stabilization of institutions to the degree that they themselves become institutionalized. For this to happen, understandings need to be continuously validated. Validation takes place in encounters with other people deemed authorities (i.e., through recognition), as the result of an evaluation of the merits of understandings in orienting action (i.e., in corroboration), or by agreement with already existing understandings (i.e., by resonance). These validations, too, can at least partially become institutionalized. Just imagine the ways in which our understanding that we are in fact the bearer of a particular name is continuously validated through deeply institutionalized forms of address, administrative documentation, and so on. In part, the very institutions that are stabilized by particular understandings increase or decrease the likelihood that a particular validation will occur. What we obtain, then, is an image of society as a thicket of social processes that wherever they are stable, that is, institutionalized, buttress each other; wherever some are changing, others will be affected, possibly even creating cascading change effects. We have therefore a unique way of making sense of both, apparent stability and catastrophic failure, which followed in the case of GDR socialism on each other's heels.

Methodologically this means we should focus our investigation on processes of co-constitution between formed understandings and other kinds of institutions. These processes of co-constitution take the form of a dialectic where they remain open. They do so where processes of validation remain open-ended, where they are allowed some degree of play, which is to say, where they are not fully institutionalized. Such openness is important in situations of social change necessitating an adjustment of understandings and institutions to changing circumstances. However, processes of co-constitution can also be short-circuited, that is, closed onto each other. We will see in the course of the investigation that institutionalizing validations is not simple, especially in the case of resonances (because of their long-term temporal horizon and their inertia) and in the case of corroborations, which can only become institutionalized to the degree that they are effectively remade in the image of recognitions. We shall see that some meta-understandings, epistemic feeling patterns, ideologies, and practices make short-circuiting much easier. In the case of GDR socialism, short-circuiting was prevalent, because its self-politics was driven by understandings emphasizing mobilization at the expense of critique. How this came about historically is the topic of the next chapter.

THE EMPIRICAL AND THE THEORETICAL—
A NOTE ON METHOD

Consequent Processualism and Ethnography

Adopting the meta-theoretical framework of consequent processualism has profound consequences for the study of institutions. They need to be understood in terms of the interconnected flows of actions and reactions that form them. However, much of social-scientific analysis has taken to reifying institutions. This is done, even where lip service is paid to the ontology of institutional formation, most notably in Durkheim's highly influential *Rules of the Sociological Method* (1982) and the various kinds of sociological structuralisms that have systematically built on it. There are several reasons for this. First, as Durkheim's text makes clear, there is a particular normative understanding of what proper science is about that is inspired by the phenomenal success of the natural sciences in the nineteenth century. It proposes that legitimate scientific objects are things that are independent of the human imagination. Accordingly, the condition for the possibility of a true science of the social is taken to rest in strictly limiting analysis to the causal relations among different kinds of social things. Thus Durkheim analyzes how one particular form of institutions, most importantly forms of social organization, "cause" other kinds of institutions, most notably particular forms of solidarity (1997) or categories of the mind (1995). With a few (albeit notable) exceptions, he is not interested in the distributed action-reaction flows that alone can transport an effect and thus "cause" one institution to have an impact on another. The whole Durkheimian tradition has in consequence developed a penchant for fetishizing institutional arrangements.

The second reason for reification is its promise of parsimony in explanation. Talking about "classes" or "states" or "organizations" as collective actors reduces the complex, distributed flow of effects in a myriad of actions and reactions into a much more simple analysis. Under certain circumstances, treating institutions as if they were things is a justifiable analytical shorthand, just as it is a necessary, and by no means necessarily problematic, shorthand in everyday life. But even then it is important to develop an ethnographic imagination (Glaeser 2005) that allows us to retranslate institutions into the processes that form them. Where we cannot do this, we have no way of validating our analysis, because institutions appear to us only in the actions and reactions of people in real time and space. Without their retranslation into interconnected action-reaction flows we can also neither say what institutions (and our analysis) mean for the life of people nor can we propose courses of action that could either help to maintain or change institutions should we desire to do so. Thus, without an ethnographic imagination, we end up with a meaningless sociology of shadows, a theater of "collective actors," of "forces" or "variables," or worse, still, a mere exhibition of "structures" set up not as a means to the end of a better comprehension of social *life*, which also offers hope and suggestions for how to change it, but very much for its own sake.

Against these various structuralisms, against the fetishization of institutions in the social sciences (as opposed to the everyday), the processual formation of institutions has been recovered repeatedly in the history of the social sciences as a *critical* device.[48]

---

48. A genealogy of authors who have contributed major pieces to the recovery and/or reformulation of the interactive formation of institutions could be constructed. It would include at least (here with the original publication dates): Marx (e.g., 1867), Simmel (e.g., 1908), M. Weber (e.g., 1922), Schütz 1932, Vygotsky 1934, Elias 1935, Mead 1934, Wittgenstein 1949, Goffman 1959, Austin 1962, Berger and Luckmann 1966, Garfinkel 1967, Burke 1969, Bourdieu 1972, Silverstein 1979, Giddens 1984, Latour 1999, Abbott 2001b, Brubaker 2004, and Sewell 2005.

While the institutional fetishisms of the everyday effectively undercut the very possibility of politics, academic forms make it more difficult to comprehend institutional change while serving at the same time as political ideologies. Ethnography promises a way out of this predicament because it urges the study of process (Gluckman 1967; Moore 1978). However, more traditional ethnographic conventions, above all the fixation on the immediate spatial, temporal, and social context, render the study of institution formation difficult. Luckily, in the last quarter century ethnography has come a long way in overcoming at least some of these problems by having become historical (e.g., Sahlins 1981; Moore 1986; Comaroff and Comaroff 1992). And yet, the theoretization of processes has, in my opinion, lagged behind description. This has something to do with the ways in which social scientists think about the relationship between theoretical and empirical work. One way to produce a tighter link between theoretization and description is what I have called *analytical ethnography* (Glaeser 2000; 2005). The standard lore of common procedure in social research is to begin with an interest in a particular social arena, which is then dramatized into a pointed empirical puzzle. This supposedly gets solved by mobilizing the right kind of theory, which may get adjusted, amended, or transcended in the course of solving the puzzle. Without even beginning to get into the question of whether this is in fact what social scientists do, one conclusion about this account is obvious: the empirical puzzle comes first, and theory development is relegated to the status of a side-product of the research process. It is neither explicitly given a role in the choice of the empirical arena of interest, nor is it acknowledged how much of (mostly implicit) theory goes into the formulation of the puzzle. The point of analytical ethnography is to engage questions about the social world in which we live and theoretical problems dialectically right from the start of the project. This means that the arena of investigation is chosen not just for its intrinsic interest but at least as much for the theory development potential it holds. Theory and the story, which is developed as an answer to the empirical puzzle at hand, are developed pari passu.

This confronts us with the following questions: "Why are answers to sociological puzzles stories?" and "what does theory have to do with narrative?" Driven by action-reaction effect flows social processes are contingent; their course is *principally* open.[49] This does not imply that they cannot be also highly regular and thus more predictable. However, regularity and predictability is something that needs to be accounted for by analyzing the metaprocesses that stabilize and regularize types of reactions to types of

49. For two collections of essays zeroing in on the matter of contingent development of processes from a variety of angles (e.g., ambiguity, polysemy, ingenuity, chance) see Abbott 2001b and Sewell 2005.

actions.[50] I have in the previous sections of this chapter explained how I plan to go about analyzing the stabilization of particular understandings as an inroad into investigations of institutional stability and change. Narratives are the particular form in which we have learned to communicate a linked sequence of events, and thus they are the means of choice to relate them (e.g., White 1973; Ricoeur 1984). The analytical work of picking and connecting relevant types of events out of an infinitesimally complex tapestry of happenings, of proposing systematic action-reaction links at the core of these events, and of hypothesizing how these events constitute, maintain, or change institutions is the work done by a particular kind of emplotment. Stories are composed of a number of elements such as characters, locations, actions, and events. They arrange them along the linear temporality of telling that makes visible the underlying temporal order of happenings that are related through the story. Following Aristotle (1970), the work of synthesizing the sundry elements of story into a coherent-appearing whole has been called emplotment (cf., Ricoeur 1984). Helpful for the work of constructing this synthesis are cultural forms, templates of tale telling such as genres, and, even more importantly, standard forms of emplotment. Arguably the best known among these are tragedy, comedy, satire, and romance (Frye 1957). The use of these templates as synthesizing devices relies on audiences to fill in commonplace associations between the elements of story (e.g., that jealousy can turn human beings into murderers, that fathers try to replicate themselves in their sons, etc.). The social sciences cannot satisfy themselves with telling stories in this sense. They must critically investigate the synthesizing links of story. In other words, they must explicitly reflect on the *effective emplotment* of the tales they tell, which is to say that they need to develop theories explicating the dynamics of process. The theoretization of process is possible because the chain of links from actions to reactions and institutions comes about in fairly regular ways, a fact that opens the dynamics of process to careful generalizations. These, however, must take into account that the production of links in process is contingent on local circumstances, for example, the understandings of events by participants or the wider institutional field in which action-reaction sequences are embedded.[51]

50. An illustration for the radical contingency of processes and institutions that look so stable that even the very word *prediction* feels ill applied may be in place. On the end of May Day 1989 nearly everybody in the GDR would have "predicted" that there would be a May Day 1990 resembling the one that had just taken place. Of course it was not to be. Most of us would "predict" that the next Independence Day celebrations would resemble the last. What could we imagine to happen that this would not be the case?

51. The making of such limited generalizations as effective emplotment devices is what I take Weber's (1988c) ideal-typical approach to be about.

Theory can be developed by working forth and back between using alternative effective emplotments as data-mining tools on the one hand (if a person has reacted this way then there should have been this kind of antecedent action; if a social formation has changed this way then there should be this kind of action to alter it, etc.) and the integration of these data into stories on the other. The altercation between data and theory, stories, and effective employment can come to a (provisional) end when a locally satisfying fit between story and data is achieved. In their final versions, theory and story are therefore both results presupposing each other. The story is effectively emplotted by the theory and the theory is the reflexive abstraction of successively refined stories.[52] That does not guarantee that theory and narrative are perfectly adjusted to each other. The narrative will always outstrip the theory, and theory will take flights of fancy that are not fully reflected in narrative. This is so because both constantly overshoot each other. And at one point one has to come to a stop. Science after all is an open-ended process. It lives by unruly narratives and overshooting theories. Where else would we get the ideas from for the next round of investigating social life?

Data

The data I have collected for this study originate in a wide variety of different sources. However, the main body flows from a historical ethnography of Stasi's efforts to control the peace, civil rights, and environmental movements in East Berlin during the 1980s. This historical ethnography relies on the one hand on intensive interviews with twenty-five Stasi officers, sixteen opposition members, and three secret informants. These interviews varied greatly in length. The shortest ones lasted two hours; the typical interview was conducted over three to four sessions with a total of six to eight hours of interview time; some interviews with selected key informants stretched over a whole year, totaling forty hours of interview time. There are more interviews with Stasi officers for the simple reason that there is far more published material about the lives of opposition members, including memoirs on which I could rely in addition to the interviews. On the other hand the historical ethnography builds on archival material mostly from the Stasi, but also from the opposition collected in the Stasi archives, and especially the

---

52. In the end, then, one could tell the story without making the theory explicit. However, self-consciously writing stories on the basis of effective emplotments while making the theory explicit and thus available for discussion is a central component of reflexive social scientific practices. In fact, the explicit development of effective emplotment schemata should be as much an integral part of ethnographic practices as it is typically not a part of fictional writing, where explanations or psychologizations stick out as alien to the genre.

Mathias Domaschk archive in the Robert Havemann Society, a private foundation. The interviews provide retrospective autobiographical accounts, reconstructions of daily routines, reflections on local ideologies and practices, and descriptions of events from several perspectives. The archival material supplies on the one hand propaganda material, contemporary action plans, reports about events, security assessments, training materials and textbooks, official rules and regulations, planning documents, case progress notes that were formulated by Stasi officers and other state and party agencies. On the other hand, the archival material furnishes official letters, petitions, position statements, and samizdat publications written by members of several opposition groups.

I paid close attention to matching officers, opposition members, and secret informants onto each other as participants in the same social arena. The choices were driven by what was interesting as much as by what documents could be made available and who was willing to talk. Although I have collected wider contextual information, I have in the end focused on an interrelated set of Berlin opposition groups, among which Women for Peace (Frauen für den Frieden), the Initiative for Peace and Human Rights (Initiative für Frieden und Menschenrechte or IFM), the Ecological Library (Umweltbibliothek), and the Peace Circle Friedrichsfelde (Friedenskreis Friedrichsfelde) form the core.

The advantage of pairing documentary evidence with interviews is that they form a lively commentary on each other. Documents are objectified, radically decontextualized communications. Interviews can reveal much about how these documents were made, how they were used, and hence what they mean. Oral accounts of past events are notoriously prone to constant rewriting through successive presentations. Documents can be used as effective memory props. They also provide significant clues about how the reconstruction of the past actually proceeds.

Besides these interviews and documents I have participated for a whole year in the monthly meetings of the Insiderkomitee, a group of former Stasi officers who are interested in researching and discussing the history of the Stasi and the GDR. Several members of this group have engaged in writing articles and books about the Stasi (e.g., Eichner and Dobbert 1997; Grimmer et al. 2002b). These were instructive, because here I could see former officers interact with one another: appealing to common goals, listening and commenting on each other's narratives, and so forth.

Besides the historical ethnography of the Stasi's efforts to control the peace, civil rights, and environmental movements in Berlin, I did archival research on the ways in which various other governmental and party agencies addressed the issue of dissidence. Thus, I consulted documents of the Staatssekretariat für Kirchenfragen (the governmental agency responsible for church-state relations), the central committee, and the politburo. To learn more about how the party state made sense of itself, I studied text-books and pamphlets on propaganda, personnel administration, organization and planning. More, since my study of Stasi revealed particular patterns of interaction, ways of thinking about information flows, of talking about work and the world at large, I began to wonder how typical they were for socialism more generally. This was a very important, even necessary, step for this investigation, because I wanted to see to which degree I could generalize from Stasi to GDR socialism. For this reason I have spent a lot of time reading a wide variety of memoirs available about work in socialist bureaucracies in East Germany, covering not only politburo members but also central committee bureaucrats and county administrators, artists, and scientists. This was made possible by the fact that after unification, many former East Germans felt the need to reflect on their time either because they saw themselves challenged by countless prejudices of West Germans about their former country, or because they themselves wanted to arrive at a better understanding of what had happened.

PART I

Socialism as a Self-Fulfilling Prophecy—The Party's Project

The following two chapters address the project of the party state to establish, maintain, and develop socialism in the GDR. Chapter 1, "From Marx to Conscious Social Transformation," takes a longer historical perspective. It goes back to the very roots of the state socialist project in the writings of those men the party state has self-consciously adopted as "classics": Karl Marx, Friedrich Engels, and Vladimir Ilyich Lenin. The central narrative line of this chapter follows the historical unfolding of something of a paradox. In spite of Marx's base-superstructure model that analyzes consciousness as an epiphenomenon, the actually existing socialisms of Eastern Europe have attributed central importance to ideology for the formation of socialist institutions. At least for the GDR I can show that the efforts to construct and maintain a socialist consciousness assumed ever-greater importance as a tool of politics. Once it became clear that the rearrangement of ownership structures (i.e., socialization) and work flow (the introduction of collectives), which both combine a politics of articulation with a politics of incentives, did not work as planned, a politics of education moved to the foreground. It is only a slight exaggeration to say that the party's understanding of its own project increasingly boiled down to the hope that if only everybody would internalize the teachings of Marxism-Leninism, while sincerely acting in accordance with them, socialism would realize itself in an ever more perfect way because Marxism-Leninism was the only true science of the social that has ever existed. What was required, then, of politics was to make a heroic effort to create a countrywide monolithic intentionality, which meant strengthening the one organization that could actually bring that change about (the party) while enabling it to bring everybody else on board through a systematic program of proselytization. This was seen as all the more important because socialism saw itself entangled in a mortal battle with capitalism. From these self-understandings followed logically, first, a particular kind of ethics that was supposed to compel everybody into relentless self-objectification vis-à-vis that goal of the party state, and second, a specific form of accounting for errors that carries all the marks of a theodicy. The longer historical breath of this chapter serves also another purpose. It reveals the historical and theoretical roots of central notions of actually existing socialism's self-understanding that have left deep traces in its institutional structure. Once it has become clear what assumptions the party made about the social world, it will also become much more transparent why it wagered its very own survival on the production and policing of monolithic intentionality.

The second chapter, "Aporias of Producing Right Consciousness," provides an overview of the institutional means by which the party state aimed to implement its consciousness-driven model of social transformation. I will in particular point to three prongs of the institutional fabric of the GDR that are important here. There were first the organizational principle of democratic centralism and central planning that operated like fractals through all contexts of organized socialist life. These principles were meant to create for the party the conditions for the possibility of central control while at the same time mobilizing and rallying the population behind its project. From here the party followed basically two strategies of creating a monolithic intentionality. It pursued a politics of education actively proselytizing for the truth of Marxism-Leninism through a wide-ranging, steadily increasing propaganda apparatus. However, the party state understood that for a host of reasons, the machinations of the class enemy abroad being the most important one, propaganda could also fail. More, as the key instrument of politics, propaganda was thought to be especially vulnerable to the ideological attacks of the enemy. Hence an agency was necessary that could address both the consequence of propaganda failure and that could also secure the smooth operation of propaganda itself. That did in fact become one of the central tasks of the secret police (Stasi), especially after fighting espionage became less demanding in practice after the building of the Wall. Moreover, the party institutionalized a comprehensive web of prohibitions of contact with ideas and people and thus again a politics of (dis-)articulation that was meant to buttress its own efforts of forming socialist consciousness. Among the web of prohibitions were travel restrictions, censorship, and the prohibition to form groups or organizations that were independent of the party. The forms of validation I introduced in the last chapter will serve as a handy way to think systematically through the intended effects of these policies.

One important message of chapter 2 is that the secret police was an entirely integral, within its own logic, consequent, and necessary part of the socialist project as it existed in Eastern Europe. Even though the Stasi was the institutional anchor for the aforementioned tasks, which carried with them a particular kind of habitus, it would be easy to show that this habitus, this secret police way of doing things, was in fact permeating all socialist organizations, just as propaganda and democratic centralism were constitutive parts of the Stasi as an organization. Rather than being an aberration of history, ideological policing was an integral part of the Soviet socialist project. After all, the first socialist secret police, the Bolsheviki's Cheka, was founded within weeks of Red October and quickly began to play a central role in institutionalizing socialism. In many ways, the prevalence of secret policing as a political tool is a consequence of an array of interacting political understandings. A second major intention of this chapter is to isolate aporias of socialist politics, that is, to provide an analysis of how the single-minded pursuit of the goals of the party created unintended consequences that threatened to undermine the attainment of these goals. These aporias pertain especially to the aforementioned key tools of politics of the party: central planning, proselytization, and prohibitions. Each posed a conundrum that the party within its established institutional means could not solve.

I

From Marx to Conscious Social Transformation

The young Hegelians logically put to men the moral postulate of exchanging their present consciousness . . . and thus of removing their limitations. This demand to change consciousness amounts to a demand to interpret reality in another way. . . . The youngest ones of them have found the correct expression for their activity when they declare that they are only fighting against "idle talk." They forget, however, that to this idle talk they themselves are only opposing other idle talk, and that they are in no way combating the real existing world.

MARX, *GERMAN IDEOLOGY*

As everybody knows, communist society . . . cannot be the result of the realization of historical necessity. This society gets created . . . on the basis of the deeply conscious, goal-directed activity of every single one of us.

STANDARD SOVIET PROPAGANDA HANDBOOK[1]

In contradistinction to all former social formations, socialism is created and developed by the conscious, planned action of the people.

ERICH HONECKER[2]

INVERTING MARX'S "INVERSION" OF HEGEL

Anybody who approaches the "actually existing socialisms" (Bahro 1977) of Eastern Europe with the Marxian base-superstructure model in mind and with the vague notion that socialist countries have realized some Marxian model of state and society is up for a big surprise. For socialist practices and

1. The quote is from the second German edition of a Soviet handbook on political education widely used in training party propagandists throughout the GDR during the 1970s and '80s (Wischnjakow et al. 1974, 8).
2. The quote is from the report of the central committee to the VIIIth party congress of the SED, delivered by its first secretary Erich Honecker (ZK 1971, 111). As with many key quotes from party documents it has been used as a reference point in countless other documents (e.g., ZK 1972, 18).

ideologies have de facto inverted that model. This can be well illustrated by a central passage of the program of the Socialist Unity Party (Benser and Naumann 1986, 98–169) of East Germany.

Marxism-Leninism is, in the unity of all its parts, the *theoretical foundation* for all actions of the party. Only on the basis of this generally valid scientific theory and its further creative development, is it possible to fight the revolutionary battle for the interests of the working class and of all working people. Marxism-Leninism is the *reliable compass* for creating the developed socialist society in transition to communism. The Socialist Unity Part of Germany provides *direction and aim for the conscious, planned activity of the working people*; it consolidates and *strengthens socialist class consciousness*;[3] it awakens and promotes the creative initiative of the people for the creation of the socialist society and socialist manners and customs. It is the main goal of the political-ideological actions of the Socialist Unity Party to equip the working class and all working people with the *revolutionary ideas* of Marxism-Leninism, to *explain* to them the policy of the party, to develop their *socialist thinking, feeling, and acting*, to mobilize them for the solution of the tasks at hand, and to fortify them against the influence of imperialist and *bourgeois ideology*. Every member of the Socialist Unity Party of Germany must be an active fighter at the *ideological front*. Wherever communists live and work, they will disseminate and defend Marxism-Leninism as the *roadmap for conscious action* on behalf of the interest of the working class and of all working people, they will demonstrate the superiority of socialism, of its values, and of its accomplishments. (My emphasis, 159–60)

Echoing this vision of what socialism was about, the Stasi officers who were my interview partners have all stressed the importance of ideology as the *basis* of social life in the GDR. This is how Herbert Eisner put it:

Socialism is very sensitive to ideological disturbances. The bracket that keeps the whole thing together is ideology, and if this bracket is weakened the whole system falls apart. In capitalism this bracket is money. Thus we

---

3. In what follows I will often refer to the socialist concept of "consciousness." Wherever I use the term it is in reference to its use in the socialist tradition. I use *understanding* as the core analytical concept of this study to analyze content and genesis of "consciousness." The term consciousness appears primarily as "class-consciousness," in which the term simply means that one actually understands oneself as a member of a class with corresponding consequences for action. In the course of time "conscious" increasingly came to mean that the person so qualified knows socialist theory as currently defined by the party to be a true understanding of the world. In other words, "conscious" people differentiated and integrated the world in accordance with current party doctrine leading them to act at all times in the party's interest.

always spoke of the ideological work, the party-educational work that aimed to make everybody identify with it. The idea was that I will raise my children, that I will influence the neighborhood, the parents' council at school, the national front, the association of fishermen, whatever, in accordance with party policy. We wanted everybody to internalize the policy of the party.

Now, had Eisner uttered these precise words at a party meeting during the lifetime of the GDR, chances are that he might have been censored for deviating from the party line in the direction of idealism, although it is quite clear that he more or less puts into his own words the whole thrust of the program passage quoted above. At least he would have had to acknowledge that capitalism and socialism both have an economic base and that socialism is not just kept together by ideology. However, all former Stasi officers I could talk with, alongside a great number of former party officials who have published their memoirs and even the party itself, emphasize the centrality of ideology for socialism's success.

It is, then, one of those ironies of history that central practices and institutions of Eastern European socialisms cannot be understood properly until one begins to appreciate the fundamental role ideology has played in a variety of ways in its everyday operations and in its historical development as especially more recent scholarship has pointed out (Verdery 1991; Burawoy and Lukács 1992; Lampland 1995; Kotkin 1995; Kharkhordin 1999; Halfin 2000; Boyer 2005; Hellbeck 2006; Yurchak 2006). Indeed, I shall argue, one can not understand Eastern European socialisms unless one confronts them as forms of *idealism* with strong *rationalistic* underpinnings. The irony does not lie in the fact that the people embodying these institutions and practices were idealists in the common sense of the word, or that they thought of themselves as working for a greater good. Given the harm often willingly incurred in the pursuit of this good, this is rather a tragedy of shattering proportions. The irony lies much more in the fact that these institutions and practices were idealistic in the philosophical sense that ideas were de facto afforded primacy over "material," that is, physical and social realities. In fact, socialism fetishized certain ideas. Thus, a gulf emerges between socialist practices and part of socialism's self-avowed theory, Marxism, because the latter was constructed precisely against the foil of philosophical idealism, which was not only the perennial target of Marx's and Engels's vigorous criticism but also the favorite object of their biting derision. In spite of the frequent invocation of Marx in socialist rhetoric, then, socialist practice was in an important sense very un-Marxian. It inverted the Marxian "inversion of Hegel" once more in developing what was, in effect, a *consciousness-driven model of social transformation*. In the end, Eastern European socialists were Marxists almost in spite of themselves and in a rather paradoxical sort of way. In the rest of this chapter I hope to show how this happened. The ensuing history of socialism's self-understandings, which includes a consideration of the meta-understandings that were used in producing them, would be worth a book in its own right. What follows are, in fast forward mode, what I see as highlights and turning points.

Marxian Beginnings

To get a better sense about divergences and congruencies between Marx's theory and Eastern European socialist practice it may be useful to recapitulate briefly what Marx had to say about the relationship between understandings and other kinds of institutions. As we shall see, the base-superstructure model is only one, if a strong streak, in his thought on this relationship. In the *German Ideology* (1958a) Marx famously assigns consciousness (and with it what I have referred to as discursive understandings) to the superstructure, his umbrella term for the total set of determined institutions. Besides consciousness, it also includes politics, the state, science, and the arts. He calls the determining set of institutions base, which includes the fragmentation of society into two antagonistic classes, a system of productive relations (such as property regimes) and a constellation of productive forces constituted by the integration of the social organization of production in a concrete division of labor with a particular set of skills and technologies as well as with available material resources. Arguing for a particular direction for the flow of effect, Marx asserts rather unambiguously that "life is not determined by consciousness, but consciousness by life (1958a, 27)." The explicit reasoning behind postulating a unidirectional determining effect flow from economic institutions to all other kinds of institutions is Marx's assumption that as physical creatures human beings need to reproduce themselves materially; humans have to be (whether they like it or not) above all *Homo faber* to satisfy their historically specific material needs.

Moreover, Marx sees ideas not only as a direct outgrowth of a mode of production, but he also sees these ideas as completely misrepresenting social life. In a society ruptured by the abyss of class, everybody lives in false consciousness. The reason is simple. With the help of intellectuals, the dominant class forms its understandings exclusively from within its own social position, that is, in response to its own experiences, problems, and anxieties, which is to say from one particular perspective. By universalizing these understandings grounded in the particularity of standpoint and history they do not only become apologetic but also fundamentally false. Wages, for example, are interpreted by capitalists with the help of liberal economists as market prices determined by the universal law of supply and demand. From where they stand neither capitalists nor the economist working for them can see that prices are the result of a historically specific set of power relations resulting from a particular mode of production. They could neither understand, much less admit, that it is the power inherent in an economically defined position rather than merit that affords them income and status, nor that the wages they pay amount to exploitation (or as he later [e.g., 1962b] argues in greater processual detail: that in fact they need to be exploitative if they are to remain competitive as capitalists).

Since the dominant class also has at its disposal the institutional means to impose its way of thinking on the dominated class, these ideas also become *generalized*—in capitalism, for example, through the institutions of the state and the state-run educational system. Accordingly, "the thoughts of the dominant class are in every epoch the dominant thoughts, that is, the class which is the dominant material power is at the same time the dominant intellectual power" (1958a, 46). Together, false universalization and generalization make the understandings generated by or on behalf of the dominant class *ideological*.[4] Interestingly, Marx does not move from here to conclude that these ideologies, false and misleading as they may be, might still have a stabilizing effect on the institutional order of society. For the writer of the *German Ideology* they remain without consequences, they are a mere epiphenomenon. In this sense, the term *ideology* (as opposed to science, as we shall see) has both practically and theoretically a thoroughly negative meaning for Marx. For him, ideologies are dead (but strangely not as Horkheimer and Adorno [1971] have argued: deadening) collections of symbols.

The base-superstructure argument is by no means only a feature of the early Marx's thought. The preface to the 1859 *Critique of Political Economy* (1961) provides an often-quoted formulation of the argument in summary form:[5]

> In the social production of their life, men enter into definite, necessary relations that are independent of their will. These are relations of production that correspond to a given stage in the development of their material forces

---

4. Interpreting thought under capitalist conditions as distorted on all sides puts Marx into the interesting position of having to account for himself and the truth claims connected to his theory (cf. Postone 1996). The question is not only how somebody of (auxiliary-)bourgeois origin (Marx's father was a civil servant) could begin to think thoughts that are obviously not reflective of his class position, but the question is also how anybody could think revolutionary thoughts at all. His answer is that "the existence of revolutionary thoughts in a particular epoch presupposes the existence of a revolutionary class" (1958a, 47). A revolutionary class emerges when alienation has reached such proportions that the contractions between ideology and the social life become blatantly obvious (1958a, 34).

5. It is this comparatively slender volume that has historically been the source of the base-superstructure distinction, since *German Ideology* was not published until 1932.

of production. The totality of these relations of production constitutes the economic structure of society, the real basis, on which arises a legal and political superstructure and to which correspond definite forms of social consciousness. The mode of production of material life conditions the social, political, and intellectual process of life per se. It is not the consciousness of human beings that determines their existence, but their social existence that determines their consciousness. At a certain stage of development, the material productive forces of society come into conflict with the existing relations of production or—which is just a legal expression for the same thing—with the property relations within which they have operated until now. From frameworks for the development of productive forces these relations turn into their fetters. Then starts an era of social revolution. With the change in the economic basis, the whole tremendous superstructure gets overturned more or less speedily. In the consideration of such transformations, one always has to distinguish between the material transformation of the economic conditions of production, which can be determined with the precision of natural science, and the legal, political, religious, artistic, or philosophic—in short, ideological forms in which men become conscious of this conflict and argue it. As little as one judges individuals by what they deem themselves to be, one cannot judge such a period of transformation by its consciousness. To the contrary, this consciousness must be explained with the help of the contradictions of material life, from the existing conflict between the social forces of production and the relations of production.

There has been quite some dispute about the proper interpretation of this passage, which pertains to the relationship between productive forces and the relations of production.[6] However, there is no doubt that both together constitute a historically specific mode of production that is the material base that in turn determines the superstructure, including discourse.

As behooves a passionate dialectician, Marx's thinking about the relationship between understandings and other institutions is, however, more complex than his base-superstructure model suggests (Williams 1977). The latter's place within the development of Marx's thought can only be appreci-

---

6. The issue is essentially whether one could say that the productive forces determine the relations of production, or whether there is more of a dialectical relationship of co-constitution between both. Some of the confusion may have occurred due to some stylistically well-meaning translation effort that has sacrificed accuracy with respect to the imagery invoked. Given that the text in question is Marx's effort to bring to publication at least some of the thinking he has developed in *Grundrisse* (which take the form of a long, raw thought piece), and since the *Grundrisse* themselves make it crystal clear that Marx has a dialectical relationship in mind, less ink might have been spilled.

ated if one takes into account that the origin of this model lies in his fierce polemic against the left neo-Hegelians. In fact, he feels an almost violent urge to distance himself from them, not least because they stand for a part of his own becoming. In the obsessive attempt to avoid anything that might even faintly smack of idealism, the Marx of *German Ideology* therefore drains the baby with the bath water; he is unable to conceive of a genuine action-reaction mediated dialectic between understandings and other kinds of social institutions. Nevertheless, true to his own, in the twenty-six-year-old's exhortation pronounced in his "eleventh thesis on Feuerbach," Marx aspired not just to interpret the world but also to change it (1958b, 7). And he did so not primarily by becoming a labor organizer—others were much better at this than impatient, quarrelsome Marx—but by becoming a writer and theorist. This is, after all, what he excelled in. Accordingly, Marx leaves no doubt that even his most theoretical writings must be understood as in the service of his political agenda. But how, then, does he understand the relationship between theory and political practice? Why does he think that *his* theorizing is not yet another interpretation, as futile or as misleading as those of the ridiculed neo-Hegelians?

While discussing the relationship between communists and proletarians more generally in the *Manifesto* (1959, 474), Marx and Engels already argue: "The communists [being internationalists] are therefore the most decisive, always advancing part of the labor parties of all countries. The *theoretical insight* into the conditions, the dynamics and the general results of the labor movement is their advantage over the remaining mass of the proletariat [my emphasis]." So, no doubt, understandings, including conscious, discursive understandings, have orienting power for Marx. They can inform action, even revolutionary action, and thus they can have an effect on the institutional fabric of a society. The advantage of communism, according to Marx, is precisely that its actions are highly conscious and rational. It provides a theory that through its materialist *scientific* foundations can transcend the limitations not only of local perspective but also of the delusional universalization of ideology. Scientific communism offers an ordering that can always place occurrences into the context of universal historical development.[7] Real

---

7. In the *Brumaire* (1960), Marx makes a related yet even farther-reaching move. He reasons that "human beings make their own history. However they do not make it according to their own will, not under self-chosen, but immediately found, given and socially transmitted circumstances" (1960, 119). Part of these transmitted circumstances are the understandings developed in the past and deployed in the present. They are essential for getting the action going, argues Marx, even where they are in some ways bound to misrecognize the present moment, thus involuntarily creating the comical effects (French revolutionaries in "Roman costumes") that Marx so much relishes in describing. The argument Marx makes here, especially with regard to the revolutionaries of 1789– and 1848–, is quite akin to Sorel's (1999) notion of the empowering

social science (as opposed to ideology) can be as effective in directing action as the natural science that finds its way, for example, into the production process, and that properly seen has to be understood as a part of the productive forces.[8]

In this spirit, Marx aims to show throughout his oeuvre how scientific theoretical-historical analysis can provide a road map for the actions of the labor movement. The point of such analysis is not merely to satisfy some curiosity but also to free the proletariat from its unwitting participation in the reproduction of the economic and political institutions of the time, *to the degree that this is possible under the given historical circumstances*. Marx aims to provide insights into what kinds of actions would be most effective in bringing about change within the institutional strictures of a particular time and place. In the awareness of the immense difficulties (and often plain futility) of human-induced institutional change, Marx tries to provide an analytics that helps the labor movement to decide which battles to fight and which ones to avoid in any concrete moment—including the determination of the right moment for revolutionary action.

Contrary to what one would expect from a literal interpretation of the base-superstructure model, therefore, Marx works, in many of his writings, with an implicit concept of understanding-enabled agency that has the power to form institutions. In chapter 5 of *Das Kapital* he finally sets out to develop such a theory more explicitly by describing the labor process (1962b) as an idea-directed operation. There, Marx avers that understandings are not only important in the planning phase that "ideally" anticipates the product of the process before it begins, but that they also function as a regulative throughout the process. To carry this through, Marx argues (leaning on Kant—and the Bible), that the laborer has to make himself subject to his own law and thereby transforms himself. "He develops the potentialities of his nature and subjects the play of its forces to his own command" (1962b, 192). In other words, in learning to labor, humans cultivate their own agency. And understandings are a constitutive element of this process, which leads to a simultaneous transformation of self, product, and understanding.[9]

---

myth (e.g., the general strike that will never happen and yet infuses the actors with the will to go on). He hastens to add that such productive misunderstandings were only necessary for the revolutions of the past. The proletarian revolution has to be guided by *true* understandings of the laws of historical development.

8. Indeed, Lenin (e.g., 1967e) and after him the Soviet Marxist-Leninist orthodoxy, has seen scientific communism in the form of "Marxism-Leninism" or "dialectical materialism" as a decisive factor behind the accelerated development of the productive forces in socialist countries.

9. Obviously, the kind of labor process Marx is describing here is not capitalistic wage labor. It is the kind of activity that Hannah Arendt (1998) (building on Heidegger's phenomenology) calls "work," a type modeled in Marx as in Arendt's case on the production process of a skilled

What matters here are not just discursive understandings. Marx is keenly aware that the social world in which we live always transcends the concepts we have about it. Even if rational planning is possible, it is impossible to conceive of the entire social world as rationally planned, because actual *practice* always explodes its conceptualization. Especially in the introduction to the *Grundrisse* (1983), Marx mentions several reason for this, not the least of which is that the abstraction inherent in conceptualization presupposes the plurality of concrete forms. In other words, concepts presuppose that some state or process could be otherwise, more precisely, that the actor can de facto *imagine* them to be otherwise. In this sense "gender" is contingent on the possibility that something could be either male or female; the notion of occupation is necessary only once there are several to pursue; the concept of culture can emerge only where one becomes keenly aware that people could think, feel, and act, differently, and so on. Of course, this is anything but a rejection of the link between understandings and institutions. It is rather an earlier call for a practice theory[10] and in effect a plea for the systematic consideration of other kinds of understandings, unconscious kinesthetic ones included. It is also a plea for the recognition that mercifully not all of social life is institutionalized, that besides understanding*s*, whatever their mode, there is understand*ing* as an open ongoing process.

Looking at the ways in which Marx thinks and lives the relationship between theory and activism raises the issue of his method. He hopes for, analyzes, and predicts, and in the failure of his prediction is forced to revise his theory several times in order to furnish a better road map for action. In analyzing the failures of the 1848 revolution in France, for example, Marx offers in the *Brumaire* (1960) significant improvements of his conceptualization of class and the historical forms and functions of the state over earlier writings. In the same spirit, his analysis of the ill-fated Paris Commune of 1871 (1962a) offers a refinement of his thesis of the withering away of the state, and the forms of political organization replacing the state after a proletarian revolution. This process of theoretical development in response to an analysis of real-world events, this cultivation of his own sociological imagination, leads to an impressive differentiation and refinement of his theory, the logic of which comes to be worked out with increasing rigor. However, Marx never sees reason to completely overhaul major parts of his theoretical apparatus. The core elements of his thought remain firmly in place so that

---

craftsperson who completely makes a finished product from basic raw materials. Wage labor is much more the Taylorist pure exertion of energy, which Arendt calls "work," for which the worker needs no concept.

10. Quite rightly, then, Bourdieu (1977; 1990) has taken his departure for his formulation of a theory of practices from Marx.

earlier works like the *Manifesto* or *German Ideology* can always be read as adumbrations of *Capital*.

After his initial revolution of "turning Hegel on his head," Marx works exactly in the mode that Kuhn (1962, 23–42) has described as "normal science." Even though Marx and Engels have a clear understanding of the historicity of their science (Engels 1962, preface) and the need for its continuous development, they do not anticipate or even consider the possibility of further revolutionary transformations of their social science, especially of its fundamental concepts and ontological foundations. That is, they did not expect this for the historical stage of bourgeois capitalism. They thought they had freed social thought once and for all from the funny mirrors of ideology, much in the same way that Enlightenment scientists thought they had broken out of the darkness of myth into the eternal light of knowledge. That is to say, Marx and Engels (and Lenin and the official stalwarts of Soviet ideology after him)[11] operated with meta-understandings that did neither foresee, much less welcome, the possibility of radical transformations of their own understandings.[12]

In sum, the explicit and continuous emphasis on the base-superstructure model notwithstanding, Marx works with a much more sophisticated, in its consequences, dialectical theory about the relationship between understandings and other institutions. However, Marx's dialectical reasoning has a definite boundary. In the last instance, he asserts that no matter how good our understandings are, no matter how much we have succeeded in cultivating ourselves as agents, *the course of history* will not be changed by it. As he says in the preface to the first German edition of *Das Kapital*: "Even where a society has tracked down the natural law of its motion—and it is the final purpose of this oeuvre to uncover the law of economic dynamics of modern society—it can neither jump over, nor declare as void *natural* phases of development. But it can shorten and mitigate the pains of birth" (1962b, 16; my emphasis). The choice is only that between a rougher and a gentler ride along the inevitable path of history. Marx, one of the founding fathers

---

11. Marx and Engels did not have the benefit of living through the complete ontological remake of modern physics, beginning with Einstein's special theory of relativity, that is, a revolution *within* science rather than a revolution from other forms of knowledge-making *to* science. Lenin and especially his successors did.

12. This raises an interesting counterfactual question: Might the whole fate of socialism have been a different one, had Marx and Engels allowed for such a possibility, that is, had the commitment of socialism not been to some original formulation, but to the project of an ontologically open, critical social science with an emancipatory agenda? Perhaps. Asked from the perspective of a political epistemology, the important question is why on the one hand such a meta-understanding could never take hold in the institutional center of Soviet-type party states, and on the other hand what the consequences of this particular kind of meta-understanding is for the actual generation of political understandings, for politics and self-politics.

of social scientific institutionalism, has drawn a hard line around the possibilities of human agency and immanent understandings of social processes. According to him, at least in the *longue durée* the dynamics of society do not follow an institutional but instead a "natural" logic that only communism will eventually break. The institutional order of a time is, with minor variations, ultimately the set piece of a metaphysical order that is radically (i.e., ontologically) removed from all human influence. The "immediately found" circumstances under which we make history are to a considerable degree literally *not humanly mediated.* The infrastructure-superstructure argument about the relationship between economic organization and understandings set forth in the *German Ideology* is replicated at a higher level throughout Marx's oeuvre in the superstructure of institutional spheres that are driven by the infrastructure of *natural* historical laws. And thus (as critical thinkers in the Marxist tradition such as Castoriadis 1987, or Unger 2004, but also critics of Marxism such as Popper 1966, have seen quite rightly) he performs a venerable philosophical act: that of revealing what appears as real as a mere shadow that must be investigated in the glaring light of the absolute. Marx's critical theory has with its philosophy of history a rigid metaphysical core. One could also say it has in its middle an anticritical blind spot.

This does not disqualify Marx as a theoretician otherwise full of brilliant insight. But it does mean that if one wants to use Marxist theory to guide political action, *eventually* one has to come to terms with this metaphysical core lest one succumb to the fetishization of understandings. The actually existing socialisms in the GDR never did. And this had serious consequences, for it eventually led the party state, as we shall see, to literally close the door to the world, locking official understandings into a dogmatic hall of mirrors. Yet, this did not happen out of ill will, spite, or a lack of intelligence as conservative critics have always been ready to surmise. It was a consequence of how, within the socialist movement, and then within socialist countries, understandings about the world came to be validated. Political epistemology has to show how Marx's metaphysics came to appeal and then institutionally remained action-guiding. I cannot say more about the original appeal here than this. It is not hard to see and understand the inspirational qualities of Marx's metaphysics. In dark hours (and there were many) it was a tremendous source of hope. Still the Stasi officers' enthusiasm for the socialist project is thoroughly suffused with it, especially in the immediate postwar years. More, the very success of the labor movement is inexplicable without it. Importantly however, that very success with its seeming climax in Red October was in official state socialist accounts of it always celebrated as an indirect corroboration of Marx's philosophy of history. To see how it became institutionalized, thoroughly woven into the fabric of socialist society, I have to continue my narrative about the increasing importance of ideology in socialist theory and practice.

Soviet Developments

Marxist thinkers continued to develop further the idea that sound theory must inform the struggle of the labor movement. In fact, the relationship between theory and revolutionary practice in form of poignant analysis of the present and their consequences for the revolutionary struggle was what writing in the tradition of Marx was centrally concerned with. The *Manifesto*'s vanguard party idea, which combines theoretical guidance with tight, central organization, found further development especially in Lenin's "What Is to Be Done?" (1967h). There Lenin asserts that "without revolutionary theory, there can be no revolutionary movement" (117). This had fundamental consequences for how Lenin evaluated the priorities of party work, for he argues that "the *role of vanguard fighter can be fulfilled only by a party that is guided by the most advanced theory*" (Lenin's emphasis; 118). That means for the party members and their leaders:

> In particular, it will be the duty of the leaders to gain an ever clearer insight into all theoretical questions, to free themselves more and more from the influence of traditional phrases inherited from the old world outlook, and constantly to keep in mind that socialism, since it has become a science, demands that it be pursued as a science, i.e., that it be studied. The task will be to spread with increased zeal among the masses of the workers the ever more clarified understanding thus acquired, to knit together ever more firmly the organization both of the party and of the trade unions. (119)

Elsewhere, that leads him to the conclusion that "the development of the consciousness of the masses will always remain the basis and the main content of the entire work of the party" (CW 11, 164).[13] Given the centrality Lenin affords to theory, it is also no surprise that he advocated the foundation of a central newspaper (his *Iskra*) as the most important instrument to organize, unify, and motivate the party with its otherwise dispersed local activities (1967h, part V). Stalin (1952a, III) has later summarized the Leninist position on the relationship between theory and practice in clear reference to Kant's epistemology:

---

13. From the perspective of Western Marxist thought one would have to speak about the changes in the understanding of the relationship between base and superstructure and the more positive evaluation in the works of Lukács 1968, Gramsci 1971, and Althusser 1971. However, considered renegade pieces in socialist Eastern Europe they did not lead to a positive redefinition of the concept of ideology in actually existing socialism.

Theory is the experience of the worker's movement of all countries in its generalized form. Of course theory becomes useless where it is not connected with revolutionary practice; and in the same manner, practice turns blind if it does not illuminate its path through theory.

This increasing positive evaluation of the power of discursive understandings to influence processes of institutionalization is nothing if not a consequence of revolutionary and reformist socialist practice itself. A whole series of events corroborated meta-understandings, which increasingly overshadowed base-superstructure reasoning. In many countries the labor movements were successful in effecting significant political change. Not only was the franchise in most western European countries increased to encompass eventually the entire adult population, which led to strong socialist parties, pursuing newfound possibilities through the means of electoral politics, but also legally more-protected and better-organized trade unions eventually effected real wage increases. Social legislation led in many countries to the emergence of what later would be called the welfare state (e.g., Steinmetz 1993; Wehler 2007). These improvements in the standards of living of laborers happened against the explicit predictions of Marx, who famously foresaw a process of continuing immiseration. The mainstream labor movement systematically interpreted these new institutions as the results of their ideas and their political struggle. Most importantly, however, the first socialist party–sponsored revolution was undertaken in a society that was in Marxian developmental categories at best in transition from late feudal to early bourgeois phase and therefore nowhere near the stage in which a proletarian revolution could be expected to occur and even less, be successful in the longer run. Yet revolution succeeded in Russia, of all places. Thus, Lenin's continuing emphasis on the power of the right kind of theory seemed better corroborated than ever by the very success of his and his party's theory, organization, and determination.

The formation of Soviet institutions must be understood through the interplay of a multiplicity of understanding-guided actions, reactions, and validations that I described in the last chapter. Charged with the task to form the political, economic, social, and cultural institutions of the Soviet Union, understandings about what they ought to look like played a major role in bringing them about—besides the decaying institutional context of late czarist Russia (e.g., Figes 1998). Without direct historical precedent they had to be imagined with the help of analogies. Lest I be misunderstood: by emphasizing the importance of understandings, I do not want to argue that these institutions were drafted as plans and realized as planned. For that the imaginations in question were far too vague, if still powerfully suggestive. Lenin (1967e) famously imagined the entire economy of postrevolutionary

Russia on the model of a large state enterprise such as the post office (304), indeed the entire socialist society as an "office and a factory with equal work and equal pay"(345). In search for more concrete models he famously looked to Germany's war-planning efforts as a type of state capitalism. This he argued was the first step to socialism. He says (1967k):

> Here we have "the last word" in modern large-scale capitalist engineering and planned organisation, *subordinated to Junker-bourgeois imperialism.* Cross out the words in italics, and in place of the militarist, Junker, bourgeois, imperialist *state* put *also a state,* but of a different social type, of a different class content—a *Soviet* state, that is, a proletarian state, and you will have the *sum total* of the conditions necessary for socialism. (Lenin's emphasis, 697)

It is important to note that there was neither just one understanding about what these institutions ought to look like and how, with what degree of popular participation by whom and potentially at what cost and what risk of losses in human life, the politics of forming them ought to begin. For Lenin was by no means the sole undisputed leader (e.g., Fitzpatrick 1993; Service 2002), and at least until the 1921 Petrograd strikes and the final sailor uprising of Kronstadt (Getzler 1983) the leadership of the Bolshevik party faced not only counterrevolutionary forces but also democratic opposition from without (Brovkin 1988). In fact, the revolutionary process inspired imaginations of a new society, in the arts, architecture, the sciences, and in practically all dimensions of social life, and not only by intellectuals but also by common man (Stites 1989; Rosenberg 1984). Accordingly, Lenin had to fight for his ideas, which he presented (imitating Marx) more often then not couched in a sharp polemic tone against others, including leading comrades. Nor were the institutional arrangements so stable and predictable that plans could be realized as decreed. The chaotic circumstances of a lost world war, of revolution, and of civil war made it hard to know which institutions still worked in what way and where, what newer kinds of institutions might have sprung up locally, and if so how they operated. The threat of physical violence and the lack of resources weakened or transformed understandings; it disrupted communication, transportation, and memory practices; and it deprived actors of time and the material resources necessary for action. In this way it disrupted action-reaction effect flows and therefore the reproduction of institutions. Since all institutions must rely for their own stabilization on the stability of other institutions (in the introductory chapter I used the image of a "thicket" of processes that all mutually support one another), politics is usually, under such circumstances, even harder to realize than under relatively stable institutional arrangements. Not surprisingly, then, this situation forced continuous adjustments to constantly fluctuating situations that sometimes led to outright political flip-flop movements. The contradictory agricultural policies of the Bolsheviki, using land reform, socialization, forced requisitioning, and reprivatization in short succession, are a case in point.

A necessary precondition for the ongoing possibility of politics under these circumstances was the existence of a set of relatively stable institutions that could successfully reestablish regular, distributed action-reaction effect flows, with the possibility to revive the carcass of the state to resume its privileged position as a former of institutions. Historically, this role was played by three institutions: Dzierzynski's[14] Cheka (i.e., the secret police later known under the acronyms GPU, OGPU, NKVD, MGB, and KGB; Knight 1990), Trotsky's Red Army, and above all by the party, especially its central leadership. It is the success of the Bolsheviki's vanguardism in the historical context of world war, revolution, and civil war that has, in the mind of communist leaders in the Soviet Union and Eastern Europe, *definitively* corroborated the vanguard party model as the way to organize and subsequently guard the achievements of revolutionary transformations. In socialist lore, instead of the state, the party became the master former of institutions; it became the center of constitutional politics.

There is another side to chaos, however. It is an impediment to institutionalization only to the degree that it deprives politics of the necessary support of *already existing* institutional arrangements. Along with the potential for support however, institutional obstacles to ignite and make sustainable novel formations may also come to be removed. Thus, a unique opportunity for politics emerges for players with the ability to orient themselves with the help of firm understandings and who can in spite of the disorder projectively articulate distributed action-reaction linkages across time and space, while also mobilizing necessary resources. In other words, chaotic times present a unique political opportunity for strong-willed, disciplined, tightly organized and distributed organizations. Not surprisingly, given their keen political sensibilities, Lenin and after him Stalin often skillfully used opportunities offered by chaos (Service 2002; 2005). What is more, they deliberately created disorder through organized waves of terror, precisely to destroy institutions they foresaw as impediments to their own politics. The two most famous terror waves unleashed with such intention are the Red Terror of 1918–22 and the Great Purges of 1936–38. In the first case, the bridging institutions

---

14. Dzierzynski's name is transliterated from the Russian with the usual variations. However, since he was ethnically a Pole, and since East German sources stuck to the Polish spelling of his last name, I will keep it that way throughout the book.

achieving projective articulation across space and time were again the core of the party, the Red Army and the Cheka. The target institutions were those of the state, the economy (and there especially agriculture) and the periphery of the party. For example, the party leadership utilized the civil war to establish lasting party centralization (Service 1979). Prolonged armed conflict prompted the absence of many local party leaders who served in the army. Under these circumstances the party stepped in to nominate party officers to its liking, who were then formally elected—in effect merely acclaimed—by the local rank and file. These war procedures established a practice that became lastingly institutionalized to be later legitimated as the principle of "democratic centralism." In the case of the Great Purges of 1936–38, the bridging institution was now the secret police, at that time called NKVD, which was used to terrorize the party itself into an even more centralized, now essentially bureaucratic organization in which authority is conferred exclusively by the center, expressed in rank and position, rather than, for example, by charismatic gifts acquired during the October Revolution.

It is therefore also because of and not just in spite of an almost decade long series of events shattering the institutional fabric of imperial Russia, that Lenin and Stalin managed to guide the formation of a set of political and economic institutions that in the end were quite compatible with Lenin's admittedly general ideas of what such institutions ought to look like. Understandings and politics proved crucial for the creation of the fabric of Soviet social institutions, economic structures included.[15] This does not mean that the economic conditions of Russia did not matter. However, the formation of the Soviet Union is an excellent example for how processes of institutionalization are best understood through a genuine dialectic between understandings and other kinds of institutions, rather than through some kind of base-superstructure thinking, whatever the "base" and the "super-structure" may be.

One last step in the growing concern with a theoretically educated consciousness as the basis for socialism needs to be presented here. Lenin remained persuaded to his end by the classical Marxian thesis that revolution needed to be a wider international phenomenon if it were to succeed in the longer run. Throughout the early years of Bolshevik rule, Lenin expected, and through Comintern later tried to encourage, revolutions in the major industrialized countries of Europe, especially in Germany, but elsewhere as well. He thus hoped to break the young Soviet Union's international isola-

---

15. For studies about this drawing-board-to-reality practice of socialism, see, for example, Kotkin's (1995) study of the invention and construction of Magnitogorsk, the city and its mines, and Scott (1998), with a host of further references about the collectivization of agriculture.

tion, a move he hoped would stabilize the fruits of the revolution from without. However, these hopes were dashed in a series of dramatic failures. Béla Kun's Hungarian Soviet Republic survived for little more than three months; the 1919 November revolution in Germany established a fragile liberal democracy rather than a republic of soviets; the 1920 Munich Soviet Republic was defeated barely a month after it was declared; the 1923 risings in Saxony, Thuringia, and Hamburg were crushed even before they could really begin. After Lenin's death, it was the party's left wing around Trotsky that held on to an orthodox Marxian view against Stalin who developed the notion of "socialism in one country," arguing that the construction of socialism in the Soviet Union could proceed without revolutionary support from abroad (Stalin 1952b [1926]). This mattered theoretically and practically especially with regard to the relationship between the urban proletariat and the peasants. The land reform launched on the heels of revolutionary takeover and a little later also the "new economic policy" (NEP) had in Lenin's own understanding (1967b) turned peasants *partly* into allies of the proletariat—as they were poor, working people, but partly also into enemies—because they did indeed engage in haggling and price speculation over the sale of their privately grown produce. The question of the possibility of a socialist society in which class antagonisms can be greatly reduced thus boiled down to the issue of whether the Russian peasantry could be transformed, or better: would allow itself to become transformed through the collectivization of agriculture into a rural proletariat without marshaling major resistance. Not surprisingly, then, one of the major bones of contention between Stalin and his opponents lay in the proper assessment of the revolutionary consciousness of the peasantry measured by its insight into the necessity of the collectivization. Says Stalin (1952b [1926], section 7):

> What is the *disbelief* in the victory of socialism in our country? This is above all the lacking *conviction* that owing to the state of development of our country the main masses of the peasantry can be included in the project of constructing socialism. This is, secondly the lacking *conviction* that the proletariat in our country has ascended to the command post of the economy, that it is incapable to include the main masses of the peasantry into the project of constructing socialism. (My emphasis)

Even though Stalin still employed the language of conditions in his rationale for the possibility of socialism in one country, a major reason was that if the construction of socialism was in fact the aim in the near future, there were few alternatives. Counterarguments about the impossibility of such a move were brushed aside in the knowledge that such seeming impossibilities had been overcome before with the October Revolution. With a certain right,

Stalin could see himself as the true heir to the Leninist spirit. Just as Lenin had brushed aside with his "April Thesis" (1967f) the Marxian doctrine of a sequence of two separate, epoch-making revolutions—a bourgeois revolution preceding a proletarian one—Stalin now brushed aside Marx's globalizing logic. The unlikely trajectory and ultimate success of the Bolshevik establishment of power in the Soviet Union seems to have finally led to an understanding that what mattered most in the establishment of novel institutions was firm belief, the certainty that this could be done, executed by a party exhibiting a monolithic intentionality. The reality of socialism was close to becoming a matter of a sheer will to power. And not just because the narcissistic imagination of a genuine autocrat desired it to be that way, but because the course of history rendered such a presumption plausible through a number of indirect corroborations that came to be recognized time and again in central party rituals as well as in the sacred texts people were asked to make their own.

MONOLITHIC INTENTIONALITY: A CONSCIOUSNESS-DRIVEN MODEL OF SOCIAL TRANSFORMATION

If anything, the historical significance of ideas is even more palpable in Eastern European socialisms. Even if the conditions in some countries were more akin to those imagined by Marx as the grounds on which proletarian revolutions could develop (especially in East Germany and Czechoslovakia), none of them developed indigenous revolutions triggered by the contradictions between productive forces and relations of production. In fact, Eastern European transitions to socialism were not even the result of mostly indigenous politics—as, after all, Russia's February and October revolutions had been. Instead, Eastern Europe's socialisms were the product of political, administrative, military, and police strategies and tactics carried forward by the Soviet Union, which enforced them as liberator from Nazi rule and victorious occupying power. It always did so in collaboration with local communist parties, which were, however, more or less tightly controlled by the Communist Party of the Soviet Union (CPSU) through Comintern, the third international (e.g., for Germany: Schroeder 1998; Staritz 1996). In the long run, this control worked best under conditions of military, economic, or personal dependence. That is to say, it worked where the Soviet Union became the ultimate guarantor of communist party rule through its willingness to engage itself militarily should communist party rule become threatened, where the country in question was economically dependent on Soviet supplies, and where the leading members of the Eastern European communist parties had survived persecution by spending the war in the

Soviet Union, where they were schooled (and tested for loyalty) for some potential future work in their home countries.[16]

In driving the transformations of Eastern European countries, the Soviets applied a number of lessons the Bolsheviki had learned in the context of the October Revolution, the ensuing civil war, and the initial years of Soviet rule. First, the establishment of a socialist order can succeed whether or not the conditions Marx had laid out for a proletarian revolution are in fact met. Second, the radical transformation can be successfully accomplished in a top-down manner by seizing control of the state and by remaking it under tight control of a communist party. Third, the latter has to be organized as a Leninist vanguard party that offers through its disciplined self-politics and broad base extraordinary means of engaging in politics. Fourth, the disorder and weakening of institutional arrangements created through violent conflict by hampering the webbed action-reaction effect flows constituting these older institutions can be usefully exploited for the superimposition of a new institutional order. Fifth, where such weakening has not taken place by the effects of war, and where older institutions pose a threat to the establishment of a socialist order, harassment or terror may serve the same purpose. Sixth, all of this said, violent means can be ineffective and certainly are exceedingly costly. Thus, long-term strategic goals may necessitate tactical compromises with other categories of actors. In particular this means that the establishment of a full range of socialist institutions will take time. And most importantly, the key to the long-term success is an ideologically unified, centrally organized, tightly disciplined vanguard party as the most powerful political organization with absolutely peerless institution-formation capabilities.

With the exception of Albania (which was neither liberated nor occupied by the Red Army) and Yugoslavia (in whose liberation from Nazi rule the local resistance played a major part), and national communist postures notwithstanding (as in Romania—and temporarily almost everywhere else), the Eastern European socialist governments remained militarily and often also economically (e.g., through the soft-currency supplies of raw materials and energy) dependent on the Soviet Union. Political and economic dependence typically entailed ideological followership.[17] In everyday life of the Warsaw Pact countries—with the exception of Romania under Ceauşescu (Kligman 1998; Verdery 1991)—this was visible in constant verbal tributes to the Soviet

---

16. The purges notwithstanding, which claimed a considerable toll among émigré communists as well among Soviet party members, these leaders often felt a deep sense of connection with the Soviet Union (e.g., Wolf 1998; Eberlein 2000; see also Epstein 2003).

17. See, by contrast, how the practical independence of Tito and Mao also created greater intellectual independence.

Union, as friend, as helper, as liberator, and as mentor. Friendship with the Soviet Union was celebrated as a constitutive factor of Eastern European socialism, and there is no list of socialist virtues that would not include in some prominent place the demand to maintain and develop relations with "the big brother."[18] Thus, the introduction of socialism proceeded, although with differing local input owing to the different postwar situations, in all of these countries on the basis of Soviet blueprints. In the Soviet Union the revolution had succeeded (even if few people at this time seemed to have any idea at which cost); socialism in one country had become a reality; and now the Soviet Union had beaten Nazi Germany; and thus the general slogan under which the Sovietization of Eastern Europe proceeded was, "Learning from the Soviet Union means learning to win!"

Crafting German Socialism

For Germany World War II ended in total defeat. The country had lost more than 10 percent of its population (military and civilian deaths), its major cities lay in ruins, and its industrial and agricultural productive capacities were significantly reduced. Twelve years of Nazi dictatorship had at least dislodged if not destroyed many institutions of civil society while orienting much of the institutional fabric of the country toward direction by the Nazi Party, which had ceased to exist. The sizable eastern parts of the country, East Prussia, Danzig, Pomerania, and Silesia, were annexed mostly by Poland,[19] which in turn had to cede Galicia, with its capital city Lviv/Lwow, to the Soviet Union. The population of these territories (along with the German ethnic minority in Czechoslovakia) was expelled if it had not already been "evacuated" by the Nazis as the Red Army was advancing. This created a situation where the immediate postwar population in the remaining parts of Germany was, in spite of the war losses, much higher than before the war. In combination with the destruction of the housing stock and the decline in productive capabilities this created enormous supply shortages, which were further exacerbated by the presence of several million displaced persons—in their majority slave laborers the Nazis had brought into the country. Under

18. With regard to a Western audience I should clarify that what the expression "big brother" did for many socialists in Eastern Europe has no Orwellian ring whatsoever. It could not have such a ring, as Orwell's text was typically not made officially available. This does not mean, however, that its use could not carry different kinds of ironic allusions—as in fact it often did, at least in the GDR where functionaries who had visited the Soviet Union were regularly flabbergasted by the much lower Soviet standard of living.

19. The northern half of East Prussia was annexed directly by the Soviet Union, extending the Baltic territory under its control. After the independence of the three Baltic states, this territory formed a Russian exclave.

these conditions criminality and disease rates exploded (Kleßmann 1986). Perhaps not surprisingly, German participants remember these days less as "liberation" than as "the collapse" (der Zusammenbruch), telling stories attesting to the breakdown of all common standards of morality.

The remaining central and western parts of Germany were divided into four occupational zones: the southwest was occupied by France; the southeast and the western core lands came under the control of the Americans; the northwest was taken over by the British; and the areas between the Baltic Sea in the north and the Ore Mountains in the south, between the Harz Mountains in the west and the Oder River in the east, with Berlin more or less in the center, were occupied by the Soviets. In a strange microcosmic fetishization of the capital city, Berlin, too, was divided into four occupational zones, with the French, British, and Americans in the west and the Soviets in the east. Even though the four allied powers were originally bent on administering Germany together and as a whole, each power reigned supreme in its territory, and major differences between them began to emerge not least due to significant differences in occupational policies.

The introduction of socialism into the Soviet-occupied territories of Germany was a piecemeal process driven at least as much by political expediency as by the desire of the Soviet government and German communists to establish socialism on German soil. Only in hindsight may it seem as if the various steps on the road to socialism were irreversible turning points. The reason is that it was not immediately clear to Stalin how to make best diplomatic and economic use of the Soviet Union's victory over Nazi Germany. He oscillated between hopes to get more than the share he had bargained for at Yalta and notions of a unified if neutralized German buffer zone between the two emerging blocs. Thus, many of the steps taken by the Soviets were responses to the international situation, and often enough, mere reactions to the increasing economic and political integration of the western zones.[20]

Politically, the most important steps in the application of Soviet models to Germany were these: Immediately after the war the Soviet Military Administration in Germany (SMAD) reestablished German local and regional administrations in which members of the communist party played a

20. There has been a Cold War historical controversy about the degree to which Stalin did in fact pursue an unambiguous strategy of Sovietization, or whether he seriously considered other alternatives for the future of Germany. The West German government's official line (also argued by some social democrats) was that Stalin dreamed of turning all of Germany into a satellite state of the Soviet Union. Any offer to negotiate anything else was in this vein seen as a mere tactical maneuver. The other side has always emphasized that the path leading eventually to two Germanys as model representatives of their respective blocs was a much more contingent give and take between east and west. The latter interpretation has become widely shared after 1989, even by conservative social scientists writing on the history of the GDR (e.g., Schroeder 1998).

decisive role—not necessarily everywhere in the most visible top rank, but always in the areas of personnel, security (police), mass media, and education (Schroeder 1998; Leonhard 1955). This process went hand in hand with a de-Nazification strategy that aimed at removing former members of the Nazi Party from important positions in public administration and the economy. Although SMAD allowed the formation of other parties than the KPD, they were organized—at first rather loosely—with the communists in a "united front of the anti-fascist-democratic parties." The next important step was the unification of communists (KPD) and social democrats (SPD) to form the Socialist Unity Party (SED) in 1946,[21] thus creating a large workers' party with about 1.3 million members—dwarfing its closest competitor by a factor of six.[22] In the elections to the parliaments of the five states founded on the territory of the Soviet occupational zone, the only free elections in this area between 1933 and 1990, the SED mustered on average 47 percent of the vote (Schroeder 1998)—historically speaking a respectable result and yet still much less than it had hoped for. Starting in 1948, with the Cold War now in full swing, the SED began a formal process of conversion into a Leninist vanguard party. Statehood as the German Democratic Republic followed in the fall of 1949, five months after the foundation of the Federal Republic of Germany.

Economically, the transformation began right in 1945 with the expropriation of all land holdings in excess of 100 hectares (2,471 acres) and their redistribution to small holders, many refugees among them. At the same time the property of firms whose owners were active Nazis were confiscated. In 1946 many larger corporations were expropriated by the Soviets and organized as so-called Soviet Joint Stock Companies (*Sowietische Aktiengesellschaften*) in order to service the war reparations imposed on eastern Germany. On the basis of the already socialized industry, the process of central planning was begun in 1948. The western currency reform in the same year, with its introduction of the later mythical "Deutsche Mark" (or D-Mark for short), was answered in kind in 1948 by launching the "Mark of the GDR."

21. The Communist Party of Germany (KPD) was originally founded at the beginning of the Weimar Republic as a left-wing splinter formation breaking away from Germany's main labor party the Social Democratic Party (SPD). Although some social democrats in the Soviet occupation zone had already proposed such a move in 1945, the actual KPD-SPD unification in 1946 was sponsored by the Soviet Union and succeeded only in its occupational zone, with strong criticisms of the move among social democrats in the western occupational zones. However, the unification had considerable legitimacy among significant numbers of social democrats simply because the rise of the Nazis was in part understood by them as the failure of the left to find a united voice.

22. Of these, about 620,000 were communists; 680,000 were social democrats. Among the other parties the biggest was the CDU, which reached its highest membership in 1948 with 231,000 members.

The stepwise and differential socialization of the GDR economy is best illustrated with a few statistics. By the end of 1948 more than 60 percent of the industrial product of the GDR was generated by socialized firms.[23] By 1949 this number had reached about 75 percent, slowly expanding into the mid-1950s to somewhat more than 90 percent of the industrial product. At the same time, the socialized sector employed more than 80 percent of the industrial workforce (SZS 1956, 1957; Steiner 2004, 42). In industry, this share of the socialized sector stayed constant up to the beginning of the 1970s (SZS 1970, 99), when in the context of reorganizing industrial production units into larger *Kombinate* the remainder became socialized. By comparison, in the mid-1950s still almost all of the traditionally strong artisanal sector of production (i.e., carpentry, car repair, baking, tailoring, etc.) was provided by private companies. By the end of the 1950s, artisanal production was met with a socialization wave that increased the socialist share of the gross product to 30 percent in 1960. This number climbed steadily to about 50 percent in the late 1960s with no further growth to the end of the GDR.[24] Retail trade was another area where socialization arrived only in the late 1950s, and where until the end of the GDR more than 10 percent of the turnover was still produced through private outlets (SZS 1990, 271). The land reform of 1945 led to a large increase in the number of small operators that were often very poorly equipped with capital. Thus, compared to prewar levels, the total number of farms on the territory of the GDR increased by almost 50 percent to nearly 890,000 units (SZS 1961, 419; SZS 1957, 347). These farms were then collectivized in two waves in 1952 and 1959/60. This transformation is dramatically visible in the share of arable land tilled by socialist production units of various kinds. In 1950 this number was barely above 5 percent; from 1952 to 1953 it jumped from 7 to 25 percent, growing steadily throughout the rest of the 1950s, reaching almost 50 percent in 1959 to explode to well over 90 percent in 1960 (SZS 1961, 419).

Arguably, then, economic socialization of East Germany proceeded in waves concentrated in the mid-1940s, early 1950s, and late 1950s, with a final wave occurring as late as the early 1970s. For this gradual approach there were of course not only reasons of foreign policy, but there were also important issues of internal governance that cautioned the Soviets (and part of the SED leadership) to proceed gradually with the introduction of socialism in the GDR. For a number of reasons the majority of Germans looked much

---

23. By socialized I mean here both, directly state owned and operated as well as cooperatively owned and operated.

24. The statistics show a decline of the state sector, which, however, owes itself to changes in data collection procedures that unfortunately render the time series harder to interpret (SZS 1970, 163).

less favorably upon the Soviet occupation than that of the western Allies. Older anti-Russian prejudices dating back at least to the eighteenth century when the land of the czars became the antithesis of Enlightenment and civilization, mingled with Weimar-era anticommunist sentiment to become amplified by more than a decade of anti-Soviet hate propaganda during the Nazi period. These negative historical understandings of "the Russians" and "the Bolsheviks"[25] resonated with the fear and fact of loosing property and with the initially often-violent experiences and stories about such experiences with Soviet troops (rape and looting) and the extensive war reparation program imposed by the Soviet Union on its occupational zone.

After the currency reform of 1948, West Germany's economy "took off," quickly starting to create visible wealth differentials between both parts of the country. These were particularly palpable to Berliners, who could not only move freely between the western and eastern sectors, but who often continued to work in the respective other part of the city. Thus in part prejudiced, in part scared by what had already happened, in part fearful of what still was to come, and in part lured by the new economic opportunities in the west, many people, especially those already displaced by the war, seized opportunities to move westward. Notably, peaks in the refugee numbers followed major political events, such as the formation of the GDR in 1949 (with an increase in refugee numbers in the next year of over 50 percent[26]). They also followed waves of collectivization/socialization. When the SED declared at its second party conference in 1952 that the GDR had now reached the phase when the "construction of socialism" would begin in earnest, while connecting this announcement to a massive collectivization drive in agriculture that also fed into the uprising in 1953 (Schöne 2005), the number of refuges increased by 80 percent in the following year. Since Walter Ulbricht, the SED's first leader, was reigned in by Moscow—the CPSU leadership had judged the announcement of the "construction of socialism" to be "premature"—the SED had to slow down. Thus, the collectivization of agriculture was not finished until 1959/60, again triggering a large increase in the number of refuges to 40 percent in the following two years. The refugee movement effectively deprived the GDR of valuable, often highly qualified members of the workforce who were badly needed in the reconstruction of the country. Only the erection of the Berlin Wall in August 1961—in the midst of the sustained refugee peak following the 1959/60 collectivization drive—finally put a stop to the massive loss of people. Hence, the population

---

25. The propagandistic use of "the Russians" or "the Bolsheviks" (interestingly never "the Soviets") was often heightened by the singularization of the plural into "the Bolshevik" or "the Russian."

26. Figures calculated from Diemer and Kuhrt 1994, 238.

of the GDR stabilized at a level of roughly 17 million inhabitants. Between the official foundation of the GDR on October 7, 1949, and the construction of the Berlin Wall on August 13, 1961, roughly 2.7 million people fled from east to west, that is, nearly every sixth inhabitant.[27]

I want to conclude this section with a rough comparison of the temporal patterns underlying the introduction of socialism in the Soviet Union and the GDR. In one of the first internal accounts of the success saga of the Bolsheviks, Lenin (1967b) points to the universal historical significance of the Soviet experience. Historical differences notwithstanding, other communist movements can learn "Bolshevik theory and tactics" for purposes of their own revolutionary transformations, argued Lenin. In this context it is interesting to note that there are obvious structural similarities between the highly contingent Russian progression toward socialism and the stepwise more planned transformation of Soviet-occupied Germany into a socialist state. Above all, there was, first, an immediate land reform and the socialization of big industry that had initially provided the Bolsheviks with an enormous surge of legitimacy. No doubt, a similar effect was hoped for in Germany. This was followed by a policy of more moderately paced socializations of smaller firms, of artisanal production, as well as of the retail trade that in the Soviet Union was known as "new economic policy." Finally there was the delayed collectivization of agriculture, the timing of which was in both countries fiercely debated.

Consciousness and the "Main Task" of Qualitative Economic Growth

Marx argues consistently that the possibility of communism, which is characterized by the simultaneous withering away of the state and the dissolution of any kind of class differentiation, is based on a surge in the development of productive forces well above the level attainable under capitalist conditions. The surge has to be of such magnitude that everybody can live in relative material abundance, which will allow people to contribute voluntarily to the common good according to their capabilities, as well as to take from the common proceeds according their needs (1962c, I). Unless such relative economic bliss can be achieved, claims Marx, the whole "old shit"

---

27. The strict regimentation of the freedom to move has been an integral part to all Soviet style socialist systems. East Germany struggled in its efforts to control population movements with the open border among the four sectors of Berlin (it literally took little more than a commuter rail ticket to get from one side of the supposedly iron curtain to the other), and the fact that East German citizens were automatically regarded citizens of West Germany (the FRG maintained the, in this regard, effective fiction of a single German citizenship).

(1958a, 35) of class antagonism, suppression, and exploitation would inevitably start all over again. The question that posed itself, then, was, *how* would socialism gain a productivity edge over capitalism? In search for a clue to an answer to this all-important question, Lenin (1967e) took his departure from Marx's *Critique of the Gotha Programme* (1962c). There, Marx suggests that the productive forces of society will rise with the "well-rounded development of individuals . . . ," "after labor has become not only a means to life, but life's prime want." Marx thus expects productivity gains from a transformation of humans into beings with a different profile of needs and skills. The quality of labor undertaken in the interest of personal fulfillment is the clue to the riddle.

Lenin (1967e, 340) proceeds from here to reason that the expropriation of the means of production will effect such a transformation:

> This expropriation will make it possible for the productive forces to develop to a tremendous extent. And when we see how incredibly capitalism is already retarding this development, when we see how much progress could be achieved on the basis of the level of technique already attained, we are entitled to say with the fullest confidence that the expropriation of the capitalists will inevitably result in an enormous development of the productive forces of human society. But how rapidly this development will proceed, how soon it will reach the point of breaking away from the division of labor, of doing away with the antithesis between mental and physical labor, of transforming labor into "life's prime want"—we do not and cannot know.

Why a mere structural transition of ownership should have any effect on productivity remains opaque until after the revolution. What now reveals itself as a "new form" of social life (in the same way that the Paris Commune had revealed a new form of political organization) is, according to Lenin's "Great Beginning" (1967b), a "heroism of labor" manifest in a specific "socialist discipline" that is in contrast to capitalism's "discipline of hunger" and feudalism's "discipline of the stick," "free and conscious" (212). With the proletariat's new understanding of what work is about and how it ought to be conducted, enormous increases in the intensity, quality, and duration of work are possible. Lenin argues his case with reference to reports about "subotniks" (voluntary shifts in socialized enterprises), above all a legendary one at the Moscow-Kazan Railway.[28] In addition to the

---

28. These early examples of labor heroism set the tone and provided the rational for never-ending campaigns to improve labor productivity by motivational example, that is, by transforming the mindset of the worker. Perhaps the most famous Soviet labor hero has become Alexey Stakhanov, whose marvelous feat of overfulfilling the plan by a factor of thirteen even landed

organization, skill, and motivation of labor, Lenin also expected productivity gains from other sources (1967b), in particular from economies of scale as well as science and technology. He was in particular fascinated by the possibilities of power machines and electricity, which led him to declare famously "communism—that is, Soviet power plus electrification of the whole country"(1967g, 512). Yet, the possibilities of economies of scale are by no means specific to socialism, and neither are science and technology, except in as far as they are organized, conducted, and pursued differently, that is, to the degree that scientists and engineers themselves show "socialist discipline," that is, work with a different set of understandings. In the end, then, it is the quality of labor that makes the difference. And that is seen as an outgrowth of a particularly socialist consciousness.

These lessons of the classics of Marxism-Leninism were well studied. Almost forty years after Lenin's discoveries, the SED's first secretary, Walter Ulbricht, still argued in the very same vein at the Vth party congress[29] (ZK 1959, 149): "The Marxist insight that changes in the social conditions entail changes in consciousness [documented in the previous paragraph of his speech by reference to the *Communist Manifesto*], is confirmed completely by developments in the German Democratic Republic." Ulbricht illustrates this change, emulating Lenin's *Great Beginning* in argument and style, by referring among other examples to the self-account of a worker, "comrade Christoph from the spring works Zittau (city in Saxony)," who shifted his attitude to work from what Christoph describes as "tricking your foreman" to limit output to "giving your all" corresponding to the movement from a privately owned company to a socialized one. Here was proof, Ulbricht claimed, that structural change, even if mandated, was capable of transforming consciousness, which increased the efficiency of production. This, in turn, demonstrated why socialism must be more efficient in the long run than capitalism, ultimately out-competing it. For Ulbricht, comrade Christoph, allegorizing the transformation experience of the GDR, corroborated his belief in the Marxian base-superstructure model.

him on the title page of *Time* magazine (September 16, 1935). His East German equivalent had to be—in literal emulation—a miner too. His name was Adolf Hennecke, and he worked his record-breaking, organized workers' movement to initiate a shift in 1948 (Gries and Satjukow 2002). While Lenin reports on what seems to have been spontaneous actions, he also suggested that such actions be widely used propagandistically for the reasons just mentioned. Stakhanov's and Hennecke's shifts were well prepared and part of a well-planned propagandistic effort.

29. I have selected the Vth party congress as a point of departure because it marks at the same time a certain point of completion in the development of the GDR, while it was setting the pace for the entire post-Stalinist era, in simultaneously acknowledging and overlooking the XXth party congress of the CPSU in 1956.

Yet, Ulbricht goes on to say: "But the socialization of property alone does not guarantee that new relationships between working people will develop completely. To accomplish this, education-work is necessary to trigger a political, spiritual and moral maturation of all those working not just during work time but throughout their entire common life" (111). In full agreement with Marx and Lenin, Ulbricht and his successor argue (ZK 1959, 161), "it is the productivity of labor, which is in the last instance the determinant of the victory of socialism over capitalism." Significant economic growth led by productivity gains is declared here and in all following party congresses and any number of public speeches as *the* "main task" (*Hauptaufgabe*), and it thus becomes explicitly the corroborating condition for socialism's claim to superiority (e.g., BL Suhl 1976, 15). In this spirit, Walter Ulbricht harbored in 1958 the exuberant hope to materially overtake the West during the next five-year-plan period. Corroborating signs that this was about to happen were seen by Ulbricht not only in the Sputnik but also in the other technological achievements of the Soviet Union. He extensively cites the commentary of Western observers who worried whether the West had not already lost the race for good as a recognition of his own interpretation. Propaganda brochures (e.g., BL Karl-Marx-Stadt 1961) distributed in the late 1950s and early 1960s argue for the economic superiority of socialism by comparing the historical growth rates of the Soviet Union with those of the United States, which, so the logic went, must inevitably lead to the Soviet Union's overtaking of the United States since the latter's growth rates were depicted as consistently higher.[30]

The linear causality inherent in such thought lends itself to a translation into variable-speak. Consciousness is presented here if not as the sole "independent variable" to trigger socialist transformation then certainly as the key "intervening variable" or perhaps even more as a co-determinant of successful socialist transformation. Or, to put it in terms of syllogisms: if the restructuring of the economy under socialist principles is the necessary condition, only consciousness provides the sufficient condition for a successful permanent transition to socialism (Mittag 1969, esp. 294–301). Accordingly, Ulbricht, again following Lenin's (1967b) example, was eager not only to ask party members to engage in active proselytization for socialism but also to mobilize writers and other artists to participate actively in the transformation of GDR society by helping to shape the consciousness of the people.

---

30. In addition, they try to demonstrate the moral superiority of socialism by arguing that the socialist countries, unlike capitalist ones, do not produce an internal interest in arms manufacturing by showing divergent crime statistics and a higher social service provision (time of retirement, number of physicians per head, etc.).

In 1959 the party organized to this purpose a joint conference with artists and writers significantly lodged in Bitterfeld, the hub of East Germany's chemical industry. Here Ulbricht said: "By representing artistically the novelty of socialist society, the writer can inspire individuals to accomplish great tasks. He raises the new [i.e., socialist forms] to their consciousness and thus contributes to higher achievements and simultaneously to the acceleration of the development" (Schubbe 1972, 553). To illustrate his point, Ulbricht holds up a number of Soviet authors as glowing examples for having contributed appreciably to the development of socialism in their country.[31] What Ulbricht was offering the artistic intelligentsia of the GDR was a compact: state support and influence through the opening of publication venues in exchange for the committed support by the artists for the party's goals to stimulate socialist behavior—again with the intention to accelerate qualitative economic growth. Thus, in effect he demanded a socialist literature, deeply steeped in the teachings of Marxism-Leninism that should do its bit in the overall propaganda efforts of the party to create the new socialist human being. It is precisely the focus on consciousness that made, on the one hand, artists look like useful allies and, on the other hand, as will become clear later, as potentially dangerous adversaries who needed to be kept under tight control. Much of the oscillation between so-called thaw and freeze periods in the cultural policies of socialist countries can be explained by the love-hate relationship of the socialist leaders with writers and artists, which is based on the understanding that what and how human beings think and feel is of the greatest political relevance.

In the course of GDR history, the role attributed to consciousness as a direct, and perhaps the most important, instrument of socialist politics was increasing. There are especially two reasons for this. In spite of the fact that major components of the socialist restructuring program, the socialization of land as well as of large- and medium-sized companies, were in place by the early 1960s, the expected economic gains in productivity increases and growth did not materialize. Far from overtaking the West, the socialist

---

31. Students of socialism will find here some of the favorite motivational novels of the Soviet literature that were widely translated and distributed in Eastern Europe. Gladkov's *Cement*, Granin's *The Searchers*, as well as Nobel Prize–winner Sholokhov's *Virgin Soil Upturned* (his second, two-volume oeuvre on the Don and its people after his world best seller *And Quiet Flows the Don*). In this respect it is also interesting to note how Wilhelm Pieck, the GDR's first (and only) president, has described Johannes Becher, the recognized poet, writer of the text for the GDR anthem (the melody is Hanns Eisler's) and the GDR's first minister of cultural affairs: "Stalin, the great leader of the camp of the peace loving peoples said 'writers are engineers of the human soul.' Johannes R. Becher is through his poems, songs and speeches an 'engineer of the human soul' in Stalin's sense" (quoted in Janka 1989, 9).

economies continued to lag behind. Worse, at the beginning of the 1960s the GDR entered a phase of sharply declining growth rates, accelerating—in conjunction with the socialization wave of 1959—the movement of refugees. An economic reform packet designed to increase the flexibility of the economic system was abandoned quickly after some initial gains. To the end of the GDR, there were no more major attempts to reform the mode of operation of the GDR economy. Given seemingly unalterable structures, all that could be done was an attempt to improve productivity by improving the quality of labor—its mode of conduct, skill level, motivation. In other words, the consciousness of the workforce at all levels seemed to be the key to instituting socialism. A politics of education, that is training, and propaganda seemed to be the way to bring it into the world.

The second reason for the increasing emphasis on consciousness as the key to social transformation lies in the beginning détente between both Germanys in the early 1970s. The eased travel restrictions enabling unprecedented levels of contact between East and West disquieted the leadership of the SED. The reason is simple. Along with the fast-growing penetration of Western television, more personal contacts between both countries created many more opportunities to immediately compare the economic well-being of people in both parts of Germany, thereby furnishing ordinary people with the means to validate key ideological claims. Among the leadership of the GDR the fear arose that the kind of economic development that had taken place in the GDR, a development placing a high emphasis on investment in the productive infrastructure at the expense of consumer goods production, made people discontent and perhaps less open to the world of socialism. The solution to this problem was seen in a two-pronged strategy. On the one hand the GDR economy was redirected toward the production and distribution of consumer goods. This included the use of debt-financed foreign currency to import some of the most desirable Western goods.[32] The other strategy, however, lay in renewed efforts to raise the socialist consciousness of the citizenship of the GDR. Erich Honecker, after toppling the aging Walter Ulbricht in spring 1971, said at the VIIIth party congress (ZK 1971, 111):

> In contradistinction to all former social formations, socialism is *created* and developed by *the conscious, planned* action of the people. As we all know, this is also the core of true liberty. However, only those can act for socialism who *own a socialist consciousness*, that is, one equipped with a Marxist-Leninist worldview. (My emphasis)

---

32. Shortly before Christmas 1978, the GDR even imported 1 million pairs of Levi's jeans (Menzel 2004).

Werner Lamberz, one of the younger hopefuls in the politburo,[33] narrated in an important central committee conference on agitation and propaganda the success of socialism in the GDR as a process of consciousness transformation directly affected by the party. He describes the point of departure for this transformation process in the following words (ZK 1972, 22):

> [The party] cruelly decimated by the fascists, robbed of tens of thousands of its best combatants, had to face the spiritual and moral ruins left over from fascism: human beings who were incredibly contaminated, brutalized and cut off from the truth, irate to the degree of voluntary self-sacrifice against anything communist, Soviet or socialist. . . . From this difficult point of departure, our party could arrive where we stand today because it has always considered *ideological work as the core piece of its overall leadership*, and because it has enabled its members to become active bearers of our worldview, who fight passionately and persistently to convert the word of the party into deeds. (My emphasis)

Both Honecker and Lamberz make repeatedly clear that productivity driven economic growth, "the main task" (*die Hauptaufgabe*) proclaimed at every party congress of the SED, is, in effect, a function of consciousness and by implication of propaganda. In the opening words to the same conference Honecker remarks (11): "And as we all know, the higher the consciousness, the higher the effort which will lead to economic results still in 1972 [the conference took place in mid-November 72!], and certainly in 1973." And Lamberz states a little later (36): "One is justified to say that the main task was [thanks to effective propaganda work] heartily welcomed and accepted fast by the vast majority of our people . . . the record of economic success since the VIIIth party congress is vivid testimony to this."

It is not the case that by the early 1970s the thought of a structural determination of consciousness had entirely waned. It was still celebrated as a theoretical core tenet of Marxism-Leninism. Practically, however, structural determination had given way to the notion that the workplace was indeed the most effective place of propaganda, because "there it affects the entire human being, his thinking and feeling, his insights and beliefs, his attitudes and his character" (ZK 1972, 42). What is reflected here is on the one hand

---

33. Until his untimely death in 1978 in a helicopter crash in Libya he was considered widely to be Honecker's heir apparent. In the mode of personalization typical for expected changes and/or failures in socialism (more on this below), hopes for reforms in the GDR were often projected onto Lamberz, and after his death many more reform-minded party members felt that events might have taken a different course had he been around.

the very Marxian idea that human beings are above all *Homo faber*. On the other hand this passage indexes the notion that "the free development of human beings and the satisfaction of their interests and needs is only possible in and with the community and therefore, based on the fundamental agreement between individual and collective interests aims at the voluntary integration of the individual into society" (Schütz et al. 1978, 411). The socialist collective is thus seen as a quasi-natural network of authority, the ideal location for the transformation of consciousness.[34]

Determining the Content of Consciousness

Following a historical thrust from Marx over Lenin to Stalin, Ulbricht, and Honecker, I have demonstrated that the party in the GDR increasingly worked with a consciousness-driven model of social transformation. So now the question is: consciousness of what? The answer in its widest possible sense is Marxism-Leninism. The reason is stated (for example) by the central committee document on propaganda (ZK 1972, 69):

> Marxism-Leninism is the reliable compass of our party. All revolutionary changes proceed under its influence. Proven in life and in the fire of action, the Marxist-Leninist theory is a guarantee for future victories of our just cause. It alone enables human beings to find their way in the often complicated processes of world history, to engage themselves on behalf of the interests of the labor class and all working people and to give their life deep meaning and a rich content.

Its wide-ranging and emphatic claims notwithstanding, this is one of the more modest claims about the truth-value of Marxism-Leninism. Other equally widespread statements go further, affording absolute truth to Marxism-Leninism in the sense of some sort of correspondence with the world. "According to the words of Friedrich Engels [there is no direct reference in the original] the dialectical-materialist worldview conveys the only correct idea [*Vorstellung*] of the outside world [*Umwelt*], reflecting it just as it is without any distortion" (Wischnjakow et al. 1974, 10).[35] Or, most emphatically, revealing the expected redemptive force socialism is credited with by none

---

34. The ideas and practices emphasizing the central role of the work collective are, needless to say, of Soviet origin. They hark back to traditional Russian notions of the village community, but they were worked out theoretically and experimentally by the Soviet educator A. Makarenko (see Kharkhordin 1999, esp. chap. 3).

35. Or another formulation in the standard textbook of Marxism-Leninism (Kuusinen 1960, 17): "The unshakable foundation of Marxism-Leninism is its philosophy: historical and dialectical materialism. This philosophy takes the world as it really is."

less than Lenin (1967h, 41) himself: "The Marxist doctrine is omnipotent because it is true."

Of truth, substance, and mere letters

The reason why Marxism(-Leninism) is afforded such an exalted status is an almost naive mid-nineteenth-century belief in the powers of science, for that is what Marxism-Leninism was widely celebrated to be: the first and only true science of the social. In his famous summary of Marxian thought, Lenin (1967i, 8ff.) depicts Marx (in true Hegelian spirit) as the completion and sublimation of all the best European philosophical movements of thought. In Marx's writing, thinking about society reaches, according to Lenin, an unprecedented level of sophistication that allows human beings for the first time to make valid causal explanations and to predict historical development. One of the most widespread textbooks of Marxism-Leninism has put this thought in language that I have heard often in my interviews: "Marxism has uncovered the fundamental laws of the development of society. Thus it elevated history to the status of a true science, which can exactly explain both, the character of any given social order as well as the development from one such order to another" (Kuusinen et al. 1960, 8–9). Accordingly, the socialist society was supposed to progress in a lawlike movement. These "laws," for example the increasing productivity of labor was taken to be such a law, were frequent points of reference in political discourse.

At this point in particular, two questions emerge. The first is how workers could possibly acquire this true scientific and therefore class-appropriate consciousness. The second concerns the thorny issue of proper interpretation, of what particular texts in the Marxist-Leninist canon mean in general, and how to apply these teachings to particular situations. Lenin's famous answer to the first question, clearly inspired by the *Manifesto*, was developed in his *What Is to Be Done?* Consciousness could not develop spontaneously but could only be "brought to the workers from without" (1967h, 122). A theoretically well-trained and centrally organized vanguard party was needed to organize and educate the proletariat. If anything, the course of the revolution persuaded Lenin even more that vanguardism was central to the Bolsheviki's success (e.g., 1967b). In the aftermath of Lenin's death, vanguardism came to be seen as the central tenet of Leninism (Stalin 1952a). The notorious *Short Course* of the history of the CPSU (CC 1939, 353), arguably the most important propaganda document of Soviet socialism ever,[36] has officially made

---

36. Virtually the entire East European political elite was trained with and in the spirit of this book, which was published at the end of the Great Purges when Stalin had become the undisputed supreme leader of the Soviet Union.

the vanguard party a linchpin of socialism tout court. Consequently, East Germany's SED understood itself as such a "party of the new type." Its statutes begin with the sentence (Benser and Naumann 1986, 170), "The Socialist Unity Party is the conscious and organized vanguard of the proletariat and the working people of the German Democratic Republic. . . . It leads the people on the way to socialism and communism, to the ascertainment of peace and democracy. It gives this struggle direction and goal."

It was one thing to claim abstractly that Marxism-Leninism was the only possible source of successful orientation available; it was quite another to derive from the canonized literature of Marxism-Leninism what do in any concrete situation. Thus, mediating interpretation was required to bridge that rather sizable gap. This gap was not only happily taken up by the party; its existence became the party's very raison d'être. The hermeneutic possibilities it opened were its very lifeblood, both in opening and restricting them.[37] The positivistic truth claims made on behalf of Marxism-Leninism notwithstanding, the same exigencies of revolutionary praxis that had prompted a revision of Marx's assessment of ideology led to an emphasis on the *historicity* of Marxist theory. Marx and Engels had already explicitly argued this point (e.g., Engels 1962, preface). In this context it is interesting how Stalin defined Leninism in what is in effect his (and practically the whole generation of communist leaders' trained under his aegis) *summa theoria Lenino* (Stalin 1952a):

Leninism is the Marxism in the epoch of imperialism and of the proletarian Revolution. More precisely: Leninism is the theory and tactics of the proletarian revolution in general, the theory and the tactics of the dictatorship of the proletariat in particular. Marx and Engels were active in the prerevolutionary period . . . when there still was no developed imperialism . . . in that period in which the proletarian revolution was no immediate necessity.

37. Needless to say that "Marxism-Leninism" was in practice not a static, as it may appear at first. The standard omnipresent Marx-Engels edition (*MEW*) comprises forty-five volumes, the standard Lenin edition (*CW*) also forty-five, which is to say nothing of the thirteen volumes (abandoned, still incomplete) of Stalin that had assumed the status of classics until they lost their place in the canon after the XXth party congress of the CPSU. Commenting on the XXth party congress of the Soviet Union and the secret speech of Nikita Khrushchev, Walter Ulbricht famously wrote in the SED paper *Neues Deutschland*: "One can not count Stalin among the classics of Marxism" (H. Weber 1986, 225). Of course, even the most dedicated party members, Stasi officers included, did not usually have full editions in their homes anyway, showcasing two- to three-volume collections on their living room shelves instead. What is more, however, people did not typically study from complete texts but from collections of citations that were compiled by the party for particular educational purposes. Thus, the party could select the texts it thought particularly pertinent for its current argument (cf. Bahro 1977).

In an important sense then, Stalin argues that Marx has been superseded by Lenin precisely because history has moved on and neither Marx nor Engels had the privilege to work into their theory the latest developments. The *Short Course* (CC 1939) later clarifies the relationship between these too classics by developing a set of principles. In the conclusions an important distinction is made between the "substance" and the "letter" of any classical text. What is meant by this is clearly worked out with regard to the historicity of texts:

> What would have happened to the Party, to our revolution, to Marxism, if Lenin had been overawed by the letter of Marxism and had not had the courage of theoretical conviction to discard one of the old conclusions of Marxism [that proletarian revolutions can only happen in developed capitalist societies] and to replace it by a new conclusion affirming that the victory of socialism in one country, taken singly, was possible, a conclusion which corresponded to the new historical conditions? The Party[!] would have groped in the dark, the proletarian revolution would have been deprived of leadership, and the Marxist theory would have begun to decay. The proletariat would have lost, and the enemies of the proletariat would have won. (556–57)[38]

The conclusion is that "mastering the Marxist-Leninist theory means assimilating the *substance* of this theory and learning to use it in the solution of the practical problems of the revolutionary movement under the varying conditions of the class struggle of the proletariat" (355). Since leadership in this struggle is, however, the task of the vanguard party (353), it follows that the party needs to determine what the substance of Marxism-Leninism is. The latest interpretation with regard to particular issues was commonly called "the party line."

The SED as a Leninist vanguard party has always claimed for itself the right to determine what the substance of Marxism-Leninism is for any given period of historical development. The third paragraph of its statutes (Benser et al. 1986, 170) reads: "In agreement with the historical development of our epoch, it [the party] realizes in the German Democratic Republic the tasks

---

38. Stalin identifies here his own theory of "socialism in one country" with Lenin's "April thesis," which argued that Russia was ready for a proletarian revolution. Although Lenin's explicit position about socialism in one country was opposed to Stalin's, one could argue with the *Short Course* that substantively socialism in one country is a logical continuation of the April thesis. The difference between Lenin and Stalin does not lie in the idea or practice of a historically conditioned appropriation of classic texts, but in the degree of intellectual forthrightness with which this is done. Without mentioning it, Stalin simply obliterates Lenin's explicit position, pretending there was no difference.

and goals of the labor class set out by Marx, Engels and Lenin." The formulation "tasks and goals" aims precisely at the "substance" of Marxism-Leninism defined as its true core. Rather than limiting the power of the party this "hermeneutic power," as Dominic Boyer fittingly calls it (2003; 2005, 129–32), vastly increased it; the texts of the classics, the mere "letter" in the terminology of the *Short Course*, could no longer be leveraged against the party. Worse, leveraging these texts in a way that contradicted the party automatically betrayed the immaturity of the interpreter according to the party's prevalent epistemic feelings, ideologies, and practices. The fact that the texts were seen as true only "in substance" made the party their sole legitimate interpreter. It became the arbiter of substance that is the purveyor of absolute truth.[39] For that reason, the party's main documents were treated as more sacred than the classics, because for this moment in time they came closer to the truth than the texts of the classics themselves. This interpretation of the relative import of current party texts in relationship to the Marxist-Leninist canon is substantiated, for example, by the rhetoric of authorization used by the authors of a broad variety of socialist texts from academic thesis to bureaucratic planning documents. Typically, citational preferences are given first to current party documents, then to the classics, and finally to laws, regulations, and such. It is also supported by the way boundaries between the criticizable and the sacrosanct were drawn in various kinds of verbal interactions. Before the party had formulated an explicit policy, a much wider range of questions could be asked, concerns could be voiced, or proposals made addressing a particular issue. Once the party had defined its "line," however, challenging it in public was seen as tantamount to elevating self above the wisdom of the collectivity. For the time being, then, the current party documents were treated in practice like perfect understandings of the social world, and thus they became in effect the substance of Marxism-Leninism in its presently most adequate form. More, since Marxism-Leninism was the only possible science of the social that could

---

39. Socialism has often been compared to a salvation religion with Marx/Engels/Lenin as its prophets, the party as its church, false consciousness and exploitation as states of inauthenticity much like sin, and communism as paradise, as its imperfect image of the longed-for state of ultimate redemption. If fundamentalism is characterized above all by a form of scriptural literalism (cf. Riesebrodt 1993), then socialism's stance is decidedly antifundamentalist, a move that is ultimately furthering the power of the church, which is thus allowed to appropriate the prophet for its own purposes. One of the critical insights of fundamentalism is the realization of how such moves of the churches can tempt it to engage in self-apotheosis, to which it seeks an alternative grounding in the sacrality of text. And needless to say that this fundamentalist impulse—which does not have to degenerate into full-blown fundamentalism—has always been a possibility for party-critical intellectuals. Many secret SED discussion circles in the 1980s practiced it.

correctly grasp the very nature of society, the current party documents were understood to present the truth about society as it currently existed.

Techniques of self-positioning

Given the distinction between letter and substance and the assertion of the party's right and ability to define the substance of Marxism-Leninism, the following questions arise: How, that is, through which methods did the party define the present moment? And, how did it use the classics as guides to its specific historical problematics? In other words, what were the party's central methods of self-orientation, or, in the terminology of the sociology of understanding, the meta-understandings at play in the generation of first-order political understandings? In the GDR (as elsewhere in the Soviet world), the most important document to set the general direction of the party, its "line," was the report of the central committee to the party congresses taking place about every four to five years. These reports were delivered as daylong speeches by the first secretary; they were widely disseminated via print and electronic mass media; and they subsequently played a central role in the party's life (more on this in the next chapter). The rhetoric of these texts can therefore serve as a good starting point for an analysis of the techniques of self-orientation. As we shall see, they were following meta-understandings that had already been well established by Marx, Engels, and Lenin. Three ways of producing political understandings were particularly prominent. Together they aspired to generate a dialectical movement progressing through a twofold negation to a positive determination of the present as a distinct moment on the inevitable path of history.

In a first step, the development of the capitalist world was described and analyzed. Thus the character of contemporary capitalism was revealed through an analysis of its actions, especially its aggressions (in wars, coups, the suppression of rebellions), its handling of economic crises (unemployment, inflation), its actions against its own proletariat as a class, or its policies directed against socialist countries. Via the notion that all history is a history of class warfare the present moment in socialism was then in a second step defined precisely against the present character of capitalism. This maneuver became possible through the projection of class conflict onto geopolitical constellations. In the postrevolutionary Soviet world, the main interest of this analysis was to gauge the relative strength of capitalism, to assess its potential threats, and to understand its inherent weaknesses, which could potentially be exploited to strengthen the position of socialism in the ongoing class war. In principle, this method of self-positioning in opposition to the actions of the class-enemy responding to world-historical events dates, as we have already seen, all the way back to Marx himself. Lenin, too, was following this Marxian paradigm, most famously perhaps with his "Imperialism, the Highest Stage of Capitalism" (1967c), which vies with Marx's analysis of *The Revolution in France* (1962a) and the *Brumaire* (1960) for first place among the genre-setting exemplars.

Unfortunately, none of the analysis of capitalism produced after the October Revolution matched the earlier works of Marx and Lenin in their brilliance of insight. The reasons for this decline may well be found in their mode of production. No longer was a relatively autonomous thinker or group of thinkers in charge of research and writing. Instead, the bureaucratic apparatus of a central committee was in charge while, ironically, remaining bound in its own proceedings by the very party line it aspired to set. Especially notable about this first step is the importance it affords to the development of capitalism. The October Revolution notwithstanding, it was assumed that the clock of history can still be read with more accuracy from the West. And herein lies, perhaps, one of the reasons for the cultivation of an almost obsessive westward gaze, which so characterizes the history of socialism, especially in the GDR.[40]

The second step in the process of self-orientation was the differentiation of the straight path from the many possible errant ways. This was done by critiquing, and even more typically, by opposing or attacking other theorists' writings within the socialist movement more generally and increasingly within one's own party. Again, the roots of this procedure are thoroughly Marxian. From his earliest years on, Marx's thinking thrived on an often polemic engagement with other thinkers, whom he studied in great detail beginning with Feuerbach and Bauer, then moving on to dissect and ridicule fellow socialist thinkers such as Proudhon and Bakunin, or labor leaders such as Lassalle and even Bebel. Substantial parts of Marx's mature economic writings take shape in analysis of and opposition to the classical and contemporary contributions to bourgeois political economy that are collected in the three mighty tomes that together form his *Theories of Surplus Value*. One of the first and most successful textbooks of Marxism, reputedly much more widely read than *Capital*, was Engels's *Anti-Dühring*. It defines proper Marxism point by point against lengthy quotations from the racist, anti-Semitic, and positivistic philosopher Eugen Dühring's writings, which were briefly fashionable in the 1870s.

Although Lenin has the same predilection for oppositional self-definition as Marx, he follows this strategy with a much narrower choice of opponents. In contradistinction to Marx, Lenin argues almost entirely against other

---

40. This westward gaze has a much longer history in Eastern Europe, with deep influences not only on socialism but also on the opposition against it (Kumar 1991), and it continues to be a political orientation in postsocialist Eastern Europe (Gal 1993; Böröcz 2006).

socialist writers. There is, in his oeuvre, no serious engagement with leading representatives of liberal or conservative thought.[41] Before the revolution, Lenin's major targets were opponents within the labor movement who were not members of the Bolshevik party. He understood these opponents with the help of a left-right scheme. On the right hand he saw the "opportunists" of the second international, predominantly representatives of social democracy. For Lenin their fault consisted in banking increasingly on reform by means of electoral politics rather than on revolution. On the left hand he saw "left radicals," predominantly anarchists and others inspired by their ideas. For him their fault lay in their reluctance to settle for any policy that does not conform to the very letter of socialist principles. In other words, he saw them as unwilling to engage in tactical alliances. For statist Lenin, their other fatal flaw lay in their celebration of local autonomy, spontaneity, and bottom-up procedures. After the revolution, Lenin increasingly used this by-then-well-established left-right deviance scheme and applied it to critics within the Bolshevik party, while keeping a keen eye on international developments.

Stalin finally addressed almost exclusively opponents to his rule within the party, most notably his competitors among the revolutionary leaders of the first generation: Trotsky, Bukharin, Zinoviev, and Kamenev (e.g., 1952b). The *Short Course* published right after the Great Purge became infamous because it developed Stalin's penchant into party dogma by promoting the fight against inner-party deviants to the status of a constituent principle of self-orientation:

> Unless the Party of the working class wages an uncompromising struggle against the opportunists within its own ranks, unless it smashes the capitulators in its own midst, it cannot preserve unity and discipline within its ranks, it cannot perform its role of organizer and leader of the proletarian revolution, nor its role as the builder of the new, Socialist society. (CC 1939, 359)

In view of the results of the XXth party congress of the CPSU it is perhaps not surprising that the post-Stalinist SED offers a formulation that moves away from an emphasis on inner-party enemies, instead vowing to fight more generally any kind of ideological difference or opposition (Benser et al. 1986, 171–72):

---

41. Besides a shift in the scope of interests, this has probably also something to do with changes in the very size of the socialist movement and the corresponding corpus of socialist writing, which in Lenin's time required much more specialized attention. It also has something to do with Lenin's much-deeper involvement in politics. He simply did not have as much time for his writing as did Marx. And yet the fact remains that the result was also a substantial intellectual narrowing, which is in part responsible for leading organized socialism to overlook major developments in the dynamics of capitalism.

The Socialist Unity Party of Germany contributes to the enrichment of Marxism-Leninism. It leads an uncompromising battle against all phenomena of bourgeois ideology, against anti-communism and anti-Sovietism, against nationalism and racism and against any revanchist disfigurement of Marxist-Leninist theory.

Yet, the SED, too, has continuously urged its members to maintain the unity and purity of the party and to be on the guard against "left and right deviations" (*Links- und Rechtsabweichungen*). How much this was a constant theme in party life may be glimpsed from an anecdote. Wilhelm Danziger, one of my interview partners among the Stasi officers, told me and a former Stasi colleague over a glass of wine how one fellow member of the leadership of the party organization at Halle University once made sense of the matter of left and right deviations. He reported that said colleague drew (while Danziger redrew in front of our eyes) a straight arrow up on a piece of paper adding a second arrow undulating forth and back across the first. He then pointed to one of the right-hand turning points of the undulating arrow and said, "here we were fighting the left-deviation," while touching the straight arrow in the middle with his index finger; then he moved to one of the left-hand turning points and said: "and here we were fighting against the right-deviation," tipping at the center arrow again. At this point the other officer broke out into resounding laughter of recognition. The implication is clear: rather than fighting against left (Trotskyite or anarchist "tendencies") and right ("opportunist" or "capitulating behavior") to maintain a steady course, the party flip-flopped itself, always fighting against some steady center.

The final move of self-orientation consisted in the use of these two exercises in militant dialectics in combination with a number of positive indicators to define the present stage on the movement from capitalism to communism as a particular step in the progression of socialism.[42] Among these indicators were first and foremost achievements of economic development during the past plan period. Increases in the absolute or relative volume of the production in raw materials and capital goods were as celebrated as those in the supply of apartments, durable consumer goods, and agricultural produce. Improvements in the levels of social services were taken as much as a sign of progress as increases in the satisfaction of "cultural needs" (number of theater performances, books printed, etc.). Other important indicators were signs of support of the general population for the party and its project. These were taken to speak in particular to the class structure and class rela-

---

42. Following Marx's differentiation between at least two stages of communism (1962c), Lenin (1967e) conceived of socialism as a transitory stage toward communism. This terminology was maintained until the end of socialism.

tions within the country. In this regard election results were important, as was the participation especially of nonparty members in propaganda events ranging from subotniks, to May Day parades, and national holiday celebrations. Such indicators were taken to corroborate understandings to the effect that internal class conflict was weakening. As a result of this process, the historically adequate interpretation of Marxism-Leninism was typically captured in slogans serving as general orientational mottos for the next five years. I already mentioned that Ulbricht announced the "construction of socialism" (*Aufbau des Sozialismus*) at the second party conference in 1952. At the VIIth party congress in 1967 he announced the "continuing construction of socialism" while describing the GDR as a "socialist community of human beings" (*sozialistische Menschengemeinschaft*). Honecker declared the GDR to be a "developed socialist society" (*entwickelte sozialistische Gesellschaft*) at the VIIIth party congress in 1971 and proclaimed the "unity of economic and social policy" (*Einheit der Wirtschafts- und Sozialpolitik*) at the IXth party congress in 1976 (ZK 1978). This painstaking attention to the definition of stages and their appropriate labeling is testimony to the continuing hold that Marx's philosophy of history exercised over official socialist efforts to understand themselves in a wider world.

The ultimate reason why a proper understanding of the current stage of development was so important was to yield insight into the question of what ought to be done politically. And since politics was imagined to succeed or fail with mass participation, a link was needed to connect the proper interpretation of the current stage with everyday life. This is where socialist understandings of ethics become all important.

Socialist ethics

Self-orientation in terms of militant dialectics went hand in hand with Manichaean understandings of the world. The dualism of class conflict led to a staunch us-against-them logic, with a clear, logically unquestionable *tertium non datur*! It affected notions of belonging because either somebody was a friend or she was an enemy. It ultimately produced a zero-sum game imaginary of social life because every action, every move was seen to benefit either the one, or the other of the two contending classes. This belligerent understanding of the dialectics of world history resonated deeply with the biographies of older socialist leaders in Germany, many of whom had first-hand experiences with an enemy who tried to exterminate them during the years of Nazi rule (Epstein 2003).

What was needed, in the estimation of the party, to win this battle with the class enemy was unity. The statutes of the SED claim (Benser et al. 1986, 171): "Power and invincibility of the Socialist Unity Party of Germany lie in the ideological and organizational unity and unanimity (*Einheit und Geschlossenheit*) of its ranks, in voluntary and conscious discipline, and the active and selfless work of all communists." Accordingly, the list of the duties of the party members was topped by the exhortation to (173) "always preserve and protect in any way the unity and purity of the party as the most important precondition for its power and force." Such breathless strings of pleonastic hyperboles created through the conjunction of synonymous ("unity and unanimity") or closely related ("voluntary and conscious") terms are not only a notable element of socialist propaganda style in general, but they are a good indicator of the perceived urgency of the virtues exhorted. They are also a sign of tasks still not completed simply because that which is emphatically demanded can obviously not simply be assumed as an already well-established commonplace. This impression is amplified by the sheer redundancy of the exhortation to unity itself that appeared as a veritable basso continuo of public speeches in the GDR. Finally, unity was nothing that was demanded for thought alone. After having been asked to thoroughly internalize current interpretation of Marxism-Leninism, party members were requested to "realize actively the resolutions of the party, to strengthen in every respect the German Democratic Republic, to work for a fast development of socialist production, for scientific and technological progress and for the growth of the productivity of labor." Note again the overarching goal: qualitative economic growth.

This constant appeal to unity did not only engulf the entire party but it was in the true spirit of vanguardism directed to the population as a whole. The list of duties for party members cited above continues by demanding that members must "strengthen the connection to the masses incessantly, they must educate them about the meaning of the policies and resolutions of the party; they must convince the masses that these policies and resolutions are correct and must persuade the masses to realize them; party members must learn from the masses" (Benser et al. 1986, 174). The potential audience for the members' propagandistic efforts knew no limits (ZK 1972, 76): "Our agitation and propaganda should be comprehensible for everyone and reach everyone."

It was not assumed that appropriate consciousness automatically translated into appropriate practice. Quite to the contrary, much emphasis was placed on "socialist ethics" as an important intermediary between correct knowledge and correct practice. Socialist ethics built on the postulation of an absolute good that was most frequently stated in reference to a paragraph in Marx's *Critique of the Gotha Program* (1962c):

> In a higher phase of communist society, after the enslaving subordination of the individual to the division of labour, and therewith also the antithesis between mental and physical labour, has vanished; after labour has become not only a means of life but life's prime want; after the productive forces

have also increased with the all-round development of the individual, and all the springs of cooperative wealth flow more abundantly—only then can the narrow horizon of bourgeois right be crossed in its entirety and society inscribe on its banner: From each according to his abilities, to each according to his needs (*jeder nach seinen Fähigkeiten, jedem nach seinen Bedürfnissen*)! (Marx/Engels, 1978)[43]

The key elements of this passage found their way into the program of the SED, which closes its enumeration of what communism is with the last line of this paragraph. Every schoolchild in the GDR could recite it as the definitional slogan of what communism was supposed to achieve. Given this understanding of socialism's serene goal, that is communism, Ulbricht could argue in his famous outline of socialist morals at the Vth party congress of the SED (ZK 1959, 160): "Only those act morally and in a truly humane fashion who actively commit to pursue socialism's victory, that is the end of the exploitation of human beings by human beings."[44]

Among the standard forms of moral philosophy, socialist ethics therefore belongs with utilitarianism in the class of consequentialist ethics deriving goodness from the effect of actions rather than from the quality of actions themselves (as, for example, in Kant's deontological ethics) or from notions of what it means to lead a good life (as, for example, in Aristotle's ethics of virtue). Yet the measuring rod for the goodness of an action's consequence was not Mill's question of whether it contributed to the greatest happiness of the greatest number, but the question of whether the action helped to propel society forward in the direction of communism *as adjudicated by the party*. In this sense socialist ethics offer a more sophisticated variant of consequentialism than utilitarianism by virtue of its theoretization of hap-

---

43. Propaganda efforts have frequently maintained that socialism is not too far off and that every little deed in accordance with the decrees of the party contributes to its emergence. Thus, one of the most widely available textbooks of Marxism-Leninism (Kuusinen et al. 1960) states: "The birth of this new, highest social order will take place not too far away in the future. Thus the question: 'What is communism?' is of the utmost practical interest for millions of working people. They want to know and have to know what kind of society will emerge due to their efforts, due to their daily deeds big and small, heroic and mundane" (805).

44. Interestingly, the constitution of the GDR (politically a much less important document than the party program or the party statutes, as one can tell both from its relative citational relevance and its late promulgation) states in Article 2.3: "The exploitation of human beings by human beings is permanently eliminated. What is produced by people's hands is people's property. The socialist principle 'from each according to his ability, to each according to his *contribution*' is being realized." Note how the transformation from Marx's "communism" to the constitution's "socialism" corresponds to a change from Marx's formulation "given according to needs," to the constitution's "contributions" thus emphasizing achievement.

piness as shaped by particular social constellations. And Marxism-Leninism in the interpretation of the ruling parties of Soviet Eastern Europe claimed to have positive knowledge about what happiness-producing social arrangements were. Since the party knew best what was to be done to move history faster into the inevitable *and* desired direction, everything that contributed to the realization of the party's latest decrees was deemed moral; everything hindering the realization of the party's intentions was deemed immoral. I will call this henceforth the *ethics of absolute finality*.

This ethics motivated the constant exhortations to be "partisan" (*parteilich*) or to show a "firm class standpoint" that together operated as two logically equivalent formulations of what might be called the socialist categorical imperative.[45] It "requires to approach all questions of social life from the perspective of the interests of the working class and its struggle for the introduction and strengthening of the dictatorship of the proletariat, the introduction of socialism and communism and the irreconcilable fight against the ideology and practice of imperialism" (Schütz et al. 1978, 679). In view of socialism's Manichaean dualism, applying the perspective of "class standpoint" or "partisanship" was frequently recommended as test whether the socialist project would benefit from a particular action. Here is an example from a speech that the party secretary of the basic party organization in the department XX of the Ministry of State Security gave in April 1985:

> To apply the right means, implies in our view always to ask the question: "What serves our socialist revolution, our state and our party?" Hasty and subjective evaluations which are detached from our policy will lead by necessity to mistakes and wrong decisions.

What the party therefore tried to accomplish is to persuade every citizen of the GDR, party members as much as nonmembers, to learn Marxism-Leninism and to draw from it the conclusion that a vanguard party was needed to guide them into the future of the exploitation-free and therefore just human society, an absolutely worthy good. It aspired to convince everyone that this implied that most everybody needed to learn how to realize the party's latest decrees, which alone vouched for a correct application of Marxism-Leninism to the current historical context. All citizens were asked to make the intentionality of the party their own in a movement clearly understood as a form of self-objectification, as an attunement of every single person to the absolute truth of the objective laws of history.

---

45. About the grounding of partisanship in the conception of a universal human reason, see below. In the next chapter I will show how the performance of partisanship was central to the party's self-cleansing ritual of "critique and self-critique."

Self-objectification was thought to lead to a transubstantiation of sorts: the making of the new human being. Persons who had achieved such alignment were approvingly known as *bewußt* (conscious), the state of their mind as one of *Bewußtheit* (Schütz et al. 1978, 122).[46] In effect, the party aspired to turn GDR society into a monolithic organism of social transformation built onto a monolithic intentionality devised by the party. If everybody was thus aligned, then socialism would successfully self-realize, and the movement to communism was as fast as it possibly could be.

The belief of the party in the absolute truth of Marxism-Leninism, if not in its letter than in its substance, goes a long way to explain why the party assumed that such an undertaking would eventually succeed. However, the truth of the theory itself is only the necessary condition for this to happen. What needed to be assumed as well is that every human being is endowed with a universal rationality that is able to recognize this truth once confronted with it. The Central Committee resolution on agitation and propaganda states, for example: "To the degree that human beings develop a comprehensive understanding of Marxism-Leninism, the more thoroughly they study the works of Karl Marx, Friedrich Engels and Vladimir Illitsch Lenin, the more firmly they will believe in the law of the decline of capitalism and the victory of socialism on a global scale."

Thus, Marxism-Leninism as an objective truth was thought to resonate naturally with all working people because it spontaneously reconciled their individual and social interests. Freed from domination they would naturally come to know what was the objectively correct way to understand their situation (just as Kant's human beings endowed with universal reason were compelled naturally to discover the truth of the categorical imperative in their own inner depths).

From the insight into its truth comes a particular understanding of freedom as nothing but the human capacity first to discover and then to submit voluntarily to the inevitable: the historical laws of the movement of history (Kuusinen et al. 1960, 130). True freedom is, as Honecker stated in the quotation above, the enthusiastic endorsement of necessity. The choice was to

46. There was a famous song in the GDR, promoted in the Stalin years with the title "The Party Is Always Right." Here is my translation of some of its lyrics: "She [the party] has given us everything. / Sun and wind. And she never was stingy. / Wherever she was, was life. / Whatever we are, we are through her. / . . . / The party, / The party is always right! / . . . / And comrades that remains true; / . . . / Who defends humankind, / Is always right. / . . . / The party—the party—the party." This song was sung in a wide variety of registers: ironically, sarcastically, and, romantically. The very point, however, is its existence as an officially promoted piece of propaganda. The song's refrain kept being quoted again and again, approvingly, exasperatedly, disparagingly . . .

go rationally and morally with necessity (i.e., history) or to go foolishly and immorally against it. Consequently, people living up to their own rationality, to their own humanity, were assumed to adopt the ethics of absolute finality naturally. In this way, the bifurcation of reason since Aristotle into a capacity to distinguish between true and false as well as one to differentiate between right and wrong was thought to be overcome in socialism. Consequently, socialist epistemology and socialist ethics are but two sides of the same coin.

Creativity and critique

Within the interpretation of freedom as the reasonable choice of necessity, socialist ideology placed a very high emphasis on creativity and critique. Thus the statutes (Benser et al. 1986, 172) claim that "[the party] develops the activity and the creative initiative of all members and promotes universal critique and self-critique." Clearly, coming up with the historically correct interpretation of Marxism-Leninism is a creative act, and so is the interpretation of the resolutions of the last party congress in view of very concrete problems of individual professions. What was demanded of participants in the socialist project was expressed in a handy, universally used formula as "creative application" (schöpferische Anwendung). Party members and citizens were thus likened to engineers using the general laws of science to make concrete machines and to solve concrete problems; they were seen as social engineers applying the general laws of social development to particular social circumstances. In this hierarchical arrangement, the ingenuity of the lower levels was subsidiary to that of higher levels; it could only pertain to things not yet decided or devised. What Marx did with regard to the objective laws of history, the party did in assessing their general applicability to a concrete historical problem, which in turn mirrors what every individual was supposed to do to the mundane problems of the everyday. Living under the auspices of monolithic intentionality was far from imagined as mindless order taking, but as a process of making ever more concrete choices resonating positively with more general determinations.[47] Nevertheless, given the modern cult of the genius, self-objectification was a necessary part in the arrangement. Dominic Boyer (2005, 118–59) portrays this engineering mentality in discussing the official professional norms for GDR journalists. He cites the GDR media theorist Hermann Budzislawski with the words: "The socialist journalist does not, as the bourgeois literatus does, consider

---

47. This is a nice example for the (quasi-)Hegelian character of the state socialist project. The imagination is that of a stepwise self-alienation of spirit, its becoming flesh in the decent from the abstract to the ever-more concrete.

it a degradation or an unbearable sacrifice of originality to follow the party line and to fulfill his especially complicated and singular functions as a 'cog and screw' of the unified party mechanism" (122).[48]

Standing squarely in but also moving beyond the Kantian tradition, critique for Marx (1978, 143ff. and 147ff.) was a heroic movement from insight to action that has at least two parts. First, analysis needs to transcend a mere reflection of the facticity of the present into a thorough investigation of the conditions of its possibility. This is the very path Kant describes as thinking through the phenomena to the principles of their constitution. What is new for Marx is that genuine critique must then contain the seeds to conceive the world in different terms providing guidance for actions to alter the status quo in the direction of a better world. In socialist self-understandings, this fundamental critique was achieved by Marxism-Leninism, and it was embodied in the dialectical opposition of real-existing socialism to capitalism. Thus the critical job to be done was much more modest, both for the party as a whole and for the individual. The party still needed to reflect on the appropriate general means to realize the substance, the goals of Marxism-Leninism; for the individual members this could only be the critique of the specific means to support the general means devised by the party. The creative and critical labors of the individual stood in the same relation to those of the party, as those of the party as a whole to the historical truth of Marxism-Leninism. Anything moving beyond a critique of the means that oneself had the powers to devise, to best realize the goals designated at a higher level smacked of subjectivism and was heavily censored. In effect, then, everybody within this system, the very leadership of the party included, was imagined as a bureaucratic engineering subcontractor of history.

Linguistically, this found its expression in the universal use of a form I have elsewhere (2004, 260) called the "continuous positive." The party, for example, undertook "ever greater efforts" in anything it did; people were asked to attain "an ever greater awareness" of Marxism-Leninism; positive target numbers "grew ever more," negative ones became "ever lower." Everybody in socialism needed the continuous positive in order to demonstrate that they were on target, that things progressed as planned. But what if things went wrong?

---

48. Alexei Yurchak describes this process for the Soviet Union with attention to voice: "This normalizing process followed the general principle of presenting all knowledge as knowledge that was already established. As a result, the temporality of authoritative discourse shifted into the past, conveying new facts in terms of preexisting facts. The author's voice converted into the voice of a mediator of preexisting discourse rather than the creator of new discourse" (2006, 284).

Personalizing and externalizing failure: The socialist theodicy

Closely associated to ethics are issues of accounting for failure. Socialism has developed a highly characteristic form of explaining mishaps small and large, be it the allusive misspelling of a name in a newspaper, a botched operation in the secret police, or a major explosion in a factory. The central characteristics of socialist failure accounting are these: It brackets the very possibility of asking whether the failure was caused by the interplay of institutional arrangements if such a question would have touched anything that was considered central to socialist principles. It sheltered the system as a whole and its supposed institutional anchor and guarantor—the party—from any blame for failure. In the last instance, therefore, blame was placed either on the failure of a person or on enemy interference. De facto, these two operated as the default options in concrete failure investigations. The notion of "technical failure," although used, was considered with suspicion, because it could be used to hide personal incompetence or to mask enemy interference. The category of "accident," the "concatenation of unhappy circumstances," was seen as residual.

Given that this form of failure accounting involves the defense of an absolute, it is properly addressed as a form of *theodicy*. It follows logically from a set of assumptions setting the general framework for socialism's epistemic ideology. I have already explored them in their historical context. However it is worth summarizing them here, because taken together, they constitute socialism's rationalistic core. They are: (1) The absolute truth of the *substance* of Marxism-Leninism as the only possible true social science corroborated by the movement of history in conjunction with the idea that as a science it allows for useful predictions of the future. (2) Central to this true theory of society is the insight that world history is an incessant history of warfare between a ruling class and a suppressed class, playing itself out now as the conflict between a western government and capitalist-led bourgeoisie and a global proletariat led by the CPSU and its brother parties. (3) The necessity of an internally unified vanguard party to reveal what the substance meant for the present historical circumstances, taking it upon itself to educate the masses about it. (4) The endowment of every human being with a universal rationality that would, if properly unshackled by the party, necessarily recognize the validity of the aforementioned assumptions. The party is the central linchpin in this setup. How central it is can be gleaned by what were considered to be the cardinal sins of socialist life. The list is clearly topped by what is called in German *die Machtfrage stellen*, or "posing the question of power." Indeed! Said Erich Mielke (BArch, Dy 30/IV 2/2.039, leaf 4):

The question of power was, is and will remain the decisive question of a socialist revolution and of its perspectives in the GDR. The most important condition for the guarantee of state security is and will remain leadership through the party of the working class, is the unitary and closed action of all communists in a trusting relationship with the working people. Without our Marxist-Leninist party, without its prudent, scientifically justified and mass-related politics the security of the state is unthinkable.

With party and system thus placed beyond blame, failures needed to be attributed to other sources. The prevailing strategy was personalization. It could take two principle forms. The more benevolent version imagined failures to issue from personal incompetence, which could ultimately only be seen as failure to hear or properly understand the party line, thus allowing for local perversions of the party's good intentions. In this case the culprit merely needed to be (re-)educated. This was rarely seen as an issue of mere technical knowledge. Had the person in question exhibited a clear class standpoint, then he or she would have obtained the technical education needed. What was therefore often found wanting was "resolve." Accordingly, remedies included the possibility that the culprit needed to be placed into a social situation, a work collective, that would facilitate the proper understanding of the party's intentions. Thus, when people were "sent into production" for failures, this was not just the use of a cynical euphemism covering a sense of punishment through demotion, but it was meant as a pedagogical device based on the notion of a work collective as a network of authority naturally conveying the right kind of socialist mores. People thus reformed were typically reintegrated into higher-level work.

If, however, errant persons proved impervious to reeducation it was assumed that they were possessed by a consciousness inimical to socialism. Then, these persons were enemies who needed to be fought according to the logic of militant dialectics. Thus, the human ontology of GDR socialism dealt in three fundamental categories of people, distributing them over a continuum of orientations toward the socialist project as manifested in adherence to the current party line: believers (of varying degrees of perfection in self-objectification; also called "positive people"), people temporarily in limbo (those who might be swayed either way; also called "uncertain people"), and enemies (of different degrees of opposition; very often also referred to as "negative people"). Properly understood, therefore, ideological work consisted of two complementary enterprises: positive proselytization, this is what the GDR's vast propaganda machinery was made for, and the control of adversarial, thus inimical intentionality, and this is what a significant part of the comparatively speaking equally vast secret police apparatus was designed to achieve. *No matter, however, whether failure was blamed on incomplete propaganda or the machinations of the enemy, it was almost always personalized and thus deflected from the system.* And anybody working within the system knew and feared this tendency to personalize blame. So one of the most important survival skills in this "vast post office" that was the GDR was to act like a good bureaucrat at all times, that is, to anticipate blame and act in such a way that one appeared blameless. For, of course, failures were as everywhere rampant.

An aporia of socialist identity

Taken together, the ethics of absolute finality and the socialist theodicy created a certain conundrum that can fruitfully be seen as an aporia of socialist identity.[49] On the one hand, socialism provided a powerful set of orientations. It furnished the means for human beings to endow their lives with a meaning that transcended the ups and downs of the everyday. The party promised a strong "we" that did not only present itself as a true collective subject with the ability to act politically in a major way, but it also presented that "we" as one dialogically constituted as a community of comrades bound together in a network of solidarity. Yet, the identification with the goal and the institution promising to pursue it also demanded of its members a saintly heroism in self-objectification that in cases of conflict could be tantamount to self-denial. The party placed demands on its members that were hard, if not impossible, to fulfill. In principle, all party members lapsed in light of the heroic ideal. Yet, the party was depicted as a fraternity of saints. Nevertheless, the identification with a sublime goal and membership in an equally sublime organization in pursuit of it, that also assures self-recognition as "not good enough" is not yet an aporia. What must come in addition is a further set of understandings or institutional arrangements making it hard to find a way out of this tension (e.g., by offering the institutional means to relax it through rituals of irony or atonement). Two understandings blocking the escape routes from this contradiction were important for dedicated communists (those who joined the party primarily for career reasons would not have experienced the contradiction in the first place). First, the party was successful in presenting itself as without alternatives; only *it* could achieve

---

49. This aporia is predicated entirely on a historically specific set of institutions especially on negatively resonating understandings and their ongoing validation. It is therefore not a property of socialism as an abstract idea, but of the institutional fabric that was East German and, more generally, actually existing socialism formed on the basis of the Soviet model. Only in this historical institutional sense is it meaningful to speak in this chapter and the following about aporias.

the desired goal. Besides the very concept of a unitary vanguard party, Germany's particular history was important. The failure of a split Weimar labor movement to prevent the establishment of a fascist dictatorship weighed heavily in support of any injunctions against a split and critiques that could be construed as divisive.[50] Second, self-objectification was never an achieved state, but an open process. Membership was contingent on it and thus in principle continuously subject to review. This became serious to the degree that others were willing to use apparent lapses in self-objectification as an asset in power struggles (including promotions). Therefore, committed party members felt the threat of exclusion acutely in cases where they found it difficult to support the party line without hesitation. After all, the stories of exclusion for error or deviation were a central component of party lore. So everybody knew that the promised dialogic "I"-"you" relationship among members could quickly become a monologic "they"-"I."

With no way out, committed members needed defenses against their aporetic identity. Four ideal-typical responses are relatively easily discernible in my interviews. The first consisted in "going into overdrive," as it were, by performing allegiance wherever one could in a rather ostentatious way, demanding the same of others. This way one appeared unforgiving with oneself while proving to be unforgiving with regard to the lapses of others. This response was allegorized in the figure of the "onehundredfiftypercenter." As a trope it was not only part and parcel of the efforts of ordinary men and women to make sense of the extreme and often repulsive behavior of others, but also the defense of overdrive found widespread symbolic expression in the personality cult surrounding socialist leaders. Each and every single one of them needed to be depicted as a saintly socialist hero of self-objectification. After all, in terms of the ideology, the basis of their authority, the legitimacy of their rule lay in self-objectification. No wonder, then, did the party grandees doctor their biographies to match expectations; no wonder that people who knew the truth about what had happened were perceived as dangers to the carefully cultivated image.[51] The more people cared about or were dependent on their *belonging* to the party (rather than just the pursuit of socialist goals), and the more they had to worry that their belonging might become endangered, the more they were probably drawn into ostentatious hyperperformance of self-objectification, including the possibility to tell on the lapses of others.

A second, also rather common, strategy was cynicism, often also referred

---

50. For the older generation this Weimar dilemma was still lived experience. For the younger ones, it was kept alive through continuous renarration.

51. In chapter 6, I will say more about the doctored biographies of late GDR leader Erich Honecker and Stasi chief Erich Mielke.

to as "careerism." Its logic could be phrased in the following way: Since the project is bedeviled with contradictions and nobody tries to fix them in earnest it is obviously not designed to be taken seriously. The best one could do is to turn it into a game of advancement, playing with the crazy rules to one's own benefit.[52]

A third response consisted in fleeing into the relative security afforded by the association with powerful superiors, who could offer protection in cases where self-objectification was found wanting by others. In a manner typical of patron-client relations the price was a higher degree of commitment. Clearly, superiors too needed to create their own safety blanket by associating themselves with subordinates giving their best to get the job done well. This last strategy was in many ways the emotional basis for the particular form of socialist patronage that became institutionalized as "socialist cadre politics," of which the nomenclatura-system was the corner piece.

Theoretically, at least, there was a fourth option: politics, that is, a concerted attempt to change the institutional fabric that created the aporia in the first place. That however, unless launched by a stably installed party leader, would have immediately incurred charges of factionalism and subjectivism, thus effectively undermining the effort. The alternative to that was the foundation of some clandestine circle in preparation for politics. And that was a route taken not infrequently, as especially Thomas Klein, Wilfriede Otto, and Peter Grieder have shown (1997).

Needless to say, none of these responses had to be pursued in an either/or fashion. They could be deployed strategically or enacted more or less unwittingly by one and the same person in different kinds of contexts. They could also occur simultaneously, or people could cycle through them. What is particularly interesting about these four characteristic responses to the socialist aporia of identity is that they describe a situation in which particular discursive understandings entail powerful emotive understandings that together in their interaction become constitutive for an institutional order.

CONCLUSIONS

I began this chapter with something of a paradox. While Marx's theories have some, but in the end not much, room for a constructive consideration of ideology as a central component of processes of institution formation,

---

52. Intellectual critics of socialism have often written about socialism as if cynicism was the only possible response to it, often universalizing it to a characterization of the whole population. I cannot speak for other socialist countries, but for the GDR this is certainly a misleading perspective. Perhaps it would have become more prevalent if the fall of 1989 would have led to a reinstitution of orthodoxy.

the actually existing socialisms of Eastern Europe saw the dissemination of Marxism-Leninism as a policy instrument of ever-greater importance. I tried to show, by following the development of socialist thinking among the Bolsheviki and the SED, how socialism could plausibly be conceived as an intentional project. The warrant for this intentionality was seen in the scientific nature of Marxism-Leninism as the only true theory of human society in its historical development. The success of the movement, or better perhaps the very way in which it was celebrated internally in rituals and sacred texts, seemed to corroborate its guiding ideology. No doubt, for Marx this science was historical and in constant need of adjustment—and this is how Lenin's thrust for a revolution in feudal Russia and the revaluation of ideology could be justified. And yet, in the practice of actually existing socialisms, the historicity of that science was also understood as becoming determinate in the formulation of unquestionably true laws both for history in general and for a particular epoch: by Marx and Engels for theirs, by Lenin for his, and by the party for all subsequent times. In the pathos of science there was real continuity from Marx to the end of Soviet socialism in Eastern Europe. Notably, the imaginary underlying this science as a practice is not that of a Mertonian decentralized, self-correcting, internally competitive, and hierarchy-free undertaking (Merton 1979). Instead, it centered on the cult of a genial thinker whose charisma moved on to a genial party organizer and revolutionary, to become finally (through the supposed aberration of an arrogating dictator the conditions for whose possibility were never really explored) the trust of a party as a centrally organized bureaucracy. And it is precisely the pathos of truth connected to a highest good (the just society) as something clearly and unambiguously located in a center from where it could radiate for the greater benefit of all, it is the role of the party as the warden of this truth and its agent of dissemination that gave institutionalized socialism its religious whiff.

A more nominal similarity with Marx lies in the way in which the party came to know its current historical situation. Marx's two-pronged strategy of analyzing current events and discussing the oeuvres of his opponents became institutionalized in socialism as a self-differentiation from the enemy: the class enemy without and the defeatist or antirealist within the party. Yet, these techniques became ever more ritualistic and hollow. On the one hand, the class enemy was no longer really taken seriously as somebody with whose ideas one really had to engage. On the other hand, those party members engaging in the task of distilling the substance of Marxism-Leninism for the present were members after all, and therefore subject to party discipline and in need to perform self-objectification. Thus, people working on setting the démarches for adjustments of the party line had to adhere to the party line in the first place lest they endanger their own authority as interlocutors. The result was that the originally militant dialectics of self-positioning became both less militant but also ever less dialectical.

Another continuity from Marx to the end of state socialism is the focus on production, as that which enables a better society, as that which holds the key to redemption from exploitation and alienation. Qualitative economic growth became the *Hauptaufgabe*, the main task from party congress to party congress. What was needed, then, were productivity gains, expected from (hard) science and laborer's motivation. The latter was supposed to make a quantum leap with the socialization of agriculture and industry. Now that workers knew they were toiling for themselves and for the community as whole, they were supposed to abstain from slowdowns and other techniques of manipulating the workflow on the shop floor. They were supposed to work better and harder. Yet, these expected gains did not materialize, at least not to the extent hoped for. An economic reform package introduced in the 1960s aiming at greater decentralized decision making and thus more flexibility and better performance incentives ran afoul of political resistance in Berlin and Moscow. Science, the other presumed source of productivity gains, had to wrestle with all the same problems that general production had to wrestle with: the flight of highly specialized personnel, an acute shortage of funds for necessary investments, supply difficulties, and the bureaucratic stalemate created by central party control. This science stood no chance in outcompeting capitalist science in raising productivity.

In the end, therefore, nothing came of the grand ambitions to overtake capitalist economies in terms of economic growth. In consequence, the corroboration of socialism's claim to superior economic prowess that would have ensued from such overtaking did not materialize. What remained under these circumstances as a means of politics was education. In this regard, the party's considerable experience with mass mobilization looked promising. It seemed to have worked once before in propelling feudal Russia into the industrial age, producing technology in select areas that could compete with the best capitalism produced.

In sum, then, for the GDR leadership, the struggle for socialism, the way to make it happen, was first and foremost a struggle for the intellectual and emotional identification of the people with the party and its project. The core of a successful politics was framed as a "struggle for the hearts and the minds of people." Precisely because it was built on a body of understandings taken to be validated scientifically, and precisely because that scientific body of understandings assumed a definite shape in the form of a party line through the good offices of a vanguard party enmeshed in a mortal battle, socialism's politics of education was from the very beginning staunchly monologic. Education became a didactic effort at proselytization. No matter how friendly or personally inspiring the interaction with relevant party members could be, the basic mode of interaction between the party as an institution on the one hand and its individual members and the general population on the other juxtaposed an objectified party as a world-historical agent of history to individuals urged to self-objectify. In terms of the extended Bakhtin-Buberian concepts I have introduced in the last chapter (p. 35), this can be characterized as an objectifying they-me relationship. In the long run this had considerable consequences for the ways in which the general population perceived the party and even for the very morale of the party itself. As we shall see in chapter 7, the shame and anger that can be associated with monologicity often planted the seed for paths into dissidence.

All of this does not mean that other forms of politics did not play a role. Under the name of "socialist competition" there was a politics of induction trying to tease the citizenry with incentives into the right kind of behavior. Yet material incentivization was always looked at with suspicion; it was not properly socialist—the privilege system for cadres notwithstanding—mushrooming out of control during the GDR's last decade. Considering the fact that the party pursued an encompassing project of institutional transformation requiring the participation of wide strata of the population, it maneuvered into an aporetic situation with regard to the means of its politics. For some ideological reasons, its politics of induction by material incentives had to remain limited; for other ideological reasons, its politics of education was caught up in a monologicity whose demotivating consequences the party leadership had to wrestle with but could not understand given Marxist-Leninist doctrine about the nature of human beings.

For the failures of this struggle for the hearts and minds of the people, the party had to have a security apparatus able to neutralize inimical interference in what appeared to the committed participants as the grandest project humankind had ever undertaken. Here, then, was a role for a politics of disablement and projective disarticulation. But that too was considered an unfortunate aspect of class warfare, not the center of what real socialist politics was about. How the socialist state tried to create a monolithic intentionality in the interaction between a positive proselytization and negative politics of disarticulation and disablement is the topic of the next chapter.

2

Aporias of Producing
Right Consciousness

The sovereignty of the working people realized on the basis of democratic centralism is the constitutive principle of the state's structure.

CONSTITUTION OF THE GDR, ARTICLE 48.2

It was one thing to know in theory that a monolithic intentionality, the unity and the purity of the party (and ideally of the whole population), was the best way to move socialism forward on its inevitable path to communism. It was quite another to actually make it happen. Seen from the perspective of the sociology of understanding, the party needed to control as much of the play of validation as possible to help actualize those understandings it saw as favorable to socialism and to extinguish those it saw as a hindrance. What was needed first of all, therefore, was a form of organization that would allow the party to centrally control as much of the institutional fabric of GDR society as possible. This, after all, was what it deemed "the leading role of the party" to mean: the creation of a political organization efficient in devising and projectively articulating its politics. Accordingly, the first major section of this chapter is dedicated to a brief description of the organizational principles understood by the party as assuring central control, the principles of democratic centralism and central planning. Socialist consciousness, the Marxist-Leninist way of differentiating and integrating the world, also needed to be produced substantively. As briefly outlined in the second major section of this chapter, the vast propaganda apparatus of the party conducted a politics of education. Since the party assumed that the class enemy would aim at interfering with this task, the smooth operation of the propaganda apparatus needed to be safeguarded against "sabotage" and the "soddening" influence of the class-enemies' attempts to interfere in the party's project. To this purpose the party state employed a politics of disablement and disarticulation, trying to prevent the GDR's populations from having access to certain ideas or people. More, propaganda could not be expected to do its work among "hardened enemies of socialism." The security apparatus of the GDR, with the Stasi as its central agency, was supposed to take care of this problem. Thus, the final section of this chapter is dedicated to the Stasi and the ways in which it figured into the party's project of creating a monolithic intentionality.

ORGANIZING CENTRAL CONTROL

The two organizational principles that were supposed to guarantee the party's central control were the principle of democratic centralism and the principle of comprehensive central planning. Closely connected to both was the personnel policy of the party (*Kaderpolitik*), of which the so-called nomenclatural system was a central piece.

Democratic Centralism

Following the lead of the CPSU, the SED was organized according to the principle of democratic centralism:

> This principle means that all bodies of the party are elected bottom up . . . [and] that all decisions of the higher party bodies are binding for the lower ones, that tight party discipline is enforced and that minorities and individuals have to submit to the majority in a disciplined fashion. (Benser and Naumann 1986, 184)

In effect, democratic centralism allowed higher bodies to replenish their ranks according to their own liking by proposing candidates for elections to the lower bodies without alternatives. Although the lower bodies nominally had the right to nominate candidates and to have a discussion about the merits of alternative candidates, competition was never the rule, and was virtually unheard of by the end. This was even the case for the central committee, which, as the electoral body of the politburo, nominally maintained quite some power. Democratic centralism thus fostered a peculiar socialist form of institutionalized clientelism in which those higher up actively groomed younger hopefuls for active careers. These were formally assembled in "cadre reserves," which in the case of the central committee and the politburo were also called "candidates."

Elections were in this regard barely different from the practice of staffing the nomenclature, that is, lists of positions that could only be filled with the direct approval of a particular level of party (cf. Eyal 2003; Voslensky 1984; Djilas 1983). Elections were therefore an integral part of socialist "cadre work," which placed the utmost importance on placing persons loyal to the leadership in responsible positions. Cadre politics was clearly understood as a linchpin of realizing monolithic intentionality. The direct link between objectives of the party and personnel can be gleaned from the introduction to a textbook on cadre work (Herber and Jung 1968, 9):

> The VIIth party congress of the Socialist Unity Party of Germany posed the task. . . . Under these conditions the exact scientific steering of all social processes, especially those of the economic and scientific-technological development become ever more significant; what is more, such steering becomes an unavoidable necessity in the realization of the objective laws of socialism. A main ingredient of the scientific guidance of society is the *planned development of cadres*. The success of every work depends on the right choice, the right technical and political-ideological education . . . of the cadres. (My emphasis)

There are a number of rather noteworthy elements in this passage. In keeping with the main argument of part I of the book, it states bluntly that the "objective laws of socialism" need to be realized as consciousness-driven processes. One is almost tempted to believe that the tension inherent in this formulation was at least subliminally available to the authors as they took recourse to another revealing pleonastic hyperbole, this time built from the synonymous conjunction of the adjective *unavoidable* (*unumgänglich*) and the noun *necessity*. Monolithic intentionality is reflected in the desire to steer "all" social processes under the guidance of the latest pronouncements of the party, here the VIIth party congress, and in proclaiming the particular topic of the book, cadre work, to be an essential element in its realization.[1]

The idea of central control also dominated the administrative restructuring of the GDR. Through the 1952 "law for the further democratization of the structures and procedures of state institutions," which was a direct response to the declaration of the "construction of socialism" earlier the same year, the more traditional *Länder* (states) were effectively replaced by fifteen administrative districts. With the exception of East Berlin, their boundaries were drawn with the exigencies of rational planning in mind. Consequently, they mapped only poorly onto older cultural, linguistic, religious, and political divisions of GDR territory. This effect was, if not intended, then certainly not unwelcome. It signified a fresh, socialist beginning seemingly unencumbered by custom and history. The districts were further subdivided into 227 counties, which in turn were made up of more than 7,000 communities.[2] In principle, the autonomy of the lower levels was severely curtailed, and

---

1. The title (*Personnel Administration in the System of Socialist Control Operations*) and language of the book also cannot help but betray its origin in the late Ulbricht years, when systems theory swept through the GDR.
2. The main administrative subdivisions of East Berlin, also called districts, were administratively treated like counties in the rest of the country.

they had to follow the directives of the higher ones (Hoeck 2003). The large state bureaucracies (including the Stasi) followed these segmentary subdivisions into territorial jurisdictions. They typically maintained national ministries as well as district county offices.

The organization of the party mirrored this structure. This was true not only for the segmentary organization of territory, but the party's internal organization into departments also roughly shadowed state administrative offices. The organizational structures of the ministries, for example, found their counterpart in the structure of the central committee, and so in principle on all subsequent levels. It is justified, therefore, to speak of a system of parallel structures (hence "party state"), if one bears in mind that there was also a clear hierarchy in operation that subordinated state administration to party bureaucracy. This hierarchy was further emphasized by the fact that all higher-ranking state officials were party members and thus subject to party discipline. The origins of this parallel structure lie undoubtedly in the understanding of revolution as a process of seizing the state as well as in the need, particularly in the years immediately following the introduction of communist rule (in the GDR as much as in the Soviet Union), to rely on the expertise of nonparty members. At the beginning this was simply done by strategically placing party representatives into administrative units. In the Western lore about socialism this became notorious as the "commissar system" of the Red Army, where every commander was shadowed by a political officer. Interestingly, the parallel structure was never abandoned, even when the seizure of the state was for all practical purposes completed in the sense that all central state positions were finally staffed by the party. And this was so in spite of the all too apparent inefficiencies of this system and the conflicts and ambiguities of responsibility it created. One cannot even say that the rationale was continuing control, as the important decision-making powers had effectively been transferred to the party bureaucracy that continued to control the state, but itself remained without external control. Consequently, the party became *fons et origo* of the system. This exalted status is underlined by the fact that even for the Stasi, investigating the party apparatus was taboo.

This said, the Stasi itself was a notable exception to this parallel system too. Even though the central committee apparatus had an office nominally responsible for the Stasi, the direct interference of the party bureaucracy into Stasi affairs was virtually unknown in the late GDR. The reason for this exception was probably that the party's first secretaries found in Erich Mielke a loyal Stasi chief who under Honecker did not only advance to become a politburo member, but also became one of his two closest confidants. The Stasi, like the party, controlled itself, for the party apparatus within the Stasi was ultimately responsible to the minister. This structure might have allowed the Stasi to become a state within the state. This did not happen, however, not least because Stasi officers, the minister included, were for the most part committed party members thriving in their work to realize and being held internally accountable for self-objectification vis-à-vis the party line.

Central Planning

The crux of central planning is the coordination of production and consumption across all interconnected sectors. This does not only involve the flow of goods or the provision of particular kinds of services, however. It must also involve the provisioning of personnel, its education, investments, and research. Because of the considerable duration of many projects, such as carrying out a research program, bringing an investment to fruition, or educating a workforce, planning cannot limit itself to a short-term temporal horizon. It must proceed within a time frame extended enough to calculate through the maturity horizons of at least the most important inputs. This is an exceedingly complex task not only because there are as many loose ends as there are producers, consumers, products, inputs and services, which need to be tied together into a knot that holds. It is complex because imponderables may exert pressures that threaten to untie the knot through ripple effects, straining several strings at once (Kornai 1992, ch. 7, 8).[3] More, the difficulty multiplies with the increasing differentiation of an economy because every new product requires a multiplicity of relations that need to be managed.

János Kornai (1980) has beautifully shown that precisely because of its complexities, because of its cascading levels of interdependencies, this system is only poorly understood as a *command economy*, the term that was often used as a synonym for *planned economy* in the Western comparative systems literature (see also Burawoy and Lukács 1992). The point is that requiring the cooperation of the next lower level, plans need to be negotiated. And within this process of cascading negotiation, every player has an incentive to ask more than she needs and to promise less than she could give. The rationale behind this institutionalized hoarding is not so much greed or ill will, but insurance against an uncertain future. At the end of the year, performance will be measured against the plan targets and recognition is granted for the fulfillment or overfulfillment of targets. More, since as I pointed out in the last chapter, socialism operated under the spell of the continuous positive, managers had to make sure that they could deliver on its terms, which means every year a little more. Small but steady increases

---

3. This threat of contingencies was nicely expressed by a proverbial joke: Socialism has four enemies: spring, summer, fall, and winter!

were better for career development than a whooping success, which, by raising expectations for more, could only be followed by disappointment. The general problem of hoarding resources was aggravated by what Kornai calls "soft budget constraints," that is, the fact that by and large production units could not go bankrupt. Again this had much to do with the fact that higher levels needed the collaboration of lower levels to appear successful (cf. Burawoy and Lukács 1992). The result of all of this is, as Kornai has convincingly argued, an "economy of shortage" in which especially more complex, more difficult to produce goods are constantly in short supply (cf. Verdery 1996).

Knowing about the precariousness of central planning is not only important because propaganda and secret police work was planned on the basis of the same principles as the economy, leading to the same hoarding of resources, the same demands for ever more people. The issue is much rather that, as I pointed out in the last chapter, socialism staked itself out on its economic success. In other words, the meta-understandings cultivated through the ideology of Marxism-Leninism were such that a well-functioning economy would have provided corroborating evidence for the viability and long-term success of the socialist project. Conversely, supply problems notoriously reflected back on the party and its project of creating a monolithic intentionality. Of course, the party was well aware of this. And so it tried very hard to market the socialist economy as a success story, emphasizing continuing full employment, the low prices of basic necessities such as bread, and the provision of low-rent apartments. With the succession of Erich Honecker to Walter Ulbricht as general secretary, the party also embarked on major efforts to improve the supply of highly desired consumer goods, such as jeans or television sets, to provide more tangible corroborations of economic prowess (e.g., Steiner 2004, 187ff.).

Trying to address some of the notorious problems of central planning[4] in the aftermath of the growth crisis of the late 1950s and early 1960s, the GDR began to work on an economic reform program known as the New Economic System of Planning and Steering (NÖSPL) (Mittag 1963). Its implementation began in 1964. The idea of the program was to improve the overall efficiency and to enhance the innovative capacity of the economic system by shifting to profits (rather than output) as the target variable, by cutting subventions, by giving greater planning authority to subordinate levels to increase their flexibility. To make this possible, the price-setting mechanisms had to become more flexible (Brus 2003, chap. 3). During the first years of

---

4. One example frequently cited was the so-called tonnage ideology, the fact that output was measured by weight rather than the quality of goods. Thus a perverse incentive was set to produce weight rather than a particular set of qualities, in particular, quantitative proportions.

the program, growth accelerated markedly. Nevertheless, Ulbricht began to withdraw the NÖSPL almost as fast as it was introduced. The reasons cited were: remaining difficulties in managing a disparate, maladjusted system (certain suppliers began to exploit their monopoly situation and the price flexibility to drive considerable profit margins); trade interdependencies with the other centrally planned economies of Eastern Europe, and especially the Soviet Union; as well as beginning signs of social dissatisfaction due to rising inequalities on the shop floor and potential price hikes in basic necessities (Steiner 1999; 2004). NÖSPL was already cut back in 1965, and scrapped for good in 1971. Critique came also from the perspective of what socialism was supposed to accomplish. With its more marketlike elements, the system felt like a step backward, that is, it felt too much like the Soviet Union's infamous NEP, like a retreat from the real goal of establishing a genuine socialist economy. Moreover, with the augmentation of decentralized decision making, the new system deprived the party of the possibilities to intervene directly, which was perceived as a marked decrease of its power and thus ultimately of its ability to play the "leading role" it assumed it needed to carry the "fruits of the revolution" forward on the path of a more developed socialism, not a socialism patched up with structural elements borrowed from capitalism (Steiner 2004, 132).

In this inability to carry through a reform of the underperforming economic system comes to the fore one of the ironies of intentionality of which socialism was so rich precisely because it was such a thoroughly intentional program of transformation. Perhaps one could even speak of an outright aporia of politics here. In order to avoid confusions, a clarifying remark about what I mean with the term *aporia* seems in place. If what I said in the introduction about processes of institution formation as concatenated flows of repeated action-reaction effects is correct, then politics as an intentional effort to form institutions is always in danger to become aporetic. This is so because institutions cannot simply be willed or intended; they need the active participation of others, and that might have to be negotiated rather than decreed. Therefore, wherever the goals or the means of politics are in dispute among those whose participation is important, less focused intentionally may indeed offer political advantages. Yet, this success comes at the price of becoming less fixated on the attainment of any *particular* goal. In other words, the understanding of history as an inevitably open process helps to decrease the likelihood of aporetic situations. With different self-understandings of politicians at play in various institutional settings, therefore, politics may be more or less aporetic. With changing institutional contexts, aporias can take different forms at different times and places.

The central planning induced process dynamics that entailed economies of shortage in conjunction with the party's understanding that its vanguard role necessitated extensive central planning caught the party in an aporia of politics, the *aporia of central planning*. The "steadfast" insistence on socialism as a set of definite (rather than flexible) principles has ultimately contributed to its weakening by depriving it of possible corroboration in action. Thus, the desire for control, the insistence on doing something in a preconceived particular way, has led to a distraction from the very goal that was supposed to be accomplished by that "steadfast" insistence: the enduring institutionalization of socialism. But again, and this was the source of the anxiety: in order to have socialism it might have had to be different. The catch was precisely that socialism could not be conceived as something that can take a wider variety of forms and therefore might also be an object of negotiation. Of course, the very idea of socialist principles as result of science renders the suggestion to open them to negotiation mute.[5]

I have so far based my reasons why central planning proved to be aporetic in GDR socialism on Kornai's conceptualization of economies of shortage. However, Kornai's model is ultimately based on the logic of a utilitarian calculus that is underpinning most of liberal economics. That assumption sidesteps the very question of how this calculus has taken root in practice by insisting that it is not based on historically contingent ways of ordering the world but on transhistorical, hardwired brain processes. Of course, if I believed that this were true, I would not have written this book. The question that poses itself, therefore, is why socialist managers, most of which were (the cynics apart) dedicated to the socialist project, were driven institutionally to follow through on what they very well understood as perverse incentives, acting as if they were utilitarians.[6] Put differently, why could these managers not simply have pointed to the madness of the system in which they found themselves, leading to analysis, discussion, and perhaps a successively improving reform? Or put in Hirschman's famous (1970) "exit, voice or loyalty" triad, which has been made much use of in analyzing the fate of socialism, the question is why did the managers opt for "loyalty" in the sense of playing within the stricture of the institutional framework provided rather than for "voice," that is, protest. One could also ask, why did the managers opt for a

---

5. In due time, when the archives of the Communist Party of China will be opened, it will be one of the most fascinating questions to ask: how it managed to get out of the aporia of planning. Clearly this was a gradual process. Did it learn to give up power in order to maintain it? Or did it fool itself about the possibilities of control? Or was the market never as negatively cathected as it was for the Europeans?

6. Martha Lampland (1995) has followed up on a related puzzle in Hungary, namely, the question how, ironically, through the interventions of socialism, the rural population developed an individualistic, indeed utilitarian mentality.

withdrawal from a politics of reform and for the exercise of a politics maintaining existing institutions. What we need to understand, then, is how they were led into a de facto fetishization of these institutions.[7]

In the last chapter I provided important ingredients for an answer to why insights were hard to develop into veritable reform proposals and why reforms were difficult to enact, that is, why in the end there was an aporia of central planning. These elements all had to do with the party's self-understanding, its vanguard role in pursuit of an absolute good, backed by a presumably true science, requiring the production of a monolithic intentionality that in turn went hand in hand with an ethics of absolute finality according to which managers had to self-objectify in accordance with the party line (or "paint socialism" as Burawoy and Lukács [1992, chap. 5] say). I will contribute further elements to an answer in the remainder of this chapter by revealing other components of a more comprehensive answer by pointing to two other political aporias, the *aporia of proselytization* and the *aporia of prohibition*. Further important contributions are the three ways in which the dialectical formation of understandings can degenerate into circularity, thus decoupling knowledge and world in the conclusions to chapter 4. I will show all of this in action in the third part of chapter 6, where I will analyze the discursive culture of the Stasi, which I take to be rather characteristic for the GDR as a whole, after extensive readings about work in other GDR organizational settings from the ZK to the planning bureaucracy to county-level party administrations.

PROPAGANDA

The party tried to use every contact as a potential vehicle to convince people of the truth and worth of its mission. Within the logic of monolithic intentionality, failing to engage in this politics of education would not only have undercut the potential of socialism, but it would also have been unethical. In a rather direct sense, then, the party, the state, the entire educational sector (from day care centers to the academy of sciences), all forms of mass communication (from print news media and book publishing to radio and

---

7. On a more theoretical level this means if we want to explain systems failure, it is not enough to point to incentive structures producing destructive unintended consequences. What has to be explained is why people within the system either cannot form an adequate understanding about it that might enable them to intervene, or where these understandings exist in at least rudimentary form, why they cannot be further developed and enacted in attempts at reform. Speaking of political aporias must imply an attempt to account for why a particular institutional arrangement looked from within as if it could not be altered in a more desirable direction, which is tantamount to asking why a program of reformist politics seemed unlikely.

television), and all events staged under the auspices of the party, its mass organizations, or the state were used as propaganda channels. These were monopolized by the state in an effort to enable its politics of education through a politics of articulation. Given that the party tried with significant success to control as tightly as possible all forms of human organization beyond the immediate family and the two legalized churches, this means that there was almost no environment in the GDR that was not penetrated by—and with the exception of intimate private spaces and the churches—in many cases even saturated with propaganda.

Propaganda reached citizens in the GDR through three main channels: as formal instruction in Marxism-Leninism, in the context of propaganda events, or through the mass media. Since formal instruction and the mass media were in an important sense subsidiary to major propaganda events, I will begin with a very brief overview over logic and types of propaganda events. Taken together, they provided the basic beat of the socialist calendar, lending temporal structure to public life in the GDR. All propaganda events can be analyzed as entwining two dimensions: discourse and participation. With socialism's characteristic emphasis on the former, participation was designed to support the messages with a social, emotively saturated context of reception. These contexts were hoped to validate the message through multiple, mutually amplifying recognition. Accordingly, propaganda handbooks (e.g., Wischnjakow et al. 1974) make much out of the importance of proper, meaning above all *social* reception. A brochure instructing party officers in the art of propaganda (BL Suhl 1976, 19) states for example: "The collective discussion and analysis of all resolutions is absolutely necessary to prevent subjectivist interpretations." Social reception was, therefore, hoped to facilitate self-objectification, the self-alignment with monolithic intentionality. The reception of the party's main messages within a community was also meant to help with another problem. The directives of the party were by necessity somewhat abstract. It was, for example, not immediately clear what the "fulfillment of the main task" (*Erfüllung der Hauptaufgabe*), propagated at the latest party congress, should mean concretely for the work of high school teachers, machine tool factory workers, or secret police officers. More, the propaganda training literature emphasized that the concrete realization of what has been abstractly put in the dry pedagogical style of party language would come alive in concrete application, thus furthering motivation, memory, and acceptance.

There was yet another reason why participation was thought to be very important. It was hoped that it would, in addition to the pathos of speech, help to undergird the acquisition of discursive understandings with strong emotive ones. Says the "Little Political Dictionary" (*Kleines Politisches Wörterbuch*) (Schütz et al. 1978):

The unity of thought and feeling is of great importance for the development and consolidation of socialist consciousness. Socialist formation and education is not just about the transmission of knowledge and convictions, but it is necessary as well to form and educate feelings consciously, to bring the world of feelings in congruence with thought and to provide an emotional base for theoretical knowledge.

In practice, therefore, discourse and participation were mixed, albeit in various proportions. This created on the one end of a spectrum events emphasizing complex messages with references to the classics, to party documents, to history, statistics, and world politics, which could only be effectively recognized within relatively restricted immediate participation. Since the decoding of text in these events demanded much more stringent attention, the audiences selected for participation in such events were typically constituted by particularly engaged party members; it was discourse by believers in the center of power for believers living further out toward the periphery. The news about such events was the entextualized discourse that acquired authority if not sanctity through its performance in particular party contexts and by deploying references to other sacred texts of socialism. On the other end of the spectrum were events aiming at mass participation either by directly including a very large number of people or by using still large numbers of category representatives. In this spirit, delegates of the Free German Youth (FDJ) were taken for example pars pro toto as "the youth of the GDR."[8] Mass participation was facilitated by less stringent demands on attention by reducing discourse to simple slogans dedicating the participants to a general identification with state, party, or socialism (e.g., "everything for our socialist fatherland") or to the pursuit of some goal proclaimed as that of the party (e.g., "in closed ranks for world peace"). Participatory events aimed at bandwagon effects in normalizing desired identifications, ideally triggering veritable Durkheimian effervescence with lasting motivational effects. The newsworthiness of participatory events was always just that: participation counted and/or enumerated, taken as identification with the party state and its goals. Since participation and performance were closely choreographed, they were taken to confirm what they were supposed to produce: identification and policy approval (more on this in the conclusions).

8. The proportion of any cohort organized in the two age-differentiated communist youth movements, the Pioneers (from 6 to 14) and the Free German Youth (FDJ) (from 14 to 25), was very high. In 1981–82, 86.6 percent of all relevant cohort members were Pioneers and 77.2 percent were members of the FDJ (Herbst, Ranke, and Winkler 1994, I:293).

Discursive Events

The foundational rhythm of life in the GDR was created by the party congresses of the SED, which took place every four (later every five) years.
They were the discourse event par excellence, bringing together in Berlin
elected party delegates, the party leadership, and guest delegations from the
worldwide fraternity of socialist parties. Their highlight was the report of
the central committee (ZK) to the assembly. These were read by the general
secretary from a carefully prepared manuscript that usually took the better
part of a day to deliver. In print these reports could swell to over 200 book
pages. These reports served a Janus-headed purpose. First, stock was taken
of and credit taken for the accomplishments of the previous five years. Palpable successes were attributed to the foresight and hard labor of the party
and its members since the previous gathering. Then the horizon for the next
five years was mapped out to motivate and direct members to participate
actively in the making of history.[9]

In spite of the restricted audience, and in spite of their dry manner, the reports of the central committee were very widely disseminated. They were the
constitutional document for the next half-decade. Radio and television covered them live; *Neues Deutschland* (New Germany), the party's flagship newspaper, published them the next day. They were commemorated as the primary
reference points not only for all subsequent party documents, speeches, and
resolutions, but also for any bureaucratic dossiers (such as planning documents), newspaper articles, and even university theses. In keeping with the
logic of monolithic intentionality, the reference to the party congresses ranked
above the reference to the classics or to the state's laws and regulations as the
most important vehicle of authorization in the political life of the GDR.

Another important discourse event rhythm was struck by the semi-
annual meetings of the central committee. It addressed more specialized

---

9. Imagine the scene. A large hall, one used for sporting events first (*Werner Seelenbinder
Halle*), then one used otherwise mostly for concerts (the great hall of the *Palace of the Republic*).
On the audience side of this hall: a few thousand delegates from all over the country as well as
foreign guest delegations. On the stage side: the political leadership and in its midst the general
secretary, as well as guests of honor. Long, standing ovations as the general secretary appears at
the podium. He then delivers the report, a full seven, eight hours long, read from a finely balanced manuscript. Only a lunch break interrupts the speech. Neither Walter Ulbricht nor Erich
Honecker were known as captivating orators or, for that matter, as good readers, or in any other
way as charismatic performers. The language in which they spoke was thoroughly suffused with
party jargon and would not have moved anyone who was not already a committed socialist. At
the end there were again long minutes of standing ovations, and a sense among the delegates
from far and near that they have witnessed the making of history.

topics than the party congress and provided interim reports or nuanced corrections of the party line.[10] These ZK reports also took center stage in the everyday life of the party, where they were the objects of stringently organized discussions in party groups. To these meetings members had to appear with a copy of the document clipped from *Neues Deutschland* that visibly bore the marks of their loving labor and attention (underlinings, margin comments, etc.). The party officers orchestrating these discussions were supplied with study material and argumentative aids to steer the acquisition of the text into the desired direction. Later, relevant sections of these ZK reports were regurgitated, for example, during the mandatory "party study circles" (*Parteilehrjahr*) or any kind of formal training in which the subject of Marxism-Leninism was an integral part.[11]

The shortest beat was supplied by the weekly politburo meetings (every Tuesday morning). Although its resolutions were of central importance for the governance of the country, they were typically too technical and too specialized to be of any direct value as texts for propaganda purposes. However, on certain occasions the politburo issued such documents. Speeches of the general secretary on any possible occasion, but most notably those held at his annual meetings with the district and county secretaries, were distributed and referenced widely. Finally, there were conferences of party delegates at the district and county levels; their first secretaries also delivered reports and speeches that were regionally covered and discussed. The same is true for the mass organizations of the country. In sum there was a veritable cascade of discourse events, rolling down the slopes of time, issuing from one principle source, the report of the general secretary to the most recent party congress.

Participatory Events

The most significant participatory events tried to mobilize the entire population of the GDR. On a four-year cycle these were the national and the nation-

---

10. Compare here, for example, the initiation of a "freeze period" in cultural policy by the notorious 11th plenum (compare chapter 1, p. 93).

11. For example, the high-level study circle of the FDJ addressing party members, and students with "philosophical questions," held in 1986–87 (FDJ 1986), was dedicated to the regurgitation of the results of the party congress, organizing the acquisition of the material under six themes. The first one was: "Marxism-Leninism—reliable compass in the class battles of our time," which was then organized into "key areas" (*Schwerpunkte*); the first one was: "Every generation has to acquire Marxism-Leninism under new concrete-historical circumstances." Underneath these headings the study guide is organized like an extended catechism, asking questions and giving answers. For example: "What characterizes the new stage in social development?" is then followed by a list of "arguments" with references to the report of the ZK and cross-references to the classics.

ally synchronized communal elections. Participation was quasi-mandatory and monitored. Party members fanned out in the afternoon to motivate those who had not yet cast their vote. On an annual cycle these were the May Day parades and the celebrations on the occasion of the Day of the Republic (October 7). Although less strictly enforceable, there, too, participation was quasi-mandatory and monitored through the mass organizations or the employers who typically participated in closed formation.[12] The national meetings of the mass organizations, were most notably the Pentecost meetings of the communist youth organization, FDJ, and the congresses of the Free German Trade Union (FDGB), both of which took place every five years.[13] In addition, larger socialist organizations (state bureaucracies, combines, even mass organizations, etc.) celebrated the day of their statutory "foundation" as a "birthday." On this occasion they were officially honored by others through visiting delegations of the party, while members were involved in special events in which some were given awards, the contributions to the goals of the party were celebrated, and so forth. Stasi's "birthday" was on February 8, 1950, when the Division for the Protection of the Economy was taken out of the responsibility of the Ministry of the Interior to form the new Ministry for State Security. Finally, the socialist calendar was studded with days functioning like the beads of a rosary to commemorate particular historical events (e.g., October Revolution, Luxemburg-Liebknecht murder, liberation from Nazi-rule), people (e.g., the birthdays of Marx or Lenin), or categories of people (e.g., women, teachers). They did not give rise to mass participation events but they were referenced in the news, school instruction, and the like.

General Education

Propaganda was also part and parcel of any kind of formal education. In the higher grades of high school, Marxism-Leninism was a regular school subject under the name of "civic education" (Staatsbürgerkunde). At the university "M-L" was a discipline in its own right that supplied the party with its theoreticians, the elite of which was lodged at the Institute for Marxism-Leninism affiliated with the ZK and the Academy of Sciences.

---

12. Individuals had to decide with which organization they would march: their employer or one of the socialist mass organizations arranging their leisure activities, for example, the Society for Sports and Technology or the Society for German-Soviet Friendship.

13. These meetings of the mass organizations combined the characteristics of discourse and participation events in more equal terms. Their heads typically held speeches that became reference points for these organizations' internal propaganda. Yet they also provided ample space for torchlight processions and friendly get-togethers.

Lesser practitioners not only became teachers within the system of part- and full-time party schools that functionaries had to attend as they were advancing through the ranks, but they also supplied the country as a whole with certified interpreters of current party documents and classic texts. Demand for such teachers was high since Marxism-Leninism was in one form or another part and parcel of any formal training in the GDR, mandatory for police officers as much as for doctors, for engineers as much as for lab assistants.[14] Training in M-L had particular significance for teachers of anything, since no matter what they taught, they were considered propagandists who were asked to consider carefully how their work could contribute to the fulfillment of the *Hauptaufgabe*. Thus, they designed problem sets with socialist content: the rule of three was practiced on Pioneer budget problems or on some military example, and such. In the GDR as anywhere else in the world, the current mode of governance was normalized with the help of the school curriculum. What was different is that in the GDR, this was done with a high degree of self-consciousness, highly centrally organized and with a specific goal in mind, and with an enormous attention to detail.[15]

FIGHTING THE WRONG KIND OF CONSCIOUSNESS

By its very own understandings of the world, socialism had to begin under threat and with conflict. Wherever it wanted to be, there was something else before, against which it had to develop itself and which it needed to overcome through revolutionary transformation. The proponents of the old order were expected to resist change with all possible means. Moreover, wherever socialism established itself, it had to face a vast majority of people who had grown up and lived in a different social system that had presumably shaped their consciousness. Against this old consciousness the party had to deploy its proselytizing efforts. It could not be assumed that the transformation was painless. Thus, Ulbricht said at the Vth party congress (ZK 1959, 1:150):

14. Nonmembers and members who were tiring of the relentless regurgitation of the same messages in these training sessions dubbed them "red light therapy" after a treatment method that is common all over Germany as a cure for the common cold, sinus and ear infections, etc.

15. It would be immensely useful to have figures about the relative development of propaganda expenses in the course of East Germany's history. Unfortunately, there are no such figures. The problem for such an undertaking is that propaganda was so all-pervasive that it is hard to compile reliable figures, for example, on the basis of published government budgets. It would be hard to tease out that segment of the budget for schools, the mass media, or socialist mass organizations that was used exclusively for propaganda as opposed to other purposes. The circumstantial evidence provided by the party's agitprop officers I interviewed suggests that propaganda expenses increased steadily.

However, among the various parts of the population the development of socialist consciousness does not proceed in a balanced and conflict free way. Instead, [it can succeed] only by participation in building socialism and in the conscious working through of the passé ideas and understandings of the capitalist past.

In terms of the consciousness-driven model of social transformation, the persistence of old ways of thinking and doing, even if it pertained only to certain parts of the population, posed a threat to progress:

The leftovers of the old in consciousness are not as innocuous as they may seem at first. Those who are still endowed with it typically do not show the right kind of attitude to work as well as to their duty to work for the greater benefit of society. . . . These leftovers as well as religious ideology and morals disturb our efforts to create a healthy way of life and a healthy mentality. (Wischnjakow et al. 1974)

In terms of the theoretical model I sketched in the introduction this means that resonance is seen as a problem that needed to be addressed aggressively. Since the reconstruction of consciousness through structural changes and propaganda would take time and was expected to proceed unequally, a particular problem emerged: what to do with those whose development did not keep pace, or those who even refused themselves?

Critique and Self-Critique

Ideological "weaknesses" were by no means seen as limited to the general population. To the contrary, as I have shown in the last chapter, "uncertain," "wavering," "defeatist" or "left-radical" ideological orientations were assumed to emerge in the lap of the party. The right course needed to be defined in opposition to these internal ideological problems. To deal with such problems the party's first line of defense was the instrument of "critique and self-critique."[16] Over the course of time the forms this ritual

16. Theoretically, the roots of this practice lie in Marx's acquisition of Kant's notion of philosophy as critique, that is, as a self-reflexive practice. Moreover, Engels praised Marx in his foreword to the second volume of *Capital* as ruthlessly self-critical. So self-critique came to be celebrated as a virtue of socialism in party programs, party statues, and other propaganda instruments. This said, however, the institutional origins of the *ritual* of critique and self-critique remain in the dark. Yet, the memoirs of the most famous Marxist renegades are filled with harrowing accounts of being subjected to this ritual. In fact, Leonhard (1955, 270–282, 294–301) traces the development of his own critical understanding of Stalinist practices to his first encounter with this practice. Kharkhordin (1999) makes an effort to trace it back to Russian Or-

took changed. It could come in more informal varieties in the GDR called *Aussprachen* (discussions) or in the form of party trials (*Parteiverfahren*). Yet, there is a guiding principle central to all of these forms, and it follows directly from the ethics of absolute finality that I described in the last chapter. Critique and self-critique's central idea was to demonstrate to some accused person that he or she failed the socialist duty of self-objectification. Typically, the accuser argued that some concrete behavior of the accused was purely subjectively motivated and devoid of consideration for the objective needs of the socialist project, which was shown to have suffered through the objectionable behavior. If the ritual went according to plan, the defendant's response was a self-analysis agreeing to his or her lacking partisanship. Ideally the accused felt ashamed, because he or she had thoroughly internalized self-objectification as part of his or her ego-ideal. The accusation could then build on the lingering self-doubt of the defendant to have lapsed in the one way or the other, if not necessarily as the accusation depicted it. In the more organized versions of the ritual, isolation was kinesthetically enacted in the seating arrangements confronting a sole individual with a whole phalanx of members and officials in an often-elevated position. The soiling subjectivity of the individual was thus symbolically juxtaposed to the objectified purity of the collective. For minor offenses, the credible performance of rueful self-objectification in which the accusations are accepted by the accused usually opened the path for more or less direct reintegration. Heavier offenses could lead to temporary dismissal and a trial period in some lower task, the so-called *Bewährung in der Produktion* (trial in production). Heaviest offenses could be performed in front of a court of law, which took in the 1930s, 1940s, and 1950s the form of show trials with the possibility of long prison terms and even execution. Interestingly, a prison term did not necessarily preclude later reintegration in some (typically lower) function, provided the person offered the required mea culpa or was later, after some change of the party line, found to have been unjustly tried.[17]

---

thodox monastic confession practices. Indeed, the cultural resonances are certainly plausible, and yet, it would actually be useful to trace its institutionalization among the Bolsheviki.

17. Perhaps the most chilling description of a critique and self-critique-like performance is Arthur Koestler's (*Darkness at Noon*, 1941) fictional account of "Rubashov's" (inspired by Bukharin and Radek) confession in a show trial. Even though he knows that the concrete accusations of him are fabricated, he suffers from the fact that he has subjectivist inclinations. His confession is a final act of self-objectification to help the party, which turns out to be a self-sacrifice entailing his execution. That this is by no means just fiction is well born out by what we know, for example, about Noel Field who, as an American spying for the NKVD while also helping many communists to survive in Nazi-occupied southern France, was later accused in Hungary of being an American spy. His letters from the prison show an amazing degree of self-objectification. Once released, he applied for asylum in Hungary.

Exercises in critique and self-critique were after truth. Yet it was decidedly not the truth of the story itself; it was about the truth that everybody was prone to subjectivism and that subjectivism needed to be transcended if people were to be successful agents of the party. They were a ritual reminder that self-objectification was a moving target, thus performatively foregrounding another truth: that belonging was contingent on the continuing performance of self-objectification. I should mention at this place as well that publicly performed critique and self-critique was a feared ritual, precisely because of the shaming and isolating component. Slang terms used among Stasi officers were "to go into the laundry" (*In die Wäsche gehen*) or "self-laundry" (*Selbst-Wäsche*). With its unmistakable allusions to the trope of washing dirty linen (*schmutzige Wäsche waschen*), this idiom nicely and accurately captures the fact that subjectivity was indeed perceived as polluting while underscoring the shame aspect of the procedure.[18]

Critique and self-critique might have had the potential to reconcile the often acutely perceived gap between the ego-ideal of the party celebrated in the cult of socialist heroes on the one hand and a more trite reality on the other. The *aporia of socialist identity* produced through the tension between the ardent desire to belong and the simultaneous threat to belonging might have been overcome by it. This did not happen however. The reason is simply that failures to self-objectify became a convenient tool in power struggles on every level. I will describe in chapters 5 and 6 more or less formal cases of critique and self-critique to which Stasi officers were subjected. In chapter 7 I will describe a case of a pupil subjected to a procedure that followed the logic of the ritual in detail even though it would not formally fall under the rubric. This case is particularly interesting because the pupil in question—Ulrike Poppe—sees in it a momentous experience on her path into dissidence. A comparison of these cases will show what a precarious means of addressing wavering consciousness by techniques of shaming could be in pursuit of the party's goal of creating a monolithic intentionality among its citizenry.

18. Excellent and easily accessible examples for this are the critique and self-critique of the deputy minister of culture, Günter Witt, at the 11th plenum of the ZK in 1965 that initiated a freeze period (*Frostperiode*) in cultural policy (Schubbe 1972, 1088–92). The casus belli was Witt's agreement to the production of the film *Das Kaninchen bin ich* (The rabbit—that's me), which depicts a cold, career-minded party functionary against whom the hero, a woman, develops her own character. The film was never released for circulation simply because the party insisted it exuded "negativism" in being critical without really crediting the transformation of the GDR for what had been achieved and without pointing to positive resolutions of conflict conforming to the party's intentions. A contribution to the plenum heaping scorn on Witt was titled "A firm [class] standpoint—good results" (Schubbe 1972, 1095ff.).

Policing Contact with People and Ideas

The party state engaged in a panoply of prohibitive interventions to influence the formation of its citizens' understandings. These measures can be analyzed and classified with the help of the validation forms I discussed in the introductory chapter. In this sense, the party state can be said to have aimed at managing the recognitions the citizens of the GDR received. It did so not only through propaganda but also by limiting contact with people and by restricting access to objectified understandings in the form of newspapers, books, movies, performances, architecture, art, music, and so on. Through the very same means the party state also engaged in a very active politics of memory by which it can be said to have hoped to influence the occurrences of particular resonances. Finally, the party state tried to manage the kinds of experiences people could have and thus the possibility for the occurrence of certain corroborations, for example, by tightly managing the use of public spaces as well as by monopolizing the right of social organization. In what follows I will provide a brief general overview of such measures. A detailed understanding of the interactional dynamics entailed by these policies will become apparent throughout all of the substantive chapters of this book.

The GDR party state went to extraordinary lengths in managing the contact between people with "right" and "wrong" consciousness. Since all citizens were supposed to be or become bearers of right consciousness, this meant that it tried to manage the contact between its citizens and those of other countries that were deemed to wield "negative influence." This pertains in particular to Westerners, West Germans and West Berliners, but it also pertained in the 1980s to Eastern European countries that were increasingly perceived as wrestling with infestations of damaging consciousness. It is useful to differentiate between two different levels of contact management. There is on the one hand personal contact enabled by travel, phone, or mail. On the other hand, there is the access to mass media in both print and electronic form. Let me address the former first. The freedom of movement between East and West Germany was influenced by a number of policy choices, not all of which were made with contact management in mind. During the time of Allied occupation Germans needed permits to travel or move between occupational zones. However, people moving from the Soviet occupational zone to the western zones or vice versa, were accepted as refugees. Obviously, the introduction of different currencies in both parts of Germany in 1948 made interactions between easterners and westerners more difficult. The foundation of two German states in 1949 created an entirely new situation. In 1952 the GDR began to fortify its boundary with the FRG. The actual border area was cleared of vegetation and settlements, a complex system of border control was installed including watchtowers, barbed-wire fences, minefields, and later also automatic gunning ranges. A 5-km-wide "border zone" extending inland from the actual borderline was established to make the policing tasks more effective. For this purpose several thousand inhabitants of this control zone were evacuated.[19] From then on the only hole in the Iron Curtain was the boundary between East and West Berlin. In this time the police regularly screened the trains from the GDR provinces to the capital as well as the commuter rail trains from East to West Berlin to pick out people who looked as if they harbored the intention to flee. The intention alone was deemed illegal.[20] That hole in the Iron Curtain was closed with the erection of the Berlin Wall. The border area was policed by a special force which was first organized under the responsibility of the Ministry of the Interior and later under the Ministry of Defense.

The near-complete control of the physical border went hand in hand with a strict examination process for visa applications to leave the country. In the course of time relatively free travel in the socialist world became possible. Vacations in Hungary's Balaton Lake area or at the Black Sea resorts of Romania and Bulgaria came within reach of many GDR citizens, as did hiking trips into the Polish or Czechoslovakian Tatras. However, visa requirements were reimposed on a general level or on an individual basis wherever there seemed to be a danger for the proper socialist consciousness of GDR citizens. The general visa-free travel with Poland was abandoned after the dramatic rise of the independent workers union *Solidarność* in 1981. The visa-free travel arrangements with Hungary were rescinded after it opened its borders with Austria in the summer 1989, hastening the refugee crisis of the late summer and early fall of that year. By administrative procedure (no court order was needed), citizens of the GDR could be excluded on an individual basis, without a requirement to name reasons, from visa-free travel to any country (see chapter 8, pp. 452–53).

Personal travel into countries with "nonsocialist currencies" (i.e., with freely convertible currency) was heavily restricted. After the construction of the Berlin Wall in 1961, and for most GDR citizens below retirement age, it became virtually impossible.[21] Since 1964 pensioners could travel to visit relatives in West Germany. Funds for travel had to come from abroad how-

19. For a fascinating ethnographic account about the life within this borderland before and after the fall of the GDR, see Berdahl 1999.

20. With the promulgation of the new penal code for the GDR in 1968, one article (213) was reserved for border violations and cases of "flight from the republic" (*Republikflucht*), which was punishable in severe cases (e.g., "in collaboration with others" or "with the help of a hideout"), with prison up to eight years.

21. The term *nonsocialist currency territory* (*nichtsozialistisches Währungsgebiet*, known also simply as NSW) played on the official reasoning provided by the party state that travel to the capitalist West was so heavily restricted because of currency convertibility issues.

ever.[22] With Brandt's détente in the 1970s and the conclusion of the "Basic Treaty" between the GDR and the FRG in 1972, younger people still working could apply for permission to visit Western relatives for baptisms, weddings, funerals, or even "round" birthdays. In every single case a risk assessment was undertaken gauging the likelihood that the petitioner would return to the GDR. Thus, travelers typically had to leave their close kin behind to make sure they would come back. Nevertheless, the number of journeys undertaken were increasing rapidly toward the end of the GDR. From 1986, when 1.7 million GDR citizens (among which 1.5 million were retirees) visited the FRG, the numbers exploded in the subsequent year (when Honecker finally paid his long-planned visit to West Germany) to 5 million (3.8 million retirees).

To better manage foreign travel, the GDR created the category of "traveling-officials" (*Reisekader*). This much-coveted designation marked the privilege of some employees of GDR companies and members of some organizations (such as scientists, sportsmen and women) who had regular professional business in Western countries to travel with considerably less bureaucratic hassle. They all had to undergo a thorough investigation by the Stasi evaluating their loyalty to the GDR according to a catalog of criteria that included their "reasons to stay" (*Bleibegründe*). I have already mentioned some of these, such as familial ties or a professional environment that could not easily be replicated elsewhere. In the eyes of the authorities, another reason to stay was commitment to the socialist project. The point of the Stasi's screening was to permit only those people to travel who had a near-perfect likelihood of returning.

Access to non-conforming understandings was not only managed through contact restrictions. All print products, newspapers, magazines, or books had to be licensed in the GDR. Except for minor publishing rights granted to the two recognized Christian churches, all publishing houses and printing presses were controlled by the party state. The print news media was owned and run by the party or any of its affiliated organizations, including the parties associated with the SED in the National Front. The flagship paper *Neues Deutschland* (*ND*) exercised an ideological signaling function for other media. The reason is not difficult to understand. In addition to the party's chief propagandist, politburo member Joachim Herrmann, Honecker took the

22. GDR citizens were allowed to export M 70.- (GDR Marks) only. To help East German travelers, in 1970 the FRG introduced the instrument of "welcome money" (*Begrüßungsgeld*). Simply by showing their GDR travel documents, visitors from the GDR, who were, juridically speaking for West German authorities, German citizens (a separate East German citizenship was never recognized by West Germany), received DM 30.-, since 1988, DM 100.-. After the fall of the Wall, the welcome money provided the funds for millions of GDR citizens to get a taste (and not just a look) of the consumption possibilities in capitalism.

trouble to censor content and layout at least the front page for each following day (Boyer 2005, 130). In general, interventions in editorial decisions were commonplace (Schabowski 1991b). Since this was generally known, *ND* could become the benchmark for the current interpretation of the party line for the whole country. Accordingly, any even subtle changes in the paper's tone were interpreted as policy shifts.

News reports were all centrally provided by the party's wire service, ADN (Allgemeine Deutsche Nachrichtenagentur). New book manuscripts had to pass censorial control, which could increasingly rely on decentralized self-censorship in the sense that, for example, editors at publishing houses or at periodicals decided themselves that a particular manuscript or article needed to be rejected (Boyer 2003).[23] In addition to censorship, writers, even those favored by the party, were frequently subjected to secret police surveillance (Walther 1999). Older material of questionable political orientation was largely expunged from the public libraries in the late 1940s and 1950s (e.g., Bruyn 1996, 25ff.). In research libraries they were moved to special collections, popularly known as "poison cabinets," to which access was only granted with special permission. The importation of unlicensed print material was illegal and could, depending on the exact circumstances, be punished with prison terms (see chapter 8). Censorship extended also to performances of any kind (e.g., Klier 1989) and to art exhibitions and public events more generally (see also chapter 7, p. 386).

Electronic mass media were owned, run, and controlled by the government. Yet, thanks to the relatively central location of West Berlin in the middle of GDR territory, and owing to the multiply curved and folded border with West Germany, most of the GDR was in range of regular West German radio and television stations.[24] Attempts to regulate access to Western electronic media ranged from selling equipment (receivers, TV sets, antennae) with limited reception capabilities, to monitoring the positioning of antennae on roof tops, and the screening of conversations in school yards and at work places. Party members even had to endure surprise visits at home in which the contents of kitchen cabinets could be checked as much as the position of the dials on radio receivers and television sets. Yet, to no avail. The majority of the GDR population, many party members included, was

---

23. Some fascinating descriptions of working the censorship system can be gleaned from the memoirs of writers, both those who remained essentially loyal to party and state (e.g., Kuczynski 1994), those with mixed loyalties (e.g., Heym 2005), and those whose critical engagement finally led to their emigration (e.g., Kunert 1999; Loest 1999).

24. By regular I mean that the population of the GDR did not have to take recourse to listen to West German broadcasts on low-quality medium- or short-wave dials. The West German broadcasting companies had installed high-power transmitters on the tops of the medium-range mountains forming much of the boundary between the two countries.

not dissuaded from following the Western media through any of these measures. This does not mean in the least that they did not watch GDR television, even its newscast. But it does mean that they contrasted and compared two different, at times starkly contradictory, news sources.

In the interest of controlling the occurrence of resonances, the party tried to install its own memory culture. It did so in part through the management of access to people and ideas, but in part also through the construction and reconstruction of cityscapes and the selective celebration of events. This attempt at managing memories was less radical in avoiding contradictions with preexisting understandings than, let's say, radical French revolutionaries who went as far as changing the calendar, clothing, forms of address, and so on. Yet, socialism made decisive attempts to assimilate traditions it could weave into its own positive self-narrative or revolutionary transformations toward a communist society while trying to extinguish others that in terms of the Marxian philosophy of history appeared reactionary. In East Germany this included, for example, the appropriation of "early bourgeois" classics in music, literature, and philosophy. The revolutionary bourgeois was welcome as precursor of the revolutionary proletarian, not least because historically they did not immediately compete with each other. This contrasts sharply, for example, with the rejection of the "late" or "decadent" bourgeois, which was taken as a foil against which socialism could develop. Thus Luther, Grimmelshausen, Schiller, and Goethe were celebrated through anniversary festivities, monuments, and/or museums; their works were published in handsome heritage editions that cash-strapped Westerners were eager to buy. Others, however, such as Rilke, Musil, or Mann were elided, referred to if at all in the negative. Kant, Herder, and Hegel were canonized, but not Nietzsche, Husserl, or Wittgenstein (to say nothing of Heidegger). Pöppelmann, Schinkel, and Semper were seen as exemplary architects but not Wagner, Behrens, or Mies van der Rohe. This attempt at the destruction and reconstruction of tradition is visible in the programs of GDR publishers, of opera houses and other performance venues, and last but not least in the reconstruction of the GDR's cityscapes, which are characterized by ruthless destruction as much as by pockets of careful preservation.

In an effort to manage locally produced recognitions, the party state did not tolerate the foundation of groups and organizations outside of the party's direct domain of control. Citizens were asked to participate, but they were asked to do so exclusively within the frameworks provided by the party. This prohibition to form independent groups extended to unions organized for the pursuit of some hobby (be it diving, soccer, or chess) as much as for any grouping that might in the end play a more narrowly defined political goal such as professional associations. For all of these social pursuits the SED and its affiliated parties entertained a wide array of organizations that were supposed to cover the field of possibilities. The party state aimed to be civil society as well, claiming that the distinction between the two was mere bourgeois-liberal ideology. As far as its self-understandings were concerned, the party was *the* public sphere in the GDR. The only exceptions from this carefully guarded rule were the Protestant and the Catholic churches in the GDR, which enjoyed a semiautonomous status as societies within society, under the heading of "church in socialism" (see chapter 8, p. 401).

In the enforcement of all of these prohibitions the Stasi played a leading, if sometimes only, coordinating role. At the border it was responsible for passport control. Even though the police was responsible for issuing visas, it was the Stasi who ran the security (i.e., reliability) checks on the persons who had asked for a visa. This was even more the case for the evaluation of traveling officials. Stasi became involved if people became suspect of maintaining "illicit contacts" with the West or when state authorities got wind of the circulation of unlicensed print materials. As we shall see in part IV, it also tried to learn about the formation of any conceivable enduring groups, no matter whether they were punk bands or reading circles. The Stasi was the agency chiefly responsible for protecting the party's agenda.

This massive barrage of policed prohibitions and exclusions was intended by the party to shelter its own propagandistic work from interference by the class enemy who, with its seductive tricks and corrupting promises, constantly threatened to lead the GDR's citizen astray from the virtuous path into monolithic intentionality. In the lingo of the sociology of understanding, the party did not want any competition for its carefully planned and deployed recognitions, positive and negative. Yet the results of these measures were mixed at best, possibly substantially detrimental to its own project. For one, to many citizens of the GDR, the Stasi officers I spoke to included, these prohibitions were easily recognizable as merely defensive gestures. They bared the party state's own inferiority complex, its own implicit recognition that it could at some level not compete with the capitalist West. They also revealed that at a fundamental level the state was not ready to trust its own citizens with their desires, their choices, their judgments. These prohibitions made particularly obvious the state's presumption of a tutelary role based on supposedly higher insight. Yet among GDR citizens the meaning of these prohibitions were disputed and thus, the consequences drawn from them were very different. Some people learned to accept these prohibitions as necessary to defend the socialist David from the capitalist Goliath, while others deemed them simply presumptuous.

The eroticization of the forbidden seems inevitable with so many prohibitions at play. As long as the traces of the forbidden remain decipherable and the negative recognition of the prohibiting agency visible, an intense curiosity for it may emerge. How strong this curiosity is depends not only on the imagined effect of access, but also to a considerable degree on the authority of the blocking agency. Trust in its judgment will recognize the understanding advanced by the prohibition that there is nothing to be curious about, only potential harm. In the GDR the forbidden did, as we shall see, by no means beckon all. I will introduce in chapters 5 and 6 Stasi officers who felt no desire for most of what was officially forbidden by the party state. They neither craved to see Western countries, nor did they long to read Western papers, novels, poems, or plays. This was so, precisely as long as they trusted the party's judgment unhesitatingly. Yet, the dynamics of prohibition play out very differently when the authority of the prohibiting agency appears questionable. Then every irritation or conflict with it may feed the curiosity for the prohibited. Under these circumstances, the negative recognition of the questionable authority operates as enticement to have at least a closer look at what has been removed from access.[25] This was certainly the case for the majority of the GDR population whose cravings for travel to Western countries, for Western consumer goods, for indexed literature, philosophy, and art were nourished by Western electronic mass media while they were amplified if not exoticized by the party-state's panoply of prohibitions. The first years after unification were testimony to the degree to which these cravings bordered on the fantastical, which in due time had to explode in disillusionment. Finally, yet others, seasoned dissidents among them, struggled hard to extract themselves from the Manichaean logic of the party. They aimed to make the prohibition of the party as irrelevant as possible for their own evaluation, which they shared in alternative networks of authority.

In spite of the fact that the efforts of the party to construct a monolithic intentionality through prohibitions met a variety of responses, I still think it is justified to speak here of a second aporia of socialist politics, the *aporia of prohibition*. The party state thought that it could not do without these prohibitions in order to achieve its goal. And yet, by the very fact that it felt compelled to enact them it implicitly revealed its own weakness. More, simply because it never managed to attain the status of the exalted authority it craved to have in the eyes of the majority of the population, the prohibitions also helped to eroticize precisely that which it tried so painstakingly to prevent.

The Stasi and the Ideological Enemy

The problem of uncertain consciousness was, in the eyes of the party, amplified by the fear that people without a firm partisan viewpoint embedded in a healthy socialist collective might become easy prey for the conniving

---

25. Such dynamics will be explored in detail in chapter 4. For the case at hand compare the discussion of the dialectics of recognition (p. 221 ff.).

machinations of the class enemy who never relented in his efforts at "political-ideological sabotage" (*politisch-ideologische Diversion*). Because this is a key term of socialist reasoning about its own security, I will provide the definition of the term used by the Stasi, the agency that had the primary responsibility in combating it (Suckut 1996, 303):

> With political ideological sabotage, the enemy tries to accomplish subversive goals. . . . These consist in the decomposition of socialist consciousness, or the impediment or stunting of its development, in the weakening of the trust of large groups of citizens in the policies of communist parties and of socialist states, in the inspiration of antisocialist behaviors including political crimes, in the mobilization of inimical-negative forces in socialist countries . . .

As the party saw its own propaganda efforts as a "struggle for the minds and the hearts of the people," the enemy's efforts were described in popular propaganda jargon as attempts to "sodden the minds and the hearts of the people." These formulations reveal that the enemy was assumed to work chiefly through means of consciousness deformation. Just as agitation and propaganda assumed increasing relevance as a means of policy within socialism, class warfare was increasingly understood as ideological warfare. The historical development of the Cold War from actual armed conflict through violent partisan tactics to the balance of horror of nuclear deterrence corroborated this understanding of the historical trajectory of class warfare. This is reflected again in the Stasi's definition of an enemy (document in Suckut 1996, 121):

> Persons who, either in groups or individually, intentionally develop political-ideological attitudes and perspectives that are alien to socialism and who in realizing these attitudes and perspectives engage in practical behavior provoking events or conditions that endanger the socialist orders of state and society in general or in any of its aspects.

Accordingly, socialism perceived itself as always under threat and thus in urgent need of protection through a determined security apparatus. In effect, security and propaganda were seen as the two flipsides of the consciousness-driven model of social transformation in historical times of Manichaean duality. Both were integral components of the production of monolithic intentionality.

The peacetime protection of socialism from it enemies had at least three different components. First, it was necessary to make sure that propaganda, the positive instrument of proselytization, was working as effectively as possible. Since propaganda was seen as the key to socialism's success, the enemy was assumed to attack propaganda events and channels. Second, security meant as well to develop a realistic picture of the true state of consciousness of the citizens of the GDR. Since there were almost no ethnographies or opinion surveys taking stock of the habits and thoughts of the GDR population, this task fell mainly into the lap of the bureaucratic information-gathering activities of party and state, with Stasi playing an increasingly pivotal role.[26] Third, security meant to incapacitate already existing enemies and to prevent the emergence of new enemies in the future. In all three cases, security work implied discovering "who is who?" as this was expressed in the language of the secret police; in other words, socialism needed to differentiate friend and foe to find means to react adequately (SAPMO BArch DY 30/IV 2/2.039, 58–59):

> In our Chekist[27] work we have had the experience that many sympathizers and fellow travelers of oppositional groups are people who have for various reasons temporarily come under the spell of internal and external enemies.... With the help of prudent ideological influence and in collaboration with state and social organizations we have to make every effort to bring them back to positions which are in accordance with society or at least loyal.... As far as the fanatic enemies are concerned ... we advance against them with the full force of the law. The decision whether or not to indict is in particular with respect to inimical forces a deeply political one, which has to be made depending on the overall political situation, the concrete situation of class warfare and in accordance with the overall interests of the state.

The differentiation between friend and foe, and the development of adequate means to deal with propaganda failure, were seen as central goals of the GDR security apparatus. The agency entrusted chiefly with this task was the Ministry of State Security with its fifteen district and 227 county offices.[28]

The Stasi's central position in the GDR's security apparatus was not so much the result of a direct organizational subordination of the other "security organs," after all the Ministry of the Interior presiding over the People's Police (and with it the prison system) and the Ministry of National De-

---

26. Empirical social science research that would have systematically investigated how people in the GDR thought and felt about socialism and the party was almost nonexistent. For the fate of opinion research in the GDR, see the conclusions to chapter 4.

27. Cheka, originally Vecheka, was the first postrevolutionary secret police, founded within weeks after the Russian revolution. It was headed by Feliks Dzierzynski, the official role model of all Soviet-style communist secret police agents. In honor of the Cheka and its first chief, Stasi employees, much like their brethren elsewhere in Eastern Europe, referred to themselves as "chekists" to highlight their discipline, morale, and commitment to the success of party and revolution.

28. Mampel (1996) has talked in this context quite fittingly about the Stasi as an "ideology police."

fense were completely independent bureaucracies. Instead, the dovetailing of several practices enabled the Stasi to play this central role. First, the Stasi was responsible for the security of the other agencies, including performing security checks on their personnel. By contrast, the Stasi controlled its own people. Second, the Stasi was allowed to take on the cases deemed of more immediate security relevance for party and state. This included high-profile criminal cases. And last but not least, the Minister of State Security was the only chief of a major security agency who became a member of the politburo, and who in addition ultimately belonged with Günter Mittag (economy) and perhaps Joachim Herrmann (propaganda) to Erich Honecker's innermost leadership circle (e.g., Eberlein 2000, 457ff.). In the public imagination the Stasi was *the* security apparatus, owing in part to the mystery in which it shrouded itself. Its buildings were unmarked, although most people knew where the main Stasi offices in their neighborhoods were located. Stasi officers were known in their families and in the circle of their friends to work for the Stasi, which some people also called mockingly "the firm" (*die Firma*), or "people-owned company listen and look" (*VEB Horch und Guck*). Yet nobody, spouses included, knew what exact unit they worked for, or even less, what kind of cases they worked on. Thus, shrouded in secrecy, the Stasi was, in some people's imagination, transmogrified into a mythical helper who could rectify situations an otherwise intransigent state or party bureaucracy could not or would not address; in others it could become the loathed object par excellence, standing for everything that was wrong with the GDR; and in yet others it was the butt of any number of jokes, which may in the end have actively supported its mystification (Brie 2004).

The Stasi operated as a large, bureaucratically organized secret police organization. In 1989 it counted roughly 91,000 employees on its payroll. Following in the footsteps of Lenin's Cheka, the Stasi understood itself as the effective guardian of the achievements of the revolution, that is, as "the sword and shield of the party." It was officially founded with the status of a national ministry in 1950 through a legal act that did not further specify either its duties or its rights or procedures. After being temporarily regrouped as a mere division in the Ministry of the Interior owing to Stasi's failure to effectively foresee and counteract the uprisings around June 17, 1953, it was officially reinstated as a ministry in 1955. Since 1957, Erich Mielke stood at its helm. He stayed in this position until the beginning of the velvet revolution in the fall of 1989 when, in a vain effort to preserve the party's hold on power through a rejuvenation of its leadership, he was ousted from the politburo (only weeks after he had helped to topple the general secretary) and retired as minister of state security. It was one of the last grand applications of the socialist theodicy, the personalization of blame to save the system.

Due to its legendary success in undermining West Germany's secret services, the most famous division of Stasi was arguably its *Aufklärung*, its foreign espionage division. However, the far larger part of the Stasi was concentrated on issues of internal security, which was known as *Abwehr*, or "counterespionage."[29] Internal security was organized around "object" responsibilities. Every official organization in the GDR, including all government bureaucracies, with the sole exception of the party (and arguably the Stasi itself), was assigned to a Stasi unit responsible for its security. By and large, county-level branches of larger organizations were assigned to the county offices of the Stasi, district branches were assigned to the district offices, and national headquarters were assigned directly to the ministry in Berlin.[30] Privately formed (and therefore unofficial) groups—which, given the party state's (near) monopoly over organizing people, should not even have existed—were dealt with in the official organizational context in which they emerged. Oppositional scientists, for example, were investigated in the context of the institutions in which they worked; neo-Nazi tendencies among army soldiers were handled by the division responsible for the National People's Army and so on.

Stasi units looked after the security of objects assigned to them in both public and secret ways. Stasi officers maintained open contact with their

---

29. Only about 3,800 (1989) employees belonged to the HVA, the foreign espionage service. For a distribution of employees over various departments, see BStU 1996; for employee statistics over time, see Gieseke 2000. It is difficult to estimate how many Stasi officers were directly involved in efforts to control oppositional political thought. Responsibility and support for this task was not lodged in any single department simply because oppositional activity could happen in a wider variety of "objects," i.e., organizational contexts covered by different branches of the Stasi. Nevertheless, with the "directive 2/85" (Engelmann and Joestel 2004, 432–455), the ministry's Division XX was appointed as coordinator of all such efforts, not least because, carrying responsibility for the church and the cultural sector it had accrued most of it anyway.

30. This form of organization is mirrored in the structure of the ministry: Division I was chiefly responsible for the National People's Army, Division VII for People's Police and Customs, Division XVIII for the economy, Division XIX for postal services and transportation, and most famously Division XX for youth, mass media, education, arts, religious communities, and finally the political opposition. In addition to this structure there were specialized service departments providing telephone surveillance (Department 26), mail surveillance (Department M), physical observation and bugging services (Division VIII), forensic investigations, and a so-called division of investigation (IX), which ran the interrogation of prisoners in Stasi's own jail system and also checked the legal merits of a particular case. The Stasi also provided bodyguards for the political elite, an honor guard regiment in Berlin (used in receptions of foreign guests of state), special construction services (again, mostly for the political elite), and passport control services. An excellent quick overview of the administrative structure and organization of tasks of Stasi is provided by Wiedmann 1995. The most comprehensive overview is provided in a handbook series edited by the federal agency for Stasi documents (Suckut et al. 1993–).

object, serving as official point persons for object leaders, who were supposed to report any "unusual occurrences." Officers also recruited a network
of secret informants who participated in the organization. Informants and
officers met regularly in safe houses (typically apartments made temporarily
available by individual lessees). Originally, the idea was that every object, as
an integral part of the socialist party state, was vulnerable to enemies who
might place spies or saboteurs in the object to disrupt the favorable development of socialism. Thus, activities deemed detrimental to the aims of the
party state were supposed to be discovered *in statu nascendi* and effectively
thwarted before they could cause damage. Stasi's efforts were in this sense
geared toward preventive intervention.

As "sword and shield of the party" the Stasi set itself the task to identify
all enemies of party and state. The archetypes of the enemy were the spies
who supplied capitalist secret service agencies with crucial information and
the saboteurs who, on these agencies' behest, intended to destroy goods or
impede processes that were considered essential to the development of socialism. In keeping with the centrality afforded to monolithic intentionality, the good most vulnerable to tampering was the "unity between party
and people," and in the course of time the image of the saboteur changed
from someone derailing trains or setting factories ablaze to someone who
committed ideological sabotage by spreading negative judgments about the
party, socialism, or the GDR.

Leads for finding such enemies were mostly supplied by secret informants, either during the direct investigation of unusual occurrences (accidents, graffiti, the appearance of flyers, a case of flight, unusual voting
behavior), or during routine meetings. For this reason, secret informants
were the very backbone of Stasi operations, and countless Stasi documents,
including the major guidelines governing the work of Stasi with secret informants (documents in Müller-Enbergs 1996), call them "the main weapon in
its struggle with the enemy." At the end, Stasi had about 108,000 registered
secret informants of various kinds. Work with these informants was supported by 33,000 people who were willing to supply their apartments as
safe houses or to work as couriers, and by another 33,000 informants with
whom the Stasi maintained a less-structured relationship (Müller-Enbergs
1996, 59). These numbers are impressive in the sense that at the end of the
GDR's history almost 2 percent of the adult population was directly involved
with it. If one takes retirement rates both among full-time members and
informants into consideration, 3–5 percent (depending on the assumptions)
of the adult population had at one point in their life been on active duty
for the Stasi. Of course, these numbers are much less surprising if one also
takes into consideration that before members were abandoning the SED in
droves in the fall of 1989, about 19 percent (Schroeder 1998, 393) of the adult

population were party members. Moreover, these numbers, especially the statistics on secret informants, have to be taken with a grain of salt not only because they stand for very different kinds and degrees of involvement but also because the Stasi was, after all, a socialist production unit, which recruited and registered informants according to plan. In other words, to meet targets officers recruited informants with little value for the organization. The much bemoaned "tonnage-ideology" characteristic of socialist central planning even applied to the secret police.

The Complementarity of Secret Police and Propaganda Work

The Stasi's efforts to do whatever was politically feasible[31] to "secure" the efficacy of propaganda demonstrates that its work was merely the "dark underside" of the party's project of creating a monolithic intentionality, unifying the GDR population en route to a communist society. This work involved actions aiming to ensure that the party's monopoly over sources of information was maintained to the largest possible extent. After all efforts failed, for example, to prevent the GDR citizenry from receiving Western electronic mass media, Stasi directed its efforts to help secure party control over print media. This meant first that it had to suppress publicly accessible written utterances, from graffiti and "misused wall newspapers" to any sort of unlicensed publications such as flyers. As far as officially published materials are concerned, the Stasi's attention was directed to "mistakes," which, following the logic of the socialist theodicy, could just as well have been acts of sabotage. Such seeming mistakes could be articles that came to be published, although in the estimation of the party should not have, as much as typos that added a funny or critical twist to otherwise sober socialist print. The Stasi also paid much attention to the educational sector that, as a major stage of proselytization, was thought to be vulnerable to the ideological attacks of the enemy. Thus, the Stasi routinely investigated incidents (*Vorfälle*) in which students or teachers at educational institutions of all levels made statements or were involved in activities that could be understood as antisocialist once these reached a certain magnitude or sensitivity.

The "undisturbed course" of mass events was afforded great importance in Stasi work. This is reflected in the annual planning documents of the Stasi,

---

31. As the Mielke quote on page 146 makes clear, what was politically feasible is not identical with what Stasi could or would have done if allowed free reign. For example, in curtailing samizdat publications the international political context had to be taken into consideration. Thus, Stasi tried to deal a devastating blow to the important samizdat paper *Grenzfall*, which was edited and produced by members of the "Initiative for Peace and Human Rights," only after Honecker had come back from his state visit to West Germany (see chapter 8).

which, for purposes of resource management and motivation, centered on "social highlights" (i.e., gatherings of socialist mass organizations, commemorative festivities, etc.) of national, regional, and local significance. It is also reflected in the room given to mass events in the biannual security briefings of the minister, which shed an interesting light on the reasons why the Stasi engaged in such work. Mielke's argument about the particular vulnerability and need for protection of mass events took the following path (SAPMO BArch DY 30/IV 2/2.039, 49–50):

> The powerful pleas of allegiance of our young generation to the party of the working class and its socialist State on the occasion of the communal elections, the national youth festival, and the 35th anniversary of the GDR . . . are impressive proof that we can rely on the youth of the GDR. This has to remain that way. In the face of the growing attacks on parts of the youth this implies a growing responsibility of all party organizations, the state and social organizations to increase all efforts to continue to thwart the enemy's attempts to interfere in the relationship between party and youth.

Since mass events were taken to corroborate the overwhelming unity between party and people, which in itself was seen as corroboration of the enormous vitality of socialism, they were also thought to attract the wrath of the class enemy, who would with all means like to disturb these events. Such disturbances were thought to come in two distinct forms: as classical sabotage, for example, the misdirection or delaying of trains transporting performers scheduled to appear at the event, the poisoning of food for participants, viscerally spoiling the fun for the participants, and so on; and as ideological sabotage, which might entail chanting, unfolding banners, or distributing pamphlets containing party-critical slogans that suggested the unity between party and people was not as tight as media reporting on these events proclaimed.

To prevent what it considered sabotage, the Stasi undertook an enormous range of measures. All performers in mass events had to be announced to the Stasi beforehand by the organizers so security checks could be run on each and every one of them. Anyone considered a potential risk—for example, because they were known to harbor party-critical attitudes, or because they maintained relations with such people—had to stay home. The network of secret informants was used to find out whether independent groups had plans to stage actions at events. Even if no actions were planned, it frequently happened that persons with ties to independent groups were kept under control during mass events, which meant their employers were prompted to keep them busy; in addition, key figures were put under surveillance and were, if deemed necessary, placed under house arrest or were temporarily detained on other pretexts (chapters 7 and 8 will provide concrete examples of this). Moreover, the Stasi, with the help of its network of informants, inspected the technical condition of locomotives, railroad cars, and buses used to transport participants, as well as technical equipment used during the event. Kurt Bogner, an officer involved in coordinating the security efforts for mass events, commented: "just imagine, Honecker would have grabbed the microphone and—silence!" Stasi also double-checked railroad schedules, secured key intersections in the traffic flow to and from events, and inspected the food and lodging of participants. The officers in charge of participating groups typically accompanied them, using secret informants throughout the event to learn of unusual occurrences as fast as possible. Other officers were strategically positioned throughout the audience.

In keeping with the increasing importance of "ideological work" during GDR history it may not come as a surprise that the efforts the Stasi engaged in to secure propaganda increased as well. Here are the recollections of Karl Maier, comparing the security efforts for the same event spaced almost two decades apart:

> You have to imagine, I was then, in 1961 . . . the only officer, a third lieutenant . . . who was there. That was the Pioneer meeting in Erfurt. [At] the last Pioneer meeting [1988] there was a group from the ministry consisting of 50 people. The head of the Division XX, Lieutenant General Kienberg managed the mission, not third Lieutenant Maier.

In the same context, he also comments on the logic of the Stasi's efforts to secure propaganda events:

> Let's say the publicity effect, or the danger to society, as we said, was [seen as very high] when the whole thing happened in front of running cameras or if the political intention of such large events could be damaged. If such a large event proceeded without major occurrences, then this was always counted as a large success of the MfS [Stasi]. . . . This means of course that in such times the measures of surveillance and control over people who were regarded as inimical or negative were propped up.

Maier's recollections reveal the powerful impact of certain background assumptions, most notably that of incessant and increasing class warfare. The acceptance of the argument that peaceful events demonstrated the work of the Stasi presupposes that without its protection, propaganda events would have been massively disturbed by enemy interference. Even if part of this may be discounted as the self-centric perspective of a particular bureaucracy eager to depict itself as indispensable, the very fact that such enormous security measures were deemed necessary betrays the overall feeling of threat under which the party leadership saw socialism.

Interestingly, this threat perception was not based on corroboration. Although all mishaps were systematically investigated according to whether they could be attributed to the machinations of the enemy, no such interference was, according to Kurt Bogner, proven for large public events in the 1970s and 1980s. Asked whether he had ever encountered any form of sabotage, Bogner answers: "not really." There once was poisoned food, which had been stored incorrectly, but it could not be proven that someone had done it on purpose; another time, buses were misdirected and the participants did not show up in time, and again no conclusive evidence for sabotage was detected. The bombardment of buses with water bottles or the firing of an air rifle at the audience from a nearby apartment could be traced to disgruntled youths with no ulterior political motives. The lack of corroboration becomes all the more curious if it is considered that the enormous increase in effort takes place precisely at the time in which even the overall incidences of both espionage and sabotage in the GDR decreased drastically, owing at least in part to the closure of the Berlin Wall and the much higher risk of being caught for any of them.[32]

Since elections were, as I argued above, major participatory propaganda events aiming at the hyperbolic recognition of identifications with state, party, and socialism, Stasi was involved in their preparation, conduct, and, later, analysis. As the Stasi would have investigated any disturbance of other propaganda events endangering their "political intention," inevitably a convincing performance of the unity between party and citizenry, so it did with elections. Critical utterances made public during the election campaign or the election itself, such as the distribution of flyers, or the production of graffiti, as well as instances of nonvoting, no-voting, or ballot invalidation, were considered such disturbances simply because they were thought to weaken the propaganda effect of the elections. Discussing the preceding communal elections, Erich Mielke (1984b) opened his May 1984 security briefing with regional and division heads of Stasi (a group roughly coextensive with Stasi generals) with a celebration of the success of the party. He took the usual near-perfect approval rate not only to indicate the overwhelming trust of the population in the party and its leadership but also as a token of patriotic love for the GDR:

> The high participation rate in the election and its result [the usual 99.x approval rate] are an expression of the deep trust of the citizens . . . and they reflect pride in the GDR and her accomplishments.

32. Unfortunately I cannot offer any numbers here. However, the trend depicted rests on consensus among the officers I have interviewed.

Mielke then showed himself greatly aggrieved by the occurrence of critical public statements in the context of the elections:

> In this context I would like to point to inimical-negative actions, incidents and phenomena, especially to the production and distribution of inflammatory leaflets (*Hetzblätter*) and inflammatory graffiti (*Hetzlosungen*). These actions directed against the communal elections were typically characterized by a massive slander against the state and social order, and contained in part a direct appeal not to participate in the communal elections. Territorial centers are: the districts of Leipzig with 5 incidences, Dresden with 3 incidences, and the capital Berlin with 3 incidences. The large majority of them could already be resolved. The perpetrators could be identified and arrested.

Mielke typically spoke in the tiring monotone characteristic of so many socialist leaders. But at this point in the tape his voice betrays a mixture of worry and anger. An extraordinary window onto the mindset of GDR leaders is opened by what appears in hindsight as a stark contrast between the build-up of towering (pleonastic) ("actions, incidents, and phenomena") and other hyperboles ("massive slander," "inflammatory graffiti") and the startlingly low number of actual occurrences, with a total of about fifteen to twenty cases in a country of 17 million inhabitants. If one further considers to whom Mielke is saying this, the absolute top brass of the Stasi, all party members of long standing, the aspiration level of what monolithic intentionality ought to accomplish becomes crystal clear.

How serious the Stasi took all of these instances of protest can be gauged from Mielke's exhortations to his men to learn as much as they possibly could about every single one of them through their network of secret informants. And he encouraged them to triangulate what they learned that way with information gathered about enemies of the state in other contexts and through other means. There was always the presupposition that there was an organizing hand behind all such occurrences, an inimical outside force that tried to find a hold within GDR society. Election analysis, much like the analysis of all other participatory propaganda events, was, for the Stasi, an integral part of their "who-is-who?" reconnaissance that is part of their efforts to differentiate between the friends and enemies of socialism.

The Abyss of Other Minds

The GDR leadership's anxieties about active rejection through parts of the population have not been fully captured so far. Mielke continued:

We may not overlook the fact that much like in previous elections, a not so insignificant number of enemies tried to camouflage themselves through progressive demeanor and behavior as well as through a public approval of the candidates. To discover such persons remains a preeminent political-operative task.

Here the consciousness-driven approach to social transformation begins to descend into the abyss of infinite semiosis: signs have lost their power to reference anything but other signs; recognition could be taken as such, but maybe it was not meant in that way. The hoped-for positive signals of successful propaganda reception may be faked, nothing but reflections functioning as deflections. In other words, the socialist leadership is lost in what philosophers have called the problem of other minds. How could the party state be sure to know what the people in the GDR really thought?

At this point it may be productive to recapitulate the argument thus far. Considering the appropriate consciousness as the key to success, the party engaged in massive propaganda efforts geared at teaching its citizenry new ways of thinking, feeling, and acting. Since, however, socialists had to begin with an "old" consciousness that was assumed to be hostile to the "new," and since the class enemy was expected to interfere with the proselytization effort wherever she could, and, finally, since the actual message of propaganda needed to be constantly adjusted to changing historical circumstances, the party needed some kind of measure of how successfully people had internalized monolithic intentionality. Such measures of success become all the more desirable as the expected rate of economic progress did not materialize. Since this contradicted the theory, the question was, why. Given the theodicic character of socialist failure accounting, there were really only two possibilities: the enemy or a perhaps still not sophisticated and/or comprehensive enough propaganda effort. The party also needed other kinds of success measures, especially ones that could testify that the increasing attention to propaganda did indeed pay off.

Since self-objectification remained a moving target, the party asked everybody to supply tokens of allegiance *continuously*. In reference to Marx praxeology in the *Thesis on Feuerbach*, a widely disseminated slogan was "practice is the criterion of truth" (Kuusinen et al. 1960, 124; cf. Wischnjakow et al. 1974, 106ff.), that is, conduct was seen as the best indicator for that state of consciousness that was also known as *Bewußtheit*, that is, his or her moral maturity in terms of the ethics of absolute finality. An honest, simple, modest, moderate, monogamous, heterosexual, that is, a "socialist lifestyle" (*sozialistische Lebensweise*), was evidence for it; and so was speaking publicly on all occasions with "ideological clarity"; the donation of time to volunteer actions and of money to socialist causes were taken to index its existence;

membership, active participation, and taking over a functional role in the socialist mass organizations, or better, even the party itself, was seen as proof of it. In addition, the party used its own participatory propaganda events as touchstones of allegiance. These could be the recurrent calendrical events mentioned above, where active participation was demanded and noticed. But the party also created special events designed for that very purpose. Signature collection campaigns eliciting support for a particular policy of the party are a good example (for instance, after the GDR's involvement in crushing the Prague Spring). More even than in the regular participatory events, the party clearly communicated, in the context of these policy affirmations, how much the objective circumstances of the moment required self-objectification, in this particular instance, turning them into high-stakes affairs. Refusals to offer the required token were noted with considerable vexation, not least because the publicized measure of allegiance was meant to feed back onto the hyperbolic recognition of Marxism-Leninism and the party's leading role. Consequently, failure to produce the required token created the suspicion that the refusing party harbored "inimical attitudes" (*feindliche Einstellungen*). It could be used as a piece of evidence to justify Stasi surveillance.

There was a catch, however, in the party's eager collection of behavioral signs of allegiance. Since the party so clearly signaled what it wanted, it was all the easier to fake the token it expected. Yet the situation seems, if anything, worse. Since organizations (including workplaces) were asked to show up as a collective to some such events (e.g., May Day parades), and since their leaders were held responsible for the mobilization of their members/workers, they felt compelled toward the end of the GDR to provide extra incentives for participation, such as joint festivities with free beer and such, after the event. This means that the tokens effectively collected during such events were to some unknown degree rather worthless (and party members sensed this acutely). What is true for participatory propaganda events is just as true for discursive encounters in party meetings, in the office, and the like. Here the committed use and defense of the party line was the token of allegiance signaling to others and especially to superiors that the person in question was actively objectifying himself or herself. And yet again, the mere fact that somebody had understood what was expected could not be taken for an authentic articulation of thought.

The issue emerging here is one of proper corroboration, that is, the question under which circumstances the results yielded by a particular test should have corroborating power. In modern scientific meta-understandings the validating effect of an event occurs only if it is in a crucial sense contingent, that is, beyond the particular agentic powers of the person or institution who stages it (see chapter 3, p. 200). In other words, events fail to validate understandings if one has to have reasonable suspicion that the outcome is engineered. What can happen when such doubts occur is perhaps best told by an episode in which one of my interview partners was involved. To make sure propaganda events proceeded as planned they were rehearsed. For the twenty-fifth anniversary celebration of the GDR, the communist youth movement was supposed to hold a torchlight procession that marched by a tribune of dignitaries, including not only the general secretary of the SED but that of the CPSU as well. For the dress rehearsal Stasi officers stood at the tribune in their stead, accepting the youths' tribute to party and country. Jürgen Buchholz remembers:

> We stood on the tribune when they practiced saying their piece. If you ask me whether I have ever had butterflies in my stomach: then and there [is the answer]. This whole situation was so confusing for me that I still get sick to my stomach if I think of it. It was clear to me: *I am standing on stage, not the general secretary.* Therefore the whole thing was mummery. I became aware of the whole artifice involved in the matter—but then I put the whole matter behind me.

For Buchholz, the general propagandistic claim that such demonstrations corroborated the party government for an instant flew apart like a house of cards, dragging him down into an intense state of nausea, which he surmounted in the subsequent days through the friendly reassurances of his colleagues.

The uncanny sense that there was something amiss with propaganda events as a reliable measure of allegiance nourished a search for alternatives. To get a more valid understanding of the state of consciousness of a particular person the party, therefore, needed a way to check elicited and predictably positive public performances against other supposedly less-controlled behavioral expressions. Only consistency across the full diversity of contexts was taken to be a good enough guide to judge whether the person was sufficiently self-objectifying. As Herbert Eisner, a former Stasi officer, put it so poignantly: "If the majority of the people no longer follow the directives of the party, if they no longer believe that it is worth the while to work for their realization, then we'll drown. . . . Therefore it is important that the state security really knows what and how they think." The first tool to do so was the so-called security check (*Sicherheitsüberprüfung*) (document reprinted in Gill and Schröter 1991, 295–321). It was performed on people who were prima facie supportive of the party's project, but who needed further security clearance to be promoted into positions considered to be security sensitive, such as positions in infrastructure maintenance (railroad, telecommunications, postal services). Stasi checked every potential employee and every secret informant. Security checks were also carried out for people performing in public, such as actors, TV and radio employees, or athletes. Finally, checks were performed on anyone who might officially come in contact with Westerners, no matter whether they were scientists or diplomats. Depending on the sensitivity of the position in question, the check could vary in depth ranging from a simple check of whether there was anything on file against a particular person, to elaborate investigations of the person in their respective social environments, that is, at work, in the neighborhood, and within any leisure contexts. Such investigations could be carried out entirely with help of informants, through full-time members, and with the support of the neighborhood beat patrol officer (*Abschnittsbevollmächtigter*) of the regular People's Police (*Volkspolizei*). Security checks were a routine matter for operative units and were typically performed by the Stasi office that had the object responsibility.

How, then, was trustworthiness adjudicated? I have emphasized so far that consistent self-objectification played the major role. Consequently, a first approach to assess the trustworthiness of a particular person was to check whether and to which degree a particular person displayed tokens of allegiance. Probing a person's adherence to the socialist lifestyle offered further criteria. Failing to show a firm class standpoint in discussions, having no arguments to defend party and GDR, a state known as "ideological uncertainty" (*ideologische Unklarheit*), was seen as a weakness because it was expected to open the doors for the ideological influence of the class enemy. Profligacy, especially a strong desire for Western consumer goods, sexual deviance, or addictions, were thought to make people vulnerable to blackmail, and thus untrustworthy.[33] If it was the Stasi's task to investigate, in face of the fakability of tokens of allegiance, that there was a consistent expression of a "positive" orientation across domains, it is also important to note that consistency does not necessarily mean seamlessness. Properly regretted lapses that were suitably atoned for did not necessarily harm socialist careers; instead, they could add a certain credibility to the efforts of self-objectification. The successful overcoming of a lapse makes explicit the labor involved in self-objectification (much as saints' initial sinfulness render them more credible or as slight blemishes ["beauty spots"] render faces "naturally" beautiful).

A further tool of person reconnaissance was the "operative person check" (*operative Personenkontrolle*) (document reprinted in Gill and Schröter 1991,

---

33. In general there was little awareness of the fact that the existence of the norms for a socialist lifestyle were the conditions for the possibility of blackmail. Karl Maier has reported to me how there was a reconsideration of the Stasi's attitude toward homosexuals starting in the mid-1980s, as it became clear that their marginalization in GDR society made them open to form alliances with the peace and budding civil rights movements.

323–34), which was used to investigate people who, due to concrete actions or contacts, came under suspicion of harboring "inimical-negative intentions." "The operative person check has to contribute to the timely discovery and effective control of inimical-negative actions, even where such actions are below the level of relevance in the sense of the penal code." The strategy the Stasi pursued here was decisively preemptive: rather than finding the enemy after he had struck, he or she was supposed to be incapacitated before he could really become dangerous. The ideal of preemption permeated Stasi's efforts to control party-critical actions since the mid-1970s. Critics of Stasi work after unification have noted that this orientation is precisely what makes it incompatible with a formal-rational state bureaucracy operating on the principles of legality and due process. This is undoubtedly true, but it also misses the logic according to which the socialist party state was constructed and the specific role the law played within it. The revolutionary self-understanding of the party state with its drive toward a monolithic intentionality and an ethics of absolute finality entails a substantive form of rationality, that is, one that was much more interested in the correct outcome than in the right process to get there. Bureaucratically speaking, secret police work as prevention was furthermore a consequence of the socialist theodicy and its tendency to personalize problems. In other words, if it was the Stasi's task to control party-critical expressions in public, their actual occurrence was an occasion to blame the Stasi for not having done its work properly (cf. chapter 9, p. 524). The attempt to discover a proclivity for party-critical thinking to preempt its appearance in public is fully comprehensible from within the party's understandings about itself and the world.

The conjunction of a firm belief in the necessity of a monolithic intentionality and the awareness of the uncanny infathomability of other minds had deeply corrosive effects on the institutions of socialism. For truth now came to be seen as something that will not reveal itself unless it is pursued through the clandestine methods of the secret police. The meta-understandings about other people's understandings move here from a surface phenomenology connected to a felicitous affirmation of the positive to a peculiar variety of what is known in reference to Ricoeur (1970, 32ff.) as "hermeneutics of suspicion." With some justification one could say, then, that the secret police become something of an arbiter of truth for a party that had lost itself in a semiotic hall of mirrors that relentless positive proselytization had created. Monolithic intentionality was leading straight into a *secret police model of truth*. Truth cannot be seen directly, it must be spied out. The result is what I called *state paranoia* elsewhere (Glaeser 2004, 244).

One could also say that the secret police was needed as a way out of another aporia of politics, which might be called the *aporia of proselytization*. In a polity in which the actualization of a particular set of understandings is seen as the central means to success, it is not surprising that policy aims to control it. Yet the more emphasis is placed on producing it, the more people will feel the necessity to merely perform it no matter whether they believe it or not, especially if noncompliance is connected to sanctions. As we shall see in parts III and IV, different parts of the GDR population answered to this aporetic situation in distinctly different ways. Fully dedicated officials were caught in a quandary. They were irresolvably caught between two kinds of loyalty: The assertion of party allegiance and the articulation of critiques where they saw the urgent need. Since the party leadership so clearly communicated what it preferred, they typically acquiesced, refraining from developing their insights into full-fledged understandings of the shortcomings of socialist institutions. The consequences were disastrous, as the downfall of socialism in the fall of 1989 demonstrated.

Most ordinary people lived in a kind of limbo, arranging their lives in various degrees of proximity and distance from the party's project. Since people could typically not avoid participating in the official rituals of the party state, they were, as Alexei Yurchak (2006) has described, inside and outside at the same time. Yet the degrees and the ways in which they were inside and outside varied both with personal circumstances and the particular historical and political context. These different arrangements, shifting in the course of time, gave rise to a gamut of socialist subjectivities. For the GDR of the 1970s, Günter Gaus (1983, 156–233) has described a degree of disengagement, a flight into "private niches," meaning a life split between official participation and weekends in the much-cherished garden plot. Gail Kligman (1998, 13ff.) has described the Romanian context in stronger terms as "duplicity," echoing a popular Romanian term. On the one hand, she follows Havel (1990b) in arguing that this was less a move of clever resistance as more a systems maintaining action. On the other hand, she points to the effects this had on the formation of social networks that could indeed undermine the party's intention to form a monolithic intentionality. This is precisely what happened to people who began to form peace, environment, or civil rights groups during the 1980s. Across all of these different groups within GDR society, the party's intense, single-minded pursuit of its goal ultimately undermined its attainment.

CONCLUSIONS

Eastern European socialisms constitute arguably the most comprehensive attempt ever undertaken by humankind to produce top-down, designed social change secured by overwhelming military power. By comparison, Russia's revolution was a lot more spontaneous and improvised because it had to work its way against massive internal opposition and civil war with considerable foreign military intervention, while the goal toward this change was undertaken was anything but clear. Since Marx and Engels had, in full accordance with the logic of their own self-unfolding model of history, not left behind any blueprints about the organization of socialist society on the fast track to communism, such forms had to be invented in situ by Russia's revolutionaries. Eastern European socialist leaders, however, could work from complete institutional blueprints developed in the Soviet Union, and what is perhaps even more important, sanctified by the Soviet Union. Not only was this process conscious, but also after the initial structural changes, such as the ownership in the means of industrial and agricultural production, failed to transform the understandings of local citizens as hoped for, a proselytizing politics of education became the central means to achieve social transformation. Thus an understanding of socialism emerged treating it more and more like a self-fulfilling prophecy. The more people believed, the more the party managed to institute monolithic intentionality, the more it would realize itself as a truly socialist order on the way to communism.

The process of proselytization was designed as a massive mirror hall of redundant validations leading to what Yurchak (2006) has called "hypernormalization."[34] The party's truth, the party's goals, the party's claims were spread into the remotest corners of society through every conceivable channel of communication the party could seize, flooding GDR citizens from many different sides at the same time with the same message. What they saw on television was supposed to match what they read in the newspapers; what they heard during leisure time in their garden colony was supposed to match what they heard in their work-collective. And more, what they heard about the world in which they lived was supposed to match their experiences. Propaganda, so the belief went, would slowly propel socialist societies into that blissful state in which language is unproblematically referential because it has created the reality to which it refers. Communism was arrived at when the ontological gap between word and object disappeared, when the substance of Marxism-Leninism had realized itself—practically through the power of its very *idea*. If, philosophically speaking, the method of socialism was in practice rationalistic, its ideal was thoroughly positivistic.

The economic overtaking of the West, later more simply mere qualitative economic growth, was advertised throughout the GDR years as *the* corroborating condition of socialism's superiority and vitality. Socialist leaders were initially so sure about having chosen the right path that they could invite everybody to corroborate the truth of what they were saying by the material

---

34. Yurchak also shows how this hypernormalization gave rise to a particular form of humor which could rely entirely on the repetition of that which was already everywhere. For an application to a contemporary American context see Boyer and Yurchak 2010.

circumstances of their lives. As I will show in the conclusions, this strategy backfired significantly in the 1980s when a fast-widening gap emerged between the experiential corroboration of the economy and its recognition in propaganda began to assume increasingly absurd proportions. Political world events, too, were systematically employed to corroborate propaganda claims. On the one hand, the evil intentions of the enemy were, for example, found to be corroborated by the aggressive anticommunist rhetoric and military actions of Margaret Thatcher (the Falkland's war) and Ronald Reagan (above all the military support for the Contras in Nicaragua), who, contrary to their stated intentions, did much to lend credibility to socialist propaganda claims. On the other hand, socialism was declared to be corroborated in a positive way by every decolonized territory joining the socialist block as a freshly minted nation.

If one does not believe in Marxist philosophy of history as a true account of the world, then GDR-socialism's increasing emphasis on a consciousness-driven model of social transformation in word and deed suggests itself as an attempt to perform a self-fulfilling prophecy.[35] So why did it fail? Did the prophecy not self-fulfill because its attempts to create a perfect mirror hall of recognitions were undercut by West German media and West German visitors who came to the GDR in massive numbers since the early 1970s? Did it fail because socialism never overcame its negative resonances, the prejudices against the Soviets originating in a century-old class struggle amplified by it? Or did it fail to produce *uptake*—to use Austin's (1962) term—because socialist everyday life led to experiences that could not corroborate its own claims? I have begun in this chapter to provide elements for answers to these questions with the help of three aporias of socialist politics, the aporia of central planning, the aporia of proselytization, and the aporia of prohibition. Each of these aporias describes something of an institutional Gordian knot for which the party—caught up in its own understandings of the world— found no sword. Before I can get to a more satisfying answer for why the search for a sword was futile, I need to expand the theoretical tool kit I have developed in the introduction.

---

35. Even though this concept has found its way into everyday language, it is actually of Robert Merton's coinage (1968, 475–92). Merton says he was inspired to develop it by the Thomas theorem, which I have cited in the preface (p. xxx).

PART II

Contingencies and Dynamics of Understanding—The Theory

In the second part of the introduction, I argued that understandings enable agency by providing orientation, direction, coordination, explanation, justification, and legitimation for actions. Since institutions exist in the regularization of flows of interconnected action-reaction sequences I have furthermore argued that studying the stabilization of understandings across all three modes offers a key to analyze the formation, maintenance, and disintegration of institutions. In the introduction I could only hint at the fact that understandings are poorly understood as something like a "base" of institutions, because this way of looking at the social world would overlook the fact that understanding as something we do, and more, something we do in regular ways, means that understandings are institutions themselves. In the following two chapters I will explore the contingent character of understandings as institutions, especially the ways in which they come about in regularized action-reaction effect flows. This will lead us to a set of simple, but I believe powerful, ways to think through the dynamics of understandings and ultimately the dynamics of political institutions.

Chapter 3, "Constituting Understandings through Validations" begins with a reductio ad absurdum of individualistic theories of belief as they are manifest, for example, in much of opinion research and social psychology, by revealing their unrealistic ontological presuppositions. Instead I argue that understandings are better analyzed through their constitution within three intersecting contexts. First, because understanding is indissolubly social it must always be analyzed from within the interactions with other persons. In particular the stability of understandings will be shown here in reference to Wittgenstein's late philosophy as the result of interactions within networks of authority. Second, because particular differentiations and integrations are always building on other understandings they must be analyzed in relationship to these. Emphasis will be placed especially on the fact that these relationships are highly differentiated, qualitatively and quantitatively. Third, since understandings characteristically respond to orientational needs in the real world, they must be seen in relation to its experience, and even more precisely through the experience of understandings in use. The constituting link is formed for each of these three contexts by one of the three forms of validation I have already briefly discussed in the introduction. Accordingly, most of the chapter will be dedicated to an in-depth phenomenological exploration of recognitions, resonances, and corroborations.

Chapter 4 begins with a synthetic image that will serve as a guiding metaphor for analysis I am about to undertake in parts III, IV, V, and in the conclusion. I will imagine the three forms of validation as constituting a field within which understandings emerge and become actualized. Looking at this field in temporal succession will yield a space that gives rise to the personality of a particular human being. Since this space is open vis-à-vis others, larger social wholes can be imagined as hyperspaces co-constituting each other. The second part of chapter 4 is dedicated to a systematic exploration of the dynamics of validation. The particular goal of this part is the generation of an analytical framework that can be used to track the development of the political understandings of a particular person in the course of time, while remaining expandable to the analysis of the formation of understandings in larger social wholes. I will show in this section how validation feeds back on the conditions of its own production, thus adding to a dialectical way of thinking through the dynamics of social change that I have begun in the introductory chapter with the dialectics between the various modes of understanding. This is a very important step because it allows for an analysis of the ways in which knowledge formation can become circular, with the possibility that there are understandings that feel well validated while they do in fact have no bearing on the world for which they are supposed to offer us orientation and guidance. The question that will be raised at the end is how knowledge making in society ought to be organized to prevent such circularities, which are, as I will argue in the conclusions of this book, a central piece in the puzzle of catastrophic failures of institutional arrangements.

3

Constituting Understandings through Validations

In everyday discourses we often treat knowledge as if it were an isolated independent object that sits somewhere on a shelf in our brains. And even though it is clear from the introductory chapter that I am arguing against such a perspective, it is worthwhile to dwell a little bit more in detail on what is implied in such a take on understandings. As examples for possibly isolated understandings, these will do as well as any: "Peter believes that the next party congress will bring a solution to the consumer goods crisis"; "Wolfgang knows that a vanguard party is the only way to safeguard the interests of the working people"; "Gertrud understands that one cannot run against candidates nominated by higher level party organs." Such formulations express understandings on the basis of the formula "a person understands (knows, believes, hypothesizes . . .) that something is (was, will, ought, might, should . . . be) the case," or for short, "q understands that p(x)" where "q" is a person and "p(x)" is a predicated grammatical (possibly complex) object (e.g., "the house is red" "justice is desirable" "crime should be persecuted"). In speech act theory, statements of this kind are called "propositional acts." They are that aspect of an utterance that makes a statement about the world. Even though such formulations are ubiquitous, the generalization of the underlying formula into a theory of *how* understanding *works* is troublesome because such a move relies on problematic ontological assumptions. And yet, this is precisely what a good deal of opinion research, attitudinal social psychology, and some analytical philosophy implicitly do.

Looked at it with greater care, the "q understands p(x)" formula presupposes the following. First, it implies that persons and understandings are *independent* of each other, such that "q" and "p(x)" could be conjoined or separated without changing either person or understanding. More precisely, the metaphorical imagery at play in most uses of this formula is one in which "q" is imagined as a container and "p(x)" as something that can be put into it. Independence means, then, on the one hand, that the container is assumed to remain self-same no matter which "p(x)" is lodged inside of it.[1] And on the other it means that "p(x)" remains unaltered no matter in which container (person) it happened to be placed. The generalization of the "q understands p(x)" formula insinuates, secondly, that all the propositions in the container could be neatly inventorized: the totality of our knowledge is seen as a *catalog*. Here, too, the assumption is that items would remain identical no matter what the rest of the list is composed of. Third, the formula makes no reference to any sort of *context*, most notably to any kind of doing in which the understanding would have a place. Moreover, it assumes q to be an autonomous individual whose understandings are not dependent on his or her relations with other human beings and their respective understandings. Fourth, and as a consequence of the three aforementioned independencies, the generalized formula has nothing to say about the ways in which understandings come about, are maintained, and disintegrate. It has no sense that understandings can become institutionalized. Finally, simply because it lacks a theory of generativity, the formula assumes that "understanding," "believing," and "hypothesizing" are transparent kinds of activities with universal, that is, transhistorical and transcultural, validity. These points together can be summarized by saying that a model of understanding that builds on the generalization of propositional formulas is completely static; it has no sense of the dynamics of understanding, its role in lived life, in the generation, maintenance, and transformation of social arrangements.

Unpacking the imagery involved in uses of the "person understands something" formula thus brings to the fore the reifying and isolationist ontological foundations on which it rests. They are implausible for the following reasons: (1) Understandings are constitutive of who we are as persons; they are inextricably intertwined with our selves and their meanings, that is, our identities as well our capacity to act, that is, our agency. (2) "P(x)," the predicated grammatical object of our understanding, is never quite a state

---

1. For a related analysis of the imagery underlying commonsense understandings of language, see Reddy 1993 and Lakoff 1993.

of the world but just a symbolization of a state of the world, and as such it is contingent on social practices of symbolization in context. While this has long been uncontroversial for value judgments, social formation needs to be acknowledged for all kinds of understandings, including facts. They too are made in a particular way by particular people in particular contexts for particular purposes. In disregard of these multiple contingencies, it would be incomprehensible how understandings came to be problematic in the first place. Taken together, these two reasons, for the ontological implausibility of a propositional theory of understanding, imply that persons exist to a considerable extent *in* their understandings, while understandings come into being only through concrete persons in concrete situations. (3) Understandings are not isolates, but they are deeply intertwined with the practices within which they are deployed and through which they are generated and maintained. Within these practices they are used in a multiplicity of ways: certainly epistemically, but also aesthetically, morally, socially, to feel good, look good, and to sound pleasing. They are also always related to other understandings, some of which we might be able to state under certain circumstances explicitly, others we could not even think of because they reflect such basic assumptions about the world that they have, as it were, long receded from view into a general background of presuppositions. (4) Understanding is nothing we do alone but something we do in complicated relationships with other people in direct contact and in socially and technologically mediated ways. The particular ways in which these relationships with other human beings are lived and organized has profound consequences for how we come to understand the world the way we do. In other words, understandings are institutions, and we need to learn how they come about in action-reaction effect flows. (5) Our processes of understanding are always informed by higher-level understandings about how they ought to work, how they must be procured, under which conditions and how they can be considered reliable, and so forth. In other words, historically and culturally distinct meta-understandings structure the ways in which we maintain, certify, and change understanding. (6) I pointed out in the introduction that the articulation of understandings through their role in guiding actions as reactions to other actions is formative of institutions. Thinking of understandings only in terms of propositions would therefore fall far short of what they actually do in social life.[2]

---

2. Building on Austin's speech act theory (1962) (and mobilizing the hermeneutic tradition of social thought), this generative institution-forming characteristic of understandings (usually with a limitation to discursive understandings) is often also referred to as performativity (e.g., MacKenzie 2006). Unfortunately, this use of language can lead to confusions with another important sense of the term *performance*, i.e., artfully structured action as addressed to other human beings (e.g., Herzfeld 1985; Baumann 1975; Goffman 1959). Of course, both meanings of

Simplifying this picture into a heuristic image, one could say that what we need is a way to comprehend understanding in context. Schematically, three of these contexts suggest themselves: the embeddedness of understandings in interactions with other people; the connection between any particular understanding and other understandings that the person entertaining them inhabits; and, finally, the relationship between understandings and the world at large. Since understanding is always the understanding of a concrete person in a concrete situation, we also have to trace how these three environments shape the person who is doing the understanding. I do not want to suggest that these contexts are in any real sense separable from one another. Instead, they could be thought of as the dimensions of a space in which they can intersect. One could speak in this sense of a social, a doxic, and a referential dimension spanning up a space within which understandings are constituted with varying degrees of actuality. The question arising now is *how* these contexts actually do their constituting work on particular understandings. And the answer is: they do it through the three forms of validation for which I have provided only a rough sketch in the introduction. The following three sections offer important pieces for a phenomenology of each form of validation. Since the focus of the discussion is the processual link between understandings and the social, doxic, and referential contexts, each section is prefaced by a brief discussion of pertinent major issues that have been raised in the literature about this link. Thus the social dimension is introduced by a quick review of the seminal contributions of Mead and Wittgenstein to our comprehension of human sociality. The section on the doxic dimension begins with a discussion of *meaning holism*. And the referential dimension opens with a critique of poststructuralist writers' overemphasis on the linguistic that led them to disregard the experience of the world's resistance to our interpretations.

THE SOCIAL DIMENSION: RECOGNITION

Arguably the twentieth century's two most important contributions to our comprehension how human beings are irreducibly social are George Herbert Mead's (1934) theory of self-formation, and Ludwig Wittgenstein's (1984b) argument about the impossibility of entertaining a language privately. Even though neither was primarily concerned with the concept of understanding, the bearing of their work on a sociology of understanding

---

performativity are closely related to each other, even if they are not identical. Performance as artful communication is often an invitation to produce "uptake" in Austin's sense, that is, to react to it in a particular way and thus to close one element of an action-reaction flow forming institutions. In other words: performance is often undertaken in the interest of performativity.

is readily appreciated. Mead teaches us how we can think of selves as woven from understandings emerging and tested in conversation with others, and Wittgenstein is indispensable to see why understandings need to be maintained in interaction on an ongoing basis within a connected social whole. From both authors we can learn how our inner lives are laminated on our interactions with other human beings.

Selves and Identities in Context

Orienting us, understandings form the interface between human beings and the world, as I have argued above. George Herbert Mead's *Mind, Self, and Society* (1934) provides us with a process model of how we come into understanding as an integral part of self-formation. Self is, for Mead (135–37), the capacity for reflexive thought, which requires us to be simultaneously the reflecting subject ("q") and the object reflected upon ("p[q]" in the notation used above). For him, reflection is essentially internal conversation in which we are speaker and addressee at the same time. In other words, the self can say sentences like "As a good communist I should overcome my petit bourgeois sensibilities," or "How come I love this man? He's a communist!" This faculty to reason emerges, according to Mead, in conversation with other human beings. Our status as self has its origin in an identification with our interlocutors who address us, thus creating in us the capacity to become the addressee of our own address.[3] A self is born precisely at the moment when we can begin to anticipate successfully (which necessarily means symbolically represent to ourselves) the other's reactions to our conversational moves. At this moment, anticipation and reaction begin to correspond or agree with each other for all practical purposes (if not wholly in substance, then at least in form). More precisely: the fact that the other acts as anticipated *recognizes* our anticipation; it certifies our understanding of the flow of communication. As internalization of external communication this means that our relationship to ourselves is mediated symbolically through culturally available gestures, images, and discourse. Through symbolic mediation we also attain a temporality comprising a future in symbolic anticipation, a present in action and a past in making ourselves an object, for example, by representing to ourselves what we have just done. This horizon of temporal unfolding is the basis of the peculiarly narrative character of the self (e.g., MacIntyre 1984; Nehamas 1985; Ricoeur 1984; Linde 1993; Somers 1994).

By describing self-formation in communicative attunement and its in-

---

3. "Object" here means grammatical object, or simply the recipient of communication. Within the Meadian use an object can be addressed both in an objectifying way (Lukács 1968) (as I-it or even me-it) and a more dialogic fashion as I-you (Bakhtin 1984; Buber 1995).

ternalization at a more encompassing level as "role-taking," Mead acknowledges that this process is suffused with particular understandings, some semantically explicit, others presupposed in the pragmatics of the context of interaction. There is at the very least a differentiation between speaker and listener, both understood as subjectivities capable of entering communication. Typically there are also references to the world, and the interaction builds on the presupposition that particular kinds of speech acts ("making contact," "greeting," "request," "jokes," etc.) will be properly identified by the other.[4] Such understandings informing the action-reaction effect flow of communication are rich in identifications—qualitatively differentiated links between speaker, listener, and world.[5] Recognition of these communicated identifications actualizes them, and thus self and substantive understandings of the world come to be inextricably intertwined. In other words, the self acquires meaning, an identity that positions self in the world. Being recognized as a "comrade" in conversation, where "comrade" is imbued with particular behavioral expectations of exercising a firm class standpoint and of practicing self-objectification, persons may begin to treat themselves as "comrades" by expecting of themselves what their interlocutors have expected of them all along. Eventually, they are comrades. A particular self-understanding thus comes to be actualized, informing actions, thus forming institutions.

This example highlights yet another aspect of Mead's model, which however he leaves unexplored. The communicative process is imbued with understandings about the particular *quality* of the interactional relationship— for example, as an egalitarian, hierarchical, cozy, cold, desiring, rejecting, permissive, punitive one. Following the logic of internalization this quality of the external relationship becomes the quality of the gaze in which a person looks upon him- or herself. In this way, understandings of particular forms of sociality translate into qualitatively specific forms of reflexivity. These are, then, not neutral universal modes of self-relationships, pure thought as it were, but historically contingent ways of relating to oneself and thus of thought, which accordingly comes in many shades and gradations. This has

---

4. Mead makes no effort to specify the gradual emergence of the self from birth to its recognizably selflike appearance in toddlers. Tracing this path poses exceeding difficulties, as one has to be extremely careful about what kinds of mental and communicative abilities are presupposed when, to show then how they are expanded into new terrain. However, Mead very self-consciously bases his model on simple forms of gestural exchanges. But these too have content, however simple. For a more updated developmental psychological take on self-development that has been inspired by Mead (and psychoanalysis) see Stern 1985.

5. I am drawing on the theory of identify formation processes I developed in *Divided in Unity*. This theory centers on the notion of acts of identification that, where recognized consistently, can become relatively stable identities.

considerable consequences for the ways in which we need to think about reason and the possibility of critique. If particular forms of deliberation are not practiced in interaction with others, they fail to form as a full-blown capacity of internal reasoning (cf. Volosinov 1973; Vygotsky 1978). More, the development of a particular form of reasoning in one content area does not automatically transfer to other domains of understanding (Luria 1976). This insight will be useful in exploring the question of why Stasi officers had difficulties raising particular kinds of questions why they stalled along with the whole party leadership in forming a more thorough-going critique of actually existing socialist institutions. It will also help us comprehend why dissidence did not proceed from a full-blown critique of socialism, instead developing it gradually with expanding conversational possibilities.

Mead ponders the possibility of a radical fragmentation of the self into as many selves as there are conversation partners (e.g., 142). This is an important point deserving further elaboration. I want to take it into two different, if related directions. First, seeing self in a perspective of ongoing action-reaction effect flows suggests that it is much better understood as a name, as a potentially objectifying shorthand for the process of continuing self-formation that may look like a structure only to the degree that it is continuously reproduced in a self-similar fashion as a set of qualitative identifications (i.e., a self-understanding) and a mode of thought (i.e., a self-relationship). Thus I propose to see *selves* as *institutions* in the sense that I have described them in the introductory chapter. As such, they may change in the course of action-reaction effect flows, especially as old conversation partners drop out, new ones come in and the topics of conversations and their references to the world change. Seen in this way, the self is a multiplex institution differentiated by a multiplicity of qualitatively distinct action-reaction effect sequences. Ongoing varieties of sociality map onto varieties of thought styles; the diversity of identifications deployed and recognized in diverse strands of communication congeal into diverse identities. The degree to which these modes of thought and identifications cohere is dependent on the coherence of the self-generating and maintaining conversations in which a particular person is involved.[6] Again this has consequence for the possibilities to formulate particular kinds of critiques. In any given situation, a person may switch selves, that is, use different modes of reflexivity. Their likelihood of use may also be distributed over the various contexts in which a person maneuvers. What I will take from Mead, then, is the notion of selves as always already existing in substantive understandings of the world,

---

6. A parallel emphasis on plurality in seeming unity is provided by Bakhtin's analysis of speech (e.g., 1986, 60–102; 1981, 259–422).

as operating in modes qualitatively shaped by the kinds of conversations in which they take form, as plural and thus possibly ambiguous or even contradictory, and finally as an ongoing process more or less solidly institutionalized at any given point in time.

The epistemic practices and ideologies of real socialism were not only compatible with this Meadian version of the constitution of persons by their understandings, but also the entire project of an ideology-driven social transformation was in an important sense based on it. This is not much of a surprise given the fact that Marx himself argued throughout his work that the particular form people take (e.g., as bourgeois or proletarian) is historically contingent. In actually existing socialism both the good party soldier and the class enemy were defined by how they understood the world and how they acted in it. The "new man" that socialism hoped to engender was thought to become new through the absorption of socialist understandings and socialist work practices and a particular socialist way of reflexivity that hinged upon the partisan self-objectification of the party member in light of the party's historical task as defined by its current leadership. The internalization of socialism's substance was hoped to bring about a transubstantiation of human beings. The unity and monolithicity I have described as an ideal of socialist vanguard parties in the last chapter could only be achieved by aspiring to a total party-controlled environment. In other words, the new man as a planned, thoroughly reconfigured institution was—if we take Mead seriously—only thinkable in a totalitarian society. And the more this measure would have succeeded the more self would have become unitary, with all the adverse consequences this has, for example, for creativity (see chapter 4, p. 239 ff.). Conversely, incomplete totalization could be expected to lead to ambiguities and contradictions and then to the feared "ideological uncertainties." This is precisely what the leading agents of the party state abhorred and consequently tried to prevent for the sake of socialism's self-realization.

Maintaining Understandings as Institutions

With Mead, one can argue that understandings are social in as far as they are wrapped up with the genesis and reproduction of the self in social interaction. Wittgenstein (1984b) has provided a different rationale for the irreducibly social nature of human beings with his argument that it is impossible to sustain a language privately (i.e., in isolation from society). Wittgenstein's argument inspires my own theory in much the same way as Mead's does by radically challenging the distinction between a private, mental interiority and a public, social exteriority. Wittgenstein's argument, the core of his later philosophy, takes its departure from the question of what it means to follow a rule.[7] Wittgenstein moves toward an answer to this question by wondering *how* we could possibly *know* that someone is following it. Seen in this light, the central problem becomes finding a criterion that can be used to tell rule-following from random behavior. However, the very notion of an adjudication of rule-following in reference to criteria is problematic, as Wittgenstein points out. Behavior, that is, a necessarily finite trajectory of action, can never be a sufficient reason to ascertain conclusively that somebody has followed a particular rule, let's call it R.[8] One can always argue that the person in question has followed another rule, let's call it R', which is congruous with the exhibited behavioral trajectory but deviates from R elsewhere.[9] In other words, any person who seems to act in perfect accordance with R can always suddenly deviate from R and argue that he followed R' all along, pointing to the trail of behavior as evidence. The connection to my own argument is that rule-following is about stability or replication of action across time. In the introduction I argued that where this is met with constancy in reaction institutions emerge.

Another way to put Wittgenstein's point is to say that understanding left to its own devices is adrift in a sea of endless deferments. The individual rule follower is like a smoker trying to quit: "one more cigarette" is nothing but one more behavioral instance after which quitting is just as plausible as it was before. Wittgenstein goes through a number of potential (individualistic)

---

7. The literature on Wittgenstein's notion of rule-following is enormous. There have been fierce controversies about what he meant exactly with his argument conveyed in collections of aphorisms. Much of the more recent philosophical debate as it has become important in the social sciences has centered on Kripke's (1982) interpretation and its critique, for example, by Baker and Hacker (1984). In the social sciences arguably the most prominent debate is that between David Bloor and Michael Lynch. Bloor's interpretation of Wittgenstein (1983) is central to his "strong program" for the sociology of knowledge (1991). In a nutshell, Bloor's point is that rules on their own cannot cause action. What we need is a consideration of external social factors such as interests. Lynch's ethnomethodological critique (1992) zeros in on Bloor's understanding of rules critiquing his view that practice is something external to rules, while also refuting his causalist program. Bloor has presented a revised version of his interpretation (2002 [1997]). My own account of Wittgenstein has learned from both opponents while steering an independent perhaps even idiosyncratic path.

8. Logically this problem is related to the problem of induction. See, for example, Popper 1971.

9. The following simple visualization might help to appreciate this point. Imagine a two-dimensional space in which one dimension signifies time, the other some measure of behavior. Any finite number of points in this diagram (i.e., particular instances of behavior) can be connected through an infinite number of functions (i.e., general rules), which all include the points. On the basis of the fixed set of points alone, there is no criterion by which one could rationally decide that they embody the one function rather than the other.

solutions to the problem (e.g., to think of rule-following as a disposition, or the difference that objectification in written form would make) but in the end finds that they all end in an aporia. They simply reproduce the same problem at another level.[10] Rule-following must therefore be anchored in something other than the movement of justificatory reason alone. And that other for Wittgenstein is a *practice* (1984b, no. 202):

> Therefore, following a rule is a practice. And to *believe* that one follows a rule is not following a rule. And therefore one cannot follow a rule "privately," because in this case believing one is following a rule would be the same as following a rule. (Emphasis L. W.]

Practices are for Wittgenstein firmly anchored in a relevant community that simply agrees that a rule is indeed followed (no. 241).

> So you are saying, that the agreement between human beings decides what is right and what is wrong?—Right and wrong is what people say; human beings agree in *language*. This is not an agreement of opinions, but of life form.

It is not rule-following that produces agreement, but ultimately it is agreement—indeed mutual recognition, shared understandings, a common culture—that certifies rule-following.[11] Agreement is the more basic fact.

This raises the question of what Wittgenstein means with "practices" and associated terms such as "training" (*Abrichten*), "custom," "tradition," or indeed "institution," which he uses throughout his later work in similar ways. Unfortunately, he does not define any of these concepts directly. To draw from this the conclusion that they are not important is a mistake (Bloor 2002). For he introduces related concepts of his own that are of central significance for his late philosophy. His notion of "language-game" (1984b, no. 7) emphasizes how speaking and doing are closely intertwined with each other, forming simply two aspects of one reality. Hence he argues that the meaning of speech has to be understood in use (e.g., no. 10). His concept of a "life form" has to be understood as an assembly of language games (no. 23), part intentionally fabricated, but for the most part the concatena-

---

10. The philosophical argument aside, one may wonder about empirical counterexamples. So what about the psychotic who steadfastly continues to believe in being a reincarnation of Einstein or Lenin? What about the genial inventor and the *poète maudite* hanging on to their ideas against the tides? Cursory evidence would suggest that all of these could be accounted for in Wittgensteinian terms.

11. The similarity with Durkheim's (1997, 40) formulation—that "We should not say that an act offends the common consciousness because it is criminal, but that it is criminal because it offends that consciousness"—is of course not an accident; institutions exist in agreement or better, in regularized action-reaction effect flows.

tion of unintended consequences (no. 18). In short, empirical sociality is central to his late philosophy.

What precisely have we gained from these considerations for our understanding of how rules are maintained, how understandings come to be stabilized? Three insights in particular strike me as important. The first is an ontological clarification. Rules would be misunderstood as autonomous devices that once implanted in our brain continue to function as they are supposed to. Instead, rules are institutions necessarily maintained in the process of ongoing action-reaction effect flows; other people need to certify rule-following. Says Wittgenstein (1984a VI:32): "A game, a language, a rule is an institution." I have already made use of this when I described what it means to develop processes of understanding into portable forms of understanding in the introduction. Stable mental life is social. What follows from this is that understandings not propped up by social input are subject to entropy. They will disintegrate, that is, they will be forgotten. So here is also at least one-half of an argument of why memory as the maintenance of particular understandings is social. The second important conclusion is that the stability of one process (such as following a rule) can only be understood in reference to the stability of another, ultimately even other *kinds* of process. Most notably, Wittgenstein's recurring emphasis on the very corporeality of practice (which is compatible with what Foucault [1995, 1978] has to say about disciplines) amounts to an argument that for purposes of regularization discursive understandings have to be laminated onto kinesthetic ones.[12] The third implication is that there is stability in number. This is what grounding rule-following in practice really means. We gain stability in understandings by involving ourselves in networks of relationships in which we check each other. And thus regularity is conceivable only as an intersubjective reality, an institution, which none of us controls individually even though all of us contribute to

---

12. Wittgenstein does not provide any reasons why this is so. And yet it is easy to make at least intuitive sense of it. Corporeal skills such as swimming and or bicycling are much less subject to forgetting than, let's say, our skills in calculus. In other words, the latter kinds of skill need much more "maintenance work," renewal in doing, than the former. This may very well have something to do with the organization of our nervous system. It clearly fulfills certain functions (e.g., heartbeat, certain chemical properties of the blood and the organs) without fail, and as far as we know today without social input. We also know that some of the "bodily rules" hang on other physical regularities produced outside of the body, such as night and day rhythms. The age-old literature on mnemonics (e.g., Yates 1966), as well as the social scientific investigation of memory practices (e.g., Halbwachs 1992 [1925]; Connerton 1989; Olick and Robbins 1998; Olick forthcoming), have also explored how in particular kinesthetic understandings can help to stabilize discursive ones. The most important reason, however, is a peculiarity of corroboration with respect to kinesthetic understandings that I will explore below. Kinesthetic understandings are much more easily corroborated than discursive ones.

its maintenance. The social as something distributed across people, localities, and times introduces interactionally generated force toward a common
center of epistemic gravity (Kahneman and Tversky 1982).

Wittgenstein's argument remains essentially an impossibility theorem,
showing that individuals cannot possibly do what they appear to be doing when left to their own devices. There is no autonomous reason lodged
somewhere in the depths of our brains. What is missing is the positive side
of the story, an account of *how* precisely the social can stop the regress of
rule-following. Wittgenstein merely asserts that it does. This is where the sociology of understanding with its emphasis on processes of validation comes
in. The form of validation that ties understandings to social relationships is
recognition.

Recognition

The gist of how recognition as a validating force comes about can be nicely
illustrated by quotations taken from two men who were concerned—each
in his own way—with the codification and canonization of knowledge precisely at a time when truth claims came to be interrogated more widely, thus
triggering a renewed search for a reliable basis of knowledge. The first stems
from the late 1790s sketches to a general encyclopedia by Prussian romantic
poet Friedrich von Hardenberg, who is perhaps better known under his pen
name Novalis (1993 [1798], 29): "It is certain, that my opinion gains much,
as soon as I know, that somebody else is convinced by it."[13] In the same
vein, albeit with an interest not in building but in dismantling certainty,
Samuel Johnson declared two decades earlier: "Every man who attacks my
belief, diminishes in some degree my confidence in it." (Boswell 1945 [1791],
III:3, April 1775). Novalis's and Johnson's central point is that the agreement
or disagreement between two people about a particular understanding has
epistemic consequences in validating or invalidating it. I call the effect on
validity resulting from the comparison of understandings between two
people *recognition*; where ambiguous I will qualify it as positive or negative
depending on whether it is enhancing or depreciating credibility.[14]

---

13. I have rendered it here in my own translation. In the English-speaking world it has circulated in a multiply flawed—if aesthetically more pleasing—translation quoted by Thomas
Carlyle: "My conviction gains infinitely the moment another soul will believe in it." In this form
it became the epigraph to Joseph Conrad's novel *Lord Jim*. It is a brilliantly chosen epigraph,
because the whole novel can be read as an exploration of this one line.

14. It is important to distinguish negative recognition from misrecognition. In negative recognition the ordering of the understandings is comprehended by the other, albeit rejected
as untrue, inappropriate, misleading, etc. In misrecognition, it is the ordering process that is
not comprehended by the other. If you like, negative recognition is an agonal aspect of com-

Novalis and Johnson limit themselves to discursive understandings. It is important to note, however, that emotive or kinesthetic understandings can also be recognized. A laughing response to a joke that meets other laughter may be validated through it. Conversely, persons who smile happily in a circle of sour faces will sense very quickly that their emotive expression meets with disapproval and may stop in consequence. Likewise, dancers, musicians, or soccer players will find that their movements are, in training and performance, subject to signs of an approving or disapproving nature.[15]

From the discussion of Novalis's and Johnson's aphorisms it is probably clear that recognition takes the form of an action-reaction effect flow. As long as our understandings appear tenuous to us we are probably seeking to find further validation for them. At some times this may take the form of an active search. We directly and indirectly ask people whom we suspect to have better knowledge than we do. At other times, we merely stumble upon other people's evaluation of understandings that we cannot help but notice. No matter whether a question is followed up by an answer, or whether another's pronouncement of the validity of a particular understanding is followed up by an attentive mulling over it, it takes two actors to produce the validating effect.

Networks of authority

Not everybody's communication of agreement or disagreement about every kind of understanding has a recognizing effect. Instead, we usually have a well-developed sense about who is an authority on something and who is

---

munication, a talking against each other; misrecognition is miscommunication, a talking past each other.

15. Axel Honneth (1992) triggered, with his book *The Struggle for Recognition*, a debate in political theory explaining the notion of recognition as part of a politics of identity. My discussion makes probably clear, that I mean something related and yet different with "recognition" than the two authors who have shaped the debate on the "politics of recognition" probably more than anybody else, Charles Taylor (1994) and Axel Honneth (1992). I do not want to discuss either of their contributions or the debate at any length here because their project is a very different one. Just so much needs to be said in order to avoid confusion. When they are concerned with recognition they are primarily concerned with the affirmation of an identity that is already formed (see Markell 2003 for a pertinent critique along these lines). As such the term has acquired much currency in the debates about the meaning of multiculturalism. By contrast, when I talk about recognition I am interested in the communicative processes that constitute understandings as institutions. Since these understandings can also pertain to self in the world, while understandings more generally form our interface with the world, one could also say that I am by comparison interested in the question of how identities come about in the first place (see also Glaeser 2000).

not. This was clear to Novalis (1993) as well; he continues his musings about the effects of agreement: "An authority makes an opinion mystically appealing" (29). What he means by "mystically appealing" is probably a combination of two factors. We are, in crucial ways, dependent on the opinion of others, who thus become authorities with the power to recognize our understandings. The "mystical appeal" of authority lies simply in the capacity of organized others to stop Wittgenstein's infinite regress of rule following, which is to say that authority puts the agony of doubt in suspension. And as I have argued in the introduction, doubt may be agonizing because it puts limits on our capacity to act. Here lies the clue to why, in the absence of authority, we may even listen to random others in spite of the fact that their understanding seems no more "informed," "better," or "judicious" than ours. The other reason why authority may be "mystically appealing" is because sometimes we simply do not know why the other appears to us as an authority. A self-reassured performance may be as much its source as good looks, credentials, or demonstrated expertise.

There is often more to epistemic authority, however. Our experiences of the world are often unordered, our understandings of it inchoate. In such a situation the understandings voiced by others may help to arrange them into well-ordered appearances that ease orientation considerably. Such work of *articulation* is an important source of epistemic authority, which may seem mystical, indeed, especially where it is based, as in the case of the soothsayers, on either profound empathic qualities or on hidden knowledge about the other and the world in which he or she desires to succeed. This is the authority of the guru. However, there need not be anything mystical about authority. The modern notion of expertise typically confers epistemic authority as a result of hard labor in organizations in which it is trained and subsequently certified. Yet, expertise may also derive from successful practice; many of us bring cars to repair shops not because they are certified, but because those around us swear that they have done a good job in the past. Intimacy, too, can bestow particular kinds of epistemic authority. We turn to partners, friends, or close kin when it comes to matters of understanding ourselves, other human beings, and/or issues of right and wrong. Precisely for reasons of the high degree of differentiation of epistemic authority (e.g., Abbott 1988; Collins and Evans 2007), it makes much more sense to speak about issue- and context-specific *networks of authority* as the social backbone of validation rather than of epistemic or "interpretive communities" (e.g., Fish 1980 in extension of Wittgenstein 1984b).

Taking somebody else for an authority on particular understandings in particular contexts is itself an understanding. Ideas and practices that confer authority on somebody are therefore among the most important meta-understandings organizing processes of recognition. Epistemic authority is eminently political because it can be a significant wellspring of power, as Hobbes already noted with keen eyes (1994, chap. 10). Accepting others' authority to validate our understandings means to give them the power to play a role in our making and remaking as agents. All notions of human difference (including those of race, class, gender, nation, etc.) matter in this regard because they typically distribute authority. Evidently, then, while effective recognition presupposes authority, authority itself has to be recognized. It is one of Hegel's (1986) lasting achievements to have seen this dynamic relationality of authority as at once recognizing and in need of recognition. With a philosophical analysis of the relationship between master and servant, he tries to illuminate how asymmetrical authority relationships are fatally mired in self-contradictions. According to him, the master's self-understanding as master needs to be agreed to or recognized by the servant. Yet, that agreement is worth nothing if not given by someone considered an authority. And Hegel takes authority to be constituted by the freedom to give or withhold this agreement. However, servants are not usually in a position to converse freely with their master and certainly need to guard their opinions if they deviate from those of their masters. Servitude, therefore, makes a truly dialectical co-constitution of master as master and slave as slave impossible because of a structural contradiction between the master's need for recognition, which for want of the servant's authority cannot be produced.

From this, Hegel and his followers have derived an impetus for social transformation in the direction of a liberal polity in which all are formally equal (Honneth 1992). Given the model of validation I am presenting here, this is, sociologically speaking, anything but inevitable. All that is needed to stabilize the master's belief in his superiority is the recognition of this understanding by *some* others who are deemed authorities in this limited respect. That role can be played perfectly well by a combination of two different kinds of recognition: one by peers as equal and the other by subordinates as superior. Every leader, every expert has a keen sense of the value of these dual sources of recognition—as expert certified by coexperts and as authority recognized by the less informed seeking advice. If this is so, then the liberalism seen as the inevitable outcome of the master-servant dialectic is already presupposed in it. Only if equality is already assumed in the master's need for recognition by the slave does a contradiction occur. And only then does the dynamic proceed as imagined by Hegel and his followers. The point to learn from the misfiring of this argument is simply that just like in the case of action-reaction effect flows more generally, recognitions, including those constituting authority, need not be mutual or symmetric. They can be distributed in qualitatively differentiated ways over complex networks.

There is another interesting side to the relationship between recognition and authority. Given particular meta-understandings and ways in which networks of authority are maintained as institutions, they can begin to feed on one another in such a way that knowledge comes to be certified in a circular way. If the ascription of authority is constituted by agreement in particular understandings, then disagreement about them puts authority at risk. Had Erich Honecker ever openly expressed doubt that history's path to communism is inevitable, the rest of the SED leadership would probably have found him unfit to rule. Whole networks of authority can be built on the assent of its members to a core set of understandings. At the same time, this assent endows them with authority, the right to speak up, and the right to the attention of others. Most ideology-based organizations, churches, or political parties operate this way, as do partisan media. The effect of this short-circuiting of authority and recognition can be the removal of particular understandings from critical scrutiny, while they are at the same time continuously certified as well-validated knowledge. Understandings thus maintained are dogmas. They are a common feature of social life. Culture has in this sense a dogmatic core. Enlightenment's unease notwithstanding, dogmas need not be problematic if they are well suited to guide the actions they are de facto orienting and directing. They are also less problematic if the various authorities involved in the formation of dogmas maintain a degree of independence, because they can draw sources of validation distinct from the assertion of the dogma. This was Stalin's problem with men like Trotsky or Bukharin, men who had acquired charismatic authority before and during the revolution, and who could therefore credibly entertain a critique of the currently favored party line. Finally, dogmas are easier to question when meta-understandings emerge that require that they need to be certified in more ways than through the mere recognition by members of the network.

At this point it is useful to consider the emotional dimension of agreement, which was so important to both Johnson and Novalis. Agreement with our cherished understandings makes us feel socially integrated, in touch with other people. It signals to us that we are not alone, and thus it tends to be associated with the positive range of feelings. If we consider our understandings as accomplishments, we may also feel pride; if they are just dear to us, we may simply feel at ease through others' recognition. If agreement seems paramount we may even feel elated. Universally cheered we may feel as if we were walking on water. The underlying reason for this is the link between understandings and agency, which I have dwelled upon in the introduction. No wonder then, that agreement as trigger of positive emotions is such a strong tonic for making and maintaining affirming social relations. Conversely, disagreement with a valued interlocutor produces feelings of isolation. In the absence of strong countervailing meta-understandings that shelter the quality of social relations (such as various kinds of intimacy), disagreements threaten relationships. Depending on how we relate ourselves to the understandings negatively recognized, we may feel ashamed, sad, or angry. Beyond all the rational reasons we may give for the justification of authority on the basis of agreement, there is, then, a powerful emotive process at work that can, in the absence of countervailing meta-understandings, lead to the authorization of those who make us feel good and the deauthorization of those who make us feel bad. Hence the folk and literary topoi of the seductive "pseudofriend" whose ingratiating counsel propels us into tragic failure by recognizing clay-footed understandings and the "misrecognized real friend," the value of whose uncomfortable but ultimately sound counsel we come to value far too late.[16]

Communicating recognition: Intentions versus effects

In the last chapter I presented GDR socialism as carrying an agenda of social transformation that has increasingly focused on the *intentional* transformation of people's political understandings through propaganda. The main instrument to accomplish this goal was the spoken and written word, that is, the dissemination of particular sets of discursive understandings and their subsequent repeated recognition through multiply redundant propaganda channels. However, as speech act theory (Austin 1962; Searle 1969) has reminded us, a communicative intention is neither identical with its performance nor with its reception and effect. There are many reasons why intention, act, and reception do not necessarily match up, even where the interlocutor is a competent speaker and accepted as an authority by the receiver. I will outline the most important ones in what follows because they shine a critical light on the party's project of consciousness-driven social transformation.

Agreement is communicated in fine shades and gradations in the interplay of several simultaneous levels of semiosis. Beyond literal word meaning, the minutest variations in speech patterns (word choice, grammatical

---

16. In a pioneering work Randall Collins (2004) describes a process similar to the emotional effects of agreement just outlined in terms of the generation of "emotional energy," which he links to agency. He argues that people produce emotional energy in *interaction rituals* (a term borrowed from Goffman) by rhythmically attuning to each other in bodily co-presence (47–48). This process dynamic too, claims Collins, is productive of social relationships. For that a clearer understanding of what emotional energy is—that is how it operates—would be useful. The sociology of understanding provides an alternative account, offering more clarity about how the phenomena Collins's describes come about. Rhythmic attunement is tantamount to the mutual recognition of emotive and kinesthetic understandings in performance. It will become clear in what follows (most notably through the dialectics of recognition discussed in chapter 4) how this agreement is mutually authorizing and thus productive of social relationships. At the same time it enhances agency in specific domains by actualizing understandings.

construction, stress, rhythm, sentence melody), as well as in gestures, body postures, and facial expressions, can appease doubt or raise it, affirm understandings or undermine them. In the flow of everyday interaction it is impossible to attend to and calculate in advance all the validating consequences our performances may entail. Therefore, our intentions to recognize specific understandings, even where they are absolutely transparent to us, and our performances, do not neatly map onto each other. In fact, it is probably fair to say that we inadvertently exude recognitions at least as much as we consciously pronounce them. In performative slips, such as unruly verbal concoctions, dry laughter, or sudden bodily retreats or advances, we recognize others' understandings unconsciously. Through guttural grunts, the slightest nods, and even more so by unfazed, questionless silences we affirm background assumptions about the world that have long escaped our conscious attention.[17] As the phenomenologists (e.g., Schütz and Luckmann 1984) have argued and the ethnomethodologists (e.g., Garfinkel 1967) have amply demonstrated, the recognizing character of such performances becomes perceptible to us often only in breeches against which we may act—with the Samuel Johnson in us—quite violently. In consequence, many understandings become positively or negatively recognized in performance without being thematically highlighted. Every appropriate response to an address is a recognition of the fact that we know how to address and be addressed; every laughter answering the intentional efforts to produce it recognizes a person's ability to crack jokes along with her knowledge about what is supposedly funny.

Given the multiplicity of communicative channels, attempting to control recognition across all levels of semiosis is hard labor. If at all, it can only be produced with a combination of extremely tight discipline and minute preparation. Yet we undertake this labor in particular situations, because we know that recognizing communication is productive of relationships, understandings, and ultimately of institutions. This is especially the case where our explicit situational understandings make this clear—for example, in those domains of interaction that Austin (1962) originally used as paradigm cases for speech acts, such as naming or contracting practices. Because of the awareness about consequences such situations are also fraught with particular anxieties directed at the efficacy of the performance. Almost inevitably, attempts at perfect control of potential recognition lead to rather rigid actual communications. The language of international diplomacy and tele-

17. In highly controlled communicative situations the breakthrough of deep motivations and background assumptions into controlled performance is therefore seen as a particularly interesting boon of informational value promising insight into something "real" behind the facade of make believe. In public discourses they are as "gaffes" at once celebrated and played down.

vised debates between political candidates are cases in point. Politicians in contemporary parliamentarian democracies need the skill to talk a lot without committing to much while asserting their own competence through the style of their communication. Since socialism very self-consciously placed increasing stock in the institution-generating efficacy of propaganda, and since there was hardly any official communication that was not at the same time seen as propagandistic occasion, the control over language became an obsession. A highly managed and restricted and nevertheless ubiquitous "politolect" emerged as a result.

While the actual performance of an understanding by an authority is the necessary condition for recognition to materialize, the sufficient condition is the judgment of that authority's performance as recognizing by the person whose understanding is subject to validation. Not only is this judgment as an understanding in turn subject to stabilizing recognition, but it is built on meta-understandings that require continuous validation. Although wishes clearly tinge what we hear and how we hear, wishing to interpret a statement in a certain way cannot be the same as interpreting it; wanting to hear a recognition cannot be the same thing as hearing one (to paraphrase Wittgenstein). For if this were so, we would have lost our capacity to communicate; we would have started to live in our heads. Recognition is thus always dependent on further recognition. So we have to keep asking for it—and not only because it may always be incomplete, but also because, much more prosaically, it is subject to entropy. Even though it is interpreted, it is never merely subjective. To produce the effect, it takes at least two—repeatedly. No matter whether understandings are aired in the interest of obtaining recognition, or whether comments on understandings are dispensed in order to strengthen or weaken certain understandings, the process of producing recognitions is akin to the art of rhetoric in which people try to attain a common ground to stand on in the interest of making or shaping a set of common institutions (Burke, 1969).

Recognition objectified

To a certain degree recognitions can be disembedded from face-to-face contexts. This is possible wherever there are technologies enabling the objectification of acts that others can interpret as recognizing. Potentially recognizing discourse can be objectified through technologies of writing and voice recording. Thus, we may find recognition for our understandings in books sometimes written centuries ago (Nietzsche 1976, 112); we can find them in laws and regulations, in utterances made or performances given by people we have never met and probably never will. Gestures, winks, and smiles too can be objectified through imaging techniques. Thus we may find recognition in photographs capturing the encouraging presence of those dear to us. Accordingly we place such pictures in albums or frame and hang them as constant recognizing presences in an environment where we feel we might need them. Sometimes recognition becomes further abstracted and condensed into the image of mythical figures, of gods, heroes, and saints, objectified as paintings, statues, or photographs.

If what I have said in the introductory chapter about the relationship between understandings and institutions is correct, then it is clear what enormous advantages the objectification of recognition has for the formation of translocal and transtemporal institutions. Propagandists of all sorts have used the technological possibilities to objectify recognition, and the socialist parties of Europe were no exception. In addition to distributing texts widely, the images of the founding fathers, Marx, Engels, Lenin, and Stalin (until 1956), and especially of the incumbent party secretary, were seen everywhere in public places. These were also plastered with the latest party slogans. Committed party members placed the founding fathers' images in their private homes.[18] However, recognitions based exclusively on agreements read off from objectified performances cannot really stabilize understanding *on their own*. Unless readers, viewers, auditors of an objectified performance are involved in some ongoing interaction with others in which the recognition they derive from the objectified form is recognized in face-to-face communication, they are the sole judge of their own inferences. What looms here is Wittgenstein's regress of rule-following, which can only be halted in practices embedded in corresponding networks of authority.

Objectifications with a potentially recognizing effect are connected with yet another problem for those distributing them with a particular political purpose in mind. Performances are rarely ever unambiguous with respect to the kinds of understandings they can be said to recognize. After all, the recognizing effect follows a particular understanding of another's performance. As interpretations these are necessarily variable. However, the cultivation of particular meta-understandings about how to read objectified performances is a suitable means to narrow the variability of interpretations. Of course this is precisely what the party tried to do by institutionalizing the elaborate and highly centralized system of social reception for party documents and classics I described in the last chapter.

Since objectifications can entail a use that is unintended by the authority issuing and distributing them, the sheer existence of objectifications may pose a problem. For that reason the party never just "issued" new party documents, such as party programs, party statutes, and such. It only "ex-

---

18. Stasi officers sometimes owned a ministatue of Cheka chief Feliks Dzierzynski. Some of their homes were decorated with portraits of socialist leaders.

changed" them, that is, the old versions, which if read right next to the new ones might deviate from, contradict, or ambiguate a particular new message, had to be surrendered when the new ones were picked up. In this regard the party showed considerable awareness of the potential ironies the objectification of recognition may produce. In others it remained oblivious to the unintended consequences of the mass dissemination of objectified performances intending to recognize the latest party line. It was oblivious to the fact that the omnipresence of a nonauthority or even negative authority— for this is what the party was to people not invested or even opposed to its rule—is vexing to people who cannot escape these performances. To the outsider who does not have to endure the cult of the leaders or the incessant barrage of political slogans they are typically embarrassing.[19]

Identity

The ideological and political conflicts of the twentieth century speak to a strong link between understandings and identity. The testimonies of the ideological combatants about their involvement—no matter whether liberal, nationalist, fascist, or communist—clearly demonstrate that their commitment can neither be understood as a form of simple interest politics, nor as dispassionate conflicts about the validity of political understandings. The pathos and the degree of violence underlying them can only be grasped once we recognize the degree to which these political understandings became fused with peoples' sense of who they are.

The constitution of agency that I discussed in the introduction provides a partial answer to the question of why understandings and identity are so closely associated. After all, it is our capability to act successfully and thus to have the possession of valid understandings providing orientation and direction that endows us with a sense of self-worth. Yet there are still deeper reasons. If identity is interpreted as the meaning of a self established through its connections or identifications with the world (Glaeser 2000), then the recognition of understandings containing identifications does not only constitute certainty, self, and social relationships, but also identity. Conversely, disagreements may threaten identity by spoiling identifications with people, ideas, or whatever else matters to self. Attacks on understandings are therefore often enough understood as attacks on identity.

Identity and the certainty in understanding are, however, not always in-

---

19. Here lies the reason why the hyperrealism of critical performers in the Soviet Union, and elsewhere in the former Soviet sphere of influence, could work as such a potent form of critique, as Alexei Yurchak (2006) has pointed out. The omnipresence of a nonauthority or even a negative authority is at least embarrassing if not outright nauseating.

tegrated to the same degree. There are cultural arrangements, practices, and symbolic and emotive forms that can help to distribute the constitution of self's meaning and certainty in understanding over different processes or different aspects of the same process, thus sheltering the one from the other. Such separation is a very important component of certain professions' ethos because they are fraught with disagreement. Law and science are good examples. In both, the identity component becomes ideally wrapped up in the *process* of bringing validations of understandings about, rather than in the belief in particular understandings. In other words, there are sustained efforts to institutionalize identity around the *form* of the professional practices rather than their content. A judge is taken to be exemplary, if she follows due process; a scientist is well regarded, if he applies theory and exercises method in a rigorous manner. Similarly, discursive forums that successfully foster a culture of controversial discussion shelter identity from disagreement by propounding values of positive relationships in disagreement and by rules of conduct that signal respect for all participants, for example, by adhering to turn-taking rules and conventions of polite speech as well as by countering the insidious effects of disagreement with well-timed antidotes of agreement produced, for example, by humor or attacks on common enemies.

The separation between the credibility of understanding and the meaning of self is, however, probably never quite complete, all the care of institutional differentiation notwithstanding. This is amply demonstrated by strong, emotional eruptions into otherwise sober, rationalistic discursive forums. In the professions, even the most famous thinkers and scientists have shown an "unprofessional" attachment to the *content* of their *own* theoretical constructions (Einstein's proverbial "the old man doesn't throw dice," for example). And in the courts even the most meticulous attention to process cannot eradicate completely the feeling that judges are partisans after all. The constitution of people through the validation of understandings is the basic reason why this separation is never entirely successful.[20]

The ethics of absolute finality, which I introduced in the last chapter, suggests, and I will empirically demonstrate this further in chapter 6, that socialism made not only no effort to institutionalize such a boundary, but to its own detriment it brandished such boundaries as a perversion of humanity. In consequence, attacks on socialist understandings were invariably taken as attacks on identity. Even minor critiques could be perceived as

---

20. It is questionable whether a perfect separation of identity and certainty would be desirable. The law must somehow remain in touch with issues of justice that cannot be defined in purely formal terms. What matters about scientific work is content in the end, not the process of its production. For that reason we tend to see the lawyer, the bureaucrat, or the scientist who is merely concerned with the form of their work as heartless or, and in an ethical sense, also as mindless.

intensely threatening with often-dire consequences for the critic. This was not only true for the relationship between people who identified as socialists and others who did not, but it was also true for the relationship between members of the party.

In sum, I have argued in this section for the irreducibly social character of understandings. By recourse to the work of Mead I have first shown how understandings come to be woven into the very capacity of human beings to make themselves the object of their own reflection. By recourse to the work of Wittgenstein I have then demonstrated how understandings as regularized processes of ordering are contingent on the continuous input of other human beings. In both self-formation and regularization the input of others comes in the form of recognitions. The rest of the section was then dedicated to the phenomenological exploration of recognition as an action-reaction effect flow that takes place in networks of authority relations characterized by the slippage between intentions and effects. Finally, I have considered the potential but also the problems involved with the possibility to objectify recognizing performances while closing this section with an exploration of the reasons why negative recognition is frequently experienced as an attack on identity.

THE DOXIC DIMENSION: RESONANCE

Understandings are not only constituted from within social relationships, but they are always already constituted in relationships with other understandings. In the literature the emphasis on the indissoluble interdependence of discursive understandings is called *meaning holism*. The hermeneutic tradition has from its very beginning battled individualistic and atomistic notions of understanding. Vico and Herder were strong proponents of a meaning holism. The romantics have followed in their wake. It is through their writings that concepts such as weltanschauung (literally world conception) or *Weltbild* (world image)[21] gained wide currency. Weber made the latter concept central to his sociology. Through the notion of culture, meaning holism has not only had a deep impact on the hermeneutic social sciences but also on the everyday imagination of the social. In the debates about the nature of science it has likewise left a deep mark with what is known today as the Duhem-Quine thesis. It states that contrary to the basic sentence theories of the positivists, statements are not accepted or refuted one by one, but they "come before the judge of experience together" (Quine 1951; cf. Putnam 1988).

21. "Weltanschauung" is of Kant's coinage and was fast adopted by other writers (e.g., Herder). "Weltbild" goes back all the way to the Middle Ages as *imago mundi*.

In the last two chapters, I made extensive use of meaning-holism. I tried to show how various components of Marxism-Leninism systematically built on each other. For example, what I have called the ethics of absolute finality systematically built on the vanguard party concept, which in turn is contingent on understanding Marxism as the first true science of the social in human history. What I called the aporia of socialist identity and the three aporias of socialist politics are unthinkable without meaning holism because they were formed by at least three understandings interacting with one another as a whole. In fact, socialism cultivated a strong meta-understanding that Marxism-Leninism was a "coherent, all encompassing doctrine," no part of which could be doubted without endangering the rest, thus locking the aporias in place. The various component understandings of Marxism-Leninism did not only build onto each other. The distinction of a larger social whole into two antagonistic classes, for example, partook, on the one hand, in other kinds of dualisms (good-bad, light-darkness, male-female, etc). On the other hand, it was a component of yet other more complex sets of understandings prevalent in socialism. Sets of understandings thus build, if not a system—a metaphor suggesting far too much neatness—then a more or less regular or irregular thicket of crosscutting and intersecting differentiations and integrations, that is, of understandings.

While it is undoubtedly correct that understandings must be seen in complex wholes, the conclusion that Duhem and Quine have drawn from it—that they fail in wholes—is untrue in practice. People sort through complexes of understandings, be it theories or religious doctrine, and change either some aspect of their arrangement or one or another of the components. In other words, the difference between a useful theory and a nonworkable theory is not necessarily a total revision of fundamentals, but sometimes it is just a matter of detail adjustments. This is not only true for science, as Kuhn (1962) and other sympathizers with holism have pointed out, but actually existing socialism also offers countless examples for such detail revisions.[22] Historically speaking, some of the more important revisions pertained to the social and economic conditions for successful revolution, the revaluation of the concept of ideology, and the possibility of socialism in one country. Even in total failure, useful components usually survive to be used in other contexts. This book, for instance, is an example for this, as I am still, in major parts of my argument, relying on selected theoretical frameworks developed by Karl Marx while making no use of his philosophy of history. So even if

---

22. Even the canonization of the classics was constantly adjusted, as they were never favored in their entirety, but always promoted in selective readings. Not only were Marx's early writings hard to get (even though they were formally published), but also even among his mature works texts fell in and out of favor (e.g., Bahro 1977).

sets of understandings, and a fortiori institutions, are always more than the sum of their parts, there still is a kind of modularity to the components.

Holism therefore needs modification. What we need is a concept to analyze the relationships between various understandings in a set, a concept that gives us some clues why, for example, people let go of some understandings rather than others once pressures for revision occur. It is again Wittgenstein's work (1984b, 1984c) that offers interesting points of departure in analyzing this problem. A variant of the private language argument wonders about the ways in which we attain certainty. He fences with two opponents. On the one hand, he tries to show that radical skepticism is misguided. On the other he argues against Enlightenment optimism concerning the possibility of radical critique associated with the glorious notion of individual autonomy. His main point is simply that justification as process, where one understanding is linked back to others, must come to an end somewhere, as one can continue to doubt—literally—only ad nauseam. So he famously declaims, "Rational human beings do *not* have certain doubts [my emphasis]" (1984b, no. 220). To live our lives we have to let go of skepticism, eventually necessitating a leap of faith. Just imagine you were the propaganda officer of a party group. You have to prepare a speech for which you need a number of quotations. *Neues Deutschland* just had an article with a few quotes of a Honecker speech, and some by Marx, both of which you thought might be useful. What would it be like if you began to doubt that these quotes are accurate and you checked them in the library. It dawns on you that the printed speech may contain errors of transcription and that the Marx volume you consulted might be sloppily edited, or worse, edited by the class enemy. . . . Therefore, all understanding rests somewhere on understandings that nobody *cares* to justify. This does not mean that the process of justification is not important. It just means that it is necessarily selective.

Wittgenstein suggests, in particular, two ways in which skeptical regression is halted in practice.[23] Both of these point to the embeddedness of understandings in contexts of interaction. The first operates by way of transposing the skeptic query from an epistemic to a moral key. Trusting a quotation is translated into trusting the person (or institution) who made it or who supposedly controls it. A good party propagandist might trust a Honecker quote he hears reported on an East German radio station, but he may have doubts about a quote reported on a West German station, which might turn out

---

23. Nietzsche has made a similar point before, which has found its way through Weber (esp. 1988b) into the social sciences. Wittgenstein's particular contribution to the skeptic's dilemma is the way in which he argues that solutions are typically found in practice. Whereas Nietzsche and with him Weber still assume an arbitrary break-off, a voluntaristic leap of faith, Wittgenstein offers social anchoring in hidden self-referentiality as a solution.

to be enemy propaganda.[24] Thus, the production of knowledge is typically deeply intertwined with a particular economy of trust relying on the recognition by a trustee.[25] The second way to arrest the skeptic's regress cannot be captured adequately with the notion of trust. Wittgenstein (along with gestalt psychologists, phenomenologists, and ethnomethodologists) observes that there seems to be a certain play between what he calls the "foreground" and the "background" in the sense that in the pursuit of knowledge certain issues are always explicitly problematized, whereas others, which could equally be put to scrutiny, are not. Most interestingly, people are not even aware that they could raise questions about the background. They are simply not asked, or "bracketed" as the phenomenologists say. Background assumptions are naturalized in the sense that people forget that they are formed as institutions in collaboration with others; they are essentialized in the sense that people forget that they are mere symbolizations of the world rather than the world itself. With Wittgenstein we should ask, then, how particular foreground/background arrangements come about and how it happens that issues previously problematized end up as unquestionably given and vice versa.[26]

Two characteristics of the background are to be noted. The questioning of understandings not only stops because the skeptic herself no longer has any questions, but also because nobody else with whom she is conversing does. The background as such rests on ubiquitous recognition within a network of authority. Moreover, the understanding that has first given rise to the skeptical inquiry stands in a special validating connection to background

---

24. There is the possibility that he trusts neither and that he chooses the Eastern version simply because that one may not get him into trouble once he is asked to justify his choices.

25. The sociology of science has made much of this point. Stephen Shapin's (1994) analysis of the role of social status in the production of acceptable truth in seventeenth-century England is the pioneering example for this line of research. As Shapin shows, a fact assumed exalted status of trustworthiness not least by virtue of its pronunciation by a gentleman.

26. This route of inquiry, too, has been traveled in the sociology of science, here most notably in some of Latour's writings (e.g., 1988; 1999), who follows, for example, how milk fermentation has moved from a cutting-edge research program hotly debated and contested in leading science journals to the status of mundane knowledge available in every elementary school and every kitchen as a fact-equals-world truism. In practice, both of these paths—moral translation and backgrounding—may be intertwined. Reading Adrian Johns's (1998) account of the history of the book it seems that there may be a trajectory that leads from an epistemic problem (is the person who claims to be the author of a particular text really the author) to a moral issue (a trustworthy publisher) with a moral solution (reputations of publishers) that gets institutionalized as a background assumption that can then be exploited (by fraudulent posing as a trustworthy publisher) to spin back into the other direction.

understandings. That validity-enhancing connection between understandings is what I have called *resonance*. It is the concept that helps us to lend more precision to meaning holism, because the links among various understandings can now be differentially treated as more or less strong and as of varying quality. The "whole" in meaning-holism can now be analyzed as internally structured.[27]

Resonance

With the notion of resonance I want to capture the validating force resulting from the "fit" between any two particular understandings (within the same or across modes), as well as between as of yet unordered aspects of experiences and their articulation in processes of differentiation and integration forming understanding. The key question in this formulation is, what "fit" means. Long-standing traditions in philosophy and (cognitive) psychology, from Leibniz to Piaget, seek an answer to this question in some formal logical connection that is assumed to be a representation of a universal human reason. However, the ethnographic and historical record has taught us that what is locally perceived as validity fit between understandings varies considerably across cultural contexts. There is not one, but there are different kinds of logics that have not only been mobilized historically across cultures but also within one culture to assess the quality and quantity of validness between understandings. Thus, fit, much like authority, is regulated by meta-understandings, which is to say that it is culturally variable.

In the wider cultural context of European modernity, three broad types of fit that repeatedly appear in different guises can usefully be distinguished from one another: pattern resonance, consistency, and resonance in pursuit. I will discuss them in turn in the following three sections.[28]

---

27. The structure of variously strong connections between the component understandings of the "whole" can now be used to formulate hypotheses about which assumptions can be dropped with more or less violent ripple effects.

28. Since "fit" is a matter of designating meta-understandings, this list is needless to say not complete. In chapter 5, p. 275, I will for example, introduce the notion of metonymic resonance where understandings are validated through sheer co-occurrence in a particular spatio-temporal environment. It should also be noted that some of the similarities between principles of classification and principles of resonance discussed here are not accidental. For example, Lévi-Strauss (1966) distinguishes between metaphor (with obvious similarities to what I will explore here as pattern resonance) and the just mentioned metonymy as classifying principles. Resonance builds very particular kinds of classes, namely groupings of understandings from the perspective of their validating relationship of the sort: if this is reliable, then that is too; if this is doubtful then that is as well.

Pattern resonance

In this type of resonance, validating force derives from the similarity between the formal structures of understandings. An interesting case of pattern resonance in the history of GDR governance is, for example, the 1960s passion of the party leadership for cybernetics (Apel and Mittag 1964; Mittag et al. 1969; cf. Steiner 1999). All administrators (secret police officers included)[29] were asked to present their work plans in terms of feedback-control systems. This is not surprising if one considers that cybernetic thinking shares countless similarities with Marxist thought (the latter's revolutionary dialectic notwithstanding); it stresses the interdependence of all parts, none of which can be adequately understood in isolation, thus urging a totalizing perspective. In the same sense, a statement may resonate (sound right), for example, because it imitates the prosody of another that is already believed, because it follows a particular style of presentation, or because it emulates a particular argumentative form.[30] An example of positive formal pattern resonance is provided by socialism's politolect. Written documents across a wide range of social domains became quite similar in lexical choice and style because the writers needed to authorize themselves by creating a pattern resonance between what they had written and official party speak. In other words, writers employed pattern resonance to perform the required self-objectification. Conversely, the party tried to legitimate its own rule as "*of* the proletariat *through* the party *for* the proletariat" by using popular speech patterns. In this way many socialist slogans were likened to proverbs. However, the use of pattern resonances to legitimate action can also backfire. The performances of the SED party grandees during the fall of 1989 offer many striking examples, of which Mielke's "But I love you all" and Honecker's "Socialism in its course cannot be stopped by either donkey or horse" are only the most prominent examples. The problem of these performances was precisely that in their very style they provided overwhelming evidence that the speakers seemed either oblivious to what was going on in the country or, worse, were quite willing to simply ignore it.

Pattern resonances not only occur *within* one particular mode of understanding but also *across*. The very principle behind rituals is to create such resonances. Accordingly, the spaces built or set up for their perfor-

---

29. A number of my interviewees remember with a twinkle in their eyes how in the 1960s they all of a sudden had to present their work plans in terms of systems-theoretic considerations. Some say they did not exactly know what it meant, but they saw that these plans made use of boxes and arrows in different colors—and that's what they used to present their plans.

30. Michael Silverstein (2003) provides telling analysis of the pattern resonances created by Lincoln in his Gettysburg address, as well as by "Bush speak."

mance are typically meant to produce resonances between the placement and movement of bodies and ideology (Benjamin 1983; Geertz 1980; Sennet 1996). Where spaces and the movements performed within them do not resonate with doctrine, this may prompt anxieties (for people might get the wrong idea) or the desire to redesign the space. The Renaissance hesitance of the Catholic Church to accept central-plan buildings as spaces suitable to celebrate the Eucharist is an example of this. And so is the redesign of city spaces in socialism (e.g., Flierl 1998). Another simple example for a cross-modal pattern resonance is modern politicians' "bath among the people," associating physical with moral proximity, which was practiced by socialist politicians with the same zeal and for the same reasons that their liberal-democratic colleagues take recourse to it. Another poignant example, equally shared among various forms of modern political arrangements, is the expressive use of marches, associating political action with physical movement, which often end in a central gathering linking physical with the ideological unity in pursuit of a political goal. Finally, in the last chapter I have already mentioned the ritual of critique and self-critique spatializing the usual charge of subjectivism with the seating arrangements of a trial in which a lower-sitting defendant faced a phalanx of elevated party members. The actual experience of resonance in all of these cases is contingent on a principle, that is, a meta-understanding, defining an aspect according to which similarity can be established. In the critique–self-critique case it is the culturally available superimposition of a spatial high-low onto a moral good-bad distinction that makes the resonance between discursive and kinesthetic aspects of critique and self-critique possible.

Consistency

The second type of resonance I want to discuss here is *consistency*. Its validating force is derived from the compatibility between understandings. Especially, the strong incompatibility or contradiction between an understanding whose validity is at stake with a body of understandings already endowed with credibility invalidates the former. Pattern resonance directly compares the structures internal to two understandings with each other transferring validity through similarity. Consistency by contrast demands that the understandings set in relationship to each other find a mutually supporting place within a relevant overarching order (i.e., a set of meta-understandings such as a particular form of logics). Within this order the understandings under consideration may play a different, albeit complementary role. This means also that they can be structured internally rather differently (as for example major and minor premise in a conclusion). The conduit that transfers validity is not similarity but integratability. Inconsistency is then the impossibility to reconcile understandings in view of a relevant overarching order.[31] It means that either the one or the other understanding can be part of the order but not both. The more the relevant overarching order is essentialized, the more it appears as a natural, inviolable given, the more pronounced is the resonance effect. Formal logic is such an overarching order that is often hypostasized as a natural grammar of sound reasoning. And so are literary genres or artistic styles, even though these two may make the conventionality of the order more visible.

For the analysis of resonance effects it is important to investigate the ways in which an overarching order is made situationally relevant. Since these orders are historically variant and since there are typically a number of different ones available, the relevance of an overarching order can never be assumed; it needs to be established empirically. Max Weber's *Zwischenbetrachtung* (in English known as "Religious Rejections of the World and Their Direction") (1988c) is particularly helpful to think through the conditions under which inconsistencies can manifest themselves experientially with consequences for institutional arrangements. The starting point for his considerations are phenomena such as the whole-hearted affirmation of an ethics of brotherly love during Sunday church service and the very different ethics underlying business relations the following Monday. Weber makes sense of such phenomena by arguing that we participate in different "spheres of social life." Each sphere may be organized (Weber says "rationalized") according to its own logics. Since these spheres of life are typically bounded institutionally, for example by the temporal structure of the calendar and the spatial distribution of practices, differences in these logics need not be perceived as inconsistent with each other. However, where such boundaries come to be eradicated (e.g., by a fundamentalist ideology claiming paramount consideration across all spheres of life) differences may come in into view as inconsistencies. For Weber, this new situation creates motives to change institutional arrangements. Inconsistent understandings may come to loose their validity and cease to be action guiding; new boundaries may come to be invented; or aspects of the overarching order may come to be reconsidered.

After World War II, Leon Festinger's theory of "cognitive dissonance" (1957) became widely influential. His work focuses on the question of whether "contradictions" between a "belief" and actions that are not "con-

---

31. Since inconsistency as a form of resonance is different from the Marxian concept of contradiction it is important to keep them apart. Contradiction in the Marxian sense pertains not to the incompatibility of understandings but to the incompatibility of institutional arrangements within an encompassing institutional order. It means in particular that the institutional dynamics underlying one institution undermine those of another.

sonant" with it create a motive to change either future behavior or the belief. Countless laboratory experiments conducted by social psychologists around the world have led to rather inconclusive results (Petty and Cacioppo 1996). Yet, refinements of the experimental procedures have led to an interpretation that has found wider acceptance in the social psychological literature. Subjects experience "dissonance" (for Festinger a motivating stress, "like hunger") if they have no choice but to see themselves as the agent of the dissonant action (rather than seeing themselves as forced), and if they have no means to rationalize the dissonance. This immediately raises the question, under which circumstances anybody would *accept* agency and would not rationalize the situation. So again the question of meta-understandings forming an overarching framework moves to the foreground. Due to the individualistic and acultural presuppositions dominant in psychology, however, cognitive dissonance theory has neither tools nor interest in investigating this question. In this respect, the older, Weberian framework is preferable because it highlights the question under which institutional sociocultural conditions, inconsistencies, come to be perceived thus gaining relevance. Again, the experience of consistency is contingent on meta-understandings, for example, an ethical norm exhorting people to do as they say or even more: to do so uniformly.

Enriched by the notions of meta-understandings and networks of authority, however, cognitive dissonance theory is still quite useful to think with, because it points to one of the ways in which understandings may change. In this spirit I will, in the next chapter, utilize an associated social psychological model, Fritz Heider's (1958) "balance theory," to explore some of the possible dialectics of understanding. In the last chapter, I showed that socialism had its own, substantively rational consistency criterion: the ethics of absolute finality. It was even cast into a simple formula that was supposed to help actors maintain a resolute class standpoint. Aspiring socialists were told to ask themselves who the beneficiary of their action would be—the proletariat or its class enemy. In practice this criterion was connected with far-reaching agency ascriptions, which are rooted in assumptions about the party's and by implication any believer's access to truth. The flipside of this agency ascription was a particular way to reason about failure, which I have called *socialist theodicy*. This ideological frame, embedded in the organizational structure of a Stalinist vanguard party, did indeed at times produce extreme pressures on party members to self-objectify (which sometimes also had again counterintentional consequences). By contrast, people less committed to the party and its doctrines often describe much less consistency stress because they could argue that they did not have much agency in the first place and that they were forced to act in inconsistent ways as not to face undue disadvantage.

Resonance in pursuit

The third type if resonance interprets fit as the degree to which a particular understanding furthers or thwarts an active project or pursuit. Hence I will call it *resonance in pursuit*. Understandings, no matter whether they are discursive, emotive, or kinesthetic, resonate in this sense when they fulfill wishes, help to solve problems, further the chances to accomplish a goal, assist in living according to particular principles, open or close the route to, or enhance or diminish sensory pleasures.[32] The validity of the pursuit is transferred to the understanding via the helping hand it lends to the pursuit. The SED's enthusiasm for cybernetics resonated at that level as well. The exuberant hopes for overtaking the West economically that motivated the late 1950s and early 1960s had given way to a more sober understanding of the problems of central planning. Cybernetics was hoped to revolutionize the planning process. It promised new solutions to persistent problems. It looked like a possibility to "overtake the West without catching up with it," as Ulbricht had formulated his hopes.

Resonance in pursuit has probably been the most popular take on how people come to gain certainty in particular understandings. It looms at the bottom of recurrent reproaches that humans are a credulous race. One version of it, a common vulgarization of both utilitarian principles and of the Marxian sociology of knowledge, has it that people believe what they perceive to be in their own best interest. Because desires, goals, and wishes were, over the centuries, seen as such a strong certifying tonic, explicit meta-understandings were developed to counteract their effect. They have found their way not only into Enlightenment thought and scientific pedagogy but also into good counsel to princes, gentlemen, and ladies. In the validating force of resonances in pursuit lies the wellspring of favoring reason and discourse over feeling as reliable sources of understanding. Knowledge is, in that sense, what has been gained in overcoming tempting forms of resonance in pursuit. Just as old as the fear of epistemic seduction is the counterargument of decrying the futility of generating "dry" knowledge devoid of any deeper significance for us, that is knowledge devoid of resonance in pursuit.

I argued above that the dynamics of recognition follows an action-reaction effect flow pattern—as it should being part and parcel of the process of forming understandings as institutions. Resonance too follows this pattern, however with a peculiarity of its own that has everything to do with the self as a being that is simultaneously object and subject. The action part of the sequence is easy enough to discern. The process begins with a more

---

32. Thus the concept of resonance in pursuit is closely related to Bruno Latour's (e.g., 1999) notion of proposition.

or less consciously posed question: "Does this understanding fit with what else I know or desire?" The peculiarity comes about through the fact that we are asking ourselves, not another human being. We react to our own action. It is important to see however, that this reaction typically follows spontaneously; it can not simply be manipulated by the inquiring I, that is it follows with a certain degree of autonomy. The source of this autonomy is the fact that the understandings we use as a base of comparison are not simply maintained by ourselves, but through our interaction with the world above all with other human beings. Memory is in this sense an important mediator in processes of institution formation—a fact that has haunted the socialist project in many ways.

In sum, no matter how innate pattern recognition capabilities, desires, and possibly even some form of rudimentary logic might be, there is no doubt that judgments of similarity, consistency, and desirability proceed for the larger part on the cultural grid of meta-understandings. Which of our five senses would we emphasize in making judgments of pattern similarity? What kind of rhythm or symmetry do we have in mind when we speak of "pattern"? Do we judge consistency in a logical system that is constrained by a binary system of truth values, or do we work within a more complex modal logic? Do we see desire as something evil, leading us to make every effort to transcend it in reason? Do we essentialize our senses, reason, and desires as something biological, or do we assume that they can be developed, cultivated, and refined? Meta-understandings regulate how resonances operate—with consequences for the institutional fabric within which we live.

Meta-understandings also regulate what body or bodies of understanding are relevant for resonance considerations. In other words, they establish a context of resonance. An important meta-epistemological device used for such purposes is the classification of understandings as belonging to a certain domain of social life, thus emphasizing some comparisons at the expense of others. Particularly pertinent for a political epistemology is the very act of labeling an understanding as *political* rather than *private*. In the GDR, designating something as *political* implied immediately that the understanding in question was of concern to party and state. The context of resonance was therefore the latest party policy and doctrine, its "line," its current interpretation of Marxism-Leninism. What was considered *private* shifted in the course of time, but in general only those understandings that were seen as having no bearing on public life were considered as unambiguously private.[33] Of course, the comparative mobilization of bodies of

---

33. We will see in chapter 8 how difficult it became for the party to relegate religious belief to the private realm, as the peace issue amplified resonances between politics and religious beliefs and practices.

understanding may also depend on the contingent limitations of the situation, such as location, time, the activity a person is currently involved in, and more broadly the issues a person is wrestling with at the moment. They all facilitate spontaneous comparisons. The co-presence of others, too, may make a difference as they can suggest relevant comparisons.

THE REFERENTIAL DIMENSION: CORROBORATION

To introduce the question of how the world impinges on the validity of our understandings through the success and failure of our action, I will begin by sketching the difference between a positivist and an antipositivist position. The point of this exercise is not to defeat positivism once more, but to highlight a fundamental problem with dominant forms of antipositivism. The last influential school of philosophy that has argued for some kind of unmediated access to reality through our senses is the logical positivism of the so-called Vienna circle. It maintains the notion that there are particular kinds of propositional statements, sometimes called "basic sentences," that perfectly correspond to the world. Basic sentences in their pristine purity are in this sense not made, but discovered, really dug out from under all the layers of biases and preoccupations with which we deceive ourselves about the true nature of things. And this is what members of the Vienna circle identify as the task of philosophy: the purification of language, exorcising anything in it that is meaningless in either a referential or logical sense. The ideal on the horizon, programmatically invoked by the young Wittgenstein of the *Tractatus*, is a language in which lying is impossible, a language in which our problems can be either resolved clearly and unquestionably or be discarded as the nightmares of a misguided mind. Logical positivism has become something of the great antipode of almost all philosophizing of the short twentieth century. This sense of a common enemy has, beyond all sorts of other divisions (across which the war of ideas was no less intense), created a broad consensus on the following point. Facts are always constructed by particular people in particular contexts. Alas, there is very little agreement about how it is possible to construct and still learn something valuable about a reality.

The reaction against positivism has led to strong variants of linguistic constructivism. Richard Rorty (e.g., 1989) is probably its best-known proponent in the English-speaking world. The starting point of his reasoning is a valuable critique of the correspondence theory of truth, which he argues along the following lines. Correspondence claims (such as those of the positivists) are apparently problematic and therefore need to be adjudicated. This requires criteria that must be communicated and assessed in discourse. Therefore, rather than pointing to the thing in itself, the adjudication of a truth claim made on behalf of a sentence just refers to more discourse. There is an important insight here, and I will systematically build on it. However, Rorty's claims go further. He insists that adjudication refers to *nothing but discourse.* He also argues, and this is by no means a necessary precondition for his critique of a correspondence theory, that language neither represents, nor mediates the world in the sense that it would intercede between a self and a world independent and outside of it. Instead, Rorty argues that for us as human beings both we and the world exist always already and *wholly in* language. What this implies is that there is no nonlinguistic understanding, and that there is no prelinguistic experience.

How is it, then, that people in real life make distinctions between understandings that are mere figments of the imagination and constructions that provide some useful orientation? Rorty takes up a pragmatist line of reasoning by arguing that people adjudicate understandings according to their usefulness, which—because according to him we are always already wholly in language—must be done from a perspective of comparisons between languages. If more useful, we change idioms, which Rorty (building on Kuhn 1962) conceives as something like a gestalt-switch between fundamentally incommensurable ways of seeing the world. Rorty feels no pressure to conceptualize the process of switching. There is no investigation of what "usefulness" might mean in the course of our real-world pursuits, and there is never any interest in the question *for whom* such a switch must be useful in order to let such a switch happen. For obviously we do not live in linguistic isolation. Of course, such processes are what interest me, and the theory of validation offers an alternative model. In direct contrast to Rorty, I will argue that changes in understandings may, once carried through, be very well like gestalt-switches, but that the process of getting there has much to do with a disenchantment of old understandings, which typically loose credibility first, not because alternative languages prove to be more useful, but because people begin to "bump into walls" with their current understandings, an experience that has many extralinguistic kinesthetic and emotive components, and that motivates them to look for and/or produce new understandings. Again, the problematic I have just sketched out can be illuminated by thinking in terms of validations. Clearly, Rorty argues his case chiefly along the lines of recognition. What we need is a stronger notion accounting for how we succeed and fail in practice, thus adjudicating what is useful and what is not. The notion of corroboration may help to fill this gap.

Corroboration

Analytically it is useful to distinguish a direct and a more indirect way in which our understandings can come to be corroborated. In the first case an understanding is self-consciously put into action to see where it leads; in the second case, circumstantial evidence is mobilized to see how it reflects on the understanding in question. An example may help to illustrate this difference in a flash. A number of Stasi officers have explained to me that at some point it dawned on them that party elections had become mere acclamations of candidates designated by higher party organs, and that it was in fact no longer possible to nominate candidates from below with any reasonable hope for success. The first formulation of this insight, that is, the act of symbolizing a hypothesis in response to a series of experiences, typically took shape in a context of marked dislike for the candidate put forth by the next higher level of the party organization. This prompted a kind of puzzlement about why nobody spoke up against him or her as the dislike for the candidate was suspected to be more widespread. In this way, the generalization of the dislike for a particular candidate paved the way for seeing top-down nominations as a problematic practice. There were now two ways of corroborating this suspicion. One officer did indeed make use of his statutory right to nominate a candidate in the next elections. Not only did he fail to win *any* support for his choice, but he was also severely reprimanded for his subjectivism and for endangering the unity of the party. Others feared that much and quietly inquired within their networks of friends what they had observed in elections to party offices in their basic party organizations. It is important to realize that this insight was often formulated without ever having witnessed the actual defeat of an attempt to nominate a candidate from below. The sheer fact that a series of inquiries about election events yielded the result that bottom-up nomination was, after the 1950s, unheard of corroborated the suspicion that it had become impossible. In the first case the suspicion was corroborated directly. If you like, a hypothesis was formed and it was put to the test in a focused, self-conscious action, that is, in an experiment. In the second case corroboration remained indirect—it was not directly linked to past or present actions (insofar as no candidate was set forth and defeated). Instead, indirect corroboration limited itself to the collection of circumstantial evidence.

Direct corroboration

In direct corroborations, understandings are seen as more or less successful guides for action in the same sense that a map can offer better or worse guidance in getting from here to there. By using them in action they are, in Marshall Sahlins's (1987, 145) felicitous term "put at risk." For direct corroboration to take effect two conditions need to be met. First, the understandings in question need to be seen as shaping the action performed. This connection is immediate in simple kinesthetic understandings. A particular sway of the hand succeeds or fails to thrust the thread through the eye of the needle. The action-guidance of a particular understanding also seems obvious in processes of rational planning, where an understanding is first articulated discursively before the action takes place. However, since this move involves translations from discursive and emotive to kinesthetic understandings, this link is always open to interpretation. Meta-understandings regulate what counts as a legitimate translation and what does not. Second, the action performed needs to be seen as having had a significant effect on the outcome. This seems to be most obvious in events expressly produced for corroborating purposes, as, for example, in trials, tests, or experiments. But here too, beyond customary attributions it is anything but trivial to demarcate an "action" and an "outcome" from a stream of happenings. Worse, perhaps, since the action guided by understandings is typically part of a larger set of action-reaction effect flows that jointly produce the result, interpretation is indispensable in establishing links between actions and outcomes. Meta-understandings are needed and sometimes even need to be developed to sort through this challenging task (Collins 1992; Knorr-Cetina 1999).

Given what I have said in chapter 1 about the planned, consciousness-driven model of social transformation in socialism, it is clear that direct corroboration is not necessarily limited to the small scale. Even though socialism ranks among the largest such attempts ever undertaken, there were and continue to be others, ranging from the production of planned cities or agriculture (Scott 1998) to the planned introduction of a market economy and liberal democracy in postsocialist Europe. Indeed, common parlance often refers to such large-scale planned transformations as "experiments." Socialism is often referred to in this sense as a "failed experiment" since the idea of socialism has been established as an "illusion" (e.g., Furet 1999). Within socialism, on the one hand, party documents refer again and again to the purported success of policies planned on the basis of Marxism-Leninism as confirmations of the truth of the teachings of the classics. On the other hand, policies could also be repealed if the outcomes were not as hoped. The official proclamation of the "beginning construction of socialism" at the second party congress in 1952, for example, helped to spur an increasing movement of refugees and was in consequence judged "premature" by the Soviet Union. Hence it pressured its small brother in East Berlin to repeal some of the policies connected with the announcement. And yet, it needs to be recognized that with the scale at which understandings are pitched ("bottom-up nomination of candidates is possible" vs. "socialism is more just than capitalism"), the interpretative needs for linking actions and outcomes increase dramatically.

Direct corroboration is not restricted to prospective rational action, however. In fact, putting it this way would de-historicize the epistemic ideologies and practices on which the notion of rational planning is based. It is not untypical that we experience a series of happenings as an inchoate conundrum. Yet, the like or dislike of the situations in which we find ourselves after a series of actions can provide an occasion for postmortems, or retrospections in which systematic attempts are undertaken to reconstruct happenings as causal structures that try to link what we have done, the understandings informing in these actions, and some kinds of effect. Retrospection does not have to be a linear retracing, working backward from outcomes over causing actions to antecedent understandings. Working through the conundrum of happening can begin with any known part—our good intentions, the mess or unsuspected bliss in which we find ourselves, the actions we have undertaken. This may include the consideration of understandings that were held unconsciously as deep motivations, of background assumptions as well as of understandings that have only taken shape in the course of action and therefore cannot be said to have preceded action. In fact, through retrospection we may for the first time come to see which understandings have shaped the actions in question. We are ready to admit this in everyday interactions where one can answer, "I don't know," to the question of why we have done a certain thing. In such cases, understandings have to be gleaned from a course of action that, as a muddling through, sometimes only articulates understandings in process, which we later see as having directed the action in the first place. Yet, what matters in this process is not what comes first and what comes later; what matters is that a particular way of ordering the world, through differentiations and integrations that can be seen as those de facto organizing the performance in a particular environment, has been rewarded with success or penalized with failure. What matters as well is that through retrospection understanding becomes *an* understanding (or set) that is isolated, clarified, and reified out of an infinite stream of differentiations and integrations to become transportable and deployable in another context as digested experience.

The process of retrospection reveals again the degree to which associating understandings, actions, and outcomes is an interpretative task that requires a variety of meta-understandings to succeed. Psychoanalysis, for example, is a complex of meta-understandings that helps us to reconstruct understanding-action-outcome dynamics. Current western trial procedures sometimes project an understanding-action-outcome sequence, and sometimes they just focus on parts of it. The action-outcome link is particularly important in addressing the question of whether anybody's action in particular is to blame for an outcome, for example, in cases of "criminal neglect." The understandings-action link moves to the foreground in criminal procedures where assessments of culpability are often contingent on finding a motive. This is significant, for example, in distinguishing "murder" from "manslaughter." More mundanely, cultural forms and practices helping to describe and establish understanding-action-outcome dynamics are an integral part of the many "debriefings" that have become a regular feature of organizational life understood as a rational pursuit. The forms of failure deliberations I discussed in the last chapter under the heading of a "socialist theodicy" are good cases in point.[34] For the Stasi, adjudicating whether an airplane crash was an "accident" and thus unintentional or "sabotage" and thus intentional made a big difference for what this event might have been taken to be corroborating.

This dependence on meta-understandings is what Rorty (or poststructuralism more generally) has in mind when he asserts that discourse is pointing to just more discourse. Yet, in a direct encounter with the world there is prediscursive experience in the form of sensory data often offering poignant evidence of success or failure. If I assume that there lies nothing between my beloved one at the other end of the hallway and me, and halfway through rushing to her I bump into a glass door, kinesthetic understanding gets abruptly thwarted, and there is ample immediate sensory evidence of the failure of my assumption. And before discourse picks up we typically feel something, elation or frustration, pride or shame; joy or anger. And only now does a discursive postmortem kick in, perhaps together with my worried beloved suggesting that I need a pair of new glasses. Life in late socialism offered many such immediate experiences of sudden thwarting not only of hopes but also of everyday expectations of failures that were of great significance in understanding socialism as a polity. A carefree afternoon stroll could suddenly end in front of the Wall; a greengrocer did not have the expected fruits; the drive to family in the other corner of the republic took longer and longer, because the number of potholes increased. Also, one such experience could perhaps be talked away in the company of others. But repeated experiences of this kind helped to actualize understandings that could not be rationalized away. Admittedly, all these events could do is to directly corroborate rather minor hypotheses. Yet that "firsthand" knowledge proved to be extremely significant for the *indirect* corroboration of more encompassing political understandings.

34. The whole chain is constantly negotiated in the experimental sciences, as Collins (1992) and Collins and Pinch (1993; 1998) have shown. There the issue is often whether a positive experimental effect is actually due to the aspect of the experiment that is supposed to produce it; conversely, in cases of negative results it is often argued that certain aspects of the experiment, which, according to the design intention should not have had an effect, did in the end overlay or make illegible the effect the experimenters wanted to demonstrate.

Indirect corroboration

There are a number of reasons why it is often difficult, if not impossible, to corroborate understandings directly in action. Many understandings are simply too broadly scaled and scoped to be directly testable in any meaningful sense. They cannot be tied to a systematically executable action framework whose consequences remain identifiable and attributable while working themselves out within a human time scale. Think of the claims socialism made about itself, say its insistence that it alone will lead to an ultimately desirable, just, and fulfilling human society. The problem with such claims is that they require for their execution a massive institutional transformation, working itself out over the longue durée. Much more than in any smaller scale and hence a more likely controllable test, the questions haunting any attempt to corroborate broadly scoped understandings are these: "Were the actions intended indeed the actions performed?" "Have they been executed in the prerequisite way?" "Have there been any unanticipated interferences invalidating the results?" This situation becomes compounded if, like in socialism, those interested in corroborating a particular understanding actually work with a set of epistemic ideologies and practices that make the efficacy of actions contingent on the receptivity of the historical situation. One can then always argue that either the institutionalization was not complete enough (insufficient development) or the time not ripe enough to judge conclusively that corroboration has succeeded or failed. This problem is prevalent even for socialism's "smaller" claims, for example, that it is more just than capitalism. How could such an understanding directly inform anyone's actions?

Another reason why understandings can often not be directly translated into actions is that the possible consequences are deemed too costly. Opposition members frequently debated the possible consequences of their actions, often rejecting a particular project because they did not want to run the risk of imprisonment (and the consequences this might have had for their children, etc.). So they had to draw conclusions from their deliberations of what might have happened, had they acted in a particular way rather than from the consequences of their performances. Moreover, one may simply not be in a position to perform a direct enactment because one does not have access to the resources that would be required to do so. Just imagine you have a hunch that the secret police taps every phone conversation you are making from your private phone, or that the general secretary does not really know anymore what is going on because his entourage shelters him from all negative news.

In all of these cases we may want to find *indirect* ways to corroborate the understanding in question. This means that we would want to identify understandings resonating with the one we are interested in and which could be put to the test in action. Such an effort might lead to a more limited direct corroboration. More often, however, indirect corroboration involves the conversion of the understanding-action link into an indicator-search problem. Fixing the indicator value is the outcome of the event, which is then interpreted as corroborating a larger understanding either positively or negatively. The question of justice may in this sense be translated into an issue of criminal success rates, of feeding and housing the most needy, or into a matter of the existence and possibilities of using administrative law to fight decisions of the state. The indirect method of corroboration may also be performed retrospectively. We always do so when we puzzle about the meaning of a particular historical event, features of which we read as an indicator for the veracity of a particular understanding. Thus at the Vth party congress Ulbricht could use the Soviets' successful launching of the Sputnik as a proof for the superiority of socialism, or the Anglo-French-Israeli military intervention after Egypt's nationalization of the Suez Canal as a proof of the imperialist nature of capitalism.

Epistemic ideologies and practices may designate that there are classes of understandings for which no translation into actionable understanding is available or for which corroboration is fundamentally meaningless. This point is frequently made for aesthetic judgments, and it defines the norms of deontological ethics. Thus, corroborations are contingent on a number of epistemic ideologies and practices that need to be recognized in order to stabilize. Without recognition, the proper translation from possible understanding to actual understanding, from actual understanding to action, and action to more or less successful outcomes would be open to Wittgensteinian regress. The contingency of corroborations on recognitions does not imply that corroboration can be reduced to recognition, however. Once the connections between events and understandings are more or less firmly rooted in epistemic ideologies and practices, corroborations do have a force of their own. Just because there is a more widely held agreement of how to make the connections and how to interpret an event, the event itself obtains power because the injunctions of these practices and ideologies cannot be violated at will by any single individual without invoking the censorship of the relevant networks of authority. In Kuhn's (1962) account of scientific revolutions, anomalies can only come up as an unsettling force on the firm grid of epistemic ideologies and practices that characterize what he has called "normal science." Kuhn emphasizes that such normal science is necessary to produce revolutions. Its rigidity is the very precondition for the *recalcitrance* of experience. And thus it is on the basis of particular discursive arrangements that experience can be allowed to transcend discourse.

In either the direct or indirect case, it is the result of enactment or identification of indicators that in experience creates the corroborating effect. Emotive understandings may play a significant role in signaling that the corroboration is taking place. Shame is a forceful indicator of failure; pride a powerful sign of success. And as Silvan Tomkins already pointed out by investigating the developmental roots of pride and shame (1962, 1963; see also Scheff 1990; Scheff and Retzinger 1991; Nathanson 1992; Katz 1999), these feelings are closely tied to kinesthetic experiences of continuing to *move* with the desired thrust or being radically stopped in one's track, thus abruptly breaking the flow of enjoyment. Indeed, corroborations do at some level include the validation or frustration of some kinesthetic understandings: our movements become blocked or unblocked; we meet physical resistance or we do not; we hit or miss.

Like resonance, corroboration follows an action-reaction effect format with something of a twist. The action part is straightforward. In the direct case it is the action translating an understanding into a test, and in the indirect one it is the indicator search. The reaction part is what I have previously called the outcome or the determination of the indicator's value. And there talk of action-reaction effect flows introduces awkwardness. A natural science experiment is a good example because it forces us to call nature an actor. There is no doubt that experimenters sometimes feel and act as if this were so. And there is indeed no harm if we treat nature as an actor if we also remember that it is a particular kind of actor whom we need to "interact" with in ways rather different from human beings.[35] There are two advantages to using this language. It reminds us that the reaction follows from a contingent process that is influenced, but not in a strict sense determined, by the preceding action alone. Second, we have thus found a way to talk about the role of natural processes in processes of institution formation. The development of kinesthetic understandings—what we usually call skills—is an excellent example. Learning to bike, we venture to hold ourselves in particular ways on saddle, handlebar, and pedals to which gravity "responds" in a constant fashion. It is precisely this constancy that allows us to adjust our own actions until action and reaction literally produce the skill to balance ourselves on a bike in motion. Precisely because nature is a respondent characterized by utmost regularity, kinesthetic understandings are more easily maintained as institutions than discursive ones. There is no moodiness, whim or ambiguous partiality to wrestle with. This, then is at last one reason why laminating discursive rules on kinesthetic ones stabilizes the former

---

35. Latour (1999 and 2005) speaks in this sense quite appropriately of "actants." What is missing in his work is a clear differentiation of the modes of interaction between various kinds of actors.

(see p. 175 in this chapter). This way of bringing stability into process works by supporting recognition with much less whimsical corroboration.[36]

Thinking in terms of action-reaction effect flows in the context of tests performed within social institutional settings is revealing for other reasons. The outcome is now shaped by the concatenation of many people's actions. This is still not a reaction in the traditional sense and yet the term certainly fits better than in the case of a natural science experiment. Now imagine the following. A supply side economist believes that lowering income taxes will increase the government's revenue because he assumes that people will respond to the incentive of higher returns on work by working more. The president he advises puts the theory to a test—and lo and behold the government's revenues sink! The economist is not impressed by the data, arguing that the people are merely spiting him and the president by refusing to work more. In fact he argues that in knowledge of his theory people recognized it negatively, thus making the point that the experiment is spurious. The lesson is simply that in social institutional contexts it is often not so simple to separate corroboration and recognition. The more the concatenation of reactions leads to outcomes intended by no one the closer the validating effect resembles corroboration; the more the concatenation of reactions leads to intended outcomes, the closer the validating effect resembles recognition. The experimental behavioral sciences have long known this in practice. To prevent even the possibility of recognition interfering with corroboration, social psychologists often tell stories that are meant to deflect attention from the actual research hypothesis.

CONCLUSIONS

In the introduction I proposed political epistemology as a way to inquire into the rise and decline of particular institutional arrangements. The reasoning behind this move proceeded from an analysis of the ontological characteristics of institutions as existing in regularized action-reaction effect flows. Regularity, I argued, is a continuity of action-reaction effect flows, which must be understood from the stability of that which orients, directs, coordinates, explains, justifies, and legitimizes action, namely discursive, emotive, and kinesthetic understandings. I also argued that the process of understanding becomes objectified into understandings by the three forces

---

36. I suppose this is the reason why the practice of physical skills does have a steadying effect on practitioners' identity as is often maintained in the literature on habits and mental health. Nature is neither prone to moods nor to partial feelings, making it easier to maintain our self-worth as physically skilled than as artistically gifted because the latter can not do without the recognition of others.

of validation. In this chapter I deepened this argument. I began by exploring what it might mean to consider understandings as objects, as is so often done not only in everyday discourses but also in social scientific ones. I found the ontological presuppositions of such a view untenable and then explored how understandings are constituted at the intersection of three kinds of "environments": the social, the context of action in the world, and other already actualized understandings. I found that what is doing the constituting work are three forms of validation, whose phenomenology I unfolded in the sections dedicated to each environment. One of the most important takeaways from this investigation is how the stability of one process (an understanding) must be analyzed in reference to the stability of a possible plurality of other processes (ongoing validations). Following up on this insight we will have to explore in the next chapter how we can model the interaction of various forms of validation as joint contributors to the stability of understandings. Another important result of this investigation is that the three forms of validation are not all created equal. They offer distinct sources of validation, they have a distinct poetics, and yet, corroboration and resonance remain, for their stabilization across time, dependent on continuing recognition. This is true above all for complex discursive understandings about social and political life. Their direct corroboration is scarcely possible. And as Hobbes says in the quote with which I introduced this chapter, now translated into the language of the sociology of understanding, in the absence of possibilities to corroborate understandings one has to take recourse to recognition to gain certainty. The consequence is that networks of authority and propaganda play a much larger role in the formation of those understandings that cannot easily be tested in practice. The crux is that political understandings, that is, those understandings needed to orient and direct politics in the maintenance or transformation of larger institutions, fall squarely into this category. This asymmetry of the role played by the various forms of validation has consequences for how we *should* think about their institutionalization in a polity we might find attractive. The prevalence of recognition in the validation of political understanding needs to be counterbalanced by efforts to keep recognition an open process with real epistemic value. What this involves can be gauged better after a discussion of the dialectics of validation—which is the topic of the next chapter.

4

Dialectics in Spaces of Validation

Even while . . . a person is said to be the same from childhood till he turns into an old man . . . he never consists of the same things . . . he is always being renewed . . . and it's not just in his body, but in his soul too, for none of his manners, customs, opinions, desires, pleasures, pains, or fears ever remain the same but some are coming to be in him while others are passing away . . . each single piece of knowledge has the same fate. For what we call studying exists because knowledge is leaving us, because forgetting is the departure of knowledge, while studying puts back a fresh memory in place of what went away, thereby preserving a piece of knowledge . . .

"DIOTIMA" IN PLATO'S *SYMPOSIUM*

VALIDATION SPACES AND HYPERSPACES

In what follows I will conceptualize the whole complex of understanding co-constituting processes as taking place within a space of validation.[1] Space is a

1. I understand "spaces" here as "fields" in their temporal development. The field metaphor has taken root in the social sciences as an alternative to the systems metaphor and is used to think through complex crosscutting interrelations (e.g., Turner 1974; Bourdieu 1977; Abbott 2001b). The major difference between the two is that the use of "system" is aimed at modeling co-dependencies among fixed elements that provide distinct services or "functions" to an inter-related whole (cf. Parsons 1951). Systems are conceived like organisms, or simultaneous equation systems. As trans-poststructuralists we are all familiar with the critique of the staticism (both in terms of time and constitutive components), which is more often than not implied in the uses of "system." "Field," by contrast, is invested more in allowing one to think through historically contingent co-constitutions where the elements interacting in it get defined and reshaped through the field processes themselves (cf. Martin 2003). There are uses of the field notion, however, that tend to merge with "system." This is true, for example, for one of the true pioneers in this transition, Bourdieu (e.g., 1984, 1990), because in his analysis he is focused on reproduction at the expense of transformation. The network concept has undergone a parallel reinterpretation. Classical sociological network theory is structuralist and was built on the idea of co-dependence of fixed elements; it has found its contender in actor-network theory (e.g., Latour 1999; 2005), which likewise focuses on co-constitution of its elements in flow. For a radical constitutionalist critique of structuralist remainders in actor-network theory, see Law 1999.

convenient metaphor because the intersection of its dimensions lends itself as a scaffolding to think through a series of processes operating simultaneously. In particular it allows for an integrative imagery for the social, doxic, and referential environments of understandings discussed in the last chapter. Thus it provides a framework into which I can place subsequently more detailed discussions of analytically isolated processes. Naming these spaces after validation is appropriate, because recognitions, corroborations, and resonances are the recurring process dynamics, the main ties linking all the components of the space. Remembering that validations are effects of action-reaction dynamics, spaces of validation can be seen as meeting grounds of interfering forces. Together they validate and thus actualize certain understandings for an interconnected network of people within a particular experiential and mnemonic environment. They thereby constitute people's selves, agency, and identity, and ultimately the institutional fabric of the society.

Imagining the Co-Constitution of Understandings, Persons, Events, and Relationships

Relative to one particular person, one can imagine such a space of validation as set up between three dimensions that can be given *quantitative* and *qualitative* interpretations.[2] Two of these capture the force directions for recognitions and corroborations. Resonance can be imagined for simplicity's sake as a force acting "between" corroborations and recognitions.[3] The third dimension symbolizes time and the biographical trajectory of the person in question. The space is populated by understandings of various degrees and kinds of actualization complementing and competing with one another (see figure 4.1). Taken together, these understandings form a profile, an interface through which a particular person interacts with the world at a particular moment in time. The space metaphor brings to the fore that understandings do not only exist in the selective differentiations and integrations they map but also through their situation in the space of validation and thus within the three contexts I have described in the last chapter. The spatial metaphor emphasizes the historicity of understandings as coming into actuality, be-

2. For the purposes of my argument it is important to keep in mind that the dimensions of this space do not simply deal in quantitative variation in spite of the fact that the graphs that follow look very much like mathematical graphs. The dimensions are qualitatively heterogeneous while still carrying also a sense—but in no way a precise sense—of quantitative variation. They should look more like medieval maps than technical graphs.

3. This is a reduction of the model to fit into the limits of a Euclidian mind with its currently preferred representations on paper. In principle, resonances would require a fourth dimension since its validating effect is different from recognitions and corroborations. In the model I have de facto depicted resonances as combinations of recognitions and corroborations.

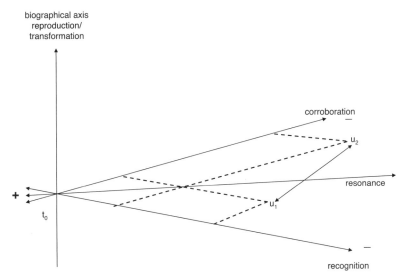

Figure 4.1. Validation space relative to one person

ing maintained and changed through changing constellations of validating forces. What it means to feel more certain in response to a particular validating event, whether or not and how it is meaningful to compare the degrees to which understandings are actualized, is regulated by meta-understandings.

In terms of the graph, validating events have two different kinds of effects. First, positive validations (i.e., affirmation as "true," "reliable," "good," etc.) propel understandings closer to the biographical axis, weaving them more deeply into the fabric of the self. Negative validations (i.e., throwing into doubt as "problematic" or rejecting as "misleading," "false," etc.) have the opposite effect. One of the horizontal axes symbolizes recognizing forces, the other corroborating ones. Resonances emerge between understandings, likewise driving understandings toward or away from the biographical axis. Understandings' proximity to the biographical axis represents their relative degree of actualization (i.e., the degree to which they are seen fit to guide action). Second, validations maintain understandings in actuality. In the absence of renewed validation an understanding gradually looses certainty by virtue of the kind of entropy better known as forgetting. In the imagery of the spatial metaphor, an understanding not renewed by validations drifts away from the biographical axis; it becomes less prominent as an aspect of that person. Thus at any moment a field of more or less actualized understandings emerges that constitutes a human organism as a person endowed with a particular profile of agentic and reflexive capabilities and conflicts as well as with a particular identity.

Figure 4.2 provides a schema for the reproduction of two different under-

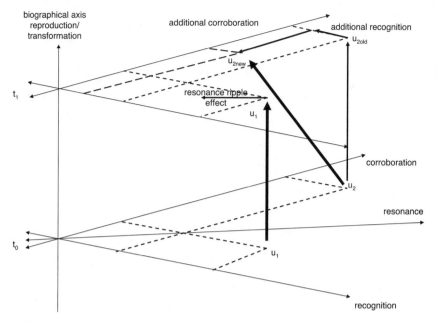

Figure 4.2. The reproduction of understandings and the transformation of people

standings (u_1 and u_2) from one moment in time (t_0) to the next (t_1). While one understanding (u_1) is reproduced through the interplay of an equivalent mix of validating forces, which keeps it at the same level of actuality (i.e., distance from the biographical axis), the other understanding (u_2) is not only reproduced but also gains in actuality through some more powerful combination of validating forces. Graphically this is represented by a movement toward the biographical axis (u_{2new}). The metaphor of the space of validation invites the analysis of ripple effects. Through resonances, these supplementary validations of u_2 may also have a further validating effect on u_1, which, depending on the kinds of resonances it has with u_2, may mean that it now is more (shown in graph as u_{1new}) or less actualized.[4] A person can now be seen as the self-similar reproduction of a certain profile of actual and possible understandings across time.[5] In other words, personhood is the institutionalization

4. Foreign language learning may serve as an illustrative example. The cognateness of two languages is a particular kind of resonance. If as a German speaker I learn French, English, Urdu, and Thai, my efforts to stabilize my French are in all likelihood also helping to maintain my English, as both share an immense set of closely related words and grammatical constructions. My Urdu will get a mild boost in reproducing the shared word stems and grammatical features of Indo-European, but my Thai as a language unrelated to the others will not benefit at all.
5. Personhood as the totality of self-similar understandings in the course of time has to be differentiated from identity, which comprises only a subset of person constituting understandings, namely, his or her identifications with the world.

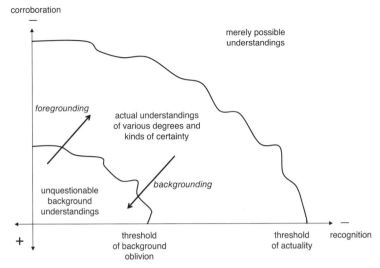

Figure 4.3. Possible, actual, and background understandings

of a profile of understandings. One may thus wish to ask, for example, "what constellation of validating forces maintains a particular person?"

The spatial metaphor also enables us to imagine the historical transformation of understandings, for example, from a mere "hypothesis," "assumption," or "hunch" to esteemed "knowledge," "fact," or "belief" and back to regretful "error," "misunderstanding," or "wishful thinking" as movements toward or away from the biographical axis. It also raises the question, what constellations of validation may move a particular understanding or set of understandings across the two thresholds that I have referred to earlier. These are first, the threshold of actuality where merely possible understandings become actual and thus action guiding and second, the threshold separating two types of actual understandings, namely those with various degrees of never quite perfect certainty from those forming the unquestionable background, where understandings recede from consciousness due to incessant, unidirectional validation (see figure 4.3). In other words, the spatial metaphor invites us to think in terms of processes of actualization, of backgrounding and foregrounding.

Economies of Validation

Thinking in terms of constellations of different forms of validation invites the question of relative substitutability among them. Substitutions clearly take place within one and the same form. A Stasi officer whose assessment of a particular situation was first recognized by his immediate superior and then by the district head is likely to be the more certain for it. Presenting one's own argument in a party meeting as recognized by one Marx quotation and substituting it for that of another may or may not make a difference, depending on how the text in question is *currently* esteemed by the party. Substituting a Lenin or current–first secretary quote for a Marx may be advantageous. The effect of substitutions among recognitions is thus dependent on the ways in which the authority of the source is evaluated. Corroborations are often substitutable too. Different kinds of tests may be deemed equally supportive of a particular hypothesis. In the GDR a person's survival in a Nazi concentration camp as a member of the communist underground was as good a credential to prove an antifascist attitude as risking one's life as a spy for the KGB. And the same holds for resonances. Highlighting the formalist stylistics in a novel was as damning a comment as pointing to the defeatism of its main character.

Substitutions also take place among different forms of validation, however. In efforts to maintain the validity of a particular understanding it is quite common to substitute recognitions for corroborations and vice versa (figure 4.4). If a particular assessment of the performance of the economy is not borne out by everyday experience, one may be tempted to find an expert to lend it credibility. A boy who cares about a masculine self-image and whose father is stingy in appreciating his masculinity may try to corroborate it instead by taking himself through a number of trials of courage. An artist whose name does not create ahs and ohs will have to win admiration through her performance. Again, the space metaphor proves to be a useful device to

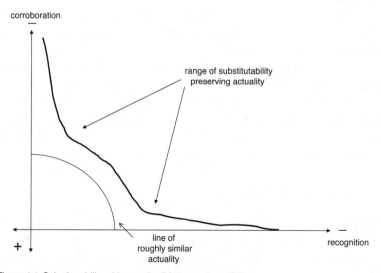

Figure 4.4. Substitutability of forms of validation and credibility

think with, now through the possibilities and limits of substitution between various forms of validation. While the substitution of one form of validation for another is possible, substitution beyond a certain point may go hand in hand with credibility losses. I have shown above how Walter Ulbricht banked in 1957 on the corroboration of socialism's claim to superiority through fast economic growth. Once this hope did not materialize, propaganda (and thus recognition) became ever more widely used and more carefully organized. This substitution worked for a certain time. Yet to remain credible, promises have to maintain a certain balance between the forms of validation. In the conclusions to this book I will discuss the effects of the creeping loss of positive corroborations in the 1980s and its attempted substitution by more recognition for party functionaries' understandings of socialism. What precisely the effect of such substitutions is on the certainty of understandings, where exactly the boundaries lie for the substitutability of a concrete validating force by another within the same category or across, is governed by the meta-understandings relative to a particular person and context.[6]

Validation Hyperspaces

The spaces of validation I have sketched in the last section were drawn in reference to one single person. What about more comprehensive social wholes, then? These can be imagined now as hyperspaces, or spaces of spaces in the following way. Individual spaces are open to environmental influences along all three axes of validation. These connect individual persons as poles of crystallization with each other in a force field spun up through their shared entanglement in thickets of authority relations (listening to each other, to the same experts, watching the same news casts, etc.) through their subjection to the same corroborating events affecting them in similar ways (war combat, unemployment, etc.) and their exposure to non-discursive environments (city- and landscapes, soundscapes and smellscapes) triggering certain resonances at the expense of others. The links between persons can in this way be both personal and communal. Everybody's directly connected to others who serve at the same time as conduits for the influences of more

---

6. The meta-understandings, which organize spaces of validation that are generated, maintained, altered, and abandoned in their own spaces. Both can partially overlap but also go beyond those of their first-order. Thus understandings refer back to other understandings; any concrete differentiation and integration of the world is dependent on others. Yet this is not infinite semiosis because these orderings are not just symbolic but are also emotive and kinesthetic. So yes, it is "understandings all the way down," but this all the way down is a heterogeneous bunch of different understandings across different modes. And this heterogeneity creates stability as understandings buttress each other like thin sticks that, connected in the right way, can create an amazingly solid edifice.

distant others. Notice that this model is not additive in spite of its modularity; it remains thoroughly co-constitutive. Individual spaces with personal, personality-shaping profiles of understandings are always already a part of social hyperspaces. Outside of these, following the logic of Wittgenstein's private language argument, individual understandings could not become actualized in continuing validation. One could say, then, that the individual spaces simultaneously co-constitute one another. We are only persons in relation to other persons. This does not mean, however, that individual spaces are created equal in relation to others. Due to their multiplex differential placements in authority networks and unequal access to experiences, their influence on others can be quite unequal too. Hyperspaces are structured by ideologies, practices, and emotional cultures, distributing authority over individual spaces and kinds of understandings in highly structured, unequal ways; they distribute access to corroborating experiences and indicators differentially; they entangle people in differing kinds of memory cultures.

The boundaries of these larger social wholes lie precisely where they fold back onto each other in the sense that across boundaries validation effects no longer entangle more persons. If we take the notion of six degrees of separation seriously, there are few places in the world that are not somehow connected to form a truly global hyperspace. Yet the relations between these individuals cannot only be highly asymmetrical, but the epistemic ideologies, practices, and emotions I have just mentioned create semi-insulated "clouds" within these hyperspaces characterized by particularly dense authority relations, shared access to experiences and indicators, as well as memory cultures. Simple examples for such clouds are professionals, such as the Stasi officers, who have a particular expertise that can only get recognized and corroborated within their secret activities, their relationships and (com-)memorative practices. In chapters 7 and 8 I will provide a narrative of how such a cloud within a larger validation hyperspace comes about as a mini civil society among dissidents within a larger socialist whole. Large social wholes should therefore be imagined as an assembly of intersecting clouds, not as a homogeneous space.

The validation model emphasizes a distinct way in which human beings and their social lives are inextricably intertwined. The classical market model presupposes the circulation of goods in one direction and that of money in the other, both forming something of a two-component social glue between autonomous actors. Classical cultural models come in two forms. One has remained within an exchange paradigm, albeit emphasizing circulating items (e.g., gifts) and logics of exchange (e.g., mutual obligations), differentiating these exchanges from market transactions. The other has looked to the dispersion of ideas and skills through mimesis enabled by various peaceful and violent structures of encounter. *This book looks above all at the flow of validation effects across individual spaces through which they are at the same time constituted.* What distinguishes the validation hyperspace from markets or other interconnected flow models is that it does not assume reciprocity or "sharedness."[7] This model does not replace the other two flow models, but it adds a different perspective that can contribute significantly to our understandings of how sociality exists and operates. In the penultimate section of this chapter I will provide a sketch of how validation figures into processes of innovation and mimetic dispersion.

In spite of the seeming complexity of the whole, the model remains economical through its fractal character, singling out a very limited number of processes that together form, maintain, or erode understandings and institutions. And yet we still do not know the processes of validation well enough for a fieldwork-ready analytic. What is missing in particular is an analysis of how the microdynamics of validation can create feedback loops affecting the conditions of their own repetition and thus the emergence of path-dependent processes. For that we need a much closer look at the dialectics of validation.

THE DIALECTICS OF VALIDATION

To comprehend the dynamics of understanding, I have so far discussed three different kinds of dialectics. (1) In the introductory chapter I have introduced the dialectic between different modes of understanding. The impetus for change is derived from the tension occurring when, for example, an emotive understanding (e.g., love for a particular person) comes to be at odds with a discursive one ("This person is a class enemy!"). (2) In the discussion on the production of the three validating forces in the last chapter, I have explained how the validating effect is in each case the result of the inflection of the understanding in something else: another person, the outcome of an event, or other sets of understandings following the pattern of action-reaction effect flows. (3) In the previous section, I have discussed the dialectics among different forms of validation, especially their economies of substitution. What is of interest in that dialectic is how, for example, a shift from maintaining an understanding by recognition to actualizing it in corroboration transforms the ways in which this understanding informs agency. In what follows, I will concentrate on the multiple effects of the three validating forces not only on the understanding itself but also on the very conditions for the possibility of future validations, this is to say, on the institutional fabric that makes the occurrence of certain validations

7. It has in this sense an affinity with Greg Urban's (2001) analysis of discourse as existing in circulation.

more or less likely. Thus a view is opened onto a fourth dialectic, that between an episode of validation on the one hand and on the other its consequence for the authority networks in which persons operate; the readiness of persons to test understandings or to find indicators; and the validity of a body of understanding persons already hold—one could also say their memory. In the conclusions, I will address the question under which conditions these dialectics remain substantively open, thus allowing for the necessary adjustment of understandings to maintain agency in changing social circumstances. By the same token, I will show how these dialectics can come to be short-circuited to degenerate into a circular reproduction of understandings that appear well founded while losing their orienting power. In other words, this fourth kind of dialectic will provide insight into self-amplifying epistemic processes that can lead to a dramatic break between our knowledge of the world and our experience of it.

The main purpose of the following sections is the development of a set of heuristics that will allow me to think through the feedback loops between the production of validating effects and the conditions for their production. An adaptation of Fritz Heider's (1958, 174–217) balance theory serves as a good starting point for this purpose.[8] It allows me to devise another set of visual metaphors as heuristics for the systematic analysis of the dynamics unfolding *along and across* the three validation axes of spaces of validation. One could say that each of them zooms into the microdynamics of a specific part of the validation space. The center of Heider's model is formed by an analysis of triadic relations, represented graphically by a triangle. Indeed, validating forces can be conceived as produced through the dynamic interplay of minimally three "poles." Two of these are the same in each form of validation: A person (P) and his or her understanding (u). The third pole is the point of inflection specific to each validating force: another person's (Alter or A) perceived evaluation of the understanding; the outcome (O)

---

8. Heider was interested in the development of general social psychological laws. He surmised that some triangular relationships among two persons and an object would be inherently stable, because they were "balanced," while others were inherently instable, exhibiting a general tendency of change toward a balanced state. While thinking the general question of stability and change through in terms of triadic relations is an old figure of thought, Heider's contribution lies principally in formalizing the relationships. I use his mode of formalization as a heuristic rather than as a lawlike proposition, because I think Heider's nomological project ultimately failed for the same reasons that Festinger's cognitive dissonance theory got stuck. They are unable to account for the cultural specifics of the situations in question that can alter the dynamics profoundly. For a brief social-psychological evaluation of Heider's research program, see Petty and Cacioppo (1996 [1981], 127–33). Originally, I have developed the framework presented here on my own as a tool to generate questions teasing out the particularities of validating situations. I am grateful to Paula England for alerting me to Heider's work.

of a practical engagement with the world shedding light on u; and finally the Person's other sets of actual action guiding or possible (known but not action guiding) understandings (marked as AU or PU) resonating with the understanding in question.

Recognition

The validating force of recognition emerges in the refraction of one person's understanding in that of another person taken to be an authority. For purposes of arriving at a simple schema highlighting the dialectical relationships, I will drastically simplify the more nuanced discussion of the preceding chapter by assuming that the relationship between each person and the understanding u under consideration can be more or less captured with "P is to some degree certain that u holds" (signified by a plus sign in the graphs) or "P is to some degree convinced that u does not hold" (signified by a minus sign). In the interest of developing useful heuristics I thus disregard for the moment that actualized understandings are constituted in what they mean to us through their validation histories within a web of resonances. This includes the possibility that these understandings may have a mixed or ambiguous validation history of which we are more or less aware. Moreover, I have assumed that the quality of the authority relationship between the Person and Alter can be summarized as either "Alter is an authority for the Person regarding the understanding u in this context" (in the graphs signified by a plus sign) or "Alter is not an authority regarding u in this context" (signified by a minus sign). So here (figure 4.5), then, is a visual metaphor that may help to think through the dialectics of recognizing events. The recognition dimension of the Person's individual space of validation cuts right through the P–u side of the triangle below (I have swiveled it to form a vertical axis pointing to the "self/identity/agency" circle that represents the biographical axis in figure 4.1).[9]

Figure 4.5 depicts a situation in which the Person can compare her evaluation of an understanding with that of Alter. In the simplest case she asks Alter (action "a." within the main triangle) what he thinks about her understanding u. Either directly or indirectly, Alter then signals agreement/disagreement with the Person (reaction "b.").[10] This action-reaction sequence

---

9. If the authority relationship is mutual, then one can also say that Alter's recognition axis cuts right through the A–u side of the triangle. Accordingly, we would look at a connector between both spaces as a part of an overarching social validation hyperspace.

10. Again, for the moment I will have to ignore the fact that the comparison of the evaluation of understandings is no trivial feat because it involves, for example, interpretative effort to settle whether different formulations of discursive understandings or expressions of emotive ones mean the same thing, or likewise whether similar expressions may not in the end occlude

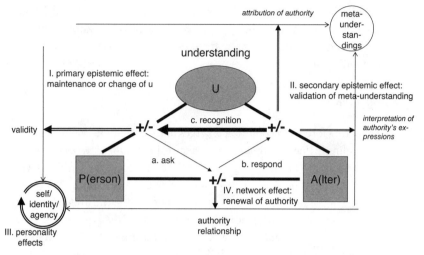

Figure 4.5. Validation through recognition

entails a number of different effects: Recognition (arrow "c.") is the *primary epistemic effect* manifesting itself in an enhanced/diminished certainty of the Person in the understanding in question. Recognition is at the same time a contribution to the institutionalization of *u* as a set of differentiations and integrations enduring in time (Roman numeral I). However, there are a number of further effects. There are first two *secondary epistemic effects*. The recognition of *u* may qua resonance change the validity of other understandings the person holds or knows about. Then, with any situation of validation, the meta-understandings that govern it may come under scrutiny as well (Roman numeral II). In the case of recognition, the meta-understandings governing the attribution of authority or the schemes used to interpret the utterances of the authority may become further cemented or they may come to be questioned. Four effects reconstitute the person (Roman numeral III). With the change in certainty comes a change in our ability to act in areas where the understanding in question is important. In other words, there is an *agency effect*. Since understandings also identify us in a particular way with the world, and since our identities are a snapshot of such links at any moment, there is also an *identity effect* (Glaeser 2000).[11] More, to the de-

---

differences, and if there are differences whether these understandings are comparable and if so in which way, etc.

11. The dialectic between recognition and authority has been noted in the history of political thought. Again with characteristic acuteness, Hobbes (1994, 52): "To agree with an opinion is to honor, as being a sign of approving his judgment and wisdom. To dissent, is dishonour, and an upbraiding of error, and (if the dissent be in many things) of folly."

gree that these understandings are not actively separated from self-making, recognizing it reproduces or undermines a particular form of *reflexivity*. Finally, by triggering positive or negative feelings, recognition creates more or less powerful *emotive meta-understandings* to consult again or shun the consulted authority in the future. These appear in addition to and possibly in contradiction to the understandings that led the Person to attribute authority to Alter, for example as an expert. This brings us to the final effect. In the validating event the very authority of Alter is on the line for renewal or change. Recognition is, therefore, constitutive of social relationships; one could say it has a *network effect* (Roman numeral IV).

With such a formidable list of epistemic, person, and network effects to consider, the question appears, whether it is possible to create a heuristic to form simple hypotheses about the likelihood and direction of effects. Such a heuristic should pay particular attention to the dynamic processes exacted by a particular episode of recognition. Figure 4.6 presents such a heuristic. It lists eight basic recognizing constellations generated by the simple combinatorial exercise of listing all possibilities to distribute two values (plus/minus) over the three relations in the triangle. The eight constellations fall into four cases with two roughly symmetrical constellations each. In what follows I will work through these four cases one by one. I will label them by their most likely effect, namely, amplification, irrelevance, differentiation, and reversal. This may appear at first as a more or less mechanical exercise. Yet, I have

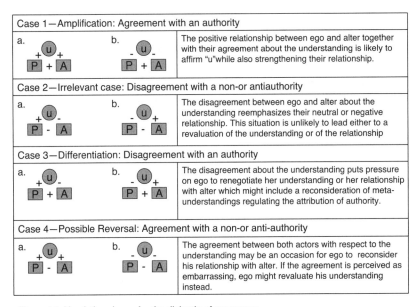

Figure 4.6. Heuristic schema for the dialectic of resonance

found working with this heuristic very helpful in analyzing validation events ethnographically. Its particular merit lies in suggesting counterfactuals, raising more precise questions of why under a particular set of circumstances certain effects have materialized rather than others. I have tried to illustrate the abstract formulations wherever I thought this would help with brief examples taken from the history of socialism.

Case 1: Amplification through an agreement with authority

In the first two constellations (1a. and 1b.), the combination of a positive authority relationship and agreement produces recognition that reproduces both understanding and authority at the same time. In this rosy situation there is no reason to question anything; understandings, social relations, and meta-understandings seem in perfect alignment with one another. As a boundary case, where the relationship to Alter is neutral, the agreement may also lead to the subsequent endowment of Alter with authority. Case one transposed onto an entire society represents the socialist party ideal of monolithic intentionality (figure 4.7). The vanguard party can be imagined to function as a "switching agent" (in the scheme a universal Alter) that brings everybody in alignment with everybody else.[12] In this way the unity of the party becomes the unity of the people. The model also offers a way to think through the power of the vanguard party concept. As long as the party really forms a strong set of evaluations within a much less organized and much less opinionated field, and as long as party members do not accept outsiders as authorities about understandings, while outsiders know party members who do indeed possess authority for them, the party stands a very high chance of succeeding with its ideal. For the same reason the party was happy enough to accept the neutrality of its citizens toward its own project. With a vanguard already aligned in agreement, everybody would sooner or later become a supporter. The only attitude that could not be tolerated was a rejecting (negative) attitude toward the state, and above all an organized one. It was seen as inimical because a switching dynamic in opposition to the state's plans was seen as possible in the form of a contaminating chain reaction.

Case 2: Irrelevance through disagreement with a nonauthority

Disagreements with a nonauthority may work out very differently under different meta-understandings. If the Person really feels indifference

---

12. This is the situation Peirce (1992, 117) had in mind as the "method of authority" for fixing belief.

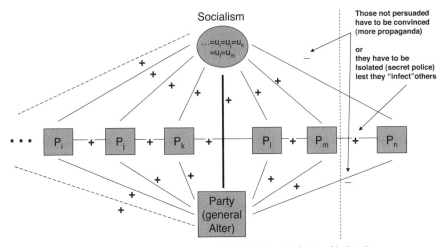

The understandings about socialism, socialist identities and forms of belonging mutually support each other.

Figure 4.7. Monolithic intentionality

toward Alter, her disagreement does not produce a negative recognizing effect; it does not produce a reason to reformulate u or to invest Alter with authority. The episode is in fact irrelevant. Yet a particular boundary case is interesting. Manichaean meta-understandings (and socialism was as I have shown in chapters 1 and 2 shot through with Manichaeanisms) tend to divide the world not into authorities and nonauthorities but into authorities and *anti*-authorities. Under these circumstances, the disagreement of an anti-authority can produce a recognizing effect ("my enemy's disapproval is automatically a sign that I am on the right track"). The consequence of Manichaean thinking is that no agreement or disagreement is ever irrelevant, leading to the hypervigilantism I indicate in figure 4.7 with the effort to radically isolate dissenters, lest they become the root cause of an understandings-switching domino effect gradually infecting ever wider strata of society with party critical attitudes.

Case 3: Differentiation through disagreement with an authority

This is the most interesting case of all and will be of central importance for the conclusions of this book. What happens when an authority disagrees? Depending on the circumstances, Alter can lose authority, either of them may adjust their respective evaluation of the understanding to suit the other, both may agree to redefine a shared understanding, or either or both may begin to doubt the principles by which authority is attributed, that is, the

meta-understandings at play here.[13] Case 3 was, in practice, even where formulated as an ideal on paper, an acute nightmare scenario for the party—at
least in all those cases where there was an official party line. It feared that
dissenting voices endowed with authority might "infect" ever more people
with their deviance, eventually leading to "fraction building" and "division-
ist" (*spalterische*) tendencies, draining the vanguard party of its power to
act. Accordingly, such voices needed to be de-authorized or isolated instantaneously (right side of figure 4.7). Historically, the reaction of the party to
case 3 scenarios was purging the dissenters by exclusion, imprisonment, and
during Stalin's purges: by assassination.

Meta-understandings that favor quick de-authorization of anybody who
disagrees with particular understandings effectively remove these understandings from critical discourse. Thus a strong tendency emerges to natu-
ralize and essentialize these sheltered understandings, which is—given the
nature of representation as aspectual translation—always also a fetishization. I have argued with Wittgenstein (1984c) in the last chapter, that at some
point fetishization is inevitable, because skepticism—and thus the very dynamic underlying case 3— has to come to a stop somewhere if we ever want
to act. The question is, then, not whether or not we fetishize but just whether
our fetishizations are currently the right ones, whether they are good enough
for what we need them to accomplish. Without batting an eyelash we are
ready to radically de-authorize anybody who doubts that the earth circles
around the sun. Yet, should Catholics consider someone anathema who
doubts the wisdom of the doctrine of papal infallibility? By the same token,
in a strikingly similar case, are socialist party members who consider anybody an enemy who doubts the wisdom of vanguardism already on the best
way to lose their grip on reality because they are caught up in unsuitable
fetishizations? Is there any *ex ante* way of telling which fetishisms are good
to have and which ones are not? All properly functioning democracies thrive
on meta-understandings that prevent people in those areas in which they
are really democratic from de-authorizing disagreeing others. Instead, they
have institutional arrangements ensuring that dissenters will be listened to

13. Goffman (1955) provides a fascinating analysis of such mutual adjustment in verbal interaction, which requires, as Goffman argues persuasively, some minimal mutual authorization.
Genuine communication is therefore always risky for the participants included. Following this
logic, folk wisdom has it that those wanting to maintain their understandings (with "tenacity"
in Peirce's [1992] words) are best off closing their ears (and by extension their eyes and mouths).
By the same token, the very address of those considered inferior to those seen as their superiors
has always been understood as an act of impudent equalization. Royal authority (as absolute
autonomy) has therefore often been protected by strict interdictions to even meet the royals'
eye. The flip side of this knowledge of mutual authorization in communicative contact is the
hope that the very act of conversing may eventually lead to a resolution of conflict.

with an open mind. This is what we mean with an "open society." Yet, to some extent openness comes to an end when action must be taken. All democracies therefore have institutionalized procedures that effectively close debate. Anybody who still disagrees after the debate has formally been ended and gets for all practical purposes de-authorized—at least for some time. Good democracies, effective organizations, and reasonable people foreground and background, fetishize and de-fetishize the right things at the right time.

Case 4: Possible reversal through agreement with a nonauthority

This too is an interesting case, for it may spring a surprise. The nonauthorized or possibly even anti-authorized Alter agrees with the Person. Should Alter thus get authority; should the Person, possibly alarmed by the unsuspected concurrence, hasten to revalue her own assessment of the understanding in question? Here is the root of the embarrassment of getting applause from the wrong side, which in socialism was used ad nauseam to discredit criticism as thinly veiled enmity. Only if the Person is wholly indifferent to Alter ("steeled" in socialist jargon) will there be absolutely no recognizing effect from the agreement. Of course, indifference has to be produced rather actively by techniques of epistemically neutering the other.[14] Socialism made a strong effort to establish the continuous demonstration of a firm class standpoint as the marker to differentiate people who should be listened to from people whose opinions should be disregarded. The very possibility that the agreement with a nonauthority may lead to a change in the quality of the relationship also captures socialism's fear with respect to tactical alliances with parts of the class enemy (e.g., the United States and Britain in World War II) against a common enemy (e.g., Nazi Germany). Communists who had spent the war years in the West were constantly suspected of having come under the sway of their host countries (i.e., attribute authority to them and thus be susceptible to what they say). They had to go to extra lengths to perform their allegiance. In the late 1940s and early 1950s all over Eastern Europe fear about communists with Western contacts was whipped up in the conjunction with the various "Noel Field–affairs" (e.g., the Rajk trial in Hungary or the

---

14. Historically, particular forms of ideological constructs dividing humanity into different categories of being were employed to accomplish this task. Common are oppositions between city-sages and country-bumpkins, teachers and students, experts and lay persons. The most radical are human ontologies employing biological markers as boundaries between categories. These assist men in their de-authorization of women, people of Western European decent to disregard everybody else, Nazis to decide which life is worth breeding and which should be murdered. Paradigms for the analysis of such cases of othering were provided by Said 1978, Fabian 1983, and Todorov 1992 [1982].

Slánsky trial in Czechoslovakia) in which communists were accused of having become agents of American intelligence services through the offices of Noel Field, who was once a member of the U.S. Office for Strategic Services (a CIA precursor) and who helped numerous communists to survive World War II in the West (Barth and Schweizer 2004). In chapter 9 it will become apparent how this "applause from the wrong side" was systematically used by the Stasi as a corroboration of inimical intentions on the side of dissidents.

Corroboration

Figure 4.8 shows the basic structure of a corroborating event. A particular understanding is investigated (typically retrospectively) in light of identified outcomes of events that potentially reflect on its validity. The relation between the Person and understanding is, as before, reduced to "is certain/ has doubts about u" (represented by a plus sign respectively a minus sign). In the case of direct corroboration, the relationship between the Person and the event are glossed as "does/does not have significant influence on the outcome" (i.e., the Person has/does not have agency) represented through a plus/minus sign. In the case of indirect corroboration the activity connecting the Person to an event is a search for the existence of indicators reflecting positively or negatively on the understanding. A plus sign means having found such an indicator. The relationship between outcome and understanding may be interpreted as "O reflects favorably (positively) or unfavorably (negatively) on u." The inflection process generating the validating force as a resultant is captured by the small triangle in the graph connecting all the plus and minus signs (Δabc). Again, this may be interpreted as an action-reaction effect flow. For example, setting up an experiment (action, a.) and interpreting its result (reaction b.) entails a validating effect (c.). This time however the reaction is produced by an impersonal environment to be interpreted by the Person.[15] The logic of this inflection is governed on the one hand by the extant meta-understandings pertaining to the link between understanding, action, and outcome as well as to the proper interpretation of the outcome. On the other hand, it has to come to terms with a potentially recalcitrant person-environment interaction.

As in the case of recognition before, corroboration produces a diverse set

---

15. This makes apparent that Wittgenstein's regress may loom here, at least for discursive and perhaps also for emotive understandings. The recognition of correct procedure in a network of authority is therefore important (Kuhn's [1992] "normal science"). For kinesthetic understandings, however, the Person's action (pushing a thread through the eye of a needle) and reaction (pulling it through on the other side) are effective and quite self-sufficient contributions to institutionalizing the skill of "threading."

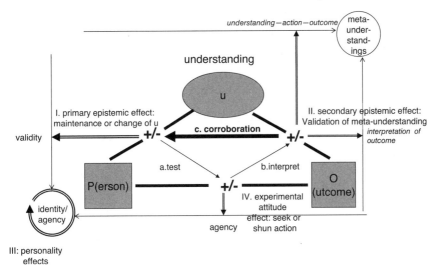

Figure 4.8. Validation through corroboration

of effects. There is a primary epistemic effect strengthening or weakening *u* (I). Thus the recognizing situation is part of the institutionalization of *u*. The secondary epistemic effects consist in the validation of other understandings resonating with *u* and the validation of the meta-understandings at play in the corroborating event (II). Then there are person effects. The Person's sense of agency will be affected as the reinvigorated or weakened understandings will rise or diminish her sense of orientation and direction. Her identity is affected to the degree that the understanding contains relevant identifications (III).[16] Most importantly, however, since the validation is likely to create positive or negative emotions, the Person will have a motive, a powerful emotive meta-understanding leading her to seek out with confidence or avoid such corroborating situations in the future. This could be called the *experimental attitude effect* (IV).

A heuristic model (figure 4.9) of case constellations can thus be developed in analogy to the one I have just discussed for recognitions. Again, the first two cases describe four stable constellations in which there is no pressure to reconsider anything. In the first case (amplification), the Person's assessment of *u* is in line with how it is inflected by the outcomes of the event. The world appears transparent and predictable. The second case describes two constellations that the Person can write off as irrelevant. In the first constellation, the event's outcome would reflect negatively upon the Person's

---

16. Unlike in the case of resonance, there is typically no effect on the Person's modes of reflexivity, unless the world of happenings becomes anthropomorphized as "speaking."

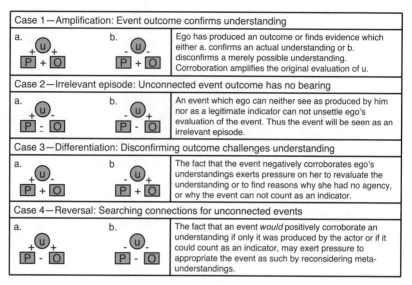

Figure 4.9. Heuristic schema for the dialectic of corroboration

assessment of the understandings in question, if she would have to see herself as the author of the event or if the event's outcome would have to be taken seriously as an indicator. Here is an example for case 2a. Official socialist doctrine maintained that capitalism had, after World War II, entered a phase of accelerating decline going hand in hand with mass unemployment (u) (e.g., Ponomarjow et al. 1984). However, in Western Europe mass unemployment quickly gave way to economic miracles, leading to historically unprecedented employment levels (O). This outcome can be disregarded because the Marxist-Leninist philosophy of history—functioning here as a relevant meta-understanding—covers an interpretation of this indicator as irrelevant for the understanding in question, because the crisis theory predicts boom and bust cycles as normal local variations on the way to inevitable doom. In the second constellation (case 2b) the event outcome's seeming confirmation of the understanding is also seen as irrelevant. Just for the sake of it somebody conjectures that "capitalism is economically superior after all" (u), offering as proof West German statistics indicating rapidly vanishing unemployment (O). Again the meta-understandings predicting boom and bust cycles as well as doubts about Western statistics readily explain why one should not be misled by such appearances and why it is thus better to ignore them.

As before, the cases of differentiation (3) and reversal (4) are unstable and for that reason of great interest for analyzing change. Case 3 presents the two constellations that negatively corroborate the Person's understandings, thus exerting pressure on him to change his evaluation of the understanding. It is the classic case of a test or a search for evidence with a negative result.

Here lies the heart, the beauty, and the power of fallibilistic epistemologies (Popper 1971). Of course, especially when this outcome is unexpected or appears undesirable, this may trigger a reconsideration of the whole corroborating situation. In order to preserve his evaluation of the understanding, the Person may feel the urge to reinterpret the constellation as one without properly corroborating power by reconsidering the links between understanding, action, and outcome. His argument might be that the concrete constellation under consideration is actually not a proper case forcing the differentiation of understandings, but much rather an irrelevant episode of the case 2 variety. He can do so by reinterpreting the relevant meta-understandings. Often this is done by adding a certain casuistry, bracketing "anomalous" cases. This is the kind of maneuver that Wittgenstein has in mind when he argues against the possibility of following a rule "privately." In the science studies literature, maneuvers that effectively explain away an "anomaly" are known as "ad hocing" (cf. Kuhn 1962). The favorite historical example is the continuous, ultimately Byzantine extension of Ptolemy's geocentric model of the universe.[17] In everyday reasoning there are proverbs, such as "exceptions prove the rule," that can be called upon as meta-understandings to save a favored understanding against countervailing evidence.

Case 4 presents another instance of a potentially dramatic reversal. The fact that the two constellations in question would corroborate an actual understanding if only the event could be seen as produced by the Person or as a legitimate indicator (the minus sign indicates they are currently not) provides an incentive to appropriate the event as legitimate. What this maneuver is supposed to accomplish is the reinterpretation of case 4 as a de facto case 1. This can be accomplished by either disregarding, reinterpreting, or in the last resort changing the meta-understandings originally at play. Manichaean understandings of the world facilitate such maneuvers greatly. They often give rise to conspiracy theories working in accordance with case 4 constellations. Socialist show-trials worked according to this pattern. The typical understanding motivating them was that the accused was an agent of the enemy. Since there was initially only irrelevant evidence (the minus sign between P and O), then one could reverse the case by suddenly finding a surprise witness or, better even, a pressed confession, that makes the evidence suddenly relevant. If this sounds like an odd case at first, consider how Stasi officer Martin Voigt described the way in which the SED handled successes and failures of the country: "Every success owed itself to the relentless efforts of the party; it confirmed its wise politics; every misfortune was the

---

17. Hallyn (1993) and others have argued that this take on the Ptolemaic system is a rhetorical move that normalizes modern Western scientific meta-understandings, thus eliding the very different scientific culture of ancient Mediterranean and Medieval European times.

work of the enemy, it confirmed his ill-intentions." He hastens to add: "That of course is no different in the West." And as if to prove the universality of his point he quotes a German proverb. "Success has many fathers; failure is an orphan." In the language of the model: the more than questionable agentic link between the Person and the event outcome is simply claimed into existence where this maneuver seems to corroborate understandings reflecting positively on the Person (case 4a).

Resonance

Resonances (figure 4.10) emerge through the fit between an understanding in question and at least one or possibly a whole body of relevant actual or possible understandings (in the graph, AU respectively PU). Resonance has a primary epistemic effect on the understanding in question (I) and a secondary epistemic effect on the meta-understandings governing the choice of the body of understandings brought up in comparison with u (II). What makes resonance special is, however, a third epistemic effect best called *memory effect*. Due to the fact that the point of inflection is provided by other understandings, the sheer act of invoking them (the action-reaction effect Δabc: search-recall-resonance) makes them subject to resonance as well. In other words, every search and recall is a component act of ongoing memorization. This is the chief reason why a dialectic ensues in the first place. As in the case of resonance and corroboration the feedback loop is amplified by the fact that the experience of resonance can be accompanied by powerful emotions with a positive or negative hedonic tone. These create a motive, leading people to either seek again or attempt to prevent similar retrieval situations in the future. Here lies the root of sentimentalism and nostalgia, but also of repression. Finally, resonance has a number of person effects (III), reproducing or altering a person's agency and identity.

The heuristic for the exploration of the dialectics of resonance distinguishes, in the by-now-familiar combinatorial fashion, eight constellations falling into four cases.[18] As before, the first two typically confirm existing directions of evaluation, while the latter two can lead to significant changes. In the first case (amplification), the Person's assessment of a particular understanding is consistent with a body of actual understandings previously

---

18. The distinction into cases requires a differentiation of the relevant body of understandings that is used to evaluate the merit of the understanding under consideration into a body of merely possible understandings (PU, that is, those we do not take to be action guiding and hence the minus sign in the graphs that will follow) and a body of actually held understandings (AU, i.e., those understandings we actually use as action guiding and that are therefore connected with a plus sign in the graph to the Person).

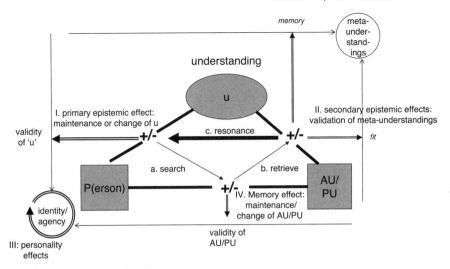

Figure 4.10. Validation through resonance

acquired. The Person's trust or doubt in *u* becomes further strengthened, as does the body of understandings invoked for comparison, which is thus moved further toward assimilation into the unquestionable background. How exactly the dynamics of the second case unfold, depends on the meta-understandings governing the process. Since the Person already harbors significant doubts about the body of understandings invoked, its incompatibility with his evaluation of *u* will be in many cases simply deemed irrelevant. If the body of understandings is part of a Manichaean setup and the Person considers it as abominable (let's say fascism for a communist), its incompatibility with a positively assessed understanding will further actualize the latter. By the same token, a mildly doubtful evaluation of *u* will turn to contamination by positive association with the despised body of understandings.[19] The logic at work here is that an understanding that is incompatible with a set of terribly false understandings must be the more valid for it.

The third case (differentiation), where a body of well-actualized understandings resonates negatively with a single understanding with a credibility bonus (e.g., because it was advocated by an authority), or where a disliked single understanding fits perfectly with a relevant subset of what we already know (e.g., the favorite thesis of an enemy), is again replete with tension,

19. An analogous dynamic obtains for a strongly evaluated understanding in question. If it is close to the Person's heart, an only mildly distrusted body of understanding can become contaminated by opposition to it. Conversely, if the understanding in question is vigorously opposed, its fit with an only mildly distrusted body of understanding will contaminate the latter.

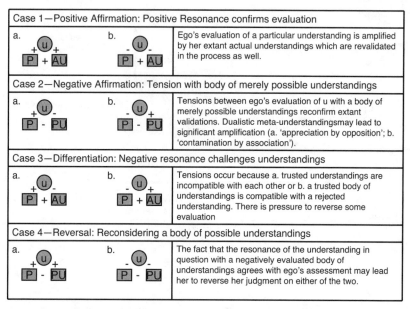

Case 1—Positive Affirmation: Positive Resonance confirms evaluation		
a.	b.	Ego's evaluation of a particular understanding is amplified by her extant actual understandings which are revalidated in the process as well.
Case 2—Negative Affirmation: Tension with body of merely possible understandings		
a.	b.	Tensions between ego's evaluation of u with a body of merely possible understandings reconfirm extant validations. Dualistic meta-understandingsmay lead to significant amplification (a. 'appreciation by opposition'; b. 'contamination by association').
Case 3—Differentiation: Negative resonance challenges understandings		
a.	b.	Tensions occur because a. trusted understandings are incompatible with each other or b. a trusted body of understandings is compatible with a rejected understanding. There is pressure to reverse some evaluation
Case 4—Reversal: Reconsidering a body of possible understandings		
a.	b.	The fact that the resonance of the understanding in question with a negatively evaluated body of understandings agrees with ego's assessment may lead her to reverse her judgment on either of the two.

Figure 4.11. Heuristic schema for the dialectic of resonance

possibly leading to differentiation. To resolve the tensions, some adjustment may have to be undertaken. There are three basic solutions. Repealing or adjusting the single understanding considered in relation to a whole body of understanding might be the easiest, especially if it is not favored for other reasons. This is in many ways what the SED leadership had done with the economic reforms of the 1960s. Here the understanding in question was that efficiency gains could be driven from decentralized decision-making. This idea, however, as it turned out in practice, was more incompatible with the vanguard party idea than the party was willing to accept simply because it lost context (see chapter 2, p. 126). This was at least one reason why the decentralization of decision-making, initially a cornerstone of the reform package, was reversed. The next step led to even greater centralization than before, yielding a seemingly happy case of amplification. The second solution to tension is arguably the most radical step. The belief in one particular understanding is so strong, so "infatuating" that it leads to the dismissal of the previously favored body, which reflects negatively on the new favorite. If magic offers the believer in science what appears to be a solution in a desperate situation, he can come to dismiss the science (or fool himself that magic is science). In the Soviet Union Lysenko's Lamarck-inspired theory of inheritance that promised a way out of the hunger crises of the 1930s led to the prohibition of Mendelian genetics, which was considered standard knowledge before Lysenko's meteoric rise (Joravsky 1970; Soyfer 1994).[20] The third solution is a critical investigation of the epistemic ideologies and practices in use. The development of the doctrine of socialism in one country is a poignant example for this kind of maneuver. Although the thesis of the necessity of world revolution was an integral part of Marx's teachings, this particular thesis came to be negatively evaluated by Stalin and others because it essentially predicted that their own revolution was not sustainable. The differentiation of meta-understandings to the effect that one has to distinguish between the letter and the substance of Marxism set forth in the *Short Course* (see chapter 1, pp. 99–100) resolved the tension. Of course, this move was facilitated by the fact that Marx had argued for the historicity of science, thus licensing the step taken.

In the fourth case (reversal) the fit of a valued understanding with a merely possible (e.g., rejected or indifferent) body of understandings may be taken for a reason to reconsider the evaluation of that body of understandings. Here is an example for case 4a. We will meet, in the next chapter, Stasi officers whom the horrors of World War II turned into antifascists. And even though they were raised to be skeptical or even hateful about socialism before the war, the self-definition of socialism as antifascism led them, among other reasons, to reconsider their ideological orientations. Case 4b becomes relevant in the context of particular meta-understandings. Where Manichaean thinking holds sway, a merely possible understanding's incompatibility with a strongly rejected body of understandings may be a reason to accept the former as valid. This is again the logic of "the enemy of my enemy is my friend" transposed into the realm of ideas. Even though this logic did not lead socialist officials to look more favorably at artistic movements rejected by fascism (e.g., expressionism) it certainly operated at the level of adjudicating the trustworthiness of single individuals.

The combination of cases 3 and 4 provides significant components of a process of religious or ideological conversion. Conversions combine a radical answer to the tensions inherent in a case of differentiation—shedding an old body of accepted understandings because it resonates negatively with a new favored understanding—with the reversal of adopting a complete new body of understandings that was previously considered merely possible. Joas (1997) draws attention to the fact that what is involved here is in fact a self-

---

20. Joravsky makes a strong case that the acceptance of Lysenko's theories cannot be explained by their positive pattern resonance with Engels's *Dialectics of Nature*, as had previously been assumed. Rather, the key to the solution lies in the fact that they resonated in pursuit of a solution to the steep decline in agricultural production following the collectivization drive after the end of NEP.

transcendence, which he sees at the very root of value formation more generally. Following the dialectic of recognition and corroboration one would have to hypothesize in such a situation that the process of self-transformation would also be accompanied by a change in networks of authority, new types of experiences, and access to new indicators. Because this process is rich in reversals that challenge established meta-understandings, the latter will in many cases have to be transformed as well. The autobiographic literature from and about communist renegades espousing some kind of liberalism is rich in such conversion stories (see also Hollander 2006). The differentiation case with which they begin is often so strongly felt because they bring the evaluation of an individual (self or a friend) into sharp conflict with the party. The fact that the liberalism renegades converted to in contrast to socialism strongly endorses decisions of conscience has certainly facilitated its adoption in spite of its previously negative evaluation.

A Note on Memory

Through continuous validation in the course of time understandings maintain their actualization; they are thus memorized. By the same process (or better, the lack thereof) others are forgotten. One could say that as organized wholes, understandings are subject to entropy. In use understandings are maintained directly. Since understandings are interconnected in resonating webs, however, even those that are not directly used may still be reproduced by resonances rippling through these webs. Yet it has to be considered that validations are not necessarily reproduced in a selfsame manner, since differentiation and reversal dynamics can lead to their transformation (more about that in the next section). This has interesting consequences for our sense of the historicity of our understandings. Unless we operate with meta-understandings that urge us to also memorize these transformations (e.g., through narrative strategies such as diary writing, giving accounts of our past) we do not necessarily know how selfsame our understandings retrieved at different moments in time really are. Through the constant play of validations, our memory is floating; the actual history of retrieving understanding covers their historicity. In consequence we often simply assume that we have always seen the world the way we do now. Memory becomes naturalized. This is the reason why adults often have difficulties understanding children. And the social scientist studying the ways in which people understood their lives in some distant past better be careful in taking people's word for it. For what interviews yield is not past understandings but understandings as they have become in the incessant play of validations. Fortunately, the validation space model presented in this chapter offers a critical tool to think through this problem. In the next chapter, opening a four-chapter sequence reconstructing the lives of Stasi officers and of dissidents, I will explain how.

ACQUIRING UNDERSTANDINGS

Until now, I have mostly spoken about the validation of already existing understandings. Thus, I have begged the question where they come from in the first place. However, I need a general framework to think through the generation of new understandings, because I claim in the end that the socialist party in East Germany institutionally disabled itself to create adequate understandings of a fast-changing social world. As will become apparent in what follows, the sociology of understanding can (leaning on American pragmatism), with the help of the notions of a space of validation and the very dialectics just outlined, make a contribution to the analysis of the conditions for the possibility to develop novel understandings.

Undoubtedly, by far the largest number of understandings we are using are not of our own making. Instead, we adopt them mimetically from elsewhere, which is to say that most of our discursive understandings originate in hearsay. Their availability in symbolic form allows them to be easily communicated and distributed. Emotive understandings, too, are often acquired mimetically through processes of what psychologists call *affect attunement* (e.g., Stern 1985, 138ff.). Little children, for example, can learn what to be afraid of and what to enjoy by falling in line with the emotions communicated by their parents.[21] Many of our kinesthetic understandings, finally, are modeled on those of others. We acquire them by being with others, by doing and moving as they do.

Mimesis

It is important not to misunderstand mimesis as a simple, unproblematic process of copying. Instead, it should be seen as involving active adaptation to individual circumstances undertaken from a particular perspective (Auerbach 1964; Gebauer and Wulf 1992; Taussig 1993). What precisely adaptation means can be illuminated with the help of the validation space model I have just presented. Typically, mimesis begins by gleaning understandings from those we consider authorities. There are several reasons why we might

---

21. That this does not work universally, and certainly not intentionally, can be attested by any parent who tried to get a child to enjoy healthy foods by staging a theatrical display of sounds and words signaling appreciation in connection with the consumption of these foods. Again, corroboration is a force to be reckoned with; it cannot simply be reduced to resonance.

want to do this. First, other people's performances may articulate our own inchoate experiences or desires. The differentiations and integrations inherent in them spontaneously resonate with us because we desire fitting understanding. The work of articulation is what we expect of writers we admire or poets we cherish, and of friends or specialists we consult. Second, we might want to be able to do what others do. It appears to us that they have been able to achieve an outcome that we too desire, and thus we are interested in attaining their kind of agency. And as we, with the help of our epistemic ideologies, practices, and emotions, articulate understandings from our own performances, we can do the same with theirs. This can pertain to the minutest of detail actions, such as validating a subway ticket in a foreign city, or to rather complex practices such as playing the piano. Third, our ambitions may be still farther reaching. We may identify more wholly with others, and we may strive to become like them. Since the mimetic acquisition of what we take to be their understandings is a rather complex task, we might begin by adopting gestures, facial expressions, inflections of voice, and the like.

Mimesis, therefore, proceeds from other people's valid appearing understandings; they enter our spaces of validation with something of a credibility advance. Now that they are there, they need to demonstrate their validity by continuing to resonate with us, that is, with the other understandings we currently inhabit. As we put them to use, they have to be corroborated and recognized in use. This has interesting consequences. The (seemingly) same understanding composed of the same distinctions and integrations may orient two persons rather differently, depending on how this understanding has become actualized and situated in a context of other understandings. A particular understandings' context of acquisition as well as its subsequent history of validation shape the ways in which this understanding becomes operative as an action-orienting and directing device. Here lies at least in part the clue to the different attitudes diagnosed by my interview partners as characteristic of particular officer generations. For the practices of party membership it made a difference whether the belief in the leading role of the party and its necessary unity were acquired during the Weimar years and tested through the Nazi period, whether they were acquired with a country devastated by the war as a background or whether they were absorbed at a time when communist rule was firmly established in a rebuilt country.[22]

---

22. The separation of pure understandings from personal acquisition remained an important part of socialist discursive practices. Stasi officers commenting on such differences—for example, between various superiors or party secretaries—have typically attributed diverging styles in the face of supposedly identical beliefs to different "personalities." This points to an interesting epistemic ideology and practice that differentiates between that which is essential (here to socialism) and that which is merely accidental. Here lies the crux of the frequent, in certain circles

We usually encounter the apparently useful understandings of others in a holistic fashion. This means that the differentiations and integrations constituting them are not fully appreciated in their consequences until they are used and validated in practice. Sometimes, we even encounter understandings in such a compacted form that the process of mimetic adaptation becomes a complex process of reconstruction of component understandings and their intricate connections. This is particularly obvious in the acquisition of complex skills, such as learning to perform jazz improvisations on the piano (cf. Sudnow 2001) boxing (cf. Wacquant 2004) or carpentry (cf. Herzfeld 2003). Here mimesis becomes a complex course of reverse engineering that oscillates between an at-first-mysterious image of a whole and what appear to be its constitutive parts. Since they can often not be gleaned outright, this path resembles redevelopment more than imitation. It is mediated by the forms of validation I have just discussed using the cues of others ("am I doing this right?"), the result of action ("does this sound/look right?"), and resonance ("does this sound/look like what I remember from the master's performance?").

Given that socialism operated with a consciousness-driven model of social transformation placing an ever-increasing emphasis on propaganda as a key policy tool, it bears noticing that, like recognition, mimesis can be encouraged, but it cannot be decreed and enforced. This can be immensely frustrating for professional disseminators of understandings, especially if they see themselves as inspired by some privileged access to a transcendent truth. The situation becomes worse if they presuppose meta-understandings

---

heartfelt, differentiation between Lenin and Stalin. The "aberrations" of the latter, since the CPSU's XXth party congress conveniently labeled as "cult of the individual" (Khrushchev 1956) or more commonly as "personality cult," are attributed to the perversity of his personality, which thus saves the essential characteristics of actually existing socialist organization, including vanguardism, which is a thoroughly Leninist and even Marxist concept. What is denied here (at least for this case) is the systematic connection between personality on the one hand and ideology and social organization on the other. Applied to the Lenin-Stalin comparison one might hypothesize, on the basis of the validation space model, that Stalin became who he was precisely because he was formed as a battle-hardened member of the CPSU, and he came to succeed because his understandings resonated with those of other leading party members whose opinions mattered. While the separation between personality and ideology is in principle a very un-Marxian move, one that is ironically made here on behalf of Marx (and Lenin), it is in fact a variation of the widely used scientific ideology and practice that urges us to explain outcomes by looking for co-variation. This method demands that the difference between two cases be explained by seems to vary across them and not by what is purportedly identical in both of them. This is only a valid procedure if what varies (personality) and what is purportedly the same (ideology and institutional context) are completely independent of each other. And one of the points of the sociology of understanding I am trying to develop here is that they are anything but independent, shedding a critical light on the method of co-variation much cherished by comparativists.

that emphasize insight into truth as the primary *motivator* for the acquisition of understandings. Searching causes for the failure of making mimesis happen is therefore a widely established practice. Suspecting lacking will or even ill will and stupidity on the side of those who are supposed to learn are old favorites—not just among proselytizers of religions divine and secular, but also among pedagogues and parents. And so it was in socialism. In chapter 1, I discussed the principles of socialist theodicy, which suggest either ideological immaturity or enemy influence as causes for the failure of mimesis to take place.

In a culture emphasizing proselytization and conversion in conjunction with incessant failure searches followed by blame and punishment, it is not surprising, that people learn to feign understanding as well as efforts to acquire it mimetically. The literature on socialism is replete with evidence about the ways in which people dissimulate the understandings expected of them in public performances. Kligman (1998, 13ff.) has described this as "duplicity," echoing a popular Romanian term.[23] The most famous account is Havel's (1990a), who tells the story of a greengrocer who puts up a sign in his shop window demanding "Proletarians of all Nations unite," not only without agreeing with this ritualistic call to world revolution but also without thinking all too much about it.[24] However, Havel concluded, the authorities who demand dissimulation are actually dependent on it. From here he drew the conclusion that "living in truth," that is, refusing to continue with dissimulation, would lead to a revolution. There is much merit in the latter part of his argument, for indeed, political institutions are maintained through the effect flows generated in such interactions. However, the front part of his argument, the clear positioning of a duality between a faked performance and true self, is too simple. Feigning requires the continuous, active maintenance of this distinction, which is not only exhausting, but it also requires the appropriate social support, as I will show in the chapters on the GDR opposition. In the absence of such support, feigning is always in danger of being the first step in what might be called a "Pascalian conversion." Replying to a friend who could not get himself to believe in God, Pascal (1931) scandalously recommended to simply *perform* belief in deeds and words, and belief would surely come all by itself. This is indeed a bril-

---

23. And not just socialism. For a vivid account of such practices in Assad's Syria, see Wedeen 1999.

24. It has to be kept in mind that the performance of understandings as actualized when in fact they are not, that is, classical dissimulation, is very much a phenomenon of social life more generally. We laugh with others about jokes we did not understand, or that we did not find funny, so as not to appear like a slowpoke or a spoilsport. At work we publicly consent to actions we do not think are right because we believe that it would be useless or unwise to do otherwise, etc.

liant observation and a very real possibility. For it to work, however, the understandings merely deployed *as if* they were actualized need to become actualized *in fact* in the space of validation. Positive recognition, corroboration, and resonance can do that work. If this is what happens, then there is feigning only at the beginning. Rather than magical, Pascalian conversion is a normal part of everyday processes. Feigning is a common part of the mimetic acquisition of understandings where the learning of one mode of understanding is supported by another that is associated but more easily acquired. People may learn to talk the talk before they know how to walk the walk or vice versa. By contrast, the maintenance of a split between "mere performance" and "true self" takes special effort and can happen only under particular structural conditions. It requires a space of validation with split occasions for experience and split networks of authority sustaining the split in understanding, preventing the Pascalian conversion from happening.

Thinking, Working Through, Practicing

My emphasis on the sociality of understanding notwithstanding, we are evidently capable of articulating novel understandings on our own. Typically, we initiate this process in a situation of need, when we feel lost, desiring new orientation, after some of our old understandings become questionable. This often takes the form of one of the tension-laden dialectical constellations I have just discussed, where some authority contradicts us, where the outcome of an event suggests that our understandings of the relevant situation are wanting or even wrong, or where one of our cherished understandings comes to stand in conflict with what we seem to know or desire. Such tensions need not be thrust upon us by the exigencies of life. We may also actively seek them out simply because we may take pleasure in solving them. What is challenging and potentially disconcerting about these tensions is that they trigger doubt; they suggest that orienting ourselves in the world is more difficult than we have assumed; and thus they make apparent to us that the range of things we can accomplish, the variety of tasks we can master, may be more limited than what we might have thought.[25] In short, tensions of validation may challenge, tease, or threaten our sense of agency and identity.

For both Peirce (1992) and Dewey (1997), such tension lies at the origin of what is commonly known as (reflexive) thinking proceeding in some

---

25. The games we find "good" or "pleasurable" seem to offer a degree of tension that is manageable, which means that we do stand a fair chance of finding an understanding that relieves them (Loewenstein 1994).

symbolic medium.[26] Clearly, novel understandings are not articulated in discourse alone. Yet, for the creative development of emotive understandings, we have no single handy term. In everyday language people often use the word *coping*, which, however, focuses more on adaptation to unchangeable circumstances than on the creative aspects of reorientation. Contemporary clinical psychologists like to call it *(emotional) processing*; and more psychoanalytically inclined writers and practitioners prefer terms building on the verb *to work*, borrowing from Freud's analysis of psychic processes as well as processes of therapeutic healing (Freud 2000a). Thus, they speak, for example, of "working through" an emotional conflict or a traumatic experience; or more specifically attached to one context, one also speaks of the "work of mourning." Again, actual uses of these constructions typically describe a movement from pathology to normalcy, once more underplaying the potential creativity involved in articulating emotive understandings. In the realm of the kinesthetic, the articulation of novel understandings is typically called *practicing*. Like its emotive counterpart the general use of this term does not differentiate between mimetic adaptation and the invention of new differentiations and integrations. Yet, besides practicing toward well-known targets already performed by others (mimesis), there is innovative practicing toward open goals: a new way to get from here to there, a new figure in ice skating, and such.

To develop a model for casting novel understandings, I will extend Dewey's (1997) schema about the moments of reflexive thought by placing it into the logic of the validation space.[27] For Dewey, the creative leap follows the awareness of tension (see above) and comes with the formulation of a

---

26. Peirce (1992, 114) says: "The irritation of doubt causes a struggle to attain a state of belief . . . [it] is the only immediate motive for the struggle to attain belief." Dewey (1997, 11) seconds: "Demand for the solution of a perplexity is the steadying and guiding factor in the entire process of reflection." For a contemporary development along pragmatist lines, see also Joas (1992), chapter 3, for an account of the situational development of creative action that adjusts goals and values and thus understandings, providing local orientation in process.

27. I have no further theoretical ambition here than to connect the validation model in a systematic fashion with the very issue of casting novel understandings. I cannot go much further because I do not have the kind of data that would enable me to produce a tenable theory of creativity. I have serious doubts that a theory of creativity that would move significantly beyond what we seem to know already could come from a historical ethnography such as this one. The simple reason is that the data density on the process of invention is far too sparse in this kind of investigation. This said, I still need the following remarks to connect the model of actualizing understandings with a notion of creative processes. I need such a connection because in the end I have to account only for a "negative case," that is, the inability of the party in the GDR to produce novel understandings of itself in a wider political environment when it mattered. For that the actualization model is sufficient.

hypothesis. Yet, Dewey does not explore *how* hypothesis formulation, the development of an understanding, comes about.[28] In this regard he is not alone. Creativity has been a notoriously difficult subject to research, and it has remained rather elusive. In spite of considerable interest in the subject spawned by the hype about life in a "knowledge society" during the last twenty years, there is no agreed-upon theory, not even a small set of strongly competing contenders, of how the process of articulating (casting, projecting, making up) novel understandings unfolds. Nevertheless, and perhaps true to the phenomenon, the literature has crystallized a few thematic focuses, attracting relatively widespread consensus (e.g., Sternberg 1988). First, innovation cannot be sufficiently described through a body of rigid rules. Second, there is a recurring emphasis on building bridges between different domains of understanding, of projecting differentiations and integrations (or the techniques for developing them) from one area into another. Many researchers concur that this maneuver typically proceeds through the good offices of tropes such as analogies, metaphors, synecdoches, metonymies, that is, through strategies of translation. Third, even though innovation is not built on logic, it is not an entirely haphazard process either. For there are "tricks of the trade," "ruses," or "shortcuts" that are more technically known as "heuristics," which can be deployed in the interest of generating insight (e.g., Abbott 2004).[29] Together this implies that insight builds on a plurality of different kinds of understandings, on diverse repertoires of differentiating and integrating techniques, and more specifically on epistemic ideologies

28. Peirce (1992, 186–99) has identified this as the problem of hypothesis formation, or "abduction," which he developed by thinking through all three possible directions of inference with the three terms of a classical syllogism: rule (major premise), application (minor premise), and attribution (conclusion). For Peirce, *induction* is a movement from attribution ("Blacky is white") and application ("Blacky is a swan") to the rule ("all swans are white") (a general law); *deduction* is the classical inference from rule ("All swans are white") and application ("Blacky is a swan") to the attribution ("Blacky is white"); *abduction*, finally, is the inference from the rule ("All swans are white") and the attribution ("Blacky is white") to the application ("Blacky is [probably] a swan"). For the Vienna circle (Reichenbach 1951), hypothesis formation famously belongs to the "context of discovery" (*Entdeckungszusammenhang*), which is sharply distinguished from the "context of justification" (*Begründungszusammenhang*), which alone is deemed accessible to logic and thus to philosophical investigation. Since then it has become commonplace to assert that there is no "logic of discovery."

29. The dialectical schemata I have presented in the central part of this chapter, for example, have served me as heuristics of discovery. Heuristics have also garnered a lot of attention in psychology, first, as practical if incomplete logics (Kahneman, Slovic, and Tversky 1982) and, more recently, as productive and economical thinking tools in their own right (Gigerenzer 2000). Yet again, psychologists pursue a universalist agenda, overlooking the possible historicity of such heuristics, which may in the end be little more than successfully backgrounded epistemic ideologies and practices.

and practices that enable playful translations across domains. This requires that the domains of understanding not be rigidly sequestered from one another, that translation is not preempted by inhibitions or taboos. More, it requires that individual practitioners are comfortable with movements between domains, that they know what it means to think, feel, act differently about something. People need a repertoire of diverse understandings and of reflexive modes. This also means that people move at the same time within a plurality of diverse networks of authority sustaining diversity. The ability to make metaphoric translations has a social root as well.

One particularly interesting source of creativity emerges in processes of translating understandings from one mode into another. Events are more or less structuring. In their flow they may differentiate and integrate the world in patterned and thus understandable ways. In a protest event, for example, some people become associated by physically moving in the same direction, facing someone or something together (see chapter 8, p. 415 ff.). By the same token, routine actions may suddenly be brought to a halt simply because there are physical barriers where there were none before. These movements in time and space or emotional episodes may become discursified. Conversely, discourses can be translated into actions and feelings. What usually is considered translation's flaw is, peculiarly, the condition for the possibility of innovation. As the translation between languages has to wrestle with the different ways in which languages are structured (e.g., by grammar, semantic fields, etc.), the translation between modes of understanding has to face the different poetics characterizing them. Every translation falls short because it misses particulars in the process of differentiation and integration. However, it may thus also clarify and add focus. Every translation may also overshoot, because it inevitably generalizes past the original context. However, understandings thus come to be applied to novel circumstances. In this way the dialectical movement between modes can—like twists on an epistemic kaleidoscope—offer surprising vistas at every turn.

Once articulated, the new, hypothetical understanding enters the space of validation. And it typically does so (like the understandings gleaned from authority in mimetic processes) with a validity credit accrued either from the articulation itself, which carries with it the promise of a sustainable ordering of the previously inchoate, or from the hope of reducing tensions between concrete validation processes. From then on, the new understanding is subject to the usual interplay among recognitions, corroborations, and resonances. In fact, the processes of thinking, working through, and practicing can be described as partly systematic, but partly also playful, even random, marches in open spaces of validation. Resonances will be fathomed, indices for indirect corroboration will be sought, opportunities for direct corroboration will be developed, and occasions will be created for the dialogic exchange of recognitions. This exploring movement is oriented by particular meta-understanding. For example: formal logic provides the tools for a systematic exploration of resonances for particular kinds of discursive understandings; workshops and conferences are organized gatherings to exchange recognitions for specified sets of discursive understandings; emotive understandings are worked through on meditative walks, in conversations with friends, in pilgrimages, and in therapy sessions. Thinking, working through emotions, and practicing are actions undertaken in the service of enhancing agency. They are social in that they engage with others, either in actual conversation producing recognitions or in imagined conversation with internalized voices producing resonances. Explorations of novel understandings are social as well because they proceed on extant grids of meta-understandings. However, they also transcend the social in any individual's unique environment of resonances as well as in the sensory experiences occurring in direct corroboration. To engage in such individual exploration, one needs both a dream space in which odd understandings are allowed to meet (e.g., Bachelard 1994; Winnicott 1989) as well as a relatively open playing field for action, a laboratory of the sort needed to test a particular understanding.

The validating effects of these explorations change the new understanding, either by leading to its actualization or to further tensions with other validated understandings that can give rise to revisions of the initial hypothesis. The articulation of (novel) understandings can thus be depicted as an interactive movement between the awareness of tensions, the development of hypotheses, and their exploration in spaces of validation. All three moments constitute processes of thinking, working through, and practicing. Without the awareness of tension, there is nothing to work from—it anchors the process by raising a more limited question or puzzle to solve, thus limiting the range of the possible casting about in the next step; without hypothesis there is nothing to work with—the exploration can only proceed from the basis of an already articulated understanding; and without exploration there is no actualization—the hypothesis would remain forever tentative speculation.

CONCLUSIONS: LOOMING CIRCULARITIES

The actual development of political understandings among Stasi officers and peace and civil rights movement activists stands in the center of the following four chapters. The analytical tools for this undertaking are provided by the validation space model and the three heuristics synopsizing the dialectics of recognition, corroboration, and resonance. What is at the heart of every dialectic is development in time. Since it is the historicity of understanding that is therefore at issue, it may be useful to summarize my arguments for it. First, the sociology of understanding builds on and elucidates the Marxian and

Mannheimian sociology of knowledge with its claims that understandings are *of* a particular time not only as a way to gain orientation and direction in the face of particular problems in a particular situation, but especially also in validating encounters with other people and events. Second, in chapter 3, I introduced Wittgenstein's private language argument to back up my claim that understandings should be analyzed processually, that is, *in* time. In particular I used his late philosophy to plausibilize that not only changes in understandings but also that their stability need to be studied dynamically. Understandings as institutions are in this sense processes that are repeated in a self-similar manner over a particular span of time. Moreover, in the last section I have argued that creativity, that is the articulation of novel understandings, proceeds through explorations of the validation space. There is an important third sense in which understandings are historical. Recognition, corroboration, and resonance can become entangled in path-dependent relationships in which validation and the institutional context giving rise to it mutually amplify each other *across* time.[30] Epistemologically this means that particular understandings and the contexts producing and reproducing them feed on one another; their relationship can become closed or circular. This is problematic, because instances of unfavorable validation may become overwhelmed by self-amplifying favorable validation. These processes may lead to understandings that may have the feel of well-validated knowledge. In the longer run, however, such knowledge may become disentangled from the realities of life, thus undermining the agency of the persons placing their trust in it. These path-dependent, epistemologically circular processes are the reason why power and knowledge stand by no means only in a mutually supportive relationship. Power, if no restrained, can stand in the way of producing useful knowledge by forcing its production into a particular form. The dialectics of validation just discussed provide the clue for comprehending how path dependence and circularity come about. In what follows I explain how this works for each of the three modes of validation.

---

30. The notion of path-dependence as it is typically used is of course only one way to think this across time historicity in what happens at a particular time depends on what happened before. With the notions of "trajectory," path-dependence presupposes some kind of feedback dynamics above and beyond the sheer inertia of movement; it is self-amplifying historicity. What I mean by that is that a particular event positively influences the conditions of the possibility that a similar event will occur in the future. Self-amplification is of course only one way to think historicity in the across time sense where what happens at one point in time is dependent on what happened before. In the last section I have described processes of articulating novel understandings as party random and partly systematic explorations of validity spaces. These explorations may or may not be path-dependent in the sense of this definition. Abbott (2001b) has proposed the term "narrative analysis" for the study of the "enchainment" of events forming sequence dependent "trajectories." For an introduction into the notion of path dependence see Pierson 2004.

Recognition easily drifts into closure. If agreement validates understanding while also establishing authority, there is the possibility that authority gets constituted via agreement to the very understanding it is supposed to validate. In the history of socialism, an increasing short-circuiting of recognition and authority becomes apparent if one compares the performance of recognition and authority in the writings of Marx, Lenin, Stalin, and the major documents of the SED. While Marx regularly created caricatures of other authors, often drenching them in derision,[31] he was also very eager to learn from his opponents. The ratio between learning and defeating was already much smaller for Lenin, although he still knew how to profit intellectually from writers taken as opponents, as evinced, for example, in his engagement with Hobson (Lenin 1961c). Stalin completely drifted in the other direction. In his writing, defeating vastly outweighs learning, thus setting the tone for the cultural life of the party in the future. Lest I be misunderstood: I am not arguing here that Stalin did not or could de facto not learn from opponents, this would be a silly claim. However, I am arguing that he introduced opponents from within and without the party, overwhelmingly as if their influence was merely negative, as if their contradictions could not but destroy resolve, ultimately endangering the accomplishments of the revolution. Worse, he used opponents as target practice while inviting others to follow suit, creating opportunities for mutual recognition in rejection of the opponent. Thus oppositional thought became radically de-authorized. Stalin's writings were subsequently taken as models of how to deal with opposition within the party, shaping the discursive culture of party life in the GDR up to the very end. The consequence was that in party life outside of small enclaves of intimacy the performance of self-objectification, the strict adherence to the party line, was the condition on which authority was conferred. In turn these authorities recognized the party line and the need for self-objectification. The party line thus became dogma. A considerable degree of narrow-minded bigotry and sectarianism was the inevitable consequence. Even though such short-circuiting had obvious advantages in sustaining the momentum of a fighting ideology for seizing power, the long-term costs were immense. In terms of the dialectics of validation, situations of differentiation (case 3) were largely excised from party routines. And thus the party deprived itself of a valuable tool to think, work through, and

---

31. To some extent, this reification of the work of others with the intent to defeat them is the professional scourge of writers caught up in the Romantic cult of genius. From the perspective of the sociology of understanding it, like its twin, ignoring the writing of others, can be seen as a particular kind of confidence game undertaken not only in the service of competition for recognizing attention but also in the interest of puffing up writers' agency and thus their ability to write in the first place.

practice creatively through its own situation. In the third part of chapter 6 as well as in chapter 9 and the conclusions I will return to this issue to show how it operated within the Stasi.

Sectarian authorization is not the only reason why recognitions can lead to self-amplifying certification of understandings. The emotional charge of recognizing events can have much the same effect by leading to the avoidance of authorities feared to disagree. This in turn may lead to the urge to compensate by the more frequent consultation with authorities expected to concur. The result can be an increasing homogenization of the relevant networks of authority. Proverbs are a vivid testimony to the fact that this is a rather common occurrence. They not only remind us of the value of friends willing to offer candid advice; they even admonish us not to take unkindly to the mere purveyor of negative recognition (or corroboration). This indicates that we need powerful meta-understandings to countervail the particular path-dependency enabled by the dialectic of recognition. And even though, for example, the party statutes of the SED paid lip service to such meta-understandings (e.g., by upholding critique as value), other meta-understandings effectively overshadowed them. Chief among them are the party's Manichaean worldview, the ethics of absolute finality, and the socialist theodicy. They directly licensed sectarian authorization and the emergence of emotive understandings that charged any behavior that could be understood or merely construed as a critique of the party line with intense fear.

Corroboration is not immune to circular validation either. If events directly corroborate understandings while understandings guide actors in events, then there is the possibility that if contingencies can be kept under control, the understanding-driven event corroborates the very understanding to which it owes is course. And people do indeed engage in a far-reaching contingency control that may in effect amount to self-deception about authorship.[32] The minutely choreographed mass propaganda events, such as youth meetings in which the policies of the party were supposedly "discussed" as well as elections that were meant to corroborate the party's direction by demonstrating "approval," are cases in point. By micromanaging and "securing" these events, measures undertaken in the hope for self-amplifying recognition, the major contingencies were systematically driven out of these events and politicians or bureaucrats could well in advance refer to their results as corroborating the party line. Thus Mielke could say in November 1984 about the Pentecost meeting of the communist youth organization taking place a *full half-year later* in the spring of 1985 (1984b):

---

32. Certain neurotics, for example, have the uncanny capability to produce the events that validate their fears.

500,000 members of the FDJ will again demonstrate their loyalty to the party of the working class and will offer proof of their readiness to contribute to the consolidation, strengthening, and defense of socialism. . . . All operative units of Stasi carry the great responsibility to discover and foil all plans, intentions, and measures of the enemy respectively of inimical-negative forces within the GDR which are directed against the preparation and execution of the festival.

The sole remaining contingencies are enemy interference and the failure of individual organizers to realize the party decrees. Controlling these two remaining sources of contingency became one of the Stasi's primary tasks. The fact that these contingencies remained, absorbing much attention, has effectively masked the contingency-extinguishing choreography behind such events. This maneuver made room for the self-deception to actually find corroborating force in the outcome of the event in spite of the fact that it was in an important sense rigged. The existence of the enemy was a necessary condition for the maintenance of a self-deceiving fiction. The Stasi and party could celebrate these events as overwhelming successes not least because they demonstrated that they could keep the enemy at bay, letting socialism run its *natural* course. The productivity movements (e.g., Stachanov in the Soviet Union and Hennecke in Germany) born out of Lenin's observation about the Moscow-Kazan railway (chapter 1, p. 90) are another good example for extensive efforts at contingency control. There, too, the outcome of the thoroughly choreographed event was used to corroborate the understanding that a lot more could be produced.

With indirect corroboration the possibilities for circularity are even larger by simply selecting events corroborating understandings in the desired direction. And again the writings both of the classics and of the party furnish interesting examples. If Marx was involved in selective readings of events, he was also forced by his opponents to comment and analyze a wide variety of events challenging his theory. In fact the *Brumaire* (1960) and *Civil War in France* (1962a) are excellent examples for how the analysis of events leads him to revise theory. Once socialism was firmly institutionalized, however, a rampant self-serving selection bias with regard to corroborating events became the norm. Neither was there ever a serious party-official attempt to look at the consequence of the successful institutionalization of welfare states in Western Europe for Marxism-Leninism as a body of theory, nor was there an attempt to deal seriously with socialism's internal challenges, such as the June 17, 1953, uprising in the GDR, the 1956 rebellion in Hungary, the 1968 Prague Spring, or the various Polish crises. Sustained analysis of the conditions for the possibility of Stalinism had to wait until glasnost and perestroika.

As in the case of recognition, emotions play a significant role in placing corroboration on a path-dependent trajectory. The fear of negatively corroborating its understanding outcomes has certainly influenced the party state's decision not to undertake systematic ethnographic or demographic research, or where it was allowed to happen, to curtail its influence as far as possible. Only from 1966 until 1978 was there an institute of opinion research run under the auspices of the ZK. Its findings were all classified documents that were never published. Nor were they used much internally for the formulation of policy. A recent reanalysis of the data suggests (Niemann 1993) that although the SED might have hoped for much more unqualified approval, the actual levels of positive attunement to the party state were significantly higher than Western critics had assumed. The GDR government maintained an institute for youth research in Leipzig that to the end produced interesting snapshots of the situation of young people in the GDR. Its results were equally classified and remained politically inconsequential (Walter, Förster, and Starke 1999). Just as in the case of recognition, only a strong set of independently validated meta-understandings can save corroboration from convenient event selection, driven not only by wishful thinking but also by the sheer desire to avoid unpleasant feelings. Such meta-understandings were, however, much less firmly established than they should have been. We will see (in chapter 9) that even the Stasi was subjected by the party to "messenger assassinations," which then became a significant problem for Stasi's organizational culture, its very modes of producing knowledge.

It is perhaps easiest to see how resonances can become enmeshed in circular validation. If the fit between new understandings and older beliefs currently in force validates both old and new, then resonance can become self-amplifying. Validation through resonance thus has a built-in conservative principle. In the absence of countervailing measures, this leads to a narrow-mindedness that is associated with provincialism and at times also with old age. Emotions do their bit to amplify this tendency. The rationalist underpinnings of socialism, the very assumption of the eternal substantive truth of a concrete body of teachings, has made this inherent conservatism if anything even more severe, because the only means to counteract it, the occasional willingness to let go of time-honored truths, was effectively preempted. This is one of the deeper reasons why de-Stalinization never succeeded; its effective cornerstone, the idea of the necessity of an internally unified vanguard party, hailed back to Marx and Lenin, and become untouchable. Apart from this "natural" effect, resonances can become circular also through the conscious manipulation of memory cultures. In chapter 2, I provided examples from the arts and philosophy. Events, too, can be made into objects of deliberate forgetting and remembering. I have already mentioned the Stalinist purges. In Germany, the suppression of the Hitler-Stalin pact was a hot issue, and in chapter 5 and 6 I will show several examples illustrating how what Olick (2007) calls the politics of memory is employed to shape resonances and thus ultimately identities and modes of reflexivity. The negative complement of a positive politics of memory is censorship, the confrontation of a person with only select understandings in an effort, again, to avoid unwanted resonances, thus helping to produce and maintain what Zerubavel (2006) calls "conspiracies of silence."

In sum, then, sectarian networks of authority, self-deceiving contingency control, selective event interpretation, selective memory cultivation, and censorship are process dynamics entangling people in circular validation. One of the reasons why they are so common in politics everywhere is that they offer real advantages at mobilizing people behind a clear, unambiguous vision of the world. The real truth is seen in the goodness of the institutional changes the politician wants to effect, not in the paltry realities of the present, which may include both the state of the political organization and the world to which it responds. This was precisely the Marxist critique of the positivist social sciences, which can never but affirm what is already there, missing the essential truth that human society is *in posse* as much as *in actu* thus misunderstanding what it really means to be human. The hope is, then, that the future will make true what is now only the discursive anticipation of the institutions politics tries to engender in the future. Following this logic, validation has to become future directed; it has to work in the service of a project at the core of which lies a prophecy hoped to self-fulfill. What appears here in all clarity is a real dilemma for politics in general. Political understandings, in as far as they pertain to the imagination of the future, can in a deep sense only be validated *in posse*, that is, as a commitment to do one's very best to achieve the institutional change taken in view. One may find indicators corroborating the hope that indeed it will be doable. And the imagined institutional state might resonate deeply with our wishes and desires. At the same time, however, knowledge of the present can have a depressing effect, making it appear as if only the present institutional arrangements were possible. In other words, political understandings *in actu*, which are much more open to validation, especially to corroboration, can lead to the fetishization of currently existing institutional arrangements ultimately disabling politics. So one may be tempted to disregard this knowledge; one may want to set hope against it; one may be tempted to merely insist on the future state at the expense of building knowledge that offers useful orientation in finding a way from here to there; one may come to a point where one cannot even properly distinguish anymore between possibility and actuality. Such a conflation is justified by social imaginaries that posit a lawlike historical development, because *in posse* is simply taken to mean not yet *in actu* (but necessarily so in the future). This confusion of the actual and the possible enabled by a firm belief in a law of history may well have been the greatest seduction to which socialism in Eastern Europe succumbed because it led to privileging mobilization over the renewal of political understanding.

Under such circumstances an eerie gap may emerge between the affirmation of particular understandings that claim to comprehend and the actual experiences of that very same world. Circular validation may create a knowledge that appears certain while being at the same time inept at providing guidance. This is what happened to socialist functionaries deeply committed to the project of the party. To understand fully what it meant to them to be caught in this gap between publicly cultivated understandings and countervailing experiences sequestered into a more or less private world, we need to understand how functionaries came to be committed to socialism in the first place. The story of how this happened is told in the following two chapters.

PART III

Becoming Socialist Men— The Stasi Officers

The following two chapters make an attempt to show how men, through the interaction of their experiences, their memories, and the discourses of the people around them, came to adopt socialist understandings.[1] I will show how they came to imagine themselves as communists ready to dedicate their lives to the party's project. The theoretical subtext of both chapters, their emplotment scheme, is formed by the validation space model I presented in the last chapter. At first it may appear hopeless to reconstruct the development of people's political understandings because validations are so much woven into the minutiae of the everyday, often operating below the threshold of consciousness. And yet, combining people's stories with an effort to reconstruct the institutionalized forms of validations they have been subjected to in their work and leisure environments offers a good enough means to reconstruct the development of their political understandings. For the analysis of institutionalized forms of validation it is important to draw on the interviews of several people who have gone through a similar socialization process while also utilizing historical studies, novels, newspapers, films, and virtually anything that promises to convey a glimpse at relevant mundane experiences at a particular moment in time.

Since most of what I will have to say in the following two chapters is based on interviews taken more than a decade after the officers' last day

1. These two chapters in no way aspire to provide a comprehensive history of the Ministry of State Security and its regional and local branches in the GDR. The most complete description of the Stasi in the breadth of its activities is provided by Suckut et al. (1993–). Very helpful is Jens Gieseke's (2000) overview of the full-time staff of the Stasi and its development. Equally useful is Wilfriede Otto's (2000) biography of Erich Mielke, which sheds much light on the Stasi through the lens of its long-term head. An insider's account is provided by a collection of essays about the Stasi's various branches written by former officers themselves (Grimmer et al. 2002b). English-language introductions are provided by Childs and Popplewell (1996) and Koehler (2002).

at work, I will begin chapter 5 with considerations about the historicity of memory and its implications for a historical ethnography such as this one. It will turn out that the validation space model offers useful means to think through perpetually reconstructed memories. The main body of the chapter is then dedicated to a reconstruction of the development of the officers' political understandings and their validation. I will trace their wartime experiences, their postwar schooling in an emergent Cold War context, their involvement in communist youth organizations, their hiring by the secret police, and their work during the late 1950s, '60s, and '70s. I will in particular pay attention to the question of how these various experiences are building on each other in an amplifying or relativizing manner. This narrative tells of boring sleuthing assignments and veritable spy-catcher episodes, of the usual military hazing rituals and the particular socialist twists they have; it reports on the officers' constant worry about people fleeing the GDR and their concomitant relief when finally the Wall went up; and it tells of a completely new set of tasks emerging slowly in the shadow of that Wall: their assignment to control oppositional activities. As a narrative strategy for this chapter I have chosen to allegorize general periods of development through the life story of one individual officer whose biography brings more clearly to the fore what appears important to me. The narrative flow will be broken in regular intervals by episodes from other people's lives to show more of the diversity of experiences.

While chapter 5 unfolds as a straightforward historical-biographical narrative, chapter 6 proceeds along an analytical logic, exploring how the officers' validation spaces came to be structured by the organization and culture of the Stasi. Three main themes will find particular consideration in this context. I will first investigate the meta-understandings that shaped the officers' attribution of authority. Three sources of authority are particularly prevalent in the officer's stories: antifascist credentials, self-objectification toward the party's goals, as well as professional expertise. In reference to a concrete case study, I will show that in cases of conflict, self-objectification dominated the other two. The development of the officers' networks of authority is the second important theme of the chapter. I will show that they became ever more narrowly focused on people who were, like them, dedicated to the socialist project and even more narrowly on other members of the secret police. Security restrictions on contact, long work hours, and the distribution of apartments and vacation spots through work are chiefly responsible for a situation in which the Stasi reproduced itself. The chapter aspires to make plausible why, in 1989, the vast majority of the new class entering the secret police academy came from Stasi families. The third main theme of the chapter is the discursive culture of Stasi, both in its formal and informal dimensions. This includes an analysis of bureaucratic strategies of communication as well as an inquiry about to whom the officers could talk about problems, issues, and questions they had. I am particularly interested in the principles that separated the sayable from the unsayable and ultimately the thinkable from the unthinkable.

5

Guardians of the Party State

We believed then that Marxism had objectively worked out the laws of human society. . . . I don't want you to have any doubt: this was a comprehensive worldview that was really convincing. It was a complete, homogeneous perspective.

JÜRGEN BUCHHOLZ, FORMER STASI OFFICER

For me the belief in the Soviet Union and Lenin's party was a sanctuary.

ERICH MIELKE, FORMER MINISTER OF STATE SECURITY

The environment in which I lived was almost exclusively a party environment. To be expelled from the party would have been my death, physically as well. . . . In the first instance I am a communist and only in the second instance am I human.

MARTIN VOIGT, FORMER STASI OFFICER

Stasi employees were committed to the idea of socialism. . . . With it we have also acquired a sense of discipline that led us to go along with everything. For me, the primacy of politics was absolute; it was law for me.

WALTER SCHUSTER, FORMER STASI OFFICER

January 25, 2001. For Berlin in winter it is a nice day—a good omen. I have an interview scheduled at 9:30 with Walter Schuster, a former staff officer in the department XX of the Berlin district office of Stasi. It is our first meeting and I am a bit nervous. Mapping officers, activists, and available files onto each other as "participants" in the same social arena has been much more difficult than I thought. Finding people whose names I glean from documents is arduous work. In a city the size of Berlin phone-book searches typically yield lists of names that remain four, five entries long even after pruning implausible residence locations.[1] Many officers cannot be found. Some may have

---

1. In general, Berliners have preferred to stay in "their" part of Berlin after unification. The exceptions to this are the high-value central locations in East Berlin, the former districts of Mitte and Prenzlauer Berg, where the renovation of government quarters and tourist attractions with their ancillary infrastructure of restaurants, cafes, and shops has encouraged investors to build luxury apartments, which are mostly inhabited by Westerners.

died, others may no longer live in the city or choose to be listed under their spouse's name. Even where I finally succeed to get the right "Peter Müller" on the phone (after having stunned several wrong ones), and even where I garner some interest in the former officer himself, I mostly fail in the end because his wife vetoes his participation in the project—or so he says. Of course this is anything but surprising. In the past decade Stasi officers have become the epitome of everything that was wrong with socialism. They have come to symbolize its inhumane face. Journalistic depictions of officers and their informants frequently play on an exoticizing imagery of quasi-religious zealotry, cynical power mongering, or sadistic and neurotic psychopathology. Employers have the right to check East German job candidates for Stasi connections; they also have the right to refuse employment if such a connection can be established with the help of the Stasi document centers. The public sector, including city services such as parks, streets, and sanitation have made it a point to present themselves as "Stasi-free." A decade after the fall of socialism, unmasking somebody's Stasi connections is still the most sensationalist aspect of working through the socialist past. The effect of the public debate is not undone by some employers who not only do not mind but probably even value former Stasi officers: private security and financial service companies above all. Accordingly, many former officers and secret informants did not want to talk. After several job changes and spells of unemployment those officers who are still working and have achieved some stability do not want to undertake anything that might possibly endanger it.[2] What worsens the situation is that some officers who once were ready to speak no longer are willing to engage in a research project such as this one because they feel that what they said before was misrepresented or presented in a disagreeable moralizing or self-congratulatory way. A small minority of former officers suspects the CIA behind my efforts and declines because even now the former class enemy is not to be assisted.[3] "Snowball sampling" is the way to go then. Therefore, I need to leave a favorable impression on Walter Schuster at this first meeting: I need to protect my relationship with the officer who referred me, and I needed to keep the option open that this new connection might eventually produce more referrals.

On the tramway from my apartment in Prenzlauer Berg, the Berlin neighborhood that was the scene of many Stasi actions, to Schuster's apartment in Pankow, I wonder about what he might be willing to talk about

2. Not that the rest of the former GDR population had an easier time after unification. However, given the public discourse about the Stasi, former officers see more readily than others a causal connection between their present problems and their past.
3. The former officers may also have reasons of their own that have little to do with their public image, among them simple time constraints and expected awkwardness.

and in what depth. I also wonder how much he might be able to remember because I am interested in circumstantially rich descriptions. After all, his first day on the payroll of the Stasi is almost half a century old, and even his last day with rank and office lies more than a decade in the past. I am much less concerned that he might actively mislead me. My ease in this respect has as much to do with the kind of data I am most interested in as with the work that has already been done by others. I do not see myself as an investigator set upon uncovering spectacular, as of yet unknown Stasi operations, or to identify secret informants not yet known.[4] I do not have to do that because the Stasi record about suppressing not only oppositional activity but also virtually any form of organized group activity not sanctioned by the state has been established by now through the conjoined forces of the Berlin state prosecutors office, historians, and members of the former GDR opposition. And even though this record is shocking in the depth and width of surveillance revealed, it also offers a depiction of East Germany's security bureaucracy that is far from the gruesome, bloodstained image many observers had expected to surface as reality. Moreover, the record is so persistent that the discovery of individual cases of physical torture, or even of political murder, would no longer alter it fundamentally. This record was largely established on the basis of the documents the Stasi has produced, as well as on the basis of the testimonies of former dissidents and of former political prisoners. What is missing from this picture is an understanding of how this record was produced by actual human beings with particular historical experiences, working in particular organizational cultures and structures.

Having to walk two blocks from the ultimate tramway stop, I was surprised to find Schuster living in a brand new apartment complex that self-consciously showcases its postunification construction date. Most of the other officers I got to know still live in the apartments they once were allotted by the Ministry of State Security. These are mostly located in so-called new building areas (Neubausiedlungen), that is, in structures assembled from prefabricated concrete panels, which have, after Stalin's death, become socialism's signature architecture. The fact that these buildings have by now typically been dolled up with upgraded facades and new bathrooms may have contributed as much to the officers' decisions to stay as the local

---

4. Or for that matter to find conclusive evidence in cases that have remained ambiguous. The two most notorious cases that have received legal clearing and yet remain rather ambiguous are that of the long-time PDS chief, Gregor Gysi, who was a prominent lawyer in the GDR (as well as the son of the prominent politician and civil servant, Klaus Gysi), and that of Brandenburg's first postunification governor, Manfred Stolpe, who subsequently served in Schroeder's government as federal minister of transportation.

remnants of their old social infrastructure and the comfort conveyed by an aspect of stability in a fast-changing world. But Schuster had obviously moved. Not a bad point to start a conversation. Schuster greets me with the, in his generation, still mandatory handshake. We sit down around the small dining table in his living room. I hesitate to describe the furnishings of his room and his clothes. Such descriptions have become a staple in denouncing former GDR state functionaries as petit bourgeois, frequently reading provincialism or narrow-mindedness into them. This way of reasoning is inherently classist. The furniture in Schuster's apartment seems all new. It, like the late GDR furniture that is still in use in many officers' homes, is in line with the aesthetic preferences of the *Facharbeiter* (qualified worker) class in West Germany. Thus Schuster's apartment is somewhat "out of class" if West German "distinctions" (Bourdieu 1984) are applied, for Schuster, after all, was a staff officer with a university diploma. It is important to remember, however, that in East Germany the aesthetic codes of the upper echelons of the working classes became universalized as standard with normative force well beyond their origin stratum (Engler 1999). What commentators are reacting to are differences in aesthetic conventions. Noticing these differences is one thing; linking them to character (in an often self-serving way) is simply an expression of prejudice.

Schuster offers me a strong cup of coffee. I gladly accept. Preferring late night work I got up too late to brew my own before leaving the house. Yes, indeed, he had lived until quite recently at Alexanderplatz, right in the heart of eastern Berlin. Alas, the progressive westernization of the whole historical inner city made him feel increasingly estranged. "I did not want to keep living there to be gazed at as a strange object by Western tourists." He, like many other East Berliners, feels crowed out from the center city (Glaeser 2000). And so he begins to make a whole number of angry comments about how unification was in effect a colonization, how the GDR is about to be edited out from the cityscape of central Berlin. "The Palace of the Republic is gone, the town hall pub is gone, so why should I stay there." These measures are so frenzied, he explains, that the new authorities were even getting rid of touristic signs pointing to the *Rotes Rathaus*, the "Red City Hall." Of course, he hastens to explain, that building is not nicknamed "red" because it was East Berlin's communist town hall, but because it is made of bricks and has been known as Red City Hall from well before the war. The new signs simply say Berlin City Hall. All of this is for him just a sign of rabid anticommunism, a hatred for anything associated with the GDR. That, of course, was to him also visible in how former Stasi officers and former secret informants were treated: as pariahs, as criminals. Stasi officers, he feels, have been especially singled out. His son-in-law, a radio officer working for the Stasi, had found employment with the Berlin park service after unification. "Nothing big" he says, "just watering plants." He was dismissed for his Stasi past. He himself feels cheated out of his rightful pension because Stasi officers receive less than other former GDR state employees.

As I enter Schuster's apartment the radio news reports on the latest reproaches against Germany's foreign minister, Joschka Fischer, whose past as a student movement radical of the 1960s and 1970s has recently come under scrutiny. Conservatives in the CDU/CSU opposition and some media outlets, above all the Springer-Press papers and the weekly news magazine *Stern*, are running a campaign against Fischer, whom they try to portray as a former terrorist unfit to serve as a major representative of the state.[5] The CDU's chairwoman, Angela Merkel, who hails from the former GDR, chimed in with the Fischer critics. Schuster takes this as a chance to berate her. "For how long do you want to criticize people for their past," he exclaims. Here, too, he sees antileft sentiment at work, and so he can now, curiously, readily identify with Fischer. That Merkel has become a vocal member of this chorus angers him especially. "This idiotic Merkel! *Bei uns hatte sie alles!*" ("With us she had everything!"), he exclaims. "She could study physics, go to work at the Academy of Sciences, she got to get her doctorate and all, and now she has this hate of the left!" He points out that she was not even a member of the civil rights movement in the GDR. The former opposition members are just as bad, he argues. Rainer Eppelmann, a leading GDR dissident instrumental in launching the peace movement in the GDR (see chapter 8, p. 406ff.), especially attracts his scorn. "First a pacifist, then minister of defense!" he exclaims angrily. One only needs to study the documents carefully (he means the Stasi's documents, including character descriptions, etc.) to see what kinds of people they are. None of them, he goes on, were able to win a seat in parliament on their own, which to him proves how incapable, how unattractive they really are.

Most officers, very much like Schuster, let me quickly in on their emotive and cognitive understandings of unification, the GDR, socialism, the Stasi, and the opposition. None left even the least bit of a doubt regarding their strong identification with party, the Stasi, and state in the GDR. For most of them, the GDR is still home and unification brought a worthwhile experiment in social transformation to a (some think temporary) stop. Yes, they acknowledge mistakes, excesses, and in retrospect wish the GDR had institutionalized a more open form of socialism. They also strongly feel that the capitalism in which they live now is not only not what they wanted, but it also shows in their eyes such blatant weaknesses that there is little doubt that the present social, political, and economic constitution cannot be anything

---

5. This was a move in a much larger campaign against the cultural and political achievements of the 1968 student movement, with clear nationalist undertones.

but a historical episode in the longer run. With few exceptions, they have little more than scorn for the members of the former GDR opposition. The overwhelming understanding of the officers is that the former opposition members suffer by and large from serious character pathologies that have made them then and make them now untrustworthy individuals. Before I can tell the history of these understandings, I need to digress briefly to note how I think such a history can be developed with the help of interviews.

(RE-)HISTORICIZING UNDERSTANDING/RECONSTRUCTING SPACES OF VALIDATION

It follows from the framework for the analysis of validation spaces I developed in the last two chapters that the officers' understanding of the GDR, socialism, capitalism, and the GDR opposition are by necessity anchored in the present. Ongoing recognition, corroborations, and resonances keep them actual while possibly also altering their meaning. The officers have always understood the merits of socialism against the purported demerits of capitalism. In 2001 (the year of my fieldwork in Berlin), however, unlike in 1988 for example, they not only have their own ethnographic experience of an actually lived life in both systems, but also they need to wrestle with the question of what socialism and capitalism are in entirely different discursive environments. The powerful organizations of state and party that once recognized their understandings are gone, and they have been replaced with a state that consistently places the officers' work in the neighborhood of criminal activity. Where the mass media once largely mirrored what they believed, they now find their most cherished understandings attacked. In consequence, the officers cannot but understand themselves and their work in the Stasi against the pictures that are currently drawn about them in public discourses. If this is so, then interviews provide no direct access to the understandings officers may have held decades ago; no time capsule has preserved them in their pristine then- and thereness. Instead, historical understandings need to be reconstructed, and current understandings depicted as those of the past need to be historicized.

Biographical interviews provide very valuable clues for such reconstructive work on two different levels. On the first level they perform a particular historicization of the past in which the ethnographer is directly involved. Most of this reconstructive work is done by the interviewee—but it is done in response to the questions of the interviewer.[6] It is not without interest

---

6. All interviewees were acquainted with the general questions I was about to ask before we met for the first time. Interviewees typically insisted that they needed time to think about these questions. Some prepared for the interview by consulting with former colleagues, with friends

to analyze the interview as an interactive production in the present for the present. And sure enough this component should not be lost sight of, but one can do more with an interview. The understandings presented as historical are also the current result of an ongoing reconstructive effort that may be analyzed not only for what it says about the past but also for how this reconstruction has come about. At times, this process of becoming is more directly manifest in the interview itself. This is often the case for consciously experienced reversals of validation that are, for their dramatic effects, eminently narratable. Interviewees directly comment on when and why they "changed their mind," why they had a "change of heart." Whether or not these reasons are post hoc rationalizations is an open question, but at least the fact of a change is consciously available. By no means is this the case for all reconstructions. This necessitates that the ethnographer learn as much as possible about the development of the interviewee's space of validation in the course of time. The understandings presented in the interview as historical need to be read for the conditions of their own possibility, as it were. To do that, the ethnographer needs to develop a sense of the environment in which the person has lived, its chances for systematically producing certain kinds of recognitions, corroborations, and resonances that work together to selectively feed some understandings while slowly starving others of sustaining validations. In part such background knowledge comes from the interview itself, by scrutinizing it for breaks in the performance, for a disjuncture of content and style, emotional thrust or narrative poise revealing understandings that seem to belong to different times because some were reproduced in a more self-similar way while others have changed more noticeably. In this way the text becomes a digging ground for an archaeology of understandings (and self).

Much of it, however, needs to come from other sources: other interviews shedding light on the same social arena as well as historical documents, texts, and secondary sources. They provide important hints about the kinds of understandings the interviewee could have reasonably been expected to have had in a particular context, which, however, are nowhere present in the interview. In the face of what is actually said, they are counterfactuals; in the face of the other historical record, they are more or less probable hypotheses about what once might have been actual understandings. The space of validation of the interviewee needs to be investigated for its pos-

---

or partners. Some consulted documents or photos they had collected over the course of the years. Sometimes questions were postponed from one meeting to the next because interviewees needed time to recollect their thoughts. Moreover, I not only asked questions, many of which were derived from the study of written documents, I also used documents as prompts during the interview.

sibility to starve or otherwise transform such insinuated understandings. Counterfactuals need to be investigated. If it seems plausible in the end that these understandings were actual for the interviewee at a particular time, an important insight is gained about the ways in which the interviewee's space of validation has wielded its effects in the course of time. While this procedure is not necessarily very accurate at the level of an individual person, it is very informative about processes of validation characteristic for particular social arenas. And this is precisely the reason why I could not have done this project by arbitrarily assembling a cast of characters without real life connections. I needed people who were interactively connected to one another.

On the second level, the interviews contain the debris of that past. Here it is important to remember that the three forms of validation preserve while they alter; they make memories after all, even if memorization is by necessity a process in which life is historicized in the refraction of progressively current validations. Our understanding that we are called by a certain name, that we have been born on a particular day in a particular place of a particular mother, is validated so frequently in so many different forms that there is little reason to assume it has shifted much in the course of time. The immediate reason why we trust this memory is that we have found it to be reliable; and it is dependable because there are powerful epistemic ideologies and practices that make the self-similar reproduction of particular understanding a central concern. Even where the reproduction of orderings is not institutionalized to such a degree, however, aspects of orderings may be reproduced "faithfully." For example, Stasi officers have, by and large, held onto the understanding that members of the peace and civil rights movements suffered from a character disorder in spite of the fact that the validation of this understanding has shifted considerably in the course of time. In the mid-1970s it was chiefly validated by what appeared to them as an unsocialist lifestyle—after all, the public campaigns against such markers were still fresh in their mind; the main source of validation, let's say in 1988, was the opposition members' sustained contact with Western journalists. There, the negative press the GDR has received in the West over recent Stasi actions surely did its bit; in January 2001, finally, the former dissidents' supposed contradictions in performance between life in the GDR and in postunification Germany (such as Schuster's comments about pacifist Eppelmann turned minister of defense) moved to the foreground amid the former opposition members' sustained activities to reveal the nature of Stasi operations in the former GDR.

SOLDIERS FOR A BETTER WORLD

The quotations opening this chapter provide glimpses of a worldview in operation. They suggest how deeply the secret police officers I could interview believed in Marxism-Leninism, and how this belief was wrapped up in strong identifications with institutions, most notably the party, the state GDR, and the Stasi. In a sense, they reflect the success of the SED to create the kind of monolithic intentionality it envisioned for the country as a whole. But why did the party's project succeed with these men? How did they come to attune their political intentionality to that of the party? How did they come to think and feel in terms of the ethics of absolute finality with communism as the goal and a strictly disciplined vanguard party as a means to achieve it? If they were remade in the image of the party, if they became "new men" indeed, then how so, and to which degree, against which odds? This chapter is the story of officers' understanding in the making where "in the making" means both—becoming and remaining once become. I will show how socialism in the guise of an idea, a person, an institution, or a setting began to be appealing to these men, and how this appeal became compelling through the mutually supporting work of resonances, recognitions, and corroborations. I will do so in the first two parts by drawing in each part more systematically on the life of one officer, while juxtaposing his development to a more general consideration of others' experience. The officer chosen to allegorize the group over a particular period of time was selected not for reasons of representativeness in a demographic sense—the use of that notion is often just the admittance that one knows little about the relevant processes—but for reasons of highlighting particularly important dynamics of validation, which are especially clear-cut in this particular case.[7]

The Lure of Socialism

Before my interview partners became members of the secret police, typically at the tender age of eighteen or nineteen, they already had heavily involved themselves in socialist organizations, especially in the communist youth movement. In fact, the demonstrated dedication to socialism in word and deed was the precondition for being considered for a Stasi job in the first place. Thus, I have to show first how these young men became dedicated to the socialist cause as it was presented to them.

Nie wieder Faschismus! (Never again fascism!) and Nie wieder Krieg! (Never again war!) are the most notable refrains ringing through the interviews with my twenty-five interview partners as they try to explain to me what motivated them to become socialists and, as socialists, members of the secret police of East Germany. With two exceptions, all of them were born between 1928 and 1938. They had consciously experienced the war and its immediate aftermath. They had to mourn the death of close kin and friends;

---

7. In this sense allegorization is following the logic of theoretical sampling. See Glaeser 2004.

they had felt the immense anxieties associated with air raids, the uncertainties associated with decampment from their city homes. A minority of them, refugees from western Prussia, from eastern Pomerania, Danzig, Silesia, and the Sudenten country, had lost their homes entirely. A few of them were old enough to have been drawn into the *Volkssturm* of the Nazis, the home defense brigades made up of males either too old or too young to fight in the regular units of the *Wehrmacht* or the SS. They remember this more as an anxiety-arising episode that, owing to the chaotic circumstances of the last months of the war, had lost any luster of adventure and honor (at least in retrospect).

Take Kurt Bogner, for example. He was born in 1935 in Leipzig, which was then the very heart of one of the most sizable and dynamic industrial agglomerations in all of Germany. Although Leipzig was, before the Nazis came to power, an SPD and KPD stronghold, Bogner's parents, the father a locksmith, and the mother a seamstress, did not have an affiliation with either one of the socialist parties or the trade union movement. However, they were, until the Nazis abolished the organization, members of the vaguely left-leaning "Friends of Nature" (*Naturfreunde*) movement. According to Bogner, they were "humanistically oriented" but "apolitical" (*unpolitisch*) during the Nazi years.

Bogner's narrative of his wartime memories conveys strong feelings of unease, insecurity, and, in the last instance, outrage toward individuals and institutions he could label Nazi. Some time in the early 1940s, the older Bogners were apparently lax in flying the Nazi flag on a holiday, which prompted a threatening comment by elderly neighbors, members of the Nazi party, to fly the flag "or they would come to regret it." His parents then warned him to guard his mouth in front of these neighbors, and to greet them always very politely, "lest his father lose his job." Father Bogner was working for a local arms manufacturer. Losing his job would have meant immediate draft into the armed forces. The young Bogner found this rather troubling and very confusing because the very same neighbors acted a bit like grandparents toward him, for example, by treating him to much-appreciated sweets for his birthday. Bogner also recalls terrifying nights in the shelter as the air raids on Leipzig began in 1943. Their house took a hit twice but their apartment was only damaged and not entirely destroyed, unlike that of his paternal grandparents who "got bombed out" and had to be evacuated from the city to a village between Leipzig and Dresden. Bogner recalls that he got so frightened of the sirens warning the population of an imminent bombardment that at the beginning of 1944 his parents decided to send him to the evacuated grandparents. The carpet-bombing of December 4, 1943, which devastated most of Leipzig's inner city, may have done its part to hasten that decision. Consequently, the young Bogner spent most of 1944 in a village he self-consciously describes, "in today's words," as dominated by a local lord and by large farmers. He also describes it as thoroughly in the grip of the Nazis, as the following episode seems to have made clear to him. The wife of the local Nazi party leader complained one day to his grandparents' landlady, the wife of the local leader of the Nazi farmer's organization, that young Bogner had failed to greet her properly in the morning. In spite of his plea of innocence, the consequence of this intervention was that he was punished by his elementary school teacher; he had to write one hundred times: "I have to greet Mrs. 'what-not' every morning with '*Heil Hitler!*'" His feelings of injustice and humiliation mingled with a troubling unease about the mistreatment of slave laborers from Poland and the Soviet Union in the village. He wondered why they were forced to wear readily identifiable badges, *Ps* for Poles and *Ost* ("East") for Soviet citizens, on their clothing. He couldn't understand why they were not allowed to eat with the Germans. All this, as he says, "burdened" him. At the end of 1944 his parents heeded his pleas to take him back to Leipzig.

Like many other successful working-class families, the Bogners had purchased a little garden plot outside of the city limits. On the way to their plot, they regularly passed a spot that in March 1943 became one of the first concentration-camp *Außenkommandos* to supply German industry with slave labor, in this case from the Buchenwald camp just north of Weimar, about 130 km southwest of Leipzig. In passing, the Bogners could see beyond the barbed-wire fences and watchtowers how the completely emaciated inmates in their striped outfits toiled away at building the infrastructure, and once the camp was completed, airplane fuselages.[8] One day, as the American front line drew close, they saw a big cloud of smoke over the camp. The older Bogner leaped onto his bicycle to go and see what was going on. He came back completely discombobulated. He had witnessed how the SS herded all inmates into buildings that they nailed shut and set on fire while shooting everybody who tried to escape.[9]

Bogner explains that this event prompted his father and him to conclude, "We have to do something! Such a system should never take root here again. We have to do something! We have to be engaged, we can no longer just watch as in the '20s and '30s." Thus, he explains, his father and mother joined

---

8. Bogner did not recall the name of the camp or the type of planes constructed there. I suspect that it was the camp known under the name "Thekla" or "Leipzig-Thekla." However, Bogner did recall that it was part of the "Erla-Maschinenwerke." And they did produce Me 109 fighters in license from Messerschmidt in Munich at the Thekla camp.

9. Margaret Bourke-White has photographically documented the massacres the SS committed among concentration camp outposts in Leipzig. Some of these pictures were widely circulated through *Time-Life* magazine. See also Bourke-White (1946).

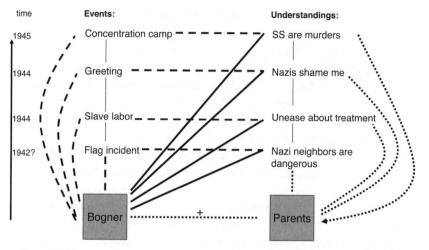

Figure 5.1. The emergence of Bogner's understanding of Nazi rule: This graph shows the complex interaction among recognitions (square dots), corroborations (dashes), and resonances (thin lines) as a progression of overlapping and mutually reinforcing validation dynamics depicted in the form of triangular relations familiar from chapter 4 (solid thick lines are major shared lines). The result is a multiply validated unease about the Nazis.

the refounded KPD even before it was unified with the SPD in 1946 in the Soviet occupational zone to form the SED, the future ruling party of East Germany. Encouraged by his parents and introduced by a cousin, the young Bogner joined the "antifascist youth" (*Antifa-Jugend*) a forerunner of the Free German Youth and its children's organization, the Pioneers. Bogner's emergence of his own understandings about Nazi rule can be schematically presented as a temporal succession and integration of a number of dialectic "triangles" of resonance, corroboration, and recognition (see chapter 4, figures 4.5, 4.8, and 4.10), which have led to a solidification of the relationship to his parents.

It is remarkable to which degree Bogner's story shows how the core socialist messages of "Never again war!" and "Never again fascism!" as well as socialism's call for "social justice" are articulating and thus resonating with his own life experiences. The emotive understandings Bogner began to develop during the war, especially those of the Nazis as an object of his fear and outrage as well as of the Nazis as triggers of his helplessness and shame, are mirrored by socialist propaganda up to the very end of the GDR. In fact, they constitute the core of the SED's claim to legitimacy (Meuschel 1992). Socialism resonates with Bogner in answering to his emerging questions about why he felt uneasy about the Nazis and wherein precisely their evil lay. In particular, socialism built a powerful bridge between questions of social justice on the one hand and the Nazi's unleashing of the world war and the Holocaust

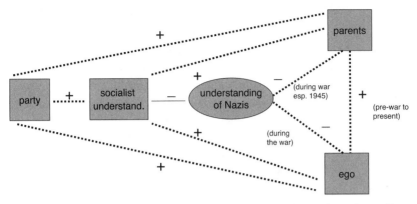

Figure 5.2. Elements of Bogner's space of validation, 1946: Bogner's negative understanding of the Nazis is recognized throughout the war by his parents (rightmost square dot triangle). Socialism as an ideology resonates both with his and his parents questions about Nazism (two triangles in the middle with thin base line). This resonance opens space for the authorization of the party, which can then on its own begin to recognize Bogner's understandings of the Nazis (two leftmost square dot triangles).

on the other. Moreover, socialism answered to his desires to be rid of the Nazi influences, including any positive connections he had entertained to Nazism, Nazi institutions, or persons identified as Nazis. What is more, socialism not only offered him the promise to fight fascism, but it also offered him a role in this fight. The party as the agency articulating these resonating understandings thereby acquires authority. Finally, it is noteworthy that key authority figures within his own social networks, his parents above all (but other relatives, too), decisively turned toward socialism as well, stetting a model while again positively recognizing his own orientation.[10] The understandings offered by socialism resonated with his own desires to make sense of what had happened during the war. The positive recognition of his involvement in socialist institutions within his authority networks began to nourish a positive identification between Bogner and socialism.

After analyzing the forces at play in the space of validation, which created a positive identification of young Bogner with socialism, it is important to investigate whether there might not have been other forces working in the

10. The positive recognition does not even have to be primarily an explicitly ideological one, although it may by default imply or engender one. His parents, for example, signaled to him "that they were very happy that he was taken care of," which simply means, as Bogner points out, that he was, for the time since he was there, "out of danger." And according to Bogner this did not refer to the possibility of a moral corruption, but simply to the very practical concern that he was not playing on the nearby railroad tracks, in the ruins of bombed-out buildings, or the nearby gravel yard.

opposite direction. After all, the majority of the German population reacted much more cautiously, in a large number of cases even with outright hostility to the Russians and their plans for a socialist Germany. In view of the Nazi's cultivation of a general fear of the Russians and their incessant propagandistic representation as inferior, dirty, and violent, in view of the even older painful left-left[11] and left-right divisions during the Weimar years, such negative resonances would not have been surprising. Moreover, the negative and often traumatic experiences many Germans had with the Soviet occupational forces did in many cases corroborate negative evaluations of Russians and the ideology they brought with them.

Bogner's narrative shows an awareness of this possibility by remarking explicitly that nobody in his family or network of friends actually suffered in any way from the Russian occupation. To the contrary, his memories of encounters with Russian soldiers are thoroughly positive, as he makes clear, especially in contrast to his experiences with American troops. Characterizing the immediate postwar situation as one of chronic hunger, in which a search for something edible was the all-absorbing task of everyday life, Bogner describes how the Americans were laughingly burning food leftovers, including sweets, the luxury item par excellence. Worse, they did so under the eyes of children (!) who had come with an empty stomach to beg for something to eat. Bogner insists that this was not only his experience, but that a number of other children were also describing very similar experiences. In Bogner's description Americans are committing an act of *annihilating recognition*, which accurately assesses the desires, thoughts, or feelings of others to use this knowledge to let them feel their utter worthlessness in denying any common human bond with them. By contrast, he describes the Russians as committing an act of *altruistic recognition* by sharing their meager rations of rice or bread with the children, a most powerful symbol of common belonging, which, as Bogner's case makes clear, communicates to others that they are worth someone's personal sacrifice.[12]

---

11. After the mainstream of the Social Democrats (SPD) supported World War I, an independent group of internationalists who later formed the communist party (KPD) broke away. This led to the dual proclamation of a republic on November 9, 1918, by Philipp Scheidemann, a social democrat, and Karl Liebknecht, a communist. After the murder of Rosa Luxemburg and Karl Liebknecht by right-wing forces with which the social democrats had aligned themselves, and definitely after 1925 when Thälmann became its leader, German communists came ever more closely under Soviet control. By the end of the 1920s the KPD was, in effect, a Stalinist organization. Seeing each other, hence, as principal enemies, the German labor movement came to be deeply split. This split, a fundamental aspect of both parties' self-narratives, had significant repercussions all the way to reunification policies in the 1990s.

12. The three other interviewees from that corner of East Germany that was under brief American occupation have very similar contrasting narratives about the American and Russian occu-

If Bogner had negative understandings of the Russians before the end of the war, and if they were initially corroborated by postwar experiences, then the forces at play in his space of validation have successfully extinguished them. There are two related moments in his narrative that point to the possibility that his understandings of the Russians might have been more ambiguous at one point. There is, first, the unprompted direct comparison between his experiences with American and Russian soldiers. And there is, second, the immediate placement of German postwar suffering at the hand of the Soviet forces (including widespread rape) into the context of the much bigger Russian sufferings during the war.[13] Such direct comparisons may be traces of later narratives and their recognizing effect. The postwar East and West German propaganda material continuously worked with precisely these comparisons. Both moves appeared to me at first as defensive, as ideological rather than experiential. However, they both may, at least in part, also have been an interview effect. Not only was I known as of West German origin, and in addition to that as a representative of an American university, but owing to what I thought I had understood about the postwar occupation, I might have looked rather startled at his account. Moreover, it has to be considered that he was also arguing in the context of prevalent, publicly disseminated understandings after unification that negatively validated and thus challenged his understandings.[14]

Bogner's narrative and the manner in which the SED legitimated its rule in the GDR are closely related to each other. There is no doubt that the party's account of its role has profoundly shaped Bogner's account of his own life. It has done so through its efforts in selective recognition, its attempt to create a memory culture, increasing the likelihood of particular resonances at the expense of others, as well as by creating experiential environments standing a higher chance to corroborate favored understandings. It is important not to misunderstand this process as a simple case of a passive subjection to propaganda, as a kind of brainwashing. The condition for the possibility of an agency to form the understandings of a person into a personality it

---

pational regimes. Interestingly, other officers who encountered the Americans in Berlin (three months later) have no such stories. The clue to the puzzle lies in changing moods of the troops and revised orders about contacts with the German population.

13. Other officers also pointed out that the incidence of Russian atrocities may have been exaggerated because socialism and the Russians created negative resonances that can be traced back to Nazi propaganda

14. This interesting moment in the interviewing process forced me to write an account of my own political epistemics, especially my own background understandings of Soviet and American occupational forces in postwar Germany. Originally I intended to add it as a postscript to this book. However, since this volume is already rather long I have decided to publish it as a separate paper.

finds amenable to its own purposes is a strong identification of the targeted person with that organization.[15] What needs to be taken into account is the dynamic interaction between resonances, recognitions, and corroborations. Recognized understandings have to resonate, otherwise the authority of the recognition-dispensing agency is at risk. In Bogner's case, for example, the equation of antifascism and socialism propagated by the SED resonated both with his wartime and postwar experiences. At the same time, however, any changes in recognitions and corroborations also affect the resonances within an existing fabric of understandings. In Bogner's case, for example, peace, socialism, antifascism, pro-Soviet attitudes, anticapitalism, and anti-Americanism become more and more an inextricable totality integrated by necessary linkages. Unless there are memory practices that mark some understandings as historical, which means within the model presented here as of past actuality, one has to be careful not to simply identify understandings presented in an interview with the historical understandings that were action guiding in the past.[16] In the first instance the interview provides an excellent account for why fifty years later Bogner still believes that socialism was an almost logical answer to his life. This does not mean at all, however, that his story is worthless as an account of why Bogner became a Stasi officer. It clearly establishes linkages between emergent understandings and real events. The development of his own understandings in the refraction of recognizing propaganda and future life experiences has probably magnified and purified some of these linkages while silencing others. While these understandings are constructed and reconstructed they are still grounded in actual experience. They are constructed and true at the same time.

Bogner is, among the Stasi officers I have interviewed, not the most typical case, but for several reasons his is a very interesting one. Not only does his space of validation combine most of the elements of his colleague's spaces, but also in many ways he represents the ideal subject of socialist propaganda. Thus, before I return to Kurt Bogner's life story, it is important to review how his beginning identification with socialism compares to that of his colleagues. No other officer had as dramatic an encounter with the crimes of the Nazis as Bogner. Although many do remember being bullied by Nazi zealots. One officer recalls, for example, how his family changed grocery stores once the owner of the one they used to frequent demanded a "Heil Hitler" of everyone

---

15. The only alternative to an active identification is a situation in which there is no alternative to the fashioning agency and identification happens by default as for example in brainwashing (Lifton 1961).

16. In interviews, such past actuality comes to the fore as a juxtaposition of different understandings in the course of time, as in "then I thought x, but then event A happened and I began to think y instead."

entering the store. This does not necessarily mean that such incidences were terribly important at the time they happened (although they may very well have been rather upsetting), but it does mean that seen in retrospect such incidences corroborate socialist understandings of fascism and its evil. It is also important to note that nobody has found his way to socialism without the help of a significant intermediary acting as an authority on political understanding. Although these were very often parents who, regardless of their previous political commitments made a decision to join the SED after the war, important intermediaries could also be other relatives, friends of parents, teachers, or fellow workers.[17] Among reestablished networks of Weimar-time communists, the influence of authority relations was often unambiguous and strong, following classical socialization models. Such officers moved from a socialist family to "progressive" schools and decisively socialist employment relations, such as the Stasi. Horst Haferkamp says, for example:

> I have often been lucky in my life. Part of this was that my father as the oldest of three brothers [all Weimar-communists] was the only one who did not die in the war. My father was a politically conscious man, . . . a member of the KPD and later of the SED. There was nothing on my way to 11th grade [when he was hired by Stasi] that could have distracted me from this path, but I have, from all sides, only received encouragement [in becoming a socialist].

For some of them, the way to socialism was almost fortuitous in the sense that they were drifting about, ultimately landing in the lap of institutions with a strong socialist flavor, in which they were made to feel at home. Wolfgang Schermerhorn had lost both of his parents, his father to the war, his mother, right after the end of the war, to pneumonia, which she was ill suited to survive after several exhausting months fleeing with four children from West Prussia to Leipzig. After a stint with foster parents and three years with different relatives who had maintained, according to Schermerhorn, their anti-Semitic and anticommunist views, keeping him from attending meetings with the communist youth organization, Schermerhorn was apprenticed to a small independent cabinetmaker in Dresden. He describes the atmosphere in this shop as exploitative and abusive because he was treated as cheap labor. After one year, friends made him switch to a large socialized carpenter's shop, where they had a separate teaching gang and masters tending to the needs of apprentices. The leader of the work gang to which he belonged as a young journeyman in the same company, a member of the SED whom he much admired,

---

17. In only one case was the father of a Stasi officer a member of the Nazi party (NSdAP) during the war. Karl Maier says, "My father became unemployed in 1930. He was a member of the NSdAP and welcomed the Nazis with enthusiasm. But in 1946 he joined the SED. I think he honestly worked through his past, and he had a lasting influence on me."

convinced him to join the party. Owing to the experience of both workplaces and his new social environment, Schermerhorn says that some of the central tenets of socialism sounded rather convincing to him. It made sense now that socialism would bring exploitation to an end through the public ownership of capital and also that the labor class ought to be the leading class because it produces all the valuables. The party articulated his experiences; socialist understandings resonated with his past, which at the same time corroborated them, thus endowing socialist institutions with authority.

Nothing seems to have been as important in connecting future Stasi officers with socialism than the sheer joy of participating in the life of socialist organizations. They provided a sense of order in the midst of chaos; they painted a bright picture of the future in a historically bleak moment; and they provided orientation where other organizations had just thoroughly discredited themselves. All officers describe an enormous enthusiasm sweeping through these organizations at the end of the 1940s and the beginning of the 1950s. This was not exactly a revolutionary ferment (though they had discussions about the question of whether they could count as revolutionaries!) but something very nearly like it in its mobilizing sweep, in its heartfelt hopes connected with a new departure, and in its firm belief in its success. Says Horst Haferkamp recounting his school experiences:

> We had strong, emotionally colored experiences of community (*Gemein-schaftserlebnisse*) then. Just to give you one example, which has not for nothing stuck in my memory. Somehow the song "build up, build up, build up, Free German Youth build up" surfaced and we sang it, without the encouragement of any teacher . . . in our break, again and again, the whole class, with such an enthusiasm, we were really euphoric.

Walter Schuster, who hails from a poor labor-class family in western Thuringia, describes how workers were rebuilding their factory. With tears in his eyes he is expressing his pride at a kind of newfound agency in the following words: "We have made our own things. We were building a power station. One would have never known that simple people who were part-time farmers could do such things." Besides pointing to the enthusiasm he felt at work in the reconstruction effort, his wording points directly to another reason why socialism resonated with him: it promised to rectify the long-standing and heartfelt injuries of class. It pledged to give to common people what was their due not only in terms of better resources but also in terms of respect, which included access to higher education and subsequently better positions in the social pecking order. Quite a number of officers reported that their parents, too, would have liked to do something else with their lives. Unfortunately, some did, in their younger years, hold little more in stock than humble working-class occupations. And thus they reminded their sons that they were given an opportunity that capitalism before had withheld from them. This is an interesting case of what might be called complex super-ego validation. The desires and hopes of the parents become those of the child through the usual processes of identification (Freud 2000d, 505). The promises of socialism resonated in pursuit of these desires, which were then also explicitly recognized by the parents. They were ready to give this recognition, however, because their own experiences were first articulated by socialist understandings, which were, through the advancement of their own sons, also corroborated as promises kept. Validation thus came at the same time from within, from without, from intimate authorities, and from social institutions.

Ernst Stellmacher, born and raised in the industrial heartlands of Saxony, describes how in the factory where he was a worker and leading functionary of the FDJ they formed the first youth brigade. This was an assembly team that consisted entirely of young people and that worked side by side the older, hierarchically structured teams. Vividly he recalls the enthusiasm with which young people involved themselves in these then-rather-radical new forms of organizing work life. A decisive part of all of this is a very deliberate policy of the new socialist authorities to dedicate extra resources to young people, to make them feel welcome, and what is perhaps more, to make them feel important in bringing forth a just social order. As the examples I have just described make clear, these claims to a better, more just life could become immediately corroborated by the experience of different work conditions, and, as we shall see, a very favorable set of career opportunities. In educational institutions, the communist youth organization was given considerable influence in organizing almost all extracurricular activities, by being consulted over students' and teachers' promotions, and eventually even over grades.

Students who were functionaries of the FDJ often thoroughly enjoyed these activities and the recognition that came with the function. Several officers describe how busy they became in this role and also how the curricular aspects of school could not only take second seat to the "social-political involvement" (*gesellschaftspolitisches Engagement*) but also how such activities could, much like sports, also compensate for less-than-satisfying academic performance in building self-esteem. Since they knew that their activities were encouraged by the new political order and were deemed important, this also gave them a sense of independence from and a sense of power over their teachers—especially if they were known not to be communists.

What all of them emphasize about their social-political involvement is the joy of acting in unison with others and the idea of belonging to a community of like-minded people. This community was, however, not simply one of conviviality. The experience and renarration of the officers' immediate past; their vicarious identification with German communists persecuted during the Nazi time as well as with the heroes of the victorious Soviet Union;

and their newfound belief in a teleological and Manichaean philosophy of history presenting as a science forged their experience of community as one of fate. The feelings emerging out of these activities at the local routine level were not directly like Durkheim's effervescence, not quite as intensive, but they had some of the same energizing effects of giving everybody the sense of being a member of a universal brotherhood.[18] This was then amplified by their participation in mass-propaganda events such as the World Festival of Youth, or national meetings of the Pioneers or the FDJ, which had, to the enjoyment of the participating officers, obvious effervescent qualities. The officers have pointed out that the effect of these events were specially pronounced because there were, at that time, not all too many alternatives to this kind of merrymaking.

The officers are describing a very interesting pathway on which political understandings are formed, actualized, and, in the last consequence, backgrounded. Very common desires for companionship, pleasure in society, and the acknowledgment of personal worth serve as starting points. The party provides an organized social context in which these desires can be met through the participation in sanctioned practices. This process of articulation creates a complex interlinking of kinesthetic and emotive understandings: the practices are enjoyed, one might become fond of the location where and the institution in which they take place, and one grows to like at least some of the people with whom one interacts there. Since the other participants also enjoy these activities, the participants begin to recognize one another's understandings and thus others' emergent selves and identities. Since these practices are, however, systematically linked as well with discursive understandings, that is, with ideological messages, these may begin to resonate at first simply because they are heard at the same place and at the same time at which the happy feelings of community occur. Moreover, this enjoyment of practices, places, and people typically authorizes at least those participants who are perceived as enabling one's own good feelings. Unless otherwise managed through authority-mediating social arrangements (for example, of parents or valued friends), this emerging authority can now spill over into domains that have only secondarily something to do with the original desires.[19] The systematic connection of the desire-fulfilling practices

---

18. Collins's (2004) notion of "emotional energy" accounts for the fact that Durkheimian effervescence comes about in shades and gradations while being generated both in elaborate rituals and in many everyday interactions.

19. Some opposition members, for example, participated in the activities of the Protestant Youth organization and the FDJ. In these cases parents were often attempting to manage the domains for which these organizations and their leaders would obtain authority. Needless to say that such efforts can also backfire, to the detriment of the authorities who undertake such

with ideological messages facilitates this spillover into an explicitly political domain. Subsequently, these authorities can then recognize and, in the long run, form political understandings. Finally, through a micro-macrocosmic identification enabling the identification of global characteristics of the political from local circumstances, the emotional satisfaction derived from participation in activities and events sponsored by communist youth organizations, could directly corroborate claims of what life in socialism is like. The fact that there is hardly an ideological organization from churches to trade unions to social movements that do without extensive efforts to create resonances for their political messages by association through the co-occurrence with happy feelings, points to the potential effectiveness of this process for the actualization of its political understandings in members. This process of creating resonances by association is also a nice example of the interdependence of discursive, emotive, and kinesthetic understandings.

After this comparison of Bogner's pathway to socialist organizations and understandings with that of other officers, I can now return to his story. As soon as Bogner had joined the socialist youth movement, identifications with socialism and its institutions were continuously recognized. In other words, their recognition was institutionalized. To a significant degree this was recognition by privilege granted in the form of selective access to education and jobs, by which the new powers could reward demonstrated belief and active commitment. In Bogner's case, such recognition was at first indirect, operating through the identification with his father's success. With the help of his Friends of Nature acquaintances and through the affiliation with the party, the older Bogner could embark on an administrative career, leaving his blue-collar background behind.

What is more, the good use of privilege can in turn bring admiration, which is, of course, nothing if not another form of recognition. Recognition can thus beget more recognition, functioning like a form of capital. Feeding onto itself it can create a self-amplifying, belief-consolidating effect.[20] Bogner remembers how proud he was of his father who got "called" (*berufen*) to the labor office and began to counsel recent middle school graduates (including the younger Bogner's own classmates) on career opportunities.[21] Due to

---

management efforts. The dialectic of resonance always puts authorities at risk in negotiating the value of understandings.

20. This is well known from reputation games, be their participants academics, financiers, or talk show hosts.

21. In socialism it was always a matter of particular dignity to be "called to," (*berufen*) "delegated to" (*delegiert*), or "charged" (*beauftragt*) with a job or position. The point in using these expressions was to emphasize that one did not apply out of the presumption of individual qualification, but that one was selected as qualified (and thus recognized) by the party or an organization representing it. Accordingly, the use of these expressions with respect to one's occupation

father Bogner's work, the family became quickly known and respected, as the younger Bogner remembers. Soon enough, he personally came to enjoy recognition through privilege. After eighth grade (the end of mandatory schooling at the time) Bogner received an opportunity to continue with his formal education at an *Oberschule*, a college prep school. Bogner is well aware of the fact that he owed this opportunity not only to his grades but also to his class background as well as to his and his parents' political orientation. Like his father "he was given a chance" and drew from this recognition not only joy but also a keen sense of obligation.

Recognition is pleasurable for the receiver, and pleasure resonates by answering desire. Bogner savored his activities with the communist youth movement. He marvels at the camping trips into the country, which otherwise the family could not have afforded; he fondly remembers the social activities, such as helping the elderly. Given how much he enjoyed participating in the youth movement, it is perhaps not surprising that he was further recognized by being asked to take a position of responsibility with the movement; he became the head of a group that was coextensive with his class in high school. From then on he organized the activities that others might have found pleasurable, thus affording him their gratitude and respect while also corroborating his sense of being good at this. Responsibility, as long as it entails agency, is a potential for successful action and thus further recognition.

By the beginning of the 1950s, therefore, Bogner found himself on a self-reinforcing trajectory of recognition and resonance that every successful career affords. And there were many young people his age who felt exactly the way he did, and who were happily traveling along similar paths. With this feeling of enthusiasm for socialism also came an interesting change in meta-understandings. Bogner and others emphasize the pleasure of being with like-minded people; they still talk of the advantages of attending "progressive" (which means forward looking because socialist in orientation) schools and being taught by "progressive" teachers. Authority became, in this context, more and more defined by commitment to the party and its ideology. This was hastened along by another development. The introduction of socialism into the GDR did not proceed without protest and more or less passive resistance. Not only had many Germans been active Nazis with decisively anti-Soviet attitudes, but the Soviets also began to expropriate private property, first from people with known Nazi ties, and later applying across-the-board size limitations to privately held property. Moreover, the Soviets appointed loyal communists to as many leading positions as possible. The consequence was the beginning of a mass exodus of people, which until

---

was typically connected with a sense of pride—much in the same way that in capitalist liberal democracies the winning of a competition is a matter of pride.

the building of the Berlin Wall made almost 3 million people abandon their homes in Soviet-occupied Germany and later the GDR to flee to the West. None of Bogner's relatives or close friends was among them. This context of conflict led very quickly to a pronounced *we* versus *them* mentality: "who is not for us is against us," became the dominant battle cry. *Tertium non datur!*

The world historical events at that time indirectly corroborated Bogner's suspicions about the evil machinations of the class enemy. The Korean War was proof. And so was the GDR worker uprising of June 17, 1953. Bogner had a much-liked cousin who was a worker in a factory. She told him that the newly established production norms that triggered the demonstrations were impossible to fulfill. So, he concluded, there was a real kernel of worker's dissatisfaction and concern. But then he saw with his own eyes how demonstrators stormed the Kulturhaus (cultural center) in Leipzig, broke the windows, threw out typewriters and chairs, and set fire to the building. The Kulturhaus was an icon of the local labor movement. Built during the Weimar years, it became a workers' debating club, meeting place, pub, fun spot, and a union house. Bogner says: "Only the Nazis closed it, and it was opened again in 1945." Could it really be, Bogner asked, that workers would destroy their own house? So he became convinced that the whole demonstration was clearly hijacked by people with counterrevolutionary intentions. Corroborations and resonances together thus support the official party line. Bogner also supported rearmament in the GDR. At the beginning he argued about it with comrades in the youth movement; he took his "never again war" seriously. But then he too agreed that East Germany had no choice after the West had taken the first step. Again, in both of these cases doubts could be relativized within his authority networks, and relativization was grounded in corroborating events. When the Stasi asked him to join in 1954, Bogner felt honored for being asked and signed up. He was nineteen.

SECURITY BUREAUCRATS

None of the officers I interviewed had planned on a Stasi career. All knew that the secret police existed; some had heard about particular actions because the Stasi was then still involved in "public relations management" (*Öffentlichkeitsarbeit*). Yet nobody had an idea what exactly the Stasi did, that is, what different kinds of work it was involved in, what life in the various branches would be like, or why it should be particularly desirable or for that matter undesirable to become a Stasi officer in general or a member of any branch in particular. Such knowledge was considered, to the end of the GDR, top secret, and the officers themselves learned much about the organization as a whole only once they advanced very high up or once it was finally dissolved. Moreover, even if one of them should have wanted to, one could not apply for a Stasi job. Self-applications were regularly discarded as security hazards. Instead, the Stasi cherry-picked and approached the people it wanted. What they were looking for is not only deep dedication to the socialist cause, as evidenced by a continuous active involvement in the communist youth movement, but also people whose immediate social network looked as if it would not question or endanger this commitment. Close ties to Westerners or people who were regarded as harboring "inimical-negative" attitudes to the party state were disqualifying, as were "lifestyle choices" that were deemed to increase the vulnerability to blackmail, such as homosexuality, indebtedness, alcoholism, or gambling. For all of the officers I interviewed, therefore, their Stasi career began with an unexpected call by some official or the other, most likely the director of their school, or an older higher functionary in the youth movement. Upon arrival they were told that there were "two gentlemen" (*zwei Herren*) who desired a conversation with them. These gentlemen then typically identified themselves as Stasi officers.[22]

Beginnings

Not surprisingly, then, all officers harbored other career ideas before the Stasi approached them. Many had already shown a strong interest in the armed forces (until 1955 the paramilitary "barracked People's Police"), often because they considered this a particularly patriotic career choice (which does not exclude the possibility that especially those attracted by the navy also felt the romantic appeal of the sea). Others were set on quite different careers. Kurt Bogner, for example, had already applied to study economic planning; Horst Haferkamp, whose life-narrative I will use as an allegorizing anchor for this section, was eying philosophy. No matter what, however, working for the Stasi was not only presented to them as an honor, a deep sign of the party's trust to them, but also as *the* mission the party had in stock for them (*Parteiauftrag*): this was going to be their position in class warfare. When Haferkamp was called out of class in the eleventh grade to meet two Stasi recruiters, they began their conversation with the question:

> whether I would be ready to work for the party after the final exams. And there I have said yes, without any discussion at all what this was about in detail and whether one could earn money that way. It was for me in accordance with my education and my political convictions a great honor to be asked and there was only this answer. And it was for me entirely unimport-

---

22. In a few cases conversations began under cover, yet these seem to have been occasions in which the Stasi's interest was aroused for other reasons and recruiting emerged as a possibility along the way.

ant if it turned out that I should have become a mountaineer, a member of the foreign service, or a miner.

Not everybody remembers being quite as unwavering as Haferkamp. Many conferred with people they trusted, with parents or the friends of parents. These, however, not having enough hard information either, and since they were typically as committed to socialism as the candidate, could only make vague suggestions that secret police work was important and that the candidate might want to say "yes."[23] Horst Stellmacher, entering at a slightly older age and with much more professional experience, used the Stasi's call to escape another party mission, namely that of becoming a full-time functionary of the communist youth movement. The publicity involved in this task always made him uncomfortable. The mixture of the quasi-public recognition afforded them by the state (for their capability and trustworthiness) and the appeal to act in accordance with their publicly avowed principles, and thus to recognize themselves through deeds in their recognition by the party, did the trick. They signed on.[24]

For almost everybody I could talk with, their work at the Stasi began in the role of an "undercover investigator" (*verdeckter Ermittler*), which means they were typically made to participate in the kind of security checks I mentioned in chapter 2. Endowed with official ID cards from other government agencies, trying to convince their more or less unsuspecting interlocutors that they were in fact not who they were, that is, young, completely inexperienced Stasi officers they were sent out to question neighbors or colleagues about the habits, thoughts, and activities of a particular person. For some officers this kind of work was merely boring and they took it as one of those things one has to go through to move on. That meant in a large number of cases advancing to officer school, which followed for some in a matter of weeks, for others their attendance was planned for the foreseeable future. Some officers found in this investigative work a nice reprieve from the stress of the final exam year at high school; for yet others it resonated with some of their curiosities in bringing them in contact with people they might have not met otherwise, for example, with prostitutes.[25] Finally, there were officers for whom this kind of work, with its secrecies, already signaled that they

23. In part the lack of knowledge led to helpless statements. Jürgen Buchholz, for example, reported that his father said "that [Stasi] is the same thing as the Gestapo [Nazi secret police]—just the other way around [purportedly meaning: this time fighting for the good]."
24. I am working with ultimate self-selection sampling here: I don't know of anybody who was approached and rejected it.
25. Although this aspect was quite straining for some who were taken aback by the frequency of explicit jokes among their colleagues or by contacts with people at the margins of society.

belonged to a small elite that was much better informed, much deeper in the know than average citizens or even other party members.

For quite a few, this low-level investigative work came nevertheless as a shock, because they felt forced into "misstating the truth." Martin Vogler recalls: "I hated it, I was supposed to pretend that I worked for the senate [the city government of Berlin]; I approached this work with real horror and I was close to giving up." Karl Maier, too, remembers: "I didn't like the conspiratorial aspect of it." However, such negative resonances with perceived moral duties were in most cases overcome by a mixture of different kinds of rationalizing recognitions. These ranged from the pragmatic invocation of proverbs such as "all beginning is difficult" to the concrete evocations of more positive resonances by appealing to vibrant "defender of the fatherland" images. After all, paternal friends or older colleagues argued that the class enemy was working with just such measures, leaving them no choice but to retaliate in kind. This was class warfare after all, not child's play.

In this context it is interesting that the question of lying rose twice to prominence in my interviews with former officers while their wives were present. They participated because they felt intrigued by the opportunity to catch up with aspects of their husband's past about which they felt they did not know enough. Both wives were party members; one was a teacher, the other a physician working for the Stasi. In each instance the officer explained how he worked "under cover" appearing to represent some other agency, to which their respective wives responded in unison by saying "you mean a lie." Their husbands reacted in exactly the same way, too, both in terms of the emotional tone of their response—with indignation—and in terms of the argument they made to defend themselves. Peter Wagner retorted that he did not want to digress into a lecture about the necessity to work under cover in secret service contexts. He insisted he would have had to give up his job right there and then if he had considered what he did a form of lying. Horst Haferkamp said: "The important thing was that it has to serve the cause of the working class, . . . And if it does not, it is no good, and if it does, it is ok." With these answers, the officers have both in effect taken recourse to arguments in terms of the ethics of absolute finality. Needless to say that honesty was propagated as a value in the GDR. However, the point was to understand that it could not be a value per se. Instead, it was important to learn when to be honest and when it was better not to be.[26] My point is simply that absolute finality did not come "naturally" but needed to be practiced

---

26. Accordingly, the long list of duties in the statutes of the SED (Benser and Naumann 1986, 1) exhorts members to be merely "sincere and honest vis-à-vis the party," only after the principles of absolute finality have become abundantly clear. In the "socialist ten commandments" (ZK 1959, 160–61), which was addressing a wider citizenry, honesty is not mentioned directly at all but

and recognized in everyday life in part against that resonance with older thinking (here: setting honesty absolute) that was so frequently denounced as an impediment to socialist development.

Officer School

The next step on the career ladder was entry into the officer school. This is therefore a good moment to review quickly some important problems of recruitment and training that the Stasi faced during the mid-1950s. The party paid much attention to recruiting politically reliable people into the Stasi, which meant that it displayed a strong preference for people with a labor-class background who had shown a strong commitment to the socialist project in some function, and also that no former members of fascist security agencies would be considered. The pool of qualified personnel was very small indeed. In it were mainly people who had gained relevant experiences in the Weimar-KPD's intelligence apparatus (M-Apparat), in some function for the communist international, in the Spanish Civil War, or in some Soviet military or intelligence agency. Communists with such backgrounds were immediately earmarked for leadership positions. All three ministers of the Stasi, Wilhelm Zaisser (1950–53), Ernst Wollweber (1953–57), and Erich Mielke (1957–89), and a number of the first-generation leadership personnel belong into this category. Weimar communists incarcerated by the Nazis in high-security prisons or concentration camps who have had experiences with underground KPD work were often taken into the immediate postwar police service as well and were, since 1950, also employed in Stasi leadership positions.

The emphasis on political reliability implied that the Stasi had to recruit its rank and file, especially for local and regional offices, from an applicant pool whose members were not really qualified for such work; by and large they had neither the formal qualifications nor the kind of life experiences that might have predisposed them to becoming effective secret police agents. This led quickly to a number of problems. In a conference between SED security experts and Soviet councilors with Walter Ulbricht it was remarked in particular that Stasi employees lacking formal training and/ or experience showed considerable deficiencies in recruiting and working with highly qualified informants (Gieseke 2000, 187). Thus, Stasi launched a qualification campaign that took a two-pronged approach. It aimed at recruiting candidates with a higher level of formal education (meaning twelve years rather than the then-still-quite-common eight or nine school years), and it aimed at improving the system of internal training. The latter led

---

seems to be subsumed under an exhortation to live "decently," which again comes late in the list (number 9) and after the contribution to the realization of socialism have been featured first.

ultimately to the stepwise upgrading of the Stasi's school in Eiche, a small village outside of Potsdam on the southwestern city limits of Berlin (Gieseke 2000, 187–97). The development of this school is an interesting index for the progressive formalization and bureaucratization of the Stasi. Up until 1955 the school offered only intensive short-term training sessions ranging from a few weeks to a yearlong course. From 1955 onward it offered full two-year officer training courses; in 1966 it was recognized as a diploma granting "law school" that, starting in 1968, acquired the right to grant doctoral degrees as well. In 1984 it began with full four-year officer training courses.

This school in Eiche is where most of the officers in my sample were headed sooner or later. More commonly they attended as full timers; some, however, were deemed so irreplaceable by their superiors that they were only allowed to become correspondents. Eiche produced feelings of elation in some officers. Georg Assmann said:

> One got the feeling of belonging to a socialist elite, or better perhaps to an avant-garde. In the center of it all was the education to see oneself as a member of a community, a collective . . . as an active part of a whole. One felt as a part of that force that propelled the GDR toward becoming a better society, all the more so since there was ample literature about the short-comings of capitalism.

Even though most officers agreed that such feelings and thoughts were part of the Eiche experience, all in all it was a hard time for those who went there in person. For the first three months they were not allowed to return home, and later they could do so only every four weeks, for what amounted to a mere twenty-four-hour stint for many. Initially, they were not even allowed to leave the barracks. After a few months they could do so in larger groups under the guidance of an officer, and even as seasoned students they could only go out in a group of three. The officers remember their time in Eiche with that peculiar retrospective pleasure in survived hardship that derives from the eminent narratability of an unusually intense but luckily closed life episode. Their stories resemble those told by military draftees elsewhere. And yet there is something special about them. Some of the merely silly, innocuous, or otherwise trivial actions leading to public reprimand or punishment are not presented as injustices but rather as personal failings that were met with an adequate response.

Take Jürgen Buchholz. In his last year of high school he worked for a couple of weeks as a farmhand. He used his salary to have a suit tailored out of a rarely available mouse-gray corduroy fabric that he had the good luck of finding somewhere on the market in East Berlin. That suit, its fabric, the way it was buttoned, as he says, "in no way resembled current GDR fashion." Wearing this suit and a pair of crepe-soled shoes, which were considered dernier cri at the time, albeit Western too, he was seen at a dance event by one of his fellow students. The fact that he wore such attire was immediately made public at the wall newspaper of his study group at school. In a specially called meeting of the communist youth movement, wearing such clothes and shoes was censored as petit bourgeois. Buchholz agreed to this assessment in an exercise of self-critique.

As I pointed out in chapter 2, the ritual of critique and self-critique aimed at producing shame for failure to self-objectify. For the shame affect to set in, the person needs to agree on some level with the accuser. Where shame does not materialize because the accused does not agree with the accuser, anger is often the more immediate response, which may be followed by sadness about the isolating aspects of the procedure (Tomkins 1963; Scheff and Retzinger 1991). So I asked Buchholz whether he could remember how he felt in the proceedings in which he was censored as a petit bourgeois. He insisted he had no bad feelings about it either then or afterward. Of course, this is surprising because most communist renegades (e.g., Leonhard 1955, 270–82, 294–301) have left us rather gruesome accounts of their experiences in critique and self-critique during the Stalin years. It is also surprising because Buchholz had just so lovingly described the suit and the way he got it. Yet, as if in answer to my expressed puzzlement, he quite vividly remembered another "funny thing," as he put it, that he was not promoted that year either. And here at last it seems as if he displaced his patent disappointment to an exact statement of related facts. He pointed out that this cost him every month dearly in salary. Instead of 570 Marks he received only 525. He also noted that he was, although among the better students, one in a group of merely four out of a total of more than one hundred students who were not promoted. He then attributed his nonpromotion to the fact that his group organizer knew that his mother ran a little shop and that he was therefore, strictly speaking, not of proletarian origin. Yet, according to him, this too did not trigger any resentment on his part. It was true after all.

Another interesting case is that of Horst Haferkamp. He explains how upon arrival the entire group of newcomers was divided into "study groups" of twenty-five students, each of which were, militarily speaking, platoons. To remind new arrivals of Stasi's character as a "military organ," students at Eiche, contrary to normal practice, wore a uniform, marched to lunch, and so on.[27] Every study group was assigned a classroom in which most of

---

27. As one might expect of a secret police organization, its officers typically wore plain clothes. Exceptions to this rule were the passport control units as well as division II, which as a whole had the National People's Army as its object. For festive occasions officers wore dark suits and ties with their medals, and only for very rare occasions did they wear their dress uniforms. The monthly military training was conducted in fatigues.

its instruction took place. Three students in every platoon were selected as platoon leader, party secretary, and coordinator of studies. Haferkamp assumed the role of the latter and became good friends with the holders of the former two offices—a fact that may have as much to do with their shared responsibility as with their common origin in the region around Leipzig. One of the key tasks of the study organizer was to keep all notebooks about secret service subjects under lock and seal (literally). This practice seems to have been driven as much by the desire to inculcate a certain discipline in handling classified information as by fear that this was a possible leak for important Stasi secrets. Another was to collect and submit every Monday all platoon members' study plans for the impending week. In these plans the students had to fill in, around the fixed lectures, their hours of "self-study," which had to take place in the assigned classroom:

> We scrupulously controlled this among each other. If people did not minimally register for self-study on two evenings for at least two hours then we considered them to be lazy bums who needed to be dealt with through the means of the party. And really good were those who came to 55 to 60 hours of total work time per week. Those were regarded as the "conscious" (bewußt) ones.

One day, Haferkamp and his friends, while registered for self-study, were caught playing skat in their room, arguably Germany's most popular card game. The trio of functionaries "got beaten up verbally for this," that is, they were officially and publicly reprimanded. And again my question of whether he got angry with those comrades turning him in: "I wouldn't even call them informers. We didn't act in a party-adequate manner and if somebody else would have taken that liberty we would also have 'beaten him up.'" However, his wife added to our conversation at this point: "One thing is quite certain, you were quite angry then!"

Both cases reveal an interesting formation of understandings in terms of the ethics of absolute finality. They are interesting pieces in the archaeology of a socialist, or better perhaps, a partisan, person. What both stories reveal is that it took emotional and discursive labor to achieve self-objectification. In Buchholz's case this labor shines through in the cracks between the ostentatious denial of emotional hurt and a dispassionate attention to minute detail. Haferkamp's words form a seamless account of perfect self-objectification, the labor of which becomes transparent only in his wife's intercession. The pointer to a process of critique and self-critique makes available a very common practice of person formation that was used in widely varying degrees of formality. In terms of the sociology of understanding, it operates through the mobilization of a massive negative recognition, the effect of which is supposed to strengthen superego in its conflict with ego. Superego then has to speak, publicly affirming the negative recognition of ego, which ideally moves ego to reconsider his or her understandings, leading to an identity in which the ego-super-ego conflicts are greatly diminished. In this way ritualized self-objectification (as in critique and self-critique) put the finishing touches to (or reinvigorated) conversion to socialism. This also resulted in a more acute sense of self that was corroborated in successfully overcoming subjectivism and thus as more adept at representing socialism as a body of ideas that was in turn affirmed as an immense source of value (Joas 1992, 10).

What both cases reveal as well is the production of a consciousness that emphasizes mutual observation and enforcement of the party line. Personal allegiances, friendships, intimacy, all considered bourgeois forms of sociality, were not supposed to interfere with the primary allegiance to the party. Ideally, intimacy between people was the product of shared allegiance. Mielke expressed this again and again in speeches to his men by asking them to practice "comradeship" (based on self-objectification) not "camaraderie" (putatively based on subjectivist likes and dislikes). Many officers and other functionaries of the party have expressed their surprise in how fast the social fabric of the party and that of Stasi colleagues disintegrated after the dissolution of first the Stasi and then the GDR. However, this is precisely what one would expect of networks built on the ethics of absolute finality. The breakdown of person-forming institutional arrangements doing their work through organized validation leads to subsequent changes of personality, unless some countervailing institution takes its place.

First Assignments

Leaving Eiche, the officers were reintegrated into some unit of the ministry or of the district and/or county administrations—typically the unit that has recruited them. Arriving there, they were assigned their first "object responsibilities," that is, organizations or parts of organizations for whose security (as understood by the Stasi) they became responsible. This meant that they had to introduce themselves to the leaders of these objects as the Stasi's point person in charge of security. Since these objects included hospitals, publishing houses, or whole branches of universities, the officers (many of them barely twenty years old) were faced with much older, much more experienced leaders of these organizations as counterparts. Horst Haferkamp recounts how he braced himself for the first encounter with the director of a research laboratory that became his first object:

> I scratched my head and began to think really hard and then I cheered myself up by thinking this: I said to myself, I am the Stasi, he is a professor and director of a lab. Could you become a professor and direc-

tor of a lab? Yes you could (laughs), not today and not tomorrow but in principle you could. Could he become a Stasi officer? Never (laughs), completely unsuitable, much too stupid (laughs), not intellectually, but politically! So why should you fear him? . . . In my entire life [until then] I always had to conduct conversations with professors wearing an expression of credulity; but now I stood for something, in this case a ministry!

Most officers have stories of this kind. The prospect of such encounters was at first frightening but then also exhilarating as they felt they were charged with a responsibility that made them appear as equals of sorts, if not in some sense even as superiors, in spite of the age difference, because the category of political allegiance was opening up a whole new sphere of value. Another officer expressed this sense of a basic equality in terms of expertise: "He is an expert in his field, which happens to be medicine, I am an expert in mine, which happens to be security." These encounters filled most officers with pride, especially once they had overcome their initial anxieties. The organization that lent them power led them into situations where they had to be recognized at least formally by others, people who until recently would have looked as if they were operating on a much more elevated plane. Now they faced each other as equals—at least that's how the officers came to see it. Moreover, they were encountering people whom most of their parents would never have stood a chance to meet on a formally equal footing. Thus the bond was strengthened between the organization they represented and self. With the imprimatur of the Stasi they were now important. Their cards identifying them as officers of the Stasi became tokens of recognition for their newfound, indeed exalted, value.

The fact that theses organizational leaders had to meet with them does not imply that they welcomed these young Stasi officers with open arms, or that they took them particularly seriously. In fact, the officers' stories are shot through with hints that the heads of their objects—especially if they did not have a party background—did not particularly care for their security concerns. In the best case they thought it was silly, a nuisance really, stealing their time. In the worst case they took the security concerns of the Stasi officers as a pretext to snoop around their turf or even to put them under surveillance, which they did not welcome at all. Haferkamp tells how his predecessor in another laboratory, which he soon took over from him as his second object, was almost thrown out by the director when he introduced himself. He remembers his colleague's account of the director's words as: "I too think calm and order and security are very important, and I am sure you can very productively contribute to it by not disturbing us in our work." Haferkamp continues:

You must remember that in the 1950s and '60s the SED wasn't quite in command yet in the Academy [of Sciences]. The old professors, who were established from before 1945 and who had a scientific reputation also were politically quite powerful [in their respective units]. . . . We couldn't quite say "fist in face" I will teach you! No, no, in such cases we just withdrew to our hearth to huddle with each other about what to do next.

The choice of metaphors here underlines the epistemic force of their interlocutors' doubts about the meaningfulness of their role as security agents. These doubts had to be overcome through the warming recognition of their growing identifications with the party, the state and Stasi work within their own authority networks.

Thus it was all the more important that through their own work they should be able to corroborate their understandings. And thus Haferkamp said:

All that changed soon, about a year later, when we locked up the first spy from his [the director's] lab who had worked for an American [secret] service. This of course strengthened our position vis-à-vis him and the entire lab now that we didn't have to say there might be someone with evil intentions and could instead point out "you had an administrative director who was a spy." . . . now nobody could say anymore we just make that up, that problem with security.

Easing the task of explaining to the leadership of their objects why their work was significant was as important as being able to tell just that to themselves. At the same time they furnished the Stasi through these cases with a repertoire of stories that could be told time and again to corroborate claims about the acuity and violence of class warfare.

Corroborating Work Experiences

So here, then, is the story of how Haferkamp caught "his" first spy, which he tells, needless to say, with gusto. The story proper begins with Haferkamp taking over the four secret informants his predecessors had recruited among the lab's employees. The quartet was of varying quality or "caliber." One informant, a secretary, had been recruited as a means to atone for some minor criminal act, the charges for which were dropped in a peculiarly socialist version of plea bargaining in exchange for regular information. As all officers never tire to point out, informants recruited under pressure, were typically lacking independent drive, and were therefore rather ineffective. So it was with this secretary ("she could have been my mother") who more or less kept Haferkamp up to date on the gossip in the lab and skipped as many meetings with her guidance officer as she could possibly find excuses for. One of the other three, however, was deemed so valuable that there was some hesitation at first as to whether "greenhorn"[28] Haferkamp could really be entrusted with guiding him. Yet his boss insisted on it "or else he might just as well send him packing." The informant's code name was "falcon";[29] he was the head of research of one of the institution's four or five departments. Already in his early fifties, he was significantly older than the director, who was something of an early highflier (a clue, perhaps, to why the "falcon" might have engaged in Stasi work in the first place). The meetings between Haferkamp and his secret informant were at some level rituals of virility: smoking a pack of Orient, then the GDR's most expensive cigarette brand while drinking a good half bottle of cognac (both courtesy of the Stasi) was de rigueur. Haferkamp was keenly aware that keeping up was part of being accepted across the wide age difference.

One day in late 1958 Haferkamp was called by his somewhat cantankerous boss, whom he—as he explains digressing from the main storyline—respected greatly because he had taken part in an insurgency fighting the Nazi army in World War II. The boss asked him to bring all of the object's documents along. This was then still possible, Haferkamp explains, because they were rather lean then in comparison with what they were twenty years later. As his boss began to leaf through the files, he stumbled across information they had gotten from another unit that caught his immediate attention. The institute's administrative director had been seen late in the evening in a somewhat intoxicated state at Bahnhof Friedrichstrasse (the commuter rail station handling the transit across the then-still-open border with West Berlin). Haferkamp's boss looked up, saying: "Why haven't you put this guy behind bars yet?" Haferkamp had seen the piece of paper but did not think it was significant. His boss, however, felt it was good enough to launch a formal investigation for suspicion of treason, and this is what Haferkamp hurried to do.

Haferkamp instructed "falcon" to become better friends with the administrative director of the lab, a task in which he succeeded to the degree that he could collect evidence that the administrative director, at this point well into his seventies, began to ship more and more of his belongings to West Berlin in an apparent attempt to flee. Once the apartment was emptied to such a degree that this fact alone constituted enough evidence to prove the

---

28. The German equivalent expression is *junger Dachs* ("baby badger").
29. Since code names were chosen by officers or their informants they can occasionally shed a revealing light on underlying emotions: here, obviously, the hope that the informant be useful in what is basically understood as a hunt, by either the informant, his first guidance officer, or both.

intention, a felony in the GDR, the Stasi arrested him and his daughter, who, although in her early thirties, still lived with her parents.

Searching the house, Haferkamp and his colleagues found at first nothing of note that could have proven espionage, such as photographs, documents, radio equipment, or code lists. However, in a corner of the kitchen where the householders kept odd bits and pieces, Haferkamp zeroed in on an inconspicuous slip of paper with nothing more than a phone number scribbled on its face. Suspiciously, the first two digits revealed that it was most certainly a West Berlin number. Running this number against the Stasi's registry revealed that this was a number used by an American intelligence agency. Whatever became of the case Haferkamp only knows from hearsay. Although he had personally arrested the administrative director, he was not involved in the interviews conducted at the Stasi's jail and or the trial itself. Apparently the administrative director confessed quickly, implicating two more people, and was sentenced to fifteen years in prison. He did not know what kinds of secrets he did betray or even could have betrayed.

Spy-catcher stories are important for the consolidation of Stasi officers' understandings of their work and its place in the socialist project. Direct participation in such actions corroborated Manichaean understandings of class conflict. The romanticized stories about them provided a recognizing rationale for their work, which thus became an object of pride. Officers who had a hand in a success were given formal recognition and were awarded with premiums or medals or by promotion. Narratives of successful actions could also be used by superiors to request more effort from other members who were less successful. They were used for training purposes, both to demonstrate the validity of socialist ideology and to discuss particular kinds of techniques. Until 1961, the Stasi used selective episodes to produce road shows in which it presented itself to a larger public in an effort to legitimate its own existence and the further-reaching claims of the party regarding the hostile intentions of the class enemy. Although such stories are a constitutive part of many officers' pre-1961 direct or more often indirect experience, they are not as common as one might think given that this is what *Abwehrarbeit* (counterespionage) was supposed to be about. They are exceedingly rare for the time after 1961. The reason was in plain sight: the Wall. But before I can discuss the officers' relation to the Wall, I want to discuss a case of sabotage, the second type of criminal activity the Stasi was supposed to thwart or clear up once committed.

The identification, arrest, and conviction of saboteurs had a similarly corroborating effect on Stasi officers' understandings of socialism, the position of the GDR in the world, and of their own role as successful guardians of the party. Sabotage demonstrated to them that enemy action in the GDR could cause considerable damage to the socialist project. Here is Haferkamp's story of how he (in close collaboration with a colleague whom he credits with the key idea) caught "his" only saboteur. The Academy of Sciences was building a brand new institute for physical chemistry. One Monday morning the workers returned from their weekend away and found all electric wires cut level with the wall on a whole floor, in ten to twelve rooms that were destined to become lab rooms. The damage was considerable in as far as the walls had to be reopened for rewiring, which caused a delay in completing the building. The same morning a young man in his early twenties failed to report for work at the construction site. As it turned out, over the weekend he had fled to West Berlin. He emerged as a prime suspect in this case. "For us it was quickly clear, if not yet proven in a juridical sense, that it could only have been him." The background knowledge that led them to this conclusion was that although every East German fleeing to the West could claim citizenship, those able to prove that they were persecuted by the state could become recognized formally through a document whose name Haferkamp remembers as "C-slip," which entitled its holder to more assistance (for example, in securing an apartment).[30] He argues that this fact was propagated via Western media throughout the GDR and especially by the RIAS[31] radio station.

So they set out a trap, which basically consisted of making their suspect feel unsuspected. They told the young man's parents, whom they had interviewed after his disappearance, that they had identified the perpetrator and it wasn't their son. Thus calmed the son returned one last time from his refugee camp in West Berlin to meet his parents, bid them proper farewell, and possibly take along a few things more. This was what Haferkamp and his colleagues had waited for, and they arrested him in front of his parent's door. He confessed and was sentenced to several years in prison. The pride of having played an important role in this action is still audible in Haferkamp's voice.

This story is particularly interesting for the conclusion Haferkamp drew from it then and that he still believes now. He argues that this story is proof

that our contention that the damaging of the GDR was organized from over there (drüben) was not in every case correct, but it was in principle correct. One shouldn't think about this in too simple a way, assuming that everybody [doing damage here] had his [Western] guidance officer who told him what

---

30. Already in 1950 the Federal Republic passed the "Law for Emergency Admission" (*Notaufnahmegesetz*), according to which people fleeing the GDR for political reasons obtained particular assistance such as unemployment benefits until they obtained work, assistance with finding and paying for a regular apartment outside of the refugee camps, and paid airfare from Berlin to West Germany (Heidemeyer 1994).

31. RIAS is an acronym standing for *Rundfunk im amerikanischen Sektor* (Radio in the American [occupational] sector [of Berlin]). In GDR rhetoric it was the epitome of enemy propaganda divulged by mass media.

actions to undertake against the GDR. This process worked via the media, and we were therefore also correct to say that RIAS is a radio station disseminating inflammatory speech [*Hetzsender*], that is, an agency undertaking sabotage against the GDR. What they have said has affected the head of this young man in such a way that he allowed himself to be made a criminal, because he thought he could secure this way a better starting position for himself over there. And this wasn't even stupid, because this is how it really was.

No doubt then, the episode also corroborated emotive understandings about the class enemy as heinous and worthy of hate. The significance of Haferkamp's conclusion lies in foreshadowing the way Stasi officers later thought (and often continue to think) about the members of the GDR opposition as guided if not directly then indirectly from abroad. But it also highlights how deeply entrenched the model of a consciousness-driven social transformation has become in explaining human behavior. Since he knew that socialism tried to influence the minds of its citizenry through mass-mediated propaganda to accept a particular understanding of the world, he assumed that Western media would do the same. And just as the East was centrally organized and coordinated in this effort, so must be the West.

The Berlin Wall as Relief

In this story and in many previous ones, the boundary between East and West plays a significant role. The much longer boundary between both countries, stretching over hundreds of miles from the Baltic Sea in the north to the Thuringian and Bavarian forests in the south, had already been made virtually impenetrable in the early 1950s. Owing to the formal sovereignty of the four allied powers of World War II, however, the boundaries within Berlin remained open. That is, until August 13, 1961, when the Wall was erected to bring the free movement between both parts of Berlin to an abrupt halt.

This open boundary in Berlin was a continuous source of problems for Stasi officers not only because it facilitated espionage and sabotage actions, but also because people in the officers' object responsibility continued to flee the GDR, leaving behind painful gaps. Officers all investigated cases of "desertion from the republic" (*Republikflucht*),[32] not least because it might involve "trafficking in humans with intentions inimical to the state" (*staatsfeindlicher Menschenhandel*). Since the officers were deeply invested in the

---

32. Literally, the word means "flight from the republic." However, it is built on the model of the German word for "desertion" (from the military), *Fahnenflucht*, which means literally "flight from the flag." Since its use was always meant as a moral condemnation, as will become clear in an instant, the translation "desertion from the republic" is more accurate as it more adequately carries the moral weight of the charge.

socialist project, and since they also identified with their task to secure a particular object, they tended to perceive every case of flight as personal defeat. Horst Haferkamp expresses these feelings with the following words.

I personally didn't scare off these people (laughs) but they were in my domain of responsibility. And if somebody ran away here [from his domain] it was different than if somebody fled from someone else's domain of responsibility. In this sense it was quite a defeat, this is difficult to explain because irrational factors play a role here too, even if in particular cases one could understand some of their motives, if they had been treated badly . . . Yet the fact remains that for me they were traitors too. I don't want to hide this, even today. These were people who in their majority left for base reasons, because one could live materially better over there, at least for the moment[!] . . . Among professionals such as doctors this was contemptible because it always affected patients.

Besides abandoning people, an argument heard also for teachers, the most often quoted reason why officers thought that fleeing the GDR was immoral is that the refugees had all enjoyed the privilege of obtaining a good education in the GDR, just to capitalize on it in the FRG by obtaining better paid jobs.

The official version of why people abandoned the GDR was again that the enemy in the West tried to solve its labor shortage problems by actively recruiting GDR citizens. Officers speak in this context of outrageous "recruiting campaigns" (*Abwerbungskampagnen*). Letters from people who had already fled to those still in the GDR, whom they encouraged to follow suit, are often quoted as evidence. And so is the fact that the FRG did much to lower the cost of transition by not only providing every refugee from East Germany with citizenship and accordingly with the right to work but also by running a system of "transition camps" (*Durchgangslager*). These camps gave refugees a place to go and provided help in establishing them in the West.[33]

---

33. The transition camps also served the secret services of the United States, Britain, and France as well as that of the Federal Republic of Germany as a screening device. On the one hand they wanted to learn something about the GDR; on the other hand they aspired to filter out potential spies. Especially during the 1950s there was quite some fear in the Federal Republic of becoming undermined with communists, or at least communist thought, potentially playing a significant role during strikes. When in 1956 a prominent member of a GDR block party first fled to the West only to return later to the GDR, he fueled a discussion about the logic behind the Law of Emergency Admission. The Federal Ministry for Refugees answered thus (in the paraphrase of the weekly *Der Spiegel*, May 16, 1956, 18): "Rescinding the law of Emergency Admission would lead to a further depopulation of central Germany [i.e., the GDR] increasing the stream of refugees to the West to an undesirable extent. In addition, in case of an economic crisis sources of social unrest would be increased by the unconsciously communist thought of the refugees." The fear of ideological infiltration was of course mutual.

However, the Stasi was also keenly aware that there were by no means just "pull" reasons in the form of opportunities and hopes, realistic or not, that led people to flee, but that there were also homegrown "push" reasons that made them want to go. Karl Maier's first object upon graduating from Eiche in 1958 was the Ministry for People's Education, whose main responsibility was the GDR's system of K-12 education. He recounts how they began to undertake systematic efforts to stem the tide of teachers leaving the country. The basic idea was to remove what they called "conflict situations" seen as decisive causes in people's decisions to flee by using the Stasi's possibilities to cut through ordinary bureaucratic pathways of conflict resolution. Secret informants everywhere were supposed to spot the people who were dissatisfied and looked as if they might jump ship. The reason was not to begin criminal procedures but to see what could be done to keep people in the GDR, for example by talking to the headmaster.

Maier also recalls how the minister at this point had the idea of producing a propaganda brochure, not, and this is the real novelty, based on socialism's understanding of history, but grounded in interviews with returnees (of which there were also some) about the conditions in the West and why it was preferable to stay in the East, difficulties notwithstanding. Thus the Stasi conducted interviews that it presented to a professor at Humboldt University who was supposed to write the brochure. However, the "measure of August 13, 1961," as the building of the Wall was known in official GDR lingo, made these plans obsolete. The Wall brought a sigh of relief to all officers I interviewed. Literally overnight they were discharged of a considerable professional burden, which too was in effect a constant, gnawing epistemic nuisance, all efforts at rationalization notwithstanding.[34] The GDR's official designation of the Wall as "antifascist bulwark" may sound quite cynical from the perspective of someone critical of the GDR. To state and party functionaries fully committed to the socialist project, however, it sounded rather accurate given how they thought and felt about the class enemy to the west, given the kind of agency and will they attributed to him for wreaking havoc in the GDR.

The building of the Wall was a watershed in the GDR's history. It fundamentally changed the rules of the political game domestically and inter-

34. How significant an event in the officers' life it really was became only fully apparent to me by attending a 2001 meeting of the *Insider-Komitee*, a group of former Stasi officers talking about, investigating, and writing about the history of the Stasi, which was dedicated to the building of the Wall. Not only was that sigh of relief clearly audible four decades removed, but it was also a uniform sigh. The officers reconfirmed in community that "there was no other way for the GDR then" (*Es gab damals keinen anderen Weg*), and they also agreed that the ten to fifteen years following were perhaps the best time the GDR ever had.

nationally. Domestically it brought consolidation of sorts. People could no longer live their lives with half an eye to the West, thinking "if push comes to shove, I can always leave." By increasing the cost of fleeing to include a gamble on one's very life and by making it virtually impossible to flee in complete family units, the movement of refugees from East to West came, for the time being, to an almost absolute stop. However, this benefit of keeping people also led to what in retrospect would end up to become the GDR's most egregious human rights violation: the attempted and all too often successful assassination of anybody who tried to cross the border in defiance of it, a policy that ended up costing hundreds of people their lives. In the longer run this proved to be a burden for international relations as well.[35] In the short run, however, the Wall undoubtedly strengthened the GDR's position because it literally forced its recognition as a partner in negotiations.

CONCLUSIONS

The officers' political epistemics, their understandings of socialism, the GDR, and its perceived enemies, are presented by them as direct responses to their experiences of and their questions about Nazi Germany and World War II. This reconstruction of the genesis of their political understandings clearly bears the traces of the party states' historicizing recognitions that have continuously shaped and reshaped their memories of their own experiences, thus molding them in the image of the party's prescribed understanding of the past. This does not mean, however, that these remembered understandings should be understood as "fake." Understandings can only become stabilized and thus memorized in reconstruction. Moreover, for the historicization to proceed as it did, the understandings recognized by the party had to resonate on some level, while the war experiences could in retrospect be taken to corroborate them. This whole process was a systematic selection and consequent disambiguation of earlier, less clearly structured understandings in highly structured spaces of validation.

---

35. The estimates for the number of deaths at the Wall (around West Berlin) and the increasingly fortified "intra-German border" vary widely. The following figures indicate deaths until and since August 13, 1961. The Berlin state prosecutor's office, which led the juridical investigation into cases of government crime after unification, lists 270 deaths directly attributable to the use of firearms or the explosion of mines by the GDR border troops. The Berlin state police's former office for the investigation of government crimes lists 431 cases since the foundation of the GDR, including deaths at the borders with Poland and Czechoslovakia, which could be classified as "politically motivated." The count of a private initiative lists all deaths of people who have died "in consequence of the GDR border regime" which includes suicides, accidents with firearms etc. Its counter has arrived at 1,008 deaths (August 22, 2003), at www .chronik-der-mauer.de/begleitung/statistik/todesopfer.html.

But it was by no means just the ongoing commemoration and invocation of fascism and the war alone that continued to validate the officers' understandings of socialism, the GDR, and its position in the world. Their work experiences were just as important. Here their own but also their colleagues' initial successes in identifying spies and saboteurs corroborated socialism's Manichaean claims about an ever-increasing class warfare in which they had a vital role to play. The construction of the Wall in 1961 rang true for other reasons: it deeply resonated with their desires to rid themselves of the more or less shaming experience of having to account for flight in their domain of responsibility. Without exception all officers I spoke with welcomed the Wall. The fact that the GDR picked up economically after 1961 corroborated the decision to build the Wall retrospectively. Now the state that they so ardently desired to succeed looked more than ever as if it had a real chance to deliver its promise. In their memories, therefore, the Wall was a new beginning.

After the Wall spy catching receded as a source of corroboration for their political understandings; efforts to control oppositional activity slowly began to move into the foreground. The Wall which had put a stop to many Cold-War-style operations, helped to further oppositional activity because the exit option as an outlet for discontent was no longer as readily available. Political events also served to corroborate the officers' worldview, albeit only indirectly. Without exception, the officers saw the Prague Spring as a counterrevolutionary movement that had to be crushed if socialism was to survive. The increasing international recognition of the GDR, which was enabled by the rapprochement between both Germanys, gave them the impression that the GDR had finally arrived, that it was taken seriously on a worldwide scale. There were other indicators that this was indeed the case. Throughout the 1970s the supply of apartments and durable consumer goods in the GDR increased sharply. The foreign policy successes seemed to be mirrored by appreciably better economic performance. At the same time, Vietnam and the continuing arms race made them more certain that the West did indeed harbor imperialist tendencies and was willing to wage war wherever its interests seemed to be at stake. No doubt, the return to Cold War rhetoric by the U.S. president, Ronald Reagan, and by British prime minister Margret Thatcher, the Falklands War, and later Nicaragua, continued to make this point for them. In the face of what they perceived as a manifest military threat, the emerging GDR peace movement seemed to undermine the military resolve of the "camp of peace" to the undoubted advantage of the "camp of war."

If these appear like one-sided interpretations of historical events by the officers, one must ask how they were sustainable. To understand how, one has to turn to the networks of authority in which these events were discussed and endowed with meaning and in which particular interpretations of them began to look certain. I will do this in the next chapter.

6

Stasi Culture—Authority, Networks, and Discourses

If somebody would have rebelled politically [within the Stasi] we would have isolated him immediately, just to make sure he doesn't defect to the enemy. A life outside of the Stasi was unthinkable.... Who works for us [MfS] lives with us; the MfS was my entire life ... we expected that everybody behaved like a Chekist all the time.

MARTIN VOIGT, FORMER STASI OFFICER

When we got married I said to her [his wife] that my work [for the Stasi] would always come first and second too and then there would be a big gap and only then came everything else.

PETER WAGNER, FORMER STASI OFFICER

At the beginning of the politburo meeting of October 17, 1989, a mere ten days after the ill-fated fortieth anniversary celebrations of the GDR, prime minister Willi Stoph asked general secretary Erich Honecker, to resign. In the ensuing discussion about this proposal, Erich Mielke, the minister of state security, is reported to have said to Honecker something along the lines of, "Erich, if you do not step down I will tell all and then many people will be surprised" (Schabowski 1991b, 105; Pötzl 2002, 324).[1] Later in November it was rumored that Mielke had in his possession a "red briefcase" in which he kept documents about Honecker. The existence of such a briefcase was later ascertained by the GDR state prosecutor's office, which subpoenaed it. Quickly both pieces of information were connected in public discourse leading to the suspicion that Mielke wanted to blackmail Honecker into resigning. Many people, my interview partners among the Stasi officers included, began to wonder what Mielke could have known and proven about

---

1. As with all politburo meetings (again following CPSU customs, as I have learned in personal communication with Sheila Fitzpatrick) there is no official verbatim transcript that would have reliably captured who said what to whom and in which order. However, several participants have reported extensively on this meeting. Yet there remains some uncertainty about the exact words.

Honecker that, if published, would have stood to discredit him so much that he might have had to resign. What was at stake in this politburo meeting was authority: the authority of the general secretary and the authority of the party. In fact, Stoph's call for Honecker's resignation was a desperate attempt to save the institutional authority of the party by de-authorizing the person who had been at its helm for almost two decades.

Authority is the topic of the first part of this chapter. If we want to understand how particular understandings become stabilized, are maintained, and decay among a particular set of people, we have to investigate the structure and dynamics of the authority networks in which these people operate. I will begin this task by exploring the principles according to which officers have learned to ascribe authority over their political understandings to others. I will also describe how the structure of their networks of authority was influenced by the organizational cultures and structures of Stasi. Finally, I will analyze the discursive cultures that characterized these networks because the very precondition for understandings to be recognized is that they are allowed to emerge and develop in interaction.

AUTHORITY

Officers' commentary about the judgment of their colleagues, their superiors and subordinates, their evaluations of public figures and of people they have investigated, as well as their assessment of the mass media and other sources of information sheds light on the question of whose understanding about what they took seriously and for what reasons. In other words, such commentary helps to reconstruct the ways in which they apportioned authority to other human beings and/or to the institutions they represented. One particularly interesting class of test cases for such authority evaluations is delimited by opposition coming from within the party. Such cases may lead to conflicts between different criteria of authority ascription, which then need to be weighed against each other. The two cases I will consider in the longer excursion that follows, that of Robert Havemann and of Wolf Biermann. They are interesting because they represent people who have gone through a change of understandings. Both started their careers as prominent supporters of the GDR party state. And subsequently both became icons of oppositional life in the GDR. Before discussing the cases of Havemann and Biermann, and the ways in which Stasi officers have interpreted them, it is useful to look at two earlier cases of intraparty opposition. A comparison between them and Biermann and Havemann will make apparent a particular trajectory of the discursive culture of the party with significant consequences for party-run organizations the Stasi included.

Excursion on Prominent Cases of Intraparty Opposition

The open border between both parts of Germany, together with West Germany's refusal to recognize an independent GDR citizenship, implied that those people who felt socialism to be insufferable could leave the country without many of the more traumatic consequences that refugee status usually entails. This has always had a dampening effect on anarchist, social democratic, liberal, and conservative oppositions to the GDR party state, and it left the country without better-known dissidents representing these political streams outside of the established Christian churches.

Therefore, it is not surprising that most of the leading GDR dissidents have, until the 1980s, consistently come from within the ranks of the party.[2] Encouraged by Stalin's death, in 1953, the growing discontent about the continuing shortage of consumer goods, and the opportunity created by the power struggle between Beria, Molotov, and Khrushchev in Moscow, Rudolf Herrnstadt (then editor of the flagship party paper *Neues Deutschland*) and Wilhelm Zaisser (then minister of state security) opposed the continuing rule of Walter Ulbricht. They might have succeeded in ousting Ulbricht had they not associated themselves with Lavrenty Beria, Stalin's notorious secret police chief and master of terror in the great purges. To them Beria seemed an attractive partner not so much for his fear-instilling reputation, but because he promised a different policy toward Germany that they perceived could pave the way for national reunification (Knight 1993, 192–94). After Beria's fall and execution in December 1953, Ulbricht could move swiftly to rid himself of these critics. They were dismissed from their positions in the ZK and the politburo and later also expelled from the party for "fractional activities."

Only three years later a small group of intellectuals formed a discussion group at Aufbau Verlag (literally "reconstruction press"), the GDR's finest literature and philosophy publishing house. The core members were Spanish civil war veteran Walter Janka, the press's chief executive, and Wolfgang Harich, a very young philosopher who worked there as Lukács's editor.[3] In consequence of the XXth party congress of the CPSU they demanded a process of systematic de-Stalinization in which they wanted

---

2. In view of the German debates about varieties of forms of resistance and oppositional behavior (e.g., Deutscher Bundestag 1995, Poppe et al. 1995) it is worth noting that this is not the same as saying that all oppositional activity was located in the party. Resistance activities ranged from work stoppages to silent church affiliation to the participation in the uprising of June 17, 1953.
3. Notably, Harich was also the managing editor of the GDR's only professional philosophy journal (coedited among others by Ernst Bloch), where he was (inspired by Lukács and Bloch) concerned about the extremely simplistic reception of Hegel in Eastern European socialism (Harich 1993, 34–35).

to see Walter Ulbricht replaced, not least because they aimed at German unification and wanted to win the social democrats in West Germany as potential allies (Harich 1993, 70). Naively Harich involved the Soviet ambassador who worried in the context of the Hungarian uprising more about the stability of the GDR and informed Walter Ulbricht of their plans. In a private conversation Ulbricht invited Harich to explain himself (Harich 1993 and 1999). In effect, the whole group was arrested, and two highly politicized trials were staged to intimidate critical intellectuals (Janka 1989, 79ff.; Schroeder 1998, 137–39).[4]

Both of these cases are perhaps best seen as intraparty power struggles in which different ideas about policy and tactics did play a role, though without questioning the most sacred assumptions of actually existing socialism. Yet, there is also an important difference between them. Looked at in succession they herald the movement of the center of the discussion away from the politburo to less central party organizations, and even more, to private networks of friends and colleagues. The 1953 Herrnstadt/Zaisser opposition follows the pattern of a thwarted palace coup, launched and directed from within the innermost circle of power holders. In 1956, there were sympathies for some of the ideas that Janka and Harich were discussing among some politburo members (most notably Karl Schirdewan), but the politburo never became the center of activities.[5] Something else deserves mentioning in view of what is to come next. Even though Zaisser, Herrnstadt, Janka, and Harich were dismissed from their functions (and the latter two were also tried and sentenced to lengthy prison terms) they acquiesced to party decisions without attempts to continue with oppositional activities. Even though the party excluded them they continued to hope for a change of course in the party's

4. Janka and Harich opted for very different defense strategies. While Harich thought that their plans were out in the open anyway, there was little reason to deny anything. He basically pleaded guilty and publicly thanked the Stasi for capturing him before he would have committed acts that would have brought him to the gallows. Janka, by contrast, to the end denied any kind of wrongdoing. Leading intellectuals were made to attend the trials. Among others, Helene Weigel, actress extraordinaire and Brecht widow, and star novelist, Anna Seghers, had to witness the trial in person. None of them spoke out in favor of either defendant although they were personally quite well acquainted.

5. Opposition from within the politburo was only one more time in the history of the GDR an important impetus for a change in the direction of party politics. Under the leadership of Erich Honecker—the long-time heir apparent of Ulbricht—and in close collaboration with Leonid Brezhnev, Walter Ulbricht was forced to retire (Podewin 1995, 423–55; Frank 2002, 420–27). Originally, this was a conservative move against Ulbricht's economic reforms and the beginning rapprochement with West Germany. Subsequently, this led to a brief thaw in cultural policies and a shift in economic politics from capital investment to the production (and importation) of consumer goods.

politics including their own rehabilitation while working respectively as translator, archivist, film scriptwriter, and editor.

With Robert Havemann and Wolf Biermann, a new type of intraparty critic emerged. Even though they were relatively prominent cultural figures, they were even further removed from the centers of power. More importantly, they began to critique fundamentals of Marxism-Leninism, most notably the leading role of the party. And this is probably also the reason why they did not respond to the repressions of the party with silence, but they continued their critique. In other words they opted for a life as dissidents. This is the beginning of the end of what Kołakowski (2008, 1153ff) and after him Michnik (1985, 135ff) have dubbed revisionism (cf. Joppke, 1995, 61–65) in the GDR—at least at the level of prominent party members (Klein et al. 1997). Havemann was a member of the KPD and a chemist who earned his PhD in 1935.[6] Right after the Nazis came to power in 1933 he joined a resistance group. In 1935, when most of the members of this group were arrested, he escaped their fate because his ties to the group could ultimately not be proven. In 1943 Havemann cofounded another resistance group with the illustrious name "European Union." Among other things the group helped to hide Jew's in Berlin. Just months after its creation, however, a Gestapo informant exposed the group. While the death sentences of his friends were swiftly carried out, his own execution was delayed time and again because former colleagues managed to have his research declared "vital for the war effort." Accordingly, a laboratory was established in the notorious Brandenburg (the city) prison where he could continue his work. There, Havemann pieced together a little radio that helped him to learn about and inform his fellow inmates, among them Erich Honecker, about the advancement of the Red Army. After the war he joined the SED, describing his commitment to communism retrospectively in a way that poignantly captures the degree to which he had internalized the ethics of absolute finality:

> Then I was of the opinion that a good comrade can be told from the speed with which he can grasp and publicly defend the new, wise insights of the party. The poor uncertain comrades, however, could be told from their disagreements voiced in immodest arrogance and from asking absurd questions that were better left unanswered. The worst comrades standing already with one leg in the camp of the class enemy, however, were those poor fellows who dared critiquing leading comrades of the party, perhaps even critiquing the leading comrade. Today the state of mind in which I was in then appears to me as outright ridiculous. Then it was not at all. It was self-evident for a

---

6. Apart from the biographical notes Havemann has published, the best source on his life to date is the biography penned by his late wife Katja (Havemann and Widmann 2003).

good communist. We had decades of hard struggle behind us. In one phase of this struggle, which was a battle for life and death, I had participated in the antifascist German resistance. My best friends had died in this struggle. The collapse of Hitler's hated regime was a great victory for our good cause. This was achieved under the leadership of Stalin. My liberation from prison, my life, my mind—I owed everything to the party; I owed it to Stalin.[7]

The revelations of the XXth party congress of the CPSU, however, came as a shock to Havemann. In particular, he wondered what had produced his own credulity to such a degree that even he, an accomplished scientist, accepted the party's advocacy of Lysenko's genetics or its condemnation of Pauling's theory of chemical resonance. His answer to this nagging question was unthinking obedience, the absence of critical dialogue. His party-critical engagement reached a first apex in his 1963–64 lectures at Humboldt University in Berlin, which were fast becoming a major attraction, appealing to a wide range of listeners including members of the *corps diplomatique*.[8] They were later published in the West under the title "Dialectic without Dogma?" (Havemann 1964).

At the same time that Havemann took up the real existing socialism argumentatively, a young poet and chansonnier, Wolf Biermann, began to scrutinize it in his songs and poems. Biermann came to the GDR only in 1953 at the age of sixteen. He hailed from Hamburg in West Germany, where his parents had been communist activists, and where he, following their political example, felt increasingly out of place, endlessly fighting with his noncommunist classmates in high school (Rosellini 1992). Biermann's father, Dagobert, was a longshoreman. He used his position in the harbor to spy out Nazi supplies for Franco. Caught, he was first sentenced to a prison term. As a Jew he was subsequently murdered in Auschwitz.

Young Biermann began his career in the GDR supported by the system, mentored by none less than Hanns Eisler.[9] He then wrote propagandistic

---

7. Quoted from, "Ja ich hatte Unrecht: Warum ich Stalinist war und Antistalinist wurde," printed originally in the West German weekly *Die Zeit*, May 7, 1965 (reprinted in Jäckel 1971).
8. Among others, Mikhail Voslensky was among the audience; he later became well known in the West through his book on the Soviet *nomenklatura* system (1984).
9. Hanns Eisler was a student of Arnold Schönberg's, a close collaborator of Bertolt Brecht's, and later one of the first victims of McCarthyism in the United States. Returning to Germany, he composed the new national anthem for the GDR to the lyrics of Johannes Becher. He was one of three rather prominent children of Viennese neo-Kantian philosopher Rudolf Eisler. His brother, Gerhart, joined the communist party of Austria after World War I and became a journalist who wrote for leftwing media. He took over several Comintern functions, came to be imprisoned in both France and later in the United States, where he came under the investigation of the House Un-American Activities Committee (HUAC). He eventually be-

songs celebrating "the good people / good for the new epoch" (Biermann 1991, 41–47) while encouraging young men to join the National People's Army. "Dear boy there are Lords / who arm for war / against worker's states / and thus my advice / join our troops!" (36). Yet, soon he came into conflict with the official cultural policies of the GDR, and he dared to publish "The Wireharp" (Biermann 1965), a collection of "ballads, poems, and songs" in the FRG after he could not find a publisher in the GDR. The reason becomes apparent to any reader who advances to those poems where he offers a direct critique of people and practices that he feels have ossified his socialist dreams. A good example of Biermann's signature candidness is a poem titled "reckless nagging," which at first suggests that he is chastising "subjectivism" by beginning with the lines "I, I, I / Am full of hate." But it then builds up to a "you / want to preach communism to me / while you are the inquisition of joy. You / drag souls to the stake. You / tie longing to the wheel. You! / . . . / Go shaking your heads at my wrong attitude / but Go!" to end unabashedly with a celebration of intimacy against party tutelage: "I am wrong, ok / I am sleeping with my wife / and she knows my heart."

At the 11th plenum of the ZK, Biermann was made an exemplar of defeatism. Delivering the report of the politburo and thus featured as Ulbricht's heir apparent, Honecker said (Schubbe 1972, 1078):

> We are not in favor of a superficial reflection of reality. But we are concerned with the partisan perspective of the artist in the political and aesthetic evaluation of our reality and thus with the active help in the depiction of conflicts and their resolution in socialism. The orientation toward a litany of mistakes, deficits, and weaknesses is supported by groups that have an interest in sewing doubt about the policies of the GDR . . . Wolf Biermann belongs to these groups. In a collection of poems [the above-mentioned "Wireharp"] published by the West Berlin Wagenbach press he dropped his mask. . . . With cynical verse written from the perspective of the enemy, Biermann does not only betray the state which has afforded him an excellent education, but also the life and the death of his father who was murdered by the fascists.[10]

---

came the director of radio broadcasting in the GDR. Their sister, Ruth Fischer, was a founding member of the Austrian communist party and later a leader of the left wing of the German communist party in Berlin. Stalin made sure that she was expelled from the party, to make way for Teddy Thälmann, his man in Berlin. Ruth eventually also migrated to the United States, where she became, in a twist of history that Charlie Chaplin called quite rightly Shakespearean, an important witness of the HUAC proceedings against her two brothers (Epstein 2003, 91–99).

10. Biermann responded to this charge, as behooves a bard, with a "Singing for My Comrades," published in West Germany as well as in an anthology with the title (echoing Heine) "Germany: A Winter Tale" (Biermann 1972, 66): The first verse begins: "Now I chant for my comrades all / the song of the revolution betrayed / for my betrayed comrades I sing / and for the comrades betray-

Havemann and Biermann were crucibles for the legitimacy of the GDR as "the antifascist Germany." Both were victims of fascism, and both were in or had been primed for central positions in the GDR's official intelligentsia. It was therefore painful for the party state that precisely these two turned away, not, in their own words, from socialism as an ideal but from the actually existing socialism called GDR; they criticized and mocked—test of tests—the leading role of the party. Fast isolated, they became friends. In 1976, Biermann was allowed to go on a concert tour through West Germany, during which he repeated his critical songs on television (for the first time reaching a GDR-wide audience); the party state reacted with fury, stripped him of his GDR citizenship, and thus denied him reentry into the GDR. The measure instantaneously backfired. More than one hundred writers, actors, artists, and other prominent members of the GDR intelligentsia signed a petition on Biermann's behalf. Among them were such prominent authors as Stephan Hermlin, Stefan Heym, Christa Wolf, Sarah Kirsch, and two of the GDR's most popular actors, Manfred Krug and Armin Müller-Stahl.[11] Following Biermann's expulsion, Havemann was put under house arrest for almost two years. Havemann and Biermann profoundly inspired the peace and civil rights movements in the GDR during the 1980s.

Left Opposition as Authority Test

The appearance of these two foreshadowed a completely new type of casework that the Stasi was asked to address. When Stasi battled Western organizations fighting the GDR such as the "east office" (*Ostbüro*) of the social democrats, the "battle group against inhumanity" (*Kampfgruppe gegen Unmenschlichkeit*), the "investigative committee of liberal lawyers" (*Untersuchungsausschuß freiheitlicher Juristen*) (Fricke and Engelmann 1998), various religious groups (including the Jehovah's Witnesses), it dealt with the prototypical class enemy: the bourgeoisie and its allied organizations. Havemann and Biermann heralded a new left opposition that had roots in the party but radically broke with it in the end.[12]

In spite of a clear rejection of political behavior not aligned with monolithic intentionality, which also gets immediately moralized as bad, the ques-

---

ing / the great song of treason I sing / and the still greater song of the revolution / . . . . The second verse then begins with the lines "I sing for my comrade Dagobert Biermann / who became smoke from the chimneys / who was resurrected stinking from Auschwitz /."

11. This episode led to constant struggles in the GDR writer's union and led eventually to a veritable exodus of GDR artistic talent.

12. This stands in marked contrast to Herrnstadt, Zaisser, Janka, and Harich. When the latter was rehabilitated officially in the fall of 1989 when the SED was still in power, he gladly accepted one of the highest orders the GDR could bestow (Großer Vaterländischer Verdienstorden).

tion of possibly winning the "stray soul" back was always there and discussed. Thus former Stasi officer Wolfgang Schermerhorn says:

> Biermann pretended to be a communist but at the same time he massively attacked GDR society. This contradiction, which time and again arose in oneself and which was reflected in his texts, was dominated by the thought that he is a dissembler and hypocrite, that he produces himself and craves to be admired. This view was informed by the most diverse operative and political insights, which we had won over the years. . . . As I read the texts, the first ones, I thought, gosh, this guy is good, it should be possible to reeducate him. But then I had doubts that we as the Stasi could accomplish such a thing.

If outright political action in defiance of monolithic intentionality persisted, however, the concern for "reintegration" dropped quickly from the picture. The officers moved swiftly to unambiguous rejection, reacting indeed as Havemann in the quote above explained he himself would have reacted before the XXth party congress of the CPSU. Former Stasi officer Jürgen Buchholz:

> In any case, Biermann was by conviction a dangerous enemy of actually existing socialism.[13] And anybody protesting against his forced emigration automatically sided with Biermann . . . and thus they had to be put under surveillance too.

In a similar fashion, Martin Voigt spoke about Havemann:

> For me the case was unambiguous. Havemann used Western media to voice his opinion and thus he no longer had the right to be recognized as a communist. For me this was a principle: whoever opens himself up in this way to Western media automatically supports their agenda. Therefore it was never a question for me that he was an enemy. I couldn't see in him somebody who wanted to reform socialism, even if that is what he said about himself. To me an imperfect attempt to realize socialism on our side was still better than the perspective to loose a version of it—improved by Havemann—to the West. . . . Fact is he was much applauded from their side, and it was clearly not their project to improve the GDR, but it was their declared goal to annihilate the GDR. And an organ like the *Spiegel* [West Germany's most important weekly news magazine] has never made any bones about the fact that this is what it wanted to do.

Three moves in particular are characteristic about this reasoning, which describes Stasi logic about the opposition not only in the cases of Havemann

---

13. Note the retrospective appropriation of the oppositional Rudolf Bahro's term "actually existing socialism."

and Biermann but also in pretty much all opposition. First, there is a certain structural identification between East and West. Just as socialism verifiably creates a monolithic intentionality that unifies everything into a functional whole, capitalism is assumed to be involved in an analogous move. Within this context news media become mere "organs" of a larger whole that is centrally organized and has a clear historical goal. Then there is the *tertium non datur*, the imagination of the dynamic between East and West as a zero sum game. Consequently, any cooperative contact with the West (literally any of its institutions) is, unless explicitly licensed by the party, a deal with the mortal enemy; the offender thereby unfailingly corroborates his or her inimical intentions and loses any right of belonging.

Up to this point, the officers reason deductively from the minor premise of an event—a particular kind of contact with the West—and the major premise of fundamental socialist doctrine, which I outlined in chapter 1. However, this ideological solution to the issue was apparently not completely satisfying either. Stasi officers have sought ways to corroborate their picture of antisocialist dissidents as veritable enemies by throwing a bad light on their character. This means first and foremost that their antifascist credibility had to be destroyed. For Biermann this meant to accuse him of not living up to the heritage of his father. In Havemann's case, the obvious starting point for such considerations was the fact that he had twice escaped the fate of his friends in resistance groups. Accordingly, all officers I have talked with and who were somehow involved in his case found the suspicion anchored in the repeated deferral of his execution sufficient ground to raise questions about his character. This need not even be the outcome of central briefings to this effect. Their reasoning follows the pattern of discreditation typically employed by vanguardists, making use especially of one background understanding. A rational person who has really absorbed the truth of Marxism-Leninism as the only possible science of the social cannot possibly betray that truth again unless he or she falls either prey to enemy influence or suffers from a character disorder. However, the Stasi never found anything of substance with which to slur Havemann in this way. Secondarily, both Biermann's and Havemann's "antisocialist lifestyle," especially their alleged promiscuousness (for which there was hard proof, the officers eagerly point out), was mobilized to show that they were indeed thoroughly bourgeois characters (who therefore did not deserve their respect). The final corroboration in such cases came with dissidents' political activities after they were expelled to the West. Now, the officers thought, came the proof of their real political convictions. Havemann never had to pass this test. But Biermann, in the eyes of all officers I spoke to, failed miserably. Although he remained critical of the FRG, they pointed out that he had not continued to agitate for his beliefs as would have behooved a true communist. Among my interview partners only one showed regrets that Havemann and Biermann had become the objects of investigation and harassment.[14]

The officers' evaluations of Havemann and Biermann show a number of potentially contradictory ways to construct and deconstruct authority. There are, first, both dissidents' antifascist credentials. Havemann was publicly celebrated as a "fighter against fascism," and Biermann was known to have suffered through the Nazis' murder of his father in Auschwitz. Second, there is the degree to which either can be described as furthering the socialist cause, which was ultimately assessed in terms of their willingness to live by the ethics of absolute finality, that is, the degree to which they were ready to perform self-objectification. As I pointed out before, self-objectification includes consideration of a number of other behavior characteristics, such as faithfulness in marriage, diligence at work, the adherence to a particular dress code, and temperance, which are moralized through their classification as socialist. Finally, there is their expertise in their respective fields: Havemann's merit as a chemist is considered, as is Biermann's talent as a poet and performer. Havemann was one of the celebrity scientists of the GDR. Not only did he hold the according appointments (professor at Humboldt University, director of a research institute, member of the Academy of Sciences), but he also was prominently featured as one of the authors of *Weltall, Erde, Mensch* ("Space, Earth, Man"), which was given to all youths participating in the youth consecration ceremonies (*Jugendweihe*), a socialist rite of passage held at age fourteen. Biermann was initially not well known among Stasi officers. However, those concerned with his case became familiar with at least some of his poems.

The officers' evaluations of Havemann and Biermann reveal that antifascism, self-objectification, and expertise were considered to be the three main springs of authority. They were, however, not necessarily seen as independent or equally important. In the following two sections I will discuss how they were evaluated in comparison to each other.

Antifascism and self-objectification

The attempted depreciation of Havemann's antifascist credentials after he became a major critic of the party and Stasi's efforts to find documents that could prove he was a traitor to the socialist cause during the Nazi years may

---

14. In another case, however, one officer, Martin Voigt, personally apologized to Stefan Heym that he had been the object of investigation. The reason: Heym became a member of the reformed communist party, PDS, after unification and was one of the directly elected candidates sitting in the first united Bundestag. In the eyes of Voigt he lived up to his commitments. He passed the test that Biermann failed.

sound surprising at first. However, in view of the fact that in Marxist-Leninist theory socialism and antifascism were seen as two sides of the same coin, it is less so. Since fascism was interpreted as a developmental stage of capitalism, and since in its own Manichaean understanding socialism was anticapitalism, socialism was by definition antifascism.[15] A nonsocialist or even "another socialist" opposition to fascism had no place in this ordering (except as a kind of misguided, retrograde nostalgia).[16] Antifascism is thus not only a personal claim to authority but also an intellectual and institutional one. The GDR presented herself consistently as the "antifascist Germany";[17] the SED claimed antifascist credentials as a party qua historical ancestry as the successor of the KPD battling the Nazis in Weimar Germany, as the brother party of the CPSU who led the Soviet Union to defeat Nazi Germany under enormous sacrifices, and as the party of German men and women active in the resistance against and victimized by the Nazis (Meuschel 1992, 29ff.). While it is the personal example that is consistently foregrounded by the officers in their interviews as authorizing state and party, this does not mean that in GDR times they read these accomplishments in an individualist fashion. They clearly understood the party, the solidarity of its members, and the link with the Soviet Union as enabling conditions of individual acts of resistance against the Nazis.

In this context it is important to recall that among the members of the first politburo all had antifascist credentials. They had worked in the Ger-

15. Historically speaking, this claim is of course quite problematic. First, it has no way of accounting for the labor-class support for the Nazis, including the fact that communist resistance, notwithstanding many Weimar communists, did in fact join the NSdAP. It also overlooks how the KPD at Stalin's behest refused to collaborate with social democrats who were interpreted as "social fascists" and almost as vigorously fought as the "class enemy," which means that the left vote in Germany (unlike in France a little later) was effectively split, which made it much easier for the Nazis to assume power. Finally, this simplistic equation conveniently overlooks the Hitler-Stalin pact, including the fact that the Soviet Union had no qualms about sending German communists who had fallen politically out of favor right back to Hitler's concentration camps. Discussions of these historical matters were, needless to say, taboo in East Germany.

16. See, in this regard, the article *"antifaschistische Widerstandsbewegung"* ("antifascist resistance movement") in Schütz (1978, 46–48). The commemoration of antifascist resistance in West and East Germany took radically diverging paths. In the GDR, the men around Stauffenberg who had conspired to assassinate Hitler on July 20, 1944, mattered as little as the other conservative resistance groups around Goerdeler, the Kreisauer Kreis, or even the liberal Munich group White Rose. Conversely, official narratives in the FRG have typically treated the communist resistance to Nazism with the same sleight of hand, and there is to this day no official commemoration of the communist resistance.

17. Within the logic of Manichaean dualism the GDR's self-celebration as antifascist was at the same time a move to discredit West Germany, which was equally consistently depicted as a continuation of fascism.

man underground or were active in organizing resistance from abroad; some were incarcerated in ordinary prisons, others in concentration camps; some had fought on the side of the republic in the Spanish civil war, others were in one way or another in the service of the Red Army or were helping to organize desertion among German soldiers fighting on the eastern front. Even among the last group of regular members of the politburo, ten of twenty-one had an active antifascist record. In fact, every member of the politburo old enough to have had one did indeed have one.[18] To the officers, the GDR was the antifascist Germany because communists were persecuted under fascism and it was governed by antifascists—and as I will show in the next chapter, this was by no means only important for the officers and other party members. Party and state in the GDR publicly underscored their antifascist commitment by publicly recognizing the contributions and sacrifices of former antifascists. There was an "International Day of Commemoration for the Victims of Fascist Terror" and an "Action Day against Fascism and Imperialist War," which was honored on January 27, the day Soviet troops liberated Auschwitz.[19] The GDR also made the resistance against, as well as the suffering from, fascism a publicly recognized status with the two official designations "fighter against fascism" and "victim of fascism." Both carried an honorary pension (more for the fighters!), preferred access to medical treatment, spas, and the preferred access of their children to education.[20]

The officers I interviewed were too young to have antifascist credentials of their own. A few of them, however, had the opportunity to participate in investigations against Nazi perpetrators. In all of these cases they rank such work among the most meaningful of their life. Peter Wagner, for example, describes as a formative experience his involvement in hunting down a former SS officer who had first raped a Ukrainian woman and then murdered her by throwing her out of a running train. It was also one of the few occa-

---

18. The precise meaning of individual contributions to the antifascist struggle of some of them is open to debate. Mielke, for example, did undoubtedly fight in the Spanish civil war. Yet some claim (as of yet without conclusive proof) that he brought the Stalinist terror into the ranks of the international brigades (Otto 2000, 74–80). Looking at Mielke's authority networks at the time he came to Spain, this is by no means an impossibility. The fact that the question of antifascist credentials creates such debates until today is further evidence of its authority-generating power.

19. Given the West German political elites very own Manichaeism and much deeper-than-acknowledged involvement in the Nazi regime it may be not surprising to learn that a day commemorating the Holocaust was introduced only after unification. The now-expanded FRG also chose the day Auschwitz was liberated.

20. Claims were investigated and decided by committees of the "persecuted of the Nazi regime" (VdN), which were integrated into the GDR social welfare system.

sions where he could tell his wife about his work. By and large, however, the officers' participation in the authorizing qualities of "antifascism" worked by identification, which was facilitated greatly by their own wartime memories. Working under the guidance of superiors who had distinguished themselves as antifascists provided opportunities for identification. Jürgen Buchholz said, for example:

> The people who were then our superiors were peerless role models. The head of the district administration, Fruck, for example. We greatly respected them, their age, they were considered to be people with a lot of political experience, who once participated in the resistance against the Nazis. People like Wolfgang Wiechert who was in a concentration camp and who resisted there; he was in the county office Friedrichshain. Karl Pioch was a Spanish civil war veteran. These were the people to whom I looked up to.

In the interviews, the officers never failed to mention the names of these antifascist role models with the utmost respect, with what appeared to me as an air of "you must know who I am talking about." Names in conjunction with the designation "antifascist" were deployed as "saying it all." As a cultural outsider I usually had to plead ignorance, and thus I began to inquire. Curiously, the officers' knowledge about what precisely the "antifascism" of a particular person entailed was typically meager. It was the recognition as such that counted. Karl Maier said: "It is not that they went peddling their stories—and we didn't ask questions either. Still, everybody knew it." Thus "antifascism" operated as a trope, gaining its significance from positive moral associations. Its content no longer had to be concretized beyond standing up against mass murder and war because it was stabilized in opposition to these two evils, which were thought to be embodied in fascism. "Antifascism" thus lost its differentiating, critical potential in a stark binary semiotic. It became the heroic against the demonic and thus so abstract that it was almost devoid of content. Yet it is probably just this abstraction into a pure unspecific goodness that allowed Stasi officers to partake metonymically in it; it commanded a kind of generalized authority, directly for the bearer and indirectly for everything and everybody associated with him.

Simply because the designation of an institution or a person as "antifascist" was such a powerful means of authorization, the designation as "fascist" was an equally powerful tool of de-authorization, if not anti-authorization. In response to the workers' uprising of mid-June 1953, which was officially interpreted as a fascist plot, Stasi began to centralize, collect, and systematize documents from the Nazi years (Unverhau 1999; Grimmer et al. 2002b, 2:464–). These documents played a role in the GDR's trials against war criminals. They were also used to embarrass West Germany's elites by showing time and again that they were also leading functionaries of the Nazi regime.[21] A number of such cases, investigated in part with the help of the Stasi, were published in the famous (to some rather infamous) "Brownbook" (Nationalrat 1965), which played a significant role in West Germany's student upheaval in the late 1960s because the information contained in it was otherwise not available in a handy printed format. These cases also played a role for the officers: they corroborated their commitment to socialism and its vanguard party.[22]

As the case of Robert Havemann shows, however, historical documents from the Nazi years could also be used to reevaluate the antifascist records of party critics. In principle they might even have come to use in exerting pressure on party members. This brings me back to Mielke's "red briefcase." It contained Honecker's Nazi "People's Court" (*Volksgerichtshof*) files, consisting primarily of his and other defendants witness statements. Thus they touch an important aspect of Honecker's claim to an antifascist record. Judged in retrospect, the critical evidence these files contain is not scandalous per se. The files just make Honecker look frailer, much less composed, and not as heroic as he had depicted himself in his autobiography (Honecker 1981). What transpires from the witness statements is that Honecker has needlessly incriminated another defendant who happened to be a young Jewish woman from Czechoslovakia about whose further fate nothing seems to be known (Przybylski 1991).[23] It will probably remain forever in the dark whether it is this material that Mielke had in mind when he confronted Ho-

---

21. One of the most notorious cases is Konrad Adenauer's administrative head of the chancellery, Hans Globke, who in 1963 finally resigned over a scandal in which his involvement in the framing of the Nürnberg race laws (and subsequent racist legislation) was made public in the GDR. There was also the possibility of using such material for blackmailing officials into doing spying work. I do not know to which extent this technique was employed. Its chances for success in West Germany were probably limited simply because the tolerance for employing and continuing to employ officials with a Nazi past was extremely high. In East Germany this may have worked, however, although it is unlikely to have been employed on a bigger scale as the Stasi much preferred to recruit its informants on the basis of shared ideological convictions.

22. There were several West German attempts to pay back in kind by unmasking the Nazi past of GDR functionaries (e.g., Kappelt 1981). There were indeed a number of high-ranking GDR officials who had once been members of a Nazi organization. Throughout the GDR's existence there were a total of twenty-eight ZK members and twelve ministers or deputy ministers who were NSDAP members (Schroeder and Staadt 1997). However, with rare exceptions, such as the country's chief prosecutor in the 1950s, leading GDR officials had not been leading representatives of the Nazi regime. Qualitatively and quantitatively there remains a stark difference between the FRG and the GDR.

23. The *Volksgerichtshof* let her go. However, it is unknown whether this was just a tactical maneuver to find further traces to more underground activists. The fact that she has not made her story public in the unlikely event that she survived the war means nothing much. Chances are that she was as dedicated to the communist cause as Honecker was (although her line of

necker. It has to be considered that throughout his career Mielke was loyal to his general secretary. Moreover, the knowledge about problematic spots in the biography of the respective other was symmetrical. Honecker is likely to have known that Mielke's publicly disseminated biography was falsified in suggesting that he had fought "side by side with the Red Army" against the fascists during World War II. In fact, Mielke shared the more typical fate of interbrigadists decommissioned after the Spanish civil war. He landed first in French internment camps and then in the Organisation Todt, where he had to perform slave labor for the Nazis (Otto 2000, 80–90).

In principle there is nothing particularly dishonorable about cracking in Gestapo interrogations, nor is it dishonorable to have been enslaved by the Nazis. The question that thus poses itself is, why both Honecker and Mielke would have to put themselves potentially on the spot by palliating their biographies. Evidently both feared that full knowledge of their past would potentially de-authorize them as leaders. An answer to this question must consider both the cultural forms brought to bear on the evaluation of biographies and the exigencies of the discursive construction of authority, which are closely dependent on each other. In part, the reactions of a wider public to the revelation of Honecker's and Mielke's biographical "blemishes" proved them right. They were both subjected to the scorn, which seems the fate of the fallen authority. Time and again the officers have used a lack in ideological consistency in the biography to de-authorize people, and both of these leaders have done the same. Inconsistency, as they understood it, was a weakness of character. However, it is also important to consider that consistent narratives provide fewer obvious docking points for efforts of de-construction. And in contexts that are, or are at least, perceived to be agonal this seems a definite advantage. Another interesting point is that the reconstructed narratives avoid depictions of victimhood. This has again something to do with cultural forms: authority is seen as agentic, it is the capacity to get things done. There seems to be shame in the passivity of victimhood that does not go away even as one can point to brute force (again: the "victims of fascism" had less privileges than the "fighters"). To the degree that agency is gendered this means that authority has to act like the archetypical male. And yet again there are discursive reasons too: the foul choices a victim may be forced to make under situations of duress are much more difficult to explain than the seemingly simple straightforwardness of heroic action. Together, the careful palliation of socialist leader's biographies as well as the scornful reaction to the revelation about this fact demonstrate once more how aporectic socialist identity was—on all levels of socialist society.

---

defense was that she got into the role of courier unwittingly). In this case she would have done nothing to compromise a leading comrade in a "brother party."

Self-objectification and expertise

The officers' depreciation of the professional qualifications of Havemann and Biermann are not their own, and in the interviews they point to published expert opinion. It is a constitutive principle of professionalism as we know it that only fellow professionals can decide who is a worthy practitioner and who is not. As such, the party systematically marshaled loyal professionals in the same field to debunk the authority of political critics or newly coined renegades. The literary scholar Hans Maier, the philosopher Ernst Bloch, and of course Robert Havemann, all celebrity practitioners of their respective disciplines as long as they were regarded as loyal citizens committed to the socialist cause, were publicly reproached for all sorts of professional shortcomings by professional peers after becoming critical of the party state. Perhaps the case of Wolf Biermann stands as the most massive attempt at destroying the professional reputation of any individual in the history of the GDR. After leading intellectuals had protested his forced exile, the party organized a phalanx of experts, which included literary stars such as Hermann Kant and Anna Seghers, to do the debunking in a series of negative assessments of his work that was published in the party's flagship newspaper, *Neues Deutschland* (Rosellini 1992; Berbrig et al. 1994).

To understand again how such debunking could possibly be credible it must be appreciated that just as socialism and antifascism were thought of as coextensive, socialism and expertise were too. Socialisms' claim to authority derived from its supposedly true knowledge of human society, which supplied the vanguard party with *the* road map to steer human affairs in the direction of a just human society. Individuals acquired personal authority precisely to the degree to which a person was recognized as supporting the party as font of morality, wisdom, and truth. Turning away from the party was understood as betraying a doubtful attitude toward truth itself, discrediting expertise even where it pertains to a domain in which Marxism-Leninism seems to make no claim.

The party state made extraordinarily prolific use of prizes, orders, medals, premiums, and promotions to mark people as role models.[24] In the ac-

---

24. Unfortunately, I have found no surveys about the numbers of honors conferred every year and their development in the course of time. I would expect that the field of such honors got increasingly differentiated during the years and that the total number of honors conferred in the GDR rose steadily over the years. Instead of hard statistics, I have the reactions of the recipients of these honors. Since Stasi officers wore their decorations on festive occasions, people got a keen sense of their frequency and import. They knew how to differentiate between at least two large categories of honors that were "in their range." On the one hand, there were what they called *Durchhalteorden* ("orders of endurance"), decorations that were "dished out" (*verteilt*) in a matter of course. Their absence was more significant than their presence. On the other hand,

companying official commentary on such formal recognition, it was typically emphasized that the person so honored had contributed in exemplary ways to the realization of the goals of the Stasi, the party, and the progress of socialism. At the level of justifying rhetoric, self-objectification was the central cause for authorizing recognition. The progress of self-objectification was also formally assessed in the regular evaluations officers got from their superiors. These emphasized both the degree to which they embodied self-objectifying ideals in their work and equally importantly the degree to which they led others in living up to them. These assessments were discussed with the officers and found their way into their personnel files. These also contained the reports on the evaluation of the self-objectification of their children, which was attributed to parents' influence and which was also sent to the personnel departments and could be reflected in promotions or formal recognitions to the officers.

This said, self-objectification needed to be interpreted; and officers found themselves in regular disagreement with their superiors about who really deserved recognition as a good socialist and who did not, which is to say that the officers and their superiors operated with different meta-understandings. All of them complained that official honors were far too often bestowed on those who were ostentatiously obsequious rather than those who really tried to advance socialism through their innovative solutions to acute problems. Karl Maier puts it thus: "Our cadre policies have not promoted the most capable people. The usual way was that people needed to prove that they had enforced a given line. The issue was not innovativeness, but model discipline, the submission under orders and guidelines." In effect, the officers accuse their superiors of separating self-objectification from expertise, where in fact they should have seen them in a much more complementary fashion. In the understandings inherent in the officers' comments on the promotion practices of their superiors, the acquisition and exercise of expertise was the proper way to help the party attain its goals. They accuse those higher up of wittingly or unwittingly cultivating a culture of sycophancy.

Typically, the officers accounted for the discrepancy between their ideal and actual practices of promotion not by pointing to systems' failure but to individual superiors who are described as suffering from one character defect or another, thus following the principles of personalization characterizing socialist theodicy. Still, their narratives also point to extraordinary superiors who behaved like ideal socialists should have in giving expertise its

---

there were "real" decorations, which often also carried a significant premium and which were "awarded" (*verliehen*) for particular merit only and for which one thus "had to stretch oneself a little bit," or, for the most "difficult" ones, that stretching figuratively had to go "to the ceiling."

due. In the eyes of the officers they carried the candle of hope in sometimes-adversarial circumstances. At the same time, reflecting on their own role as superiors, the officers reveal that the tensions between self-objectification and expertise rendered their own practices ambiguous. Martin Voigt, for example, who praised himself for systematically nourishing more critical talent, says, describing the differences between generations in the Stasi: "Where we [his generation] consented out of a sense of discipline, they [the generation of officers born in the 1950s] asked for reasons. I know that I had, occasionally, difficulties to suggest these people for promotion, simply because in the last consequence they were lacking in unconditional submission."

This raises the question, where the so acutely perceived tension between self-objectification and expertise comes from. Historically, it has its practical roots in the absence of sufficient expert knowledge among communists taking over the organizations of state and economy. The experts they found there were understood (justly or unjustly) as stalwarts of the old regime who needed to be controlled. At the same time, however, the understanding of Marxism-Leninism as a science and the emphasis on qualitative economic growth have led to a keen awareness of the need of science, technology, and expert knowledge. Given this ambiguity it is perhaps not surprising that campaigns of lionizing experts were followed by campaigns against the presumed arrogance of experts that were meant to reassert the leading role of the party. Introduction and recall of the economic reforms of the 1960s are an excellent case in point.[25]

In conclusion, among the three sources of authority discussed in the previous sections there exists a relatively clear hierarchy. Self-objectification tops the other two wherever circumstances are invoked that suggest a conflict between them. In other words, antifascism and expertise only augment authority to the degree that they are not seen in conflict with self-objectification. This hierarchy helped to disambiguate authority that was celebrated in the image of a selfless yet agentic, male warrior hero who always knew how to act in the interest of his overlord.[26] Ultimately, this hierarchization was enabled by understandings firmly equating socialism with antifascism and expertise. In other words proper self-objectification should have automatically led to proper antifascism and proper expertise. After all (as I explained in chapter 1) socialism was assumed to have overcome the chasm between moral goodness and truth.

25. For a general account centering on this ambiguity, see Steiner 1999; for an interesting perspective on how this looked from the standpoint of the first secretary, see Podewin 1995, 357–78.
26. Victoria Bonnell (1999) has documented this heroic image in Soviet posters.

NETWORKS

The dialectic of recognition (compare figures 4.5 and 4.6, pp. 220–21) closely entwines the development of meta-understandings regulating the attribution of authority on the one hand and the development of a network of actual social relationships on the other. After I have discussed the three main sources of authority for Stasi officers in the last section I will discuss the development of their social networks in this section. As we shall see, this development is best described as a homogenization resulting from two complementary movements: the deauthorization and severing of ties with people who are not committed to the party's project and the concurrent development of authority relations with people who are. Both movements were not only the result of spontaneous choices of the officers, but as we shall see, they were supported by powerful administrative practices.

Focusing Ties on Fellow Socialists

I have already indicated how as young people the later Stasi officers began to voluntarily favor association with like-minded ("progressive") people and how this gave them a sense of belonging in a political environment that was by no means homogeneous. Joining the Stasi amplified these tendencies considerably. There are several reasons for this. Long daily and weekly work hours increased on the one hand their absolute face time with "comrades of mind" (*Gesinnungsgenossen*). On the other hand, it limited their opportunities to maintain sustained contact with others. People who were directly critical of the party state were unlikely friends of the officers to begin with. But after they had joined the Stasi they were even less likely to become friends, not least because in addition to the ideological barriers there were now structural ones: such relationships could now create problems for the officers as the Stasi almost jealously guarded their contacts with the outside world.

The strict rules of secrecy were a structural impediment to the building or maintenance of heterogeneous authority networks. The officers took these rules very seriously as they saw them to be constitutive of their work and their identities ("after all we were a secret service" was a constant refrain in the interviews). They prevented them from sharing much about their everyday lives in the Stasi, and certainly nothing about the material core of their work, that is the operative tasks they were involved in. General characterizations of problems with superiors or subordinates, freed from all references to casework, is all they could get themselves to share. The rules of secrecy were already a potential strain on their relations with their wives and children, as conversations remained strangely asymmetrical. While family members were supposed to share their lives outside of the house, the officers remained largely mute. That some wives felt "locked out" of the work life of their husbands was underscored by some wives' interest in my interviews with their officer husbands. Friends, too, had to be tolerant of such restrictions, respect for which was much more likely among other functionaries dedicated to the party state. Finally, officers had to abstain from contact with people who maintained lively relations with Western relatives or friends. Since many GDR citizens, party members included, did maintain such contacts, not least because this was often the only way to obtain certain consumer goods, further limits on their networks were imposed.

In the GDR, the provision of certain key goods was organized via the workplace. Above all this was true for housing and vacations. Both in order to fill the immense housing shortage created by the destructions of World War II and to gradually update general living conditions to apartments with indoor toilets and bathrooms, the government of the GDR bet on new construction rather than on restoration and upgrading. Apartments in new developments that typically comprised hundreds or even thousands of units were distributed en bloc to various employers, ministries among them. The consequence of this housing distribution system was that the Stasi officers typically lived in buildings where their neighbors tended to be other Stasi officers or at least officers of the other *bewaffnete Organe* ("armed organs"). The system of central planning in housing construction and distribution also had considerable consequences for other aspects of life. For example, it radically changed the demographics of certain school districts, some of which ended up with a very high concentration of party functionaries or even of Stasi families. Martin Voigt remembers that the "parents collective" at his children's high school "was always dominated by Stasi officers."

Since the various employers also owned and operated most vacation homes, either singly or in close cooperation with one another, Stasi families were likely to spend their vacations in the company of other Stasi officers and officers of the other *bewaffnete Organe*. When officers broke loose from such arrangements (for example, if, like Martin Voigt, they preferred camping trips), superiors saw gaps in mutual surveillance, influence, and ultimately security, and frowned on this behavior. Finally, the Stasi and the Ministry of the Interior jointly operated a sports club, the Spielvereinigung "Dynamo," to which the officers were supposed to take both their own activities and their fandom.[27] In consequence, the private "home environment" was deeply structured by workplace relations. The officers' chances to make friends outside the three concentric circles of Stasi, the armed organs, and

---

27. The name Dynamo was again borrowed from the USSR. Dynamo was the largest sports club in the GDR and was very active in supporting the GDR's high-profile athletes.

the party were therefore limited if such contacts did not derive from their partners' contacts. This was one of the reasons why the Stasi reserved the right to reject their employees' proposed partners (more on this below).

Losing Sight of People with Other Opinions

For the officers, the positive association with the socialist project was a generative principle helping to build and maintain authority networks. Conversely, nonauthorized associations with Western organizations were driving radical de-authorization and the disruption of personal relationships. The cases of Biermann and Havemann again illustrate this point. In the publicly displayed discourses about them and in the eyes of the officers it was above all their use of Western media that delegitimized their reform agenda and their belonging to the community of communists. But not only dissidents' Western ties were threats to their authority. The officers' own ties to the West, down to every possible past visit, were of central interest in their own security checkups and in their ongoing assessment by superiors. German communists who had spent the Nazi years in the West rather than the Soviet Union were regularly, even if selectively, made the object of suspicion.[28] The officers were required to scrupulously reveal any connections to the West, including short visits and loose, occasional ties to relatives. In their pledge of obligation sealing their employment at the Stasi they foreswore any further contact with Western countries.

Georg Assmann had failed to list a visit to West Berlin in his personnel questionnaire for fear that this might endanger his impending employment.[29] When this became known he was "given the works" and was almost dismissed. Phone calls, letters, or visits that officers received from Westerners had to be immediately announced to their superiors. Kurt Bogner's son was an amateur radio operator. One day he received a QSL-card from the United States.[30] His father immediately became worried and queried his son about U.S. radio contacts. Bogner's son claimed that he had not had any. Bogner dutifully handed in the card, convinced that it was nothing but a test of his loyalty. To this day he does not know. The files of the Stasi's party organization contain a number of cases in which officers were reprimanded for

---

28. Most notorious in this respect is the so-called Noel Field affair (see pp. 225–26). How selectively this association with Field or the West more generally was used for creating suspicion can be gauged from the fact that Jürgen Kuczynski, who had direct dealings with Field, was promoted throughout as one of the GDR's showcase intellectuals.

29. He had also skipped his membership in the Jungvolk, the Nazi youth organization.

30. In such cards, amateur radio operators acknowledge successful communication, usually with reference to time, frequency, and quality of the transmission.

improper dealings with the West. Cases on record include the acceptance of gifts from relatives, attempts to secure an inheritance in the West, the failure to register each and every contact, even with relatives and more of the like.

But the difficulties could be more severe. Herbert Eisner's mother-in-law originally came from Westphalia in northwestern Germany. All of her relatives stayed behind when she moved to Mecklenburg, East Germany's Baltic Sea shore region. Eisner's personnel file documents that her connections to her Western relatives were always regarded with suspicion by the Stasi, not least since her daughter, Eisner's wife, refused to become a party member and her holding out was attributed to her mother's influence. When the Eisners moved to Berlin the personnel department expressed the hope that the new distance to the mother-in-law would make it easier for Eisner to educate his wife, leading her eventually to apply for party membership. When Eisner's brother-in-law undertook an ill-fated attempt to flee East Germany, Eisner had to explicitly distance himself from him. As soon as his mother-in-law reached the age at which she could apply for a travel permit to the West in order to see her siblings there, she did. Her first trip led to Eisner being called in to discuss the matter with his superiors. As a result, he had to agree to influence his mother-in-law to henceforth abstain from such journeys. In what amounts to one of those many tests of loyalty socialist lives could be studded with, he also had to agree that she be placed on a blacklist of people whose applications to travel would be denied automatically. Accordingly, her next application was rejected. However, three years later her next application was accepted for reasons of advancing age. But when she applied again in the early 1980s her son-in-law had to again sign a declaration that he would do his utmost to dissuade the elderly lady from applying again, and that in case of her refusal to give in, he would cut all ties with her.

This paper trail is interesting because it opens a view on the ways in which such a trivial case is used to remind an officer of his obligations while obtaining declarations of loyalty from him. Yet it becomes even more illuminating through Eisner's commentary. Neither did his mother-in-law refrain from the last trip mentioned, nor did he sever his ties in consequence nor did this fact have any perceptible repercussions. At one level, then, the whole affair was a bureaucratic formality as long as his superiors backed him and he continued to make gestures in the right direction, recognizing the validity of the concern (which he said he saw—which is the reason that he claims he never felt angry about the matter). At another level, however, his mother-in-law's travels put extra conformity pressures on him: here was a potential blemish that he had to make up for by shining otherwise. Finally, the mother-in-law did not travel as often in the end as she might have liked.

Much more dramatic still is another case. Jürgen Buchholz had fallen in love as a young Stasi officer with a woman who was, in his own assessment, very much like him, a dedicated socialist, a fact underscored by her role as a highly active functionary of the communist youth movement. Her brother, however (before the Wall was built), had apparently made an attempt not only to flee but, much worse, to also enlist with the French Foreign Legion in West Berlin. In spite of the fact that the brother had returned to the GDR, admitting in official interrogation to his attempt to become a *légionnaire*, Buchholz's request to marry his love was declined by the Stasi. The reason given to him was that this young man still posed a security hazard. Faced with the choice to continue his career or to marry her, he chose his career, a fact that, even after forty years, still fills him with considerable unease. He made sure that I would tell this story only under pseudonym. Another of my interview partners succeeded in convincing his superiors that his partner who was first rejected by the Stasi was not objectionable after all. In her case it was the Christian orientation of his love's parents that the personnel department found objectionable, again for security reasons. That the problem of the social networks of the officers' desired partners and the Stasi's sensibilities about it did not change much in the course of GDR history can be shown by quoting a speech that the party secretary of department XX of the ministry gave in April 1985 (BStU MfS SED-KL, 1206):

> There are more and more examples where young comrades no longer take a partisan position in choosing their life partners. They increasingly decide for the partner and against our organ . . . the dismissals for this reason prove this point.

In what follows, the speaker exhorts his colleagues to do more, so that these young comrades act again more like Buchholz: taking a partisan viewpoint down to the most intimate decisions.

As I pointed out in chapter 2, the SED state made active use of contact management to shape the spaces of validation in which GDR citizens moved. They could not visit the West (the official reason given was not the fear of ideological influence—that in itself would have been an admission of ideological inferiority—but the scarcity of convertible foreign exchange), and they could not buy or borrow the majority of Western publications, a rule that included periodicals as much as books.[31] However, GDR citizens

---

31. Most of the public libraries only carried books that were published in the GDR. The situation with university and/or research libraries was different. They had a "poison cabinet" that contained non-freely-circulating literature. However, what each library put into the "poison cabinet" was decided on a local basis and was, depending on the librarian in charge, handled more or less liberally. Many opposition members have told me that they had no problem, for

could receive visitors from the West, exchange mail with Western friends and relatives (including packages), and they could listen to or watch Western electronic media. If anything, these regulating limitations were even more rigorously enforced among party members, Stasi officers included. In addition to the absolute contact prohibitions with Westerners, Stasi officers were not allowed to consume Western electronic media either. Many easily internalized this interdiction. Martin Voigt, for example, says that he never even wanted to watch Western television. "Why should I?" he wonders, "it was enemy propaganda after all." Horst Haferkamp pretty much takes the same view and gives it a humorous spin: "With us it wasn't customary to tune into RIAS [Western radio station] or something like that. I have always said, 'excuse me, they are lying even with the weather report.'" When both Voigt and Haferkamp finally reached a level in their careers where for professional reasons they were supposed to attend to Western media, they found their fetishization, the obsessive attention afforded them, rather strange. Their propagandistic intention was all too obvious to them. Other officers were not as pure in the partisanship but were more worried about sending mixed messages to their children and abstained from tuning into Western channels for these reasons. A few actually did watch Western television regularly, not really quite knowing what to make of it.[32]

It was not the case, then, that a demonstrated ideological commitment was seen as sufficient ground to relax the surveillance of contacts with ideas and people, to trust that party members would, due to their ideological training and their experience in the service of the party, have the right kind of arguments, perhaps even instincts, to handle understandings deviating from the party line. Much rather, deviating understandings were treated as a continuing danger, potentially contaminating the resolve of any good socialist (compare fig. 4.7, p. 223). Thus, like other party members, Stasi officers were asked to avoid ideologically dubious publications, broadcastings, or people. The cases I cited above make apparent how deeply this concern could penetrate the private life of the officers with sometimes-painful consequences. Contact prohibitions could be outright absurd. Georg Assmann reports that in the 1960s he lived in the same house as two ladies who were active churchgoers. His superiors thought it necessary to order him not to talk to them.

---

example, getting to the publicly denounced Western European communist literature. This does not mean that being caught with a copy of the same book illegally imported from the West would not have been taken as an indicator of at least budding "negative-inimical" attitudes or even as a criminal act. See also Wolle 1998, 149–50.

32. Several officers have pointed out that the discipline in this matter was much more lax among younger officers and that this was one of the indicators for what appeared to them as a worrisome generational break.

The efforts at managing its citizen's and especially its functionaries' contact with things, ideas, and people Western led the party eventually into very controversial policies. Since in the GDR many consumer goods could only be reliably obtained with the help of Western friends and relatives, officers were effectively asked to forfeit access to such goods. For some of them, many of my interview partners included, this was not an issue. Self-objectification was so successful that they did not even desire them. The disciplinary records of the party organizations in the Stasi, however, paint a different picture. Some officers complained about their purported disadvantages, and the slew of consumption related disciplinary proceedings might have convinced the Stasi that even Chekists have soft spots when the issue comes to managing desire. The fact that contact prohibitions preempted officers' and other party members' access to Western consumer goods prompted the party to make some of these goods available in specialized stores. Since these goods cost the government valuable foreign exchange reserves, however, officers only obtained rank-differentiated access to them, leading to a system of privilege. That in turn created concerns that I will talk about later.

In sum, then, a number of factors contributed to centering Stasi officers' networks of authority on shared political understandings. The key factor was the selective authorization around a demonstrated political commitment to the socialist project, which, even when it was not fully congruent with the designation of the party itself, seldom strayed far from it, for example, to include heterodox socialist thinkers. The self-objectification the party had demanded of its members eventually became an integral part of the self; it became a part of that individual's self-relationship or mode of reflexivity. That this could be domain specific (without necessarily raising issues of betrayal) is amply demonstrated by Eisner's case. Relatives with other views were not necessarily avoided, but they were typically de-authorized politically. If some Eastern relatives were in contact with Western relatives, the officers had to be careful of how they were managing these contacts. Since officers could marry only approved persons who had undergone a systematic security check, spouses were not typically a strong source of different opinions either. Not surprisingly, the large majority of the spouses of my interview partners were party members. Some of them were working for the Stasi, typically in a "nonoperative" unit (such as medical services, payroll, etc.). Since officers worked long days, their friends were often their colleagues at work. The last director of Stasi's university in Potsdam–Eiche told me that at the end more than 90 percent of the new recruits were coming from Stasi families. Stasi was one the best ways of becoming a cast.

The development of Stasi officers' networks, which were shaped in part by their own practices and ideologies of authorization and de-authorization, led them to maneuver in ideologically homogeneous environments that tended to systematically validate the party line. With the narrowing of networks the modes of the officers' self-formation and reformation got ever more limited around typical party patterns of interaction and, consequently, typical party modes of reflexivity. This homogenization trend was broken by officers' indirect and direct contact with dissidents' thoughts and penetrating questions through their secret informants. Nevertheless, the question remains, why these networks did not in themselves fragment to produce internally more diverse environments.[33] To understand this, a closer look at their cultures of interaction is necessary.

DISCURSIVE CULTURES

If particular understandings of the world can only be stabilized through validations, and if among these validations recognitions play a central role, then the question of what can be made the subject of conversations with whom, in which form, and to what extent, becomes central for any investigation of how and why people gain confidence in their understandings of the world. To pose this question is to ask for the discursive cultures prevalent in the networks in which people interact, which must be seen in their totality, including the reception of authorized mass communications.

Stasi officers were maneuvering mostly in two interactional networks that in the course of their lives showed, as I have just argued, increasing overlap. There was first a work environment consisting of their colleagues, superiors, peers, and subordinates who also doubled as the members of their party groups. And there was, second, a house environment consisting of their families, relatives, and friends. The mass media, especially the party's flagship paper, *Neues Deutschland* (and to a lesser extent *Junge Welt*) and GDR television, permeated both of these networks. With regard to the work environment, and according to the party's rules and regulations, work life and party life should have been markedly different discursive environments organized by diametrically opposed cultures of interaction. Work relations were conceived doubly hierarchically, as military chains of command and as bureaucratic relationships of subordination. Officers were both the holders of a military rank and the incumbents of a bureaucratic position. As such they gave, received, and obeyed orders, and they were given casework, the

---

33. Abbott (2001a) has shown how such internal fragmentation occurs within academic disciplines. There, the driving force of fragmentation is an institutional incentive system that places high rewards on "innovation." Innovation, however, needs to be argued, and this seems to be best done in opposition to something that already exists. The party's cultivation of an ethos emphasizing "unity and purity" worked in the opposite direction.

progress of which they had to document and report upward. Party meetings were supposedly governed by the principle of the fundamental equality of all party members, and communications were supposed to be discussions conducted in an open, critical spirit. In other words, while the discursive ideologies of the Stasi qua security bureaucracy were unabashedly hierarchical, those of the Stasi qua party were expected to form into a cherished *communitas*.

The statutes of the SED (Benser and Naumann 1986, 175) urge party members to "expose faults fearlessly . . . to step up against palliation (*Schönfärberei*) and the tendency to get high on successes . . . fight against any attempt to suppress critique or to replace it by sweet talk or palliation." Critique was seen as an aspect of the dialectical step of the "negation of the negation," which was supposed to differentiate between what had become obsolete and needed replacement from what worked and needed to be maintained. In this sense critique was officially espoused as a motor of innovation and progress. In theory, then, the problems created by the efficiency sought in hierarchical communication at work were to be rectified by critical communications in the party group. This separation did not work, however. To delineate admissible domains of critique, to differentiate what could be said to whom, where and how, officers do not take recourse to the official distinction between party and work environments. Such a distinction would have had no real base in their social relations, since, in effect, the military-bureaucratic organization of the Stasi and the organization of the party closely mapped onto each other: the base organizations of the party were congruent with a Stasi department;[34] and a party group was typically identical to a divisional section. Thus, officers were facing their immediate colleagues as well as their direct superiors during party meetings. These functioned, then, and more often than the party might have wanted, as opportunities to work overtime.[35] Consequently, instead of employing the work/party distinction, officers worked with a crosscutting indexical distinction between "official" and "unofficial" forms of communication.

34. Some very large departments, such as the department XX of the Berlin district administration for state security with well over one hundred employees, were split in two party base organizations.

35. The difference was that the party officers were typically not identical with the superiors. Party officers were embedded in a secondary party hierarchy, at the top of which stood within Stasi a full-time party county leadership (*Kreisparteileitung*). This gave them an alternate route to work the system and thus a limited degree of autonomy vis-à-vis their immediate superiors. Rather then approaching them with a problem in official meetings, they were approached in more private conversations by officers with grievances. For a succinct presentation of the party organization within the MfS, see Schumann 2003.

The Logic of Written Communication

The most official communications were those objectified on paper. The higher documents were expected to percolate up, the more "official" they were considered to be, and thus the more officers felt compelled to perform self-objectification in the thematics and stylistics of their writing. Georg Assmann was working for many years in an "analysis and control" function summarizing and analyzing the work of others for the perusal of high-ranking Stasi and party officials. He framed something of a "law" of communicative self-performance of subordinates' communicating with superiors: "You needed to give them [the higher ranking addressees of the document] the feeling that they are in charge and that you understand their goals and work toward fulfilling them." For all planning documents, activity surveys, and so on, this implied the performance of a clear orientation toward the stated goals of the party as well as those of the ministry and its subdivisions. This was done by directly referencing pertinent party documents and speeches of the general secretary or of the minister of state security: his orders and directives. This was also done by the prodigal use of particularly socialist linguistic forms, which perhaps more than any reflect its underlying teleology: the *pleonastic hyperbole* (amplification by chains of words with similar meanings) and the *continuous positive* promising steady increases of goal-contributing and equally steady decreases of goal-undermining activities. Thus planning documents, annual reviews, and similar documents promised to engage in "conscious watchfulness" or "unyielding toughness" as well as to "exert ever more effort" (e.g., in reducing the use of gasoline), "to further increase" (e.g., vigilance, consciousness), or to "continue to raise" (e.g., the number of secret informants).

In documents reporting on the operational activities of the Stasi, the performance of self-objectification meant to demonstrate an unwavering class standpoint. Walter Schuster puts it this way: "The problem was that one had to counter at every step the suspicion that one was thinking in the same way [as the class enemy]. Everybody wanted to avoid being misjudged in this sense." Officers explain that they needed to destroy even the slightest appearance that the activities of people under investigation were regarded with sympathy, that their thoughts, their concerns might contain any kernel of truth or real interest to them. This was done through the profligate use of certain labels, unambiguously answering with revolutionary brazenness the question of "who is who," that is, who is friend and who is foe. Thus all Stasi documents overflow with the use of the designator "negative-inimical" long before it is clear what the person operatively investigated is actually up to. Conversely, descriptors used by the investigated persons needed to be used with the utmost care because they implied a certain understanding of what they are in the grander scheme of things. Thus the use of scare quotes, of "so-called," and of their functional equivalents, proliferated. The deputy minister of state security, Rudi Mittig, was reported by several officers to have exhorted his men time and again that since the GDR was in the stage of a "developed socialist society" there could no longer be any real, indigenous opposition. Domestically, the class conflict was positively resolved. Accordingly, the opposition was always an "enemy inspired opposition" or a "so-called opposition," or simply an "opposition." By the same token, since peace was declared a primary goal of state and party, and proclaimed to be with these two in the best possible hands (because they were purely motivated and knowledgeable), the independent peace movement could never be anything but a "so-called independent peace movement." According to official party doctrine, a group of people so designated could impossibly be independent (since it was surely inspired by the enemy), it could neither really want peace (because the capitalist enemy on behalf of which it was inevitably working surely wanted war to increase profit), nor could it be a movement (since the people were smart enough to see through the ploy).

Beyond all care in the rhetorical use of ambiguation and disambiguation there remained an old problem, part of which is more commonly known as "shoot the messenger" and which Vincent Crapanzano (1992, 43–45 passim) has—in reference to ethnography—called with greater generality "Hermes' dilemma," that is the difficulties involved in communicating unfamiliar, strange, or even uncomfortable news. In the language of the sociology of understanding it can be stated thus: The authoritative communication of a "fact" by a messenger inevitably recognizes this fact and thus makes it more real in the eyes of the addressee. If this fact creates at the same time negative resonances in the addressee because it is nondesirable or noncompatible with the other understandings currently in force, there immediately emerges a case three type tension, that is, someone who is taken as an authority disagrees about the evaluation of understandings (see figure 4.6). To protect the credibility of the body of actual understandings in conflict with the message, the addressee may wish to de-authorize the messenger. Worse, the messenger may attract the addressee's wrath because the messenger literally makes the addressee uneasy. The problem is heightened in a situation where the reported fact resonates negatively with knowledge afforded absolute truth. Messengers carrying as facts news that draw into question sanctified understandings, almost automatically de-authorize themselves. Who are they in comparison with eternal truths? Worse, since certainty in understanding is indeed connected to agency, the reporting of facts that draw into doubt the confidence of core understandings may always be read as destructive of agency. Add to this the self-perception of a life under acute threat in which nothing is more needed than resolve, then the communicator of uncomfortable facts is in imminent danger of being written off as a defeatist. This is exactly the danger in which the Stasi officers found themselves when they were reporting on such uncomfortable facts as oppositional activity where there should not be any or on public opinion about party and state that was not exactly the support the party hoped for and that it publicly claimed to have.

The officers acutely perceived Hermes' dilemma. They all describe the processing of information from the first recording of an "information about the meeting with secret informant xy" up to a "party information" directed toward the politburo as a practice of gradually "defusing" or "castrating" it, as they say. The Stasi had to prepare "atmospheric reports," that is, assessments about the opinions of common people "in the street," about certain policies of the party, or about certain propagandistic events. Such atmospheric reports were ordered, for example, in the context of party congresses. The data about how people thought came from secret informants since officers had no other source of information (except when they smuggled in a few phrases of what they had heard elsewhere, for example, from relatives, and what appeared to them as important). Each guidance officer therefore harvested the requested information from his informants. These were then forwarded to "analysis and control groups" (*Auswertungs und Kontroll Gruppen* or *AKGs*) officers who condensed them to write a general report for the unit in question. These were then sent upward where the reports of several units were condensed once more. Jürgen Buchholz explained how "defusing" worked by making an example:

> There was a youth festival in Berlin. Countless reports complained about the noise and the dirt. Of course you could not write this: the result had to be that the Berliners enthusiastically welcomed the youth festival. One simply picked the reports that supported that. And then one could add at the end that there have been some concerns about noise and dirt.

He had a particular word for writing these reports: he called them "Bummis," after a lullaby. Peter Wagner created a little precept for himself to handle Hermes' dilemma in his own way, characterizing the boundaries between the communicable and the incommunicable as *Was nicht sein darf, das nicht sein kann!* "What may not be cannot be."

In order to prevent the rash de-authorization of the messenger one may want to make the messenger morally irreproachable. The effective messenger of bad news is someone beyond the doubt that she might want to harm the addressee. The repeated loyalty rituals of the individual Stasi officers to the Stasi and the party, as well as the loyalty demonstrations of the Stasi as an organization to party and state, have to be seen also in this light. At least the officers felt that it was this greater unquestionable loyalty that allowed the Stasi to reveal more of the bad news than, for example, the party's internal information systems. The Stasi was also organizationally sheltered to some degree; its reporting of bad news to a local party boss did not lead to direct career consequences. Yet, the mark of independent loyalty may also lead to a bigger sense of betrayal when the news remains consistently bad as the following episode illustrates. Soon after his deposition, still a guest of the Soviet troops in Germany in Wünsdorf, Honecker granted an interview about his life (Andert and Herzberg 1990, 351). Asked about the quality of the reporting of Stasi concerning the opposition in the last year of the GDR, Honecker argued that it was on the level of the *Bild-Zeitung* ("Picture Paper")! *Bild* was and is West Germany's most notorious tabloid, part of the Springer Press empire that was not only staunchly anti-GDR but also set upon doing what it could to subvert it when it found an opportunity to do so.[36] Honecker's point was that Stasi had become defeatist; in the eyes of the general secretary its reports about the growth of the opposition were undermining the resolve of the party and thus the country. Apparently, the trust of the general secretary in his secret police was not strong enough to escape Hermes' dilemma.

Another important strategy utilized to avoid trouble in written communication was to abstain from summarizing judgment, from formulating further-reaching hypotheses, or from integrative interpretations. In consequence even high-level security briefings (*Lageberichte*) (e.g., Mitter and Wolle 1990) are written in the form of a fact digest where the underlying analysis shines through only in the selection of what gets reported and what does not rather than in an explicit argument for a particular interpretation. It is stunning to see, for example, that the annual security reports (*Jahresanalysen*) of the department XX of the Berlin district office of state security and of the division XX of the ministry abstain from a direct assessment of the concrete threat posed by oppositional activity to the power of the party. In the same vein, the reasons why GDR citizens opposed party and state were never investigated. As far as I can see there are three main reasons for this startling absence of analytical depth in written Stasi work. First, it was always argued that those higher up knew more because they received more information from more sides and thus were assumed to be much better able to synthesize data and then to draw the necessary conclusions. Second, it was assumed that those further below were "ideologically less mature,"

---

36. Much as the Stasi officers spoke about the GDR opposition only as "opposition," Springer papers made it a point to refer to the GDR only as "GDR," for it argued that East Germany was neither representing Germany, nor was it democratic.

which means that their judgments were less trustworthy.[37] Georg Assmann summarizes this distrust: "Those higher up did not trust those further down with their assessment. That's why they wanted to know everything, down to the last little detail." Third, the formulation of hypotheses or summarizing interpretations harbored even more danger of appearing to violate the party line than descriptions, and they were thus studiously avoided.

According to all of my interview partners, writing reports became more complicated in the course of the years, because "one had to be more careful." In other words, self-objectification had to be performed more self-consciously, which means that the forms signaling adherence to a firm class standpoint were employed more liberally. That this was by no means only true in Stasi officers' official writing is attested by Mary Fulbrook (1995, 73), who has compared intraparty communication in the 1950s and 1970s, concluding that "the rhetoric of reporting becomes ritualized: the structures are standard the phrases jargonized, the contents increasingly predictable."

Oral Workplace Communication

Case-related conversations with superiors were official too, the more so when third parties were present. Most officers describe their former superiors as intolerant of contradiction in such contexts. The most blatant case in point was Erich Mielke himself, who was famously autocratic and irritable, always ready to verbally assault anybody who did not live up to his expectations.[38] The tape recordings of his security briefings with his generals typically end, after he has spoken for several hours, with his question: "Comrades, are there still any questions?" And the answer is silence, which sometimes prompted him to make comments to the effect that he will see from their actions how well they have understood him, and that in any case they will get a written version of the talk he just gave, and that his orders, even the

---

37. I have described this phenomenon elsewhere (Glaeser 2004) as a part of a generalized distrust that radiated from the center of the party state to its periphery, which I have called "state paranoia."

38. There are countless episodes about Mielke in this regard. One particular style of demonstrating to subordinates that they were wanting was his incessant pursuit of detail knowledge. One officer reported that while driving through his territory he was asked why at 11 p.m. at night there was still a light burning in a church, another was asked why the grass in an irrigation ditch was not cut yet, a third how many visitors there were annually paying homage to the Soviet Memorial (*Sowjetisches Ehrenmal*) in Treptow, and another time visiting the same memorial with the same officer how many steps there were up to the gigantic statue of the Red Army soldier. And the minister liked these answers "bellowed like a shot from a gun" (*wie aus der Pistole geschossen*).

old ones, deserve being revisited and studied, and so on. Mielke's autocracy was inscribed in the very form in which he addressed others: whereas everybody else (at least officially) addressed him with the inimitably state socialist *Genosse Minister* ("comrade minister"), using the polite third person plural, he addressed everybody else in the Stasi using the colloquial second person singular in conjunction with the last name, a form of address that is reminiscent of a master-apprentice or landowner-tenant relationship (and thus his slip at his one and only parliament speech on November 13, 1989, with which I began this book).

While few other superiors enforced a similarly stark symbolization of hierarchy through forms of address, the officers in the interviews agreed that there was a hierarchical line between an upper and a lower tier of officers that was symbolically marked in a multiplicity of ways. It was captured in the distinction between "leaders" (*Leiter*) on the one hand and everybody else on the other. In practice this distinction emphasized administrative position (department head and above) rather than military rank. For many officers it was associated with a significant cultural break within the organization, because in their eyes it stood for differences in habitus. In the ministry and the Berlin district administration, "leaders" had their own dining hall where they were served food (rather than fetching it cafeteria style) that they could order à la carte (rather than selecting from just a few daily choices); they enjoyed special parking privileges at lots near the building in which they worked; they had access to special stores; they were treated to (or cajoled into—depending on one's individual tastes) hunting expeditions, and so forth. All these privileges were justified with the achievement principle, in spite of an enduring discourse of equality (cf. Merkel 1999, 231–37). It is thus not surprising that for many officers, the line between leaders and others was also the line between the Spartan simplicity of what socialism ought to be and its corruption in a new master habitus, which climaxed in their eyes in the chauffeured Western limousines (mostly Volvos) at the disposition of the Stasi's generals. Whereas the line between leaders and nonleaders was symbolically overdetermined, all key administrative rank differentiations came, as in all hierarchical organizations, with their own little privileges (even section leaders got their own offices, had primary access to secretarial assistance, etc.). In this way the "official" at work was demarcated in a host of different and indexical ways.

The omnipresence of hierarchical differentiations in Stasi work environments was reflected in discursive styles. In general, arguing with superiors about casework was seen as an acutely career-endangering move. Martin Voigt condensed this insight into a maxim: "One does not contradict a prince." What is more, officers consistently describe the Stasi's discursive culture as becoming more autocratic over the years. Decision-making processes in casework are said to have been more inclusive in the 1950s and '60s than they were later in the 1980s, a time for which they are described as much more top down. This may very well be a consequence of the higher ideological sensibility of casework against political movements as compared to the more traditional secret service work of catching spies and saboteurs.

Party meetings followed the same logic of indexical official/nonofficial distinctions as well. Meetings in the base organization, which could comprise entire departments, were much more official and hierarchical than party group meetings, which typically included only a section. Within party meetings at any level, organized discussions around the table were more official than coffee-break conversations. By and large the workplace rules translated into the party sphere. Herbert Eisner characterizes the limits between the sayable and the unsayable as following the discourse of the party:

> Attempting a critique was as if you would throw a bucket of water upward. There were no really critical discussions. One simply could not talk about party resolutions. Once a line was decided it was decided. Discussions about mistakes were also avoided. One always insisted that circumstances had changed.

In effect, then, all those themes covered by the party could only be discussed within the margins set or left open by the public discourse disseminated by the party. The participation in official discourses therefore required a clear understanding of these margins. Where one did not know them one was better served to remain silent if one could afford to say nothing. Discussing mistakes had to be avoided altogether because one could be reproached for having "internalized the arguments of the enemy." The general line of the party was that there ought to be "no discussions of mistakes" (*keine Fehlerdiskussionen*) as they were deemed to do the work of the class enemy in undermining the necessary resolve of the party.

But even those areas not explicitly covered by the party in official resolutions and such could be tricky terrain if they were of ideological relevance (or could be construed as such). Jürgen Buchholz remembers:

> There was a foreign policy journal by the name of *Horizont*. It was about international political life, a strictly socialist publication. There was an article about the development of the working class in advanced capitalist societies. The article claimed that in Italy workers bought machines to produce in direct dependence on the market. Thus there was information about the development of the working class. But such things never played a role in the discussions at party meetings. In retrospect one would have to speak

of stagnation. I have not even tried to thematize this [article], although I should have liked to.

Buchholz and many others felt that only those things that were in the discussion anyhow could be brought up. A question like his about the development of the proletariat in other countries would have immediately touched unchartered terrain. Nobody, including the party secretary of the group who always received additional ideological training, would have known to which conclusions such a discussion should have been steered, and so it was avoided altogether. In consequence, Stasi officers felt that their party meetings were boring, endless repetitions of the same. This does not mean that they rebelled—they were party soldiers after all; if it took this to defend their socialism, they would put up with it.

Nevertheless, the representatives of the party organization were unofficially told that meetings were felt to be stifling. In a speech to officers, the secretary of the base organization of the ministry's department XX explained, for example, that it should be entirely legitimate to ask questions such as whether the GDR does not involve itself too closely with the class enemy (in reference to increasing trade and credit relations with West Germany, for example), why the party leaders' meetings with Western representatives at the Leipzig Spring Fair should be reported on so widely in the media (while those with other socialist leaders received scant attention), or why the media reported so late on allowing a large number of people to leave the GDR for the FRG. He then continued (SED-KL, GO xx, April 17, 1984):

> We take it to be an important goal of our party work to communicate to all party members that it is safe to ask such questions; to respond to them in a sensible and in a partisan manner; and not to allow that comrades asking such questions will be confronted with blame. If we assume that the basic organizations of the party are the political homes of our comrades, then we have to make sure that this is actually the case. Where else could comrades work out convincing arguments if not in party collectives. Of course in doing so we always consider that our comrades participate actively in producing these arguments and do not simply ask questions.

"Simply asking questions" was considered a frivolous, disruptive pursuit. The arguments that the comrades were supposed to produce were reproductions of those of the party. Ideally, the meetings followed the format of a catechism. The goal remained fixed, only its rationale needed to be rehearsed. The party secretary illustrated his point with sample questions that could not be more innocuous because they were posed from a schoolbook class position interrogating the tactics of the party, which under particular historical circumstances strayed from schoolbook doctrine to better serve the cause of the labor class. And, indeed, officers had such questions pertaining to the schmoozing with the class enemy. They puzzled about why on earth the Shah of Iran, whose secret service they knew had murdered Iranian communists, would be awarded an honorary doctoral degree from Humboldt University. They wondered why the GDR had to offer taxicabs and hotel rooms to West Berlin once the IMF, that instrument of imperialism, met there. Of course they knew about their country's dependency on oil imports as well as about foreign currency shortages, but they also felt that these in particular were issues of honor.

Far from venturing criticism freely, then, the boundary between the askable and sayable and the unaskable and unsayable had to be negotiated continuously and from setting to setting. What happened when this boundary was overstepped? In January 1989, participating in a conference for party functionaries, Karl Maier got angry about papers from the 7th plenum of the ZK that praised the mass-media policies of the party. Mass media were Maier's hobbyhorse, and he had long harbored ideas about allowing a more open, that is, a more realistic news reporting. He strongly felt that the party was losing support throughout the country because the media had long lost their credibility, for example, by continuously reporting plan overfulfillment in production while everybody experienced continuous shortages, which seemed to increase rather than decrease in severity. So once the conference passed a motion to "enthusiastically welcome" the plenum papers he begged to disagree, venturing the hypothesis that the ZK had overstepped its own jurisdiction by making decisions that only the next party congress had the authority to pass. He wanted a discussion that became impossible, however, with the formulation and publication of a renewed line.

Maier felt tempted to venture this hypothesis because he, like many other SED functionaries (and most of the officers I spoke with), was placing great hopes in the next party congress. In fact, he fervently desired that it would bring a leadership change and with it some fundamental corrections of the course the party had charted. And yet the level of complaints reaching the party by then had reached such levels that the party, instead of opening itself to increasing dialogue, started a "campaign against grumblers and grousers" to enforce party discipline. Maier's comments fell into the beginning phase of this campaign. And so he went through what can only be described as the typical party dissenter's experience so often portrayed in the literature. Maier's question was enough for the party secretary to initiate a party trial against him with the intention of dismissing him from the party and from service in Stasi. Maier says it was a strange experience. He knew the people involved in the trial. Most of them would have easily consented to what he had said in a nonofficial conversation among colleagues worried about the ever-more-visible economic and political problems in the GDR.

Yet as participants in the trial, none lent him the least bit of support. The line was that "all decrees of the party are binding for every party member," and that he had violated that duty that is prominently featured in the party statutes. Herbert Eisner, who participated on behalf of the party in Maier's trial, explained that nobody helped him since everybody jumping to his assistance would have subjected himself to the same reproach. More, he explains, it might have possibly even worsened the case by making it appear as if there were a whole splinter group in formation. Nothing was more sacrosanct than the unity of the party. Accordingly, everybody had to perform self-objectification even though unofficially many of those involved had signaled agreement with Maier before. Maier felt pressured to "recant like Galileo Galilei," a suggestive comparison given that Maier's critique was far from coming close to touching the ontological or political core of Marxism-Leninism. He merely critiqued current policy. Yet, he did not feel like caving in right away, something had crossed a threshold within him too, and he felt it was time to be more stubborn, at least for a little while. In the end he was saved by the intervention from the deputy minister of the Stasi, sparing him a full recantation, as Maier proudly recalls:

> This whole thing became a ritual. I have then conceded to have said the right thing at the wrong time and the wrong place. Had I been dismissed, I would of course have forfeited the possibility to wield influence. My core thought was, there is no use fighting windmills.

I pointed out in chapter 3 that the "being in the know," the feeling of sitting in a position from which more influence could be fielded than from others, was a powerful motive for sticking with the party, even in times of crisis. His resignation into the institutional character of party culture, the renewed keen awareness that politics is difficult if not impossible, is interestingly captured in comparing the path of action he chose not to take, that is, insisting on a discussion of Don Quixote's proverbial battles against windmills. In his account, the proverb functions as a meta-understanding, which effectively fetishizes the institutional fabric of GDR socialism. In considering the significance of this event, it has to be remembered that this affair was entirely internal to the Stasi. In fact, it was internal to division XX of the ministry. The interactions were those among colleagues who had known one another for years, and each and any single one of them had demonstrated loyalty to the party and the Stasi over decades, and yet as soon as a slightly more controversial issue was brought up, the question of loyalty appeared like a bat out of hell! Officers were allowed no lapses of self-objectification in official contexts. The fetishization of the party and its line and the concomitant resignation of its members were the consequences.

This does not mean that the Stasi was uniformly autocratic. Perversely, perhaps, precisely because it (like many other organizations) was not uniformly an autocracy it was bearable. Officers all remember with fondness the occasional superior they have had in the course of their careers whom they credit in the interviews with creating a more collaborative work atmosphere characterized by trust and mutual respect that enabled more extensive delegation and self-responsibility. They also typically describe themselves as willing to further critical discussions within their own realm of responsibilities. Undoubtedly, superiors, from section leaders onward across the various functional and territorial divisions of the Stasi, had some leeway to institutionalize locally more open or more closed forms of discursive cultures. On the basis of comparing notes with friends and family, both during and after socialism, officers working in the area of the "political underground" (*Line XX*), from the Berlin district administration as well as from the ministry, claim that discussions among themselves were a lot more open than those in other divisions. The reason they state is simply that they had to address the issues raised by the opposition members as well as the concerns of their secret informants who were not easily placated by standard propaganda formulas.[39]

In effect, the officers prided themselves for having had lively and critical "unofficial" or "off-the-record" discussions. Werner Riethmüller insists: "Those in higher political functions would have been stunned about our conversations." Horst Haferkamp seconds this but then also brings into view the line that bounded all discussions, official or unofficial:

I have to say that it is not the case that among each other we did not have conversations about such things [e.g., the deteriorating economic situation in the GDR]. I mean people who were close to each other, people who got close through work, who trusted each other. This went all the way to pointed conclusions that something needed to be done. I don't say that here to fashion myself retrospectively into a resistance fighter—I have no intention to do that. Such considerations all ended with the thought that we had no illusions about a third way, an illusion that was harbored by many in the fall and winter of 1989/90. . . . For us it was always clear, and the historical development after '89 has proven it, that there is only "red" or "white" or maybe I should better say "black-brown." Anything in between won't work. This much was clear to us. Changing the power as it was installed in the GDR, warped and contorted as it was in parts, would inevitably mean that they [the "black-browns"] would come to power. And we

---

39. It is noteworthy that members of the espionage division of Stasi (*HV A*) make much the same claim against the rest of the organization. Their argument mirrors that of the division XX officers: they had to deal with their spies who were exploring the world of the enemy.

were so happy that they had not been in power since 1945, and we certainly did not want them ever again. And thus all thinking in alternatives came to an end.

There was a saying that worked much to the same effect. It goes: *die DDR ist die beste DDR die es gibt* (The GDR is the best GDR there is).

CONCLUSIONS

This insistence on the possibility of critical discourse, with its dramatized conclusion of "something needed to be done," echoes through my interviews. Attempts to fill this formula with content, however, did not lead very far. By and large the critique exhausted itself by stating that there are problems in several domains of social life ranging from the situation of the economy and the newly swelling tide of refugees to the handling of the opposition. These were problems the officers were wrestling with in their daily work. Not unlike the "fixers" employed in factories who were cherished for miraculously producing goods officially unavailable with the help of their personal networks and ample cunning, the Stasi often tried to play the role of the party's universal helper. They attempted to fix acute local problems through their wider access to information and officials. The range of problems the Stasi officers tried to fix is astonishing even if they ultimately had to concede, with regret, that the means available to them as secret police were insufficient to tackle any of them. They tried to fix supply problems by short-circuiting information flows otherwise blocked by red tape. And yet they could do so only to a moderate degree since their own internal secrecy requirements limited the flow of information. They tried to procure instruments and material ingredients for scientists, even going so far as stealing them from the class enemy in the West. They tried to stop the loss of man- and brainpower using their force of secret informants to identify persons whose discontent grew to a degree that they were willing to apply for the permission to leave the country. They tried to move away obstacles to the well-being of the disgruntled by involving their bosses and party secretaries.[40] But for every one of those rare incidents where they succeeded there were many more where they were absolutely powerless. As Ernst Stellmacher put it: "We could not magically produce bigger apartments or shorten the wait list for a car either." And they tried to control the gradually rising levels of oppositional activity. Although they managed to know what was going on, their attempts to con-

---

40. This is, among other things, what Mielke meant in his short speech before the People's Chamber with the comment that the Stasi contributed to the economic development of the GDR.

tain the movement were as doomed as their attempts to improve the supply of goods, or their efforts to stem the tide of those willing to flee the GDR. The officer's conclusions about their failures were uniformly that these were problems that had to be resolved at a political level, not contained by the secret police. Pointing out correctly that their weapons were dull in shaping institutional developments on a larger scale and that instead a wider political approach was needed is the extent to which their criticism went. By themselves they had few recommendations about how to improve matters. Karl Maier's ideas about the liberalization of the media went further than anything else I have heard. Yet, Stasi officers' ideas could not develop because their networks of authority were extremely restricted. Thus their hopes for change were pinned on a "biological solution" to the stalemate of the party, that is, on a younger generation of party leaders who they hoped would take over at the next party congress, the XIIth, scheduled to take place in 1991.

The officers' accounts of what they could talk about and where, might suggest that they lived in a bifurcated world. To play by the system they said one thing, yet they thought another. However, to speak in the Stasi officers' case of "duplicity" (Kligman 1998) would overstate the degree of duality and the depth of the schism in their world, which probably went no deeper than that of every other "organization man's" (Whyte 1956). They had a deep stake in making the GDR work, they by and large identified with its ideology and with its practices, and in the interest of the whole they put up with the system's "quirks," which they inevitably, following the logic of the socialist theodicy, attributed to incompetent persons. Moreover, that second world outside of the official one was comparatively small. Rather than being an independent alternative world, it was a set of question marks appended to the world of official understandings. If this was the price to have socialism rather than capitalism, so went their reasoning, they gladly paid it. Said Martin Voigt:

> The Stalinist Model has only worked with this incredible party discipline. I am a very loyal comrade. I have always followed all movements of our party. This was the only chance to keep our cause going. Every questioning would have led to a faster disintegration. During GDR times I have thought much about the question of how much diversity we can afford, and I have come up with an image. One can get the water out of a boat by scooping it out or one can rock the boat. People like Havemann wanted to rock the boat, and I saw that they immediately received assistance from the political enemy; they thus bore the mark of Cain. . . . A bad socialism is better than none. Of course this idea in the end hastened our decline.

The officers' practices and ideologies of constructing and validating authority centered on the party. Even if other modes of authorization may have given them pause, occasionally threatening to undermine the seamless monolithicity of authority, in the end self-objectivation almost always pre-vailed. The networks in which the officers maneuvered, too, were increas-ingly centered on the party, with membership and commitment to the so-cialist cause as central organizing features. In part this was an effect to their liking, after all it is troublesome to interact with people who disagree with us, but it was also an effect of organizational practices such as the distribution of housing and of vacations through workplaces. The limits of the sayable and questionable were ultimately negotiated in view of what in socialist jargon was called "the question of power," that is, the capacity of the party to hold onto power in the GDR. Through its principle of democratic centralism, its hermeneutic power to articulate a unitary and coherent historically apposite interpretation of Marxism-Leninism, the party was fixated on its leadership. No wonder, then, that the officers and other party members waited through-out the crisis of 1989 for "the redeeming words" from the party leadership showing the way out of the country's problems.

This brings me back to the politburo session of October 17, and its the-matization of authority. Assuming that the authority of the diviner and pur-veyor of truth carries with it the responsibility to deliver authority if needed, the general secretary had visibly, to all party members, failed that test. To prevent the authority loss from infecting the party as a whole, the politburo had to act. The question of why the measures it took failed will be investi-gated in detail in the conclusions of the book.

PART IV

Disenchantment, Disengagement, Opposition—The Dissidents

I have to introduce this part of the book with a caveat. Just as the last two chapters have not aspired to present a comprehensive history of the GDR's Ministry of State Security, so the following two chapters make no pretense of telling an encompassing history of the peace and civil rights movements in the GDR, or even in the more limited space of Berlin. Such an endeavor would explode the possibilities and the intentions of this book.[1] Instead, I will allegorize in individual life stories the dynamics of the political understandings of GDR citizens, who have come to oppose the state, providing initial guidance and inspiration for the citizen movements (Bürgerbewegungen) in the fall of 1989. For the ensuing narrative I needed to focus on a few groups in Berlin (albeit some of the most prominent ones), and even within them I needed to focus on a handful of individuals. Moreover, resistance to the state comes in many shades and gradations, ranging from the refusal to attend to the party state's propaganda, the sourcing of information from non-state-sponsored sources, or the avoidance of participation in large propaganda events, to the casting of an invalid ballot at election time, the spraying of a party-critical slogan at a wall, and the participation in actions of a civil rights group. And even though the focus of the analysis in this book is on movement activists, that is, on people who have gone much further in their resistance than the vast majority of the citizens of the GDR would have ever been ready to go, the dynamics of their trajectory can tell us something about a broad variety of resistance behavior, because they did not become sponsors of samizdat publications over night. Instead, it was what the movement members have consistently called "a slow process" that led some people to go

1. For overview studies, see Torpey (1995), Joppke (1995), Choi (1999), and most comprehensively, Neubert (1998). Wolfgang Rüddenklau's early account of the Berlin scene is still very worthwhile reading (1992). Useful collections of individual perspectives are provided by Deutscher Bundestag (1995); Poppe, Eckert, and Kowalzcuk (1995); Gehrke and Rüddenklau (1999); and Neubert and Eisenfeld (2001).

ever further, while others stalled or changed course. The logic of that trajectory, if analyzed with the help of validation space model, reveals the coemergence of political understandings of networks of authority and of events. Following this trajectory shows how dissidence is only poorly understood as a rational clash of preexisting opinions or even ideologies. Rather than being a cause of dissident action, well-articulated dissident understandings are the result of a journey that often takes its departure from deeply embodied experiences, from emerging kinesthetic and emotive understandings rather than from discursive ones.

Analyzing how such a trajectory crystallizes out of the contingent mess of history within the institutional fabric of GDR society is also important because GDR dissidents come from the most diverse backgrounds, stretching the full gamut from families fully dedicated to the socialist project to others that have always kept their distance to SED rule, nurturing a spirit of opposition at least within the perimeter of their home. What they share primarily is not a range of values over some demographic variables that, locked into a model, could together "explain" the variance of a "dependent variable" called "dissidence." Instead, what is common to them is the dynamics of understanding that propelled them through a long series of events in the context of changing networks of authority from diverse starting points into the same direction.

Chapter 7 focuses on the earlier parts of these trajectories from school experiences up to the moment when people began to form discussion circles while trying to organize critically engaging programming in official performance venues—that is, the so-called cultural opposition. Chapter 8 continues this thread with the formation of peace groups, their cooperation with church parishes, and therefore their access to vital resources of the Protestant church. These resources included assembly halls, duplication equipment, and organizational capacities that enabled at first more regional but then ever more encompassing countrywide intergroup networks. Finally, it accounts for the groups' growing attention to civil rights issues and the foundation of samizdat publications reaching a larger, more geographically dispersed audience. I will show in the end how the group's life, its oscillation between the politics of public action and the self-politics of group and network formation, led to the emergence of a small but active civil society. This also sheds light on the usefulness of the validation space model to analyze the emergence (and by the same token the dissolution) of public spheres.

7

When Someone's Eden Becomes
Another's Purgatory

Only in community with others has each individual the means of cultivating his gifts in all directions; only in the community, therefore, is personal freedom possible. In the previous substitutes for the community, in the State, etc., personal freedom has existed only for the individuals who developed within the relationships of the ruling class, and only insofar as they were individuals of this class. The illusory community, in which individuals have up till now combined, always took on an independent existence in relation to them, and was at the same time, since it was the combination of one class over against another, not only a completely illusory community, but a new fetter as well. In the real community the individuals obtain their freedom in and through their association.

MARX, GERMAN IDEOLOGY (TUCKER, 197)

In the middle of the 1970s we founded an opposition group with friends from school. The group was the spiritual and political conclusion we drew from our studies. It was impossible to know, if one did not hope; one could not hope, if one did not do anything. To find out where things stood, one already had to act. In a thoroughly intimidated environment we had to construct a new political worldview. . . . Whence should the grain of sand have known whether it was in the desert or at the beach.

KLAUS WOLFRAM (GERHKE AND RÜDDENKLAU 1999, 99)

The "enemies" of the GDR were made by nobody more effectively than by the GDR herself.

THOMAS KLEIN

An account of the gradual formation and transformation of political understandings among later activists of the peace, civil rights, and environmental movements in East Berlin during the 1980s forms the main body of this chapter. The sequencing of relevant experiences, the articulation of understandings, their subsequent corroboration in contingent events, their recognition in changing networks of authority as well as the various resonances they invoke will provide the underlying structure of the narrative. The chapter will conclude with a critique of liberal understandings of oppositional activity. Before I will introduce the people through whose life stories I will allegorize the dynamics of understanding typical for many people, however, I will take time to describe the place in which a good deal of this development took place: Berlin's fabled Prenzlauer Berg neighborhood. Three reasons motivate this attention to space. The most important one is this. The neighborhood, its concrete spatial configuration, its geographical location within the cityscape, as well as the particular form of its architectural build-up played an important role in shaping the movements. Location and architecture impinged directly on the formation of understandings; they played an important epistemic role. The second reason is to provide the reader with a sense of place for the location where the activists lived, met, and staged a good number of their actions. This is all the more important for this book because the neighborhood was also the place where many of the relevant actions of the secret police took place. Finally, the history of Prenzlauer Berg, projected into the present, is a very apt means to address the situation of the activists after unification and thus the context in which I have conducted my interviews with them.

PRENZLAUER BERG—THE SPACE OF DISSIDENCE

Three epistemic effects of space (Sewell 2005, 365) can be distinguished analytically. First, the built environment is ordered, that is, differentiated and integrated in a particular way. Therefore it can be read as a set of signs or a text, as petrified discourse signaling who built for what purpose at what time. Since space forms the general backdrop of all of our life, the dimensions, colors, arrangements, scents, and sound qualities of built environments are prone to trigger resonances with scenes long past, thus evoking emotions or, more characteristically, moods. In this way, the built environment may begin to mean or express, for example, wealth, power, beauty, security, familiarity, despair, loneliness, destitution, disorder, and so forth. Second, the built environment contextualizes, enables, and constrains particular actions. It does so, for example, by offering undisturbed spaces for repose and reflection, by encouraging or discouraging the encounter of and communication with different kinds of people, and by serving as a stage for action more or less suitable to present it to particular audiences.[1] Third, building on the other two processes, the built environment can also facilitate or hinder processes of institutionalization by mediating particular kinds of actions and their projective articulation. The built environment thus becomes directly political.[2] At the

---

1. In *Divided in Unity* (Glaeser 2000) I show how East and West Berliners read built environments in search for the clues about the nature of the polity in which they live. This is possible because that polity is seen as the regulator and, in conspicuous ways, the builder of this environment.
2. Unlike the built environment, natural landscapes are not political in the sense that I defined this term in the introduction. However, as political thinkers have realized for a long time, they

crossroads of meaning, action, and institutionalization the built environment can be made to signify, and practically enhance or diminish, particular ways of being human.

Prenzlauer Berg's meaning as a text has been closely connected to its history. Like much of what we know today as Berlin, it was only settled in the last quarter of the nineteenth century on a minor hill—the remnant of a glacial moraine—about a mile northeast of the old city center. It was then that the newly appointed capital city of the second German empire began to precipitate as a major metropolis from an uncontrolled chain reaction between nation state politics, industrialization, and imperialism. These processes fed on large quantities of immigrants, who all needed housing in accordance with the means they were afforded.[3] Within that period of frenzied growth, Prenzlauer Berg was developed to accommodate a cross-class population. The hopeful petite bourgeoisie was lodged in relatively spacious street-front apartment houses sitting atop ground-floor shops. Their facades were garnished with stucco implements or brickwork, suggesting Classicist, Baroque, Renaissance, Gothic, or Romanesque origins. Public buildings and churches, erected alongside the new housing complexes to administer and minister to the new inhabitants, were executed in similarly historicizing styles. These facades appear as if they attempted to clad a radically uncertain present in the settled garb of a nostalgically reassuring past. That these were only appearances, however, was only too obvious to the inhabitants. In the larger blocks, the central gateway of the front-houses typically opened to a cul-de-sac system of increasingly smaller and consequently ever more poorly lit and aired courtyards. Here were small craft shops of all sorts, and the modest to squalid, typically overcrowded dwellings of the proletariat. These infamous *Mietskasernen* (rental barracks) are living proof and petrified symbol of industrial revolution misery in Berlin.[4]

Prenzlauer Berg's mixed-class building topography survived the air raids

---

often have profound political consequences, for example, by instigating or preventing competition (Locke), enabling or disabling trade and communication (Smith), or making certain mentalities more likely than others (Montesquieu).

3. This is how Berlin's population grew: 1810, 170,000; 1848, 415,000; 1871, 823,000; 1881, 1.3 million; 1890, 1.9 million; 1900, 2.7 million; 1910, 3.7 million. Today, Berlin has 3.4 million inhabitants.

4. Even if not designed with this purpose in mind, it strikes me as a rather ingenious arrangement for the perpetual stretching of capitalism to house the petite bourgeoisie, the proletariat, and the lumpens side by side in that way to instill a fear of falling as much as the hope for better things to come. For Berlin, the front-house/courtyard housing system is one of the key spatial synecdoches of the late nineteenth century. It is the missing counterpart to Benjamin's "arcades" (1983) among the spatial chiffres capturing nineteenth-century life.

and the battle of Berlin relatively unscathed. Yalta's caprice made it part of the Soviet-occupied zone. Pulled along by economic necessity, the socialist city-planning ideology quickly moved away from the ideal of "workers' palaces" in the form of decorative and historicizing "national styles,"[5] an ideal with which at least the front-houses of Prenzlauer Berg might have been quite compatible. Instead, planning began to favor the industrial version of modernist architecture placed on open fields to provide the very air and light so sorely missing in Berlin's original proletarian housing complexes. In part for ideological reasons and in part for practical considerations, then, Prenzlauer Berg and similar historical neighborhoods came to be literally written down by keeping repairs to an absolute minimum. The idea was that once uninhabitable they would be razed and replaced by new construction projects. In consequence, Prenzlauer Berg's structures not only saw their paint chip and their stucco crumble under the joint assault of the seasons and Berlin's bituminous coal–fired ovens, but also many a backyard wing, structurally weakened by infinitely deferred maintenance, became uninhabitable in the course of the next decades, and beginning in the 1970s were slowly demolished. As proper socialist employers were beginning to offer their employees the much-touted fruits of socialist development, apartments in new building developments sporting central heating and running hot and cold water in bathrooms located within the dwelling,[6] Prenzlauer Berg's population dropped from approximately 250,000 in 1950 to less than 150,000 in 1990.[7]

Bohèmification by Default

The consequence was a politically efficacious social sorting process. Only the economically and politically weak—since least well connected to the socialist project—remained, while people less enchanted with GDR socialism began to move in, largely driven by the sheer availability of this least-desirable housing stock, often trying to escape provincial life and/or ordinary socialist careers, they were lucky to find anything at all in a city that was notoriously short of apartments (Feix 1999). The result of this sorting process was that potential dissidence found a spatial home. On the streets,

---

5. The Berlin exemplars of such grandiose but also solid and relatively generous buildings are those along Karl-Marx-Allee (formerly Stalin-Allee).

6. By contrast all the apartments in Prenzlauer Berg needed to be heated with coal-fired ovens, while many of them only had shared toilets in the hallway.

7. The population of Prenzlauer Berg reached its apex in the late 1920s with roughly 325,000 inhabitants. It was considered one of the most densely populated areas of any big city. The population declined during the 1930s as better-designed housing became available for workers.

those taking issue with the GDR—embodying their political understandings by choice of hairstyles and clothing—could see more of their own kind. At least in Prenzlauer Berg they did not seem to be the vanishing minority that they were in statistical terms. Their sheer co-presence was mutually recognizing of their apartness from the socialist project; to some degree it was even normalizing their otherness. The emergent alternative "we" had spatial roots in a crumbling neighborhood.

The new immigrants were undoubtedly enchanted by the neighborhood's decidedly presocialist aura, by one another's very presence, as well as by the conspicuous absence of socialist officialdom. The front buildings' expansive, high-ceilinged rooms and the proximity to center city and public transportation made them not only great party spots on which friends from all over Berlin could converge. They also offered spaces large enough to stage performances, such as readings or discussions, that is sorely needed space for singers, writers, and thinkers whose access to official venues had been blocked. Large apartments are in effect private spaces convertible to public uses. This employment of space is something hardly imaginable in the tightly economized rooms of the new building complexes erected for the larger part on the sandy fields of Berlin's outskirts, as well as on the ruins of war and neglect.[8] And thus the spatial foundations for the emergence of the various fabled Prenzlauer Berg "scenes" emerged, which made this particular neighborhood a hot spot for Stasi officers who not infrequently developed a visceral dislike for both the physical space and its inhabitants.[9]

Even though dissident groups were scattered throughout Berlin, Prenzlauer Berg not only became the area with the highest concentration of inhabitants participating in state-independent political activities, but it also became the home of some of its most important and most active dissident groups, such as Women for Peace (Frauen für den Frieden) in the first half and the Initiative for Peace and Human Rights (Initiative für Frieden und Menschenrechte or IFM) as well as the Environmental Library (Umweltbibliothek or UB) in the second half of the decade.[10] During the final years of the

---

8. These often contained spaces for social functions, but they were officially controlled through the house communities.

9. For a charming and, in GDR terms rather unconventional, portrait of Prenzlauer Berg's general population, see Dahn 2001. Published in the GDR the book says nothing about the artist or political dissident scene, but all the more about its workers, the unusually many small shopkeepers, and their life. Interesting portraits about lives in the artist scene can be found in Felsmann and Gröschner 1999.

10. The UB was located in the basement of the community center of the Church of Zion, which is just outside of the boundaries of Prenzlauer Berg, administratively speaking in Mitte. From the standpoint of social geography, however, it is undoubtedly part and parcel of Prenzlauer Berg.

GDR, Prenzlauer Berg groups issued the most important GDR-wide sam-izdat publications, the *Grenzfall* and the *Umweltblätter*. At the same time, some of its key members continued to maintain contact with SED reformers while interfacing intensively with other non-parish-based as well as parish-based groups in Berlin and elsewhere in the GDR. They maintained contacts with dissident groups in Eastern Europe, especially in Warsaw, Prague, and Budapest, as well as with the Greens in West Germany and the peace move-ment in Western Europe. Thus the political scene in Prenzlauer Berg was arguably Berlin's and perhaps even the GDR's most important nodal point for non-SED dissident activities.[11]

Post-Wende Gentrification

Toward the end of the 1980s small numbers of Western tourists arrived in the area either in search of political and/or artistic expression authenticated by state suppression and isolation from market forces, or they came to get what might pass for a firsthand experience of socialisms' economic inepti-tude and political authoritarianism. In the hectic months of socialism's final disintegration, Prenzlauer Berg became a household name to Easterners and Westerners alike: to some degree it became the real, and to a much larger extent, the symbolic home of the velvet revolution. It is thus not surprising that after unification the area was a primary target for gentrification. The historicization of the place in combination with a building ensemble that, in its consistency is quite rare in war-torn Berlin, provided ideal preconditions. The impediments to gentrification, such as the thorny issues of ownership and restitution as well as Germany's somewhat more protective law gov-erning tenancy, were eventually overcome; generous capital city rebuilding subsidies added further incentives. Thoroughly renovated and upgraded with modern amenities, the building ensemble of Prenzlauer Berg began to appeal to certain contemporary understandings of stylish living that aim to root the appearing breadth of a cosmopolitan present in the supposed depths of local history. Accordingly, Prenzlauer Berg increasingly teemed with boutiques, galleries, restaurants, and cafes, peddling wares and meals from all over the world to its educated upper-middle-class clientele.

Some of the former GDR opposition members who lived there before unification opted to stay. Others felt the urgent need to leave. Both decisions are intimately connected with what Prenzlauer Berg has remained—in a decreasing number of pockets a cheap area to live in—and has become—a chic upper-middle-class neighborhood with increasingly (for Berlin any-

11. The other two locations that matter most are Jena, especially during the late 1970s and early 1980s, and Leipzig during the last few years of the GDR.

way) upscale rents. This social division is not unconnected with the personal issues that tore dissident friendships asunder after unification. The crux is that former GDR dissidents have not, with some exceptions, become an integral part of the postunification political or economic elites of unified Germany. Instead, a sizable number of former dissidents have remained marginal, even if this renewed marginality might be much more bearable now, lacking the chicanery, tutelage, intensive surveillance, and the threat of incarceration of the older one.

The story of renewed marginalization of GDR dissidents in postunification Germany does not follow the familiar plot of an uncontrollable revolution devouring its children in a process of self-radicalization. To the contrary, its central plot rests on a sober revolutionary genie who could be called back into the bottle by the first agency that was able to make a credible promise of affluence, order, and liberal rights. In its course it gladly abandoned those from whom it had drawn its initial inspiration because they wanted to go further, endeavoring yet again to experiment with new social forms. With few exceptions, therefore, the GDR dissidents' political life peaked in their active participation in the revolutionary transformations of GDR society in the half-year between September 1989 and March 1990 (Torpey 1995, chap. 6). They formed GDR-wide movements and contributed to the organization of demonstrations that prepared the way for the demise of Erich Honecker and, soon after, the party itself. In the direct aftermath of the fall of the Berlin Wall, they were involved in founding new political parties; they became members of roundtables and commissions dealing with the socialist past; they were elected members of parliament; and for a short time they even served as ministers and chiefs of large bureaucracies. Yet, already the March 18, 1990, elections came as a chilling shock to most of them. These first and last free elections in GDR history amounted in large part to a plebiscite over form and timing of German unification. The alternatives furnished by the constitution of the Federal Republic were unification by simple accession or unification by reconstitution (Jarausch 1994, chap. 6; Maier 1997, 1995 ff.; Glaeser 2000, chap. 2). The majority of dissident group members, adherents of a truly democratic ("third way") socialism, spoke out for reconstitution. They felt that unified Germany could benefit from the experiences of the GDR and that this experience should somehow find its way into the institutional fabric of the unified nation. However, this path, together with the dissidents' moralization of life in the former GDR, was soundly defeated at the ballot box in favor of the much-quicker unification by accession that projected the entire legal-administrative, political, and economic order of West Germany onto the territory of the former GDR.

If they wanted to remain in politics after unification, dissidents had to make the gigantic leap into the unknown territory of what was de facto West

German electoral politics. Since the parties they had founded garnered only marginal electoral success, they had to pursue ambitions for political office within the well-established Western parties, their structures and culture. At first, these parties were quite willing to place a good number of former dissidents on safe-list positions during the next electoral period at the communal, state, and national level. With easily recognizable Eastern faces among their candidates, these parties hoped to gain advantage among the Eastern electorate. Moreover, the GDR dissidents carried with them the aura of what many commentators then saw as the first successful revolution on German soil. Western parties were eager to partake in this aura.[12] By the mid-1990s, however, the parties had woken up to the fact that dissidents rarely contributed to electoral success in the new Eastern states and were thus much less willing to make room for them on party lists. Therefore, many former dissidents dropped out of the game: exhausted, defeated, or even appalled by what they had experienced.

With electoral politics becoming an increasingly difficult option, the question was, "what now?" Since many former dissidents could not complete their formal education in the GDR, while others had been kept from working in their professional fields for a long time, their employment prospects were often even bleaker than those of ordinary GDR citizens. Yet, the country had another role in stock for at least some of them. Instead of politicians in the present, they (were) turned into what might be called "politicians of the past." In that double meaning of this expression, they were honored for what they did and they became sought-after eyewitnesses of GDR history, commentators on all things GDR and its proper memorization. After all, they were victims of a dictatorship; they had resisted and shown civic courage under adverse circumstances. And thus they were, what the vast majority of Germans in East and West were not, but should have been under publicly espoused political ideals.

With this, their very own biographically acquired qualification, a number of possibilities were open to them after unification. Under the rubric of "political education" a whole sector of organizations was founded in West

---

12. Germany has always suffered from a serious revolution-envy based on the understanding that true, deeply rooted democracy is built on a successful liberal revolution à la England, the United States, or France. Given the influence Hegel had on the German social imagination, as Boyer (2005) has shown, this popular modernization-theoretic take is perhaps not surprising. While it seems to me that this argument suffers fatally from a misguided teleological understanding of the development of human society, this view contributed to seeing GDR dissidents as the revolutionaries who could vouch for the authenticity and legitimacy of the new "Berlin republic" that could thus successfully and finally dispel the specters of Germany's past by becoming a "normal nation."

Germany after World War II by the state, the churches, the parties, and the unions of workers and employers for the express purpose of instilling the political virtues displayed by the dissidents into citizens of all ages. The idea was (and remains) that a politically educated citizenry would meet a new Hitler with resistance rather than compliance. The luckier ones among the former dissidents became full-time employees of such organizations.[13] Others found within such organizations time-limited employment for lectures, seminars, or projects on a fee for service basis.

With the demise of the GDR the political education sector was considerably expanded. Not only did every single one of the new states need its own set of institutions, but there was now a new kind of past that needed to be *bewältigt* (worked through): "the second German dictatorship" as the GDR is now called with historical legerdemain. In this context the formation of one federal-level and five state-level Stasi document centers is significant.[14] The heads of all of them are former dissidents with varying centrality within dissident groups. It is their task to make available Stasi documents to everybody who had a Stasi file, above all, the dissidents themselves. These centers also answer to employer inquiries about Stasi ties of potential employees.

13. Those affiliated with the Protestant Church in East Germany, ministers above all, stood a much better chance to secure such full-time employment, not only in directly church-affiliated organizations but also in state organizations. Sociologically speaking, it is quite easy to develop any number of hypotheses about why this is so (e.g., proven track record of disciplined work in another recognized organization, institutional networks, ideological preferences, and above all the link between the church and the established West German parties). Alas, these West German preference schemes left non-church-affiliated dissidents in limbo.

14. The establishment of the Stasi document centers followed on the heels of a fierce debate about whether or not to open the files at all, and if so under which conditions to whom. A certain compromise solution was found with the federal law concerning Stasi documents (*Stasiunterlagengesetz*). In practice, three categories of people are distinguished: 1. Private persons without Stasi connections. Any personal information about this group is restricted and will be censored unless this person consents to making his or her file available for a particular purpose. 2. There are "people of historical significance" whose privacy rights are more limited by the public's countervailing rights to know what was going on. 3. There is anybody with official or documentable unofficial ties to the Stasi. Their files, even personnel files, are free for everybody with a legitimate research interest independently of whether this person has been sentenced for his or her Stasi activities or not. This debate has been refreshed as former chancellor, Helmut Kohl, damaged by party finance corruption scandals, tried to block access to his files in an obvious attempt to manage his short- to medium-term reputation. He succeeded, and the law about access to the files of "persons of historical significance" had to be reformulated. In response to these debates and the federal law all of the five new states with the exception of Brandenburg have created their own Stasi document centers through which the files of the Stasi district and county offices are managed.

They undertake research on the history of the Stasi, they edit Stasi documents, and they support journalistic and academic research about GDR history. A few prominent dissidents have found permanent work there.

Finally, there are a number of new memorials (for example, the former Stasi jail in Hohenschönhausen, and the former Stasi headquarters at Normannenstrasse) and foundations that are dedicated to research and education about the socialist dictatorship. And again it is the lucky dissident who has found full-time employment in such organizations. Most have to content themselves with project-based work. Either in the context of such work relations or otherwise on their own account, many former dissidents started to engage in historiographical endeavors, editing documents, writing memoirs, or even researching and writing scholarly articles and books. Thus, through permanent employment or project work in organizations of political education as well as through their writings, former dissidents have exerted a continuing influence over the perception of the former GDR in unified Germany. That is a role that former Stasi officers begrudge them, because the former dissidents command public attention for their descriptions of their own political suppression in the GDR.

THE EMOTIVE AND PRACTICAL ROOTS OF DISSIDENCE

I am on my way from my field-site home near the Water Tower to my meeting with Ulrike Poppe, a founding member of both Women for Peace and the Initiative for Peace and Human Rights and thus one of the core figures of the non-parish-based dissident groups in Berlin. She lives around the corner at Kollwitzplatz, and to get to her I pass right through the heart of the French Quarter,[15] the touristy center of Prenzlauer Berg. I walk past the "Pasternak," a well-known postunification hangout whose original East-meets-West aspirations are still manifest in its Cyrillic and Roman signs as well as in its hearty borscht. The Kosher Restaurant next door, with its regular, eerily popular live klezmer music, has become a favorite destination where the hopes for a renewed Berlin Jewish life must confront the reality of heavily armed police officers guarding the adjacent synagogue. Poppe has moved since our last meeting, and so she quickly shows me around the new place. She is delighted to live now, after all these years, in a beautiful, fully updated

---

15. This nickname refers to the street names of the wedge between Schönhauser Allee and Prenzlauer Allee, which originally commemorated the Prussian victory of 1871 over France. For example, newly (re)incorporated Alsace-Lorraine was placed on the map of the imperial microcosmos that Berlin was taken to become through a Straßburger, Kolmarer, Mühlhauser, and Metzer Straße. Other street names honored Prussian generals of that very war.

and renovated apartment. Pointing through the kitchen window she explains that the old backyard houses have been torn down, making room for a spacious yard that all inhabitants of the front house can use. Unlike other former opposition members, Poppe has landed on her feet after unification. She has a full-time job organizing adult political-education events for the academy of the Protestant Church in Berlin. She has been part of the old Prenzlauer Berg and she is part of the new.

Outrage at the Abuses of Power: Ulrike Poppe

After settling down in the kitchen with a bottle of wine I try to get the ball rolling quickly by asking a bit awkwardly how she became opposed to GDR socialism. I learn that her family background did not in any easy way push her in this direction. In fact, her grandmother had benefited from the efforts of the new state to find teachers after the war. Her father was a party member. He had studied Slavic languages and history at the venerable University of Rostock on the Baltic and became a staff historian at the academy of sciences. He met his future wife as a fellow student in Rostock. And although she was not a party member, she moved on to work as a translator for the president of the GDR's association for the blind. Poppe's sister produced a picture-perfect GDR career. After being a model high school student, she became a top medical student and a successful prize-winning researcher, and she was a party member (Poppe thinks mostly for practical reasons, though). And even Poppe herself started out as an involved member of the communist youth movement. In sum, Poppe was surrounded by authority figures with some kind of positive relationship to the socialist project.

This does not mean that her familial environment consisted of uncritical believers. One of her favorite uncles eventually fled to West Germany. Her mother was not in the party in spite of her close ties to functionaries, and she successfully defended her noncommitment with the help of her superiors once she was pressured to join. Poppe also reckons that her father was disillusioned by party and state because de-Stalinization got stuck in superficialities, but he was shy about taking more radical steps simply because he loathed the idea of possibly losing his work at the academy (in an area of research then considered to be politically of low priority). He also eagerly watched Western news programs with his daughter with the express purpose of cultivating critical-thinking capabilities. Father Poppe encouraged her to scrutinize arguments and evidence for any major political claim. In fact, he was an authority who taught her to be critical of authority.

The hypocrisy of teachers

Poppe begins her narrative of becoming critical of the party state thus:

> Hmm, I would say this was a very slow gradual process. As a child at school
> I was outraged by the hypocrisy of the teachers. I knew that at home they
> were watching Western television [from their own children who also at-
> tended the same school], but at school they preached that one must not do
> that, that this [Western television] is the class enemy. Pupils were punished
> if they told that they watched Western television and, depending on their
> position, the parents of these pupils got into trouble at work. And that's of
> course the reason why many parents demanded of their children to lie. . . .
> Later of course we did it [talk about Western TV] anyway and we just
> learned to be careful in class. However, it destroyed the credibility of the
> teachers.

This beginning may be surprising. Probably the majority of GDR citizens
experienced tensions about their interest in Western electronic mass media,
and most of them more or less quickly and more or less painfully learned
what to talk about with whom in which context. Reinhard Weißhuhn, a
close associate of Poppe's in Berlin dissident circles, calls such tensions and
the lessons learned from them, "a constitutive feature of political socialization in the GDR."[16] It was equally common in the GDR, especially among
youths, to accuse functionaries of hypocrisy. More, even in Western Europe
and North America, high school students explained their protest activities
with the hypocrisy of their teachers (and parents or anybody beyond the
age of thirty). In other words, charging authority figures with hypocrisy was
part of an international youth culture. The question is, therefore, how such
a widely spread phenomenon could actually become the starting point for
a dissident career.

One way to answer this question is to look for distinguishing circumstances. Poppe was not just outraged that she had to wrestle with demands
she did not want to fulfill, that she had to manage the conflict between the
rules of her home (and possibly her own desire) and those of the state. She
was angry because she knew for a fact that those enforcing the norm (her
teachers) violated it. The issue for her was not only the pain of being forced

---

16. Most of the Stasi officers I have interviewed did not face this problem simply because they
felt little desire to watch Western television until they had reached a certain level of hierarchy
and were officially asked to do so "in the interest of staying abreast of enemy propaganda." Another group that did not have to wrestle with this issue were the inhabitants of the Elbe valley
upstream from Dresden who resided in the shadow of Western transmitters. For this reason,
this area was also known as "the valley of the naive" (das Tal der Ahnungslosen).

into a self-denying situation by a more or less abstract state that claimed to have abolished such forms of alienation. She faced an obvious abuse of power by identifiable and self-declared agents of the state who posed as models while violating the norms they claimed to uphold by the regular use of punishment and humiliation. Moreover, to understand the variety of reactions to the Western media problem, it has to be considered that the degree to which it was made an issue varied from district to district, from school to school.[17] In Poppe's assessment the driving force behind the particularly harsh climate prevailing in her school was the principal, whom she describes as a staunch believer ("onehundredfiftypercenter") who was ostentatiously concerned with the socialist purity of his institution. Poppe went to school in Oranienburg, a small town just north of Berlin, a fact that has also contributed to her knowledge about the private life of her teachers.

This said, the harsh climate in her school and the small town transparency of hypocritical claims do not sufficiently distinguish her case from others who did not become involved in dissident activities. Poppe's school did not become known as a breeding ground for future dissidents. A more promising answer to the question of what began to push her in a direction eventually leading to dissident actions lies in her hint about a "slow, gradual process." What mattered is the emergence of particular understandings in response to a *series of events*, the context of their occurrence as well as their sequencing. In the interview with her, the deeply emotional and personal ring in her statement about teacher hypocrisy becomes fully comprehensible just a few minutes later, when Poppe describes how as a nine-year-old she had to part with her best friend who also sat next to her at school. The surprise building of the Wall on August 13, 1961, caught her friend's parents off guard while visiting West Berlin.[18] This situation posed a tough choice for them. They could stay in the West, leaving their daughter for the time being with her grandparents and

17. Reinhard Weißhuhn, a longtime participant in various dissident scenes and later a central figure of the IFM, reported about such a regional variation of norm-enforcement. While he lived in Karl-Marx-Stadt (now Chemnitz) the afternoon meetings of the young pioneers seemed to be deliberately organized on the very same afternoons as the instruction in religious education organized by the Protestant Church. In Weimar, where he moved at age eleven, religious education was not taught in competition with the pioneer afternoons, it was taught to his great surprise in school! This eased his life considerably because he eagerly attended both.

18. Even though there were rumors that the GDR leadership intended to close the border between East and West Berlin, Ulbricht famously declared during a press conference on June 15 that "nobody has the intention to erect a wall [between both parts of Berlin]." In Western discourses, the discrepancy between this statement and the actual erection of the Wall a mere two months later has always served as evidence for the cynicism of the GDR leadership. Against this interpretation, historians have pointed out (Podewin 1995, 347ff.) that Ulbricht might still have harbored hopes at this point to come to a "contractual solution" of this problem. The outlines of such a

hoping to get her out as soon as possible. Alternatively, they could go back right away, risking that they might never be able to visit again or even less settle in the West. They opted for the former. And luckily, their bet paid off. One year later the GDR authorities let Poppe's friend (and other children in the same situations) join her parents on the other side of the Wall. Poppe wanted to stay in touch and began to write letters. However, they were all returned as undeliverable, a fact that she says "deeply saddened" her. Thus, she began to understand the Wall as the direct cause of some of her pains, a physical barrier thwarting desire to be in touch with and to be physically united with her friend. Living in sight and sound of the Wall, the barking dogs, the star shells, the occasional gunshots all of a sudden had a very personal and frightening meaning. The violence of the forced separation from her best friend began to be associated with an awareness of the violence of the GDR border regime. The hypocrisy of the teachers, their public upholding of rules they broke in private, resonated negatively with Poppe's pain of personal loss. And thus, in a palpable way the teacher's hypocrisy raised the issue of the meaning of sacrifices the socialist state asked of its citizens. It is remarkable in this context that in her memory she places her first perception of this hypocrisy at around the time she lost her friend.

When Poppe was about fifteen or sixteen, she and two classmates engaged in what turned out to be a veritable, if unwitting, experiment in political knowledge-making. Enthused by the ideal of political participation through discussion, the trio resolved to write a letter to the People's Chamber. The time was 1968 or 1969, Poppe no longer remembers when exactly. It is important, however, to recall that this was a time of considerable political upheaval. The Prague Spring was either blooming or was already militarily crushed; the Ussuri crisis (a Sino-Soviet border conflict) was imminent or still on everybody's mind. The trio desired answers to three questions, two of which Poppe recalls: First, if China and the Soviet Union are both communist countries, then how come they could not remain friends? Second, revealing the still lingering pain from the returned letters to her friend in West Berlin, if the party still pursued a policy of German unification, and it said it did, then how come the GDR maintained strict controls on the intercourse with West Germany? As soon as the father of one of the two classmates, also a party member, heard about the letter, he preemptively went to the head of the local school district to tell him what was in the offing.[19] The district head

---

"contractual solution" are, however, rather unclear. There is no doubt that for economic and political reasons the SED needed and wanted the boundaries between both parts of Berlin closed.

19. He rightly feared that the letter might be read by those higher up as a provocation or at least as an indication that something was amiss in the school district. In either case, the reaction anticipated of the party state tended to develop cascades of blame in accordance with the prin-

immediately called in the homeroom teacher to reprimand him severely. That teacher came in turn to Poppe's father to get some more clues of what was going on. Poppe remembers bits and pieces of their noisy conversation behind closed doors. She remembers her father saying to the teacher: "just calm down, they are just kids!"

The ensuing events ended with the expulsion of one member of the letter-writing trio: the boy, who was also active in the Protestant youth movement and whose parents were both not members of the party. The other two got away with a warning because their party member parents appeared to provide the guarantee that the children would be steered back to a path of socialist virtues. The reasoning for this decision was given in a class meeting in the homeroom at which the representative of the school district, the director of the school and the homeroom teacher were present.[20] When nobody said anything in defense of the boy who was to be dismissed, Poppe, who was, after all, an equal part of the censored activity, publicly reminded the homeroom teacher that he had in private confided in her that he too thought expelling the boy was much too harsh a punishment. Poppe remembers that thus challenged, the teacher's head turned fire-red and that he banged his fist on the table declaring that he would not tolerate such an offense against his socialist fatherland. In response to this attack Poppe, burst into tears and had to leave the room. "I was totally shocked by this reaction because I did not anticipate it."

"To this day," Poppe says, "I am ashamed about the event." However, the reasons behind her shame have changed. At the time of the incident she clearly felt the force of isolation; probably she was also ashamed about the fact that her friend got dismissed while she walked away with impunity. The fact that she never tried to make contact with him afterward lends support to this interpretation. She remains ashamed, however, because today she wonders how she could have been politically so naive as to betray her teacher's trust. The differentiations and integrations central to shame as an emotive understanding follow a characteristic pattern. Shame is typically triggered by an authority's negative recognition of an action that is read as revealing a person's identity

---

ciples of socialist theodicy in which higher-ranking officials would accuse lower-ranking ones of not living up to their duties. At the lower end of this chain were the teachers and of course the parents. The father's reaction must therefore be understood as an effort to perform right consciousness, which was probably also connected with the hope that the letter could somehow be intercepted early on to prevent the cascade from developing in the first place. Instead, his contact with the school district official forced the latter to perform his right consciousness too, thereby at least contributing to, if not perhaps even triggering the cascade at a lower level.

20. Even if this event would not have been called critique and self-critique, it still followed both the intention of that ritual in reasserting the party line, as well as parts of its procedure, for example in making use of shaming tactics.

as defective with regard to an ego ideal that is valued by both ego and the censoring authority (e.g., Tomkins 1963, 185ff.; Wurmser 1998, 40; Nathanson 1992, 197ff.). Thus, shifts in shame constellations, that is, changes in triggers, authorities, ego ideal, and ranges of actions that are potentially shameful, are of high analytic value regarding fundamental, immediately self-related understandings. The shift that Poppe recounts nicely illustrates a major transformation in her political understandings of herself in relationship to GDR socialism. While her adolescent shame is still so clearly predicated on her desire to belong, her adult shame is predicated on her superior insight into the workings of the socialist system with which she no longer identifies.

Another aspect of the school episode deserves attention. The kinesthetic performativity of events like the homeroom meeting are epistemically important too. In chapter 2 I discussed the spatial setup of a critique and self-critique meeting where the accused is, like in a court room, spatially and thus kinesthetically juxtaposed to party, state, and, ideally, the people. After her homeroom teacher's acoustic efforts to demarcate insiders and outsiders, Poppe had to literally run away from the scene, setting her in opposition to "them." In events, it matters who takes in a person kinesthetically as "theirs" and who marks them as outsider. In the theory of socialist practice, the isolation in critique and self-critique is followed after a (reflexive) hiatus by a reintegration into a work collective where the defendant has to prove him- or herself, thus becoming again a member of the socialist community. Poppe was certainly taken in by her family and her closer friends. But vis-à-vis the institutions linking her to the project of the state she felt herself henceforth marked. Her persistent shame shows that any naive security in belonging had come to an abrupt end. This was underscored by the fact that her relationship to persons important to this integration, for example, her homeroom teacher, had changed fundamentally. In this way the physical dynamics of events creates orderings, that is, kinesthetic understandings that can subsequently—depending on their integration through validation—lead to transformations in other modes of understanding.

Rock and roll and the party state

Poppe describes the hottest and most prevalent point of contention at school as "lifestyle issues."[21] Many young people in the GDR tried to "catch up with international youth culture," as she puts it. They listened to beat

21. For an analysis of the similar appeal of Western popular culture on youth in the Soviet Union, see Alexei Yurchak (2006, chap. 5). Even though "the West" emerged in both youth cultures as "imaginary," as Yurchak says, it is still important to see how much more tangible that "West" was for people in the GDR.

music, young men tried to grow both their hair and their beards, and members of either sex wore jeans. All of this was regarded with much disdain by the GDR leadership, which throughout the 1960s denounced this music, clothes, and body imagery as "decadent bourgeois," the style of the class enemy and therefore profoundly antisocialist. At school Poppe remembers that showing up with Western shopping bags, jeans, or long hair got people reprimanded, if not punished in the case of repetition. Yet in spite of these strong negative recognitions of their own lifestyle preference by school officials and usually by parents too, in the evening she and her friends were regularly listening to Western radio stations so they could talk about it in school the next day. On the weekend they organized parties or went to dance events where the bands had to maintain a quota for music from socialist countries all the while playing Western hits. This is how she describes what to her was the apex of the confrontation between young people's lifestyle choices and the state:

> On the twentieth anniversary of the GDR . . . there was the so-called "RIAS-canard."[22] The RIAS announced that on October 7, 1969, the Rolling Stones would give a concert on top of the Springer building [the headquarters of the conservative West Berlin Springer Press, located directly at the Wall].[23] We didn't really believe it, but it was nevertheless the signal for a particular type of youth in the whole of the GDR to flock to Berlin. Most were already taken out of the trains and didn't even get to the capital. And we drove to Spittelmarkt [closest square in East Berlin] to look from there at what was happening at the Springer building. But then there were already communist youth movement formations marching in closed blocks, and we were caught right in the middle. And then they [the police] appeared with water cannons and dogs and people got arrested. I could escape in the last minute. . . . On Monday, we always had roll calls, the names of all those were called who got themselves arrested. . . . And they had to step forward and they got

---

22. Poppe uses the official GDR designation of the event. The German Historical Museum in Berlin has a picture of a 1954 Leipzig carnival procession in which one truck displayed a large "RIAS-canard," at http://www.dhm.de/ausstellungen/kalter_krieg/bild/b_069.htm. I have not found anything about how this particular RIAS piece came about—as a joke of an individual journalist, or as a planned piece of disinformation. In the latter case it would be interesting to find out who contrived it and how it got to be placed.

23. Axel Springer built his headquarters directly at the Wall near the Wall Museum and the Allied Checkpoint Charlie so that his journalists would be reminded constantly of what they were writing for—and against. Much like the Stasi, who used quotes around expressions like independent peace movement (see chapter 6, p. 325), Springer had his papers refer to the GDR in quotes. Taken together, this is a good example for the linguistic precipitation of what Mannheim (1995) calls partial ideology.

reprimanded for having fallen prey to the lies of the class enemy, thereby proving how politically immature they really were and thus not worthy to study at a socialist school. I don't know anymore what happened to them, whether there was more than the public reprimand, but I don't think so. It was bad enough. And I stood in my row, trembling, but happy that I didn't belong to them [the reprimanded].[24]

This event is interesting for the state's starkly performed negative recognition of young people's musical tastes and leisure preferences. It is also interesting again for the kinesthetic and emotive ordering emerging through the event. Kinesthetically, the state literally places itself in front of the young people, not only physically keeping them from following their desire, but also making itself an object of fear by arresting many. Those arrested were first isolated from their friends, effectively splitting the group that was thus shown to have no protective power. The arrested were then publicly shamed in their high schools, again splitting them from their friends. What people further made out of these emergent kinesthetic understandings depended very much on how they resonated with previous experiences and how they were talked about in networks of authority. The state's physical confrontation, shaming practices, and threats of further sanctions may have persuaded some not to take such risky action in the future. For others it may have become the basis of solidarity not least because the event is eminently narratable. Poppe was glad she was not singled out and shamed this time. But she clearly knew that she might just as well have been.

Path dependence and institutional defetishization

The socialist state in its various institutional guises did not content itself with offering mere opinions about a staggeringly wide range of matters, that liberal observers would consider private. Grounded in its missionary goal of radical, consciousness-driven social transformation, and armed with Marxist-Leninist theory, it instead had outright teachings on even minute aspects of everyday life that it made every effort to disseminate through its various propaganda channels. Through its acute attention to the mundane, the party state politicized (in a narrow sense) understandings that could have remained merely aesthetic. For Poppe, a significant number

---

24. The events surrounding the "RIAS canard" were formative for other future events as well. Vera Lengsfeld (2002, 40–42), one of the most active members of the Friedenskreis Pankow who also went to see what was happening, likewise narrowly escaped arrest. She reports about the detention of large numbers of youths in the excavation for the new buildings on Leipziger Straße.

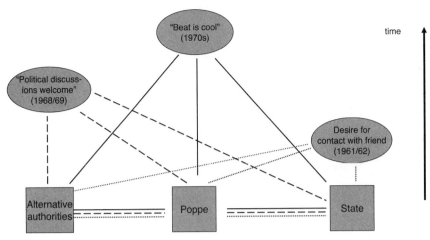

Figure 7.1. Competition of recognitions in Poppe's authority networks: Poppe's biography is characterized by a succession of episodes in which the state (mostly negatively) recognizes some of her most valued understandings (three successive recognition "triangles" to the right). Given her other sources of authority, however, the state's negative recognitions can be counteracted (three "recognition triangles" to the left). The form of the lines (dotted, dashed, solid) are specific to the event.

of the party state's teachings on everyday pursuits—for example, those on the insidious influences of the Western class enemy working their way through personal contact, electronic mass media, or forms of music, dress, or hairstyles—operated as negative recognitions of some of her most cherished understandings (three of which are represented in figure 7.1). However, it is also important to see that for Poppe the state's recognitions were by no means all negative. For example, the party's appeal to be politically active and conscious positively recognized Poppe's self-image as a political being. Thus, for adolescent Poppe, state authority was first ambiguous and then became increasingly negative. The authority of her parents, with whom she fought incessantly over the same lifestyle choices that the state disapproved of, was ambiguous too. Yet, as far as overtly political matters are concerned, she also felt the unwavering support of her parents. As with many other adolescents, especially of her generation, peers played a large, steadily increasing role in the structure of her authority networks. However, these peers were as powerless as she was when she needed active support against some measures undertaken by her school. In sum, then, none of these three distinct sets of authorities simply dominated the others across all domains. Instead, they partially overlapped and partially contradicted one another in what they were willing to recognize positively and negatively. For Poppe, as for others, this heterogeneity of her authority networks was the precondition for the development of a certain degree of independence.

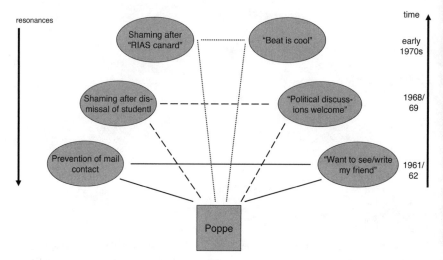

Figure 7.2. Negative corroboration of Poppe's understandings: Poppe's biography is characterized by a succession of episodes in which the state produces events that are intended to negatively corroborate some of her most valued understandings. In the course of time these episodes and understandings evoke one another, that is, they resonate.

Ambiguities and contradictions afforded her an opportunity to think, work through, and practice novel understandings.

The state did not rest at dispensing verbal forms of recognition through its general propaganda machine, however. In accordance with its self-understanding as a political educator, it self consciously produced emotionally and kinesthetically meaningful events to directly evaluate, punish, or laud actions. In as far as these events evaluated actions negatively, they were molded on the ritual of critique and self-critique even if they were not necessarily called that. As I pointed out before, their central script was the demonstration that a person or group of persons had acted in a "subjectivist" manner, thus undermining the transformational agenda of the party, and by consequence the public good. Directly censoring actions, these events were no doubt intended to negatively corroborate undesirable understandings (figure 7.2). From Poppe's case it is apparent that with these censoring events the state often undermined understandings it seemed to officially endorse by means of propaganda, thus opening itself to the charge of self-contradiction or even ill will. In Poppe's story this is the case, for example, with her critical questions to the People's Chamber, a move that was not only enshrined in party documents (see chapter 1) but also one that was continuously endorsed propagandistically. Yet once she put the party's encouragement to become critically involved into practice, it led to intensely disagreeable censoring activities of the state that she could not but understand as punishment.

In order to accept such censoring events as corroborations, they need to be understood as "natural" or quasi-automatic responses of a system that cannot but react in this particular way. In other words, the interpretation of these events as corroborating is contingent on institutional fetishization. Precisely to the degree, however, that these events are de-fetishized by "debunking" them as staged by a particular agency, which had a choice of *if* and *how* to bring them about, they assume the character of recognitions. Experientially, this marks a shift from "this is what happens if I do *x*" to "this is what *they* do to *me* if I do *x*." Thus, the authority of the recognizing agency comes in view; it can now be questioned, challenged, or denied, but also of course supported.[25] Recoding a corroborating event as an instance of recognition therefore involves something of a gestalt switch in epistemic ideologies and practices. This entails significant political consequences because a generalized, impersonal, dislocated, objective world is transformed into a world populated with particular, localizable, intentional agents who can be addressed.

To some degree institutional de-fetishization is part of growing up. As we age we realize in a slowly expanding horizon how the social world around us is actually made by human beings in their interaction. In this sense, de-fetishization is—as I argued in the introduction—the very precondition for politics. Yet, people take de-fetishization to different lengths. This is a fundamental problem in any sort of political mobilization. What to some seems well in the purview of human agency (especially their own with respect to seemingly more powerful actors) is taken by others to be quite beyond it. Here lies at least one source of political apathy, as Nina Eliasoph (1998) has argued in studying political mobilization in a U.S. context. As we become involved in work life the balance of what we see as the effect of individual intentions (and thus recognizing) and the unfathomable workings of a system (and thus corroborating) may shift yet again.[26] Sobered by our failures to effect change our earlier assessments may appear as overly optimistic, as "youthful" or even "immature."

For Poppe, as for other later dissidents who were at one point rather sympathetic to the party's agenda, recoding events that seemed corroborating as recognizing was a gradual process. It was facilitated not only by the heterogeneity of her networks that supported conflicting understandings but also by a particular form of political imagination that was cultivated in 1968 youth culture: the vague belief that a better social world was possible

---

25. A good example for the reverse reaction is Haferkamp's and Buchhholz's response to censoring activities during their officer-training course at Potsdam-Eiche (see chapter 5, pp. 282–84).
26. Dominic Boyer has demonstrated fluctuations of what he calls, borrowing from Hegel, "spirit"—a shorthand for the ability to effect change—and "system"—the resignation into circumstances—in the course of German history.

if people only acted less rigidly, with more of an open mind, more respect for others' freedoms, and with more love. This understanding was strongly and multiply corroborated by the grief young people were given by their parents and the state for participating in this youth culture. Of course, this imagination also undermined the party state's Panglossian claim to have realized the best possible world given the historical circumstances and the laws of historical development.

Overall, therefore, Poppe's experiences with the state increasingly took the form of a continuing conflict with an authority (case 3, figure 4.6). In principle, such conflicts could have been resolved in either of four ways: First, the events at issue could have quickly become insignificant. This did not happen, not least because the state made its validating claims in conjunction with existential threats and thus in rather stark, impressionable ways. In due course, these effects began to resonate with one another. With every new instance, therefore, the memory of previous, similar instances was refreshed. Second, Poppe could have altered her understandings to be in alignment with those of the state. Yet, her network of authority was diverse and ambiguous enough not to jump unequivocally to the rescue of the state and its project. This means that the recognitions coming forth from her immediate authority network did not parallel those of the state, thus lending them the kind of unshakable authority that the party state tried to achieve (as in the case of the Stasi officers discussed in chapter 5). Third, she might have wanted to persuade the state to change its understandings. Evidently this is something she tried to do (and would later as a self-declared dissident continue to do) even if her endeavors went on to fail for all the obvious reasons. Fourth, she could begin to de-authorize school, state, and party, the institutions standing for state authority. And this is what Poppe ended up doing (not necessarily as a conscious choice), at first more hesitatingly so, but then ever more forcefully. The cultivation of alternative networks of authority within a strong youth culture helped to ease the way. Her schooling in critical thinking—working here as a relevant meta-understanding—which was promoted by her father, contributed its bit. Moreover, this move was facilitated by the fact that she caught the official authorities in acts that, according to their own openly avowed epistemic ideologies and practices, should have been considered de-authorizing. The hypocrites were supposed to be among the class enemy, not among fellow socialists. Finally, all events resonated with one another and amplified one another's memory at the expense of possibly more favorable memories of the socialist project. Thus the outlines of a new understanding emerged. She had repeated evidence now that the official socialist project ran at cross-purposes with her own understandings. The seed was sown for reading the actions of the state as corroborations of more critical understandings of the state.

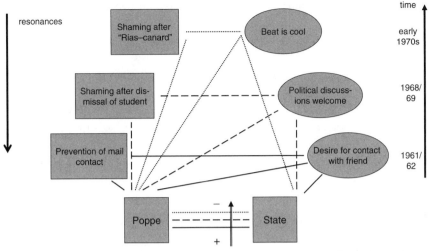

Figure 7.3. The combined dynamics of validation de-authorizes the state: Since the events intended to negatively corroborate Poppe's understandings can be attributed to the state as author, they interact with the verbal recognition of these understandings by the state. Together the "triangles" of recognition and corroboration form validating "trapezoids" showing the corroboration in the top left triangle of the trapezoid and the recognition in the lower right (line forms indicating time). In Poppe's case the combined effect of the various validation dynamics leads to a gradual de-authorization of state institutions.

It bears notice that this path was anything but inevitable. In fact, it was highly contingent. Had she grown up in a bigger place, she might not have known about the television preferences of her teachers, or her school might have handled the whole TV issue much less confrontationally; her best friend's parents might not have been in West Berlin on that day in August 1961; she and her friend's parents might have waited to see what would happen in response to the letter to the People's Chamber, which might have also landed on the desk of a wise old comrade responding to the children as children; the flu might have kept her in bed on the day the Rolling Stones were supposed to play, and so forth. Yet, the GDR being the GDR, it *systematically* produced the *possibility* for the kinds of experiences she had. More, simply because of the dialectics of validation, Poppe soon found herself on a path-dependent trajectory. Her networks did not prevent the dynamic self-amplification of recognition and authorization; this made her more prone to participate in events that stood to corroborate negatively the understandings the state would have liked her to hold. While the conservative principle built into resonance first worked in favor of the state, its force tipped at some point to favor an increasingly state-critical trajectory.

At the end of her high school years, Poppe was not yet a dissident. Instead of having readily symbolized critical understandings of the party state she more or less knew that her old understandings of being an integral part of the socialist project did not work anymore. What she needed were symbolic forms, a language, to articulate especially the emotive understanding that she and the party state had somehow ended up on opposing sides. But this was only to happen in the context of new networks of authority that she started to build as a university student living in Berlin's Prenzlauer Berg scene. Poppe specifically sought out that scene because she was actively in search of people who had experiences similar to her own. It is the sharing of similar experiences, connected with similar *emotions* (desires for particular musical styles and clothes, similar feelings of isolation, shame, anger, outrage), and the already accomplished or acutely perceived threat of marginalization that created a specific kind of solidarity between them.

Different Beginnings

How does Poppe's path into dissidence compare with others' who were active late in the peace and civil rights movements of the 1980s? Interestingly, their starting points vis-à-vis the socialist project were scattered across the social landscape. Like Poppe, a number of them hail from the households of functionaries (e.g., Thomas Klein), some even from families in which fathers were members of the "armed organs," officers in the National People's Army (Vera Lengsfeld), or even in the Stasi itself (Irena Kukutz). Some had become party members when their parents were *not* affiliated (Wolfgang Templin). Yet others started their lives in more party-distant corners of GDR society. In the remainder of this section I will present the beginnings of four rather different dissident careers, each characterized by a different social starting point and different tensions to manage.

Family dissidence: Jens Reich

Jens Reich, more than ten years Poppe's senior and another prominent representative of the movement, answered the question of how he came to be opposed to the party state during a public lecture he gave at the Technical University Chemnitz (Jesse 2000, 27):

> I grew up in opposition against this country. Already in 1945 I lost my grandfather to Stalinist terror. Well into the 1950s the dominant political motif in our family was fear of the Russians and in particular fear of their German auxiliaries. We were raised to suppress any political statement in school.

For Reich the dominant early political understanding of GDR socialism was one in which the relationship between him and his family on the one hand and the socialist party state and its Soviet guarantor on the other was demarcated by fear, an emotion that demands distance. This understanding might have had earlier roots (in an anticommunist sentiment of whatever kind); if so it was most forcefully corroborated by the fate of his grandfather. And it is thus that Reich says he grew up in opposition to socialism. For decades this was an opposition that did not find much voice or action *outside* of the family (Reich 1992) and private networks in which it was maintained through recognition. In fact, the public silence allowed Reich to pursue a career in a professional niche that was intellectually demanding and politically sheltered because it did not require party membership. He became a scientist, a molecular biologist to be precise. Reich participated first in the secret discussion-circle culture that was so typical for the 1970s and involved himself in the peace and civil rights movements in Berlin during the 1980s.

Protestant double binds: Wolfgang Rüddenklau

Opposition in the sense of a feeling that party and state were somehow on one side while oneself and intimately related others were on the other is most common in the Protestant milieu, in the families of ministers and engaged parishioners.[27] While this (mostly private) opposition through birth into a particular family acquired in the course of time the characters of a personal choice, others were literally bullied into this position by the party state. This had much to do with official campaigns against the church and its members, which at certain times and locations could take rather crass forms. Wolfgang Rüddenklau, one of the two key initiators of the "Environmental Library" (*Umweltbibliothek*) grew up in a little village in Thuringia as one of two sons of the local minister:

> The principal of the school in this village was the eminence grise of the whole area. He was an SED boss who dominated the entire area. . . . And I and my brother were the hostages in this school. . . . I was constantly beaten up by the kid of a comrade, who obviously enjoyed the goodwill of the teachers for this.

He and his brother were systematically marked as *other*. Rüddenklau remembers that they had to sit in the backmost bench in the homeroom, that they had to walk with the "social outcasts" on the way to physical education classes, and the like. He characterizes the entire situation in which he grew up as schizogenetic, as a classical double bind. As he frames it, being the child of a Protestant minister, one was automatically a traitor to the cause

---

27. For a brief characterization of the relationship between the Protestant churches and the party state see chapter 8, pp. 401–03.

of the working class in the eyes of the system's representatives. Had one become a socialist one would have become a traitor to one's father's house. Even though this might even have been desirable for gaining some autonomy vis-à-vis one's father (who in his case was anything but warm and caring), it would not have really helped either because one would have always carried the stigma of being a traitor to one's family. Rüddenklau's situation improved only by moving to a Protestant boarding school. There, however, the very same lifestyle issues that brought Poppe and her friends into conflict with state-run schools triggered, if not surprisingly then still ironically, very much the same responses in this Protestant establishment.

Unreasonable demands: Reinhard Weißhuhn

The large majority of the members of the peace and civil rights movements in Berlin during the 1980s were more than anything else formed by the conjuncture of two historical processes, which are commonly metonymized by the year in which they both culminated: 1968. Attracted by Western youth protest culture, its theoretical grounding in various nonorthodox, neo-Marxist social theories, and its physical embodiment in particular music and clothes, the later dissidents followed, with hopeful attention, how the Prague Spring burst open, just to become nipped in the bud a little later by Soviet military intervention. This connection comes poignantly to the fore in the recollections of Reinhard Weißhuhn. He was born in 1951 in Dresden. His father was a journalist and a functionary in the Christian Democratic Union (CDU), one of the block parties affiliated with the SED. The CDU's ambiguous status as a co-opted (former) class enemy translated via his father into conflicting demands on him, which he describes repeatedly as "schizophrenic." His parents had a definite preference for Western radio stations (no television in his early youth) and would play nothing else at home. At school he learned quickly that they were not supposed to "listen West," and so he found ways to behave as if they were not. And thus to him school became the place where everyone just pretended to say the truth, which more soberly seen could be found at home and with the Western radio stations. With the preferences of his parents in view, the clash of authorities led to an early de-authorization of school. He calls this "the schizophrenic experience that constituted the identity, the very being, of a classic GDR-citizen." He asserts that he found this problem more strange than disturbing or vexing and says, "I learned to live with it. That's just how it was." Yielding to the dual pressures of school and home he became an active member of both the communist and the Protestant youth movements. Accordingly, he participated in both rites of passage, the communist youth consecration ceremony and in Protestant confirmation.

Keeping on course in this dual track development was not always easy. In the industrial city of Karl-Marx-Stadt (Chemnitz), where he spent his early years, the "battle against the church" (*Kirchenkampf*) was still in progress. Weißhuhn recalls that the communist youth movement aimed to hold its meetings at exactly the time the Protestant youths were gathering, which led the latter to move their meeting time to another afternoon just to find the communists following suit. This created an ideological cat and mouse game—or so it appeared to him—designed to force people to choose sides in the battle for the "heart and souls" of the people.[28] Although he was caught right in the middle of it, he again learned to adjust. Faced with two authorities (partially embodied in the same person speaking with two voices: his father), which placed contradictory demands on him, he tried to satisfy both.[29] He did not remember this as particularly stressful—perhaps his heart was in neither the communist nor the Protestant youth organizations.

It was only after he had successfully learned to bypass the trap wires set in the force field between home and school, between Protestant and socialist indoctrination, that his real troubles began. And that had something to do with the fact that he began to care deeply about certain lifestyle issues:

Then puberty began and coincidentally the Beatles started up. And then came the whole shebang with the hippie culture and Bob Dylan . . . long hair, jeans, beat music. . . . The state offered every possibility to gain an identity in opposition to it. And we used even the minutest of these possibilities. . . . We tested boundaries. How far can I go without being thrown out of school? And so one learns. To put it pointedly: that was about fractions of inches of hair length. These are of course just little games, but quite important ones for a youth in puberty.

It was then also that television became important. One could see everything now. One didn't just hear the music, but one could see as well how long the hair had to be or could be. And all this political romanticism started . . . the student movement [in the West]. Rudi Dutschke [one of

28. It is important to note that either side counted "fundamentalist" functionaries in their own rows. That there were more conciliatory representatives on either side as well can be gleaned from the next footnote. The roof organization of the Protestant Church in Germany issued an advisory about the "incompatibility between socialist youth consecration and confirmation" on February 7, 1959.

29. It was only once his father was transferred to Weimar for disciplinary reasons (Weißhuhn thinks owing to unwelcome commentary about the Hungarian uprising of 1956) that his situation, ironically, drastically improved. Local circumstances prevailing in Weimar, including a much more ingrained local bourgeoisie and perhaps also a lower degree of class-injury on the side of labor, had enabled the Protestant Church to hold its meetings in the public school buildings!

the most prominent leaders of the West German student movement] was my man. I didn't fully understand against what precisely he was, but I was against it too. It was also totally irrelevant that this was elsewhere. It was the spirit of resistance that mattered, against everything that was established, against all these traditions, these ossified, rigidified, philistine hierarchies that I experienced as well. It didn't matter that on the one side it was capitalism and here socialism. It was all the same.

This was also against the police. They too interfered with long hair. They snatched people from the streets and schlepped them to the barber. To me the state appeared in the guise of *VEB deutsche Schallplatten* [the GDR's leading, state-owned record label]. They wanted to issue a Dylan record. This must have been somewhere around '67, '68. One had successfully told them that Dylan was the other America. Then these shitty Americans provoked the Tonkin incident to have a pretext to bombard North Vietnam.[30] That was the end of Dylan. That was my first, decisive encounter with the state. I can't describe dramatically enough how I felt then. This was a key event for me, revealing the relationship between my desires and the demands of the state. This was deprivation of liberty, the stunting of development.

Then came Prague and that was really another key event. I was glued to the German-language service of Radio Prague, since January '68 because I wanted to know what was up there and whether they would manage. I have experienced liberalization and democratization as urgently necessary. That's how far I got with my long hair. My little sister woke me up on August 21, 1968, to tell me: "They have invaded!" "Enough! I am out!" That's what I said to myself. And I tend to think that from this moment on I operated only tactically . . . [I behaved] as if I was not totally opposed, as if I was only set on reforming the one aspect or the other, but I was certain that this won't work. . . . This system is not reformable.

Part of this tactical operation, was his continuing involvement in the communist youth movement, which Weißhuhn enjoyed because of the rec-

---

30. Here Weißhuhn's memory fails him somehow. The so-called Tonkin incident supposedly took place in 1964, and the corresponding resolution was passed by the U.S. Congress in the same year. Therefore, either the timing is wrong and the episode depicted here took place earlier, or the timing is right but the presumed cause was another East-West tension. It is just as plausible, however, that the thaw-freeze dynamic in cultural policy (see chapter 1) put an end to the plans. It could also have been the interaction of both. Thus, a plausible scenario would be that the project was canceled after the initiation of a new freeze period at the 11th plenum in 1965 (see chapter 1) and that officially the Tonkin resolution was used as a pretext.

ognition he received through it. He was even elected to an office, however, not because he was a particularly staunch believer but because "like my father I talked back." This general support by his classmates is in part contrasted and in part conditioned by the school's negative recognition of his lifestyle choices, which he provoked in countless little cases of "boundary testing." While his adoption of hippie iconography reflected his own desires, their public flaunting also served as an experiment in locating himself in a wider social whole. He endeavored to find a strategy that would allow him to express what he saw as his authentic self while still finding acceptance within the institutions of the state. Already quite versed in sublating the apparently contradictory, he managed to never overstep the boundaries while apparently having it both ways (in many ways much like his block-party father).

Weißhuhn offers two episodes to illustrate how he managed to be in and out at the same time. From a certain age on he found the ideological indoctrination offered at school "unbearable." This was so not because he had any fundamental misgivings about Marxism-Leninism, but because he found the level at which it was taught insulting to his intellect. One episode he recalls vividly is a confrontation with one teacher who tried to introduce the class to the principles of Marxist anthropology. He remembers the gist of what the teacher presented as the proposition that humans evolved from the apes through labor.[31]

> The discussion got heated, thus I had to read the book. . . . The only possibility to fight back without running the danger to become punished right away was to beat them with their own weapons. For that purpose one had to play fool and clothe one's critique in the form of questions. "Tell me, is it really true that?" . . . "I don't understand this?" . . . I read this book and asked questions until he [the teacher] did not know anymore what to say. I have repeated this tactic later again and again.

The second episode of being in and out also illuminates why Weißhuhn's memory of Prague is particularly vivid. When the class returned to school from their summer vacations, at the end of which the invasion had taken place, he found one of his friends imprisoned. This friend was a sportsman who was accomplished enough to take part in international competitions, in

---

31. In case the reader wonders: This is not what textbook-level Marxism-Leninism teaches. The interested reader finds brief accounts in the entry "Mensch" in Schütz et al. 1978 or Kuusinen et al. 1960, chapter 1. Yet both of these texts are addressed to the educated adult reader. The point here is neither whether the teacher got it wrong or whether Weißhuhn remembers correctly, but rather the kinds of conclusions he drew from this confrontation and similar ones.

the context of which he started to befriend a Czechoslovak competitor. During the hot summer of 1968, one of the friend's letters to his Czechoslovak pal was intercepted by the Stasi. The content of this letter led to his indictment for "inflammatory speech directed against the state" (*staatsfeindliche Hetze*). As was common practice in such cases, the classmates were asked to distance themselves from him. The task to draft a resolution to this effect fell on Weißhuhn and the other two youth movement functionaries in the class. The homeroom teacher who had the overall responsibility that a satisfying job be done supervised their undertaking. The trouble was that they did not really know what they were supposed to distance themselves from. None of the details of the case had been divulged to them. They had no idea what their friend had written to strike the ire of the Stasi. So they wrestled hard with the formulation, especially since one of the trio was a "staunch believer" who had to be cajoled into accepting even slightly critical wording. In the end they agreed an on a face-saving and authority-placating subjunctive formulation, asserting that they would distance themselves from their imprisoned classmate had he in fact committed a crime. This was accepted and Weißhuhn was proud of his Svejkian "survival skills."

Weißhuhn presents one of the clearest cases of what Gail Kligman (1998) has called duplicity as a habitus, as a socialist survival strategy entertained in ironicizing self-awareness. Not least owing to the circumstances after unification that were all but favorable for former GDR dissidents, this irony is still very much part and parcel of his demeanor. Weißhuhn found a sense of personal dignity and freedom by ironically playing with institutional rigidities, which at the same time he learned to accept as a given. Later, Weißhuhn learned to move beyond this attitude to actively engage in politics—if with *ziemlichen Kopfschmerzen* (considerable headaches), as he says.

For Weißhuhn, the significant duality between what one would do and say in public and what one would do and say in private did not lead to anger at hypocrisy. Instead, he saw it as an essential skill that people, he and his family included, had to practice in order to survive socialism. However, what he emphasizes in his narrative is the outrage for being taken a fool in this context, which for him is an intense, primarily aesthetic displeasure.

Artistic *communitas*: Irena Kukutz

Kukutz was born in 1950. Her father, the offspring of a poor farming family, hails from a small village by the Elbe River near Magdeburg. Like many young men and women of his generation he saw in socialism a chance to better his own lot. Born in 1929, he had participated in the last months of the war as an antiaircraft artillery assistant (*Flakhelfer*). After the war he joined first the People's Police and then, with its foundation in 1950, the Ministry of State Security. Kukutz's mother was a refugee. She started to work again when her firstborn was in fourth grade. She was ambitious and climbed the social ladder; she went from being a simple shop clerk to becoming the head secretary of the GDR's minister for agriculture. Both parents were, in accordance with their work, members of the SED. Since they spent relatively little time at home, Kukutz not only had to contribute significantly to the upbringing of her younger siblings, but she also developed close relationships to people outside of her family.

> There was at this time [she was about eleven] a young woman whom I loved very much [later identified as Ulrike]. She started an independent culture group with us children at school. . . . I am surprised today that my parents allowed this to happen. Her parents were opera singers and they sang with us and danced, and we performed in Catholic nursing homes . . . and the old people were enthusiastic and we were enthusiastic about our work. . . . They lived in a huge apartment in an old building. There was a grand piano, parquet floors, bay windows, double [height] ceilings. I still remember when I came in there this was a different world. I always felt that my world was too narrow. I even felt this when I was a child, living in a one and a half bedroom apartment with five people and one never had a room to oneself. That was terrible.

This interview snippet offers a poignant example of resonance in pursuit. People who espouse understandings of the world that are markedly different from official socialism assume authority because they meet deep, probably barely articulated, desires. And the difference between these worlds is marked stylistically in habitus and space. The political need not even be explicit here, it follows from the aesthetic and/or the erotic simply by stigmatizing the desired as other and different and officially undesirable (in accordance with the aporia of prohibition). Says Kukutz:

> When she [the woman who ran the group] and her parents left the country with a permit, I would have loved to stay in touch with her. You see, I loved her like a big sister, and she loved me too. But I was not even allowed to write to her, I was not allowed to do anything, and thus I was for the first time really angry with my parents.

While in Poppe's case the abstention from contact was enforced by the system, Kukutz's parents had to enforce this rule on their own account because their daughter's relationships with Westerners could have spelled trouble at work. The contact prohibition was only one aspect of a family organization that centered on her parents' work requirements. That organization demanded sacrifice, discipline, and asceticism—in short self-objectification—in the service of "the good cause" (*die gute Sache*), that is socialism. There were the routines emphasizing the secrecy, importance, and dangerousness of her father's job. In the aftermath of the Hungarian uprising these once found a dramatic expression when he showed her the pictures of communists hung from lanterns with the commentary that this is what the class enemies would also like to do with him and his colleagues if they were ever to come to power again. The family never visited West Berlin while the boundaries were still open; and in the same spirit they abstained completely from attending to any Western mass media. Kukutz took these taboos very much to heart:

> I was educated in a very state-loyal way . . . visiting West Berlin to go shopping or something like that was totally out of the question. . . . Even I by myself would have never turned the dial to see whether we too could receive Western channels. That was totally unthinkable . . . these were enemy stations and if you listen to them you will become contaminated, the bacteria will invade your brain to multiply there. [she laughs] I really believed that. When I finally realized that this was all just hypocrisy, I was totally shocked.

As so often, this realization came in adolescence. When she was about sixteen she went to visit an uncle who lived in the southern part of the GDR. He was an officer in the National People's Army and an SED member who had so far presented himself as a firm believer. After his own young children were safely put to bed, he let his niece in on their family routines: they would now watch Western television but would never tell the kids lest they blurt out their secret at school. She did not trust her ears when she heard that; she was, in her own words, "totally shocked" and felt that her uncle betrayed his children. In the same breath she tells how just a little later the following conversation unfolded with her mother:

> My mother's motto was to "stay on course," which is, given her biography in which she often had to compromise, to adapt in order to succeed, easy enough to understand. Then there was some injustice in school and I worked myself up terribly about it. I will never forget this in all my life. We walked from here [her school in northern Prenzlauer Berg] to the commuter rail station at Prenzlauer Allee. We walked side by side; I was in a rage and wanted to fight against what had just transpired at school—I don't know exactly anymore what it was. She says to me, "Oh well my child you will also learn to keep your mouth shut if you can't really do anything anyway, if the only thing one would do is to hurt oneself." . . . Then I didn't say anything. I just said to myself: "You will not learn that!" And that is how it began.

For her, these episodes revealed that asceticism in the consumption of things and ideas, in making and maintaining friendships, and in the expression of thoughts had nothing to do with the sublime logic of the "good cause," the pursuit of the ideals of socialism. Instead, behaving in these ways was simply following the cunning of careerism. In spite of all of this, Kukutz says she remained apolitical until that fateful early autumn in 1968, when everybody, country up country down, was asked to sign declarations of allegiance agreeing to the Soviet intervention in Czechoslovakia. Kukutz had at that time a much-liked homeroom teacher whose subject was German and who taught his pupils a lot about literature. He refused to sign the support declaration circulating among faculty and students and was promptly dismissed. The class (Kukutz included) decided to fight for him, but to no avail.

> For me the consequence was this: I said to myself, if this state needs to spoil the life of someone who stands by his convictions and actions, by kicking him out of his profession, then something is fundamentally wrong here. And this is how I have argued vis-à-vis my parents why a candidacy for the SED was out of the question for me.

The reaction of the party to this rebellion was predictable. The party followed the principles of the socialist theodicy by personalizing the blame. Even though both the teacher and the pupils were identified as failing to act in line with the party, the teacher was seen as the root cause of the problem. The students' "immature" protest against the teacher's dismissal confirmed the correctness of the party's decision. Accordingly, with the dismissal of the teacher plain ideological incompetence or possible enemy influences were removed. Since the students had apparently not absorbed the teachings of the party in the way they should have, a firm ideological hand displaying a clear class standpoint was deemed necessary to steer the students back into the fold. Hence they were assigned a staunch believer as their new homeroom teacher. From the epithet Kukutz uses to describe her—"socialist bitch superior" (*sozialistische Oberziege*)—some of the effects off this move may be gleaned.

A few summarizing conclusions comparing the four brief vignettes are in place. Pathways into dissidence could start from almost any understanding of the socialist project cultivated in very different networks of authority. For staunch believers the journey often began with disappointed idealism. Quite commonly, this happened as a shocked reaction about incidences of hypocrisy, abuse of power, or incompetence, that is, as a crisis of a particular authority triggered in a situation of strong disagreement (case 3, figure 4.6, p. 221). However, the realization that one was fooled, that somebody assumed to be an authority should never have been taken for one in the first place, is immediately also a negative corroboration of the meta-understandings governing the attribution of authority. By unsettling meta-understandings, however, a crisis at first limited to particulars can now quickly become generalized. The nagging question is: "if I erred here, how can I be sure that I do not err there either." Under certain circumstances, the crisis of authority can become a more fundamental epistemic crisis.

An isolated incidence of an authority crisis does not necessarily amount to much, however. It is the rare believer whose idealism is not tried, who never has cause to doubt a particular authority or even his or her meta-understandings. What matters is how such a crisis is handled within persons' spaces of validation. Single incidences of crisis can easily be rationalized away as aberrations. Such a move is typically supported by meta-understandings embodied, for example, in the personalization of blame characteristic of socialist theodicy or in proverbs emphasizing the irrelevance of odd cases, such as "the exception proves the rule." The composition of networks of authority within which the incidence is discerned is of the utmost importance. In the GDR, the more homogeneously attuned a person's network of authority was toward agreement with the party, the more easily the crisis was overcome through the correcting recognitions of peers who affirmed the validity of meta-understandings attributing authority. The biographies of the Stasi officers discussed in chapter 5 offer several examples in which crises were rationalized away within their homogeneous, party-centric networks. The future dissidents, however, lived typically within much more heterogeneous networks of authority that did not support rationalizing tactics.

Whether or not an incident of crisis of authority emerging over strongly actualized understandings will spin into a wider epistemic crisis also depends on the frequency and sequencing of crisis events. The less often crises occur and the more they are spaced apart, the smaller the chance that more negative understandings of the party and its agenda resonate with one another across time. The possibility of such crises to occur was distributed differently over different social contexts and their participants. With Marshall Sahlins (1981, 33ff.) one could say that they were characterized by different "structures of the conjuncture."[32] These make particular kinds of clashes or tensions and thus crises of understanding more or less likely. For example, unsettling corroborations of public ideology are more common where common practices deviate perceptibly from com-

---

32. Sahlins never gives this concept a concise definition. For a systematic discussion and further development of this concept, see Sewell 2005, 219ff.

monly espoused norms.[33] In the GDR this was especially the case where people who publicly touted (or by profession needed to tout) the norms of the party were unable or unwilling to stick to them in practice for want of belief, because of unresolved and unrecognized ambiguities, or out of sheer cynicism. Of course this is almost a definition of hypocrisy. And the meta-understandings cultivated in the youth culture of the 1960s and 1970s further inspired and encouraged people to identify and condemn cases of hypocrisy.

For those growing up in a familial environment with strong reservations about or even explicit opposition to the socialist project, the movement to dissidence required the maintenance of this position in the course of time, most notably through the trials and tribulations that parental authority faces during puberty. For the Protestant milieu the propaganda apparatus of the state was much less of a challenge than alternative youth culture. Of course, not all GDR-critical family situations, not all church contexts reserved about or opposed to socialism were such that the children wanted to remain identified with their milieu of origin and its political preferences. Occasionally, the state could act as an alternative. After all it was "the other side" to which one could escape. So it should not be surprising that the Stasi succeeded, for example, in recruiting a number of secret informants among church officials, ministers, and priests. That such a move was not necessarily made easy by the state is nicely illustrated by Wolfgang Rüddenklau's reflections on the possibility of such a move, which I discussed further above.

Between the two extreme paths in relationship to the socialist project, unquestioning support and uncompromising rejection, there were any number of shades and gradations of ambivalent or conflicting understandings about the socialist project. There were critical party members, mixed families where parents leaned in opposite directions, families who carved out a block-party niche, others who participated only in some mass organizations, and finally people who remained largely unaffiliated. These situations were highly individual, biographically contingent mélanges of sympathies and antipathies, of submission and rebellion, of acts based on

---

33. If one wants to make sure that frequent participants in such situations fraught with negative validations do not begin to question their old understandings, one has to either choose people with firm beliefs who maneuver in powerful networks of authority that dispense recognitions strong and frequently enough to overcome the negative validations emerging in these situations. Where such a network does not exist it is often created, for example, in the form of a band of professionals dealing with the "toughness" of these situations through a strong esprit de corps that gains its energy from the challenge of negative validations. The party talked in this context of "steeling" members who had frequent contact with the class enemy. See also the section on secret informants in chapter 9.

considerations of principle, and others based on sharply calculated expediencies. From these amalgamations of understandings, children could again move to either extreme to become staunch believers or dissidents. By far the largest part of the population, however, remained in limbo. And some of them succeeded in turning this messy situation of powerlessness into a Svejkian art of survival in adverse circumstances. As vividly attested by countless political jokes, success at this game could confer a real sense of accomplishment.

In sum, then, the roots of dissidence do not lie at the intersection of demographic variables or in consistent "framing," or even in a worked-out ideology. Instead, they lie in the *dynamics* of understandings created by their successive positive or negative validation, which in the interplay between corroborations, recognitions, and resonances across kinesthetic, emotive, and discursive understandings create slowly hardening oppositional identification of self and state. This journey could start almost from any position in GDR society. Consequently, a markedly different understanding of socialism is not the cause of dissidence, but it emerges within this dynamic.

THE FORMATION OF ALTERNATIVE NETWORKS OF AUTHORITY

No matter whence, dissidence implies action. This, however, presupposes not only the understanding that something is wrong but also the belief that something *must* be done, and even more importantly that something *can* be done. Such understandings, moreover, cannot just float around as vague possibilities; instead they must become actualized, that is, positively validated in the course of time. While it is thinkable that single transformative events have such a strong corroborating effect that large parts of existing networks of authority can be thrown into altered patterns of recognition, it is much more common that lasting changes in understandings are buttressed by significant transformations in the composition of networks of authority. Within a broad range of social backgrounds in the GDR during the 1980s, the possibility of influencing the political system as it had established itself seemed an outright impossibility, least of all by dissident action. The reason is simply that all of these backgrounds are characterized by various arrangements with the political status quo ante, which dissident action by definition tries to unsettle. People who grew up in self-declared oppositional families often resigned themselves to a niche existence; believers could perceive action only within the institutional matrix of the party; and those who had in all ambiguity struck some compromise solution for themselves desired nothing less than to unbalance that hard-won arrangement. Thus, in order to become dissidents all of them had to break with the understandings of the past. This happened gradually, in discernible steps characterized by the dissenters' formation of ever larger, and at the core, deepening networks of authority that became an alternative to existing authority networks.

Intimate Beginnings

In all accounts of the former GDR dissidents, adolescence played an important role in breaking with authorities.[34] This break was further facilitated by their coming of age in the heyday of the globe-spanning protest and liberalization movements of the late 1960s that promulgated an active anti-authoritarian ideology.[35] This was, however, not just a simple move of de-authorization. Much like youths elsewhere, young people in East Germany began to revalue established authorities as *anti*-authorities. This means that their recognition was in a way appreciated by youths if, however, with a negative sign. The agreement of an anti-authority has the validating effect of a dis-agreement of an authority and vice versa. What is involved in this move is a replacement of established epistemic ideologies and practices by newer ones that regulate the accretion of authority differently. Thinking in terms of anti-authorities is always partial. Thus for this revaluation of authority to succeed the young women and men engaged in it had to find new authorities, effectively validating their changing meta-understandings. In part, youths in the GDR (as elsewhere) accomplished this transfer and revaluation of authority by aligning themselves with cultural icons such as musicians (e.g., Biermann in the East, Bob Dylan in the West), student

34. This makes puberty in those societies in which it is culturally recognized as a life-course stage with accelerating individualization (and often corresponding peer group formation) a regular epistemic breaking point. This issue has occupied sociologists since Comte as "the problem of generations" (see especially Mannheim 1964).

35. Some of the dissidents also read books emphasizing anti-authoritarian education, such as A. S. Neill's work on his Summerhill school. Perhaps no writer has captured the moods of youths and their elders in the GDR better than Reiner Kunze, whose prose sketches, *Die Wunderbaren Jahre*, found an avid readership in the GDR in spite of the fact that his book could only be published in the West. He captures this anti-authoritarian, anti-conformist conformism in the beginning of the following excerpt (1976, 219): "Fifteen: She wears a skirt which can't be described. Even one word would already be too long. Her scarf by contrast resembles a double-train. Slung with ease around the neck, it drapes shin and calf in full width. (She would have loved to have a scarf knit by two grandmothers for full two and a half years, a woolen Niagara Falls of sorts. About such a scarf she would say, I think, that it captures her sense of life [*Lebensgefühl*].) Together with the scarf she wears sneakers autographed by all of her male and female friends. She is fifteen and does not care for the opinion of very old people—that's all people beyond thirty." Needless to say that this sketch captures much of the mood of the same West German generation as well, and not so surprisingly, the book was a success in West Germany too.

movement leaders (such as Dutschke or Cohn-Bendit), anti-imperialist warriors (Che Guevara, Ho Chi Minh), and the like, while beginning to accept one another as relevant authorities in the peer groups.

The question is not only one of the relative distribution of authority over people but also one of granting them jurisdiction over various domains of understandings. Unquestionably, issues of popular culture, clothing, music, and hairstyles constituted a domain that could be transferred to cultural icons and peers. The cases I have recounted above make clear, however, that this does not mean the network of authority that formed around these lifestyle issues had any jurisdiction over other matters as well. As the cases above illustrate, they quickly broke down on conflict-ridden political issues, and as almost all of my interviewees point out, the more so that career considerations moved to the foreground (for example, at important biographical junctures that required certification or admission). This also means that although many former dissidents appreciated the lifestyle community, they also often had to realize that if they began to draw political conclusions, if they really wanted political conversations reflecting their experiences, most of their classmates could not act as authorizing partners. Thus the intense lifestyle sociability was sometimes paired with intense feelings of loneliness and isolation. Many later dissidents attributed the political silences of their classmates to fear, reading the lifestyle protest as an indicator for potential political protest. In fact, they thus read the recognition they received for lifestyle understandings as recognitions of their emerging political understandings. This may have helped them to feel less lonely. I suspect that this belief was one of the sources of their later understanding as dissidents that they were speaking for a silent majority. They were almost brutally disabused of this notion in the elections of March 18, 1989, which revealed their assumptions as a "consensus-fiction" (Hahn 2000, 85ff.).

At school the later dissidents often had the good luck of winning a friend with whom they could politicize, thus laying the social foundations for alternate symbolic political understandings about GDR socialism. Also, family could continue to play a role not least because much of the edge of the protest could be directed against the state in addition to parental authority. Thus Poppe could continue to talk politics with her father even if they clashed violently about her desire to stay out past his idea of what constituted a proper curfew for a young woman. She also had longer political conversations with an uncle, a prominent professor of Slavic languages, who later fled to West Germany. And she found a lover in a much older physicist who was very critical of the GDR party state. He too became a refugee. At his Protestant boarding school, Wolfgang Rüddenklau found a lover with whom he shared an interest in particular forms of music, which segued into political and philosophical discussions. Reinhold Weißhuhn "theorized" with his father and one other friend at school, who was, as he says, the only one who was really politically interested. Even before he could finish high school this friend got himself arrested. He hoped that this would get him out of the GDR through a short stint in prison, counting on the readiness of the GDR to sell and the willingness of the FRG to buy him as a political prisoner for hard currency.

Sometimes these friends maneuvered in a social milieu significantly different from what the former dissidents had known through family and school. Irena Kukutz, for example, fell in love with a government-critical young man with a bourgeois family background. His father ran a small independent printing business. Says Kukutz:

> [He] had lived with his parents in Schmöckwitz, in an art nouveau villa standing on a plot with direct access to the water. His parents had no taste, but one still saw the remainder of this [bourgeois] culture. And it reminded me of Ulrike who sang and danced with us, whose parents were opera singers [see p. 371]. . . . [Later] he lived in an apartment shared with others [*Wohngemeinschaft*] . . . and maneuvered in a completely different circle of friends. There was a totally different atmosphere there. I had not the slightest idea that such things even existed. He tried to provoke me, and we talked about everything, "Is there a God?" "How do you see this or that?" "Have you read this?" This was for me the realization that there is a world apart from mine. My world was a closed world, a walled-in world. I have not dared to enter other worlds. There was a magic boundary for me. . . . Here was the railway-line and then there was my school and beyond began the taboo zone [that's where the heart of Prenzlauer Berg begins and where she was very active soon after].

This quote brings to the fore a flow of resonances that once began with Kukutz's desire for warm open relationships. Earlier, this desire was answered by the privately organized sing and dance group at school (by "Ulrike" mentioned in the quote) just to be disappointed again by the group leader's move to West Germany and her parents interdiction to maintain contact. This older relationship was echoed in the relationship to a new lover and his environment. The intensive new contact with this "new world" fundamentally changed her perspective on life. It surely influenced her plans for university study. Kukutz's school, probably counting on her family background, aimed to persuade her to become a teacher of Marxism-Leninism, which at this point to her was an outrageous proposition. Instead, she opted to study ceramics, the arts being a field that interlaced with the circles in which she now moved. At the very end of her studies at the academy she met and became intimate friends with Bärbel Bohley. Kukutz had just lost a child, and this friendship began to soothe her pain:

With Bärbel Bohley I started to make some trouble in the neighborhood. We complained and wrote petitions to the mayor. Why is the standard route of foreign guests of state through town [Protokollstrecke] freshly painted and dolled up like a Potemkin village, while we don't even get the most essential repairs done for our houses. . . . We started to make photos at the communal level and we threatened to send them to the papers. . . . That's how we started to get involved.

The common search for political understandings and deliberations about the possibilities of political action quickly moved to the center of Kukutz's and Bohley's friendship. This interview snipped shows how this search began literally "in front of their doorstep," with palpable everyday experiences. Space, concretely the decrepit state of Prenzlauer Berg, became a metaphor for the state of the polity (see also Lengsfeld 2002, 45). This had the advantage that understandings about the state tied to their experiences were immediately sensually accessible, that is, investigable and subjectable to some corroboration. By contrast, aspects of government activities that did not produce consequences in everyday experiences were, due to the state's monopoly over information about itself, much harder to investigate.

Intimate friendships segued into the formation of looser networks of people with related experiences. Poppe's entry into Prenzlauer Berg illustrates this point. During her high school years Poppe began to work in a steel mill just outside of Berlin. One reason was to be financially a bit more independent of her parents, but the even more important rationale for the job was to "flee the well-protected bourgeois environment in which I grew up. I wanted to get to know life as it really was." The experience was taxing, the work heavy, and the workers rejected her because they did not take her and her likes particularly seriously; as mere sojourners they were predestined for "higher" occupations. After she had passed the final school examinations, Poppe moved to Berlin. She urgently wanted to move out of her parents' home and she wanted to live in the city. Since the regimented atmosphere of a student dormitory had no appeal to her, she had to find something on her own. Two theology students she had met at the mill arranged for her to move in with an elderly woman who lived in a small one-room apartment on the ground floor of one of Prenzlauer Berg's backyards. There was barely any light, the walls were humid and moldy, and the old lady proved to be mentally unstable. Thus Poppe spent as little time as possible in her room; instead she hung out at friends' places. A little later she got a black-market one-bedroom apartment.[36] It was on the ground floor too, and again dark,

---

36. The logic of this problem follows the familiar outlines of an economy of shortage (Kornai 1980; cf. Verdery 1991, 1996). Since apartments were centrally distributed and difficult to come

but this time at least the toilet was in the apartment. This small place became the meeting point for all sorts of people for what seemed to her like an unending string of parties and discussions.

In Berlin I came into circles of people with students dismissed for political reasons from university, others who didn't even get in, these were all critical people. But there was also an overlap with a semicriminal milieu. The common denominator was that all of these people rejected the standardization, the subordination under a norm, something we felt subjected to quite forcefully. These were all people who wanted to live their own lives. This was much more a protest attitude concerning lifestyles than something that was directly political. But of course these two things have to be seen together since the state politicized culture. Manners of dress were immediately interpreted politically . . .

The geography of Prenzlauer Berg made all of these friendship circles mesh into a wider network of people in conflict with official GDR life. It is here, in relative quarantine from mainstream socialist society, that they began to construct an alternative world and a set of understandings that was markedly different not only from the officially propagated understandings of the party state but of the apolitical population. Throughout party state critical circles in the GDR the Prenzlauer Berg milieu came to be known as a refuge. The neighborhood's call went through personal contacts, first and foremost to smaller local scenes in the provinces, above all, to Dresden, Leipzig, Weimar and Jena. There, it reached Reinhard Weißhuhn, for example, who went to Berlin with the express idea to live in Prenzlauer Berg, which had not quite become San Francisco's Haight-Ashbury but the closest thing to it anywhere in the GDR.

While the interlacing of personal networks was facilitated by the colocation of key protagonists in Prenzlauer Berg, it is important to remember that many key players in the GDR peace, civil rights and environmental movements in the 1980s got to know each other through the good offices of the only open oppositional figure in the late 1970s with national name recognition: Robert Havemann. This has much to do with his former official celebrity status as a star scientist and antifascist, and the official GDR's need to relate to the discrepancy between hero and fallen hero. That in turn was attractive to Western media covering his case, which thus came to be known throughout the GDR. For this reason, people who wanted to be in touch with alternative circles often went to Havemann first.

---

by, nobody wanted to give up an apartment if they were not absolutely sure that they would not need it anymore. In effect, they were hoarded like raw materials and labor in industry. This created a black economy for apartments in Berlin that required personal contacts comparable to those needed to obtain building materials or other hard to come by goods.

Peter Grimm is a good example. He was born in 1965 and was eventually one of the youngest, but also one of the most active, members of the Initiative for Peace and Human Rights. His parents had some distance to GDR socialism, but like Weißhuhn's had made their peace somehow. His father was a member of one of the block parties and was the director of a sawmill. What angered Grimm in school were the declarations of allegiance that he and others call "rituals of submission" (Unterwerfungsrituale), they explicitly demanded them to agree to something they found disagreeable. Still in high school he teamed up with a few friends who thought like him. "Sometime we thought we should get in touch with people who are something like opposition in the GDR. And of course the name Havemann came directly to mind, and he did not live far." However, access to Havemann's house outside of Berlin could only be gained by passing checkpoints where one had to register, and thus the friends got cold feet. Once they had finally summoned enough courage to go for it they learned of Havemann's death. They came to his funeral instead, impressed by the immense security machinery surrounding it, and kept in touch with his late wife Katja. This was their entrée to the larger world of GDR dissidence.

The "Cultural Opposition" and Conspiratorial Circles

Books not officially available in the GDR because their content was deemed antisocialist and dangerous fueled the discussions in friendship networks such as those forming in Prenzlauer Berg. The scarcity of these books, the rituals of their circulation, the difficulties involved in obtaining the more obscure titles, the awareness of being near to committing a political crime circulating them, their promise to initiate the reader into a clandestine fellowship of savants rising above state-mandated ignorance, all lent these books enormous appeal. They had a quasi-sacred status. No title in particular was seen as the Holy Grail, but there was something of a canon of what one was supposed to have read as a competent interlocutor. Each new forbidden title carried with it the promise of making a genuine step toward a better understanding not only of the GDR polity but also of one's own self in it. The party state's effort to monopolize the production and dissemination of understanding, its stark Manichaean divisions of the world into absolutely true and absolutely false simultaneously mapped onto the morally good and bad, created a desire to know in people who suffered from the party's categories and their practical consequence.[37] It

---

37. Incidentally, I think this desire to understand the social and/or political is not unlike that which motivates many social scientists, themselves often marginalized in the one way or the other, to become professional students of society.

also triggered the need to have that emerging understanding confirmed by others.

For the emerging dissidents the puzzle was socialism, why it operated the way it did, and particularly why it seemed unable to live up to its own ideals. Because most dissidents maintained socialist sympathies, the answers were not sought among modern bourgeois critics of socialism, such as Arendt, Popper, or Hayek, or among political theory classics that could be leveraged for a critique of the Soviet system, such as Montesquieu, Locke, or Tocqueville. Poppe commented on this issue that the whole political environment to which most critics oriented themselves was left leaning and that an orientation toward the liberal (or neoliberal) classics would have felt decisively retrograde. Thus the answers were first and foremost sought among critical or "fallen" communists, renegades or critical socialist thinkers outside of the Soviet sphere of influence. Substantively, clues to the answers of what was wrong with socialism were thought to be found in what it repressed: the parts of history it made short shrift of or obviously misrepresented, the literature it de-emphasized or did not allow to circulate freely. The various purges, the Gulag system, and the Hitler-Stalin pact were of greatest interest. There was a feeling that somewhere on the way a great idea had turned sour and that doing better in the future was about going back to the fork in the road where the wrong turn was taken. The roots of this intellectual program in dialectical historical reasoning are obvious.

Thus at the very top of the list of texts exchanged were works by Wolfgang Leonhard, Czesław Miłosz, Arthur Koestler, Milovan Djilas, Evgeniia Ginzburg, Nadeshda Mandelstam, or Alexander Solzhenitsyn. Orwell's *Animal Farm* and *Nineteen Eighty-Four* were also widely read. Among the more theoretically inclined texts, nonorthodox communist writers were especially popular. Here the GDR's own critical writers, Robert Havemann and later Rudolf Bahro, were most important, if sometimes only as icons. And so were texts by critical Eastern European communist theoreticians such as Leszek Kołakowski, Western European neo-Trotskyites such as Ernest Mandel, the Euro-communists, or the lesser and noncanonical classics such as Bakunin, Luxemburg, Trotsky, or Bukharin. In the 1980s it was also the dissident literature from Poland, Hungary, and Czechoslovakia that garnered much interest—with Václav Havel topping the list. Finally, the circulated readings included novels of East German and East European writers, especially the work that was not published in the East, such as Wolf Biermann's collections of poems, Stefan Heym's *Collin*, and Reiner Kunze's *Die Wunderbaren Jahre*.

People desiring a more serious, more organized discussion of such works or a more systematic critical reappropriation of the communist classics or of other more theoretical texts (Hegel was popular) typically founded or joined study circles. There were basically two routes to accomplishing this.

One was the attempt to use party-accredited forums for this purpose. This had the advantage of reaching a much wider audience and the possibility of obtaining halls for readings, concerts, and panels. The obvious disadvantage of this form was that plans for events required approval and that whatever was done or said during the event was in direct public view of the party, which would surely monitor such events. In the case of dislike the party could interdict future events. In consequence the organizers had to censor their own events. The other possibility was to organize smaller groups that could gather around somebody's dining room table. In this case there was no audience, which mattered insofar as the question of political impact was important to many involved in such circles. The advantage of small circles was that meetings could be organized more secretly, the range of readings could be wider, and the limits between the sayable and the unsayable owed themselves to group dynamics rather than to state sanctions.

Thomas Klein, later one of the key figures in the Friedenskreis Friedrichsfelde, was successively engaged in both kinds of efforts: organizing more critical events in public venues and in secret discussion groups. Klein was born in 1948. His father had, to the dismay of Klein's grandfather, joined the Nationalkomitee Freies Deutschland (NKFD)[38] during the war and came back from Soviet captivity a communist. Klein's grandfather remained in the West while his son moved East with his family to become a functionary in a GDR ministry. Klein spent much of his free time as a child with his grandparents in West Berlin while going to school and living in East Berlin. He liked both places for different reasons and thus developed a more critical understanding of both sociopolitical systems. This said, his ideal was a different kind of socialism since he considered questions of social justice absolutely central. However, in spite of his general socialist sympathies he never thought of joining the party. "Joining the SED would have meant that discussions would have been squashed right from the start via the enforcement of party discipline. This means the pressure would have started already before one could even have done anything." Yet somehow he felt that the communist youth could still be used as a venue to organize a more critical discourse:

38. The NKFD was a Soviet-sponsored organization founded among German exile communists and POWs that tried to persuade German troops (via German-language radio and flyers) to surrender and to form a resistance movement to topple the Nazi government of Germany. Perhaps its most famous recruit was general Friedrich Paulus, who went into Soviet captivity with the remainders of the German VIth army after the battle of Stalingrad. To have been a member of the NKFD was considered an antifascist qualification in the GDR, and former members often moved on to career positions in the GDR.

[As a student of mathematics at Humboldt University] I got myself elected into the FDJ leadership and became secretary for agitation and propaganda. And during the regular annual study cycles [official political education program] we started to read Ernest Mandel and Che Guevara, and all that stuff that was more than dangerous. I had a sense of that [danger] but really how dangerous it was I did not know.

Eventually this open form of organizing nonconformist discussion groups led the university to retract its already signed employment contract with him for the time after his graduation. Luckily (and in his estimation by an administrative mistake) he got a job at the Academy of Sciences instead, and there, unfazed by the consequences of the first attempt (and unaware of the fact that the Stasi was already on his heels), he continued with his critical communist youth group work. In an undated, unsigned summary report about his activities drafted by department 2 of the division XX of the Stasi ministry his activities are summarized thus:

[I]n his function as FDJ secretary at the institute he organized a discussion forum with Stefan Heym; on 21. Nov '76 he wrote a letter addressed to the president of the council of ministers protesting against the expatriation of Wolf Biermann; at the beginning of 1977 he organized a reading with Klaus Schlesinger. In the context of the discussion, which was prepared by loyal social forces, Schlesinger's reading was criticized especially because the characters he was drawing were untypical for socialist society. . . . In March 1978 he together with . . . took over the task of producing a wall newspaper on the occasion of the Brecht anniversary. The wall newspaper had to be removed because the selection of Brecht quotes constituted an affront to the socialist state.

Klein's work in the FDJ signaled to a group of SED party members around Bernd Gehrke who were also working at the academy and who had formed a conspiratorial group that Klein shared many of their concerns and that he was eager to act. And so they invited him to join.

In the aftermath of the SED's propaganda disaster caused by Biermann's forced expatriation, the Stasi expanded its systematic observation of both the open and the secret groups and systematically cracked down on them. In Klein's case the open group had rallied about one hundred signatories to protest the expulsion of critical writers from the board of the Berlin writers' association who had protested Biermann's forced expatriation. A considerable number of the signatories had also agreed to work together on the practice of *Berufsverbote*, the systematic use of employment monopolies to ban people with critical understandings of the GDR from practicing their profession.[39] Klein thinks that this effort at organizing people on that scale was too much for the Stasi.

Klein and some of his friends had for a long while collaborated with neo-Trotskyites and left wing social democrats in West Berlin. They had employed the services of a young seemingly sympathetic Latin American film student as their courier because he could use his foreign passport to move freely between East and West. The trouble was that the Stasi employed him as well—as a secret informant. In the absence of evidence sufficient for an indictment and under pressure to act, the Stasi framed Klein and his partner at that time, Jutta Braband. They arrested Braband red-handed as she was retrieving the reading material smuggled in and deposited by the Stasi informant. Klein was subsequently arrested and both were faced with a choice: sign an application to leave the GDR, which would have been instantaneously granted in the country's then current mode of ridding itself of its critics perceived as nothing more than thorns in its flesh, or face persecution under the foreign espionage provisions, which carried extended prison terms. Klein explains that both of them had to weigh whether the state could possibly succeed with the espionage charges given that the only usable evidence was manufactured by the Stasi. Both knew that the GDR was on a slow track of increasing legalization and expanding autonomy of the judicature. The 1950s situation in which the politically desirable outcome of legal proceedings could be produced at will was over. So both refused to sign the application to emigrate and their gamble paid off. Klein ended up with a sentence of one and a half years (nine months for Braband), ten months of which he spent in isolation at Stasi's jail in Hohenschönhausen, the rest at Bautzen II, the GDR's feared political prison.

Many of the later leading members of the peace and civil rights movement took part in what has been called in retrospect the *Kulturopposition*, the "cultural opposition." Like Klein they would try to become active in some official venue to showcase critical songwriters, authors, films, or thematic lectures

---

39. The dismissal of the Berlin board of the Writers' Association (*Schriftstellerverband*) was the occasion to address this entire issue, which was by no means a problem just specific to the GDR or Eastern Europe. The West German Social Democratic government launched in 1970, in collaboration with the states, the so-called *Radikalenerlaß* ("decree against radicals"). Employees of the West German civil service, teachers above all, were hence investigated by routine checks with the West German State Office for the Protection of the Constitution (in some ways the West German equivalent of Stasi's department XX), whether they were, in effect, loyal to the "Basic Law," West Germany's constitution. In the context of this law thousands of members of West German communist parties and organizations were effectively excluded from becoming civil servants. This law was drafted under the impression of violent left-wing terrorism, which began to shake West Germany in the early 1970s. Klein's initiative had the West German *Radikalenerlaß* as much in mind as the increasing East German practice.

and discussions. Poppe, for example, tried to participate in the youth club-council in Mitte to influence its programming. Weißhuhn was involved in a film club in Jena. If they did not belong among the organizers, they often participated in the events organized by like-minded people active in youth clubs, culture houses, and similar such venues. Perhaps the most famous venues in Berlin were the House of Young Talents in Mitte district, the youth club in Weißensee, and the Box at Boxhagener Straße. In the former two the songwriter Bettina Wegner's series *Eintopp* (dialect for "stew") and *Kramladen* ("Dollar store") were particularly popular.[40] The opportunity to use these official venues came about through the "thaw" in cultural policies accompanying the transition from Walter Ulbricht to Erich Honecker as general secretary of the SED. Organizationally, this opportunity was enabled on the one hand by the fact that many youth clubs/culture clubs were keen to cast attractive events that would make them look active and alive. And since on the other hand the state (with the exception of the church) held a monopoly over the physical public sphere, more people were willing to strike the kinds of compromises necessary to make something happen in these places. For a brief window of three to four years this worked rather well. Alas, after the Biermann debacle these possibilities were all systematically closed again by tightly policing the programming of youth clubs and such around the GDR.

Biermann's expatriation had a considerable mobilizing effect among people who had run into conflict with the state. There are several reasons for this. First, this move made clear that the hopeful signs emitted by Honecker upon taking over from Ulbricht did not lead to any systematic changes. Instead, it dawned on people that Honecker's first years were a mere episode and that the crackdown on the *Kulturopposition* constituted a downward turning point in the familiar thaw-freeze cycles of cultural policies in socialist countries. In the words of Irena Kukutz:

> With Honecker we got the feeling that this is a new departure. We thought, oh now things will turn to the positive, and we had hopes that we could now intervene without being censored right away . . . that critique was desired. And then we started to be critical and we were told not only that our critique was not needed but that we had no reason to criticize anything: "We don't know what you mean everything is in perfect order"—and one can see for oneself, nothing works. One feels then that one is just spinning, it was just another sigh of relief followed by a tightening of the reins, and everything was as before. That's a kind of double disappointment.

The second reason why the Biermann expatriation had a mobilizing effect is that the 1968-generation lifestyle conflicts generated experiences that made

---

40. Wegner was then the wife of aforementioned writer Klaus Schlesinger (p. 385).

it easy for many people to identify with Biermann's fate no matter what they thought of his work. This effect may have been amplified in some cases by the fact that as an irreverent singer he resembled the cultural ideal of the time more than anyone else. Publicly martyred, Biermann became the symbol for their plight. Finally, expatriation as a tool of political control also instantaneously provided the ingredients for serious criticism of the state; it certainly did not necessitate any antisocialist sentiment. The general point, a very simple common denominator for a wide range of people, was that expatriation was not an acceptable policy.[41]

Thus the expatriation of Biermann created enormous resonances, and a relatively large number of people decided to take their private disagreement public by either writing or signing letters protesting it. Biermann became *the* cause to associate over disagreement with the state. Interestingly, the politburo was unable to learn from this propaganda debacle, and it extended it by first harassing and then letting go of some of the artists who were active in the protests. Within the course of only a few years, the GDR lost some of its best artistic talent: the writers Jurek Becker, Reiner Kunze, Sarah Kirsch, Erich Loest, and Günter Kunert; the actors Armin Mueller-Stahl and Manfred Krug, to name but a few. Again, isolating (expelling) dissenting voices was seen as the apt way to produce monolithic intentionality, which was deemed indispensable to withstand the assault of the enemy. And thus the mass exodus of intellectuals with the accompanying "no-loss" refrain echoing through the official GDR media anticipates the much later mass exodus of ordinary GDR citizens that climaxed after the opening of the Hungarian-Austrian border in the summer of 1989.

The crackdown on the tender bloom of a more independent cultural scene in public venues after the Biermann expatriation triggered some resignation but also a considerable degree of spite. If public spaces were closed—some began to think—why not convert private space to public use? Ekkehard Maaß, Bärbel Bohley, and Gerd and Ulrike Poppe endeavored to make their apartments and their garden plot outside of Berlin available for readings, especially by younger critical writers who had no outlet in the GDR. The size of the living rooms in their Prenzlauer Berg apartments made this possible.[42]

---

41. See on this point as well, Berbig et al. (1994), who document the party's and the critic's reaction to Biermann's expatriation. As one might expect, the defenders of the party policy in the association of writers argued exactly as the Stasi officers did in the case of Robert Havemann: in view of the enemy, who will mercilessly exploit any cracks within the socialist camp, every socialist must self-objectify by taking a clear class position. Whoever does not, no longer belongs.

42. Stasi suspected that space had something to do with oppositional activity, if in a different way. In a document from the division xx department 2 of the ministry from September 6, 1979, it is insinuated that Poppe and his wife moved to a new apartment not because it was spacious but because the number of access points to the house and the number of staircases by which the

Between April 1981 and September 1982, Stasi counted nine readings in Ulrike and Gerd Poppe's apartment. In 1982 the readings followed each other in almost monthly installments. According to the Stasi the number of participants ranged between twenty and one hundred, averaging fifty to sixty participants per reading (MDA, OV "Zirkel," xx/2, September 11, 1982). Not even Prenzlauer Berg living rooms could accommodate that many people. As Ulrike Poppe remembers, people stood in the hallway all the way into the kitchen and speakers transmitted the reading from one room to another.

Such meetings were not only used to read (more or less political) poetry or prose, but to engage in political conversations as well, to offer and solicit recognition for particular understandings but also to mobilize participation in (and thus again recognition for) particular actions. This could not have been done while using SED-controlled spaces. Freed from the self-censorship that the cultural opposition needed to exercise in party controlled venues, the activists could experiment with more radical expressions in private spaces converted to public use. The Stasi became worried and began to infiltrate the scene with secret informants. Here is an example for a privately staged public reading, which was connected with a political discussion and the mobilization for a political issue. Importantly, the topic—peace—heralds things to come, that is, the emergence of a GDR peace movement that I will discuss in the next chapter. The artist whose poems were treated to a private public hearing was Sascha Anderson. Curiously, he was also one of the Stasi's top informants. He reported on September 22, 1979, about a reading in Gerd and Ulrike Poppe's garden plot. He informs his Stasi interlocutors that Robert Havemann was among the participants soliciting signatures for a letter addressed to Leonid Brezhnev proposing the demilitarization of both Germanys as a measure to make Europe more peaceful. This letter, he tells his guidance officer, also prompted a discussion about German unification. To the Stasi the letter and discussion proved the dangerous nationalist and anti-Soviet tendencies prevalent in these privately organized readings (MDA, OV "Zirkel," xx/9, September 22, 1981).[43]

Private reading and discussion groups meeting secretly were more common in the 1970s than in the 1980s. Many people who later joined the Initia-

---

apartment could be reached would make surveillance more difficult (MDA, OV "Zirkel," vol. 1, p. 103). This interpretation is derived mostly from Stasi's conviction that any kind of opposition in the GDR was instigated and directed by foreign secret service agencies, which would, the Stasi assumed, make sure to find an "operational base" suitable for clandestine activities.

43. The Stasi was not alone with this judgment. Western commentators denounced similar proposals launched in West Germany as dangerous "Finlandization." The arguments were analogous. The demilitarization of both Germanys was seen as ill-conceived nationalism merely helping the opponent by weakening NATO. Incidentally, the Havemann-sponsored letter is one of the earliest documents of the independent peace movement in the GDR (Weißhuhn 1995, 1854).

tive for Peace and Human Rights were active in such circles, among them Reinhold Weißhuhn, Ulrike Poppe, and her husband Gerd, better known in the scene as "Poppow."[44] These circles were put under tremendous pressure by the Stasi after 1976—that is, at least those that the Stasi knew about, such as Bernd Gehrke's group. Others dissolved as key members were leaving the GDR for West Germany. A number, however, survived the Stasi's control efforts into the 1980s. The conspiratorial procedures had their benefits if no secret informant was among the initial participants. Ulrike Poppe and other former dissidents describe most of these circles as geared toward intellectual concerns with very little immediate practical relevance for the concrete po-litical and social problems of the day. However, she says, one circle in which she participated was different, geared toward concerns with primary and sec-ondary education, the mass media, and housing policies in the GDR. Most impressive to her was an analysis of the group's host, an architect, who had investigated the housing situation in Berlin. The architect had come to the conclusion that the construction of new high-rises would be superfluous if the government invested into the rehabilitation of older housing structures. The pragmatic approach of this circle resonated with her in a way the merely theoretical ones never did. This does not mean that she did not cherish a theoretical argument, but she felt that discussions geared to everyday life problems in the GDR garnered far too little attention. The women among my interview partners have also pointed out that there was something of a gender bias in these discussion circles. Their "male" regard for the theoreti-cal arguments for the limits and possibilities of revolutionary change had little tolerance for the "female" question of how to cope with and/or counter, let's say, disrespectful birthing or educational practices in the here and now. Thus women felt often out of place, relegated to the margins of these circles. The Stasi pressures on these reading and discussion circles combined with the dissatisfaction of some of the participants with their format and a new political issue—peace—led some members to experiment with a different organizational and thematic format. Given their relative marginalization in the discussions, it is not surprising that women led the way. How so, I will discuss in the next chapter.

CONCLUSIONS

This chapter shows (and the next will expand on it) that even if social origins might have some predictive value as an indicator of who would eventually

---

44. In this context it may be noteworthy that the Poppes' joint Stasi files were registered under the cover "circle" (*Zirkel*), because this is the environment in which they became known to the Stasi.

support or reject the party state's project in various ways at different moments in time, they do not explain the formation of particular sets of political understandings that orient action. As children of Stasi officers became vocal opposition members so did children of protestant ministers become secret informants. Indeed, pathways into oppositional activities could begin almost anywhere, from every conceivable political and social position within GDR society. They could take turns into new directions at different moments in the life-course of individuals; they could swing first in the one direction and then back. True, some such origins were seemingly more likely than others. And yet it is precisely the focus of this study on the seemingly less likely dissidents (the unreligious participants in the peace and civil rights movements in Berlin during the 1980s) that helped to bring to the fore the kind of process dynamics that in the course of time form particular kinds of political understandings. They are only seemingly less likely because probability is always estimated with regard to a base. And my point is that demographic variables can be quite misleading as a base if one wants to comprehend the lived dynamics of social life, such as pathways into oppositional activities in dictatorships. Sociologically speaking such variables are black boxes that mask rather than reveal process dynamics.[45]

Concurrently, I have argued that what shaped peoples' development were the dialectics of validation at play in each and every single person's life course. Indeed, it was quite possible that brothers or sisters from the very same family, attending identical educational institutions, ended up with different positions with respect to the party's project. A central aspect of this dynamic was how what happened came to be interpreted in relevant networks of authority, which in turn exerted considerable influence on what would happen next. That is to say, emerging dissidence depended on what happened; it depended on how what happened resonated with what one already knew emotionally, discursively, and kinesthetically and thus on what had already happened; and it depended on the order in which happenings followed each other. In the words of several opposition members I spoke with, "it was a slow process" that could become path dependent through the process dynamics I outlined in the conclusions to chapter 4. These path-

---

45. This does not mean that statistical analysis is meaningless per se. However, it tends to reify certain categories for reasons of data availability and that an analysis based on these data hides process dynamics. Recently there has been more attention among quantitatively oriented scholars to such issues emphasizing the articulation of "mechanisms" (cf. Hedström and Swedberg 1998; Bunge 2004; Hedström 2005). Because this literature offers no conceptual tools with which to think about the historical formation of what they call "mechanisms," instead often favoring biological approaches, I do not use this term here; I use *process dynamics* instead (Glaeser n.d.).

dependent trajectories could, as one can glean from a comparison between opposition members and Stasi officers, develop in either party-critical or party-supportive directions. The various dialectics of validation could also play out in such a way that people remained forever in a kind of limbo: neither too close to the socialist project nor too far, neither committed nor opposed, eternally waiting for the next round, just getting by. And it is probably fair to say that such limbo describes the situation of a majority of the population in the GDR.

One could also say that pathways into supporting socialism or opposing it were highly contingent. For the purposes of this book this means dependent on the distribution of validating experiences of various kinds across places, social contexts, and time. The emergence of pronounced unidirectional trajectories rested on the local possibilities for particular kinds of experiences and their repetition. Much importance accrued in this context to sustained encounters with particular kinds of people with their ideas and their feelings. Ongoing contact with specific ideas objectified in the form of books, newscasts, and so on were also significant. Even the layout of buildings and neighborhoods mattered by mediating the access to ideas, people, and physical indicators about the quality of governance, and thus by increasing the chances that certain kinds of validations would occur. In Prenzlauer Berg the economic failures of socialism, for example, were more palpable than they were in any of the new neighborhoods. The likelihood of encountering expressions critical of official GDR socialism in words, hairstyles, or clothing items was also much higher there than elsewhere in Berlin.

What holds for Berlin, holds for the country as a whole. The chances that certain understandings were validated were much higher in some contexts than in others. For example, if trivially, there were more local party organizations to join than opposition groups. While the former were distributed almost evenly over the whole country, the latter were spatially clustered in only a few places. In the house of a protestant minister there was a much higher chance to encounter somebody with ideas critical of socialism than in the household of a Stasi officer; there were more opposition groups in Berlin or Jena than in Rostock or Magdeburg. Finally, contingencies of validation were *temporally* differently distributed over the history of the GDR. Importantly, the "measures of August 13, 1961," as the erection of the Berlin Wall was known euphemistically in official jargon, kept critical or disgruntled people literally locked in place. Deprived of a more or less easy exit option, serious dissatisfaction was now more likely to be voiced in the GDR.[46]

---

46. I am making use of a vocabulary that was introduced by Hirschman (1970). He later applied it to the case of East Germany's dissolution (1993). Coming from an analysis of market behavior, Hirschman made the general point that the likelihood of voice should increase with

More, the increasing availability of Western electronic mass media made comparisons, and thus the occurrence of particular kinds of recognitions and the possibility for certain indirection corroborations, more likely during the 1980s than they were during the 1950s or '6os. Another example for temporally distributed opportunities of validation is the supply of goods and services that fluctuated significantly across the forty years of GDR history. Thus visible "proof" for the government's failure, or the signs that the socialist model would eventually deliver what it promised, were more readily available at some times than at others. Finally, in the same vein, all socialist countries went politically through what were locally known as "thaw" and "freeze" cycles. That is to say, their readiness to welcome critique fluctuated with some regularity, thus producing temporally highly specific profiles of validation.

Another important conclusion of this chapter is that the beginnings of dissidence can scarcely be comprehended as the result of differences in already well articulated discursive political understandings between an individual and the state. In other words, people did not as a matter of course come to oppose the socialist state because they compared the state's publicly endorsed understandings to their own, finding the former in whatever way deficient and in need of change. Contrary to the party state's own understandings, then, dissidence was not in the first instance an ideological conflict. It only became one in the course of time, in good measure (as will become clear in the next two chapters) owing to the state's very own interventions. These were crucial ingredients in the formation of the political understandings of the members of the Berlin peace and civil rights movements.

This insight not only throws a critical light on the socialist party state's ef-

---

the possibility of exit. In a statistical analysis of data on protest events and emigration rates, Steven Pfaff (2006) modifies Hirschman's argument to posit a u-shaped relationship between both "variables," taking account of the trade-offs between the signaling effects of exit (encouraging protest) and the network-destroying effects of exit (making protest events more difficult to organize). Thus Pfaff posits that at first the incidence of protest events (accumulated from official records) increases with exit (emigration rates) to fall subsequently. Strangely, neither Hirschman nor Pfaff have systematically explored the period before the construction of the Wall, which contradicts both hypotheses. Exit was then indeed the alternative to voice. As we shall see in the next chapter, during the 1980s the possibility of exit gravely undermined voice, and the state systematically used it in an attempt to silence dissident voices and also a wider population thoroughly dissatisfied with socialism. While the latter failed miserably (in synch with the Hirschman hypothesis), the former almost crushed the dissident scene. The crux is that there are different kinds of exit (forced vs. voluntary for example) meaning different things in different contexts. What matters is not a rational utility calculus based on abstract variables, but sets of historically specific understandings which can vary significantly in the course of time .

forts to understand itself, but it also throws a critical light on *liberal* theories of the nature of political opposition with their emphasis on free speech and the articulation of divergent opinions. Indeed, in North Atlantic democracies, a liberal social imaginary has become normalized as the dominant folk theory of the political process (Taylor 2004). This includes an understanding of oppositional activity as "speaking up," or "speaking one's mind" as a consequence of "disagreement." The celebrated democratic hero is, in this image, the man or woman who musters the civic courage to publicly stand by his or her opinion, telling truth to power. This view not only overlooks other forms of oppositional activity or even resistance (e.g., Poppe, Eckert, and Kowalczuk 1995; Deutscher Bundestag 1995) and political contention (McAdam, Tilly, and Tarrow 2001), but it also misconstrues its own object: publicly voiced disagreement. Pointing out where these misconceptions of liberalism lie is especially important, because both Western observers (e.g., Joppke 1995; Schroeder 1998) and in part also Eastern critics of socialism (e.g., Havel 1990b) have written about oppositional activities from a decidedly liberal perspective.[47]

Two well-known shortcomings of almost all liberal theories are especially important in the present context. Both of them have deep roots in the natural rights imaginaries of liberal thought and its human ontology, which ascribes an essentially fixed and universal nature to human beings as rational individuals. First, in presupposing particular forms of understandings as exogenously given, they assume the fundamental transparency of the political as far as its central processes are concerned. Rather than having to form understandings of various degrees of certainty and thus actionability through conversations, experiences, and action, actors are assumed to always already have a well-formed understanding ("opinion"). In other words, typically, liberalism fails to problematize the formation of understandings as such; it is blind to the contingent processes that generate and actualize them in more stable institutional form, thus sidestepping questions of political epistemology. After what I have said about the relationships among understandings, agency, and personhood in the previous chapters, one could also say that the central problem of liberalism is never to be genuinely puzzled by human beings.

Second, along with the failure to look at understandings and a fortiori

---

47. The interesting difference between Eastern and Western liberals is that the former have typically come to their critique through the kinds of experiences I describe in this chapter and the following two, generalizing their understandings into a programmatic call for action. For them, transparency was an achievement even though in retrospect they elide the process of getting there. The latter, by contrast, project academic and folk understandings about political forms onto social actors. More on the reinvention of liberalism in Eastern Europe in the next chapter.

personhood and identity as the preliminary consequence of some process, the liberal model also underplays (and in extreme cases entirely disregards) the sociality of understanding, especially its actualization in networks of authority. It not only assumes the political as transparent, then, but as transparent to *individuals*. Both of these assumptions, the naturalization and essentialization of understandings, lead to seriously flawed accounts of the effect flows in the emergence of dissident groups and their institutionalization. One consequence of this is writings about the GDR opposition that explicitly or implicitly blame the movement members for holding on to notions of a socialism with a human face, when, according to these writers, they should have long known that this was an illusion (e.g., Joppke 1995).

I have argued theoretically and through the empirical cases at hand, by contrast, that stable, clearly articulated discursive understandings are typically only the result of social activity, the consequence of the play of the various forms of validation refracted in networked discourse. At least initially, solidarity was built for most future dissidents more on shared emotive, kinesthetic, and prereflexive discursive understandings, on common experiences and stories about them. The political become more transparent to them only by thinking and emotionally working through experiences in community with others.[48] Put differently, the political comes to be understood to the degree that human beings assume a more defined identity within the fabric of social life. In the case of the (later) members of the East Berlin peace, environment, and civil rights movements, the formative experiences were confrontations with authorities that were in the course of time increasingly depersonalized and seen as parts of an overarching institutional whole: the socialist party state. Only in a second step did ideological positioning begin to play a role. Once articulated, ideological positioning was not only directed against the state, but it also began to play a role in the further differentiation, changing allegiances, and shifting alliances within the opposition movements. In sum, before one can associate over differences in opinions, one needs to form and continue to maintain them. To say that people become opposed because they disagree is thus at best a half-truth, at worst a post hoc rationalization, because people also come to disagree because they find themselves opposed (excluded, marginalized, shamed).

This view on the shortcomings of liberalism from the perspective of po-

---

48. Recently, emotionality has received more attention in the social-movement literature. Good entry points into this research are Goodwin, Jasper, and Polletta (2001) and Gould (2009). Unfortunately there is no unifying framework underlying this research, except for the emphatic assertion that emotions do matter. Nevertheless, many authors who have made room in their analysis for emotions explicitly or implicitly take issue with the cognitive biases and instrumental nature of the "framing approach" (e.g., Snow et al. 1986). I obviously share this concern.

litical epistemology has consequences for how we should think about human rights. In keeping with liberal assumptions, discourses on human rights emphasize the freedom of opinion and free speech as the central core of personal freedom rights. However, if the criticisms just advanced hold, the freedom of opinion (i.e., understanding) makes sense only within a positive freedom to engage in epistemically relevant practices. This presupposes access to the means to either directly or indirectly corroborate understandings as well as the existence of a network of authority with suitable characteristics in which emergent understandings can be recognized. We need an experiential and social environment in which we can form our understandings of the political world by thinking them through, working them through and practicing them. The GDR peace and civil rights movement members show this as much as the Stasi officers I introduced in chapters 4 and 5. Their operative work literally threw them onto critical insights, but they could never really develop them because they had no one to talk them over with in any depth. Their critique was exhausted in daring hints that "something had to change," which all too often found their only hope by invoking a "biological solution" to the problem of party leadership. In view of the officers' experience it becomes apparent that the freedom of association is important. Some officers might have cultivated a wider network of authority in the absence of the contact restrictions imposed on them by their employer. And yet, for others personal inclinations and the demands of the Stasi were not far apart. This makes clear that the freedom to associate alone does not provide for the possibility to discuss freely what people feel the urge to discuss. Given the dangers of the circular formation of understandings I outlined at the end of chapter 3, such freedom to form understandings exists only within institutional environments in which the disagreement by a person does not lead to de-authorization, where lived life is allowed to challenge our understandings, and where ideas are not simply dismissed because they question received wisdom, in other words, in institutional environments where *negative* validations are taken seriously. The freedom *of* opinion must be a freedom to *form* opinion.[49]

It is not particularly surprising that the practice of opinion polling that is

---

49. At first glance this may look exactly like the point Mill (1992 [1859], chap. 2) has made with his passionate plea not only for the toleration but also the serious consideration of uncommon understandings, which he argued should always be allowed to be produced in plurality. However, Mill assumes that understandings are mostly formed by isolated, autonomous individuals. Discussions are, for him, only a means to sort the better from the worse understandings. The public domain functions as a marketplace of ideas from which individuals can freely borrow. In effect, Mill does not theorize the process by which understandings come to be discussed and how the one or the other understanding may prevail (and as he admits: not always the true ones). Ultimately, this is so because Mill does not have an adequate concept of the social of persons as constituted in society.

central to political processes in modern mass democracies follows the liberal predilection for essentializing and naturalizing understandings (Bourdieu 1979). After all, opinion polling is, its scientific rhetoric notwithstanding, a certain version of liberalism put into practice. Perhaps it is more surprising that the academic research on social movements has in wide parts followed suit. While the "resource mobilization" (e.g., McCarthy and Zald 1977; Tilly 1977) and "political process" (McAdam 1982) perspectives have brought into play at least a systematic consideration of social structures at various levels of analysis in critique of the earlier psychologistic "collective behavior" tradition" (e.g., Smelser 1962), they have not systematically considered, let alone theorized, the dynamics of political understandings in social movements. This is surprising in the sense that both "resources" and "political opportunities" (the core notion of the political process model) require interpretation.[50] In fact, had the movement literature worked with a constructivist framework, systematically thinking movement life from the interactions and experiences of those engaged in it, they could have avoided the analytic dilution of the notions of "resources" and "opportunity" (cf. McAdam 1982, 32; Gamson 1996, 276). By exploring how human beings come to understand what resources they need, where they would find them, and how they could use them, as well as how they understood the political process, their position within it, and thus where they thought they could intervene with what chance of success, they could have avoided the open-ended (and ultimately rather futile) cataloguing of objectively defined resources and opportunities.

The further addition of the framing concept (putatively borrowed from Goffman 1986 [1974][51]) to the dominant model was a major step forward in the consideration of meaning as a central dimension of social movements (Gamson 1992; Snow et al. 1986). Yet, even though the literature produced an almost bewildering variety of types of framing (Ford and Snow 2000), mirroring the potentially infinite situations in which meaning-making plays a role, the questions posed here as those of a political epistemology have generally received short shrift. The issue of why particular ways of articulating movement legitimation and goals may or may not resonate with potential

---

50. By contrast, in his analysis of the art of politics, Machiavelli was already concerned with the interaction between *fortuna* (good luck, but as such: opportunity) and *virtù* (capability, in principle, anything one can do to prepare oneself to be able to see and seize an opportunity once there which can also mean: made). The literature on opportunity structures is ridden with an objectivist approach to its key concept. Many of the confusions about the definition of *opportunity* could have been avoided with a hermeneutic, institutionalist approach to the topic.

51. Goffman, borrowing from James, Schütz, and Bateson, intended something much more specific with "frame" than what those borrowing from him have made of it: a synonym for meaning.

recruits and members has been posed, but has remained rather undertheorized. The question of how people come to join one another in founding groups has again been flagged as important but has garnered little theoretical reflection. In fact, major parts of the social-movement literature have exhibited a decidedly structural bias, as especially Jeff Goodwin, Jim Jasper, and Jaswinder Khattar have noted (1999). Indeed, the for a time near hegemonic mainstream social-movement literature has succumbed to a strange reification of its main categories. However, because the authors writing in this tradition were genuinely interested in making sense of the real world, which always seemed to escape these categories, they first added new categories (to "resources" was added "political opportunity," which then was enriched by "framing" and "mobilization") and then they broke down each of their main categories into numerous subcategories that seemed to better reflect the realities they were trying to describe. The mainstream movements literature therefore developed as an open-ended catalog of "factors" to be considered in research that needed to be updated ever so often for the general readership. A genuinely dynamic, dialectical approach that focuses on co-constitutive relationships between political understanding, and other political institutions promises a new perspective on social movements.

This chapter was mostly concerned with the question of how young GDR citizens came to understand themselves as living in opposition to the state-socialist project—at least as it was conceived by the party. The next chapter traces how this basic understanding came to be filled with changing political content, shaped and transformed in time through activists' life in their newly established and changing networks of authority, as well as through the experience of their political actions, both in the open-endedness of their execution and in the responses of the state.

8

Forming Groups, Organizing Opposition

Every new form [of action] we found, the first public appearance with banners, posters and flyers in the yard of the Resurrection Church, speaking there publicly, was something new, something that previously seemed unimaginable. Then came the participation in demonstrations, the production of samizdat and thus step by step we fought for things taken for granted by those who have grown up in a civil society.

ULRIKE POPPE

THE NEW COLD WAR TRIGGERS A NEW PEACE MOVEMENT

On December 12, 1979, NATO decided to deploy new medium-range, nuclear-capable weapons systems in Europe while offering the Soviet Union nuclear arms reduction talks—NATO's infamous "double resolution" (*Doppelbeschluß*).[1] Widely seen to foreshadow the end of détente, which had prevailed throughout much of the 1970s, this decision triggered deep, transcontinental fears of a new nuclear arms race leading to nuclear war and the annihilation of humankind. Thus, the double resolution became the birth hour of a new peace movement as a mass phenomenon, especially in West Germany but also in other western European countries (Breyman 2001).[2] Concurrently, in the GDR, too, the peace issue garnered much new interest in the party as well as in a wider public beyond the party's

1. Its notoriety derives from having split several West European societies into staunch supporters and vigorous opponents. In Germany the split ran right through the Social Democratic Party, the senior partner in the governing coalition under chancellor Helmut Schmidt, who was one of the architects of the double resolution. The division in the party and conflicts with the coalition partner resulting from it are in part responsible for the fall of Schmidt's government in 1982 and the ascension of Helmut Kohl to the longest chancellorship in postwar Germany.
2. In the FRG this also offered a new goal for the anti-nuclear-power movement, which had to come to grips with the second oil price shock and the concomitant difficulty to press its agenda at this particular historical juncture. The anti-nuclear power-movement was in turn a more

organizational reach. The party therefore saw this rising popular interest in peace with mixed feelings. On the one hand it promised possibilities for popular mobilization; on the other hand there loomed the threat of losing control over the peace issue. As I have pointed out already, the maintenance of peace was presented as one of the two primary goals of the party state. The presupposed capacity of a Leninist vanguard party to do more for the preservation of peace than anybody else (owing to its radical disconnection from the capitalist profit motive) was a cornerstone of the party state's self-legitimation. The GDR even used the epithet *Friedensstaat* ("state of peace") to describe itself—and by Manichaean implication its class enemy as a *Kriegstreiber* ("war monger"). The Western peace movements, however, were perceived as allies by the GDR government. Consequently, the party media depicted its foreign policy as making the world a safer, more peaceful place. NATO countries' claim that the deployment of newer Soviet medium-range missiles in Eastern Europe was an unprovoked, unilateral, and hence essentially aggressive, act to gain an edge in the arms race was indignantly and brusquely rejected. When the Soviet Union invaded Afghanistan on Christmas Day, 1979, that is, within days of NATO's double resolution, a new Cold War phase was in the making, which was further amplified with Ronald Reagan's election to the U.S. presidency in the fall of 1980.

Like many Western Europeans, a significant number of people in the GDR did not want to leave the peace issue to those governing. In the early 1980s, peace groups formed in the perimeter of Protestant parishes. Erhart Neubert (1998, 464) estimates that by 1983 there were about one hundred such groups throughout the GDR. This was by no means a mass movement (and thus very unlike its Western counterpart), and yet as a party-independent political phenomenon it was much larger and much more broadly based than anything the GDR had seen since the uprising of June 17, 1953.

At the beginning, the GDR peace movement broadened, building in personnel and organization on older peace activism. Particularly notable among these earlier initiatives are the efforts to find alternatives to outright military service for conscientious objectors (Neubert 1998, 299ff.). Since 1965 men refusing military service were given the possibility to serve as "construction soldiers" (*Bausoldaten*) in units specially formed for this purpose. This practice entailed, seen from the party's perspective, unintended, even detrimental consequences. Pooling conscientious objectors led to the formation of new networks of authority based on the strong agreement over some fundamental understanding the party state did not share. The harsh disciplinarian environment in the army's construction units also ignited a direct sense

issue-oriented and policy-focused continuation of parts of the student movement of the late 1960s and early 1970s.

of solidarity among its recruits transcending their ideological differences first in the experience and then in the narratives about common suffering. Not surprisingly, then, a number of construction soldiers kept in touch after their service, and some tried to organize in an effort to improve the lot of their successors (Eisenfeld 1999). They did so by lobbying the churches to intercede with the party state. Construction soldiers were also among the first to establish regular regional and countrywide peace meetings.

For a wider audience, the peace issue became a direct concern with the GDR government's 1978 decree to make military education (*Wehrkunde*), in the form of classroom instruction and practical exercises, a regular subject in all ninth and tenth grades of GDR schools. The introduction of *Wehrkunde* came on top of a creeping militarization of instruction by defense-related excursions, readings, problem sets, and projects, which had long been a cause of concern for parents with pacifist leanings (e.g., Kleßmann 1995). Therefore, the establishment of *Wehrkunde* served as a crystallization point for existing questions and misgivings about the role of the military in GDR society. Parents with only loose links to the church began to renew these. Vera Lengsfeld writes (2002, 134):

> The church became immediately flooded with inquiries from worried parents who wanted to spare their children the experience of military education. Under these circumstances the church was forced to act. In tough negotiations the church leadership won the state's concession that children of religious parents could be exempted from military education. Immediately, thousands of parents remembered their almost forgotten church affiliations. Parishes were, for the first time in a long while, literally swamped with new members.

Because it was hard for nonreligious pacifists to find one another, the churches acted as mediators. This led to the formation of church-based parent groups in which secular pacifists participated. Mandatory military education also prompted nonreligious parents with pacifist leanings to seek out alternative paths of education for their children. These, however, existed solely under the auspices of the churches. The results were renewed and new links between religious and nonreligious GDR citizens concerned about peace. Before I can continue to explore the expansion and consequences of these links, it is important to at least sketch the relationship between the Protestant churches and the party state in the GDR.

Church in Socialism

Since the party state saw itself only on the way to a communist society (and not quite there yet), it expected a certain degree of nonconformism, for which the churches promised to furnish an organized and thus controllable outlet. Since the party understood religion as a misrepresentation of the world, which resulted from unrecognized social dynamics and contradictions, it fully expected religion to disappear with socialism's progress. It interpreted the practice of Protestant or Catholic Christianity[3] as an *individual* and essentially private form of worship whose common practices must be kept from having a wider political significance for society as a whole. Accordingly, churches were expected to function first and foremost as places of worship. The party state also remembered that the more aggressive confrontation with the churches in the early 1950s, during that phase of class warfare it called *Kirchenkampf,* proved counterproductive. The harassment of Christians had aggravated the refugee crisis while proving to be a continuous source of tensions with West Germany. These are two of the reasons why the GDR leadership took a more conciliatory stance toward mainline Christian churches. Another one was the party's understanding that the GDR had reached a phase of historical development in which the domestic class enemy had for all practical purposes disappeared. Moreover, relying on their traditional network of charitable organizations and financially supported by their Western sister institutions, the churches in the GDR had become significant providers of social services. They contributed to the infrastructure of hospitals, kindergartens, and nursing homes. In keeping with an understanding of Christianity as an idealistic antecedent of socialism, the state tolerated these charitable activities. In the same spirit, the SED acquiesced to the churches' claim to a genuine, religiously motivated peace mission. Long before the resurgence of the Cold War, the Protestant churches had institutionally anchored this claim by celebrating peace services.

The changing relationship between party state and church can also be traced through the changing legal forms in which the church was constituted. During the early years of the GDR the Protestant churches remained organized within an all-German roof organization. Especially for staunchly anticommunist church leaders this was one way of delegitimizing the GDR as an independent state. The building of the Wall in 1961 rendered this form of organization increasingly cumbersome, however. It also furnished moderate leaders with an argument that the care for Christians in the GDR required a GDR-specific roof organization. In this spirit the Federation of the Protestant Churches in the GDR (Bund der evangelischen Kirchen in der DDR, BEK) was founded in 1968. The situation of the Protestant churches in the GDR was now officially characterized as one of a "church *in* socialism" (*Kirche im Sozialismus*), rather than a church *against* or *beside* socialism. Both the form of organization and the new formula of self-understanding

---

3. Other churches, such as the Jehovah's Witnesses, were by contrast not accepted and accordingly persecuted as organizations inimical to state and socialism.

reduced the tensions between the Protestant churches and the state considerably. In 1971 the GDR government officially recognized the BEK. The result was something of a state-church compact within which the churches maintained a high degree of autonomy to regulate their own affairs. The state guaranteed that it would abstain from interfering with worship and related activities while the churches agreed to abstain from politics in confrontation with the state (Besier 1995, chap. 2). This agreement was based on the de facto acceptance of the Lutheran dual-world theory distinguishing sharply between secular and spiritual authority (the implications of which were widely discussed among Protestant Christians in the GDR). This compact was neither to the taste of zealous Marxists nor to that of more radical Christians who remained aware about the competing claims their respective ideologies were making about truth and its implications for everyday life. As we shall see, throughout the 1980s the state-church compact came under strain through the new collaboration between church-based and independent peace and later also civil rights and environmental groups.

The Peace Issue Links Church and Nonchurch Groups

At the beginning of the 1980s, the situation for the state with regard to the peace issue started to change along two interfacing dimensions. First, pace activities within the Protestant church found new, translocal forms of organization creating symbols and links opening the church further for secular peace activists. Since 1980 parish-based peace groups began to organize so-called peace decades. These were ten-day-long local meeting and action periods synchronized nationally by using common biblical mottos and common logos. The first motto, *Frieden schaffen ohne Waffen* ("creating peace without weapons"), became, thanks to its prosodic qualities, its internal rhyme, and trochaic meter, the peace movement's signature chant. The first peace decade was also the origin of the famous logo "swords into plowshares," which emblazoned centrally distributed working materials (Neubert 1998, plate XVII).[4] Transformed into a sew-on badge it became *the* symbol

---

4. The initiative for these peace decades came from the Protestant Church of the Netherlands, which started to hold them in 1976. The Protestant churches in both East and West Germany began to organize them in 1980. They ended in the "Day for Prayer and Repentance," an important traditional Protestant Church holiday. Thus they became a fixed part of the liturgical calendar. The peace decades did a lot to make the groups within and across countries pay attention to one another. For example, the GDR's first motto, *Frieden schaffen ohne Waffen*, was promptly taken over in the subsequent year by the West German churches from where it penetrated the whole movement. The sew-on badge, "swords into plowshares," likewise became widely distributed not only across the GDR but also in the West. The peace decades de facto laid part of the groundwork for a national and transnational network of recognition.

of dissenting opinion in the GDR. Its public display in any form came to be persecuted by the state (Neubert 1998, 401–2; Havemann 2003, 335–40).[5] By successfully carving out shared identifications, manifest in discursive, emotive, and kinesthetic understandings, the groundwork was laid for the next step. Carried by the enthusiasm of parishioners, the first regional and then GDR-wide meetings of peace activists came to be organized under the auspices of the church as well. They were variously called "peace workshops" or "peace seminars."

This qualitatively and quantitatively new dimension of peace activism within the church dovetailed with a second development. Since the beginning of the 1980s, *nonreligious* peace groups formed throughout the country. The organizational core members of these groups had previously collected experiences in a variety of state-critical venues, in the cultural opposition, by participating in reading and discussion circles, or by organizing and/or frequenting privately staged public readings or concerts. In addition, the issue of peace generated interest in people who previously had no contact with GDR-critical circles. Importantly, these groups operated outside of church supervision and thus beyond the church-state compact. And yet, parish-based groups in select localities, often encouraged by younger, more radical ministers in cities such as Berlin, Halle, Jena, Leipzig, and Dresden, began to interact with and support these nonreligious peace groups by letting them use their infrastructure for jointly sponsored initiatives.

The emerging peace movement's operation at the margins of the state-church compact, in the space between a large semicontrolled and thus legal, and much smaller uncontrollable nonlegal institutional domain, created unprecedented political opportunities (McAdam 1996, 1982). On the one hand, this interstitial operation facilitated the emergence of a range of phenomena: the movement's significant increase in size; the gradual transformation of parts of it into a civil rights movement supported by the publication of samizdat writings; even the radicalization of a small group from concerning itself with issue-focused, limited interventions to a full-blown opposition advancing a critique of the political system as a whole. These developments would not have been possible for a fully parish-based movement, because the more radical voices within the church would have remained more iso-

---

5. It has been often noted that the state's attempt to eradicate the public display of this symbol is rather ironic because the logo visibly depicts a sketch adapted from a bronze sculpture donated by the Soviet Union to the United Nations in 1959. Sometimes this is interpreted as cunning on the side of the initiators. The irony works the other way round as well. After all, the sculpture serving as model for the logo was executed in the heroic socialist realism characteristic of high Stalinism; as such it became an object of intense emotional identification for an anti-Stalinist peace movement.

lated and because its operations would have been more controlled by the church-state agreement. Nor would it have been possible for a fully church-independent movement, because the church offered vital resources in terms of legality vis-à-vis the state; contacts to the Western churches and mass media and thus protection; large spaces for public meetings and events; access to duplication technology; and finally and not less importantly, access to a variety of nonstate jobs that could provide crucial means for survival. The opportunities for a growing net of dissident politics could emerge only in the gray zone that allowed the exploitation of the institutions of the state-church compact without being overly restricted by its constraints. On the other hand, the interstitial mode of operation created considerable tension among all actors involved: the church hierarchy and local ministers, laypeople and secular peace activists.

A critical communist and a courageous reverend set an example

The personal links between church and nonchurch activists grew in alternative sociotopes such as Prenzlauer Berg, the critical fringes of universities, and through youth-cultural venues. The initiating symbol for this new kind of church-secular activist interaction was the collaboration among Protestant minister, youth pastor, and former construction soldier Rainer Eppelmann and doyen and central node of oppositional activity Robert Havemann (Havemann and Widmann 2003, 314–35; Eppelmann 1993, 173–228). Eppelmann had garnered considerable attention from Berlin's alternative scene and Stasi alike by celebrating "Blues Masses" in his church. The idea for these events came from self-taught guitarist Holly Holwas, notably another former construction soldier. The Blues Masses enjoyed an ever-widening appeal, reaching several thousand interested visitors coming from far and near (Eppelmann 1993, 141–69).[6] They combined music, sermon, and staged productions of everyday scenes touching on political issues. Havemann, impressed by Eppelmann's courage and energy, introduced Eppelmann to the West German media through coordinated open letters to Brezhnev and Honecker and a video-recorded discussion partially broadcast by Western television stations.

---

6. Between the summer of 1979 and the fall of 1986, Eppelmann and his collaborators managed to organize about twenty blues masses. They began at Eppelmann's own Samaritan Church, soon had to include the nearby Church of the Redeemer, to move finally to the Resurrection Church to accommodate the steadily rising numbers of attendees on larger grounds. They attracted mostly poorer young people with only loose ties to mainstream society, people who called themselves "dropouts" or "punks" and who were labeled by the security and social service agencies, not only of the former GDR, as "antisocial."

Inspired by the enormous success of the "Krefeld Appeal" of the West German peace movement, which demanded that the NATO double resolution be repealed, Havemann and Eppelmann drafted a "Berlin Appeal" (e.g., Haufe and Bruckmeier 1993, 263–64; Eppelmann 1993, 190–92), demanding to convert if not all of Europe then certainly both Germanys into a zone free of nuclear weapons.[7] They brought their appeal within the reach of ordinary citizens by adding peace-pedagogical proposals, for example, to outlaw war toys and to stop the practice of military parades. They picked up the title for the appeal, "Creating peace without weapons," from the first peace decade in the hope that the church might help in distributing the text throughout the GDR. Yet the church could not be persuaded, even though officials had contributed suggestions for the improvement of the text. Accordingly, the authors of the appeal had to find signatories within their private networks. Together they managed to tally up more than seventy initial supporters. The state's reaction followed promptly. As Havemann was already under house arrest, the Stasi apprehended and interrogated Eppelmann, and the prosecutor's office opened preliminary proceedings against him according to article 99 of the penal code of the GDR: "treacherous transmission of information." However, after swiftly organized international protests and at the intervention of the church, Eppelmann was freed after only two days in jail. The charges were dropped. Nevertheless, the initial signatories of the Berlin Appeal were all investigated and interviewed by the Stasi. However, the party state did not want to burden the ongoing Conference on Security and Cooperation in Europe (CSCE) negotiations with a significant human rights issue on their hands. Thus, Havemann's strategy had paid off. His understanding that the best protection for dissident activities is publicity obtainable via Western media was corroborated by the events, and some of the members of the peace and later dissident movements of the GDR had learned an important political lesson. To explain the state's reaction to the Berlin Appeal, in his memoirs (1993, 187) Eppelmann says:

> Manfred Stolpe [then a high-ranking administrator in the Protestant Church and likely a secret police informer] explained later, that the state reacted so nervously to the Havemann-Eppelmann team, because they sensed the "pincers of the counterrevolution." The SED worried that the isolated Marxist-inspired resistance would team up with the only organization which was not completely controlled by the state. As much as the rulers

7. Incidentally, this was also the beginning of a more national, German-German thinking on security issues that apexed later in ideas of a "security partnership" between both countries. Eastern European dissidents and observers looked at such ideas with skepticism if not alarm (e.g., Feher and Heller 1986).

feared Havemann, they were even more afraid of the idea that loners could find a connection to some oppositional basis.

In sum, the agreement on the understanding that a new arms race constituted a considerable threat not only to world peace but also to the very existence of humankind enormously facilitated the formation of networks of people and groups that, through the mutual recognition of their commitment to the peace issue and the opposition to their respective governments and its logics of deterrence, became authorities for one another. Within the GDR, the peace issue facilitated the formation of alliances between individuals and groups that before would have hardly felt much attraction for one another, most notably Protestant Christians, critical Marxists, and democratic socialists. Just as important as the new connections between diverse groups within the GDR was the emergence of an international network of peace activists that transcended the Iron Curtain. Here the common understanding created a mutual focus of attention, the willingness to watch out for one another's well being, and the eagerness to learn from one another, not least in the interest of performing a kind of international interaction that differed markedly from the threat-posturing and conference negotiations of international diplomacy.

WOMEN FOR PEACE—THE FIRST NON-PARISH-BASED PEACE GROUP IN BERLIN

In the remainder of this chapter I will often refer to specific "groups," most notably Women for Peace, Initiative for Peace and Human Rights, the "peace circles" in Friedrichsfelde and Pankow, as well as the Environmental Library. I will use the term *group* not in a sociological but in an everyday, local sense. That is, I will call *group* what my informants have called *group*, or often synonymously *circle*. To understand what is implied in this term, it is important to see that these groups had often little to no formal structure. The parish-based groups had at least a common locale, an address, and an addressee in the minister. Through the minister and the church council they had access to the resource of the parish, most notably the church building itself, the meeting facilities, a telephone, perhaps even reproduction technology, weekend retreat spaces, access to higher church officials, and the like. By contrast, the non-parish-based groups met in frequently changing private apartments. They had whatever personal resources their members could bring to the table.

The absence of formal structure among non-parish-based groups was in part choice and in part necessity. It was choice in as far as it set them apart from the bureaucracy and central control of the party state. It was necessity in as far as formal organization would have given the state more of a legal leverage to persecute them. Both parish and non-parish-based groups understood themselves as principally open discussion and work groups pursuing common interests. They did so in contradistinction to the clandestine reading groups that operated more on the model of revolutionary cells. There was typically no formal leadership, which is not to say that there were no differentiations with respect to centrality or authority. But who was and was not central could change in the course of time. It depended on reputation, a track record of party-critical activities, but even more so on initiative, on the desire and capability to make things happen by hard work, perseverance, or connections.

There was also no formal membership in nonparish groups, which is again not to say that these groups had no boundaries. Who was and who was not "in" depended on who came to the meetings; who came was dependent on who knew where and when the meetings took place. Personal introductions were de rigueur. Also, membership was not exclusive; many people worked in several groups at the same time without too much regard to the fact that some of these groups were based in a parish while others were not. When following the narratives of my informants, I attribute actions to a particular group; this neither means that every member identifying with this group participated, nor that people who were not typically associated with this group did not. Actions emerged often as freely floating projects initiated by a few individuals who could come from one or a few groups and then involve members of various groups. In principle, participation was voluntary, not least because each and every one had to decide whether he or she was ready to shoulder the risks involved. Attributing actions to one group or another, therefore, designates the source of the initiative and/or the preponderance of membership. In sociological terms, then, groups were more like clusters, areas of connections with higher density within scenes, local and increasingly regional, national and later even international networks. Nevertheless, groups did have a distinct identity; they developed distinct cultures of interaction, and members identified with "their" groups.

Two petitions and the network-creating powers of mutual recognition

The first significant non-parish-based peace group to appear in Berlin was Frauen für den Frieden (Women for Peace) (Kukutz 1995; Neubert 1998; Bohley 2005). The formation of this group followed a very concrete historical event: the promulgation of a new military service law on March 25, 1982. According to this new law, women could now in times of crisis be drafted into the National People's Army. The virulence of the peace issue, the occasion of this new law, and the relative dissatisfaction with the all too theoretical concerns of most still-existing discussion circles dominated by men, prompted a number of women in East Berlin to found the women's group. They thus followed the example of similar Western groups that had precipitated from the encounter between feminism and the peace movement. In particular they were inspired by Western groups of the same name that proliferated throughout the continent starting with a Danish initiative (Kukutz 1995, 1291).

Ulrike Poppe, Irena Kukutz, Bärbel Bohley, and Katja Havemann, late Robert Havemann's wife, were among the founding members of this group in Berlin. At the same time that they launched their group in the capital city other women came together in other parts of the GDR for similar kinds of purposes.[8] Their first move was to write a flurry of individual petitions to governmental agencies protesting the new law by questioning its wisdom (April 1982). Irena Kukutz remembers how they got started:

> Everything pointed in the same direction, and at this critical juncture it became clear to us, now the time has come to *do* something *as women*. It is already enough what they do to our men [military service requirements]. And then the men wanted to instrumentalize this issue for their own purposes. They wanted to tell us how we should approach the issue. We worked hard to keep them out and to say that this is our problem and we are formulating our own texts and these texts will look different from your texts. . . . Then we said let's do individual petitions [*Eingaben*: a statutory instrument available to GDR citizens]. I will send one, you will send one, and then let's see what kind of an answer we are getting. And the only one who got an answer was I. . . . This answer was written by the Ministry of Defense and it was of course less than satisfying [because it did nothing but reiterate the party's position].

The lacking response of the state was, although not unexpected, still disappointing. In fact, the state's studied silence strongly corroborated the women's understandings that they were not taken seriously as citizens, making them wonder what they could do to change that. Thus their action proved to be a significant exercise in political knowledge-making, affording them hard data about how the state operated, which motivated them to move forward. Says Kukutz:

8. The Stasi was later worried about the possibility that these different groups might become unified in some organized way under the leadership of Frauen für den Frieden in Berlin, which was then in addition to the surveillance of its chief members investigated as a group under the alias *Wespen* ("wasps"). For a Stasi estimate of the potential number of participants, see Kukutz 1995, 1344, document 2.

Well, we said there is this wonderful law allowing petitions, and let's just pretend we are a house community. We are not collecting signatures here, we know that was forbidden, but we can make another petition. Then we sat down to write a common petition and we'll state again clearly what we mean. And then we just did it. There were seven women, most of them I barely knew . . . and we formulated a common text. And then we started to collect signatures among our acquaintances. And suddenly we had about 150 signatures and we got scared that this could be too much.[9] We originally thought it would be just us and perhaps the one or the other woman. Yet that so many would come together, because every woman said, "I still know this woman and that who would also sign," this was a real snowball effect. So we suddenly realized that many women were just waiting, that somebody would come along with something like this and they were happy that they could sign this. Others hesitated because they sensed that this could lead to difficulties.

The exhilaration about the wider response to their actions still reverberates through Kukutz's voice. The step from participating in discussion circles to writing down their own position to communicate it to the state, that is, the movement from talking about the party state to talking back to it was an important turn on the way to becoming a dissident. It was a kind of political "coming out" similar to what other would-be dissidents had experienced with their public protests against Biermann's expatriation. What is more, the mutual encouragement to coordinate individual action gave way to work out something together as a group.

The new collective petition entextualized and thus objectified the mutual recognition of the women for a set of shared understandings through a collective voice breaking through in the incantatory use of the first person plural in conjunction with the category "women" (Kukutz 1995, 1351, document 7). The letter begins with the circumscription of the category "women" as an irreducible plurality—as being religious, or nonreligious, with or without children, and so forth. From here the letter proceeds to a forceful proclamation of unity: "*We women* want to break through the cycle of violence, and we want to withdraw our participation in all violent forms of conflict resolution." The text then continues, through the seven-fold reiteration of "we women," to project (and certainly in the hope for uptake to constitute) a universal feminine subject calling into existence a public (Warner 2002): "*We women* do not see military service as an expression of equal rights. . . . *We*

9. Because their initiative looked now more like a forbidden public collection of signatures among strangers rather than the petition of people intimately acquainted with each other.

women see the readiness for military service as a threatening gesture. . . . *We women* feel especially called upon to protect life, to support the old, ill, and weak persons. . . . *We women* believe that humanity today faces an abyss and that the accumulation of further weapons will lead to an insane catastrophe [my emphasis]." Thus the signatories see themselves authorized to speak not as universal citizens but as women gifted with a special nature, differentiated by special experiences, and burdened with a special responsibility.[10]

The projection of a universal female subject calling into existence a public (Warner 2002, 67) was at the time of writing a rather daring assumption. Yet it was already more than a mere fantasy. It was enabled by recognition, first by the fact that the women knew themselves in unison with similar women's initiatives around the world, and second, by the fact that they had found one another to talk, write, and agree or disagree. For all the participating women I talked with or whose published narratives about these events I could access, the experience of community was perceived as empowering. Their meetings helped to clarify their emotive and discursive understandings about the party state and their role in it, thus contributing significantly to their formation as political agents. Their understandings became further stabilized and their ability to act was strengthened by the positive echo their petition found among friends and acquaintances. What emerged here is the group's inspiring (if historically probably false)[11] understanding to speak for a silent majority in the country.

What the women got from the state in response to their petition was not what they had hoped for. As always in such circumstances, Stasi investigated the identity and personal context of all the signatories (Kukutz 1995, document 9). Subsequently, a large number of them were asked to attend individual *Aussprachen* (i.e., problem discussions) with a handful of party state officials. The guidelines for these talks were worked out by the Stasi, and in cases it judged as important enough, Stasi officers, under the cover of some

---

10. Especially from an American perspective, the self-authorization of the women in the idiom of difference feminism is quite startling. It is important to understand this voice on the basis of the gender politics of the socialist state, which has emphasized women's labor participation while at the same time maintaining a traditional image of women as mothers, householders, and emotional caretakers (cf. Borneman 1992; Ferree 1993). The voicing of protest in terms of difference feminism makes particular sense if it is considered that, as Gal and Kligman (2000 chap. 3) argue, discourses systematically juxtaposed a feminized private sphere against a masculinized public. For the consequences on opposition groups as women's groups, see Myra Marx Ferree (1994), the useful documentation of Samirah Kenawi (1995), and the dissertation of Ingrid Miethe (1999).

11. My judgment in this matter is based on the devastatingly poor election results of the former dissident groups reorganized into electoral platforms in the March 1990 elections.

bureaucratic alias, participated actively in these *Aussprachen*. Party state officials saw in these meetings an opportunity to signal to everybody involved how they looked upon endeavors such as this collective petition. They hoped that the combination of an unmistakably negative recognition of the action at hand along with another firm explanation of the party line on matters of disarmament and peace, as well as an indication of the potential consequences of such actions in the future, would sway many signatories to recant their signature or at least to abstain in the future from similar activities.

For the Stasi these meetings were a unique opportunity to assess the political attitudes of a particular person. This is to say, in Stasi lingo these conversations afforded possibilities to "differentiate" the signatories from one another, to get a sense of "who is who" with regard to their overall position toward the socialist project in general and more specifically with regard to the activity at hand. My interviewees among the Women for Peace group told me that depending on who actually conducted the various conversations the tone of the interviews differed considerably. Here is an excerpt of the Stasi report on the conversations with Beate Harembski (Kukutz 1995, 1354 [MfS, XX/2, January 31, 1983/zö-fu]). This particular conversation was held at the personnel department of her employer (Park of the Young Pioneers), including a Stasi officer identified to her as a representative of the city council participated in the meeting.

> The uttered opinions of H. make it clear that she only used arguments which she knew well from her circle of acquaintances. They have their foundation in the *desire* for peace, without ever giving serious consideration to the question of the causation of wars and the nature of imperialist politics. For her, both military blocks are identical. In the conversation the wrong interpretations of the possibility to draft women exhibited in the petition were corrected. Arguments which disproved her interpretation of the military service laws were acknowledged only hesitatingly. . . . At the end of the conversation H. was confronted with the question of responsibility vis-à-vis the education of the children entrusted to her [as a gardener she worked with a youth group]. She was told that it would not be tolerated if she acquainted the children and youths with pacifist thought.

The document illustrates how one Stasi officer thought he had to convey to his superiors content and progress of the conversation with Harembski. He felt compelled to leave no doubt about the class positions of everybody involved in the 1 hour and 40 minute encounter. This includes the indirect showcasing of his own "politically conscious" evaluation of the act of petitioning, which he identifies as an immature, ill-informed political act that is devoid of the requisite theoretical background understanding of international politics.[12] Yet, the document also gives us some sense about the atmosphere that has prevailed in the "conversation." The party members had to steer the exchange to a particular preset result that could only consist in the affirmation of the quasi-naturalized party line. Accordingly, at least in their write-ups, the party's representatives had little leeway to present themselves as open and involved in a genuine *conversation* rather than in a didactic exercise conveying the position of the state once more. As a relatively unified group they faced a single "other" whom they had to treat as somehow insufficient or naive and who was supposed to come around to their position of superior insight. Finally, the document shows that the threat of consequences was very real. It ends with an evaluation of how feasible it would be to lay off Harembski (seen as unrealistic by the officer). Nevertheless, she, much to her chagrin, lost her youth group and thus a significant source of joy in her employment.[13]

In two ways these meetings epitomized state-citizen relationships in the GDR. On the one hand they were still characterized by an effort to "win back" a citizen for the party's project; ideally this required agreement, even identification with a pregiven rationale, although a more passive collaboration was ultimately acceptable to the state. Yet, quite as everywhere else in the GDR, the process of alignment was never a process of negotiation; it could only happen on the party's terms; the individual had to self-objectify, blending fully into a preexisting institutionalized framework. On the other hand, more or less obvious threats were used to deter people from actions the party saw as detrimental to its project. A few cases notwithstanding, this two-pronged strategy backfired. The meetings resonated with previous didactic, rationally monologic encounters with the state, and thus they simply corroborated activists' critical understandings about the GDR.[14] For most

---

12. Lest one may be tempted to settle too quickly on the "ideological blinders" of the Stasi officer, it is worth remembering that many West German judges adjudicating the merit of cases of conscientious objectors at about the same time were assuming the moral justification of NATO's position vis-à-vis the Warsaw Pact with the exact same self-righteousness, often looking at the position of pacifists with the very arguments and ultimately the very same contempt.

13. I hasten to add that by no means all of the talks proceeded in the same atmosphere, their central planning notwithstanding. Some women remember them as rather relaxed. I suspect that the atmosphere varied not just with different personalities, but more importantly, also with the bureaucratic need to document what happened and thus with the composition of the party group facing the women. The presence of a Stasi officer certainly influenced the dynamics of the conversation in a more formal direction.

14. In a further *Aussprache*, Bärbel Bohley faced her interviewer with the fact that he was merely threatening her without any intention of engaging in a real conversation about the substantive issues. So she demanded to be referred to someone higher up with whom she could really enter

women, the effect was a motivational push to go on. In fact, the interest in the continuation of the group among the signatories was so overwhelming that the original group had to suggest that additional women's groups be founded because it could not possibly accommodate everybody. The most important result of the action was perhaps that it corroborated to the women that something can be done, that they are actors indeed.[15] Says Kukutz:

> For us this was a real push forward. One knew, now I have gone so far, I can't take this back, you can't make yourself invisible again, you can't say this happened by accident. And thus it was clear: now one does not have to pretend anymore, we have to continue. The need to continue was there. The pressure on everyone was enormous from having been made to feel so disempowered for such a long time. So we said, we have to go out, we have to create a public for this problem, we have to mobilize people, we have to find allies.

Gaining understanding from moving across Alexanderplatz

A good year later, on October 17, 1983, the Women for Peace were ready to launch their next big initiative. To this day, this action in particular remains in the fond memory of so many (but not all as we shall see) of its members. Within the context of a "peace week," the West Berlin Women for Peace had called upon women to dress in black or purple on that day as a sign of mourning and to participate in a "memorial walk" (likened in flyers to that of the "Mothers of the Plaza de Mayo" in Buenos Aires) at Kurfürstendamm— the Western city's central business district (Kukutz 1995, document 14). The East Berlin women aware of the Western activities planned for a parallel action in their part of the city, which they thought should also address the fact that their original cause—the petition against the draft of females—was still not answered to their satisfaction. The fact that the GDR's recruiting offices had started to perform medicals on potential female recruits provided further motivation to take the new military service law once again as the occasion for action. By explicitly linking themselves to the Western event, they also wanted to fulfill a long-held dream to make a common statement underscoring that the rift characterizing the renewed Cold War was not just one between the two military blocks, but also one that on both sides separated governments from ordinary people. Accordingly, about forty women planned to send individually worded letters by registered mail to the district

---

a conversation (MDA, OV "Bohle," "Aktennotiz über ein Gespräch mit Bärbel Bohley" undated, source undeclared).

15. On the importance of experiences and discourses of self-efficacy for social movements, see, for example, Gamson (1992, chap. 4) and Eliasoph (1998).

recruiting office, declaring that they would refuse to heed a draft. The idea was that the women, likewise dressed in black, would converge from various corners of the city on Alexanderplatz, East Berlin's central square, to dispatch their letters at the same time from the local post office.

Kept abreast by secret informants, the Stasi knew early about the group's plans and tried to thwart their realization in the scale and manner imagined by the women. The group members identified by Stasi as the leaders[16] were warned in the morning by Stasi officers appearing at their door under cover of some other administrative function that their actions stood to violate the city code on public events. They were also shadowed. For some activists, the Stasi managed to arrange that they would be kept busy at their workplaces throughout the afternoon. The Alexanderplatz post office was warned in advance about the event and was instructed to hold the letters. To control the event at the location, Stasi dispatched a considerable number of officers to demonstrate presence, to clandestinely photograph the participants, and to temporarily arrest at least some of them (MDA, OV "Bohle"; BfS Berlin, xx, October 15, 1983).[17]

The participating women experienced the event very differently depending—literally—on how it, or even more accurately, how *they* went. Ulrike Poppe dispensed with the black dress, because she felt its symbolism was too heavy handed. She was one of the women who was warned in the morning. At that point, however, she was already too seasoned a dissident to be so easily dissuaded. Together with her husband, Gerd Poppe, she had to her credit several years of organizing readings in their apartment—complete with repeated attempts by the state to deter her from this practice. In fact, she fully expected shadowing and, fearing temporary arrest, she thought of ways to trick the officer surveilling her. In the afternoon, at the appointed time, she managed to escape her shadows on a bicycle handed to her by her husband at a red traffic light, sending the officers scurrying to their car. Upon arrival at Alexanderplatz, the Stasi tried to arrest her yet again. Luckily she found herself next to two friends, and when an officer in plain clothes

---

16. Tellingly, many Stasi documents from this time still presume that men were pulling the strings in the background.

17. In the interviews the women speak of a massive presence of the Stasi on Alexanderplatz. Documents from Berlin's district office indicate that sixteen officers of department xx were involved in the operation. This department investigated many (but not all) members of Berlin's dissident scene, including Bärbel Bohley who was seen by the Stasi as the leader of the group. For that reason they also talked about it as the "Bohley group." The documents (e.g., Kukutz 1995, document 15) also make clear that there was a significant involvement of the ministry's division VIII as well as the Berlin district office's department viii. The "VIII"-line was specialized in a range of surveillance techniques, such as shadowing people, overt and covert house searches, the installation of bugging devises, etc.

tapped on her shoulder from behind, she started to scream that she was being molested. The three women linked arms with one another and managed to flee into a nearby café, into which the Stasi did not dare to follow because they apparently feared provoking a scene. From the public phone in the café the women called husbands and friends who had in the meantime gathered at the agreed postaction meeting point, the artist Bärbel Bohley's atelier. Some of these friends, Irena Kukutz among them, returned back to the café to support their beleaguered friends. An official of the Protestant church (see footnote 20) was also informed by the women. He eventually came with his car to escort Poppe, Bohley, and Havemann out of the café and back to their apartments. Poppe remembers:

> Just the fact that we could prevent arrest by forming a chain has given us the feeling that we can defend ourselves and that this action was important even if its publicity effect was limited . . . it still was better than nothing. What we did was a constant testing: What is possible? How far can we go? How strong are we? How strong are our opponents so to speak? Who is on our side? Afterwards, on the one hand interested people came to us, and on the other hand there were always people saying, well that is becoming too dangerous now and who ceased to participate.

Irena Kukutz also experienced the event as enormously empowering. She had taken her son along as a "protective shield against the Stasi," calculating correctly that the secret police would be hesitant to take children into custody. Thus she managed to move across the square into the post office and back to Bohley's atelier. Kukutz remembers that she enjoyed the co-presence of the women in the public sphere as a recognizable group. Following up on my question of whom they had in mind as the addressee of their action she explains that they did not count on communicating a message to bystanders or even to the office of military recruitment as she anticipated that letters would be confiscated. Instead, she experienced it more as a communication among the women, with the state represented by the secret police.[18] Kukutz recalls:

> It was sufficient that we saw each other: ah, there is another one in black, and there comes yet another with her letter, that was beautiful. . . . This did us good. . . . It was such a victory for us, when Mr. Stolpe [a church official][19] came to pick up Ulrike and to bring her home. [laughter] Past the Stasi guys!! We should have liked to show them "thumbs up"!! Well,

---

18. It is quite possible that Kukutz's interpretation is colored by the reading of her own Stasi files, which makes clear in retrospect who the involved actors were and who pulled the strings.

19. Here Irena Kukutz may err. In my interview with her, Ulrike Poppe named Werner Krusche as the church official who led the women out of the café. Katja Havemann (Havemann and Wid-

that was quite an action, which created strength and a kind of cohesion: we concluded together we can really do something. That's quite an experience; if somebody is alone they can come and catch her, but if we can do this together, if we can even get some support to the scene, that was different. And they [Stasi] knew sure well, if this, if this has consolidated, then it is much more difficult to crack it up.

Bärbel Bohley summarizes her take on the events (2005, 43):

> We were creative, we had many ideas, our ideas were daring, provocative, and we almost always hit the nail on its head. We could not keep ourselves from laughing under the eyes of the Stasi. Quite to the contrary, in spite of all the anxiety it was a wonderful feeling to challenge authority. We sat inside, in the warmth, we drank wine, we had new ideas, thought up new plans and "they" had to stand out there in the cold, waiting and waiting. . . . At this time we felt almost invincible and sheltered in a large network, because many human beings in East and West thought like we did.

More commonly the members of the group experienced the Alexanderplatz event as energizing; it validated their sense of agency, that is, their understanding that they could act successfully even in the face of adversity, and it also corroborated their understandings of the nature of their group as successful and protective. However, the epistemic effect of the participation in the event could also be the precise opposite, as Beate Harembski's narrative makes clear. She was very much looking forward to the group's action on Alexanderplatz, which she meant to "celebrate," as the women's group had become, as she says, an "emotional home" for her. She felt that she had finally arrived after a long, lonesome search for a deeper human connection. For this special day, she decided to wear her great-grandmother's black taffeta dress, which she describes in very loving terms. Arriving with the commuter train a Alexanderplatz from her workplace in Treptow she immediately beheld Stasi officers who demonstratively followed women whom they recognized as participants in the event:[20]

> To me it became clear that it was very probable that we would not get out of here unscathed. This isolated us from each other. What mattered was sheer survival. . . . I realized I wouldn't be able to get out of this situation anymore,

---

mann 2003, 362) concurs with her. The narratives also diverge about who, in addition to Bärbel Bohley, Ulrike Poppe, and Katja Havemann, *initially* fled from Stasi officers into the café.

20. The planning documents for the Stasi action reveal an interesting change of strategy that is worth mentioning here, because of the effect it produced. In the initial plan drafted by department xx of Stasi's Berlin district office (BfS), the women were to be photographed clandestinely for purposes of identification. The women, however, report that the pictures were taken ostentatiously.

I would not be able to sink back into the status of an unknown entity. ... I was the first then to leave the post office because I felt locked in. ... Somehow, two women came along with me, one with a stroller and yet another, and I came out there with a "puffed-up chest." That is a feeling that has grown in the course of time, that is a metaphor. [It means] I stand by my convictions—this means not like a weight lifter, but straight out and in all clarity: here I am. ... So we went up to the Alex[anderplatz], and the three of us strode along until this situation came about where somebody tapped my shoulder from behind with the all too well known phrase "your ID please, follow us for the clarification of facts!" Well, and this was quite a shock to me, and intuitively I tried to stay with myself, in this moment I only looked to the floor, because I wanted to stay with myself, and I only saw the tips of the Stasi guy's shoes, and I was very strong, very calm. But I had to hear in the same moment, as he said to me "follow us" how the steps of the other two women moved away. And there were a number of such situations that led me to feel that if the turnaround in '89 [*die Wende*] would not have occurred, I would not have survived all of this much longer, I have to say this very clearly . . . I experienced this [event] very strongly as isolating, because now it was clear that we all *individually* had to come to terms with what we had dared to do. I clearly felt that the other women tried to save themselves, while they abandoned me.

A.G.: So just the opposite of many others, Poppe and Kukutz for example?[21]

B.H.: Yes, I felt exposed and abandoned.

For Beate Harembski, the course of this event corroborated suspicions of her own vulnerability. Her arrest (in comparison with the other women's escape from it) resonated positively with her prior experiences of isolation. She was one of the few signatories to the common petitition who afterward had to face more serious consequences.[22] She felt acutely that in either case the group could not offer protection. One must ask at this point why Harembski, as compared with others who had also faced not so uncommon brief apprehensions, sometimes even repeatedly, took hers more seriously—in fact, precisely in the way that the Stasi hoped? Why is it that she could not read the fact of her quick dismissal as a victory? After all, she was not taken to the Stasi jail at Hohenschönhausen for investigation, she was not confronted with the prospect of an indictment, carrying with it a potential prison sentence. The answer for her was "not yet!"

To understand this, one has to study the deeper biographical resonances

---

21. After the fall of socialism many of the participating women met to talk about their experiences with this action. So they were well aware of their different feelings.

22. She lost the right to teach youth groups as a gardener working at a Pioneer facility.

evoked by the consequences of her political actions. Harembski describes her childhood as a long period of continuing social isolation. This was not so much due to the fact that her labor-class parents tried to isolate the family from wider GDR society because they deplored socialism. Instead, Harembski felt isolated within her own family due to permanent tensions with and fear of her autocratic father. The power dynamics in her family also prevented a more intimate relationship with her mother and brother. When she became deeply involved in competitive diving (egged on by her parents, especially her father), her eminently stressful, increasingly sport-centered life increased her isolation while trapping her in even more authoritarian relationships with coaches and functionaries. After winning the Berlin youth championship for her age group, she began to attend a special school for children with the potential to compete nationally and internationally in sports. There, the individual divers were mercilessly pitted against one another by an authoritarian trainer. Once more, recognition and belonging were made ruthlessly contingent on the fullfillment of norms. From this experience she drew the conclusion that strength and protection had to come exclusively from within herself. And it was her own effort to free herself from these contexts that made her feel more in control of herself and happier. Although she had a deep longing for community, she, unlike Poppe, Kukuktz, or Bohley, had never in the same way experienced sociality as a solution to her problems, as a means to manage and work through the tensions of life. Tragically, her partner at the time, Mario Wetzky, proved to be a secret informant, who has contributed his share to her feelings of stress and insecurity at the time. And so it is perhaps not surprising that both actions of Women for Peace together led Beate Harembski to disengage from the group in the months to follow.

What comes to the fore in the Alexanderplatz episode in general, and through the comparison between these two divergent types of reactions to the same event in particular, are the epistemic dynamics created by translations between modes of understanding. The women's discursively available notion that they should have the right to perform their protest was translated into a pattern of movement, the planned action. However, on the day of the action, the Stasi tried to block their movement, literally trying to clip the activists' sense of their own ability to move act.[23] In Poppe's case they tried thrice. Yet, each time she could overcome or sidestep the obstacle. Thrice she had to face her fear of the agents of state, which she just as often conquered with an accompanying feeling of, first, relief and then joy and

---

23. Katz (1999, chap. 1) makes a related argument about translations from kinesthetic to emotive ordering processes. His case are drivers who become angry because they feel their movement blocked by others who cut in right in front of them.

pride about her own success. Retranslating these kinesthetic and emotive orderings into a discursive one, she concluded not only that she *should* have the right to express her political understandings publicly, but also that she *could successfully* take this right if she only dared to exercise it. Says Poppe (Havemann and Widmann 2003, 371):

> There was an axiom that Robert Havemann has performed for us: to live and take rights as if they were already granted. Even if there is no freedom of speech, we take the right to communicate our opinions freely.

And it was Havemann's axiom that was de facto corroborated by the flow of the Alexanderplatz event. Moreover, the fact that Poppe could interlock with fellow demonstrators, the fact that she was rescued by friends in the group and escorted out of the situation with the help of connections to church officials, immediately corroborated understandings that the group and these connections provided a workable security blanket. The kinesthetic and emotive understandings in performance were retranslated into a discursive ordering simply by narrating the event to each other. Since the women came through the same movement in space, through the same performed ordering of the world, to the same conclusion, first kinesthetically and emotively, but then also discursively, they could recognize this very insight for one another, thus amplifying its validity even further. While the event corroborated the fact that they were gifted with political agency, their discourse, their laughter about it, further recognized that they did. Finally, this event resonated with previous similar events: that they had sent a common petition signed by 150 women, that some of them had managed to organize public readings in private apartments in spite of the state's attempt to stop them, and so on. If the sense of agency that was constituted by these prior experiences was waning, then the new action reproduced it at an even higher level.

For Beate Harembski, just the opposite was true: ultimately she could not overcome the obstacles placed in front of her, she was not rescued, but abandoned. And her feeling of isolation was emphasized by the fact that the others did not recognize her experience. Yet that corroborated her much older self-understanding that ultimately help can only come from self, not from others. If the aforementioned women concluded from their successful movement across Alexanderplatz to go ahead planning more oppositional activity, she drew the opposite conclusion from her thwarted movement.

The dialectic of politics and self-politics, of actions, networks, and identity

The institutional development of the peace, and later also that of the civil rights and environmental movements in the GDR, can be described as constituted by a dialectic. One pole is formed by actions, such as the ones I have discussed in the previous two sections. These actions are directly addressed to the party state and increasingly to a wider domestic and international audience as well. They are political in as far as they are geared toward the transformation of institutions above and beyond group or movement. The petitions and the Alexanderplatz event hoped to contribute however minutely toward a renewal of political culture while remaining thematically connected with distant hopes to effect the repeal of the new military service law. The other pole consists in group meetings and encounters with and presentations to other groups. This pole is concerned with self-politics, that is, the institutionalization of group and movement as a socially and spatially distributed, local, regional, national, or even transnational network capable of affecting projective articulations with the aspirations of institutional change.[24] Political actions built the backbone of a groups' ongoing self-narrativization. Political actions signify what the group is about, what it is working toward, why the exertion of so much energy, why incurring so much personal risk, is worth the while. They are also the ultimate basis, the pivotal point of reference, for the presentation of groups to one another. This is not to say that self-politics, especially organizational, psychological, and technical know-how about how to set up and maintain a group, did not also attract a lot of interest. Politics and self-politics were intimately connected in a society such as the GDR's because the very act of founding groups and networks independent of the party state was a genuine political act. The actions of the women's group were also aiming at emancipating themselves as political actors, at proving to themselves that they were viable as a group with the potential of engaging in more political action in the future. Self-politics was in this sense politics within a shorter temporal horizon.[25] However, in the longer run, interactions concerned alone with self-politics and reflections about it are doomed to self-referentiality. The novelty effect of having founded and successfully maintained a group as a foundational political act is bound to wear off. In the absence of further outward-looking political action the group would end up being mostly about itself, eventually raising the question: "what for?"

Conversely, the scale and scope of action and with it its potential impact on target institutions is dependent on the degree of self-institutionalization of group and movement as a network, for this is where its capacity for pro-

---

24. About the constitutive importance of translocal networks for oppositional movements in Eastern Europe, see also Osa (2003) for Poland and Glenn (2001) for Czechoslovakia.

25. It is above all the work of Alberto Melucci (1996a, 1996b) which has drawn movement scholars' attention to the important issues of self-formation, the formation of a collective identity, and meaning in social movements.

jective articulation comes from. And that in turn is grounded in the degree to which certain political understandings are actualized. The processes of validation responsible for this actualization of understandings are asymmetrically distributed over outside action and inside network and identity formation. At their very best, actions offer corroboration; meetings thrive on recognitions. In consequence, actions, networks, and identity grow together; self-politics is dependent on politics and vice versa.

Forming GDR-wide networks.

More than a year elapsed between the first and the second major action of the Women for Peace, between the group petition and the Alexanderplatz event. This does not mean, however, that the women were idle in between. Quite to the contrary. They worked feverishly to participate in and organize meetings with other groups. Interest in Berlin's Frauen für den Frieden was not restricted to the capital city alone. They received invitations to present themselves and their work at smaller and larger meetings throughout the GDR. They gladly accepted these invitations even though preparing for them was very time-consuming, as they needed to work out in group discussions who they were, what they wanted, what they had in fact accomplished, and where they were going (cf. Melucci 1996a, 70–78). For example, they presented their work in the Berlin Resurrection Church's peace workshop of July 3, 1983, which was organized by the parish. The minister of this parish was Christa Sengespeick (now Sengespeick-Roos), who had joined the group. Secret informant (IM) "Martin," alias Mario Wetzky, then Beate Harembski's live-in partner, reported about the workshop (as did a number of other IMs). His guidance officer summarized the IM's report in the following way (MDA, OV "Bohle"; BfS Berlin, xx/ 2, July 11, 1983):

> He estimates the number of participants at around 2,500 people. In sum he thought the participants were split into several groups. The tone of the material presented was characterized by an aggressive antistate pacifism. Remarkable was the openness with which the participants presented themselves. The direct political effect of the various actions was hard to assess. What was apparent, however, was the joy of the participants to find themselves among so many like-minded people. Especially in that he sees a mobilizing effect for the negative forces [i.e., the workshop participants].

Since good informants knew what their guidance officers needed to hear, who in turn had a keen understanding of the relevance structures of their superiors, this report indicates how the Stasi feared (if not in these conceptual terms) the network-generating effect of shared understandings, of mutual recognition and its feedback on the validity of particular understandings. Through the party's propaganda work, the officers were familiar with the feedback loop between the experience of community and the actuality of understandings.

Thanks to Reverend Sengespeick's involvement, the women could now more easily return the invitations received from other groups, thereby contributing their bit to the formation of countrywide networks. For September 17, 1983, the women's group invited others to a "parish day—'Women for Peace'" at Berlin's Resurrection Church, which was attended by 400 to 500 people from all over the GDR. The participants split up into a number of working groups, discussing the militarization of schools and possible alternatives, the necessity of a national peace service as a replacement for military service, the political use of foe-images, the futility of civil defense in the context of a nuclear war, and related issues. The Stasi saw in this meeting a "renewed abuse of a religious event with the intention to form reactionary church and other negative inimical oppositional groups (MDA, OV "Zirkel"; MfS, ZAIG, Information 311/83)." For the women, these presentations and invitations helped to expand their personal networks.

The organizational template for the gatherings of the peace movement was inspired by the annual meetings of ministers, administrators, and laypersons of the Protestant churches in the GDR (*Kirchentage*). Peace movement meetings typically combined elements from religious services with a set of parallel thematic workshops, presenting the results of their discussions at a plenary meeting. There were also booths displaying posters and other written materials that provided information about various groups' work. An important step for the GDR-wide networking of peace groups was the 1983 Berlin gathering, under the motto "concretely for peace" (*konkret für den Frieden*, or shorter, *Frieden konkret*), that was organized by Reverend Hans-Jochen Tschiche. In 1981, Tschiche had called for the formation of a network of peace initiatives that would,

> in a concrete manner, lead to real steps toward peace. . . . For a number of reasons—following political calculus as well as tradition—it cannot be expected that the whole of the church in the GDR dedicates itself publicly to this task in a manner radical enough to meet the realities of the GDR. I know from a whole series of letters that there is a variety of local initiatives addressing the peace issue without there being any exchange between them. I therefore propose to form a brotherhood composed of lay persons and church employees uniting under the motto "peace concretely." (Cited in Neubert 1998, 474)

Henceforth, these gatherings came to be organized through an elected "continuation committee" (*Fortsetzungsausschuß*) that until 1989 managed to stage annual meetings that steadily grew in size. The first meeting took place in 1983 in Berlin. It represented about thirty-seven groups, mostly from the Berlin area. The 1986 meeting registered 120 groups from all over the GDR, and in 1988, two hundred groups exchanged their ideas (Neubert 1998). Although these meetings remained under the auspices of the Protestant Church, even though Stasi made repeated efforts to restrict them to religious purposes, and in spite of the fact that the church tried to comply to some degree, *Frieden konkret* became arguably the most important connection point for peace and civil rights activists from all over the GDR. Its significance lay precisely in creating contacts beyond the mediating offices of the church hierarchy, thus enabling the activists to projectively articulate their actions to an ever-greater degree on their own.

Frieden konkret makes for an excellent study of how such an organization, as it grows and becomes more effective politically, faces extraordinary challenges concerning its self-politics. A constant point of contention among various activists became almost naturally how far-reaching the claims made about the GDR and the demands put to the party state should or could actually go, without unduly endangering the enterprise as a whole. In other words, the issue became more to which degree and how *Frieden konkret* should actually become the organizational platform for a more encompassing oppositional movement. In the course of time it became clear that it could not possibly play this role as long as it was organized under the auspices of the church. Accordingly, in the fall of 1989 as the opportunity arose, and the need for church protection vanished rapidly, most of the more involved members sought to form other organizations capable of projectively articulating and coordinating the actions of multiple actors across time and space. Thus, *Frieden konkret* played no formal role in the fall of 1989 (Neubert 1998, 794). The all-important collaboration between the official church and nonchurch dissidents had run its course. For the further development of oppositional activities it was too much of a straitjacket. It should not be forgotten, however, that people's address books were filled with names, addresses, and telephone numbers of people and institutions they had encountered through the good offices of *Frieden konkret*. The discursive culture and meeting habitus acquired at *Frieden konkret* and similar more local gatherings continued to color the new election platforms emerging in the fall of 1989, until these were absorbed into the West German party system and the strictures of parliamentarian work in a mass democracy after the March 20, 1990 elections.

Forming contacts with the Western peace movement.

Just as important as the formation and cultivation of an ever-increasing and intensifying network of peace activists in the GDR was the institutionalization of relations with foreign activists, journalists, and politicians. Above all, the relationships with a handful of the leading members of the West German party Die Grünen (the Greens) became central to the peace, environmental, and civil rights movement in the GDR. As a party, the Greens were founded 1980 as an up-shoot of the environmental and anti-nuclear-power movement in West Germany. However, from the birth hour of the new peace movement, the Greens became deeply involved with it, while organizationally becoming one of its major pillars in West Germany (Markovits and Gorski 1993). The fluidity and interchange between the Western antinuclear power and the peace movements was guaranteed by a significant overlap in personnel. In March 1983, general elections had to be called early in the FRG because the SPD-led government of Helmut Schmidt fell apart, not least because of profound disagreements within the Social Democratic Party concerning the merits of NATO's double resolution. Surfing on the political import of the peace issue on a raft made of their party's movement connections, the Greens managed to float over the 5 percent vote threshold into the Bundestag. A minority of leading members of the Greens was eager to develop relationships with the peace, civil rights, and environmental movements in East Germany, while at the same time not shunning contacts with the GDR government. This strategy followed directly from the self-understanding of many peace activists as participants in a "block-transcending" movement that tried to overcome the confrontational style of international politics by practicing multilevel trust-building dialogues in the interest of insuring humankind's very survival in a new peaceful world order (Knabe 1995; Weißhuhn 1995).

Because the mainstream of the West German peace movement rejected the double resolution, the GDR government tried to associate itself publicly with it, for example by celebrating its achievements in the East German mass media. At the same time, the Stasi undertook major efforts to clandestinely co-opt the Western peace movement by planting secret informants in crucial positions[26] and by using the services of the DKP, the "German Communist Party," which was very active in the movement.[27] Therefore, it was only logical that Honecker wanted to receive a delegation of the Greens. And this was so in spite of the fact that in May 1983 a handful of leading Greens, among them Petra Kelly, Gerd Bastian, and Lukas Beckmann, had provoked

---

26. Perhaps the most prominent case is that of Dirk Schneider who became the Green's parliamentarian speaker for intra-German affairs (*deutschlandpolitischer Sprecher*). He contributed significantly to vilifying party members who maintained contacts with the East German peace and civil rights movement (Knabe 1995; Weißhuhn 1995).

27. The DKP was the West German successor organization to the KPD, which was outlawed in 1955 as "unconstitutional." It was financially dependent on the SED and was eager to do the latter's bidding.

the GDR leadership by staging an illegal minidemonstration at Alexander-platz. For just a few minutes they could unfold placards reading "swords into plowshares" and "nuclear disarmament in East and West" before they were arrested and promptly released. This event, widely broadcast via Western media, was meant to signal solidarity with the peace movement in the GDR whose representative were not allowed to leave the country for a European disarmament meeting in West Berlin.

The Greens were interested in a meeting with Honecker because they saw it as an apt means to showcase their dialogic, anticonfrontational approach to international relations. The meeting took place on October 31, 1983. However, the delegation did not just return straight to West Berlin. Petra Kelly and her partner, the former Bundeswehr (West German armed forces) tank-division commander turned peace activist, General Gert Bastian, and the other members of the delegation, desired to finally meet in person with representatives of the East German peace movement. Thus, they scheduled a series of encounters with individuals and groups that took place in people's apartments or, in Bärbel Bohley's case, in her atelier. During these meetings the participants wanted to get to know each other personally. But they also wanted to put the final touches to the planning of another joint East-West action. On November 6, identical appeals for disarmament were supposed to be submitted simultaneously to the American and Soviet ambassadors in Bonn and East Berlin. The action involved wider circles of peace activists in East Berlin as well as the Protestant Church whose mediation was called upon to obtain the official toleration of the action by the state (Weißhuhn 1995, 1868–71). However, the Stasi managed to thwart the Eastern part of the action by hindering all participants from reaching the embassies.

The fall meetings of 1983 were the beginning of a long series of contacts between Eastern peace activists and a handful of Green parliamentarians. In the course of time, these contacts proved to be an important resource for mobilizing international pressure to protest against travel bans against Eastern activists or to lobby for their release from jail.[28] These Greens, along-side a number of journalists accredited in the GDR, were also not shy about using their protected status to transport books, printing equipment, and whatever else was needed in support of the dissidents' work across the bor-der. Beyond the immediate practical help the logic of effects springing forth from these contacts was pinpointed by a 1983 letter from Reverend Rainer Eppelmann to the speaker of the Bundestag faction of the Greens, Lukas Beckmann (cited in Weißhuhn 1985, 1866):

28. For example, at the October 31 meeting with Honecker they lobbied for the release from prison of Katrin Eigenfeld, an important "Women for Peace" activist from Halle (Weißhuhn 1995, 1867).

Much will . . . depend on how seriously we are going to be taken abroad, how often we are going to be referred to, how often we are going to be invited, how often foreign friends of peace will ask those who govern us about their relationship to us. Moreover, what is important as well is international solidarity, the production of the impression that we are important for the growth of the West German peace movement.

Eppelmann thus expresses the hope that the continuing recognition of the Eastern peace movement by Western political parties and by the Western movement will signal to the GDR government that it can not harass the Eastern movement without consequences for the country's relationship with these Western organizations. Eppelmann also sees clearly that this link can only work to the degree that the GDR conceives these Western agencies as authorities. For a moment, it may have looked as if this authority of the Western peace movement and the Greens was lost after the Bundestag consented to the deployment of new American medium-range weapons systems. However, this was not the case. For a number of reasons, the SED began to pay increasing attention to what the capitalist world thought about the GDR. In part this had much to do with pragmatic considerations as the GDR became ever more indebted to Western lenders. This is not all, however. The GDR's craving for Western recognition runs deeper, still. It is also the consequence of the party's Manichaean ideology, its self-mythologization as a socialist David who set out to defeat the capitalist Goliath farther to the west, and of its proclamation that victory shall be declared on the basis of economic superiority. As the corroboration of the aspired superiority became ever more implausible, the GDR elites increasingly took recourse to recognition as a means of self-validation. Ironically, that recognition became more valuable if it did not come from the Eastern brother countries, but from the Western class enemy. We will see, especially in the next chapter, how it is the actual, feared, and imagined impact of dissident activities on the recognition bestowed upon the GDR that especially provoked the ire of the state. That this situation was not just born out of the increasing interest calculus of the 1980s can even be traced to the political parts of the penal law of the GDR, which are very much concerned with the impression of the GDR in foreign countries and what GDR citizens could do to affect it negatively.

In sum, the peace groups in East Berlin rapidly increased their alternative networks of authority within the GDR and outside the country to groups as well as to prominent Green politicians in West Germany. This expansion gave them the feeling of being part of an international movement of like-minded people, engaged for a common important cause. These networks provided them with a public for the discussion of their ideas and the presentation of their actions, for which they found local, national, and international recognition. This was very important, as peace activists' forced marginalization at home often led to the weakening of older networks of friends and family and colleagues at work. Often this was the case because they were no longer allowed to practice their professions (e.g., Gerd Poppe, Thomas Klein), or because they more or less voluntarily abandoned their formal education (e.g., Ulrike Poppe), or left jobs they no longer found satisfying (e.g., Reinhold Weißhuhn). These new alternative networks were central for the formation of changing understandings of socialism.

Setback and a new victory

Beate Harembski's premonition of real danger following her temporary arrest on Alexanderplatz was confirmed only two months later. On November 22, 1983, the Bundestag, the FRG's lower house of parliament with its conservative majority elected earlier that year, declared the arms-reductions negotiations with the Soviet Union failed. In keeping with the logic of the double resulution, this pronouncement paved the way for the deployment of American medium-range cruise missiles and Pershing IIs on West German soil. In an eleventh-hour effort, the East Berlin women's group tried to support their Green friends in Bonn with a telegram, read out loud by Petra Kelly in her speech to the assembly, that pleaded with the Bundestag members to vote against the deployment of new weapons systems. To make their appeal more tangible, the Greens distributed pictures taken by East Berlin's Women for Peace. They showed East Berlin children as the putative targets of the new NATO missiles.

The Bundestag's decision for deployment threw many members of the peace movement into a depression. For years they had tried to stop the arms race. They had spent countless hours of their leisure time in meetings, often at the expense of their families and at the cost of personal tensions; they had taken actions posing considerable risks not only to their own careers but also to their social existence; in many ways they had risked themselves. And yet they had obviously failed to achieve their immediate goal, and they perceived this failure acutely. Indeed, their growing self-understanding as political agents, which had only recently become more stable, was negatively corroborated through this decision. Freya Klier, theater director, actress, and peace activist, caught the mood of the moment in her diary (1989, 51):

> Thus, this year was not only a Luther year and a Karl Marx year, but it became also the year of the missiles. Total resignation. "Making peace with the weapons of the weak"—nothing much came of it. And yet, the movement was impressive. Not only in the West, we too got involved under much less favorable conditions. In our peace circle the number of Stasi guys is increas-

ing. It looks as if we had become a case study for their strategies of dissolution. . . . Many of my friends are worn down beyond measure, asking for permission to leave the country. All night discussions: why leave, why stay?

This feeling of powerlessness in spite of best efforts was amplified by rumors among East German peace circles that NATO's deployment decision would be followed with a crackdown on peace groups in the GDR since the party state's diplomatic reason for constraint was now gone. The credibility of these rumors points to the groups' analysis about the sources of their improbable success, which in their eyes might have given them a false sense of security. And, as always when a cherished understanding is corroborated negatively, hope lies at first in the cultivation of resonanaces of past achievements, in the scouting for indirect corroboration previously underplayed or overlooked, and in the mutual almost ritualistic recognition of alternative understandings. The hope is that together these validations generated from within the group might be capable of restoring the sense of agency drawn into question by the negative corroboration. The looming uncertainty, the premonition of arrest, but also the hopeful turn toward friends far and near comes to the fore in a letter Bärbel Bohley wrote in November 1983 to the West Berlin group Women for Peace (Kukutz 1995, document 16, 1374):

> During the last last year many women came together to resist their incorporation into the armed forces. We had the experience that it is possible, even in the GDR, that isolated individuals can form a community. Together we have developed imagination and courage, and they cannot be banished from the GDR anymore, even if some of us might sit in prison today. . . . State security [Stasi] errs if it believes that there are ring leaders in the peace movement that one only has to throw into prison to enjoy peace from peace. An ever-increasing number of human beings do not want to live anymore in the shadow of missiles, do no longer want to deceive themselves with civil defense exercises. . . . It is impossible to lock them all up. Perhaps it will no longer be possible that 500 women can meet . . . but many more women will find ways to resist.[29]

Barely a month later, Stasi caught the New Zealand peace activist Barbara Einhorn as she was leaving the GDR. She had visited East Berlin to collect materials about the women's group whose activities she aimed to portray in an English publication. The four women who had met with her to supply her with these materials were arrested for suspicion of "treacherous transmission of information" (*landesverräterische Nachrichtenübermittlung*), accord-

29. Although this letter was written three days before the Bundestag resolution, the fact that the Bundestag would vote for the deployment of missiles was already patently obvious.

ing to article 99 of the political part of the penal code of the GDR punishable with prison terms of between two and five years. Two of them, Jutta Seidel and Irena Kukutz, were released quickly. Against Bärbel Bohley and Ulrike Poppe, however, preliminary legal proceedings were opened and they were kept in jail. At the same time Stasi shut down the private day-care center the Poppes had started in collaboration with other families in an abandoned storefront in Prenzlauer Berg.

Even though the arrest did not come entirely unexpected, as I have just indicated, it shook the women's group to the core. Christa Sengespeick-Roos remembers (1997):

> We were afraid Bäbel Bohley and Ulrike Poppe would be deported to the West. . . . We . . . barely dared to meet in private apartments anymore (44). . . . We too waited for our apprehension. Each of us did so differently. One took her lotion to be important as not to acquire wrinkles behind bars; another urgently needed her own pair of slippers. My nightmares were directed to the need of going to the dentist in jail. Each of us had acquired a substitute fear to be better able to face the real one (46–47).

Nevertheless, after six weeks in jail (including Christmas and New Year's), both women were released and the charges against them were dropped. As soon as it was clear that the two women would not be released after the familiar one- to two-day period in temporary custody, friends and family mobilized national and international protest. They did so with the help of Eastern church officials, established contacts with Western journalists and Western politicians. They in turn used both public and diplomatic channels to exert pressure on the GDR government. Shortly before Bohley and Poppe were eventually released, members of the group pondered turning up the pressure for their release by organizing a hunger strike in Berlin's Resurrection Church. However, this idea was dropped at the recommendation of the church leadership, which indicated that such an action might only hinder diplomatic efforts.[30]

The Stasi used these efforts of the activists to mobilize domestic and international support to investigate who alarmed whom when, how, and with what effect. They aimed to collect information that could be used for a trial; but they also wanted to learn more about the movement's mode of operation to be better able to undercut such communications in the future.

---

30. Somebody in the East Berlin peace movement with contacts to Western journalists spread the rumor that Poppe and Bohley themselves had begun a hunger strike in prison. This politics of false information for the purpose of attaining a particular political goal was later fiercely debated among peace activists. The two women's purported hunger strike had nothing to do with the plans of their friends outside prison to begin a hunger strike in Resurrection Church.

Throughout the time the two women spent in jail, as well as directly after their release, the Stasi also recorded how various members of the group reacted emotionally to the unfolding situation. The alarmed preparations of other women for a potential arrest were recorded with as much interest as the reactions of the prisoner's family.[31] For example, after the release of the secret informant, Sascha Anderson (secret informant "Fritz Müller"), one of the best-known figures within Prenzlauer Berg's literary scene, informed his guidance officer that Lutz Rathenow, a competing poet, systematically compared the arrest of members of a punk group with that of Bohley and Poppe, coming to the conclusion that publicity alone led to the latter's release.[32] This is also the conclusion the women themselves drew. Robert Havemann's strategy of performing protest in sight of a wider national and international audience was corroborated anew. What looked like a devastating blow to the group at first, proved yet again to have the contrary effect—at least on the leadership of the group. For others, however, it corroborated suspicions that the group's activities carried more risks than they were ready to take on. A sorting process was set in motion, leading some to continue and others to drop out of the women's group that resembled the one I have already described in the context of the Alexanderplatz action.

Finding a political voice in night prayer

Christa Sengespeick-Roos says (1997, 45) that during the imprisonment of Bärbel Bohley and Ulrike Poppe she imagined organizing a "political night prayer" once the two women were released. Political night prayers are a form of religious service that emerged in West Germany's protest culture after 1968.[33] After Poppe's and Bohley's liberation, the women's group set out to

---

31. For example, in the "Information über die Reaktionen auf die Inhaftierung von Poppe, Ulrike, Bohley, Bäbel u.a." (MDA, OV "Zirkel"; MfS, XX/2, Berlin, December 15, 1983), Stasi records the relatively calm and analytical reactions of Poppe's husband. Such characterizations could later be used for the production of character profiles depicting Gerd Poppe as a "professional" with the insinuation that this was attributable to the fact that he worked in the service of some Western intelligence outfit (see next chapter).

32. Compare MDA, OV "Zirkel"; "Tonbandabschrift: Information zu Uricke [sic] Poppe und Bärbel Bohley," MfS, XX/9, Berlin, 1 February 1984. Dissident groups in other parts of the GDR also experienced Western publicity as safety enhancing. See, for example, the interview with Roland Jahn in Kowalczuk 2002a, 137–47. There he tells how a report in one of West Germany's most prestigious political TV magazines about a wave of arrests in Jena in 1982 led to the release of all those imprisoned. He concludes: "This was an incredible victory. It was very satisfying and it showed us: publicity, publicity and again publicity" (141).

33. The idea dates back to an initiative of Protestant theologians Dorothee Sölle and Fulbert Steffanski, as well as to writer Heinrich Böll and others who wanted to celebrate a "political

plan the first of what would become a series of four events. One remarkable aspect of these events is that they constituted a self-conscious effort to expand the counterpublic (Warner 2002) that the women had established in their group meetings and through their participation in peace movement network events to a new level of openness. They connected this invitation to expand "their" counterpublic with the hope to help with the formation of a wider solidarity among participants. The organizers promised a space to think, work through, and practice political understandings within a wider public.

This is how Christa Sengespeick-Roos describes central aspects of a weekend meeting at a church-owned retreat dedicated to the preparation of their first political night prayer (1997, 47):

> In the little wooden church in Hirschluch [location of the retreat] we sat on the floor to find a rhythm for our lamentation [after "Something in the Air," a tune from the soundtrack of the movie *The Strawberry Statement*]: "Come all, let us lament, / it is high time, / we have to scream, / lest we are overheard." We drummed and knocked. Each of us tried to find her own lament. We read them aloud to each other and we assisted each other in formulating them.

Beyond the mutual authorization by agreeing on comparable kinesthetic and emotive understandings in the joint performance of rhythmic laments, it is noteworthy that the use of popular music from the 1970 student-movement cult film during the preparations created significant resonances to the time of the women's political coming of age in the context of 1968.[34] Thus, important biographical and historical-political resonances with older emotive, discursive, and kinesthetic understandings were created, which also gave rise to a sense of belonging.

The first night prayer of the Women for Peace took place on the evening of May 23, 1984. It lasted for almost three hours and according to the Stasi was attended by about 350 people, mostly interested women, but also by two

---

service" at the national meeting of German Catholics (*Katholikentag*) in 1968. When this service was put on the program at 11 p.m. they ironically dubbed it "political night prayer." From 1968 to 1972 political night prayers were celebrated monthly in Cologne's oldest Protestant church after the Catholic archbishop prevented their celebration in any of Cologne's far more numerous Catholic churches. Sölle describes them in the following words: "They consisted in political information and its confrontation with biblical texts, a short speech, a call for action, and finally a discussion with the parish" (1995, 71–72).

34. *The Strawberry Statement* tells the story of a reluctant Columbia University student protester who is drawn into the student movement by falling in love. The most famous title of the soundtrack of *The Strawberry Statement* is arguably "Something in the Air," a title that was subsequently used in a number of film soundtracks—I suspect precisely because it creates resonances with the *Lebensgefühl* (sense of existing) of a whole generation at a particular moment in time.

church officials, employees of the U.S. embassy, two Western journalists, and of course a number of Stasi informants. In many ways it followed the format developed during the retreat. In her opening remarks, Reverend Sengespeick introduced participants to the practice of lamenting as an ancient biblical practice in which especially powerless women can find expression for their suffering. Moreover, she argued, by articulating their suffering they can contribute to a revitaliztion of public life in dire times. This, she suggested, is possible because the articulation of suffering creates community and constitutes a first step to regaining meaning and thus orientation in life. Following the idea that the lamentation as a description of the present needs to be connected with intercessions as a sign of hope, the service had two main parts framed by shorter sermons, readings, and music. In the first part, twenty-seven women and three men presented their individual short laments to the congregation, each followed by the signature verse of the event ("Come all, let us lament . . .") sung by musicians to the tune of "Something in the Air." As the tune was well known to the congregation, the audience could easily join in the singing while also accompanying it with rhythmic knocking against the benches. Together, singing and beat combined into a chorus of recognition. Sengespeick-Roos says (2006): "Even today after 23 years, I still have this rhythm in my ear. . . . It was very impressive."

About half of the laments were carefully prepared by the women in dialogue with others, where the emphasis was helping each woman to find her "authentic" individual voice. The other half of the laments were spontaneously presented in the church by the audience. In addition, the attendees had the opportunity to affix their personal laments in written form to a "wailing wall" (*Klagemauer*). In content, the laments were rather different. Some spoke about personal anxieties and problems, such as tiredness and the lack of meaningful time with children. Others used their laments to make connections between personal problems and policy issues ranging from health care and education to national defense. Yet others lamented about the political state of the world, especially the unequal distribution of income and the arms race. The second half of the evening consisted of twenty-one individual intercessions, of which five were offered on behalf of political prisoners. These were the most direct indictments of socialism as a political system offered during the evening. Many others expressed hope for the ability to do the right thing, to resist, speak, or act up. In between both parts an old Reformation-age church song was intoned, calling upon Germans to wake up to set aright contemporary perversions of justice and judgment. This was followed by what the organizers called "agape meal" (en lieu of the Lord's supper), which the congregation celebrated by eating lard sandwiches arranged in the shape of a missile.

Seen from the perspective of a political epistemology undertaken in terms of the sociology of understanding, this first political night prayer is very interesting. It offered a vehicle for the transformation of subjective worries, fears, and grievances, of personal discursive, kinesthetic, and emotive understandings into political, discursive ones. The catalyzing agent in this transformation was, where it worked, a jointly celebrated ritual. As with all rituals, the enabling condition is the kinesthetic understanding of unity, which is provided by the spatial sequestration of participants from an outside world—here through the walls of a church—as well as by the simultaneous involvement in the same activity—here singing and rhythmic knocking. These kinesthetic orderings can, especially through synchronized movement, directly lead to an emotive understanding of we-ness through mutual authorization in agreement. What helped here tremendously is the shared and thus mutually recognized resonance of the music, which triggered, in many of the participants, the same fond memories of the 1968 youth culture. Thus the recalled we-ness of a nostalgically refracted past could be projected onto the present. The central epistemic dynamic of the ritual proceeded on the basis of the mutually authorizing kinesthetic and emotive we-understanding. It worked through recognition of discursive-emotive understandings of seemingly personal woes and wishes on two different levels. First, each individual presentation was recognized through the chorus of singing and knocking. Second, and probably equally importantly, the articulation of understandings by others through a public presentation recognized similar understandings held by members of the audience who might have never said them aloud and in some cases may not even have articulated them before.[35] Politically speaking, this process validated the constitution of a "we" outside of the parameters set by the party state. Equally important was the joint transformation of seemingly personal ailments into social ones, a movement that could ultimately trigger questions about their insitutional causes, thus paving a way to their politicization through defetishization.

To say that the women celebrated their first political night prayer as a resounding success would be an understatement. They were ecstatic! The very fact that they had managed to pull this event off and bring it to such a successful conclusion was the agency-validating antithesis to Poppe's and Bohley's incarceration in winter. After it was all over they gathered in the church to dance through the night to the rhythm of drums. The feeling of

---

35. The analysis of multimodal understandings through interlocking forms of validation offered here bears again some similarity with Collins's (2004) account of the production of what he calls "emotional energy" through "rhythmic attunement" in a ritual focus. Both can be read as constructivist accounts of collective effervescence. As I see it, the advantage of the analysis in terms of understandings and their validation offers a process dynamic to comprehend transformations of agency, authority, social networks, and identity.

total political paralysis had given way to a renewed celebration of political agency. For the Stasi, however, following the logic of Manichaean thinking, the women's gain was the party state's loss. It interpreted the event in all of its components as "directed against the foundations of the socialist political order, consisting in assertions pessimistic in tone carrying implicitly the character of demands" that were judged as "attacks on socialism"; they saw the organizers of the event as "negative inimical forces." The Stasi documents leave no doubt that their authors wanted to communicate that the very idea that socialism could be the source of sufferings as presented in lamentations and intercessions was simply preposterous. The Stasi judged the event as so important that the ministry's analytical branch (ZAIG) wrote a "party information," that is, a report sent on to the party leadership, in this case to Honecker and three other members of the politburo to inform them specifically about this event. As measures to prevent the repetition of such an event, the Stasi suggested exerting pressure on the Church to prevent the "political abuse" inherent in such services in the future. Such "abuses" were seen to endanger the relationship between church and state in the GDR.[36]

Carried by the of success of their first venture, the women aimed at a second political night prayer in a little more than a month. This time the idea was to feature expressions of hope more prominently. They chose the parable of the sower (Mark 4:3–20) as a the biblical anchor for formulating an antiphonally presented meditation over hopes fulfilled and dashed; this preceded the presentation of twenty-three individual wishes. After pronouncing his or her wish each speaker placed dirt into a bucket as a sign of her hope. Although the second night prayer looks at first glance very similar to the first one, perhaps even more successful if the number of visitors (Stasi estimated 500) is the right indicator, the women report universally to have been very disappointed by this second event. The question is "why?"

A close comparison of the individual contributions to the first and second events shows interesting differences.[37] Not only were there far fewer spontaneous participatory statements in the second event, but also their content had changed in interesting ways. The new texts were more limited to personal narratives; references to politics were more indirect and less daring. This does not mean that there was no political effect in the mutual recognition of these publicly articulated hopes. Yet the narratives of the participants show that the epistemic effect of the ritual was more mitigated than during the first night prayer. Moreover, the music that was chosen the sec-

36. The evaluation uses standard formulas. They are cited from an "Information" (MDA, MfS, ZAIG, Nr. 221/84).

37. I would like to thank Christa Sengespeick-Roos for making a recording of this event available to me.

ond time around came from the repertoire of the contemporary Protestant Church song literature. This music was mostly unkown among the participants, who in their majority did not regularly attend church. Accordingly, there was no rhythmic knocking, no widespread chiming in, helping with the formation of a sense of we-ness resulting from the mutual authorization. And indeed, judging from the Stasi reports there is no doubt that from the state's perspective the second event was seen as much less provocative. In a party information report, Stasi wrote:

> ... the organizers of the event were keen to prevent open attacks on the political and social order of the GDR. They tried to give the event a stronger religious character. They refrained from instigating provocative actions, such as the erection of a wailing wall which can be used to post "opinions."[38]

What had happened? Following the party state's urging, the church, in part represented by the secret informants in its midst, did exert pressure on the women to cut more individual (and therefore less controllabale) forms of expression to a minimum and to stay closer to standard liturgical practice. More, Christa Sengespeick-Roos remembers (1997, 141) that Manfred Stolpe, in all likelihood a secret informant,[39] warned her before the second event that what they had done during the first political night prayer violated the penal law of the country, counting out the possible prison terms for each woman. He suggested that the whole group might get arrested right after the next night prayer. Sengespeick says:

> I went home [after a meeting with him in preparation of the second night prayer], barely seeing the sun. I worried about my daughter. . . . The anxiety which you [addressed to Stolpe] instigated in me, I seemed to have transmitted to the others. We sang more harmless songs.

---

38. MfS, ZAIG, "Information 3377/1984, quoted from Kukutz (1995, 1314–15). Note also the use of scare quotes.

39. Manfred Stolpe was the administrative head of the Union of Protestant Churches in the GDR (Bund des evangelischen Kirchen in des DDR, or BEK). Unlike the cases of other representatives of the Protestant Church, for example, Bishop Gienke, Günter Krusche, or Reverend Gartenschläger, the question of his collaboration with the Stasi has never been resolved entirely. To this day he denies having worked as a secret informant, and there are no documents that unambiguously prove that he has. The usual written self-obligation is missing, as is a proper informant file. Yet circumstantial evidence about what he knew and when strongly suggests that he did work as a secret informant. These uncertainties in no way impeded his political career after unification. Perhaps they even furthered them. He joined the SPD, became a much liked governor of the new state of Brandenburg, and later, with less political fortune, joined Chancellor Schröder's cabinet as minister of transportation.

In fact, the church leadership made a concerted effort to cancel the event altogether. The night before, it called a meeting of the Resurrection Church's parish council, which was visited by several representatives of the church leadership. The council however, backed its minister and the event could go on as planned.

The traces of the state's efforts at intimidation transmitted by the church leadership are clearly visible in the altered structure and content of the second political night prayer. The all too apparent danger led the women into conscious and unconscious strategies of hedging. Not surprisingly, then, the first event appeared more like an agency-affirming creation of a free public sphere, while the second, especially in comparison with the first, made the intimidating presence of the party state all too palpable in tone and in the content of the messages as well as in the choice of music. Hence their considerable disappointment. This created tensions among the various members of Frauen für den Frieden, especially between the minister on the one hand and central founding figures of the women's group, like Ulrike Poppe and Bärbel Bohley, on the other.

Sengespeick-Roos reports that after the second event none of the women came to her to even shake her hand and or to say anything. They just left. She says, "for the church I was one of the women, and for the women I was a representative of the church. I was caught in between and felt abandoned." Some of the Women for Peace began to see where the limitations of liturgical forms under the ultimate authority of the church and its particular state-church compact lay for any effort to create a counterpublic. They wanted more. Says Ulrike Poppe:

> This political night prayer is a form in which Christians can do justice to their this-worldly responsibility . . . but for me this should not have been the only form, and others thought likewise. It is a form with a limited public appeal.

The tensions among the participants notwithstanding, this was not yet the end of the political night prayers. Nevertheless, a year of self- and other politics, of discussions in the group and negotiations with the church, was necessary to launch another one. It took place in May of 1985 and thematized Trümmerfrauen, the women who, after World War II, cleared away the rubble from the bombed-out German cities (Sengespeick 1997, 100–112). The Stasi reports about this event make clear that it had provocative potential in touching on several taboos. By questioning the motives of women participating in the removal of debris after World War II, the third night prayer called on its participants to question the heroic foundation myths of the GDR that are epitomized in the first line of its national anthem "resurrected from ruins." Using rubble as a guiding metaphor, the texts and performances

of the evening suggested that such myths alongside institutional arrangements form something of a historial debris that has to be removed to open
fresh vistas on a brighter future. In a collective performance reminiscent of
the previous two night prayers, the removal of debris was again enacted with
"bricks" made of discared cardboard boxes carrying party propaganda slogans as inscriptions, such as "The party is always right," "If you want peace
prepare for war," or "Chemistry creates wealth, beauty, and bread." These
bricks were piled up in front of the altar. In leaving the church the participants were supposed to turn themselves into *Trümmerfrauen* removing the
"bricks," thus gradually opening the view onto a brighter future signified by
the altar. This event featured no spontaneous declarations from the participants. It was scripted throughout, if with considerable cunning as a Stasi
report remarks (Sengespeick-Roos 1997, 111): "It is the intention that every
participant who removes a piece of debris will present a reason for doing so.
However they will use already published texts for this purpose to create an
appearance of legality."

The last event in this series took place in June 1987, another two years
later, in the context of (but not programmatically included in) the annual
meeting of Protestants in the GDR (*Kirchentag*) as well as the 750th anniversary celebration of the city of Berlin. The theme this time was the sense of
alienation in one's own city. The biblical anchor was the Babylonian captivity
of the Jewish people. Everybody could understand through a meditation
on the 137th Psalm ("By the rivers of Babylon . . .") that the constantly self-
praising city forcing its citizens to chime in to this incessant and thus alien-
ating self-adulation was the GDR; everybody could understand that the Jews
in captivity were the GDR citizens, longing for a different home, a different
state. In the middle of the nave the organizers had erected a tower of Babel,
which they deemed also a "tower of power," which in yet another symbolic
performance they eventually disassembled to open the view onto the choir
of the church with the altar set up for another agape meal.

EXPERIENCE TRANSFORMS PART OF THE PEACE INTO A
CIVIL RIGHTS MOVEMENT

There is hardly ever only one reason why a particular institutional form
gives way to another. It is also hardly ever the case that older institutions
simply disappear completely. Instead, institutional transformations often
lead—at least in the short- to medium-run—to a greater plurality, a wider
field of institutional arrangements. So while Frauen für den Frieden lived
on, by 1985 some of its most active members, especially Ulrike Poppe and
Bärbel Bohley, were eager to try something new. For one, the peace issue had
lost considerable steam. NATO's double resolution was a concrete political

measure that could be used to mobilize people. It provided them with a concrete political goal that was interpretable as significant and attainable within a manageable temporal horizon. With the deployment decision this goal had vanished without a plausible successor.

Moreover, the peace movement had transformed people's understanding about what successful opposition work might look like. Thus many men active in more or less clandestine theoretical discussion circles began to look for new ways to get involved. Many of them had initially smiled somewhat condescendingly upon the women's initiative.[40] But once it had moved to center stage, something of a political Venus envy set in. Then, there were, in the meantime, members of a younger generation deeply frustrated by the party state who looked for ways of coming to terms with their situation. They were born in the early to mid-1960s; they never had a career in the GDR; and they had none of the reverence for socialism as an ideal that members of the 1968 generation (born mostly in the late '40s and early '50s) still harbored in their hearts. They were also willing to risk more than older activists who had to take into account their partners, children, and established networks of friends. These younger hotheads found an increasingly open ear among older activists. Finally, the activists' experiences during the last couple of years, the very reactions of the state (or lack thereof), and the Stasi's efforts to keep them at bay through a mixture of intimidation and harassment with the ultimate threat of imprisonment and exile, had revealed, with ever-greater clarity to most participants, what kind of a political system they were living in. In fact, their lives as activist could be characterized as a series of political experiments that yielded political knowledge otherwise not obtainable with such clarity and certainty. These experiences generated topoi for a powerful narrative of suppression, well corroborated by countless events personally experienced.

Because a vocabulary of rights became increasingly available, which was no longer primarily carried by Western, Cold War rhetoricians but by authorized others, the reflection on these narratives directly forced the issue of human rights. This authorized rights discourse had several mutually amplifying sources. First there was the immediate fact that peace had come to be talked about increasingly as a right and that activists began to reflect on the relationship between external and internal aggression and external and internal peace. The second source of a legitimate rights discourse was the dissident movements elsewhere in Eastern Europe, most notably Charter 77 in Czechoslovakia and Solidarność in Poland. The third important source was the continuing hope attached to the CSCE process, a central piece of

---

40. In their initial evaluation of the potential of the women's group, dissident men, the Protestant Church, and Stasi all echoed one another in their patriarchical prejudice.

which was the human rights charter. And finally, it bears mentioning that the Greens brought with them a language of rights geared toward emancipatory politics that was free of liberal Western Cold War rhetoric. Most importantly, however, the rights discourse made sense in light of the dissidents' own experience of marginalization and persecution.

In addition to the obvious freedom of speech, three human rights issues galvanized their interest. First, the freedom to travel became a heartfelt concern. Since the peace movement understood itself as "block-transcending," the more prominent members of GDR peace initiatives were regularly invited to attend meetings in Western Europe. The Stasi, regularly screening the mail of the key figures it had under surveillance, carefully registered such invitations and made doubly sure that travel visas were not granted.[41] While this was no less then expected by the activists, the invitations, transforming abstract desires to visit Paris or Rome into concrete projects central to their identities, made the issue all the more vexing. When, however, the state also started to restrict their travel to the neighboring Eastern European countries, with whom contacts had also expanded, they got really alarmed. Their sense of being "walled in" became heightened.[42]

The second human rights issue of high practical relevance was the freedom to choose one's profession. Through various means the state kept a number of highly qualified activists from practicing their profession. Among them were, to name but a few, the mathematician Thomas Klein, the physicists Gerd Poppe and Martin Böttger, the philosopher Wolfgang Templin, and the painter Bärbel Bohley. Others had given up their educationally adequate employment voluntarily because their workplaces became sites of the disciplinary state interventions. Examples are Reinhold Weißhuhn who gave up his job as city planner and Vera Wollenberger (now Lengsfeld) who gave up her work as an editor for children's books. Yet others did not even complete their education because they found the prevailing atmosphere unbearable. At the same time, however, the state forced everybody into some kind of employment. According to state ideology, work constituted membership in the political community (Kohli 1994). In this sense the constitution of the GDR speaks (much like the central party documents) of the "working people"

41. In this particular case this measure was apparently not driven by the desire of the state to prevent the possible flight of peace activists. Quite to the contrary, the threat of prison terms was often used to force people out of the country. The point was, rather, the party state's attempt to monopolize the representation of the peace issue for its own Peace Council (Friedensrat).

42. Travel rights remained a double-edged sword for many activists, because they always feared, rightly, that some GDR citizens might only join them to get into conflict with the Stasi, in order to find themselves eventually released into West Germany. Their struggle consisted in staying, not in leaving the country.

(*Werktätige*), where liberal Western constitutions would speak of "citizens." Consequently, the GDR not only knew a right to work, it also knew a duty to work.[43] In the case of unemployment, one of the jobs offered by the authorities had to be eventually accepted. Violations could be punished by prison. Accordingly, many had to accept employment that was decisively below their level of education. Gerd Poppe found work as a stoker in a public pool; Thomas Klein became a cost accountant for a furniture factory, and so on. For many dissidents the only way out of the state imposed dilemma to either acquiesce to the political demands connected with a meaningful career or to accept the potential drudgery of menial work lay in seeking work for the churches.

The third human rights issue that their activism had foregrounded was the freedom of information. How would one even know how many missiles, tanks, and soldiers were deployed? How would one know how the people of the GDR really felt about issues of peace and rearmament? How would one know how people elsewhere in the world thought about such issues? How could one know with sufficient degree of certainty what the environmental consequences of the armament industry really were? In all of these cases one had to take the government's word for fact; one had to accept the claim of the strategic necessity of secrecy given the East-West confrontation. All independent attempts to acquire such information were dangerous because they could immediately come under the suspicion of espionage. By default, then, one had to rely on Western media electronically broadcast or smuggled in print across the border. However, Western information about GDR-internal affairs was more than sparse. This dearth of independent information was particularly painful because the state systematically used its informational advantage as a tool of domination. It demanded obedience due to better oversight (which unfortunately could not be shared for secrecy reasons).

In a country such as the GDR, where the state systematically suppressed political activities outside of its own control, any independent citizen movement, no matter what its substantive aim, would eventually be pushed toward featuring human rights concerns centrally.

The Initiative for Peace and Human Rights

Arguably East Berlin's most significant civic rights group, the Initiative für Frieden und Menschenrechte (Initiative for Peace and Human Rights—also known by its acronym IFM) emerged as a result of a conflict within a wider field of peace activists who became interested in human rights issues. Since this conflict is illustrative of processes of network differentiation within the

---

43. Article 24.2 of the 1968 constitution states: "The right to work and the duty to work constitute a unity."

dissident scene in East Berlin, which went hand in hand with a differentiation of political understandings, I will begin this section by recounting it in greater detail.

In preparation for the Berlin peace workshop in 1985, members of various groups began to think about organizing a weekend seminar to discuss human rights issues. They presented this idea at the workshop and found much interest, so they set to work in the late summer and early fall of that year.[44] In the process they could convince Reverend Hilse of Treptow's Church of the Confession to offer the parish's facilities for the seminar. From the beginning, the collaboration proved more difficult than expected. There were a wide variety of opinions about how the topic of human rights should be explored. Two poles emerged in the course of the discussions. One set of people tended toward a rather concrete problem-centric approach inspired by the work of the Czech dissident group Charter 77. They were interested in the actual human rights situation in the GDR, basing their understandings of what human rights are on the UN declaration and the Helsinki accord of the CSCE process, that is, treaties to which the GDR was a signatory. Others favored a more theoretical and historical method to tackle the issue. They were interested in the very emergence of the idea of universal human rights at a particular historical juncture and the role this idea has played in politics ever since, including its use as a weapon in the Cold War. What they clearly wanted to avoid was the simple normalization of liberal freedom rights they saw as a sure way to reinstate an unproductive "East" versus "West" dichotomy.

The content of the seminar was not the only divisive issue, however. Organizational questions such as whom to invite proved even more contentious. Some people were eager to invite Western participants (especially members of the Green party) and to allow Western journalists as observers. For them this was not only a way to reach a broader GDR audience via the Western electronic mass media, but they also felt that such an invitation would increase their own security. Others were of the opinion that a seminar with Western participants on human rights might not only lead to a much less interesting discussions, but that it was also an unnecessary provocation of the state, which might pose considerable dangers to the participants. They feared in particular that the presence of Westerners would keep potential

---

44. This is not the first time that human rights were critically debated within the GDR. In consequence of both the GDR's accession to full UN membership in 1973 and then the Helsinki Process with its final documents, both of which made the GDR a signatory to human rights charters, a discussion ensued, for example, in Protestant Church circles. However, and in light of what follows significantly, the church abandoned its human rights work and internal debate in the context of its 1978 agreements with the state (Neubert 1998, 356–59).

participants who still had real jobs from attending for fear of exposure (Rüddenklau 1992, 51–54).

In spite of these differences the seminar was scheduled for the weekend of November 23/24, 1985. Yet, a mere week before the event, and at the behest of the church leadership, the parish council orally retracted its support, because it claimed to be in the possession of information that participants had invited Western journalists and peace activists and were also about to use the seminar as a launch pad for a GDR-wide civil rights group modeled after Charter 77. Most likely (I have no documentary proof for this point), the Stasi had gotten wind of the ambitions and hopes harbored by some of the organizers through its extensive network of secret informants. They presented this information to the church leadership as proof that it was being "abused for political purposes," and that it thus stood to violate the state-church compact. It probably demanded that the church cancel the seminar in an effort to prevent an impending public relations disaster for the GDR government. It is likewise not implausible that somebody warned the church leadership, which, in anticipation of considerable trouble with the state authorities, intervened in the interest of smooth state-church relations.

On the day of the canceled seminar, activists convened in Wolfgang Templin's apartment to discuss how to proceed. It was decided to continue with the preparation for a seminar, albeit with a more clearly structured organizational team (Rüddenklau 1992, 52). Three activists were elected to serve as speakers and to write a protest declaration to the church. These were Peter Grimm and Ralf Hirsch, two members of the younger generation of activists, and Wolfgang Templin, an older, highly regarded activist who started his political life as a member of the SED. All three leaned thematically toward a pragmatic approach also favoring the invitation of foreign guests. In a protest letter to the church they declared (Peter Grimm says "not quite truthfully"), that the information aired by the church as reasons for canceling the seminar were unfounded.[45] In late February 1986 the speaker trio now called itself "speaker group of the 'Initiative Peace and Human Rights'" (clearly mimicking Charter 77)—they formally addressed peace circles about the state of affairs in preparing the seminar. Thematically they announced that practical human rights questions would constitute the core of the seminar, and that they were aiming at GDR-wide work discussing the human rights situation in the country. A few days later two West Berlin radio stations spread the news that an "Initiative for Peace and Human Rights"

---

45. Several of my interview partners pointed out that they certainly wanted to form a permanent group. This could not be said publicly, however, because no church would have taken them in, and they needed a venue for such a seminar that only the church could provide.

had formed in East Berlin.[46] No doubt, the speaker trio had informed them via Roland Jahn, a GDR refugee living in West Berlin.

Predictably, content and form of the announcement triggered an angry response among activists who favored a more historical, theoretical, and strictly domestic approach to the seminar. They felt that these documents were drafted and circulated with neither their input, nor their approval. They felt faced with a fait accompli aiming at their own marginalization within the preparatory group. Another (it turned out final) meeting, called at the end of February to reconcile the differences, exploded in mutual accusations and further entrenchment with the result that the rift became now institutionally cemented. The dissenters walked out of the meeting and went on to prepare a protest resolution (dated March 6, 1986, reprinted in Rüddenklau 1992, 56–60) in which they depicted their view of what had happened paired with the accusation of massive foul play on the side of the speaker trio and their supporters. In this resolution, they too made thematic proposals, which this time focused on theoretical questions such as different notions of democracy and the historical development of the concept of rights. Henceforth, there was an "Initiative for Peace and Human Rights" (Peter Grimm, Ralf Hirsch, Wolfgang Templin, Gerd Poppe, Ulrike Poppe, Bärbel Bohley, and others). And there was *Gegenstimmen* ("Counter-Voices"), the group of dissenters chiefly drawn from two peace circles: Friedrichsfelde (Thomas Klein, Reinhard Schult, Silvia Müller) and Pankow (Vera Wollenberger and Wolfgang Wolf).

There has always been a question of the Stasi involvement in this split. The Stasi reports about the final meeting suggest that on both sides, secret informants (typically not known to one another) were busily contributing to the divide. However, these interventions were (with the possible exception of Wolfgang Wolf's) by no means decisive. The documents do not reveal any concerted Stasi action aimed at intentionally creating this division, even though splitting groups was a tried Stasi technique. Since such a maneuver would have involved several departments in the ministry and the Berlin district office, it would have in all likelihood left a paper trail. Moreover, all the involved persons I spoke with agree that the split was in the last instance caused by their own substantive disagreements.

---

46. This was the third response of the preparatory group. It named the previous circulars "document 1" (dated November 16, 1985) and "document 2" (dated December 18, 1985—an open petition to the synod of the Protestant Church) respectively, implying its own status as "document 3" (dated January 24, 1986) (MDA, "Menschenrechtsseminar 1985/86"). "Document 2" is also reprinted in Kowalczuk 2002a. A reprint of "document 3" can be found in Rüddenklau 1992, 55–56.

The emergence of an irreconcilable split can be understood by looking at the whole process of negotiating the content and form of the human rights seminar as the intersection of the individual organizers' spaces of validation. In talking (and fighting) with one another they formulated and through mutual recognition actualized understandings by working and thinking them through. In the end, two articulated, disparate understandings about substance matter, organization, and the intention of the seminar prevailed. Indeed, one could say that an emergent version of liberalism (which would at that time still have been shy to call itself that) was facing versions of critical Marxism. Each supported a distinct vision of what dissident work could and should be.[47] Surely, these ideas were floating through the discussions right from the beginning. But they were by no means as clearly actualized in particular persons as they were at the end of the process. In a sense, some critical Marxists learned that liberalism was not where they wanted to go (clearly surprised that old friends all of a sudden wanted to travel that route), while others learned that even though they might have once endorsed a critical Marxist perspective they no longer felt that it was particularly helpful in coming to terms with the situation in the GDR at this particular moment (wondering ever-more impatiently why others were clinging to it). Concurrently, with the articulation and actualization of understandings, social networks came to be reconfigured along new lines of agreement and disagreement. Some older connections endured. They built centers of crystallization around which new alignments took place.[48]

47. Labels such as "liberal" or "Marxist" have to be used with circumspection here, lest their use occlude more than it illuminates. First, it has to be noted that in either group there was certainly still a spectrum of perspectives. Second, the version of liberalism in question would have nothing to do with Western economic liberalism. It also has no link to the ontological individualism I criticized in the conclusions to the last chapter. Yet it emphasized classical liberal points such as the importance of a political civil society as a space of deliberation and negotiation between different understandings of the world and different interests. The "critical Marxism" that was at issue also no longer had much to do with the revisionism of old, the idea that communism can be reformed from within the party alone. That revisionism died in 1968 was a shared opinion among the protagonists in this conflict, following Kołakowski (1971) and after him Michnik (1985, 137). However, especially Thomas Klein, who worked simultaneously in the peace movement and in party-critical closed discussion circles, hoped that the country could be moved forward through an alliance between these two separate worlds (Klein 1995; Klein, Otto, and Grieder 1997, especially part II).

48. I wish I had been present to study the split as it occurred ethnographically. Alternatively, it would have been nice to have a dense historical record through which one could describe this process in much greater detail. Interviews are only a poor substitute for participant observation; people remember more clearly where they stood at the end of this process than what happened in between.

Seen in retrospect, the alignments taking place during the organization of the human rights seminar seem auspicious if one considers the political affiliations chosen by the various participants after 1989. The "liberals" came to associate themselves overwhelmingly with the Greens, whereas many of the "critical Marxists" continued in left-wing formations. Yet, the emergent ideological differences should not be overplayed as cause for the split. For the purposes of a seminar on human rights they could have easily been combined. What probably mattered more are particular emotional understandings and the resonance by which they came to be further actualized during the discussions. The most passionately disputed aspect of the seminar was the involvement of Westerners. Everybody was aware of the fact that the organization of such a seminar posed serious risks of criminal persecution. Yet there were very different opinions about what could be done to make the participation in this project safer. Central figures of the group of critical Marxists had spent time in prison. On the basis of manufactured evidence, Thomas Klein was sentenced to one and a half years in prison for his contacts with a West Berlin group of Trotskyites; Reinhard Schult was imprisoned for eight months for the distribution of illegal material. By contrast, the IFM members around Ulrike Poppe and Bärbel Bohley had experienced their connections with Greens and Western journalists as safety enhancing, because they could quickly mobilize international protest after they were jailed. The same measure that was connected for one group with intense fears was connected for the other with the hope of relieving them; and either group had strong corroborating evidence for their take on the security issue.

How did both groups fare with their efforts to organize seminars on their own? Not unsurprisingly, the ("liberal") IFM did not find any minister who was willing to shoulder the risk and had to abandon their plans rather fast. The critical Marxists (less ironically than it may appear) managed to organize a seminar that took place in the fall of 1986—very much on the church's terms. As we know now, it was made possible by a church administrator (Krusche) and a minister (Gartenschläger), who were both secret informants. Of the three main papers delivered at the workshop, two were from Stasi's clandestine helpers. Foreigners were of course not admitted. Even if the fact that the seminar took place at all was universally welcomed and celebrated as a success, many participants voiced their unhappiness about the program precisely because concrete human rights violations in the GDR were not centrally addressed.[49] Nevertheless, the organizers of this seminar

---

49. For contemporary reviews of the human rights seminars, see Rüddenklau 1992, 86–89 (which then appeared in the *taz*, a Western paper close to the Greens). Another much shorter

decided to stay together as a group, hence calling themselves *Gegenstimmen*, in obvious reference to the split with the IFM.[50]

The division of the preparatory group for a human rights seminar into two competing groups was by no means the last schism among dissident groups in Berlin. *Gegenstimmen* splintered anew merely two years after its own breakaway founding. In the foreground of the anteceding dispute were again questions of secrecy and publicity (Rüddenklau 1992, 194–95). The "Environmental Library" (see below) expelled a whole set of its activists, who then formed a new group that endeavored to coordinate environmental activism throughout the country (Jordan 1995, 38–40; Rüddenklau 1992, 178–80). Since I have made so much of the importance of networks of authority for the stabilization of understandings, one may wonder about the epistemic effects of such ongoing fragmentation. The networks of activists were already so large then that they could accommodate competing groups with relative ease. In fact, if anything, the competition among groups was an impetus to come up with more interesting actions. The diversity of groups and their competition about actions was also a continuous stimulant for discourse; it provided excellent occasions to think and work through understandings as long as the protagonists in the conflict kept authorizing one another. Even though every conflict and even more so every break was first accompanied by heightened self-politics, distracting the groups from action, the actual split typically made self-politics also more efficient—at least for some time. Finally, the groups did not typically become hostile enemies. Activists knew that their situation vis-à-vis the state was so weak that they could not afford not to work together where this made strategic sense. And so they did. But this was a marriage of necessity. With the demise of the party state in 1989 the old groups fragmented beyond recognition.

Two early initiatives in which IFM participants played a key role were constitutive for the group in setting its tone internally and projecting its image to others. These two actions are, like the split of the preparatory group for the human rights seminar, testimony to the changing political understandings among leading dissidents in the peace and civil rights movements

---

review (which seems to be a shortened version of the taz article) appeared in the third issue of the samizdat paper *Grenzfall* (see below), which is reprinted in Hirsch and Kopelew 1989.

50. As always, the translation of names chosen for their rich allusions is difficult. The most common meaning of "Gegenstimme" in German is "nay" in voting procedures. In music it is a voice juxtaposed to another. The further fate of this group is interesting. It created its own samizdat publication, *Friedrichsfelder Feuermelder* (Friedrichsfeldian Fire Alarm), in competition with *Grenzfall* (see below). Before the first issue appeared, the Stasi produced and circulated a complete fake first edition later known as the "zero number."

in Berlin. In fact, they amplify the magnitude and consolidate the direction of change. The first was the "Appeal on the Occasion of the UN's Year of Peace" (dated January 24, 1986) (reprinted in Kowalczuk 2002a, 153–55). Its preparation went hand in hand with "document III." It demands political steps toward the practical enforcement of human rights in the GDR, especially the freedom to travel; the repeal of key norms of the political section of the penal code that can be used to limit human rights and an amnesty of everybody sentenced under these norms; independent candidates at local and national elections; the freedom of association; the right to refuse military service; and public answers by the government to appeals like this one. The second action was the petition to the XIth party congress of the SED (dated April 2, 1986) (reprinted in Kowalczuk 2002a, 189–200). It moves decisively beyond everything previously demanded or critiqued in writing to the government of the GDR by the Berlin activists. It begins by posing the "power question," as SED members would have called it, by refuting the SED's claim to represent the people of the GDR. More, it argues that in view of its organizational form as a Leninist vanguard party bound by party discipline, it never even *could* represent the people in its diversity. From here, the petition moves on to demand a plural, open society in all sectors of social, political, and economic life in the GDR in accordance with the declaration of human rights. It expresses the expectation that an open society would also contribute to more effective, efficient, and innovative governance. The petition closes with a list of human rights violations that the signatories claim to have knowledge of. In effect, then, the document questions the legitimacy and logic of actually existing socialism from an unabashedly liberal perspective. This was not lost on other members of the peace and civil rights movements. Thomas Klein, a vocal proponent of Gegenstimmen wrote a sharp critique of the petition, to be published a year later in a samizdat publication.

Samizdat

The availability of techniques of projective articulation is central to the emergence of social movements as translocal phenomena. Even at the very beginning of the pathways into dissidence, access to nonconformist ideas through personal contacts were typically mediated by forbidden books, radio, and television programs. Telephone and mail played an important role in coordinating meetings that would be used to build personal networks. These meetings grew, throughout the period I have covered here, in scope from local to regional to national and international connections. At the beginning the church was the all-important mediating agency. It was the only organization in the entire GDR other than party state affiliates that had command over large meeting spaces, its own print media, duplication technology, and organizational communication and resource distribution channels. By contrast, church independent groups on their own had to rely on personal contacts to spread the word; they had no more than their living rooms as meeting spaces; and typewriters and carbon paper were the only means of duplication. Therefore, links to the church significantly increased their potential to projectively articulate their ideas and to call upon others to join into their cause.

The interplay between church-independent activists, their sympathizers within the church, and their supporters in the West facilitated the formation of regular samizdat publications in the mid-1980s. These publications allowed the activists to reach a wider, geographically dispersed and larger audience. The formality of written contributions and exchanges of opinion performed in front of a public also forced a certain qualitative shift in their interactions. Writing forced self-positioning moves within debates to become more reflexive.

Two of these samizdat publications became especially important among dissident circles in the GDR. The *Umweltblätter* ("Environmental Leaves"), edited among others by Wolfgang Rüddenklau for the *Umweltbibliothek* (Environmental Library), was not only the longest-running publication with the most issues (thirty-two between 1986 and 1989) but also the paper with the largest number of copies printed per issue (up to 4,000).[51]

The institutional basis for the extraordinary success of the of the *Umweltblätter* was the decision of Reverend Simon of the Church of Zion to provide refuge for the peace and environmental circle that had become homeless after the collaboration with another parish broke down. With its new rooms in the basement of the Church of Zion's community center, the group started to realize a long-held dream of creating an "environmental library" (*Umweltbibliothek*, locally known also as *UB*) as an information center for peace circles about environmental degradation. They were furnished by the West German Greens and others with books and later on with print technology and supplies. Inspired by other samizdat publications, they decided to issue an information bulletin they settled on calling *Umweltblätter*. Since the group was officially part of a parish, they were legally covered by the state-church compact that allowed the church to produce its own information media as long as the circulation was kept within its perimeter. Samiz-

---

51. The circulation of samizdat publications was typically a multiple of the print run, because the same issue was typically shared by many readers. Certain articles might also be further duplicated via typed carbon copies.

dat publications produced under the auspices of parishes therefore bore the prominently displayed note "for church-internal use only."

The first important church-independent samizdat publication to appear, inspiring many others to follow suit, was *Grenzfall*,[52] edited by Peter Grimm, Peter Rölle, and Ralf Hirsch in loose connection with the IFM. It appeared in seventeen issues (mostly before 1988) with a total print run of up to 800.[53] It understood itself as an information bulletin about human rights issues in the GDR and other Eastern European countries. Since the IFM had no church affiliation, *Grenzfall* was an illegal publication whose production carried considerable risks for its organizers. Except for the narrow editorial group, no member of the IFM even had the faintest idea where the printing equipment was stored and where and when it was printed. Moreover, printing locations and press storage were shifted in the course of time to make discovery more difficult. Ironically, the man who proved indispensable in running the aged press was Rainer Dietrich, a secret informant. Probably for reasons of political opportunity—Erich Honecker wanted to visit the FRG—the Stasi took its time to make a serious attempt to bust the press. Yet, once the visit (fall 1988) was over, the Stasi moved. Through its informant Dietrich it arranged for *Grenzfall* to be printed once in the rooms of the Environmental Library albeit on *Grenzfall* equipment.[54] The Stasi's idea was to arrest the producers red-handedly in the production of an illegal publication and to use the occasion to also exert pressure on the church to close down the *UB*, thus dealing a mortal double blow to Berlin opposition groups. The Stasi's plan did not work out. Several contingencies interacted in such a way that the Stasi ended up "catching" the *UB* staff printing *Umweltblätter*, the more or less legal publication "only for church-internal use." Sure, they found *Grenzfall*'s equipment, but due to an oversight they forgot to impound it together with a central piece of equipment (the very one the secret informant had designed and used to such great effect). In consequence, the corpus delicti was inoperable, which led the prosecutor to rule it inadmissible as evidence to open criminal procedures. All those arrested had to be set free. The initiated criminal investigations were annulled. This occurred while activists set in motion an entirely unprecedented outpouring

---

52. The title *Grenzfall* is richly allusive. In one direction of literalness it could be translated as "boundary case," in the other as "falling boundaries." After the second issue its logo became a tollgate with beaver-style gnawing marks in its middle and new twigs sprouting from the gate's dead wood.

53. Kowalczuk (2002b) provides a very useful overview of samizdat publications in the late GDR. The numbers are his. They are emended from Neubert 1998, 756–66.

54. This was an important precaution because the Stasi could have easily demonstrated through its forensic specialists that an illegal publication was produced on a machine in possession of the church.

of solidarity events within and outside the GDR. Reinhold Weißhuhn of the IFM concluded in the *Grenzfall* issue appearing with only a delay (Hirsch and Kopelew 1989, 141):

> It is difficult not to tumble into a euphoric state given the course of events in the last ten days from 24 November to 4 December. This is how impressive the results and experiences were. And why shouldn't joy be wholly appropriate. For the first time in the now already longer history of emancipatory movements [in the GDR] something of its vital power and magnitude showed itself. This was no longer an isolated act of self-affirmation, and even less the breakdown after a tough defeat. . . . This time there was resistance . . . broad, spontaneous solidarity, from punk to bishop, from Wismar [Baltic seaport] to Großhennersdorf [small town outside of Berlin].

For the Stasi and the party state the ingenious double blow had turned into an unparalleled disaster.

Grenzfall aimed to document human rights violations and to provide opposition groups with a medium by which they could inform one another about their work. It was also supposed to provide a space for political commentary on current affairs. *Grenzfall* was not primarily meant as a venue for longer, theoretical disquisitions. In fact, it was the reporting about group actions in combination with depicting the state's reactions to them as human rights violations that made *Grenzfall* effective. Projectively articulated by samizdat and Western electronic media, the actions of the groups (carried out in accordance with the rights granted through the GDR's accession to international treaties) and the reactions of the state became performances in front of an ever-wider audience. This marks an important step in the development of the meaning of *oppositional action*. An action that taken on its own would be a hopeless, if not even absurd, attempt at politics because it stood no chance of ever impacting the institutional fabric of society becomes through mediated performance an apt means of politics. Like the seventeenth-century science experiments conducted in front of audiences (which also no longer carried any particular scientific, but all the more political, value), the actions of dissidents increasingly became experiments in political epistemics. They bared the human rights situation in the country and the character of the political system in the GDR. And just as public science experiments helped to spin a new moral narrative with the scientist as hero, conquering nature and ignorance, so did the dissidents' actions lend themselves to moral narration. Yet, whereas the self-descriptions of the seventeenth-century science performers were given to a wholly romantic idiom, later assimilated by socialism and touted ad nauseam, the actions of the political experimenters increasingly ventured into the picaresque. In this way they provided a hopeful gloss on their narrative's basic structuring device, the victim-victimizer dichotomy. Let me call this political strategy, this "weapon of the weak" (Scott 1985), this "tactic" of the powerless inserted into the "strategies" of the powerful (de Certeau 1984), the *ecce homo strategy*. It is a form of what Michael Biggs (2003) calls "communicative suffering."[55]

A good number of *Grenzfall's* articles tell about the opposition's old, well-rehearsed types of action. There was the steady stream of petitions that were shown to be either systematically ignored by the authorities—in violation of the law and against the state's insistence that petitions provided an apt means of political participation—or they were shown to receive answers that quite obviously did not take the concerns of the petitioners seriously. Thus the party state was performed as antidialogic—again: against its publicly cultivated self-image. In the very first issue of *Grenzfall*, for example, the IFM explained that its petition to the party congress remained (with two exception) unanswered (Hirsch and Kopelew 1989, 3). The second issue addressed a petition about the Schönberg landfill, which received vast amounts of refuse from Western countries, including, presumably, hazardous materials. The suspicion of the activists was that the GDR leadership squandered the health of the population for hard currency to alleviate the severe economic crisis. The state's response was reported in some detail to show its absurdity. The article concluded: "It became apparent again, that the GDR authorities are neither willing nor capable to enter into dialogue with church-based or independent ecological initiatives. What is supplied [by the state in answer of the petition] are mere trinkets, valuable only with regards to their comical effects (10)."

The activists sensing the power of the ecce homo strategy started to engage also in calculated provocations. Irena Kukutz explains that the trick was to think of perfectly legal actions that the state wanted to prevent from happening in spite of its own laws and regulations. For her, the Alexanderplatz action (described above) is an example for such an action. What came to be known as the "flying to Prague action" that she initiated with Bärbel Bohley is in her eyes an even better exemplar. The idea was that a number of activists with and without travel restrictions would book a flight to Prague for the same day and the same flight, while having themselves *accompanied*

55. In contradistinction to the more typical rational choice approach that focuses on the infliction of cost, Biggs emphasizes the communicative aspects of the performance of suffering. He argues that suffering signals both commitment and what he calls deprivation. Biggs has developed his insights in relation to forms of protest that involve extreme suffering, namely self-immolations (2005) and hunger strikes. Building on Biggs, I am emphasizing the fact that while dissidents could not effectively research the human rights situation in the country they could perform it, thus articulating and communicating understandings in action. The performance of suffering has an epistemic effect in corroborating a particular insight into how particular institutions operate, thus raising fundamental questions of morality and legitimacy.

by journalists on the day of the flight to document what would happen. Seventeen activists booked a flight for Interflug IF 254 on April 24, 1987. As anticipated, none of them reached the Golden City. During the days before their putative departure, they were warned that their action constituted a misdemeanor, and/or they were notified through various means that their flight had been canceled. On the day of the action they were all apprehended. Some right at their door, others on the way to, or at, the airport. They were also immediately released. The next *Grenzfall* ("5/87") reported what had happened in the form of a satire entitled "Only flying is more beautiful." It also carried an open letter to the general secretary protesting the travel limitations and a complaint in verse by Martin Böttger to the police precinct that had (probably illegally) issued a warning to him that flying to Prague constituted a misdemeanor (Hirsch and Kopelew 1989, 55–57). The subsequent issue of *Grenzfall* carried the official letter of complaint of four of the activists against the fines (between a third and half of an unskilled workers' monthly salary) they had been issued for violations of ordinances. The ecce homo strategy could obviously be used in a cascading manner.

Even though the Stasi's move against *Grenzfall* did not succeed as planned, it deeply wounded *Grenzfall*. The fatal blow came with the arrest and engineered temporary exile of several prominent IFM members in the aftermath of the Rosa Luxemburg demonstration (Templin, Hirsch, and Bohley among them). Yet, *Grenzfall*'s example was picked up by others, and samizdat became an integral and ever more sophisticated part of oppositional life in the GDR. In a roundtable discussion among several former dissidents involved in the production of samizdat publications, Stephan Bickhardt and Gerd Poppe captured the importance of samizdat with the following words (Kowalczuk 2002a, 116):

BICKHARDT: Around *Grenzfall* and the IFM there emerged a way of life (*Lebenskultur*) that I found inspiring. The most important aspect of it was, however, that a whole domain [of life] was freed from taboos. First, I can write something myself; second, I can write about injustice; third, I can publish it; and fourth, I can connect this with a joy of life. *Grenzfall* was a breakthrough for this new way of life. Politics was commented on briefly and injustices were called by their name. For the very idea of a civil society *Grenzfall* opened a gate, which motivated many to become active as well. . . .

POPPE: The real cut [with a politically acquiescent past] was action, doing as such that went so clearly beyond the talking in seminars. Those who created such publications did everything on their own: for the most part they wrote the texts, they stenciled them, duplicated and collated the sheets, they stapled them together, and then they made sure that these booklets were distributed in the entire country. This activity—in its multifacetedness—was also a push for group solidarity and the development of personality. These booklets were incredibly important for network building among GDR opposition groups.

BICKHARDT: You don't know what happens to your ideas if you print 100 copies. A society emerges and it is the one in which you would want to live. This was an incredible feeling.

CONCLUSIONS

"It was our foremost goal to create a counter-public" (*Gegenöffentlichkeit*), said Ulrike Poppe to me. And this is also how many other former dissidents are describing their work. One could say that they, alongside their dissident friends elsewhere in Eastern Europe, have "reinvented civil society" (Mastnak 2005; cf. Arato 1993; Cohen and Arato 1992; Olivo 2001; Pollack and Wieglohs 2004; Jensen and Miszlivetz 2006). It was a small civil society to be sure, but it had begun to live the kind of political life the dissidents desired for the country as a whole. There was an increasing plurality of voices; there was "freedom" breaking through "in endless meetings" (as Francesca Poletta 2002 has so aptly called it following one of her informants) on a smaller and larger scale supported by an ever more lively scene of samizdat publications distributed in print and even electronically.[56]

I have narrated the formation of this small public sphere as a consequence of the developing dynamics in intersecting spaces of validation. In these, understandings, social networks, identities, and memories emerged together, formed and reformed by the dialectics of validation. In particular, I have told this story along two intertwining dimensions. First, I have emphasized expanding and differentiating networks of authority in which political understandings could be aired and challenged, articulated and recognized. Second, I have shown how political actions increasingly took the character of experiments, whose outcomes were suitable to corroborate understandings about the GDR, its governing party, and its ideology. Let me retrace this development through its most important steps. In the last chapter I demonstrated the importance of intimate relationships with one or two friends. I have not met a single opposition member for whom such personal relationships were not a decisive step on the way to dissidence.

---

56. After an attempt to create an illegal radio station failed in the fall of 1986 (Neubert 1998, 633), a West Berlin radio station was supplied with material for regular broadcasts. Through Western electronic media, and its contacts to Western journalists, that small society even radiated into wider GDR circles.

Intimacy allowed for the experimental articulation of understandings that was freed from the weight of indexing identity in performance. Only thus could understandings be thought through, worked through, and practiced without risk to belonging or social status. Intimacy operated not so much as a refuge from reality, but as the condition for the possibility of understanding reality in the first place. It endowed people with the means to resist the other-imposed definition of the world by opening a space in which people could form their own understandings.

These close relationships typically led to the participation in wider circles of friends or acquaintances in a marginalized, nonconformist milieu such as Prenzlauer Berg. This milieu supplied opportunities for like-minded people to meet and to form smaller, more exclusive groups. These in turn tried to make contact with similar groups in Berlin and other parts of the country, leading to the formation of regional or even national networks. While it was possible in the GDR to form smaller groups, translocal networking was almost unthinkable without the help of the church. It was the only organization that could legally maintain a countrywide infrastructure of communication and meeting places outside of the party's control. In principle, networking through the good offices of the church was a possibility only for groups that worked on issues the church understood to be in its purview. The peace issue was therefore a formidable vehicle for creating alliances between religious and secular activists. The larger meeting spaces available in the church also allowed groups to reach a wider, nonorganized audience, which was not necessarily ready to give the time and to incur the risks that active participation in one of the groups entailed.[57] With growing networks, understandings and their recognition could come from more diverse and geographically more distant people. The dissidents' frequently voiced sense that they were speaking for a silent majority of the GDR population seemed corroborated by the increasing echo their actions and events created.

Up to this point recognition proceeded mostly in face-to-face interaction. Objectified, situationally disembedded recognition was only available in the form of circulating dissident literature, which, however, was similar in different places, creating common points of reference. The next step con-

---

57. The church has sometimes been criticized for not having played as active a role in accommodating dissidents as it could have. Morally speaking, such criticisms are plausible. However, sociologically speaking, the church could never have played the supportive role it did through the efforts of individual, engaged ministers if it had not been an ambivalent organization. The church's state-conformism was the shield behind which nonconformism could bloom. I am not arguing that this was a deliberate strategy. At least not for the church as a whole. However, I am arguing that this is how it worked out in terms of institutional dynamics. The dissidents could hide behind the backs of the loyalists.

sisted of expanding the reach of face-to-face meetings into the production and circulation of samizdat publications such as *Grenzfall* and *Umweltblätter*. Where the face-to-face projection of understandings was limited to a few hundred people (the number of people who could fit into a church), the more important samizdat publications could in the end reach audiences of several thousands through the continuing circulation of every single issue. Samizdat and connections to Western media also provided the grounds on which the ecce homo strategy of performing the state's suppression could become effective. Moreover, through the mediation of samizdat, the actions of others became as examples more readily available for emulation by others. Plans to engage in similar activities could become indirectly corroborated through success elsewhere. The accessibility of action narratives in print gave them a reality that mere word of mouth could never achieve; many people could access the exact same source and could do so repeatedly. What also mattered is a particular epistemic ideology that privileges the validity of the written over that of the spoken word.

The widening of these networks of authority also allowed for their internal differentiation. It made possible more pointed articulations of arguments, because with more people differences were more likely to meet in recognition by others. The increasing plurality of voices and groups made it possible for more people to associate themselves in agreement. As long as state socialism existed, this was not a real danger to the solidarity among the groups. In the fall of 1989, the small, networked groups finally gave way to the formation of national parties and electoral platforms.

Group life was not just about recognition and the cultivation of particular kinds of resonances in a local memory culture, however. Just as significant is the fact that the groups have undertaken actions in the form of petitions, protest events, and samizdat publications. These actions were veritable experiments in political knowledge-making. In fact, the responses of the state to the groups' actions became the most significant source of information about the state and the way it operates. At the same time that activists made an effort to alter the institutional fabric of social life in the GDR (in however small a way), they gained important political knowledge. In other words, actions functioned as political experiments that helped to articulate and corroborate political understandings. In particular, I have emphasized here that this process of learning was characterized by a dialectic among various modes of understanding. I have especially pointed out that kinesthetic and emotive understandings often paved the way for later articulations in discursive form.

This sheds some light on the debate about how the reinvention of civil society, the establishment of a party-independent public sphere, proceeded. There has been a bit of a controversy over the relationship between the multiple concepts that have been used, such as the designators *parallel, independent, second*, in combination with *society, public, culture*, and such (Skilling 1989, 157–58) and the actions of the movements (Mastnak 2005, 337). By posing the question, "which one was first, concepts or actions?" the literature has created a bit of a chicken and egg problem. The analysis conducted here in terms of the sociology of understanding suggests that the relationship between both is co-constitutive. The concept would not take on the meanings it did if older conceptualizations (e.g., revisionism) had not failed to provide satisfactory guidance, and if the new ones did not resonate with the experiences of the group. Once coined, however, they provided orientation and direction for further action, the success of which positively or negatively corroborated the concepts. A central element of this co-constitution of practice and theory was oscillation of group life between the poles of politics and self-politics, that is, the effort to produce institutional effects outside of the group or movement and efforts to reflexively stabilize, widen, expand, or transform groups and the movement. This dialectic helped some groups to realize that the mediated performance of the drama of group action for national and international audiences—accompanied by Stasi intervention, which demonstrated human rights abuses—was the most effective way of doing politics in a dictatorial country that at the same time craved for international recognition.

If the transformation of the spaces of validation can be described from the perspective of changing networks of authority and experiences produced through action, it can also be described in terms of changing understandings. As far as discursive understandings are concerned, this can be documented at least to some degree by comparing documents the groups drafted at various points of their dissident careers side by side. Since there are so few documents left from the earlier work of dissidents, one has to draw on interviews as well, especially on commentaries people make on one another's development.[58] In the broadest ideological terms one can see how many activists who earlier leveraged unorthodox Marxist theories to analyze and criticize the GDR acquired a successively more liberal language—their continuing rejection of capitalism notwithstanding. The timing of this transformation is different

---

58. People often destroyed documents for security reasons. What we have left is typically only what left the desks and homes of activists and what entered the files of the Stasi. Samizdat has vastly increased the density of available texts. Since they appeared only from the mid-1980s onward, the records for the late 1970s and 1980s are very thin. The reports of the secret informants about meetings of the groups are only to some degree a substitute, because the Stasi officers cast in their own words what they thought their superiors needed to hear of what their secret informants had told them. In interviews there is a tendency to project one's later or even current positions into the past, where documented differences are quickly written off as mere strategic maneuverings. Yet people are often more critical observers of other's transformations.

for different people, yet from the mid-1980s onward many of them came together to formulate new documents with a markedly more liberal tone. This overall ideological transformation went hand in hand with related changes. If the activists initially addressed the state with their writings, using the legal instrument of a petition, they increasingly addressed each other as much as the state. This "each other" became ever bigger, expanding in the fall of 1989 to the citizenry of the GDR as a whole. The subject position also betrays an interesting development. Addressing the state first as individuals, they went on to address it as a collective, often thought to represent a whole category of people, if not "the silent majority" of the GDR population. By 1989, now knowing themselves as members of a plural civil society, they spoke on behalf of their respective groups. Thematically, the understandings transpiring from the documents move from single policy concerns to ever-broader issue areas, and then to a critique of the system as a whole, which subsequently also became more of a program about what a new society should look like. In part these transformations are the consequence of strategic necessities (e.g., security concerns) and strategic possibilities (e.g., of reachable audience). Yet, it has to be remembered that both perceived necessities and possibilities shaped the discussions leading up to a document and thus the deliberation, working through, and practicing of understandings.

Not only the discursive orderings of the world changed. Emotively, the trajectories of moving into and through dissidence were accompanied by shifting degrees and kinds of fear. Jointly organized political actions could increase or decrease fear and so could major policy shifts. And yet, here too the social situation with its characteristic everyday challenges and demands as well as the development of the networks of authority in which dissidents were lodged mattered. To the degree that they were still lodged within a meaningful career trajectory with associated colleagues and friends, the fear of losing their work was paramount. After their marginalization, working in low-income jobs, living in undesirable apartments, slowly acquiring a new friendship network among other marginalized people, such fears were no longer of much concern. But then, children made a big difference. The fear of seeing them transferred to some state-run orphanage in case of parental prison terms could be overwhelming. The ebb and flow of oppositional activities, their success and danger, could dramatically change how and to which degree the state was feared. With several successful mobilizations of solidarity in a row, fear could abate. Such emotive swings are also characteristic with respect to activists' work. Periods of intense depression altered with almost giddy hope, depending on how the actions went.

Kinesthetically, part of the dissidents' trajectory can be described as a slow conquest of the public space for their political action. Experientially, spaces that were "the party's," "closed," "taboo," became "theirs," too. Constitutive for this acquisition was the surprise and joy in carrying out a physical movement either unimpeded or, perhaps even better, outsmarting the impediments. Thus politics was carried from behind the walls of private apartments first into churches and church compounds, then into the streets. If the Alexanderplatz event was a kind of political coming out in this regard for many women participating in the action, so were human chains between the American and the Soviet embassies for others. Every little new success in this regard mattered. In 1987 peace activists participated in the Olof Palme march with their own placards—something experienced by many of them as a major breakthrough (e.g., Lengsfeld 1992, 81–83). The attempt to do likewise during the Liebknecht-Luxemburg demonstration in January 1988 led to a wave of arrests and forced exile.[59] The apex of this transformation was the fall of 1989 with its large Monday demonstrations, to say nothing of the fall of the Wall and its consequences.

Likewise remarkable is how political action acquired new meanings. At the beginning, dissidents often took action along statutory paths: they did what they thought they were supposed to do as involved members of the communist youth organization, as politically aware students, even as members of the SED. They asked critical questions, made critical comments, became active in organizing readings, wrote wall newspapers, and so forth. Retrospectively these actions appeared "naive" because the addressee in no way reacted as statutorily described—answering questions, delighting in critique, engaging in dialogue. Thus they realized that they had been entrapped in literalist understandings. And the realization that the world was not as described in words also created a moral abyss. Hence, action became an experiment, probing what this world was like in fact. The reactions of party state agencies came to be seen as much better indicators of the real state of the world than the written word of propagandistic self-descriptions or the letters of statutes and laws. Hence, political actions in accordance with the law were undertaken with an ironic distance as a safety blanket. On these

---

59. The Olof Palme march was a peace march organized by the state leading across the entire GDR. People could locally march along. Berlin peace groups used the opportunity to participate with their own placards. To the activists' own surprise, the authorities tolerated this. The idea to participate in state organized venues, transporting one's own message, resonated with the activists' involvement in the Kulturopposition during the 1970s. The successful participation in the Olof Palme march encouraged activists to try the same strategy at the annual Luxemburg-Liebknecht demonstration, a cherished ritual of the Socialist Unity Party commemorating the murder of both communist leaders in January 1919. There were fierce debates among the activists whether it was wise to participate again with their own placards. In the end, groups decided to leave it to every member to decide whether to participate or not. Some did, carrying a poster with what is arguably Luxemburg's most famous quote: "Freedom is always the freedom of dissenters."

grounds the insistence of taking legal political actions could become asser-tion of an identity, a matter of self-respect in a warped world. This might at first have had a purely individual meaning. Yet, the self-asserting *I* eventu-ally needed another to validate this identity, and thus action could become the basis of community, of a new network of authority. The experimenting and self-asserting *I* became a *we* and by necessity action became performa-tive, addressed to another and subsequently narrativized. With the expan-sion of networks, with the emergence of a small public enabled by meetings and later techniques of mass mediation, the performance of action and the reaction of the state could become what mattered. The ecce homo strategy was born as a political move. The accent of attention in politics shifted from the action that had long lost any promise of real institutional consequences besides being an (albeit important) ingredient in self-politics to the com-munication of action and reaction as a means to form and validate critical political understandings.

And so my retelling of the emergence of dissidence in Berlin during the 1980s has ended with the formation of a small public sphere that enjoyed a significant degree of autonomy vis-à-vis the party state and its project. Using the sociology of understanding as an effective emplotment scheme of this narrative, as the theory accounting for its formation, leads us to an analytical definition of a public sphere as the socio-experiential environment in which the formation and transformation of political understandings takes place. A *public sphere* is constituted by the significant intersection of individual spaces of validation. Its boundaries fall in place with the boundaries of vali-dating effect flows. Any particular person is, with regard to a particular set of understandings in a particular situation, a participant in the public sphere vis-à-vis any other participant, if he is an authority for that person and is not de-authorized by that person in case of disagreement. Opportunities to cor-roborate particular understandings in practice either directly or indirectly are an integral part of public spheres. Understandings are part of this public to the degree that they are resonating with other understandings within it. In other words: a public sphere is enabled by epistemic ideologies, practices, and emotions to embrace contradicting recognitions, corroborations, and resonances (i.e., "case 3 situations," see chapter 4).[60] This conceptualization of the public sphere aims first and foremost at the analysis of *actual* processes of articulating and validating understandings relevant to politics and thus the formation and transformation of institutions. It does not presuppose a

---

60. This definition has obvious affinities with Jeffrey Alexander's recent theoretization of the "civil sphere" (2006) in its emphasis on the institutional enablement of continuing solidarity in possible contradiction. Just as obviously we have arrived at the centrality of this point through very different argumentative and theoretical means.

unitary public sphere. Depending on the fate of what kind of institutions we are interested in, we would necessarily find different sets of institutional assemblages constituting the relevant public sphere. The primary interest of this conceptualization, therefore, does not lie in postulating a public sphere as separate from other spheres, notably the state or the economy. In the case of the East German sphere of dissidents it matters to see, for example, to which degree the public constituted in the way described above depended on state intervention (and its publication as an instrument of maintaining networks of authority) on a particular form of economic life (which made basic provisioning relatively easy) and the Protestant church as a set of institutions separate and still connected to the state.

The tale of the creation of a public sphere with significant autonomy from the party state could also be told in a slightly different register. Many later dissidents tried to do politics within the frameworks offered by the party. They wrote petitions, asked questions, got involved in discussions. And yet they had to realize that in the longer run there was no space for politics other than the incessant affirmation of the party line, which for them was tantamount to institutional fetishism (if, of course, not in these terms then still in effect) and thus the death of politics. So they learned to look elsewhere for actively engaging in politics. The struggle between various party-independent, more or less oppositional groups was about the most effective means to do politics under the given circumstances. And here some came to discover a kind of liberalism *après la lettre*. They saw possibilities for themselves in the creation of publicity domestically and internationally. Others saw better chances for politics in a style that remained acceptable to reform-minded forces within the party, even if they too were of the opinion that launched from within the party alone political projects stood no chance of realization. To make better sense of these choices in context it has to be remembered that nobody believed in the possibility of anything like the quick disintegration of socialism that then, during the fall of 1989, was about to happen in front of a perceptive audience giddy with the newfound possibilities of politics.

PART V

Policing Understandings—
Reproducing Misunderstandings

The following chapter describes and analyzes the means used by the secret police to control the formation of dissident groups and their activities. In keeping within the questions posed by political epistemology while using the methods provided by the sociology of understanding, I will interpret these efforts of the Stasi as a particular form of politics undertaken with the intention to prevent, hinder, or undo the formation of party-critical institutions. These efforts were oriented and directed by the party state's political understandings about how dissident activities come about. Taken together, these understandings form a theory that sees dissidence as an elaborate scheme of the class enemy in the West to undermine the GDR. In keeping with its major component parts marked by the Stasi's own acronyms I will refer to this body of understandings as "PID/PUT/'opposition'" theory. The first part of the chapter is devoted to the exploration of this theory and its institutionalization in rules and regulations as well as in actual practices. I will then explore how this theory acquired credibility among party officials and Stasi officers within the international context in which it was developed and the first cases to which it was applied.

In the second major section of the chapter I will investigate the methods of intervention inspired by this theory to control dissident thought and action. These methods formed part of a repertoire available to the Stasi for their bureaucratic "case work." I will discuss the rules and regulations governing the circumstances under which cases could be opened, how they were supposed to be conducted, and how they could be closed. I will pay particular attention to the method of "decomposition" that aimed to prevent the formation of dissidence by altering the self and other perceptions of activists, by "organizing failures," by spreading rumors to sew distrust among groups or individual movement participants, and so on. The sociology of understanding will prove useful to evaluate under which circumstances the method of decomposition had greater or lesser chances to succeed.

The final main section of the chapter will address the fact that the Stasi perceived and acted upon the world predominantly with the help of part-time secret informants specially recruited for this purpose. Not surprisingly this created a host of principal-agent problems. The full-time agents of the secret police had to find, motivate, and instruct suitable part-timers to gather the information needed while inducing them to engage only in actions the Stasi deemed acceptable. Analyzing the relationship between the Stasi's guidance officers and their informants will finally lead back to the fundamental issue of this book, the question of how socialism produced knowledge about itself and how this knowledge informed actions to maintain its institutional order, that is, in the language of political epistemology, to engage in self-politics. Building on chapters 7 and 8 I will show in particular how the application of PID/PUT/"opposition" theory systematically misconstrued the phenomenon of dissidence, thus depriving the party of insights into its failed policies.

9

Attempting to Know and Control the Opposition

We have always worked from the assumption, the deputy minister was very insistent on this point, that in the GDR, that in a developed socialist society, there could not exist such a thing as a genuine opposition. All there was, was a so-called opposition, which was in reality an antisocialist political underground, inspired and directed by the class enemy. And that of course we could not tolerate.

MARTIN VOIGT, FORMER STASI OFFICER

UNDERSTANDING PARTY-CRITICAL ACTIVITY

Building on Lenin's *The State and Revolution* (1967e), orthodox Marxist-Leninist doctrine evaluates the notion and practice of political opposition positively, if two conditions prevail. Opposition must take place within the context of a bourgeois political order, and it must be mounted by the suppressed class, ideally in the form of a communist party. What generally is called in liberal societies "opposition," that is, a party or parties represented in parliament but not in government, is not acknowledged as a real opposition at all. Instead Marxism-Leninism debunks such "opposition" as mere theater, staged in the interest of the preservation of bourgeois class domination. For no matter which party might happen to rule in a parliamentary democracy, social democratic parties included, the bourgeois social, political, and economic order is left untouched and revolution is excluded as a political possibility. In the analysis of Marxism-Leninism, the acknowledgment of the bourgeois order as unshakable by all accepted political parties is seen as the very condition for the toleration of "opposition" in the first place. The result of such an arrangement is inevitably the perpetuation of exploitation made slightly more bearable by stimulating false hope for change through the next government. Real opposition carrying the hope to end exploitation, must aim at revolution.

Within the context of postrevolutionary, socialist societies, however, the party state's self-understandings had no room for opposition. The "Little Political Dictionary" (*Kleines Politisches Wörterbuch*) (Schütz et al. 1978, 652) echoing Martin Voigt's words above, says:

> In socialist countries no objective political or social basis exists for an opposition, because the working class—in an alliance with other working people—is the class which exercises power while being at the same time the major productive force of society.

Real opposition has already done its necessary work. Thus the party concluded from its premises about the progressive historical development of political orders that anything that might appear in socialist societies looking like or calling itself "opposition," that is, an organized critical agency juxtaposed to the party, must by necessity be a creation of the class enemy aiming at counter-revolution. And given the historical situation, given that "developed socialist societies" by the 1960s had overcome the class enemy within, the real enemy came from without, first and foremost in the shape of the governments of bourgeois countries, but also in the form of their economic, political, and cultural elites and their associated organizations such as mass media corporations, political parties, trade unions, and churches.[1]

The PID/PUT/"Opposition" Theory

During the 1970s and 1980s the Stasi and the party operated with one particular overarching framework to make sense of understandings that deviated from the party line. This framework was also used to guide the Stasi's attempts to suppress the expressions of such understandings while at the same time justifying their actions. The core concepts of this framework were the notions of "political-ideological diversion" (*politisch-ideologische Diversion* or PID) and "political underground action" (*politische Untergrundtätigkeit* or PUT), which taken together formed a theory about the historically specific threats faced by the GDR from the capitalist class enemy. Political-ideological diversion is posited in this theory as a post-1961 class-war strategy of the West to destabilize the socialist world by way of inspiring seditious political underground activities in countries allied with the Soviet Union that can be presented by the people engaging in these activities as well

---

1. A reminder may be needed here: by rejecting the institution of an opposition in the form of an organization outside of and juxtaposed to the party with critical intention, the necessity of critique was by no means rejected. To the contrary, major party documents point to the necessity of continuing critique and self-critique as a vital motor of socialist development. However, in the eyes of the party, real critique implied making a positive contribution, which could only come from active participation, from within a position of responsibility for the socialist project, and thus needed to be lodged firmly within the party.

as by their Western supporters as an "inner opposition." The intentions of this strategy are captured in the words of the Stasi's handbook on "Definitions for Political-Operative Work" (reprinted as Suckut 1996, 303):

> to corrode socialist consciousness, respectively the disruption and prevention of its development by undermining the trust of wide parts of the population in the politics of communist parties and socialist states; to inspire anti-socialist behavior up to the commitment of political crimes; to mobilize inimical-negative forces within socialist countries; to develop an inimical, ideological basis of persons in the socialist countries for the inspiration of political underground activities; and to provoke discontent, disquiet, passivity, and political uncertainty among broad circles of the population.

Stasi assumed that this war was planned and guided by "centers of political-ideological diversion" (304–5). Among these it counted government ministries, military, espionage and other security agencies, as well as the main Western political parties and their associated foundations. In the trenches this battle was fought, according to the Stasi, mainly by secret service agencies and the mass media. Underlying this list of centers of political-ideological diversion is a syllogism by analogy. The Stasi imagined the enemy to be organized and to operate through means that were not dissimilar to its own, centrally coordinated efforts. The Stasi made extensive use of trade representatives, foreign correspondents, frequently traveling scientists, and athletes as informants for its own purposes.

The means by which the organizers of PID were assumed to inspire PUT in the GDR are these: the propagation of misleading ideologies, "in particular modern revisionism, social democratism and nationalism" (Stasi directive 2/71, p. 5); the infiltration of disinformation about socialism, the party, the GDR, and the Soviet Union; and the spreading of "decadent life-style images" propagating consumerism and individualism (the directives mention beat music, religiosity, star cults, and movie clubs). These measures were assumed to give rise to a "field of activities" among GDR citizens conducive to the development of political underground actions. This field of activities was thought to consist in (378):

> Discussions with negative and inimical content over a longer period, in particular circles of persons and groups who become the targets of the enemy. There, the shortcomings, problems, and developmental difficulties of socialism become the constant object of discussion; the fundamental propositions of party politics and of the government are questioned; the arguments used by the enemy in his political-ideological diversion are simply adopted and dissipated; and permanent negative political discussions on the basis of anti-socialist literature not licensed in the GDR are

conducted. In such circles of persons and groups, politically and ideologically unclear pamphlets are written and distributed whose content misrepresents Marxism-Leninism and the fundamental propositions of the party.

The Stasi assumed that the aforementioned enemy centers would use such activities to organize them into an "antisocialist platform" with counterrevolutionary intentions thus producing fully fledged political underground activity (377). According to Stasi's theory, that platform, the result of capitalist countries' interventions, would then be presented by the enemy to the outside world as a genuine "inner opposition" legitimated in terms of bourgeois ideology (303). According to the theory, this labeling allowed the enemy to discredit legitimate defensive state action against the political underground as a human rights violation.

It is easy to see how PID/PUT/"opposition" theory,[2] as a complex of discursive understandings, could pull a range of emotive understandings in its wake. Seen from the moral perspective of the Stasi officers, the operation, if true (and the officers I interviewed had—with few exceptions and caveats—no doubt it was), was nothing short of outrageous. The plot mapped out by the theory amounted to the capitalist countries arrogating to themselves the roles of prosecutor and judge in a trial over socialist countries, for which they planted the evidence. In the eyes of the Stasi officers, PID/PUT/"opposition" class warfare revealed the fundamental moral character of all the actors involved. Capitalist agencies were seen as betraying, besides their arrogance, also their utter cynicism by using GDR citizens as cannon fodder for ideological warfare. The theory revealed domestic PUT carriers as either naive, as the enemy's useful idiots, or as depraved enemies of the people. In these moral understandings associated with PID/PUT/"opposition" theory lie the roots of the intense scorn the Stasi officers felt for dissidents. For the Stasi officers PID/PUT/"opposition" theory did not only reveal the moral abyss in which the class enemy dwelt, but it also shone a light onto the vulnerability of socialism. The cause of this vulnerability was seen in accordance with the socialist theodicy in imperfect propaganda work. The conclusion that was drawn was to step up the efforts at creating a monolithic intentionality. Stasi-minister Mielke said (BArch: Dy 30/IV 2/2.039, leaf 35):

The aggressive political-ideological work, adapted to the exigencies of the moment of every . . . party group, remains the alpha and the omega of the

---

2. "PID/PUT/"opposition" is a summarizing shorthand of my coinage—it was not used in this synthesized form by the Stasi. Even though there was no unifying name for the various components, the theory was applied to the world as a coherent body as the examples that follow will demonstrate.

effective preventive combat against political ideologial diversion in all of its apparent forms.

The causal structure of the theory follows the plot of revengeful persecution in which capitalism is the villainous actor against which socialism as a victim has to fight for her right.

> In the context of his crusade, the enemy uses all his political, military, economic, and ideological means to intensify his fight against and to damage socialism in every conceivable way. He will try to cause phenomena of economic destabilization, he will undermine, weaken, and destroy the foundations of socialist societies, he will try to develop an internal opposition . . . and he will try to dissolve the unity and the oneness of the socialist community. (leaf 7)

This figure of relentless persecution had deep cultural resonances with the story of socialism as the self-liberation of an exploited, that is, unjustly treated, class of people. And needless to say, for the older generation, Mielke and Honecker included, persecution was not abstract but a very real, potentially mortal condition of their earlier lives. PID/PUT/"opposition" was seen in this light as a perfidious move of the old, capitalist persecutor to cheat its victim once more.

The Historical Emergence and Institutionalization of PID and PUT

To outsiders, PID/PUT/"opposition" theory may sound like a conspiracy theory. After they gained access to their files, the members of the peace and civil rights movement whom I described in the last two chapters have reacted with amusement, disbelief, or even anger to their description by the Stasi as BND- or CIA-directed PUT-carriers. They felt they were given some part in a strange fantasy play, that they were robbed by the Stasi's analysis of their political agency and personal judgment. Perhaps even more interestingly, the documents have yielded no proofs for the operation of the process dynamic central to the theory: the inspiration, organization, and guidance of oppositional activities by Western secret service agencies.[3] Rather than writing Stasi's theory off as a cynical form of knowledge in the service of a violent will to power, it is important to learn why, for the party members and Stasi officers, this theory rang true, if perhaps not in all cases always in

---

3. This does not mean that none of the dissidents ever had contact with Western secret service agencies. It also does not mean that none of them ever would have cooperated with BND or CIA even if most would have shuddered at the mere thought. What it does mean, however, is that typically neither the motive to start or join dissident activities nor the organization of these activities can be accounted for by foreign secret service interventions.

its entirety, then certainly in important parts. And that it did, historically speaking, ring true is beyond any doubt, as my interviews with Stasi officers have made sufficiently clear. In fact, a frequent response to my question of why in writing their assessments they kept leveraging the charge of secret service involvement in spite of the fact that there was no direct evidence was that the truth will finally be known once the Western archives are open.[4]

Although components of the PID/PUT/"opposition" theory, such as the words *diversion* and *underground*, are part of the bedrock of secret service terminology, the theory as depicted in the last section has crystallized in response to historical developments. Starting in the late 1950s, the party and the Stasi adjusted their understandings of the dominant modes of enemy interference in the domestic affairs of socialist countries *away* from an emphasis on the use and/or threat of physical violence *toward* social and psychological means of shaping understandings. The plausibility of PID/PUT/"opposition" theory as the master understanding and organizing framework for Stasi's domestic operations (*Abwehrarbeit*) should therefore be understood from within the historical context in which it has taken institutional form. A number of developments have interacted in such a way as to make this strategic repositioning appear necessary and the theory itself increasingly validated to the Stasi. The growing certainty about its correctness insured the progressive refinement and institutionalization of PID/PUT/"opposition" theory (through directives, orders, training materials, etc.), which in turn yielded a growing set of case material for the further corroboration and elaboration of the theory.

The initial impulse for the development of PID/PUT/"opposition" theory can be dated with some degree of accuracy to the 1956–57 power struggle between first secretary Walter Ulbricht on the one hand, and Stasi minister Ernst Wollweber, politburo member Karl Schirdewan, and other leading comrades in the *Apparat* on the other. In February 1956, the XXth party congress of the CPSU posed a serious challenge to Ulbricht. Khrushchev's secret speech condemning Stalinist leadership practices furnished his opponents with arguments to brand his autocratic leadership style as "Stalinist" giving their long standing critique of the GDR leader a powerful boost of legitimacy. In spite of signals from Moscow that a leadership change in Berlin would be rather welcome, Ulbricht's opponents did not manage to organize their efforts, however. Ulbricht could therefore neutralize his critics in a piecemeal fashion. To unseat the Stasi minister, he employed a controversial order of Wollweber's in which the latter made an attempt to centralize the

---

4. I have little doubt that these archives would yield *some* corroborating evidence for the Stasi's theory. I have also no doubt, however, that it would fall far short of explaining dissidence in the GDR.

flow of information from the Stasi to the party leadership (Engelmann and Schumann document 1, pp. 355–56).[5]

To unseat the Stasi minister, Ulbricht employed a controversial order of Wollweber's in which the latter made an attempt to centralize the flow of information from the Stasi to the party leadership (Engelmann and Schumann document 1, pp. 355–56) as an occasion to launch a devastating critique of the work of the secret police (document 2, pp. 356–65). One of Ulbricht's main charges was that the Stasi was far too focused on foreign espionage and counterespionage, paying far too little attention to "ideological softening" (358). What Ulbricht had in mind with ideological softening were not only the developments leading to the uprising in Hungary as well as the strikes and unrest Poland in the same year, but also the signs of a freer and more critical intellectual life in the GDR in the aftermath of the XXth congress of the CPSU. Falling prey to the hopes of the moment, the Humboldt University philosopher (and SED member), Wolfgang Harich sent a manifesto proposing a "German way of socialism" to the Soviet ambassador in Berlin. In it he proposed nothing less than Ulbricht's demission and the creation of a unified neutral Germany (see pp. 298–99). He was promptly arrested together with others with whom he had formed a loose discussion group about political, philosophical, and literary topics. So here was corroboration, or so it seemed to orthodox party stalwarts, for Ulbricht's thesis of ideological softening, not just in Hungary and Poland but also right among SED members in important propaganda functions.

Mielke's fear of ignorance and its institutional effects

Chiefly involved in dismantling Wollweber were two members of the late GDR's leadership troika: young Erich Honecker, who as head of the SED's security commission served as Ulbricht's attack dog in the controversy, and Erich Mielke, at the time Wollweber's deputy who acted as Ulbricht's man within the Stasi's leadership (cf. Otto 2000, 230ff.; Pötzl 2002, 68–69; Otto 1990). Mielke had provoked Wollweber's controversial information flow

---

5. The reasons why Ulbricht's opponents have failed in spite of rather favorable circumstances are rather unclear. Frank (2001, e.g., 271) attributes Ulbricht's success entirely to personal characteristics, Wollweber's frail health, Schirdewan's indecisiveness, and most notably differences in the drive to power between the main protagonists. Much like Stalin after the removal of all of his peers, Ulbricht emerged from these struggles more powerful than ever. In fact, he became the uncontested leader of the SED until he was almost seventy-eight years old and his heir apparent, Erich Honecker, overthrew him. Institutionally, Ulbricht left a fatal legacy. In cementing his position, he cemented that of his office as the general secretary of the party. In the GDR at least halfhearted efforts at de-Stalinization created the conditions for a re-Stalinization of the country, personality cult and all.

order by handing Ulbricht the text of Harich's "platform" before giving it to his own boss. After Wollweber was forced to resign, nominally for health reasons, Mielke succeeded him, having demonstrated his loyalty to Ulbricht and Honecker.

No doubt, Mielke, who had by now seen two Stasi chiefs tumble over tensions with Ulbricht after they were critically weakened by their inability to uncover in a timely fashion party-critical activities, learned his lesson well.[6] Throughout his tenure as a minister he was obsessed with taking precautions that would preclude being caught in a state of ignorance about party-critical activities in the GDR. Mielke's behavior in interactions with his subordinates and his speeches suggest that he suffered from an intense fear of being caught off guard in ways comparable to his two predecessors. The acuity of this fear was probably exacerbated by the fact that even though Mielke actively participated in the downfall of both of his predecessors, it is very unlikely that he felt any guilt over his involvement. Calling his actions "disloyal" would have betrayed, in his eyes (and that of any other properly self-objectified communist), a petit bourgeois consciousness. There is no doubt that his actions can be well justified in terms of the ethics of absolute finality. And as I have shown in chapter 6, Mielke made many explicit efforts to exhort his men to internalize this ethics as the only one befitting a true Chekist. In fact, he probably had what Max Weber called (in relation to Calvinist ascetics) a "pharisaically good conscience."[7] But he knew also that anybody who would help to topple him under comparable circumstances would have a similarly good conscience. The source of Mielke's intense fear is most likely a double identification with both leader and challengers. As a secret police professional, Mielke knew how difficult it was to know of all party-critical activities, and he knew that those toppling him if he did not know were doing the right thing.

From the perspective of this historically generated fear complex, a whole range of Mielke's character traits begin to look less like mere personal viciousness and more like emotive understandings sustained within a particular set of institutional arrangements. These emotive understandings became in turn, due to Mielke's powerful position and long tenure, constitutive of particular institutional arrangements within the secret police. My interview partners among the Stasi officers have told me, for example, how Mielke was deeply feared for his habit of pestering his employees with incessant,

---

6. In 1953 then Stasi minister Wilhelm Zaisser fell as another rebel against Ulbricht because he had failed to warn the party about the 17 June worker uprising (besides being an ally of Soviet secret police chief Beria, see p. 298).

7. It certainly helped, in this respect, that Ulbricht framed Wollweber's order about high-level Stasi-party communications in terms of placing Stasi above the party.

often trivial (or mysteriously important) detail questions, implying that they ought to know literally everything (e.g., chapter 6, p. 328 n. 38). These incidents look as if Mielke had to continuously reproduce the "primal scene" of his fear complex in which he witnessed and participated in the humiliation of the two Stasi chiefs before him. By demanding knowledge of his subordinates they did not have, he identified with the role played by the general secretary in the dismissal of his two predecessors. In this identification with the center of power which always had the right to demand information regardless of how realistic such demands were, he survived the knowledge quizzes he staged always coming out on top. At the same time, however, he had to identify with his railroaded employees because the ignorance of his men was, if push came to shove, his ignorance. Thus, his fear needed to become their fear if he was to survive. Intended or unintended (perhaps a peculiar mixture of both), Mielke's "quirk" had an institutional effect. His questions produced a never-ending stream of smaller and bigger humiliations among his subordinates, the very fear of which helped to institutionalize a "we need to know everything" attitude among the organization as a whole, leading to formulations in orders and directives, in speeches and commentary aspiring to comprehensive control. This is visible in formulations such as the ones I have cited in chapter 2 (pp. 153–54), or the following one, coming out of a foundational PID/PUT/"opposition" directive (4/66, in Engelmann and Joestel 2004, 157–73).[8] The issue here is the contribution of Stasi to prevent occurrences of PUT in the future:

> With the means of the MfS we have to contribute to foil *all* circumstances and conditions in the education and formation that contribute to the misguided development of youths [my emphasis].

As so often in such formulations, the totalizing effect of the qualifier, *all*, is carried on by the use of two subsequent pleonastic hyperboles. No doubt, seen from the outside, such formulations can be easily denounced as megalomaniac. It is harder to say why they appeared reasonable to contemporary actors. Total knowledge seemed the only way out of an emotionally untenable position. Not surprisingly then, aspirations to comprehensive knowledge and total control lace Stasi discourses, and since the officers found themselves, through the process dynamics described, in the same boat as their minister, they sounded reasonable to the degree that they resonated with their very own fears.

---

8. This whole psychological complex is nothing if not a heightened version of what ordinary party members had to face in the process of self-objectification where they were equally caught in the tension between telling on others and being told on with regard to lapses. I have described this phenomenon as aporia of socialist identity in chapter 1.

Resonances with ideology and work

Historically, the institutionalization of PID/PUT/"opposition" theory can be traced along the lines of significant directives, orders, and instructions.[9] Right after taking the helm, Mielke steered the organization in this new direction through his regular speeches to Stasi's "collegium" of division and regional branch heads (Otto 2000, 252). Within a year of his inauguration, in 1958 Mielke issued a circular instructing Stasi units on the "defense against the ideological diversion and underground activities of the right wing social democratic leadership as well as of its eastern offices."[10] From then onward, the directives, orders, and instructions on PID/PUT/"opposition" follow in regular succession, elaborating the theory as well as the organizational, tactical, and strategic means to combat it, thus transforming the theory into the cornerstone of Stasi's domestic operations against nonconformist thought and action. Milestones on the way are: 1960, the first general directive (82/60); 1966, another one specifically dealing with youth (4/66); 1968, an order demanding the establishment of departments dealing specifically with mass media as conduits of PID; 1971, the directive about the treatment of "antistate inflammatory speech" (2/71); and finally, necessitated by a surge of movement activities, the 1985 "directive on the preventive averting, discovery, and combat against political underground activities" (2/85)[11] as summa and apex of all previous work on the issue.

Needless to say, this development would have hardly taken place at the mere impulse of the party leadership alone, even in a Leninist vanguard party state such as the GDR. The PID/PUT/"opposition" theory appeared to make sense of the circumstances as defined by the organization, and it kept resonating with the party's and the Stasi's self-understandings. Socialism's general Manichaeism was the basis on which it could grow. Its fundamental friend/foe ordering describing the interactions between both sides as war with zero sum qualities provided PID/PUT/"opposition" theory with deep resonances among the fundamentals of Marxism-Leninism. The theory also resonated with the contemporary interpretations of Marxism-Leninism, which shifted attention from structural transformations to political-

---

9. The Stasi was a military bureaucracy governed by "orders" (*Befehle*) typically regulating a singular action (e.g., opening or closing a unit, taking a particular course of action), by "directives" (*Dienstanweisungen*) regulating recurrent work procedures, and "instructions" (*Ausführungsbestimmungen*) further specifying directives. The Stasi named and referred to orders, directives and instructions by running number and year. I will keep to this practice in what follows.

10. The original document has never been found; all we know is the title (Suckut et al. 1993– [2004], 128).

11. Except for the order instituting department 7 within the XX-line work of Stasi, all of these documents are reprinted in Engelmann and Joestel 2004.

ideological work, that is, propaganda. Thus Stasi's theory looked like the right lesson learned from the fundamental orientations provided in texts such as the reports of the ZK to the party congress or key speeches of the general secretary.

Moreover, the building of the Berlin Wall in 1961 shifted the dynamics of everyday Stasi work. Outright Cold War–style espionage and sabotage that characterized much of the late 1940s and 1950s were more difficult to carry out under conditions of nearly hermetically sealed borders. Accordingly, they became comparatively rare. One might have argued under these circumstances that the domestic operations of the Stasi could have been significantly scaled back. There are other reasons that might have made a rollback seem opportune. The Wall closed the "exit" option for the GDR population dissatisfied with their lives. People now had to adjust to the circumstances as best as they could. Flight became extremely risky and displays of "loyalty," however shallow and or mellow, became part of a cautious everyday routine. Finally, Havemann and Biermann notwithstanding, in the 1960s there were as of yet no signs of domestic opposition that seemed to require a large secret police apparatus to watch and control. Stasi had no inkling yet that the Wall helped to produce a new challenge, taking form hidden under Minerva's feathers. And yet, nobody of any importance seems to have argued the case for a reduction in Stasi personnel at that time. Instead, the secret police enjoyed its fastest growth during the two decades in which PID/PUT/"opposition" theory was formulated (Gieseke 2000, 545–55). In fact, it was the refinement of the theory that provided the rationale for why this had be so. It also created a bridge between the main directions of earlier and later Stasi work by continuing to attribute central significance to foreign espionage agencies, preserving the professional identity of an espionage/counterespionage organization that was already well on its way to becoming a secret political police bureaucracy, or to what Mampel (1996) has called fittingly an "ideology police."

Indirect corroboration by international events

PID/PUT/"opposition" theory was indirectly corroborated by international current events. A collective of former Stasi generals says (Grimmer et al. 2002a, 58):

> In contradistinction to the Federal Republic, the GDR was from the very first day on threatened in its very existence. . . . Policy determining forces in the FRG never left any doubt that it was their foremost goal to destroy that German state [the GDR], which had arrogated to itself the power to touch the capitalist system of property ownership and exploitation.

While the threat emanating from the capitalist West was seen as permanent, its character was assumed to take historically specific forms. Immediately after World War II, at least until the end of the turbulences of 1948 (Berlin blockade, communist seizure of power in Czechoslovakia), the likelihood of direct military confrontation between the United States and the Soviet Union was seen as very high. This assessment built on the assumption that the imperialist powers found it difficult having to wrestle all of a sudden with a Soviet Union that had, thanks to its victory in World War II, become stronger domestically while at the same time growing into an eminent international power. Says the *Geschichte der Kommunistischen Partei der Sowjetunion* (History of the Communist Party of the Soviet Union) (Ponomarjow et al. 1984, 643):

> The USSR was, at the end of the war, politically stronger than at the beginning. The unity of people, party, and government had firmed up, the authority and the moral political prestige of the Soviet state had grown, and its international influence had augmented considerably. Without its participation [the Soviet Union's], no important question of world politics could be solved completely.

On the other hand, capitalism, so went the reasoning among communist parties in Eastern Europe, had to wrestle with the dissolution of its imperial possessions around the world and with domestic crises, all of which might lead to external aggression as a response to domestic woes. However, so the party's logic, the United States and its allies had to give up their plans, as it became apparent that such a war stood little chance of succeeding thanks to the military preparedness of the Soviet Union (ZK 1978, 75). However, a military intervention was seen as increasingly less likely after 1949, when the Soviet Union advanced to the status of a nuclear power. In consequence of these assumed shifts in the geostrategic situation, the West had to learn to accept "postwar realities," that is, the existence not only of the Soviet Union as a socialist state but also the existence of a corona of new socialist countries surrounding it, and, increasingly in the rest of the world. Hence, so went the reasoning, the enemy had to shift its strategy from a "hot" to a "Cold War."[12] Containment (Truman Doctrine) partly achieved through economic

---

12. This does not mean that military intervention was ever entirely ruled out. It only means that it seemed increasingly less likely to happen in the heart of Europe. "Imperialist military expansion" was carefully followed around the world. The Korean War, the French war in Indochina, the Suez crisis, and later the American Vietnam War were seen as evidence of continuing military aggression and the readiness of the capitalist world to fight a conflict with arms wherever it saw this as the most likely means to succeed. However, these confrontations seen over a longer period of time were also seen as a long war for global domination, which capitalism was slowly

assistance (Marshall Plan) was seen as the Cold War's first set of strategies. Besides western and southern Europe, the United States tendered economic aid to eastern Europe as well. Of course it had to be rejected—according to the party—because taking it would have implied economic dependence, the implementation of structural adjustments to the liking of the donors, and thus an end to political self-determination (155–56). Since the United States' strategy was thus successfully thwarted, at least as far an Eastern Europe was concerned, the United States and its allies had to shift gears again, this time betting their stakes more on whipping up popular discontent within socialist countries, aiming to foment local rebellions (e.g., 350–58). According to official doctrine, this strategy was defeated in 1953 in the GDR and 1956 in Hungary and Poland. In consequence, the capitalist world had to bid farewell to violent means of undermining socialism. Instead, it was forced to rely increasingly on ideological and cultural means to subvert the Soviet Union and its allies in Eastern Europe. The most palpable effect of this new form of assault was the "counterrevolutionary movement" of 1968 in Czechoslovakia, which aimed, in the guise of "reform communism" or "socialism with a human face," to induct Czechoslovakia into the capitalist order.[13] The international meeting of communist parties in Moscow in June 1969 tried to draw conclusions from Prague. The final communiqué exhorted the member countries to pay more attention than before to the defense of ideology. The urgency of this task and the correctness of its general direction was for many party members corroborated by the fact that capitalist youth culture was sweeping through the GDR and other countries of Eastern Europe, a fact that was palpable to them in Eastern European youth's demand for blue jeans and rock and roll.

The era of détente that was introduced in Germany with the election of Willy Brandt to the chancellorship in 1969 fit, according to party and Stasi, right into this new strategy of the West to soften socialist resolve by spread-

---

but surely losing as more and more countries did not only attain independence, but became (at least nominally) socialist. The reports of the first secretary to the party congresses are good sources for the changing assessments of international affairs. The official history of the SED to which this section is referenced basically provides a thumbnail view of these reports seen from the perspective of the early 1970s, the time in which the mature body of PID/PUT/"opposition" theory was formulated.

13. The official GDR discourses on what came to be commonly known in the West as the Prague Spring are a good example of the logic of the Manichaean *tertium non datur* (see chapter 1, p. 105). Either a country was socialist and allied with the Soviet Union, or it was capitalist and allied with the United States. There was absolutely no space in between, even though the world was full of "in between" examples: Yugoslavia, China, and Albania had left the Soviet orbit without entering the U.S. one. The nonaligned movement in the third world would have offered a whole set of cases escaping the seeming rigor of the *tertium non datur*.

ing liberal ideology and capitalist consumer culture. It was a paramount goal of Brandt's *Ostpolitik* to "alleviate human suffering" (*menschliche Erleichterungen*) created by the arbitrary division of Germany into two antagonistic parts (Ash 1994, 127). And central to that was the creation of more possibilities for the inhabitants of both Germanys to visit and communicate with each other. Even though détente was generally welcomed in the GDR, it was, also seen as posing completely new challenges to the security apparatus of the country. Proof for the ultimately aggressive character of détente was found in Willy Brandt's slogan for *Ostpolitik*, which was *Wandel durch Annäherung* ("change through rapprochement"). For the party this slogan revealed the same old goal of toppling socialism, if this time "clad in velvet gloves" (or on *Filzlatschen*—"carpet slippers"). A strategy paper drafted at Stasi's university stated (JHS 001–255/I/76, 10):

> He [the class enemy] always wants to convert the unfolding process of normalization into one of liberalization; he wants to create a necessary link between the policy of détente and the erosion of socialism.

What the Stasi feared was that the enemy attempted to

> undermine the essential characteristics of socialism "from within" and to ultimately replace it via demands for a democratic socialism or a political pluralism and thus to replace freedom and socialist democracy by imperialist unfreedom by the grace of capital. (14)

Détente led to the "Basic Treaty" (*Grundlagenvertrag*) between the FRG and the GDR. It created new possibilities for travel between both countries while also facilitating the expansion of trade, the mutual participation in sports events, and scientific exchanges. In the estimation of the Stasi, these new contacts posed a considerable security threat for the GDR. More, they discovered in it a new Cold War tactic dubbed "inimical contact policy." The Stasi's handbook defines its purposes in the following way (in Suckut 1996, 219):

> by abusing contacts the enemy wants above all to increase the efficacy of its political ideological diversion; it wants to disturb and hamper the progressive development of all areas of society and inspire persons to commit actions inimical to state and society as well as crimes.

In other words, the Stasi feared that the new contact possibilities would operate as a conduit for PID resulting in PUT.

The party-state's fear of being publicly criticized for human rights violations connected with the demand for political reforms must also be understood in the context of the country's efforts to gain international recognition. Until the late 1960s the FRG tried to assert the claim that it was the only legitimate representative of the German people. It tried to enforce that claim by threatening to cancel diplomatic relations with any country officially recognizing the GDR. During the 1970s and '80s, when the GDR finally achieved more widespread international recognition, the GDR leadership feared that the PID/PUT/"opposition" mechanism could hamper its trade and credit relationships with hard currency countries while also weakening its position diplomatically, for example, during the CSCE process.

A paradigm case: Wolf Biermann (again)

A paradigm case for the PID/PUT/"opposition" theory became the entire cascading complex of actions and reactions surrounding the forced exile of Wolf Biermann (cf. Rosellini 1992; Pleitgen 2001; Berbig at al. 1994, documentation; see also chapter 6, p. 301ff.). His case and others like it gave rise to a further differentiation of the theory's vocabulary through the category of the "influence agent," which was defined in the following way (HA XX/AKG 8.4. 1976. In Walther 1999, 106–7):

> They are camouflaging their inimical activities through progressive declarations and analogue comportment, careful tactical behavior and compromises with the line of the party. In this way they create, maintain, and expand their influence and room to maneuver as well as their potential to have long-term decomposing effects. Their unmasking is made more difficult through their countless positive statements respectively their generally loyal behavior, and it is only possible by an even deeper penetration into the enemies' secrecy.

The Stasi formed the category of "influence agents" in obvious analogy to their central category of secret informants (see below). The Stasi (and other party-state bureaucracies) applied the theory to the Biermann case by arguing the following: Even if Biermann's early critical pieces might not have been directly inspired by Western enemy centers (see above), these soon seized the opportunity created by a conflict between Biermann and the party to build him up as a carrier of PUT in the GDR. These enemy centers encouraged him to go further with his critique by offering to publish his poetry and music in West Germany, and by lionizing him as a serious artist to be discussed on the arts and culture pages of newspapers, in university seminars on GDR literature, and the like. Analyzing the text of his poems and songs in temporal sequence, the party and the Stasi tried to demonstrate his conversion into an influence agent by showing how they became much less directed against capitalism and much more at socialism and its internal problems (Berbig et al. 1994, 289–90). Biermann's books and records produced in the FRG and illegally infiltrated into and circulated in the GDR were seen as inspiring more PUT.[14] For the Stasi PID/PUT/"opposition" theory was corroborated when Biermann teamed up with bête noire Havemann and both became leading figures of identification for critical young people in the GDR, indeed building an enemy center on its territory. More, as assumed in the theory, the outlawing of his works, the prohibition to perform, became a cause célèbre in West Germany, exemplifying to the GDR's enemies human rights abuses in the GDR, which served them at the same time as proof for the sorry state of socialism more generally.

With Biermann's denaturalization (probably inspired by Solzhenitsyn's deportation) the PID/PUT/"opposition" mechanism simply spun into its next cycle. In the Stasi's eyes, the events corroborated the theory once more. Western politicians condemned the GDR's decision. Their opinion was echoed dutifully by the Western media, triggering solidarity declarations by many organizations. Yet, as predicted by the theory, Biermann's denaturalization was decried in the East as well by friends and colleagues, concerned artists, and citizens who drafted and signed a petition against the party-state's decision (Berbig et al. 1994, 70–71). They sent this petition not only to the party paper *Neues Deutschland* but also, and this was seen as the proper index to the true nature of the act for the Stasi, to the French wire service AFP. For GDR officials it was of no interest that they did so in the well-justified fear that *ND* would never publish it anyway. In the West German media the petition was given priority treatment, and so the GDR population learned about these events once more through Western media. For party and Stasi this demonstrated again that a dense network had grown between PUT carriers within the GDR and Western enemy centers such as publishers, the media, universities, action committees, and such. And so, following the PID/PUT/"opposition" logic, Stasi arrested two petitioners it had under observation for a longer time (Jürgen Fuchs and Gernulf Pannach) while opening several new "operative procedures" (see below) against several other petitioners (Walther 1999, 107). At the same time, the party engineered the expulsion of several of the signatories from the Writers' Association while punishing the party members among them with sanctions ranging from reprimands to membership cancellations. In the absence of recanting their protest in an act of self-critique, which the party hoped for as a result of intensive "discussions" (*Aussprachen*, see also chapter 8, p. 411) by officials with the better-known artists and writers among the signatories, these punishments amounted in practice to a prohibition to practice their respective arts in the GDR. In other words, they were condemned to share Biermann's fate of isolation and professional death in public.

---

14. An interesting document testifying the logic I map out here in action is "Analyse über gegnerische Angriffe im Zusammenhang mit Erscheinungen der politischen Untergrundtätigkeit," issued by HA XX/OG, dated December 15, 1977.

Ultimately, the party decided to let petitioners leave the country too in an effort to sever the linking bridges of the PID/PUT/"opposition" mechanism. The ensuing exodus of artistic talent was widely read in West Germany and by many critical observers in the GDR as a political declaration of bankruptcy. As many of the later members of the peace and civil rights movements in Berlin during the 1980s have testified, the Biermann affair was in many ways as important as the crushing of the Prague Spring in moving them along their path into dissidence. Even though the departure of Biermann and so many well-known writers and artists had at first a depressing effect on the organizers of the cultural opposition and other budding dissidents, the long-term effect of the Biermann affair was one of encouraging further critical action. After all, the government actions corroborated existing critical understandings while providing a stream of occasions to articulate new ones.

The discourses around the Biermann affair within the party, the Writers' Association, and in newspapers makes clear to which degree the PID/PUT/"opposition" theory had not only become Stasi's main doctrine but also a key component of the party state's self-understanding and self-presentation widely disseminated through its many propagandistic venues. At the Writers' Association party meeting dedicated to discussing Biermann's denaturalization as well as the protest letter against it signed by numerous well-known intellectuals (Berbig et al. 1994, 71–90), members defending the party leadership and/or attacking the petitioners made frequent use of parts or even all of the PID/PUT/"opposition" paradigm. One witness of the meeting, Karl-Heinz Jakobs, recalls the president, Günter Görlich, making the following argument (1983, 107):

> In the course of 1976 the FRG had continuously aggravated the ideological confrontation [with the GDR] to gain a good starting position at the Belgrade conference [of the CSCE process]. She [the FRG] has done everything to prop up a civil rights movement in the GDR and to incite innocuous citizens to flee the country. Right before the federal elections, Kunze's book *Die wunderbaren Jahre* was issued. It is rather peculiar, that the "Bochum Initiative" working under the slogan "freedom of speech—freedom to travel" operated with the support of politicians like Bahr, Eppler and Schütz, as well as the GDR-traitor Heinz Brandt and anti-communists like Dutschke and Flechtheim. The poet under consideration here [Biermann] has offered himself as the tool of provocation.[15]

---

15. The transcript of Görlich's speech has been lost. Reiner Kunze was one of the foremost poets of the GDR. As previously mentioned, his *Die wunderbaren Jahre* could only be published in West Germany and became a cult book both in the East and West. The Bochum Initiative

Admittedly, Görlich was a Stasi informer and his speech was, if not directly instructed by Stasi, then probably drafted in agreement with the politburo or high-ranking Berlin party officials. And yet, Anna Seghers, the good conscience of GDR literature, although disturbed by the party's measure to expel Biermann was equally disquieted by the petitioner's transmission of their letter to Western news media. The tenor of many of the contributions of the party supporters was that regardless of how Biermann got to his thinking, there was in the end no doubt that objectively speaking he did the bidding of the class enemy, and if he was indeed a communist worthy of the GDR, he would have never allowed for this to happen.[16]

In retrospect, most Stasi officers I have spoken with see the handling of the Biermann affair as a disaster.[17] And yet, as a series of interconnected events it provided at the time indirect corroboration for PID/PUT/"opposition" for them. What mattered most in this regard is that Biermann, once in West Germany, did not visibly act on his claimed communist allegiances; he did not emerge as a major voice criticizing capitalism. Instead, he seemed to be settling into his role as a GDR critic; ergo—there was no doubt for most officers that he objectively furthered the case of the class enemy. Even the few who say they had second thoughts about the morality of denaturalization say that Biermann's behavior in exile proved the theory rather beautifully. He did what carriers of PUT are supposed to do: feign allegiance to be all the

---

lobbied for Biermann's right to travel. The three mentioned politicians were left-wing social democrats. Heinz Brandt was an SED functionary coming under attack since 1953; he fled in 1957 to preempt his apprehension. Rudi Dutschke was West Germany's most famous student leader in the 1968 movement. Ossip Flechtheim was an ex-communist, professor of political science associated with the Frankfurt school.

16. Compare here the arguments of the Stasi officers in relation to Havemann (chapter 6, pp. 303–6), but also the discussion among members of the Berlin peace movement of whether or not Western representatives of parties and media should be invited to the human rights seminar (chapter 8, p. 446).

17. Kurt Hager (1996, 337) provides the following account of how the decision to denaturalize Biermann was reached. I cite it here at length because it provides a very useful glimpse at the workings of the politburo. "When he [Biermann] picked up his passport in the Ministry of Culture, as was the custom, he was certainly exhorted to fulfill his duties as a citizen and to do nothing against the interests of the GDR. He used the concert to perform very critical songs about the GDR and its leadership. This concert was transmitted by Western television. The Ministry for State Security taped it and transmitted it to the politburo. There were excited utterances about Biermann's attitude and about the Ministry of Culture, which had given him the permission to travel to Cologne. In this emotion-laden atmosphere the idea came up to expatriate Biermann. Without previous collective council the Ministry for State Security received the order from Erich Honecker to exercise this expatriation in collaboration with the Ministry of the Interior. As the minister for culture, Hans-Joachim Hoffmann, remembers, we learned about the execution of this measure through the *Aktuelle Kamera* [main TV news shows]."

better able to do their destructive work. West German politicians, human rights activities, the media, also did what they were supposed to do: unjustly denounce the GDR for a self-protective measure. The escalation of the affair was further proof for the truth of the theory.

The peace and civil rights activities as PUT

The Stasi systematically subsumed the peace and civil rights movement under the categories of their PID/PUT/"opposition" theory. The movement's activists were classified as "negative-inimical forces"; its actions as "political underground activities." Its network-building efforts were interpreted as plots to "organize inimical platforms"; its connections to Western journalists, party members, or GDR refuges living in the West were classified as "backward linkages" to "centers of political-ideological diversion." Western media reports about state actions against any of the groups were described as attempts to market a "so-called inner opposition"; the resulting human rights critique was a "massive attempt to interfere in the GDR's domestic affairs," which was regularly used to discredit the GDR in international negotiations. This interpretation of the 1980s is pervasive throughout the Stasi's paper trail. Various elements of it can be found in every guidance officer's report about his meeting with informants; they are present in the documents opening or summarizing the progress of case work, and in the summarizing briefings handed to the Stasi's or the party's higher brass at various levels.

This uniform application does not mean, however, that the Stasi did not differentiate among various members of these movements as well as between their sets of various relations and their actions. In accordance with the human ontology of actually existing socialism that I described in chapter 1 (p. 113), participants were categorized as spanning the gamut from mere "fellow travelers" who were, ideologically speaking, just confused, to "fanatical, hardened enemies." Actions and groups were differentiated according to the danger they posed within the PID/PUT/"opposition" theory's logic, that is, ultimately with regard to the security hazard seen in them. In general, the more public and the more linked to the West a particular action was, the more dangerous it was thought to be. Danger assessments also varied with the current foreign policy situation of the GDR.

Further corroborating evidence for PUT was seen by the Stasi in the way in which actions were planned. Any of the groups efforts at secrecy—the use of code in phone conversations, strict conspiration with regard to the print locations of samizdat, the use of technology to find the Stasi's bugs hidden in apartments and telephones, conversations in the park to escape bugged apartments, and the smuggling of literature or worse of printing and later computer supplies and technology—were systematically read as hints of the groups' secret service–like organization, their beginning professionalism in counter-revolutionary activities attributed to the supervision by Western agencies. Just to provide a taste for the language of these documents, here is a longer translation of a "brief" (*Information*) about the situation after Stasi's attempt to catch the *Grenzfall* crew red-handedly printing the illegal publication on church premises (see chapter 8, pp. 449–51):[18]

> The so-called hard core of the negative inimical grouping of forces in the capital of the GDR, Berlin, to which the following notorious fanatical enemies belong . . . has come to the insight, that the state is not ready to tolerate violations of socialist law and that it intends to rigorously persecute violations of the law. They also had to learn that the state with all clarity intends to limit the action space of these groups which they tried to expand further.

The Stasi's report about the lessons drawn by the movement members from the state's actions had no factual base. It is an interesting example of rhetorical palliation characterizing even Stasi reports to political decision makers (compare chapter 6, p. 326). All the anxieties connected with arrests notwithstanding, by the time this report was written, it was clear to the activists mentioned in the brief as "hard core" that Stasi had blundered the action in a major way. In fact, they felt awash in the solidarity of people expressed in vigils and solidarity addresses around the country (see chapter 8, p. 450). The report continues:

> Starting from this base, they [the activists] react with confrontational counter measures [e.g., vigils] to prevent the situation from developing to their disadvantage as well as to press further claims. In doing so they unconditionally follow the line prescribed by external enemies, fulfilling the tasks set by them [the external enemies]. They collaborate closely with correspondents of Western media accredited in the GDR as well as with political forces from the FRG and West Berlin which have come here in this context. (There is certain knowledge, according to which several persons belonging to the hard core maintain contacts with employees of imperialistic secret service organizations.) The domestic inimical-negative forces pursue the following goals. Using the initiation of legal proceedings against Rüdden-

---

18. ZAIG, 454/87, November 30, 1987: "Information über die aktuelle Situation im Zusammenhang mit der Durchführung rechtlicher Maßnahmen zur Verhinderung der weiteren Herstellung des sogenannten Informationsblattes 'Grenzfall.'" The document existed in twenty-five copies, and it was distributed to Honecker, several other members of the politburo, to the state secretariat for church affairs, the interior minister, and the leaders of several Stasi departments.

klau [editor of the *Umweltblätter* arrested in the action] and other persons, they want to attain a country-wide solidarization effect among so-called alternative groups and they want to bring together similarly minded people and sympathizers and want to confirm their space within the domain of the church. . . . In addition, the following intelligence proves the close collaboration between domestic and foreign enemies.

What follows is a short list of visits: by a prominent left-wing green politician (Ströbele) who supposedly promised a PC with peripherals as well as by a member of the board of the West German biennial Protestant Church conference (*Kirchentag*) who putatively donated several hundred Deutschmarks to the environmental library. Further proof is seen in the role played by the editor of a West Berlin radio station in spreading information about the vigil, who is presented as associated with the West German conservative party and with two members of East Berlin peace circles. The report goes on:

> In close collaboration with Roland Jahn/West Berlin [a Jena dissident forcibly exiled in 1983] they receive information about what is happening at the Church of Zion, and they aim to influence the leadership of political parties in the FRG to undertake official steps against the actions of GDR state organs, with the particular intention to question in public the credibility of the GDR's "politics of dialogue."

Thus, this example unites all elements of the PID/PUT/"opposition" theory in making sense of a concrete political situation. And again, the theory not only structures the interpretation and actions of Stasi. The fact that the theory seems to make sense of the events appears to corroborate PID/PUT/"opposition" theory once more.

Significant further validation of the theory was derived from emotional resonances. Even where some of the officers could identify with some of the goals of the movement members, they universally felt strong disdain for most of the activists themselves. Their descriptions frequently characterize them as unkempt (bearded, long-haired, unwashed), abusive of alcohol, sexually promiscuous, undisciplined, and/or unwilling or unable to follow a career of hard work. In short, the activists, many of them with university degrees or disrupted university studies, were not seen as worthy of the socialist state's considerable investments in them. And so, for the Stasi officers the activists were the antithesis of what a good socialist was supposed to be like. And again, PID/PUT/"opposition" theory made excellent sense of this antipathy. In socialist understandings there was nothing viler than a spy working for an imperialist secret service. They were viler even than a capitalist exploiter.

Failures of understanding

Ironically, nothing validated PID/PUT/"opposition" theory more than the movement members' use of what I have called the ecce homo strategy (chapter 8, p. 452). The "Prague flight action," with its attempt at getting the state to perform its suppressive means under the eyes of the world, offered proof for the secret police that their theory was right. And yet, this strategy was not concocted in Pullach, Langley, Bonn, or Washington. Instead, the movement members themselves developed it, partially in response to the state's and perforce the Stasi's very own actions. Indeed, especially the Stasi officers emotional reaction to movement activists poses the question of whether they and their comrades did not see that it was their own interventions, their heavy-handed attempts at producing a monolithic intentionality, their extremely didactic, monological approach to human beings, and then their efforts at increasing marginalization, surveillance, and harassment that contributed significantly to forming the activists and their understandings of socialism. There is no doubt that the governments and many important organizations, probably also the majority of the people in West Germany, Western Europe, and northern America wanted socialism to go away. There is no doubt that the Cold War was fought from both sides with violent means. And perhaps there was even one or another dissident in East Germany who maintained for whatever reason relationships with the BND or the CIA. There might even have been plans among BND or CIA agents to organize embarrassments for the East German government by making human rights violations visible to the world, détente and the normalization of German-German relations notwithstanding. And yet, no class enemy was needed to bring about an opposition in the GDR. The causes for its emergence lay first and foremost in the everyday practices of socialism itself.

Today, several of the Stasi officers I interviewed readily concede this point. They agree that PID/PUT/"opposition" theory diverted attention from considering domestic causes of dissidence. Yet, while the men were still officers and fully integrated into the routines of their Stasi work, only a few of them harbored, and much less publicly raised, doubts about the validity of the complex of propositions I have called PID/PUT/"opposition" theory. For the large majority of the officers the theory rang true. They saw that the ultimate locus of causation was, for the most part, seen west of the Iron Curtain. In fact, the theory felt so well validated that the catalog of master's theses and dissertations at the Stasi's university (in Förster 1998) contains not a single item that critically evaluates the use of the theory in dealing either with Biermann or any other kind of oppositional activity. Instead, the catalog brims with treatises that are written to support, expand, and illustrate the basic model. Given the Stasi's extensive foreign espionage capabilities, putting the theory to empirical scrutiny would have been relatively easy, or so it seems. That this never happened is not just owed to the fact that the PID and the PUT side were dealt with by different wings of a secretive bureaucracy. The point is the theory was not seen as problematic; no need to scrutinize it rigorously ever manifested itself because the theory felt all too well corroborated; it had become part and parcel of the Stasi's and the party's background understanding of the world.

This is not to say that there were no critics of PID/PUT/"opposition" theory among the Stasi officers. There was, in fact, no shortage of officers who looked at the theory with a good dose of skepticism. Wilhelm Danziger reports that especially in the ranks of the foreign espionage division the theory was more widely questioned than elsewhere. There is some plausibility to this claim even if one discounts the common feeling of superiority among espionage officers over their counterespionage colleagues. After all, the theory rests on a syllogism by analogy that attributes to the institutional fabric of capitalist countries forms of interaction that are not unlike those in socialism. Officers with extensive foreign experience could more readily see that this assumption was false. Yet, the discursive culture of the Stasi (and party) prevented any systematic elaboration of critical insights, questions, and disquieting hunches that might have attached themselves to the theory. Because the theory had such deep resonances with fundamentals of Marxist-Leninist doctrines, because it dovetailed so well with general policy shifts, it could not easily be subjected to public scrutiny. Such a move would inevitably have been read as an attack on the binding party line, as an expression of lacking discipline and resolve, probably even as an alarming sign of "softening" and thus a betrayal of Chekist ideals. Questioning it in public might have been followed with a dramatic loss of authority. As much more minor cases indicate (see chapter 6, pp. 331–2) in the absence of recantation, it would probably have been sanctioned with measures as grave as expulsion from the Stasi and party and thus with a loss of one's entire social network. In consequence, critical officers shared their unease only with trustworthy friends and otherwise kept it to themselves. Furthermore, in the absence of opportunities to explore the validity of their doubts in a systematic fashion, they could never be sure how far their hunches really carried (in most cases certainly not far enough to warrant taking major risks).The effect was the production of a constant stream of recognitions and indirect validations of the PID/PUT/"opposition" theory, thus solidifying it more and more into background knowledge. At the same time, negative recognition was systematically held back. The Stasi was caught in what Noelle-Neumann (1980) has described as a "spiral" and Zerubavel (2006) a "conspiracy of silence." And so the Stasi's seemingly well-validated theory did its bit to ossify socialism. The party's shield became all too eagerly wielded, a shovel helping to dig its grave.

SUBVERTING SUBVERSION: KNOWING AND FIGHTING PUT

Given the causal structure of the theory, the most logical point to fight PUT would have been to fight PID. Short of a revolution in the capitalist world, however, the best the GDR party state could hope for was to investigate where the enemies' intentions with PID were going and to occasionally disturb its practice. The reconnaissance work abroad increasingly fell into the responsibility of the Stasi's *Hauptverwaltung Aufklärung*, the foreign espionage wing (Eichner and Dobbert 1997; Wolf 1998; Großmann 2001; Knabe 1999). Using its informants in the West as "influence agents" (rather than mere spies) this department occasionally intervened directly in West German politics with the intention to shape outcomes. Arguably, the Stasi's most spectacular action in this regard was bribing two conservative members of the Bundestag to abstain in the 1972 no-confidence vote against Chancellor Willy Brandt (Wolf 1998).[19] If such interventions were done not always with the primary intention to fight PID (as in the case of "saving" Brandt, which might have been primarily undertaken for reasons of access to the chancellor since the Stasi had managed to place one of their top agents smack in the middle of Brandt's office), then the motive to weaken the enemy's capacity at waging ideological warfare was never far off either. The publication of the famous "Brownbook," listing the Nazi involvements of leading West German politicians and administrators, can be understood as an effort at undermining the authority of the presumed carriers of PID. Another important coup was Stasi spy Dirk Schneider as a speaker of the Berlin Greens (Alternative Liste), who did his utmost to steer the Greens away from full support of the peace and civil rights movements in East Germany.

With the options to fight PID at its source quite limited the next line of defense was to fight its reception in the GDR. Here, contact restrictions with people and ideas matter. For comrades the party was eager to impose these even when it could no longer do so for the population at large. Where contact could no longer be managed, shaping the interpretations of what had transpired offered a second line of defense. Someone who was "conscious," or "ideologically steeled," exhibiting a "firm class standpoint," someone who was embedded in a true socialist collective while most of his or her urgent problems were addressed and taken care of was thought to be quite impermeable to the "softening" efforts of the enemy. So again, propaganda, more

---

19. In the end the measure was less consequential than it might have been because general elections a few months later returned Brandt to office with a much stronger parliamentarian base, thus also popularly legitimating his détente policy. Brandt's resignation two years later, in which the discovery of the Stasi spy Günter Guillaume in Brandt's office played a role, was rather seen as a disaster by Stasi (Wolf 1998).

propaganda, and the improvement of propaganda were emphasized as a constantly increasing need.

In the eyes of the Stasi, two parts of GDR society were particularly vulnerable to enemy interference. First, where propaganda did not catch on, people were seen as in danger of drifting into that field of discourse and actions that could be developed into PUT by the malicious interventions of the enemy. There were a few institutional domains or social milieus that were seen as in continuous problematic relations with the party-state and therefore belonging to this field by definition. Religious communities were among them, as were people with the expressed desire to emigrate from the GDR (*Ausreisewillige*), and so were, for example, gays and lesbians who had to lead a marginal existence in GDR society. Second, the Stasi identified targets that were seen as particularly valuable to the enemy. The whole state sector was assigned to this category, as were the institutions of propaganda, especially the mass media, and the secondary and tertiary sector of education. To a certain degree, the organizational structure of Stasi, its changing differentiations into particular lines and sublines, reflects transformations in threat analysis for these two parts of society (Auerbach et al. 2008). For example, the XX-line of work within the ministry and district and county offices emerged as the center of anti-PUT activities and was formally charged with coordinating PUT-related Stasi work (directive 2/82). The initiation and/or rededication of particular sublines reflected the assessment of problematic milieus (e.g., XX/4 was responsible for the church, XX/9 for PUT in general) or high-value targets (e.g., XX/2 was responsible for the state, XX/7 for the mass media).

The final and most elaborate directive about PUT (2/85) states the tasks involved in combating it the following way (in Engelmann and Joestel 2004, 435ff.). The key areas for the officers to address are described as:

> [the] timely *discovery* of the plans, the intentions and the measures, means and methods of the enemy, especially those of the secret services and their legal bases in the GDR . . . [the] furnishing of legally valid proof that inimical forces are guided by secret service organizations . . . the *preventive averting*, discovery and fight against all activities respectively intentions of external enemies and of all inimical forces within the GDR [my emphasis].

The last point about "preventive averting" is further elaborated, guiding the officers to prevent, in particular, the formation of social networks, the public appearance of groups, the formation and maintenance of contacts with individuals or organizations in capitalist countries [labeled in espionage jargon as "backward-linkages"], the "abuse of churches," the "abuse of the possibilities inherent in cultural-artistic means of expression," and finally the "penetration of state facilities and of social organizations as well as the abuse of these facilities and organizations as well as of their public events."

Casework

How, then, did the Stasi begin its "operative work," investigating and combating PUT?[20] In spite of the Stasi's enormous volume of case files, this did not happen by a "comprehensive system of surveillance covering everyone everywhere" (*flächendeckende Überwachung*), as is often surmised, especially in the popular literature on the GDR and its secret police.

Starting

Only when behaviors seemed to fit the PUT matrix in a particular historical moment did the Stasi become active (occurrences that would have been considered negligible at one time could be considered noteworthy at others). The attention filters officers used were filled with substance in briefings at various levels that would alert them to new Stasi directives, a critical speech by a leading functionary, the special security concerns of an imminent major propaganda event, a state visit, or changing international constellations. The Stasi's PUT casework was largely person-centric, starting from a suspicion about an individual.[21] Leads from which officers worked came typically from their network of secret informants (who needed such briefings themselves to know what they were supposed to look for). Leads could also come from other ongoing investigations, such as security checks (directive 1/82, in Gill and Schröter 1991, 295–321), other state bureaucracies, party organs, even from concerned citizens. If the case seemed significant enough the officer in charge would start an "operative person control" (*operative Personenkontrolle* or *OPK*) in consultation with superiors according to directive 1/81 (in

---

20. In what follows I can only provide a rough overview over the regulatory framework guiding Stasi casework. A pioneering work showing Stasi's casework in operation is Joachim Walther's *Sicherungsbereich Literatur* (1996). For the various sub-branches of the Stasi, BStU's multi-volume *Anatomie der Staatssicherheit* (Suckut et al. 1993–) is very useful. For the XX-line, see in particular Auerbach et al. 2008.

21. The Stasi also investigated ordinary criminal cases if they were deemed relevant to the security of the state. Officers have noted that this casework proceeded in a different fashion. Crime investigations began with the certainty of a concrete act (which could be political too, such as painting a slogan at a wall), to find the person who did it. PUT investigations began with the suspicion that a person harbored party-critical ideas that might lead to party-critical (possibly criminal) actions.

Gill and Schröter 1991, 322–45).[22] If this process yielded suspicious circumstances pointing to behavior falling under the political part of the penal code, then an "operative case" (*Operativvorgang* or OV), according to directive 1/76 (in Gill and Schröter 1991), was opened. The leading members of the peace, civil rights, and environmental movements in Berlin during the 1980s were all investigated under the regulations of operative cases.[23] However, not all people participating in the work of these groups were investigated. Those deemed less significant by Stasi were investigated and pursued through an operative person control, or they might not have been dealt with as an individual case at all while being nevertheless registered and observed within the context of the groups.

The stated goals connected to the conduct of operative casework consisted of the collection of legally usable proofs for a political crime, to stop the negative effects of inimical behavior, to remove conditions supporting the genesis of inimical behavior, and to gain reconnaissance of the plans and actions of imperialistic secret services and other inimical centers (Gill and Schröter 1991, 373). That Stasi was a thoroughly bureaucratized organization can be gleaned from the fact that these goals were pursued *through* the production of orderly case files kept in accordance with written rules and regulations. In other words, the regulations offered understandings (even if they were not the only ones) on the basis of which actions were planned, discussed, and recorded, because the Stasi officers as proper bureaucrats were held accountable for their actions in accordance with directives, orders, and instructions.

The operative case file always begins with an "initial report" (*Eröffnungsbericht*) that details the legal norms on the basis of which the investigation takes place.[24] It also lists the suspicious circumstances supporting the

22. In order to avoid misunderstandings I should point out here that the administrative instruments described in what follows were not only geared toward fighting PUT. Instead, their wording was kept general so that they could be applied to potentially all kinds of actions considered to threaten the security of the GDR, among them the classic espionage, sabotage and terror, as well as ordinary crime with a state security dimension (e.g., arson against a government institution, the murder of high ranking state functionary, etc.).

23. Reading the files of operative cases constituted the backbone of my archival work, for the most part conducted at the Matthias Domaschk Archiv at the Robert Havemann Foundation in Berlin. Among others, I have read the files of OV "Zirkel" against Gerd and Ulrike Poppe; OV "Bohle" against Bärbel Bohley; OV "Korn" against Thomas Klein; ZOV "Wespen" against "Women for Peace"; OV "Verräter" against Wolfgang Templin; and more cursorily: OV "Leitz" against Robert Havemann.

24. The relevant norms could be expanded or changed in the course of the investigation, however. In training materials the officers were exhorted to use the flexibility (i.e., the substantive

case, and it includes a first "action plan" (*Maßnahmeplan* or *Operativplan*). In regular intervals, the progress of operative procedures was summarized in "interim reports," which would also explain changes in the strategy of casework, actions pursued, and so forth. Otherwise the body of case files was made up of reports conveying information about concrete Stasi actions, above all about the meetings between guidance officers and secret informants, but also protocols of observations, of telephone or apartment bugging operations, of mail surveillance, or of open or clandestine apartment searches. To the degree that secret informants obtained them, they may also contain copies of the writings of dissidents, petitions, lectures, or articles for samizdat publications. Since one and the same report could be relevant to a host of different operative cases, these reports were shared with other relevant Stasi units.[25]

Closing cases

In the context of the peace and civil rights movements, most operative cases ended (if they ended at all) in either of two ways.[26] Formally, closure by opening legal procedures (*Ermittlungsverfahren*) leading to a trial and a sentence was foregrounded. Seen in this way, the collection of evidence that would prove that the pursued person[27] had committed a crime under any

---

rationality) of socialist law. The directives leave no doubt that the point of an operative procedure was to remove dangers to the public security and order of the GDR, in the case relevant here, to prevent PUT and to use the law creatively to that end.

25. There has always been considerable friction in this regard between different branches of the Stasi. The collaboration between directions in ministries and regional offices did not work as smoothly as the case-leading officers and their superiors should have liked. This could be problematic as different members of one and the same group could be pursued by bureaucratic units sharing superiors in line-responsibility only at the highest rank. Herein lies one of the reasons why various units liked to keep control over their sources of information, which means that they employed many more secret informants than they should have needed to obtain the information and the influence they did.

26. The other possible finalizations suggested by directive 1/76 are the recruitment of the operatively pursued person as an informant, the use of the case material for blackmail in nonsocialist countries, the transfer of the materials to party and state with recommendations for security-improving policies, as well as other non-Stasi-related sanctions.

27. The choice of a single proper verb describing Stasi's relation to the persons who became the object of their cases poses some problems. The Stasi's own word, *bearbeiten*, means really "to casework." The German word also has suitable overtones, for it also means "to treat in order to change" (as a craftsperson would with material) and by metaphoric extension "to try to change somebody's mind." Much of the literature on the Stasi uses the word *verfolgen* in the sense of "to persecute," which has deep ethical resonances. Even though this is quite correct from the perspective of the opposition members, this does not reflect the self-understanding of Stasi

of the provisions of the political ("special") part of the penal code of the GDR would have been in the center of the casework.[28] At least as far as the members of the peace and civil rights movements are concerned this was, however, not the case. The formal closure of an operative case through the opening of legal proceedings was rare. There are three reasons why this is the case. First, under the political circumstances of the 1980s the party often decided against trials as it feared international repercussions that would outweigh the gain from weakening dissident circles through the prison term of any of its members. In the last chapter I mentioned several cases where legal procedures were initiated by the Stasi but were dropped at the behest of the party after domestic and international protests. It has to be remembered in this context that socialist law still followed in the last instance a substantive form of rationality. The directive 1/76 (Gill and Schröter 1991, 394 and 395) expresses this clearly in the demand that "the closure of operative cases has to serve the political interests of the GDR . . . with every closure, those closure possibilities must be determined that yield the greatest security-political utility." This is to say that the drive toward a comprehensive, monolithic intentionality had to govern Stasi casework as much as it had to govern the production of screws or the self-objectification of every single party member. Even where Stasi managed to provide legally sufficient grounds to proceed with a trial, politics often effectively closed off this venue, leaving Stasi officers with the frustration of an open case.

Second, providing the legally required evidence was not always easy given the methods with which the Stasi was working. The greatest handicap in this sense was that the reports provided by secret informants could not be used in legal proceedings without blowing their cover. This would have burned an important source, and the Stasi would have thus broken a pledge to their informants never to make their work public. Occasionally, the Stasi tried

---

officers. At the same time, the verb "to investigate" does not capture the ways in which the Stasi destructively intervened in peoples' lives.

28. That code was overhauled in 1968 with further amendments in 1974, and both the text of the law and the commentary on it have absorbed the PID/PUT/"opposition" theory. In response to contacts with Western organizations or persons, outright espionage (§§ 97, 98) was typically not brought into play as a reason to launch an operative case. However, the milder forms of "treacherous transmission of information" and "treacherous spying activity" (§§ 99 and 100) were indeed used, as was, more commonly, the paragraph regulating "unlawful initiation of contact" (§ 219). In prosecutions of publicly performed critiques of state and party, "inflammatory speech against the state" (§ 106) was regularly invoked; less common was "public disparagement" (§ 220). For the prosecution of the formation of groups and networks "anticonstitutional union" (§ 107) and "union for the pursuit of illegal goals" (§ 218) could be used. If enough evidence had been collected (assessed by the Stasi's legal department IX), legal preliminary proceedings would be opened by the state prosecutor's office.

to get out of the conundrum imposed by using secret-informant-generated evidence by planting evidence to frame the person under investigation. The case of Thomas Klein, which I discussed in chapter 7 (p. 386) offers a case in point.

The third reason why legal closure was rare is that the GDR underwent progressive legalization throughout its history. The notions of substantive rationality came increasingly in conflict with a legal-formal rationality that emphasized proper process. In the 1980s the GDR still had no system of administrative justice or a multitier legal review system. So it would be quite premature to speak of a "rule of law" or "due process." However, the GDR was also no longer simply an *Unrechtsstaat* (state operating with disregard for legal procedure), as much of the popular (cf. Kocka 1999, 17; Jarausch 1999, 63) German literature on the GDR claims. In fact, the officers I have spoken with have universally reported that the requirements for legal proof were becoming more stringent in the course of time. Stasi had its own legal department investigating the legal merit of cases submitted by operative departments for consideration of opening legal procedures. An interesting case that speaks to these higher requirements with regard to the quality of the evidence supplied is the Stasi's sequestration of the inoperable printing press in its search of the environmental library (pp. 449–50) which was dismissed by the prosecutor as unusable evidence. There is no doubt that in the 1950s and or even in the 1960s nobody would have cared for such "details."

Decomposing people and groups

The second form of closure envisioned by the Stasi was called "decomposition" (*Zersetzung*). It is the method that garnered the attention of the public after the GDR's fall. This is not surprising, because its practice fits Friedrich's (1956) popular model of totalitarianism, which garnered a lot of renewed interest in the immediate aftermath of the GDR's dissolution. The hallmark of his model is his emphasis on secret police terror as a constitutive element of the political institutions of a country.[29] And in spite of the fact that post-Stalinist socialism cannot adequately be described as operating on the basis

---

29. Arendt's (1968) theory of totalitarianism is often lumped together with Friedrich's because both try to identify totalitarianism as a state form and because both link totalitarianism to the practice of terror. However, what Arendt has in mind with the term *terror* are not concentration camps and gulags (even though they can be its consequence) but the institutional complex I have differentiated into absolute finality and monolithic intentionality in chapter 1. Writes Arendt: "Terror is the realization of the law of movement; its chief aim is to make it possible for the force of nature or of history to race freely through mankind, unhindered by any spontaneous human action" (465).

of mass terror, the Stasi's technique of decomposition was certainly a form of terror. In contradistinction with the mass terror that early totalitarianism theories have in mind, however, this terror was wielded against a select few. Moreover, it did not work with physical threats to life and limb, but operated with social and psychological means of influence. Here is how the directive 1/76 describes it (in Gill and Schröter 1991, 389–90):

> Measures of decomposition are to be directed toward the creation as well as the utilization and the amplification of contradictions and disagreements between inimical-negative forces through which they can be splintered, paralyzed, disorganized, and isolated, so that their inimical-negative actions including their effects can be preventively averted, essentially reduced or completely stopped. . . . Measures of decomposition are to be used especially if the casework has yielded the prerequisite proofs for the commitment of a political crime or of an ordinary crime *while the operative case cannot be closed through criminal procedures, because of political or political-operative reasons in the interest of realizing a higher social utility.* (My emphasis)

The document continues to explain that measures of decomposition also have their place in operative casework where the opening of criminal procedures are quite likely, if decomposition can actually help to reduce the inimical-negative behavior.

What strikes me as noteworthy about this placement of decomposition as a means of control into a wider context of Stasi practices is the contradiction that emerges between the drive toward increasing legalization and the kind of legitimacy it affords on the one hand and the Leninist assertion of the absolute primacy of the party's current goal that has to be pursued if necessary through extralegal means on the other. Decomposition had no legal status as a regular sanction of the state, and if it did, it would have undermined the state's legitimacy. One could put it yet differently: decomposition is the attempt to generate power in a situation where it faces legal and reputational constraints; it is an attempt at politics (the destruction of a budding set of institutions) where its publicly available means are deemed insufficient; it is ultimately an attempt to reassert sovereignty in a nonsovereign environment. How so, becomes clearer as the directive becomes more concrete in spelling out the range of means envisioned (in Gill and Schröter 1991, 390–91):

> Proven methods of decomposition to be used are:
>
> · systematic destruction of public reputation, standing, and prestige on the basis of the connection between true, verifiable, and discrediting as well as untrue, credible nondisprovable, and thus equally discrediting information;
> · systematic organization of professional and social failures to undermine the self-confidence of individual persons;

- generation of distrust and mutual suspiciousness within group, groupings, and organizations;
- generation respectively utilization and amplification of rivalries within groups, groupings, and organizations, with the help of the goal-directed use of personal weaknesses of individual members;
- busying groups, groupings, and organizations with their own internal problems with the goal to limit their inimical-negative actions;
- local and temporal disruption respectively limitation of mutual relationships between the members of groups, groupings, and organizations on the basis of valid legal norms, for example, through the utilization at their workplaces or the assignment of work at distant places.

Decomposition was above all a method to undermine the agency of supposed PUT carriers. To research and teach how this could be done, the Stasi's university in Potsdam–Eiche maintained chairs in "operative psychology" (Behnke and Fuchs 1995). In the introduction I argued that agency is enabled by the conjunction of understanding and resources. Since understandings are always social (as I have shown in chapter 3), one can accordingly analytically differentiate between three fundamental approaches to decomposition: epistemic manipulation, interference with social relationships, and resource deprivation. The first, the more prominently featured approach in the above quotation, encourages officers to interfere systematically with the spaces of validation of individuals or of groups as a whole. It proposes the manipulation of the quality and quantity of validations available to certain discursive, emotive, or kinesthetic understandings. It also offers as a means of manipulation the introduction of new understandings, which, if actualized, stand a chance to undermine the life of the group. Finally, it advocates the manipulation of processes of thinking through, working through, and practicing. The second aims at manipulating people's reputation and the level of trust characterizing their relationship. The deprivation of resources as a third method to limit or destroy agency comes more prominently to the fore in the last item on the list. The resources that matter here most are the time somebody has at his or her disposition to meet and to engage in action, the space that groups need to meet and/or to perform their action, and finally the means to communicate, that is, to projectively articulate actions across time and space. Interestingly, money or income played a more limited role in the power calculus of decomposition, because the state had to offer employment while essentials such as rent and basic foodstuffs were comparatively cheap. If one could live with little and had no children to feed and clothe, income ceased to be an existentially menacing point of intervention.

Using the sociology of understanding as a structuring device, I will provide in what follows a quick survey over Stasi's measures of decomposition.[30] I do so keeping in mind that in the following section I will discuss the efficacy of these measures, which requires a theory of *how* they have operated. It should also be kept in mind that measures of decomposition were often not applied singly, one after another, but in combination and over a longer period of time.[31] Certain individuals who were consistently identified by the Stasi as the leaders of PUT activities in Berlin—Wolfgang Templin, one of the founding members of the IFM, is a good example and so is Rainer Eppelmann, pastor of the Church of the Samaritan—were subjected to a whole barrage of such measures (Pingel-Schliemann 2002, 294–300; Eppelmann 1993, passim). Finally, it is important to keep in mind that not all members of particular groups were treated uniformly.[32]

Among the tools of epistemic manipulation the easiest and most widely used strategy was to use the network of secret informants *to recognize understandings selectively* to affect their actualization in the desired direction. Where informants were unsuitable for such a task because the risks of blowing their cover were deemed too high, anonymous letters or phone calls could be used. Here are some characteristic examples. Informants were, irony of ironies, under standing orders to raise security concerns among the activists, thus feeding other members' existing anxieties; they were asked to raise doubts about the group's ability to carry through a particular action, thus amplifying other activists' self-doubt, and all of that under the guise of care and thoughtfulness. The technique of selective recognition was also used at larger open events taking place in lecture halls, churches, or performance venues to steer the atmosphere in a desired direction, for example, by cheering the contribution of more party-friendly speakers while meeting those of critics with icy reserve. For this purpose Stasi used "social forces" (*gesellschaftliche Kräfte*), as this was far too risky a strategy for moles placed within the group. In

30. To some degree I will list measures of the secret police, which the officers themselves would not have labeled "decomposition." Yet even in their own use the concept was blurry. Following the Stasi's logic I will include in it all of their activities that intentionally interfered with activists' lives to end activities Stasi interpreted as PUT.

31. For an overview covering cases of variants of decomposition from all over the GDR, see Pingel-Schliemann 2002.

32. Although this may well have been intended in theory, the documents I have been able to consult do not suggest that this was a deliberately carried out strategy. Pingel-Schliemann (2002) argues that the level and intensity of means of decomposition unleashed against an individual were more dependent on the personal inclination of the individual case's leading officer and the willingness of superiors to support such measures. Based on my interviews and the cases I have studied in depth, I can only support this conclusion.

the simplest variant, these were prebriefed secret police cadets, in more complex ones (involving more coordinating preparations), comrades from the local party organizations were involved. Well-targeted recognition could also be employed to amplify opposing opinions between fractions. In the group splitting I discussed in the last chapter, selective recognition was employed. In particularly disturbing cases, children were mobilized through pressures in school to influence their parents in a more conformist direction.

Secret informants also deliberately *planted understandings* that were likely to have strong resonances with preexisting, potentially destructive beliefs or desires. This was the idea behind combining existing with new information, amplifying the validity of the old in combination with lending credibility to the new. In this way, secret informants were used to feed ambitions, misgivings, or desires that could lead to friction; they were amplifying mistrust as well as aesthetic and moral discomfort of one member with another. Rumors were planted, most commonly about a person's link to the secret police, which was building on the group's hunches that they probably had moles in their midst. Another tried and tested means of planting understanding used especially against Protestant ministers, was spreading lies about persons' sexual life (e.g., suggesting infidelities, dissipation, or perversion) or about inappropriate levels of alcohol consumption. These were often backed by planted corroborating circumstantial evidence, such as retouched photographs, sexual toys, or strategically placed liquor bottles. The effect the Stasi aimed at with these measure was the destruction of the targeted person's self-confidence by creating shame-saturated events and/or the erosion of this person's authority in the eyes of other network members, thus ultimately destroying the operability of the network by depriving it of nodal figures.

Manipulating corroboration was also employed as a tool of decomposition. Most notably, the secret police managed to prevent people from obtaining a desired job or place at an educational institution. It arranged for people to be fired or dismissed. Stasi also influenced performance reviews, grading, and decisions to send somebody to continuing education or to an international conference. Decisions to have a manuscript for publication accepted or rejected or to award a particular research project to a particular person, could all be influenced by the Stasi in the interest of molding the targeted person's understandings. Where such measures caught their targets unaware of their entanglement in the Stasi's web of machination, they were meant to confirm doubt about their own abilities. Where people knew who was responsible for their misfortune, the "organization of failure" was meant to shape people's assessment of risk involved in party-critical activities. With the same intention, the Stasi often flaunted its presence in front of residences, on the way to and outside of events, to enhance movement members' fear that surveillance was inescapable. They tried to smother actions at people's doorsteps to confirm activists' anxieties that the Stasi knew everything and that they were ready to take action and certainly would not let them do what they wanted to do. If people could not be prevented from attending, the Stasi might also try to suffocate a wider participatory event by providing the majority of the audience. The political night prayers I discussed in the last chapter were, from the second one onward, strongly frequented by the Stasi's social forces attempting to corroborate the group's frustrations about not being able to conduct events as planned and to reach a wider audience in the GDR. Finally, the Stasi even broke into apartments, not just for searches, but to show that they could, with impunity, do as they pleased in this regard. All activists I spoke with found this measure particularly insidious because it confounded basic kinesthetic background understandings about the boundaries between inside and outside, control and contingency, safety and risk.

The manipulation of corroboration requires a high degree of environmental control. What helped the Stasi enormously in this respect were the means available to it in a centrally organized state oriented toward a common goal by the membership of most significant actors in the same Leninist vanguard party. Even though the Stasi had no formal authority to issue directives directly to other branches of the administration or the economy, it produced a formidable track record of organizing workplace pressures on dissidents. These were often facilitated by employees who were co-opted as secret informants and on whom the Stasi could rely as their own influence agents. The Stasi's success is also owed to the willingness of employees in their role as party members to cooperate with their comrades from the fabled secret police. After all, the Stasi could take for granted a basic agreement among comrades about the dangers of political diversion that were prominently discussed in general propaganda. A further reason for workplaces to comply with the Stasi's requests was that they did not want risky troublemakers among their ranks who could potentially endanger the productivity of their work collectives or attract unwanted party attention by creating a stir around some ideological issue. In either case this would have entailed blame of leaders for lax discipline or unsuccessful ideological work.

The *control of resources* available to dissidents offered another set of means for the Stasi to try their hand at decomposing dissidents and groups. A necessary resource for action is time, and so the Stasi tried to deprive activists of the time to engage in oppositional activities. Prison terms mark the extreme end of such measures. Keeping dissidents employed was at times also chosen as a means to keep them busy. The Stasi learned in the course of time that activists' underemployment in nondemanding jobs was detrimental to their intentions. It gave activists time to think and to prepare actions; and perhaps even worse: it left the activists with dissidence as their main career.

By contrast, meaningful employment offered at least some leverage for intervention. Time was also restricted on a smaller scale. The Stasi tried to keep activists from getting vacation time granted for days of planned actions or for the attendance of meetings in other cities. Another way to limit time availability was to let groups slide into excessive self-politics. Security concerns or tactics could potentially be discussed ad nauseam. Secret informants could delay the completion of tasks they were assigned. Activists were at times busied by yet other means. Stasi would place ads in periodicals in the name of a dissident with the offer to buy or sell particular kinds of goods with the effect that the targeted activist had to busy him or herself fending off buyers or sellers on the phone or worse even, at the door. A variant of this measure consisted in ordering repairs the dissident never thought of undertaking.

Space is as necessary as time to bring about action. After the party state's own performance venues became definitely closed to more critical programming after the Biermann denaturalization, the Stasi tried to dissuade activists from staging readings or concerts in their own apartments by fining them for the violation of city codes after repeated injunctions. Such fines could quickly reach the level of a monthly salary. The Stasi used the state's compact with the Protestant Church, as well as its network of secret informants among church officials, to induce local ministers to refrain from providing church spaces to dissident activities. Other resources that mattered were those the movement members needed to projectively articulate their actions, that is, especially means of communication and transportation but also the organizational capacities of the Protestant Church. As far as the technological means of communication are concerned, the Stasi had to balance two opposing rationales. On the one hand, severely curtailing dissidents' means of communication would have limited their ability to coordinate even such simple things as meetings. On the other hand, their use of telephones offered enhanced means of surveillance, more simple to carry out than, for example, bugging apartments. Apparently, the Stasi gave preference to the surveillance aspect and sometimes provided telephones to dissidents more quickly than to ordinary citizens. Stasi also monitored the personal correspondence addressed to activists. Knowing or at least suspecting comprehensive surveillance, they had to use personal couriers for important messages they did not want the Stasi to know anything about, or they had to begin encrypting what they transmitted via monitored channels. Finally, the secret police attempted to constrain the physical mobility of activists. I mentioned that many peace and civil rights movement members could, from a certain point on, no longer freely travel even to Eastern European countries. Activists working in the provinces could be prohibited from traveling to Berlin. In at least one case I have come across (Eppelmann 1993, passim), Stasi tried to immobilize a person by tampering repeatedly with his car.

In sum, then, the Stasi tried to influence almost all aspects critical to the formation of dissident institutions: understandings and their validation, resources necessary for action, the means of projectively articulating actions across space and time and with it the size and shape of networks. Given that these efforts were in theory rather encompassing, two questions emerge: "were there any limits to these efforts?" and "how effective were they in fact?" The following two sections provide some answers to these questions.

Were there limits to decomposition?

Particular officers and departments in the Stasi were not content with the means of decomposition provided to them through directive 1/76. Well documented is the case of section 4 (responsible for church affairs) of department XX of the Berlin district office of Stasi, which saw itself as a kind of PUT-fighting vanguard. Owing to security lapses and secret informant activities deemed problematic by superiors, it was investigated repeatedly by the ministry's "central group for analysis and information" (ZAIG) (BStU MfS-ZAIG 13748).[33] Department XX of Stasi's Berlin district office was deeply steeped in efforts to control Berlin's ever-expanding peace, civil rights, and environmental movements. Among others, section 4 of department XX had taken on Rainer Eppelmann as well as his blues-mass collaborator and IFM member, Ralf Hirsch. During the 1980s many, perhaps even most PUT-casework leading officers, were frustrated about their difficulties with closing cases. After all, their ability to bring casework to an end was a formal bureaucratic yardstick for personal and organizational performance reviews even though it was quite clear that PUT cases were unlike others. As I mentioned above, the possibility to close cases through the initiation of legal procedures became increasingly blocked for political reasons. At the same time, however, the regular means of decomposition just described did not produce the desired effect either.

These frustrations ran particularly high in Berlin, where the size of the problem strained the Stasi beyond its organizational capacity. Still, the officers were charged with the task of stopping PUT, and they took this very seriously. Since they found the means available inadequate to achieve the goal set for them, they began to think of ways out of what they perceived

---

33. The material presented in this file is interesting for other reasons, too. It provides insights into Stasi's bureaucratic culture, including the competition between various departments. It also shows how some individual Stasi officers could use their powers to their own advantage by stealing from the perceived enemy, here the Protestant Church. Interestingly, the same officers who were particularly active in coming up with violent means of decomposition sought to reward themselves with illicit material privileges.

as stalemate. Hence, several of them began a personal crusade, planning further-reaching and better-coordinated measures of decomposition. Plans were made to criminalize dissidents by smuggling goods they did not buy into their shopping bag or by feigning robberies in such a way that movement activists were implicated; physical assaults were concocted and even the ultimate became thinkable: the provocation of accidents entailing the potential death of the victim (Eppelmann 1993, 188). Typically, superiors further up in the chain of command refused to provide their agreement to such extreme measures for the obvious reason that substantial physical harm, to say nothing about the death of any of the well-known peace and civil rights movement activists, would have entailed a major public relations disaster for the GDR.

In consequence of the Stasi's internal investigation, a change of leadership personnel ensued, and the operative officers were relieved of their work with informants. This case nicely illustrates how ultimately decomposition found its boundary in its utility to the overarching goals of the party. The officers have told me that they had limited discussions among themselves about the moral standing of certain means of decomposition. Some argued that communists, Chekists of a socialist secret service, should, in contradistinction from imperialist secret services, not do certain kinds of things (BStU MfS-ZAIG 13748, 68). Such discussions also occurred in the context of invetigating and harassing communists such as Biermann and Havemann. Indeed, there were elements of deontological reasoning in socialist discourses. While I have no doubt that there were such considerations, I suspect that if there had ever been a serious confrontation between the logic of goals and the appropriateness of means, the latter would probably have lost, because the former would have had much stronger resonances with doctrine as well as with the ways in which careers in socialist organizations were negotiated.

The effects of measures of decomposition

I have shown in the last two chapters how important the formation of alternative networks of authority was for the emergence of dissident identities and political understandings. I have also placed great emphasis on the experience and celebration of successful actions as a constitutive part of activists' trajectories into dissidence. Since measures of decomposition aimed to interfere with such crucial moments in the formation of dissident institutions, the question that poses itself is whether decomposition worked. The detailed analysis of a case may help to shed light on the conditions for success or failure of measures of decomposition.

A fine example for the ways in which Stasi tried to subvert the institutionalization of oppositional activity by measures of decomposition is its attempt to paralyze the Berlin group Frauen für den Frieden by en-meshing it in infighting during the late winter of 1983/84. The arrest, the opening of preliminary legal proceedings, and six weeks of jail for Bärbel Bohley and Ulrike Poppe derailed the group's activities by spreading fear. Although the imprisonment of the two women fundamentally destabilized processes of institutional maintenance by significantly altering understand-ings about the risk involved in the group's work, the arrest itself is not what Stasi meant with decomposition. Yet, the situation resulting from the arrest provided the Stasi with a docking point for a measure of decomposition. When it became clear to other group members that Bohley and Poppe were arrested because they had, unbeknownst to almost all other group mem-bers, met a peace activist from New Zealand who wanted to write an article about the them in an English publication (see chapter 7, p. 429), a number of members felt betrayed, even ruthlessly put at risk. This led to an emotional argument between various members both before and after the release of Bohley and Poppe from jail (Kukutz 1995, 1310). As set out in directive 1/76, the Stasi's secret informants were asked to watch the groups they spied on for any possible rifts. Simple character incompatibilities, conflicting ambi-tions, sexual jealousies, divergent interactional styles, ideological frictions, anything that could lead to distrust or even open animosities among group members was of great interest to the Stasi. The informants were for that rea-son asked to provide ongoing character assessments as well as atmospheric reports about the state of the group. In the case of Frauen für den Frieden case officers saw the discussions about the moral valence of the secret meet-ing between four members of the group with a Westerner as a possible ful-crum for an intervention with the potential to place groups onto a path of destructive self-politics. Through its top-secret informant Monika Häger (IMB "Karin Lenz") and others, Stasi was well informed about the group's anxieties and controversies surrounding the arrest of Poppe and Bohley.

In mid-February the Stasi set out to exploit its clandestinely acquired knowledge for its intended work of destruction. As so often in the Stasi's op-erations of decomposition, the methods used stem from the classic repertoire of intrigue. Some Stasi officer in collaboration with a secret informant—the latter was important to produce a text in an authentic sounding register—concocted an anonymous letter for circulation in the women's group. Enti-tling the letter "impulses" (*Anregungen*), it was distributed to group mem-bers in the style of a circular placed directly into their mailboxes.[34] The letter indirectly charged Bohley and Poppe with an "arrogant leadership style,"

---

34. The original letter is lost. Most members of the group threw it away after it became clear to them of whose pen it was. All references to its content are from other documents citing it directly or indirectly.

as evidenced by their high-handed clandestine meeting with the foreign peace activist. As insinuated by the anonymous letter, this meeting revealed significant asymmetries of information (and by implication: power) in the group. Tellingly, the letter also took position against considerations floating around at that time to associate the group more formally with the Protestant Church in an effort to better protect its members from Stasi actions. This was controversial in the group as it was clear to most members—who were overwhelmingly secular in orientation—that activities planned and conducted under the auspices of the church were once more subject to authoritative approval and de facto restricted by the church's complicated compact with the party state.

On February 16, 1984, Lieutenant Jäger of the department 2 of the ministry's division XX, the likely author of this measure of decomposition and the guidance officer of secret informant Monika Häger, wrote a report about a meeting with her in which he characterized the effect of the letter on three members of the group who had met two days earlier in Beate Harembski's apartment. All four participants (especially the three not working on behalf of the Stasi) are depicted as agreeing with the basic propositions of the anonymous letter. The officer describes how the informant (the likely coauthor of the letter) chimed in with this sentiment by calling the dynamics of the group as having arrived "at ground zero." Through this recognizing intervention, she thus nudged the interaction even further in the direction of the result desired by the Stasi. The officer claims that the conversations of the evening and the letter have encouraged the three women to seek an open confrontation with Poppe and Bohley during one of the next meetings. The report concludes:

> The source [i.e., the informant Häger] is of the opinion that the letter's content and time of distribution will probably deepen the extant contradictions in the women's group.

In other words, the guidance officer and his informant are reporting an emergent success of an implemented measure of decomposition to the higher-ups in the Stasi hierarchy.

Nine days later, on February 25, 1984, officer Jäger reports about a report[35] of his informant about a conversation she had the day before with Ulrike

---

35. Although the language in what follows may sound awkward, it is important to keep in mind to which degree the case officers were actually removed from the persons they investigated. Sometimes it would be tempting to add a little number in superscript to the verb "to report" in order to indicate through how many links a particular occurrence was reported. To say in this notation, if an informant reports[1] (that is, something he or she has directly witnessed), the guidance officer reports,[2] and the case officer or analyst summarizing these reports[2] actually

Poppe about the letter. Therein, Poppe is depicted as hesitant about what to make of the letter. She is said to have emphasized the importance of a democratic atmosphere in the group but also to have shown considerable anger toward the letter by burning it upon receipt.[36] Another two days later, with the help of a bug installed in the apartment of Lutz and Bettina Rathenow, the Stasi eavesdropped on a conversation between Bettina Rathenow and Ulrike Poppe. The two have, according to the eavesdropping protocol,[37] led a frank and open discussion about what was going on with the group during Poppe's imprisonment. Rathenow is said to have assured Poppe, by pointing to the language of the letter, that she has no doubt that it must be a Stasi fabrication. Perhaps not so surprisingly, then, Stasi officer Jäger had to report yet another two days later about the account of his informant Häger concerning a meeting she had attended on February 27 with a larger group, which this time included Bohley and Poppe. This report makes clear that the Stasi's effort to decompose the group created a temporary friction at best, and that the positive assessment of the anonymous letter's effects were premature. Even though Jäger reports that the evening began with an open airing of the conflict, several members, including the secret informant, are said to have calmly defended the necessity of some measure of secrecy within the group. Three other members close to Poppe and Bohley, among them Bettina Rathenow, are credited with the suggestion that the letter was a Stasi forgery launched to divide the group, thus taking a position against the claims made in the anonymous letter. The Stasi report suggests that after several members of the group had declared in the meeting to have destroyed the letter for this reason, the correct interpretation seems to have prevailed in the discussion. This does not mean that the conflicts were not taken seriously. Quite to the contrary, according to the Stasi report, the women proposed more common activities to get to know one another better on a more personal level. Clearly the women were eager to engage in trust-building exercises. In keeping with its PID/PUT/"opposition" theory the Stasi, however, interpreted the women's plans to get to know each other better as an effort to differentiate friend from foe (using the Stasi's own term—"who-is-who reconnaissance"). One member of the women's group

---

reports.[3] Needless to say that the informant often only reports[2] or even reports[3] with consequences for everybody further down the stream of information processing.

36. MDA, OV "Zirkel" MfS XX/2 "Bericht zum Treff des IMB "Karin Lenz" am 24.2.84" dated 25.2.84.

37. Since, as every ethnographer knows, verbatim transcriptions are incredibly time consuming, the Stasi's department 26 (interestingly always set in Arabic numerals), the unit responsible for eavesdropping operations, has typically provided only summarizing reports about the verbal exchanges recorded on tape. One can therefore not assume that the language reported by the Stasi was in fact the language used by the spied upon persons.

proposed that the women could meet weekly at the sauna in a public pool. That proposal was apparently acknowledged by Ulrike Poppe with the wry comment: "Women sweat for peace." The rest of the meeting was dedicated to the organization of future activities. At the end the report has to implicitly acknowledge the failure of the decomposition measure while still trying to make good of it:

> In the estimation of the source [Häger] Poppe and Bohley did no longer appear as much in control [of the group] as before their internment. In both [women] the absolute demand to lead is no longer so clearly discernible.

Here is a concrete example of how Stasi tried to selectively validate those understandings floating around in the group that served its purposes best. It did so with the help of the anonymous letter, recognizing certain understandings that were deemed to have been corroborated by the course of events and that obviously had considerable resonance with what a number of women must have felt or thought already. This resonance is the real kernel from which the operation could proceed, lending the anonymous letter its initial credibility. The Stasi also used the direct commentary of the secret informants in the discussion to actively steer understandings in this direction.

From the Stasi's perspective, these interventions would ideally have been sufficient enough to propel the dynamics of the group along a self-reinforcing trajectory of destructive self-politics. The reasons why this did not happen reveal the limits of decomposition measures as techniques of control. In chapter 4 I argued that all recognitions of understandings are precarious because in voicing them the status of an authority is potentially put in jeopardy. This means that neither the letter nor the oral interventions of the informants could be worded in such strong terms that they would have risked losing their authority. In fact, the necessity of continuing secrecy forced the Stasi to ambiguous interventions. Monika Häger, the informant in question, for example, had to counterbalance indirect insinuations that Irena Kukutz might be a Stasi spy with assistance to Poppe and Bohley, justifying their restrictive information policy. Finally, the effective application of selective recognition presupposed authority. With only a few exceptions (e.g., Wolfgang Wolf, Ibrahim Böhme), however, secret informants were not among the small group of most authoritative figures in movement circles, even though many of them advanced to important second-tier positions. The reason is simple. As activists have pointed out to me time and again, authority within the movements came with a track record, with ideas for action and leadership in carrying them out. However, the Stasi did not want their secret informants to take the initiative. They were typically not employed as agents provocateurs; given the political circumstances the radicalization of the movements could not be in the interest of the Stasi since trials were unlikely to come forth anyway.[38] Accordingly, except for those informants who seem to have pursued their personal agenda, in playing their double role as secret informant acting within the Stasi's rules of engagement they could not advance to first tier group leadership positions.[39]

The problem with selective recognition as a tool of influence was amplified if the recognizing agents were readily identifiable as agents of the state. This was typically the case with the Stasi's use of "social forces," who were often enough recognizable as party members by linguistic register, habitus, and dress. Thus identified they typically became anti-authorities for the activists. As far as recognitions are concerned the epistemic effect of the action thus achieved exactly the opposite of what it was meant to accomplish. What the Stasi could do in the most extreme cases was to literally inundate an open group with the presence of social forces. The effect was produced in such cases not through selective recognition, but by corroborating the fear that party-critical work was futile anyway. The Pankow peace circle was, for all practical purposes, dissolved in this manner (Lengsfeld 1992).

The case of the anonymous letter to the women's group still holds other lessons. In principle the method of planting destructive understandings is limited by the understandings already actualized in the group so that they can enjoy plausibility through their underlying resonances. Since such understandings are often emotive rather than discursive, they take empathy to discover with sufficient precision. With its anonymous letter to the women's group the Stasi had calculated correctly. Its claims obviously hit a raw nerve with the feelings of a significant number of group members. And yet, the discursive culture prevailing in the group enabled the women to work constructively with disagreements. In particular, they resisted the de-authorization of other group members in the face of contradicting recognitions. This success at defusing subversion has an institutional and more contingent basis. Institutionally, the women's resolution of the conflict was enabled by a number of closer, even intimate friendships that offered spaces

38. One of the last acts of Monika Häger as a secret informant was to write a short analysis of how to improve the work with secret informants in the Stasi. There too she argues that informants should be allowed to become more active to acquire authority within any group (1989 passim, especially 25).

39. This can be argued, for example, for Wolfgang Wolf (alias "Max") who was a vocal member of the Friedrichsfelde peace circle (BVB, AKG, April 12, 1989). It can also be argued for Ibrahim Böhme (alias "Maximilian") who became an important member of the IFM (Lahann 1992, 209–27) after its near breakdown in 1988 (see below). In the Prenzlauer Berg's poetry scene, Sascha Anderson (IM "Fritz Müller" or "David Menzer") and Rainer Schedlinski (IM "Gerhard"), played a similarly active, and in the Stasi's view, ambiguous role.

for the open discussion of the accusations. Multiply crosscutting ties between the women prevented the polarization of the group into two antagonistic camps. History also treated the group favorably precisely at this moment. The release of Poppe and Bohley gave everybody a sense of relief, of common purpose and of success. In the end, both friendships and common goals were fortified through the debunking of the Stasi action. What the Stasi intended to destroy found itself to be strengthened.

The Stasi did not fare much better in other projects of decomposition. Unlike in the case of the letter, the measures were frequently devised so clumsily that after the initial discombobulation gave way to reflection, the fabricator of the trouble was easily and quickly identified as the secret police. In such cases the Stasi typically achieved the opposite of what it wanted. What worked in the Stasi's favor, however, is the fact that people, at least at the beginning, did not think of the secret police first when something disquieting had happened to them. Who would imagine that the secret police took the trouble to rearrange one's desk or the photographs on the wall? In the face of sexual blackmail, who's first thought is of the security forces of one's country? The Stasi relied on the fact that common purposes and common narratives notwithstanding, the members of the peace, environment, and civil rights movements hailed from different social milieus where trust first needed to be built against habit. The Stasi could also rely on structural or institutional fault lines. Tensions between ministers and their congregations are not uncommon, especially if the former is young and associating her- or himself with punks and such while the latter is made up chiefly of older and more sedate members.

Resource deprivation would have been a more effective tool for the Stasi had the party state not decided to grant the churches institutional autonomy. The church did, time and again, provide vital resources for dissidents. Within limits, it could even provide meaningful employment. Many of the Stasi officers were painfully aware of how the existence of the church limited the efficacy of their actions, their ability to control the movements. My interview partners were all angry about the "constant abuse of the church." Hence, the many efforts of the Stasi leadership to confine the church to matters spiritual. And it might have succeeded had the church not been so differently organized from the party state, in the sense that at least in Berlin-Brandenburg it granted lower levels of organization, most notably the parishes, a high degree of autonomy. The ire of officers is discernible in the measures of decomposition they had designed for ministers, which in viciousness are comparable only to those against former party members. In view of the party's project of creating a monolithic intentionality, the church became an island, nourishing difference, and at its margins, dissidence. It was not quite the Trojan horse that the Stasi at times imagined it to be with its PID/PUT/"opposition" theory. Yet it was a shelter for people who saw themselves as different and who refused to assimilate.

Real reality shows as alternative forms of control

With the route to criminal persecution closed, with the applicability and effectiveness of decomposition limited, and with forced exile as an option disappearing, the Stasi needed new ideas. Individual officers engaged in some preliminary discussions about how to more effectively control critical thought and critical activities. With a vocabulary developed in response to phenomena that postdate the GDR, one could call these "real reality shows." Karl Maier says, "Since we could not escape the formation of an opposition, why not create one ourselves, which we could control from beginning to end?" Wolfgang Schermerhorn reports about similar thoughts with regard to writers who could no longer publish in the GDR: "Projects were developed in department XX/7 which aimed at busying these writers by commissioning collected volumes through the Aufbau publishing house." None of these thoughts went very far, not least, perhaps, because these officers or their superiors sensed that such measures sat ill at ease with the positivism of party ideology, or because, the party's incessant intentionality notwithstanding, they sensed something of the eerie uncontrollability of institutions that do after all seem to have a life of their own. And what, then, if through whatever dynamic the real reality show dropped its showlike existence to become really real?

STASI'S MAIN WEAPON: THE SECRET INFORMANTS

Stasi's attempt to control the "political underground" was primarily work with and through secret informants. In many directives, orders, and instructions, the Stasi honored their clandestine helpers with the epithet "our main weapon." Indeed, secret informants were the Stasi's main tool for gathering information of any kind: they stole blueprints of Western technology; they provided accounts of production problems in factories; and they told on the political opinion of fellow citizens. Secret informants—in official Stasi jargon, "inofficial employees" (*inoffizielle Mitarbeiter* or IM)—were also the Stasi's main device for directly intervening in particular processes of institution formation: they were mobilized for efforts to improve the productivity of a factory as much as for destroying the self-confidence of a particular person. Having a few good IMs was crucial for the career of an operative employee in the secret police. In the words of former officer Martin Voigt: "A [Stasi] employee lived off two, three good informants." The reputation of entire departments was contingent on the quality of their informants, on the department's ability to know what was going on and to inform those higher up before anybody else could. Accordingly, the Stasi paid much attention to improve its recruitment and systematic employment of secret informants. Most directives regulating operative work contain a major section outlining the implications of work with secret informants, and many key directives were entirely dedicated to the recruitment and guidance of secret informants.[40] Directive 1/79 (in Müller-Enbergs 1996, 305–73) set the framework for what was to be considered good work with informants for the 1980s. Through the ways in which it urged officers to recruit and handle informants effectively, the document reveals how the Stasi understood the people on whom the success and failure of its work was so crucially dependent.

Recruiting underground dwellers

The directive reminds officers that the motivations for collaboration with the secret police among potential and actual informants varies widely and that officers therefore need to adjust their recruitment strategies and the manner of interaction and collaboration with informants accordingly. The fact that the Stasi employed roughly 180,000 informants of all grades and kinds coming from diverse social, educational, and professional backgrounds underscores this point. The Stasi officers I interviewed were all at one point in their careers more or less successfully involved in recruiting informants for whom they became what is known in English spying argot as "handlers," or in Stasi lingo as "guidance officers." They were all familiar with the intricacies of working with informants. Considering the motivation of their own informants the officers agree with official teaching materials that forced recruitment based on blackmail was relatively ineffective. Such informants typically worked to rule and frequently they blew their cover intentionally to end their relationship with the Stasi. Recruitment based on material interest or other more personal motives (such as revenge) were considered more effective but also tended to create a dynamic that could be at variance with the intentions of the Stasi. All officers complained that they often were wasting time with ineffective, not properly motivated, or even unmotivatable informants whom they should have quickly abandoned. Sometimes it was clear from the beginning that the collaboration would be a tedious affair. And yet, the officers were wrestling with recruitment quotas that forced them to maintain full rolls. Like every other production unit in the country they had to fulfill (or better, overfulfill) the plan.

---

40. The standard work outlining the development of the Stasi's work with informants from the beginning of the organization in 1950 to the end in 1990 is Müller-Enberg's introduction (1996, 5–154) to his edition of the major directives and orders dealing with informants.

Comrades, that is, other members of the party, were much more responsive targets for the Stasi's recruitment efforts than other citizens. The directives see in "convictions" (*Überzeugung*), that is, belief in the feasibility, goodness, and justice of the party's project and of the Stasi's role in it, the best basis to establish a productive relationship with an informant. The former officers confirm this by pointing out that there was never a shortage of suitable informants where party members could take over this role. However, the party-critical circles in which the Stasi did take a particular interest scarcely offered possibilities to recruit informants on the basis of their convictions. Under these circumstances the directives foresee two possible recruitment strategies: "the prying out" (*Herausbrechen*) of current members as well as the "infiltration" (*Heranführung*) of suitable candidates. According to the officers the former strategy was a total failure. Indeed, the operative case documents show repeatedly that officers attempted to recruit movement activist but failed. This is not surprising given the experiences that have given rise to an involvement in peace or civil rights groups in the first place and the social networks in which activists moved.

As far as the peace, civil rights, and environmental groups of the 1980s are concerned, infiltration was quite successful by contrast. It was facilitated by the fact that unlike the discussion and reading circles prevalent in the 1970s, the peace, civil rights, and environmental groups defined themselves as counterpublics that were in principle open to new members. Yet, the strategy of infiltration still faced particular difficulties. The Stasi afforded work in this area the highest political priority. For this reason, they placed great importance on recruiting reliable, ideologically firm, and diligent men and women. The need for qualified personnel was further emphasized by the consideration of PUT as a secret service–like operation habitually weary of moles. Ideally, therefore, the Stasi should have liked to use tried and tested comrades for this task. This was unrealistic, however, for the following reasons. The Stasi had to find people who were in fact infiltratable, which is to say that they had to look like the other activists in some crucial respects. To blend in, they needed a plausible story about their desire to become involved. More, this story needed to be verifiable by the movement members, in core components at least. Creating such a story credibly embodied by a particular person is what the Stasi called "building a cover" (*legendieren*) Plausible carriers of a cover needed to have an educational background to match that of the group's members. They needed to be willing to spend extraordinary amounts of time within the movements while also working a job resembling those of other activists. In other words, they needed to be capable and willing to accommodate to the group member's habitus. Taken together, these conditions implied that potential candidates could not be holders of demanding career jobs that required their full attention and/or people with families, lest they risk alienation from their children and partners. "Tried and tested comrades" (*verdiente, zuverlässige Genossen*) had both a habitus and a vita, which would have made their sudden involvement in something the party officially decried as subversive rather unlikely. They would have reeked of "Stasi mole." So the officers went on the lookout for comrades who looked as if life in the GDR got the better of them, that is, people with either a real career break, a sudden fall from grace, or others who were willing to have such a break stage-managed.

When I speak of secret informants on the next couple of pages, I have a very particular kind in mind, which is typical of spying work among dissident movements but not representative of the category of secret informants as a whole.[41] The request to become a secret informant was in many ways similar to being asked to become a full-time employee of the secret police. It was not something candidates pondered before they encountered the possibility. Instead, at the particular moment the proposal dropped into the candidate's life it offered a possibility for a new self-understanding. To be acceptable it had to resonate on some level with extant self-understandings. Here are six short biographical sketches of secret informants whose real lives offered the Stasi possibilities to blend them with a cover story to plausibilize the informants' introduction into dissident circles. For Monika Häger, for example, the Stasi's offer was the call to a special commission by the party

---

41. What I will have to say in this section of the book is based on thinner empirical grounds than my reporting on the full-time Stasi officers and the opposition members. In the year I spent in Berlin, I managed only to find three informants operating in the dissident scene I was studying who were also willing to grant me an interview. For two more relevant informants there exists either a book-length printed interview conducted by former dissidents (Kukutz and Havemann 1990) or a book-length biography by a respected journalist (Lahann 1992). The informant covered in the first of these books, Monika Häger, had become, pursuant on the publication of this book, so often interviewed by journalists and television crews that she was no longer interested in speaking with me. The second, Ibrahim Böhme, had died before I entered the field. Another possible interviewee (Wolfgang Wolf) had in the meantime moved abroad and was only occasionally in Berlin. Yet, in his case I can rely to some extent on a biography written up by the Stasi (BSTU, BVB, AKG 12) in conjunction with the commentary of movement members and guidance officers familiar with him. Other important informants had disappeared seemingly without a trace. Not only did nobody know where they lived, not even whether they lived, but even countrywide phone searches ended nowhere. There is one further autobiographical account of a well-known informant, Sascha Anderson, which however, is, owing to its literary style dealing in multiplex metaphors and allusions, barely usable for my purposes. Even though Anderson was a central figure in the literary scene in Prenzlauer Berg, he was rather marginal with respect to the peace and civil rights groups. All positive leads in the end owed themselves to contacts that the former peace and civil rights activists had built after finding out that they were informants. In what follows I have altered the names of my interview partners only.

that she had been longing for. The Stasi's call gave her the feeling that her commitment to the party was recognized. And if the fact that she was a lesbian might have stood in the way of a more official party career, her sexual preferences proved an asset for this particular calling. So, she felt special when the Stasi knocked at her door. she felt needed in a way she never did growing up in an orphanage, abandoned by her mother and her grandparents. The fact that in taking up the party's commission she had to give up her work in the editorial department of the publishing house Junge Welt, where she was in part responsible for paper toy kits of war implements, did not bother her. She felt honored to be given a chance to fight against the enemies of the country she loved more than anything else. The fact that officially she had to be expelled from the party to make her story of pacifist refusal to work on war toys credible did not faze her either, since she was to be secretly readmitted with all the more honors. For the secret police she was the ideal candidate: motivated, clearly committed, free to make this task the center of her life, and easily endowed with a credible cover.

Philip Kaminski (named changed) had become a teacher. His dedication to the party's project, his ease at working with young people, the signs of appreciation he had received from functionaries, made him hopeful of a significant career in the communist youth movement. However, his work with students also made him realize that he was gay. Caught in a relationship with a minor (only a few years his junior), he was sentenced to a prison term and thrown out of the party. Having assisted the Stasi in prison with a case of right-wing violence, they called again after he was released. For Kaminski this was a way to remain connected to his old life, and maybe also a way to insure himself against future unjust treatment. For the Stasi he was attractive now precisely because his vita showed the kind of break that lent itself to the production of a credible cover. A case in some ways similar to Kaminski's is that of the above mentioned Monika Häger (Kukutz and Havemann, 1990). Abandoned by parents and grandparents, she grew up in an orphanage where she dedicated herself to the socialist cause. Her extraordinary commitment, her particular biography, and the fact that she too was homosexual made her a prime candidate for the Stasi's infiltration efforts.

Wolfgang Wolf, Ibrahim Böhme (Lahann 1992), and Manfred Winkler (name changed) had nowhere near the linear party conformist development that Häger or Kaminski had undergone. They were dedicated to socialism to be sure, but to a socialism that was not always in line with how the party liked to understand it, and thus each of them had run into trouble with the authorities of state and party. Winkler, son of a Weimar-era communist mother with bohemian tastes and close ties to painters and intellectuals, had an uncanny knack for getting embroiled in historical upheaval, or from the perspective of the party, to find himself at most suspicious time-space knots. Visiting Berlin from his native Saxony to interview for a job as a teacher, he got embroiled in the June 17, 1953 uprising, landing him in a West Berlin refugee camp, where he, barely out of school, dreamed of starting all over again as a lumberjack in Canada. Being too young for the Canadian recruiters he ended up mining the Ruhr Valley for coal while, to the chagrin of his employers, spreading enthusiasm for his communist ideas as a union organizer. Married to a West German comrade, he eventually returned to Leipzig. Back home he again became active as a union representative fighting against the privileges of management in the company he worked for. This did not go down all too well with the local party apparatus, however, where he earned the reputation of being a quarrelsome and unruly comrade. Always on the lookout for opportunities to be in touch with the big wide world he befriended the first Cuban students who came to Germany in the mid-1960s. Through them he became interested in Chinese socialism just at the time when such interests came to be frowned upon by the party leadership. A packet with brochures sent to him from the Albanian embassy (then a Chinese ally) got him into serious trouble. Worse, even though banned from traveling to Czechoslovakia, he got caught in Bratislava just as Russian tanks were rattling in. Even though the ensuing chaos allowed him to sneak back undetected across the border, the careless telling of his tale in a pub finally landed him in prison. Luckily he had to stay there only for a relatively short period of time thanks to the connections of his mother and the post-1968 overcrowding. To him, the Stasi's call in the 1970s created echoes of spy novels, and never shy to embark on an adventure, he was happy to oblige, all the more so since the first task seemed interesting enough: visiting openings of art exhibitions, readings, and similar events at Western embassies.

Werner Müller (name changed) was approached by the Stasi with an entirely different profile of work in mind. He had just begun to study philosophy and economics with vague notions that he would pursue a career in some official trade or policy function that would take him abroad. In the context of these plans, the request to work for the Stasi seemed to him as a test of loyalty and beyond that simply as part of the deal. When these original career plans did not come to fruition his connection to the Stasi lay dormant, simply because he lost his relevance for the secret police's foreign espionage operations. This changed years later when he was working for the academy of sciences in the department of critical Marxist philosopher Peter Ruben (Rauh 1991). When Müller was dismissed from the academy and thrown out of the party alongside Ruben, the Stasi approached him again, this time with domestic spying work in mind. He appeared as a perfect candidate for Stasi's efforts to introduce informants into Berlin's dissident circles.

The cases of Wolfgang Wolf and Ibrahim Böhme are more obscure. The unsteady lives of both men, moving in and out of intense professional and/

or personal engagements and similarly intense quarrelsome breaks, suggest that both might have suffered from what psychopathologists now call bipolarity. It appears that both had signed on to working with the Stasi as a means to realize their dreams about a proper socialist society. They were excellent informants for the Stasi, but they also played their own games in which they (with naive grandiosity) hoped to use the secret police as much as the Stasi expected to use them.

At least five of the six secret informants under consideration here were at some level very lonely people. Häger's longing for a mother and a friend were constantly disappointed. Kaminski lost most of his friends during his time in prison. Müller had always been a loner. Böhme, who typically managed to place himself in the middle of a corona of fans who were charmed by his unconventional, quirky character, was also ready to drop them at a moment's notice, throwing himself into new relationships seemingly with the same abandon with which he had entered the ones he now severed so abruptly. And even though Winkler seemed to be always in love, always with friends, he too abandoned lovers, friends, and family, it seems without much hesitation. This loneliness was constitutive of their new roles, which did not leave them the time to manage other intensive or extensive networks of social relations. It was important for their work as informants that they would not miss anyone too much and that others would not miss them all that much either when the informants spent several weekday evenings and most weekends in the company of the people to be spied upon.

With the exception of Kaminski, none of them had anybody but their guidance officer who knew both sides of their existence. Therefore, only their guidance officers were in a position to recognize the goodness of their self-understandings as spies. More, as they lost other ties, the officers also became vital links to their own pasts, their real biographies rather than their cover stories presented in meetings with the movement activists. In some cases, as for Monika Häger, this led to intensive relationships with their guidance officers, who appeared more and more friendlike. In other cases this led to tensions, because the guidance officers were unable to strike the kind of rapport the informants wanted or even needed. Then other satisfactions moved to the foreground, such as the constant reminder that they were important (why else would secret police officers want to meet them in the middle of the night in some car?). Werner Müller says that he very much enjoyed the fact that he could determine when the meetings were taking place. For once, he felt in control. Böhme and Wolf seemed to have enjoyed their intellectual superiority over their guidance officers, which afforded them the feeling that in the end they knew better than the party state!

This situation created a remarkably skewed social world, a very unique authority network structure. On the one hand the informants had frequent, long, and intensive contact with a set of people who were supposed to be anti-authorities. Yet they ate with them, drank with them, laughed with them, played with their children, listened to music together, and seemingly shared their opinions and their feelings. On the other hand, they met one single officer, often several times a week, who for the most part was not a friend, a buddy, but in crucial ways knew more about them than anybody else. That officer had to remain a bureaucrat, even if he also once in a while cooked for them, received them with coffee and sweets at their meetings, but who had, after all, a job to do, a report to write that had to follow a particular script to satisfy his superiors. The informants were thus sandwiched between people who thought and acted like friends even though they were supposedly enemies, and an officer who was a comrade, who, qua rules and regulations, was not supposed to become a friend or even an intellectual partner because his eyes had to remain fixed to the particular goals of the casework.

The secret informants' most peculiar social situation helps us to understand a curious phenomenon. After the dissolution of the GDR, when the former informants were asked by the former dissidents why they had betrayed them, the informants often said something to the effect that they had only partially betrayed the activists, that they had in fact done both, work for the groups in which they participated and work for the secret police. They described their situation as "thoroughly schizophrenic," or as "full of contradictions." When the Wall fell and the Stasi was dissolved, most of them were relieved that their double life came to an end (not quite anticipating yet the ostracization that was soon to follow).

In living and breathing with the movement members, these had, perhaps imperceptibly at first, often become authorities for the informants. The activists' recognitions began to count, and they began to transform the informants' understandings. The Stasi was aware that what anthropologists call "going native" was a constant danger of their informant's work. Therefore, guidance officers were asked to impregnate their informants with a firm "foe image." They were asked to convince them that the activists were dangerous carriers of PUT, threatening the socialist project. For example, Häger was told by her guidance officer that Gerd Poppe had once said that "if matters were ever to change again, they [presumably the Stasi officers and their informants and leading party members] would all be hung." Yet, such explanations did not satisfy all informants, and if they did for a while they lost some of their credibility in the course of time. Winkler, Müller, and Kaminski say in unison that they tried to raise doubts with their guidance officers with regard to the Stasi's assessment of the groups' dangerousness for the GDR. They all read the movement members as desiring a reform of socialism as it was—and that a reform was necessary, they themselves had no doubts. Most of their guidance officers rigorously blocked such conversations, and so the informants dropped the theme. And yet the informants drew their own conclusions in response to this, building tension, new feelings, and old commitments. Winkler says when there were group meetings he always volunteered to do the kitchen work or watch the children so he would not even have the possibility to hear something he could betray—a self-interpretation that Ulrike Poppe confirms. Kaminski fell into the habit of leaving the meetings early, before they had drawn to their culminating conclusion, with the excuse that he had to get up early for his job—something even his guidance officer constantly bemoaned. And Wolfgang Wolf felt by no means limited by the directives he had been given by his guidance officers, proposing and participating in activities of the groups apparently as he saw fit. This met the ire of higher-ranking officers, ultimately leading to the investigation of his case. So each individual informant created something of a comfort zone, something he or she felt he or she could still defend while not severing ties with the secret police, an ultimate step none of them was ready to take (even though it would have been easily done by simply blowing their cover, which in turn could have just as easily been depicted as a regrettable mistake vis-à-vis the Stasi). The consequences of such a step seemed too dramatic, because it threatened to deprive them of all that lured them into informant work in the first place.

CONCLUSIONS: MIRROR HALL CONSTRUCTION IN ACTION

The picture I have painted of the Stasi's work to control the peace, civil rights, and environmental movements in the GDR is bleak—not just seen from the perspective of the movement members who became subjected to state terror in the form of decomposition, but also seen from the perspective of the Stasi and the party state. My central argument has been that the Stasi and party were entangled in a theory of oppositional behavior that prevented them from understanding oppositional activity in such a way that they might have enabled themselves to fight its causes. In fact, the Stasi never made a concerted effort to empirically investigate the phenomenon of dissidence. If the party state deemed it so important—and there is every reason to believe it did, given its self-understandings as an ideology-driven project of social transformation as well as the enormous efforts that went into suppressing it—then the question of why the causes were never investigated in greater depth is central. In fact, I would argue it throws into relief the party state's political epistemics, the ideologies and practices that governed its knowledge-making capacities about itself and the world and thus ultimately its capabilities to engage successfully in politics and self-politics.

Given that the party state systematically discouraged social scientific inquiries into such matters—the Institute of Opinion Research started under Ulbricht was closed by Honecker again (Niemann 1993), and the surveys of the Central Institute for Youth Research in Leipzig were routinely ignored[42]—the Stasi appeared literally as the lender of last resort for the production of reliable knowledge about GDR society. The Stasi defaulted into this role also because party leaders have from the very beginning rightly distrusted the party's own information system as palliating. So the question remains of why the secret police never produced a more thorough investigation of dissident activity. If asked, the officers reply that they were a secret service agency and not an institute of sociology. This answer has to be taken seriously, because as a secret police they always had a particular task defining a perspective and only particular kinds of methods at their disposition. And yet, their secret informants were participant observers of a particular kind. More, the Stasi's directives, orders, and instruction manuals regularly exhort the officers to investigate the causes and enabling conditions of PUT.

For a better understanding of the process dynamic behind the Stasi's failure, it is instructive to follow the wording of the demands to investigate causes more closely. Directive 4/66 asks, quoting a resolution of the central committee, to "overcome the causing factors" of PUT. And directive 6/86 demands the

> uncovering of facilitating conditions under which inimical-negative forces can become effective. Among others [the uncovering] of leverage points for inimical-negative forces in connection with shortcomings of political-ideological work, in the work of state and economy directing organs, of combines and of production facilities; [the uncovering] of inconsequent or false implementations of the party's directives as well as of laws and other legal norms; [the uncovering of] insufficient exhaustion of the possibilities of socialist law and of its politically undifferentiated application. (in Suckut 2004, 437)

Two aspects of this text strike me as particularly notable. First, the existence of "negative-inimical forces" is simply presupposed. Second, the facilitating conditions under which they can become active are seen exclusively in

---

42. The Central Institute for Youth Research (*Zentralinstitute für Jugendforschung* or ZIJ) in Leipzig was founded in 1966 under the responsibility of the Council of Ministers. The results of its survey research were considered with great caution within the party and vigorously rejected wherever they contradicted party doctrine. Like those of the Institute for Opinion Research, its contributions were not considered as "positive" enough, providing one-sidedly "negative" images of the GDR youth. In the course of its existence the range of what it could research about and how it could publish were more and more curtailed. Nevertheless, efforts to close it down did not succeed. Most publications were treated as secret; some were destroyed Walter, Förster, and Starke 1999; Herbst, Ranke, and Winkler 1994, 1209–11).

a lack of the proper implementation of the right path mapped out by the party. In other words, the search for causes and facilitating conditions has to proceed within the parameters set out by PID/PUT/"opposition" theory and the socialist theodicy. The question that cannot be pursued, much less publicly discussed, is whether the party line, whether the institutional order of the party state, is of such a kind that it produces a self-distancing of individuals from the party. Put differently, the causes and facilitating conditions are always already understood in a particular way; they are clearly lined out by the PID/PUT/"opposition" theory; party and Stasi were always already in the know. This is also one of the reasons why the character studies the Stasi undertook of dissidents with the help of informants appear so utterly mechanical, emphasizing from one case to another the ever same elements, covering diversity and nuance with pleonastic-hyperbolic categories such as "inimical-negative." And this in spite of the fact that the Stasi's regulations incessantly called for the "differentiation" of the movement members. In the end, this merely boiled down to finding out who bore a grudge against whom and why, as well as who had what kind of quirk that could provide a leverage for decomposition. There was no need for real curiosity in people qua people. So in the pursuit of "causes and enabling conditions," all that could possibly be found were either faults in the proper implementation of the party's line or sources of enemy interference. In the case of wanting implementation, people need to be "further qualified," by more party training, by "more effective political-ideological work." In the case of inimical intention, the person so designated needed to be isolated to protect the socialist edifice that was thought to be so vulnerable to ideological infections of all kind (see figure 4.7). Stasi and party were not really looking for an independent direct corroboration of their theory. What they required from everybody participating in the knowledge-making process was the recognition of the always already known, which was at the same time the *conditio sine qua non* for acquiring and maintaining authority for everybody with a career stake in the GDR. And on that basis the party demanded the search for indirect corroboration of the already established truth. Anything that could be found to draw doubt on that knowledge was refuted as divisive, the presentation of it as playing the game of the class enemy in undermining unity and closure of the party.

One could argue that socialism's epistemic ideologies and practices assumed that the direct corroboration of the theory had already been achieved. After all, Marxism-Leninism was taken to be a science. History had proven it right. To be sure, M–L was taken to be a living science, one that required adjustment. And yet, just as a properly deduced lemma of a formal theory is true if that theory is true, so was the adjustment of Marxism-Leninism for the present true because it was deduced authoritatively. PID/PUT/"opposition" theory was a lemma of Marxism-Leninism adjusted to a particular historical situation by the agency authorized to do so, and as such it had to be true. And because the authoritative participation in the adjustment of the theory required the recognition of the fundamentals of the theory as true, a full-blown review of fundamentals could never take place.

Further evidence for the dogmatic closure of the theory can be found in the patterns of interaction between the secret informants and their guidance officers, as well as in the culture of discourse by which the officers could communicate their results to their superiors. Guidance officers were asked to be attuned to the personal problems of their secret informants and to develop the capacity to adjust to their style of communication and interaction, but in all substantive matters they were warned to stay in control of the meeting. The informant was supposed to report facts responding to the questions of the guidance officer. These questions were systematically geared toward finding the information that was important to fill the data-entry slots of the theory. The stereotypical application of the theory also comes to the fore in the "informational need assessments" guidance officers were asked to write up in regular time intervals. After all, their bureaucratic task was the closure of a case either in the form of a trial or in other forms of a cessation of the PUT activities.

Some secret informants, however, wanted more than simply to fill the blanks in their guidance officers' questionnaires. They tried to start discussions about "what was going on." Manfred Winkler, for example, tried several times to convince his guidance officers that the peace movement was ill-understood as a group of people with "inimical-negative intentions." Werner Müller and Philip Kaminski made similar efforts, yet abandoned these rather quickly once they saw that their guidance officers were not interested in such debates. Nevertheless, some guidance officers humored such discussions to a certain degree. Their inability to control what they were supposed to master began to frustrate them, and thus they started to harbor doubts about the Stasi's approach to nonconformist thought. They felt that it could not hurt to hear the informants' perspective. They also needed to maintain excellent rapport with their key informants, and if such discussions seemed to help with motivation, then why not. Their ability to entertain a more exploratory discourse had definite boundaries however. In the end they were constrained by the same framework of understanding that they tried to superimpose on their informants. They had no time to let themselves be drawn all too deeply into such discussions. After the meeting they had to write up a report that in style and content had to fit the genre, meeting the expectations of their superiors. And as such it had to contain the relevant factual information, and relevant was whatever fit the theory.

Everything else had to be dropped if officers did not want to endanger the proper progress of their careers. Peter Wagner says:

> Look, had I written up exactly what my informants told me, my superiors would have scolded me: "What kind of an informant have you got here? He does not have a firm class standpoint. Your political education of that informant sucks."

And in-kicked the merciless logic of socialism's ethics of absolute finality with its peculiar theodicy that was felt so intensely by the officers as a "culture of blame." This reaction of the superiors is no mystery if one considers that for them too it was of overriding importance to be well endowed with "fact"-studded reports written up in the PID/PUT/"opposition" framework that they could then send on to the political decision makers who were keen on maintaining interpretative sovereignty (or what appeared as such). In a perfectly indexical order, those higher up were always supposed to know more and thus know better now to pull the various strings together. Everybody all the way up was caught in the need to self-objectify in light of the extant party line.

Even in the politburo, conformism as a blame-avoiding strategy set the culture of discourse.[43] Here is Alexander Schalck-Golodkowski's account (2000, 144–45). As a Stasi officer in special use (OibE) he worked in the politburo's economics commission and acted as the country's chief deal maker:

> Typically one began with the presentation of success stories. Of course one could not avoid talking about problems. Yet, then one had to be careful. Problems were no good. For how did they come about? One incurred the danger of becoming blamed oneself. Even more disagreeably: the leadership of the party tended to take the presentation of problems as criticism. The worst was to appeal to a politburo decision if something had gone wrong. Of course that happened in real life and everybody knew it. The party-

---

43. It took me a while to understand this. I initially and somewhat naively began to read up on politburo discussions of security matters because I had an image in my mind that somewhere there was a level of "initiates," the innermost sanctum of the party, where people finally got out of the lingo of permanent affirmation in the interest of self-authorization. I was in search of a place where people led, if not entirely open then at least rather controversial, debates that would do away with the worst form of palliation. But there was no such level. The imperative of mobilization and motivation through affirming right consciousness prevailed everywhere. We have no knowledge about how Honecker talked to Mielke, Mittag, and Herrmann, the members of his innermost circle. But my suspicion is that their talk was seamlessly steeped in the performance of the ethics of absolute finality while remaining weary of the socialist theodicy and its blame culture.

leadership wanted to decide everything of importance. If however, the decision proved to be wrong, the person who drafted the original resolution was held responsible. Thus the method of collecting signatures . . . became widely spread. To insure themselves, everybody paid attention to getting as many signatures of carriers of responsibility as possibly. The secretary general opened the discussion: "does anybody have something to say about this?" Then everything was possible, long or short comments, approval or rejection. Only one thing never occurred: an open controversial discussion. The politburo was concerned about presenting a unitary position.

The striking parallels between Schalck-Golodkowski's memories about the discursive culture at politburo meetings and those of the Stasi officers about that of their organization are testimony to the pervasive influence of the ethics of absolute finality. Yet, if there were no real discussions in the politburo one might surmise that there were instead plenty of informal discussions "off the record" outside of the official meetings in which not every word counted. After all, the politburo members were living together in a settlement built for this purpose in Wandlitz, just north of Berlin. However, this was by no means the case. The memoir literature as well as the accounts of life in Wandlitz provided by those who were involved in organizing it indicate that everybody pretty much lived a reclusive family life there. Wandlitz seems not to have been the place were politics was made. It was only a place where elite politicians slept. The politburo meetings were the real thing.

Honecker's accusation in the fall of 1989 that Stasi's reports about the civic discussion forums suddenly mushrooming everywhere in the country (in Mitter and Wolle 1990) had reached the level of the *Bild-Zeitung*—West Germany's notorious tabloid paper—in distributing enemy propaganda offers another fascinating glimpse at the party state's discursive culture (Andert and Herzberg 1990, 351). This reaction was by no means just a clue to Honecker's character (the Stasi officers accused him of various personal deficiencies in this context, some moral, some intellectual). Instead it was an integral feature of the process dynamics of socialist institutions. This can be made plausible by the words in a similar statement made by Walter Ulbricht several decades earlier in the context of his sweeping critique of Stasi that were meant to weaken his opponent Wollweber, who was then head of the secret police. In the aforementioned meeting of the Stasi generals Ulbricht's words were summarized thus (Engelmann and Schumann 1995, 357):

The way in which the Stasi composes its information services to the party and the work that goes into it is a weakness and not just a weakness but it is harming the party. It was a way in which state-inimical propaganda of the enemy was distributed legally.

This is to say nothing less than that the entire data-gathering effort of the Stasi was undertaken in such a way that in effect the prevailing theory could only be confirmed. The farther officers were away from the field, from the spill of data that was not to be included in official reports, the more they felt corroborated by information they received from their subordinates because what they told them in oral and written form was always made to conform to the theory.

By nourishing socialism's ethics of absolute finality, the party state's efforts to create a monolithic intentionality effectively prevented the party-state machinery from learning in a bottom up way through a systematic engagement with and the recalcitrance of the world to human description. Since recognition and authority were produced simultaneously, there existed a strong tendency to recognize only well-established understandings. Since corroboration was typically conducted in such a way that the result could only affirm preexisting understandings (at least in all areas that were considered "ideologically sensitive"), experience could not be mobilized to challenge dogma. And, finally, since particular understandings, above all the resolutions of the last party congress, became enshrined as quasi-sacrosanct, new understandings were rarely given a chance to unsettle old ones. Socialism thus systematically validated its understandings of the world in a circular way. Thus, socialism came to be populated with Potemkinian villages, from the plans of the smallest production outfit to the reports of the secret police; it became a world of make believe, quasi by design. I say "quasi" because nobody, the most hardheaded orthodox party leader included, would have *wanted* an institutional order with such characteristics. And people knew about the prevalence of make believe; they knew it because they made it, or better even: felt forced to make it. And that force came about through the interaction of institutions, each willfully maintained, each seemingly a necessary consequence of Marxist-Leninist fundamentals: the relentlessly Manichaean understanding of the world, the ethics of absolute finality, democratic centralism, and last but not least the theodicic form of error accounting with its intense culture of blame as a consequence. Each of these institutions taken by itself seemed to strengthen socialism by mobilizing the party into unitary battle mode. Taken together they fundamentally weakened socialism by limiting the possibility that reform could come about through means other than initiatives of the politburo. To get into the politburo, however, one had to have a more or less flawless record of self-objectification. To become so successful self-objectification had to be written into the very fabric of the self. Once there, it was part and parcel of everyday reflexivity.

In the introductory chapter I argued that organizations are self-reflexive institutions; they have the capability to imagine, desire, plan, and execute institutional changes, which is to say that they can engage in politics and self-politics. The Stasi's task was political in the sense that it had to prevent the emergence of particular sets of institutions outside of the direct control of the party. However, as I have tried to show in the last chapter, the Stasi not only lacked understandings adequate to its political goals, but its understandings also led to actions that assisted the political strategies of the very organizations they tried to undermine (e.g., by enabling what I have called in chapter 8 the ecce homo strategy). So it is perhaps not surprising that in 1988 two Stasi generals well familiar with the situation sought an appointment with Günter Schabowski, former editor of the party flagship newspaper *Neues Deutschland*, member of the politburo, and first secretary of the SED of the Berlin district. They explained that (I wish I had the exact wording) under the given political circumstances the independent peace, civil rights, and environmental groups in Berlin could not be controlled with the means of the secret police. Instead, they argued, the problem required a political solution. That meant nothing less than that coping with the opposition was the party's task, not the Stasi's. According to Werner Riethmüller, who was one of the two officers present, they engaged Schabowski for a long time but failed to convince him to take action. Instead, he exhorted them to do their job properly. End of story. The discussion ended the thematization of problems as it almost always did. Politics had become aporetic.

What I have said here about the ways in which the Stasi created an image of oppositional activities and the interventions designed to come to terms with them mirrors similar political epistemics in other domains of political life in the GDR. The story is always the same. Local insight cannot, because of its negative resonance with the extant party line, be communicated upward. The consequence is that insight remains local and, short of resources in terms of discussion time and possibly even research, cannot be developed beyond initial hypotheses. All depictions of administrative processes within the GDR that I could find bear a startling resemblance with those I have depicted for the Stasi. Inga Markovits's (2005) study of a small provincial court found similar patterns. The memoirs of politburo members (Andert and Herzberg 1990; Axen 1996; Hager 1996; Eberlein 2000; Schabowski 1991a, 1991b), of key figures of the GDR administration such as the head of the state planning commission (Schürer 1996), the country's chief foreign currency organizer (Schalck-Golodkowski 2000), leading bureaucrats (Uschner 1993; Modrow 1995, 1996), or even SED county heads (Scherzer 1989) and other administrators and party secretaries working in the line (Zimmermann and Schütt 1994) all point to the very same process dynamics.

Let me introduce a simple counterfactual speculation. Let us assume that Stasi had discarded PID/PUT/"opposition" theory in the face of its own failure and in response to some of their secret informants' arguments that the people whom they were spying upon were not enemies of the GDR. Let us assume that instead the Stasi would have come to the conclusion that the activists' complaints were justifiable, and that they were a reaction to extremely rigid propaganda, a consequence of the inability of the party state to take human beings seriously as partners in dialogue. Entertaining such a counterfactual is not so far off given the fact that some guidance officers did begin to ridicule the rigidities of socialist institutional arrangements with phrases like "what should not be cannot exist, therefore . . . (*was nicht sein darf, das nicht sein kann*), speaking of considerable frustration. The counterfactual exercise comes to an end right here and now if we assume that saying so would have had the same consequences as it did. My point so far is that institutionally speaking the problematic element was the particular discursive culture of the party state, which had an acute antipathy to all (in the lingo of chapter 4) type 3 situations, that is, the serious attention to contradicting validations of all sorts. So we would have to assume further, then, that such discussions could be led without negative consequences and that the party state would have been capable of translating the results of such discussions into politics.

If one plays through such counterfactuals with former Stasi officers (and they do so themselves in search of answers to the question, "what went wrong where?" which many of them find quite pressing) they typically say that this would have led to a third way and that this would have inevitably led to relapse into a capitalist order. They claim then that the only socialism possible was the socialism they had. However, this argument is entirely predicated on a particular philosophy of history, on a Manichaean duality for which there is no evidence other than the success it supposedly made possible for the Bolsheviki in 1917 and the Soviet Union between 1943 and 1945. Clearly, and this is the second result of this exercise in counterfactual reasoning, under such circumstances one could not have held on to rigid ideas of particular goals and the all too simple understanding of the means appropriate to achieving them. Without a philosophy of history, which in the end justified a single goal for everyone, one might have had to concede a plurality of goals. But this does not mean that one would have to assume that there could not have been an overarching institutional framework other than capitalism to accommodate a plurality of goals. It is not even clear that capitalism is not radically monolithic in its own way, entirely incompatible with certain kinds of pluralities. All that is clear is that one would have had to look at history as an open changeable process of institutional formations and transformations and that this process can be governed from one center with one will and one goal in mind only at the cost of ultimate self-destabilization. In short, then, socialism would have had to be a different fabric of institutions, a different kind of socialism.

In 1928 Karl Mannheim wrote (in Meja and Stehr 1982, I.339): "In a situation of intellectual monopoly, the basis of thought is fixed, written down in sacred books. Thinking proceeds in terms of text interpretation, not in terms of interpretations of being [*Seinsinterpretation*]. And where the interpretation of being exists, it receives the character of textual interpretation. Thinking consists here essentially in the integration of every new emergent fact into a traditional order, something achieved mostly by interpreting or reinterpreting the fact." And further (341), "In such a situation [i.e., fast social change] the monopoly situation of the church-official interpretation of the world is not sustainable. It crashes within the tensions of an ever more dynamic society." This is what happened to Soviet socialisms within a global social context.

Paralyzing Uncertainties

A party is invincible if it does not fear criticism and self-criticism, if it does not gloss over the mistakes and defects in its work. . . . A party perishes if it conceals its mistakes, if it glosses over sore problems. . . . A party is invincible if it is able, as Lenin says, "to link itself with, to keep in close touch with, and, to a certain extent if you like, to merge with the broadest masses of the toilers. . . . A party perishes if it shuts itself up in its narrow party shell, if it severs itself from the masses, if it allows itself to be covered with bureaucratic rust.

HISTORY OF THE CPSU: *SHORT COURSE*

Critique had to be presented in words that did not question party politics. . . . Contradictions were painted over with loyalty declarations.

MARTIN VOIGT, FORMER STASI OFFICER

Among the many remarkable aspects of socialism's disintegration, three stand out: the apparent unpredictability of disintegration seen from within and without Soviet Eastern Europe; the incredible speed with which it proceeded; and it's entirely bloodless course. Taken together, these three aspects make the process look so unlikely that it might just as well have been a historical miracle. We tend to think of cataclysmic changes as triggered by visible long-term crises that make them more predictable, and we seem to know from history that rapid change is almost inevitably connected to violence. Other somewhat less recent transformations in German history are cases in point. The impending end of the second empire (1871–1918) was discussed at length in intellectual salons and corner pubs; and so was the disintegration of its successor, the short-lived Weimar Republic (1919–33). The ends of both periods were eagerly anticipated by some, much feared by others, and so much was talked and written about them that nobody was surprised when they finally collapsed. Both also ended in traumatic violence. The second empire expired in World War I and a short series of armed conflicts involving right wing and left wing regular and irregular forces. The end of the Weimar Republic saw political street violence again. And even though Germany's first republic was blown away by a bloodless putsch, the

Nazi regime succeeding it became immediately violent in suppressing the little internal resistance there was. Soon afterward, it engaged in the mass murder of the handicapped, the mentally retarded, and finally that of Jews, gypsies, and homosexuals, while waging war on the world, which eventually led to its total defeat. It is the seemingly unlikely conjunction of unpredictability, speed, and nonviolence of the GDR's disintegration that I want to address on the last pages of this book.

Central to an analysis of all three aspects of socialism's dissolution are the roles played (or as it may turn out: not played) by various strata of the party. There can be no doubt that the party state would have had the means to stop the process of dissolution by the exercise of violence. The effects might have been dire at first, but as the Chinese example shows, there was in principle no need that this would have been the end of socialist development. In Western circles this historical option was widely discussed under the epithet of a "Chinese solution" and one of its possible consequences, a quasi-communist dictatorship on a low level of economic development was also known as the "Romanian solution." The Stasi officers have told me in the interviews that there were what some called "Kalashnikov revolutionaries" among their ranks who argued for military intervention. And yet, no plans have surfaced from the archives indicating that a violent solution was ever seriously considered. In the end, not a single shot was fired anywhere in the country. And this, I argue, has everything to do with officials' changing understandings about the state of the socialist project in the GDR and even more the quality of the party leadership, especially its ability to effect positive change. As we shall see, the party was literally speechless in the accelerating crisis of 1989; it was incapable of coming up with understandings of the situation that might have proved productive for political and economic reforms. The aporias of politics I have been talking about, especially in chapter 2 of this book, had, in the face of the party state's most fundamental crisis since the June 17 uprising in 1953 (which was crushed militarily) and the refugee surge following accelerating socialization in the late 1950s (which was put to a stop by building the Wall), finally paralyzed the whole party state. Monolithic intentionality enforced in the interest of strengthening socialism had become a cancer suffocating its institutional fabric.

THE SHIELD THAT FAILED TO PROTECT

The Stasi officers I interviewed universally describe the 1980s as a time of "increasing contradictions." With this formulation they mobilize a terminology that was central to Marxism-Leninism. They leave no doubt that they mean to use the concept analytically to grasp social developments and ultimately the disintegration of socialism. The textbook version of state socialist ideology (e.g., Schütz 1978, 1013ff.; Kuusinen 1960) understands *contradiction* as a structural incompatibility within a social system. It is a dynamic feature of an institutional arrangement that necessarily leads to a conflict, eventually necessitating its transformation if self-destruction is to be avoided. Even though the officers' reference to contradictions rarely expands into an analysis of social formations whose dynamics lead to fundamental transformation or even self-destruction, this Marxist meaning of the concept always looms in the background.[1] Yet, their use of the term is also informed by broader common meanings, of which three dominate their accounts. The first everyday use of "contradiction" involves the contrasting of two discursive understandings that are taken to be incompatible because only the one or the other can be true. The second type is a variant of the first. Rather than contrasting propositions it contrasts demands that cannot be reconciled with each other. The third common meaning of "contradiction" juxtaposes discursive understandings at odds with experiences and their emotive and kinesthetic understandings. In this case, life and the description of life are at odds with each other. According to the party's ideals, according to its efforts to produce a monolithic intentionality grounded in true science and that also endeavors to harmonize theory and life, everyday contradictions were not supposed to surface in the way the officers and other GDR citizens experienced them.

The sociology of understanding offers an analytical framework for the (phenomenal) appearance of what the officers and with them other party state functionaries and even the dissidents have called contradictions. As we shall see, it also offers a means to connect the Marxian meaning of contradic-

---

1. The most important example of a contradiction in Marx's oeuvre is the self-destructing dynamic of capital (Postone 1996). In order to survive competition, capitalists need to produce as much surplus value as they can. The only source of surplus value is labor, which means that in order to derive more capital for investments employers need to employ more labor. At the same time competition drives capitalists to innovate, increasing the productivity of labor, which through crisis of oversupply leads to lay-offs, thus depriving capitalists of their source of surplus value. Ultimately, capitalism self-destructs, because capitalists cannot but slaughter the goose that lays the golden eggs: labor. Marxism's concept of contradiction has in true Hegelian spirit a constructive, even finalist side. Self-destruction opens the way for the next necessary revolutionary transformation. It is not only self-destructing but also self-transcending. Within the existing socialisms of Eastern Europe, there have been debates about the degree to which their developments are subject to contradictions. Since socialisms were seen as still in development toward communism, and since all development was based on a dialectic at the core of which contradiction did its work (e.g., Engels 1962, 20ff.), the question boiled down to the issue of whether there are antagonistic (openly fought out) contradictions in socialism or only nonantagonistic ones (solved by negotiation rather than struggle). Actually existing socialist orthodoxy insisted on the latter position (Schütz 1978, 1014); notable critics tended to the former (Ruben and Wagner 1980), which is, ironically, a more orthodox Marxist position.

tion as a self-destructive process dynamic within a particular institutional order with everyday meanings. In terms of the sociology of understanding, the claim that there is a "contradiction" can be analyzed as an articulated meta-understanding formed in response to strong and persistent negative resonances between at least two primary understandings of the same or different modes, which cannot be successfully relativized. In chapter 3 (p. 197) I argued that resonances can appear only through the mobilization of principles that enable and motivate the comparison between (the primary) understandings. The question how the attestation of "contradictions" comes about, therefore, has to investigate the actualization of such principles in historical context.

For the diagnosis of "contradictions" in late GDR socialism, it is useful to remember that in addition to the Marxist concept, everyday reasoning has become suffused with the principle of the excluded third (something is either true or false but cannot be both). The principle of the excluded third was further supported by its resonances with socialism's fundamentally Manichaean worldview and its self-understanding as a science that produces unambiguous, "correct" solution to any conceivable problem. Other important meta-understandings supporting the comparison of primary understandings across modes with respect to their compatibility derive from ethics. The demand to live truthfully in the sense of letting deeds follow words was publicly celebrated as the hallmark of a true socialist character. Not all negative resonances develop into contradictions, however. Often, they are simply not frequent or relevant enough to become a lasting bother. Moreover, networks of authority can mobilize relativizing meta-understandings to counter the epistemic effect of the negative resonance. In chapters 5 and 6 I presented several episodes in which contradictions *in posse* were swiftly nipped in the bud through relativizing conversations. The interplay between compared primary understanding and enabling meta-understanding offers a way to think through the question of why contradictions appear at particular times and places rather than others.

The Deteriorating Economic Situation

The most tangible and persistent negative resonances adding up to the experience of "contradictions" by GDR citizens were produced by the rapidly deteriorating economic situation of the country (Steiner 2004, chap. 6; Schürer 1996; Maier 1997, chap. 2). The GDR's economic woes never became part of the official public discourses. Instead, following the logic of creating a monolithic intentionality, the country's economic prowess continued to be rhapsodized as an amazing success won against the uneven odds of wartime destruction and natural resource poverty. This "success propaganda," as it was locally known, followed a small number of distinct scripts with a characteristic distribution over the calendar year. A late winter favorite was the old and tested Leninist prop of heroic effort mobilization touting pledges to reach for higher production norms by individual brigades and whole combines, leading in the case of success to plan overfulfillment. The idea of these widely disseminated reports was to challenge everybody to follow suit in what was known as "socialist competition." Toward the end of the year (sometimes as early as late summer) these pledges were followed by sagas about early plan fulfillment successes, again connected with hopes of mass mimesis. The year typically ended in a crescendo of countrywide plan-overfulfillment odes. That such success reporting hinged often enough on little more than staged shows of good will, silent downward plan adjustments around midyear, and even the rather acrobatic use of numbers was never mentioned publicly (Schalck-Golodkowski 2000; Schürer 1996).

The deteriorating GDR economy, however, manifested itself tangibly in the lives of GDR citizens. The supply of consumer goods was stagnating or even deteriorating. The shelves in the stores did not have the goods expected, needed, or at least hoped for; the queues in front of stores intermittently offering desirable products lengthened; and particular goods could only be obtained through intricate networks of informal connections.[2] This deterioration of the economic situation came as a shock after the GDR had made considerable progress in supplying its citizens with durable consumer goods during the 1970s. In that decade the share of households calling a car their own more than doubled from 15.6 percent to 38.1 percent; television sets and refrigerators became ubiquitous and washing machines nearly so (Steiner 2004, 189). In the 1980s, however, all of a sudden meat and shoes became scarce and spare parts or building materials from cement to paint were hard to come by. Moreover, the public infrastructure of the country, the network of streets and railway lines, bridges, canals and the condition of buildings began to show distressing signs of rapid deterioration owing to permanently deferred maintenance. This was leading not only to eyesores but also to delays, detours, slow zones, and safety hazards on roads and railway tracks. The negative resonances at the core of the experience of contradictions in the economic domain thus emerged between propagandistic discourses on the one hand and rather visceral, emotive and kinesthetic understandings on the other. Unsatisfied desires kept lingering, considerable efforts at obtaining necessary goods remained vain, movement on roads and tracks was slowed down, with all of this leading to increasing frustration and anger.

2. In all of these cases the negative resonances manifest themselves in pursuit of goals seemingly attainable in view of the propaganda. They also manifest themselves kinesthetically or emotively first, to become articulated discursively later. The result is a negative resonance in the form of an inconsistency between the claims of propaganda and the articulation of actual experience.

Many Stasi officers had access to information about the economy going way beyond these everyday experiences of contradiction. Their corps of secret informants in any branch of GDR society kept them abreast of emerging economic problems over a longer period of time and across a number of different organizations in industry, commerce, health care, communication, transportation, agriculture, and research. Especially officers working in leadership positions of county offices and district administrations had access to information about the state of the economy from the perspective of many different sectors at the same time. Some officers were eager to raise the awareness about the depth and scope of these problems among their colleagues. Herbert Eisner describes a tour organized by a colleague, at the time the Stasi county chief in Treptow, to inform Stasi officers about the situation in vital parts of GDR industry:

> Martin Voigt has taken us to the building panel factory [fabricating the poured concrete panels from which apartment blocks were built]. The party secretary [of the factory] was present as well. They worked in shifts, heavy work, obviously, but it was so apparent that their equipment was so run down, also with regard to orderliness and cleanliness. It was terrible. They said [in the party propaganda] the apartment problem is solved, but then they said [in the panel factory] also that they fell short of supplying 300,000 bathrooms. The economy has its laws which one cannot outwit by telling lies.

To fully appreciate the epistemic effect of this visit it is useful to remember that Honecker repeatedly celebrated the solution of the "apartment problem" as one of the most important achievements of the GDR economy. Accordingly, Honecker and other officials were frequently featured in the media officially opening new apartment complexes.

The Stasi's secret informants also told their guidance officers about the futility of the conventional propagandistic efforts to fix the problems by merely stirring up greater effort. Here again Herbert Eisner, who had worked as a Stasi analyst on the supply problems in the health sector of the GDR, remembers:

> In medicine we were doing fine until the end of the 1960s. But then, if the ceiling plaster falls on your head during an operation, these are not good working conditions. Later even basics were missing, gloves, it was terrible, [and] there you couldn't do anything anymore with [political] agitation. . . . The initial good level deteriorated further and further.

The proximate causes for the GDR's economic decline in the 1980s are relatively easy to understand. The improvements of the 1970s were effectively loans on the future in terms of both forfeited investments and excessive foreign currency credits, which suddenly began to haunt the country after the second oil-price shock (Steiner 2004, chap. 6). Rising energy costs, increasing debt service, and stagnating productivity owing to deferred investments began to interact, creating a downward spiral (Maier 1997, chap. 2). To maintain its credit-worthiness with foreign lenders, the GDR had to export whatever it could in exchange for hard currency, including foodstuffs, building materials, oil-based products, and machinery, which would all have been needed at home. Productivity growth slowed down markedly in the late 1970s since aging machinery could not be replaced, because the increasingly inefficient production of indigenous bituminous coal had to substitute for oil, and for want of materials to repair buildings and roads. The effects of this onslaught were not only visible in the scarcity and poverty of offerings on shop shelves, however, but the working conditions in many branches of industry deteriorated as machine failures increased, workshops deteriorated, and supplies arrived in a more erratic fashion.

This bleak situation was aggravated by the fact that GDR citizens had more money than they could spend. Worse, through their newly acquired television sets tuned to Western stations and increasing streams of visitors to and from the West, they also became knowledgeable about consumption levels in Western Europe and thus the increasing gap in the standard of living between both Germanys. The awareness of other possibilities created new desires. What might have passed as satisfying in the 1920s and 1930s, the formative years for much of the GDR leadership, was no longer good enough. Even the 1960s levels of consumptive possibilities became unacceptable for the 1980s.[3] Perhaps worst of all, however, in an effort to earn as much foreign currency as possible the GDR vastly expanded its network of Intershops, that is, special stores in which tourists and GDR citizens could, for hard currency, buy Western goods and quality GDR products, in other words, all the goods they could not acquire through the regular HO and Konsum shops.[4] Thus the superiority of the Western economic system was, through government action, dangled right in front of people's eyes. The impression of the emergence of a two-class, consumption-stratified society produced by the access to high-quality GDR and Western goods was

---

3. Gerhard Schürer (1999, 26), for many years head of the state planning commission, recalls Erich Honecker saying in the context of discussions of whether the party state should abandon the enormous subvention of life essentials, which started to cost the state more every year as input costs rose while prices remained relatively stable: "People need cheap bread, a dry apartment and work. If these three things come together socialism is safe."

4. HO stands for *Handelsorganisation* the state-owned chain of stores; *Konsum* was the name of the country's largest trade cooperative outlets. A second system of specialty shops offered mostly high-quality GDR products at much higher prices than those in ordinary GDR retail outlets (Merkel 1999, 243–76).

further amplified by the purchase of Western cars, Citroëns and Volvos for high-ranking functionaries, Stasi generals included. Thus, the discipline in energy consumption, the understanding demanded of ordinary citizens for the necessity of hard currency exports at the expense of local consumption needed for the victory of socialism, contrasted sharply with the increasing conspicuous consumption now practiced by the party elites, who were increasingly allowed to help themselves to some of the amenities their Western counterparts enjoyed (real bean coffee, chocolates, high-quality cosmetics, clothes, etc.) in specialty stores closed for ordinary citizens.[5]

Many rank-and-file SED members were disgusted by the new, more ostentatious system of privileges. This was also true for many Stasi officers. Although these privileges were in some sense a mere extension of those that were already well established in terms of the availability of office cars (at the top, even chauffeured), office space, secretarial support, assigned parking space, access to special dining facilities, and such, the fact that they now involved displaying the paraphernalia of the class enemy decidedly changed their quality. The performed desire and consumption for all things Western contrasted oddly with the class-warfare rhetoric. Many officers read this as a sign of increasing decadence, and there were, for this very reason, efforts in some Stasi units, for example, in the Berlin district office, to limit the conspicuous consumption of Western goods.

Stasi officers with object responsibilities among organizations involved in planning, trade, or production saw not only the empty shelves and the slowing trains, but they also witnessed how managers had to wrestle with entirely unrealistic planning goals, how they suffered from "contradictory" economic policies. They also saw how managers manipulated their performance statistics to create the impression of successful economic activity.

---

5. Alexander Schalck-Golodkowski (2000, 215) has an interesting explanation of the higher consumptive desires of the party elites, which he won reflecting on his own development: "In my opinion there is a simple reason why the consumption needs became bigger and more differentiated. Since the end of the 1970s the members of the politburo began to travel more to Western countries than in the decades before. And the variety of goods in the world of the class enemy triggered (in me and Sigrid [his wife] too) consumption demands. Especially the children and grandchildren of the politburo members developed desires for computers, video games, sport clothes. The youngsters expressed ever new wishes." I suspect that this is a very important part of the story but perhaps not even the most important one, because it leaves unaddressed the question of why people no longer felt strongly about the socialist ideals of equality and simplicity. I suspect, but I have not really explored this in my interviews, that socialism by this time had become just another modern industrial society in which a single individual had very little real possibility to shape or contribute anything of note. The point was to play and play successfully within a hardened institutional framework. And so satisfaction had to be sought elsewhere. Much like in capitalism, the answer became consumption as ersatz for action.

In the course of time this began to undermine the officers' trust in the GDR leadership. Says Horst Haferkamp:

We also received information that was not in *Neues Deutschland* or *Einheit*, such as papers given by Mittag [politburo member responsible for economic affairs] or similar people, when there was a seminar with the directors of combines on the occasion of the Leipzig Fair. And we could read that word for word, and read that this guy had nothing to say but general orientations, higher, faster, further and we have to concentrate more and such, nothing to offer, just demands to the directors . . . just nothing in terms of concepts, nothing of real expertise.

The experience of "contradictions" in the economic sphere was heightened by socialism's fundamental claim to be economically the superior system. According to the Marxian logic of history, historical stages marked by ever-higher productivity followed each other. And so, since socialism followed capitalism, it had to sport the better arrangement of productive forces. The Soviet development inspired the triumphalism of the late 1950s, and even the hopes of the 1960s to "overtake without catching up" (*überholen ohne einzuholen*) still playing with the possibility of a decisive quantum leap forward were in the meantime all gone. All comparisons had shifted toward an internal mode. And yet the overriding emphasis on the economic remained to the very end. In fact, the GDR had become a consumption-oriented society (Merkel 1999). This is where socialism had staked out its claims. And this is where in the eyes of ever more people it was failing. Says Martin Voigt: "You have to let yourself be measured by what you promise!"

Strictures of Party Life

Voigt's words make clear that what was seen as contradiction in the economy carried right over into contradictions experienced in relation to the party and its leadership. Throughout the country, all members, but especially party secretaries, were charged with the task to justify the policies of the SED. The party secretaries among my interviewees as well as the memoir literature testify to the fact that this task became more difficult during the 1980s. Here is Thea Fischer's account (Zimmermann and Schütt 1994, 36).[6] She had studied economics and was party secretary in the Berlin Brake Works:

6. Zimmermann and Schütt's informative book of interviews with SED functionaries from different walks of life, has a brilliant title, revealing, at least to those familiar with life under socialism, exactly where much of the problem lay. It is: "Any questions comrades!" (*Noch Fragen, Genossen!*). The exclamation mark beautifully brings to the fore the mere rhetorical nature of the question that closed many a soliloquy about the party line.

During the last three years of my time as a party secretary I was constantly subjected to criticism [by colleagues in the factory and higher-ups in the party hierarchy]. It became so bad that I constantly doubted myself. You think you are incapable, no good for nothing. I could not explain to people in management the meaning of many an economic policy. They were not realistic. The plans too were not realistic. If you have studied economics and you practiced it, it is impossible to palliate, to pretend that there are no problems. So I slid into ever more contradictions. And pressed as I was, I of course started to report about the terrible conditions that existed in parts [of the factory]. That in part one could only get necessary components needed to produce the whole by paying bribes or through the personal intervention of the party secretary. Then I was suddenly made out as "disaster Elli" [the last part is apparently her nickname]. And if I said how the workers think about the fact that 25 years after the [foundation of the] GDR there is still no coffee creamer, then I was simply declared to be too stupid to explain why there was no coffee creamer, barely any meat.... Every time I went to party instruction, my ears curled up, because I had to tell myself that one can't tell [what she learned as official party line] to anybody.

Fischer describes an acute conflict of loyalty between her dedication to the party and her duties as a party secretary on the one hand and the commitment to her colleagues as well as her own self-understanding as a communist and professional on the other. One of the meta-understanding enabling the experience of contradictions is the party's constant exhortation to party members and officials to be "people near," in keeping with the quotation from the *Short Course* with which I opened this chapter. The party equally exhorted its members to "demonstrate a firm class standpoint" at all times, a precept universally identified with the adherence to and defense of the party line. What comes to the fore, then, is the fact that it became increasingly more difficult be both "people near" and to "demonstrate a firm class standpoint." Such "contradictions" as loyalty conflicts became rather commonplace during the 1980s. The situation was further aggravated—in fact turned into a classical double bind conflict—by the party's insistence that it was in fact representing the people. Any hint that there was a gap between people and party would have been taken as a divisive move doing the bidding of the class enemy.

"Contradictions" of this kind did not only manifest themselves in everyday life. The 1980s were rich in events betraying a rift between people and party that official doctrine held could not exist. For example, to the population at large but also to many party members the official reaction to the Chernobyl reactor disaster in April 1986 revealed the problematic nature of the information policy of the SED. Right after the explosion, as the cloud of nuclear fallout that had arisen in northwestern Ukraine was drifting westward, spreading menacingly over Belorussia into eastern Europe, Scandinavia, and western Europe, official GDR news media remained mute. At the same time, the West German news media was busily spreading warnings about the size of the cloud, the direction of the wind, and the dangers of the fallout to people. Like their Soviet counterparts, the GDR media was keeping to the time-honored practice of hushing up disasters that could possibly be blamed on party and state. Only three days after the event, *Neues Deutschland* reported that there had been an accident causing "damage to the reactor" in a small note on page five. Even then, there was absolutely no mentioning of fallout, no warning of the vegetables that had been thoroughly contaminated (Pflugbeil 2003, 24). Worse, the vegetables the GDR could no longer sell for hard currency showed up all of a sudden in regular East German retail outlets. Once they did not find buyers there either, they were given to schools and kindergartens. Among SED members and several Stasi officers the whole affair raised questions about an all too familiar way of dealing with information and attitudes of the government toward the citizenry of the country. With the health of the citizens on the line the usual pointers to the exploitation of the disaster by the class enemy as primary reason for why it could not be reported on in public sounded eerily out of place even to GDR party members and Stasi officers.

With Mikhail Gorbachev's efforts to pull out the Soviet Union from its own economic malaise through a program of glasnost and perestroika, hope awoke that the new beginnings in the Soviet Union heralded a time of reform for the GDR as well. Says former Stasi officer Wolfgang Hartmann (2002, 182):

> We knew then that a new beginning was necessary in the GDR as well. Only that would help to close the gap between East and West especially with respect to the productivity of labor and modern technology. With mere words and palliated statistics . . . it would not close. Could an . . . impulse for change come from the Soviet Union now? That was our hope.

Instead of a new beginning, however, Gorbachev's program of renewal provoked a previously unimaginable conflict between the two foremost socialist authorities in the GDR: the SED and the CPSU. That conflict built up to a first apex in April 1987. Gorbachev had just published his book *Perestroika: New Thinking for Our Country and the World* (1987) to great fanfare in the West and keen interest in the East. In West Germany people were curious about whether the thaw in Moscow would radiate all the way to Berlin. Kurt Hager, politburo member and the SED's chief ideologist, was invited for an interview with the West German news magazine *Der Stern*. The text, apparently reviewed and approved by the politburo, made headlines when it was printed under the title "Every Country Chooses Its Solution" on April 9, 1987

(140–44), in West Germany. When it was reprinted in *Neues Deutschland* the day after, many GDR citizens had already heard of it from listening to Western radio or watching Western television. In this interview Hager answered questions aiming at the possibility of reforms in the GDR. In keeping with the title of the article, his line of argument affirmed that socialist countries have always been and still are very different from one another, necessitating different solutions to different problems. Whereas the Soviet Union's economy might currently be in need of restructuring (that's what "perestroika" means), the GDR's was not according to Hager. The performance of the GDR's economy, in particular the "unity between economic and social policy" established since Honecker assumed the leadership of the party was living proof of the superiority of the socialist system in the chief's ideologist's opinion. He argued that the GDR had avoided the plagues of capitalism like unemployment and poverty that seamlessly coexisted with the glitz of the rich. Hager's tone in the interview was confident, even reminiscent of the triumphalism of the late 1950s. In the midst of his hymn to the GDR, he uttered a rhetorical question, that become the first in a series of famous sayings culminating in the fall 1989 sequence of propagandistic misfirings that ended in Mielke's declaration of love to humankind. Hager said: "Besides, would you, if your neighbor freshly wallpapered his apartment, feel obliged to wallpaper your apartment as well?" What struck GDR observers (again including many party members and Stasi officers) like a lightning bolt was the trivialization of the necessity of reform in the GDR implied in his words. Hence, Hager came to be deflated by being referred to as "our wallpaper" (*unser Tapezierer*) or "wallpaper Kurt" (*Tapeten-Kurt*).

All the way to the end of the GDR, the very words *glasnost* and *perestroika* rumbled as taunts in the ears of politburo members, and the deeds licensed under their banner remained deeply suspect. One and a half years after Hager's interview, on November 19, 1988, less then a year before the opening of the Wall, an event occurred that marked a turning point in their relation to the party leadership for many of my interview partners. Then the politburo ordered the Soviet foreign-language news digest *Sputnik* to be removed from the postal distribution list. Since *Sputnik* could, therefore, no longer be legally mailed, this amounted de facto to its prohibition.[7] Country up, country down this measure was widely read as yet another rejection of any serious consideration of reforms in the GDR. Surely, the skepticism

---

7. *Sputnik* was edited by the Soviet news agency Novosti. It covered a broad range of Soviet press articles; it was available in several languages and was distributed in Eastern Europe as well as in Western countries. In an article titled "Against the Disfiguration of Historical Truth," appearing in *Neues Deutschland* on November 25, this measure was justified in reference to one single *Sputnik* article wondering whether the rise of Hitler had anything to do with Stalin.

toward the Soviet reform projects was not limited to the leadership of the SED. The contrast between the old adulation of Soviet institutions and the new criticism was too stark for many party members and Stasi officers even in the lower ranks. And yet, when *Sputnik* was taken out of distribution the reaction of most comrades was annoyed disbelief. Peter Wager remembers:

> They always said, to learn from the Soviet Union means learning to win. They were the great model, the big brother. And then they prohibited the *Sputnik* and Hager said: "when the neigbor puts up a new wallpaper that does not mean that one has to put one up too." That led to reflections. Since I was seventeen, eighteen, during my whole conscious experience of politics the Soviet Union was always the center. And then came these blocking attitudes, and so one asked: "What's up here?"

The continuous rejection of glasnost and perestroika, now even involving censorship of print materials from the "big brother," obviously brought the GDR in conflict with the Soviet Union, and this was a total novelty. What is immediately obvious from this statement is how the appearance of negative resonances and eventually the positing of a "contradiction" is enabled by a particular meta-understanding: the very old, incessantly recognized leadership of the Soviet Union for the entire socialist world.

The disbelief and protest of party members hit a raw nerve with the party leadership. Süß (1999, 101) reports that the central committee (ZK) received more than eight hundred letters by party members protesting the decision. Rather than critically evaluating its policies, rather than offering serious discussions, the party stepped up disciplinary measures against critics within its own ranks (Uschner in FES 1997, 17). From 1987 to 1988 the total number of party trials increased by roughly 18 percent, well above the typical fluctuations during the 1980s. More interestingly, the party penalties became much stiffer in this period. The two types of forced membership cessation shot up by 44 and 45 percent, increasing their proportion in the overall mix of penalties by over 20 percent to 5 percent of the whole.[8] The party's reaction became more defensive still. On the 7th plenum of the ZK in December 1988, the party launched a campaign against "moaners and groaners" quite obviously intended to uproot any attempt at more serious discussions about the country's situation and possible changes of policy. The protocol of the meeting of secretariat of the ZK in January 1989 states (cited in Modrow 1995, 262):

---

8. Interestingly, there was no comparable surge of party trials in the Stasi for the same period. The raw data can be found in Modrow (1995, 262–65).

With the help of the party control commission, ever more basic [party] organizations shed members and candidates succumbing to inimical inflammatory speech and demagoguery. The number of members and candidates increased who had to be removed from the party because they argued against the party line, because they negated the achievements of our socialist state, because they acted in a nonpartisan manner constantly moaning and groaning thus inflicting damage to the party, because they betrayed the GDR [fled or asked permission to emigrate].

The campaign against "moaners and groaners" was executed swiftly. In the nine months until the opening of the Wall unprecedented numbers of members were expelled from the party. Remarkably, equally unprecedented numbers of members quit.[9] In this increasingly tense situation the leadership demanded once more loyalty declarations as a tool to maintain the unity and purity of the party in the interest of maintaining its fighting spirit in an internationally supposedly difficult situation. Several of the officers reported that these efforts culminated in an attempt to make all members formally swear allegiance to the politburo rather than the party as an institution and socialism as an idea. The outrage was such that the measure had to be canceled. Many members threatened to quit should this measure be implemented.[10]

Yet, there was more to come; really more and more. In anticipation of the May 1989 communal election, church and civil rights groups in many cities and towns of the GDR started a panoply of activities of demanding more democratic rights for GDR citizens. Building on previous successes of the ecce homo strategy (see chapter 8, p. 451) some groups tried to use legal possibilities to launch independent candidates on unitary election lists. Others called for an election boycott. And once the actual election day came around, many groups endeavored, and in a few places succeeded, to organize meaningful election monitoring, by participating in the official vote counting. Still, during the election day, irregularities such as improperly sealed urns and questionable interpretations of ballots were noted and formal complaints filed. When, however, the electoral commission, directed by Honecker's ill-fated successor Egon Krenz, announced the public results the sensation was perfect. Having successfully monitored the counting of votes in all or almost all polling stations within an electoral district, the ac-

---

9. From the party statistics it is difficult to differentiate between being expelled and quitting. This is so because the party's administrators were asked to register "quitting" as "deletion," the lesser of the two forms by which somebody could be thrown out of the party (the other being expulsion). The difference between the two was relevant for possible reapplications for membership.
10. I have not seen the documents. But whatever they were, the officers remember outrage at the leadership and this is what matters.

tivists could demonstrate that the party had manipulated the results, tilting the election in favor of yes votes (Neubert 1998, 810–15; Rüddenklau 1992, 288–93). Moreover, the activists' records of election irregularities suggested that such manipulations were common practice. The monitoring activities, decentralized and yet connected, raised the ecce homo strategy of revealing the nature of socialism to an entirely new level. The human rights violations that this strategy had so far demonstrated for individual cases were through this action shown to be a systematic feature of the political order of the GDR. Once the election was over, the now-documented election fraud—the government caught in the act of cheating about its own source of legitimation—led to demonstrations in many parts of the country that the Stasi and police had to make ever-bigger efforts to repress.

The activists' demonstration of election fraud was deeply embarrassing for the party and its leadership. In the eyes of civil rights activists and the church, the reputation of the party reached new lows. Worse, however, the affair had a detrimental effect on the morale of the party, not least because it resonated with all of the other experiences I have already described. Many Stasi officers wondered why higher-ranking party officials had to stoop so low as to commit fraud for so miniscule an effect (making an overwhelming result in favor of the unitary list just a little bit more overwhelming), especially when they had been properly warned by the Stasi where and how the civil rights groups' election monitoring would take place. For party members the election fraud did not raise questions about the legitimacy of socialism, but about the ethics of socialism and about the capabilities of the current party leadership, which had blatantly failed in a situation that was neither particularly strained, requiring compromises in ethics to secure the long-term success of socialism, nor particularly difficult in any other way. Thus, the election fraud became a nagging embarrassment to many members.[11] In retrospect several officers see it as the real beginning of the end. Walter Schuster says:

We could have lived well with the real result of the election. Now they [dissident groups] had something really concrete in their hand. We couldn't shake the election fraud anymore. Always on the 7th [every month—in memory of the election day] something was happening. Most of the time we could prevent it. We simply picked up the people beforehand. Still, the measures had to become ever more expansive. But the party had nothing

11. The question remains why the results were manipulated. I think much for the same reason that other figures were fudged, too: an appearance of progress had to be created. By no means could the party fall back below previous approval ratings. This would have created disagreeable and indeed unjustified finger-pointing in the culture of blame that prevailed through the socialist theodicy.

to say. For me this was the point where I thought, the people do not do anymore what was expected of them. And then this whole thing with Hungary started . . . one felt that suddenly people talked more openly about things that were taboo before. . . . All of a sudden it became possible to present other opinions publicly and that increased more and more, the questions became more precise, discontent became articulated and so it went on.

"Contradictions" at Work

What Schuster recalls is a feeling among Stasi officers that the situation was getting out of hand, that the tools of control at their disposal did not work. This feeling had slowly built up over the last few years, when they had to realize that casework did not lead to trials and that the strategies of decomposition did not yield the desired results either. Through their extensive network of secret informants, they knew about almost all dissident activities in the GDR, which they had documented in ever-thicker case files and countless special reports to the party. To no avail. The number of people involved in dissident activities was still small—according to Stasi estimates probably no more than 2,500 (Mitter and Wolle 1990) in the entire country—but instead of decreasing in response to the Stasi's interventions, instead of slowing down, they grew slowly became more active, publishing more and more samizdat publications, holding more meetings and protest events. In 1988, Herbert Eisner remembers, a colleague mentioned to him in passing, "if all of this continues as it does now, we'll be walking around with a submachine gun in two years."

The futility of their work showed in other ways too. All officers were reporting that during the 1980s it became more and more difficult to recruit secret informants. Each refusal to collaborate was heartfelt by the officers as a rejection not only of their mission but also of the whole project of the party. At the same time, the secret informants already working for them were asking more penetrating questions in response to the increasingly tense economic and political situation. Peter Wagner says:

> You couldn't just wave the red flag anymore and march with them [the secret informants] around the block. The "red-light treatment" didn't cut it anymore. You had to think how to respond to their questions, especially since some of their questions increasingly became yours as well. So I sat often for a long time in the bathtub to think all of this through.

Other officers, too, recount how the frequent contact with secret informants, their questions, their disbelief had nourished their own doubts. The reporting about the meetings of the movement members was constantly confronting them with new ideas. At least thematically, some of the things that the movement members wanted did not sound so unreasonable to them: a cleaner environment, peace, and even more honest, more informative news media were issues they found worth pondering. Many of the officers became more open, as more and more negative validations started to raise questions about old certainties, rendering problematic background understandings; the dissident groups' topics began to resonate, while the officers' secret informants positively recognized dissident understandings. Not that any of the officers lost their faith in socialism as an idea, yet aspects of how they looked upon the world were slowly transformed. Again, Peter Wagner:

> In '87, '88 I said for the first time to my wife, I don't understand why one is so frantic about opposition. Only a few want to get rid of the GDR. One could legalize an opposition, then one could act differently and one could also be prouder in the context of the CSCE. Yet, one had to be very careful talking about such things.

This interview quote contains an interesting admission of shame about an issue the civil rights movements emphasized in their work all the time: the contradiction between the GDR's public international stance toward human rights and their domestic practices.

Not only the relatively new problem of dissident groups posed irresolvable problems for the Stasi, but also older problems from the foundation years of the country began to surface again. Hoping to cope with increasing discontent in the population, the party resolved in 1984 to allow more people to file for expatriation. The logic for this move was the very same that was applied to Biermann's forced exile. Getting rid of the people with "inimical-negative attitudes" was supposed cut their influence at home. Yet, the measure did not have the effect the Stasi and the party had hoped for. To the contrary, the measure corroborated hopes that leaving the country without endangering life and limb was possible again. In consequence, the peace, civil rights, and environmental groups were flooded with people who thought their participation in dissident activities would increase their chance of meeting a positive response to their application for expatriation. For older Stasi officers the new waves of refugees resonated with old memories, triggering the very same feelings of helpless anger they knew from the time before the Wall was built. The people who left were again the better educated, the more qualified. How these refugees made Stasi officers feel comes nicely to the fore in the reflections of Peter Wager: "Every person leaving [the country] inflicted defeat on us." The de-authorization strategies of refugees as thankless loafers notwithstanding, the negative recognition of the GDR by anybody who left was experienced as shaming by the officers. The refugees validated a brooding inferiority complex, an emotive understanding among the officers that their beloved country was falling short of expectations, the refugees' and theirs.

The refugee crisis thus spread a sense of gloom among the secret police. In his regular meetings with generals and in speeches to the troops the minister for state security pointed to the urgency of the problem, impelling his officers to make the issue a priority of their work. He exhorted them to do their utmost to prevent people from filing for the permission to leave the country. But what, asked the officers, could they do? In contradistinction to their work against dissidents, the Stasi did make efforts to understand better why people left. They at least conducted interviews with returnees,[12] and what they found was that people preferred to leave everything behind because of the economic crisis, because younger people felt that they had no career perspectives, because they felt stifled. The officers also saw that there was nothing much they could do about any of the motives that had prompted them to leave. Indeed, the issue presented itself as intractable, short of decisive policy changes. And the worst was still to come. In early May 1989, Hungary began to dismantle its border fence with Austria and finally opened its borders for regular traffic at the end of June. GDR citizens began to sense an opportunity that this was a window of opportunity to flee and one that had to be seized quickly because it might close again. Yet, contrary to expectations, the window became bigger. Hungary officially opened its border for GDR citizens in September. Tens of thousands of GDR citizens used the passage via Hungary to leave. Others began to take refuge in West German embassies, which were in principle required to treat them as if they were West German citizens (even though this was not necessarily what the government of the host country thought). The embassy in Prague became overrun by 6,000 GDR refugees and had to shut down completely. The West German government negotiated with both Czechoslovakia and the GDR for their transport by rail via Dresden to the FRG for September 30. Former Stasi officer Walter Schuster comments: "Whoever allowed this to happen did not know what he was doing." Indeed, kept abreast of the events by Western media, people tried to get access to the platforms of railway stations through which this train would pass, some with the hope to jump onto the train and all of this on television, in broad view of the whole country. The Stasi officers who had watched the development of the crisis with increasing apprehension were utterly alarmed by its end. The conclusions they began to draw from these events raised even more questions about the leadership. Martin Voigt: "What we saw was the utter incapability to come to terms with the problem of people willing to leave the country. This became a veritable social force. The attractiveness of the GDR for young people decreased steadily."

---

12. As already during the 1950s, there were always people who regretted their decision to leave, either because the situation they found in West Germany did not meet their expectation, or because they were overcome with longings for the people and places they left behind.

The Failures of Counteraction and Relativization

As always with the analysis of the formation of understandings in spaces of validation, it is important to consider epistemic forces both actualizing and de-actualizing particular sets of understandings. This way, one can avoid teleological accounts that make particular historical outcomes look as if they were inevitable. The question to ask, then, is whether there were validations at play that weakened the emergent sense that the country was caught in a tangle of "contradictions" growing in strength as time progressed. Short of direct negative validations or less frequent positive ones weakening the perception of crisis, countervailing validations can take the form of what can be called counteractions and relativizations. Counteractions affirm newly emerging understandings resonating negatively with the diagnosis of "contradiction," thus weakening it indirectly. Relativizations work through networks of authority in which meta-understandings are mobilized to show that the troubling validations experienced do not actually mean what they were taken to mean. In other words, the mobilized meta-understandings make the troubling validations appear less relevant.

For the case under consideration here, pertinent counteractions would have been signs that the leadership had understood the problems, thus beginning to undertake measures to address them. In other words, signs that there was promise that what the officers perceived as contradictions was about to decrease or disappear in the future. One such sign appeared in the summer of 1987, and it did make a splash among party members. Since 1984, intellectuals from the West German SPD and from the East German SED were holding regular discussions originally inspired by the idea of keeping the peace process going even after the NATO decision to deploy new nuclear missiles (Reissig 2002; FES 1997).[13] After several meetings, the social democrats proposed to draft a common paper candidly outlining agreements and disagreements between them while proposing rules for a continuing dialogue between East and West. To the surprise of everyone involved, Honecker agreed that the paper should be published simultaneously in the GDR and the FRG. Under the title "The Controversy between Ideologies and the Common Security," it appeared in August 1986 in both party newspapers, the SPD's *Vorwärts* and the SED's *Neues Deutschland*.[14] The piece was

---

13. For both parties this was difficult terrain as they had long seen each other as traitors to the cause of the poor, mutually accusing each other of paving the way for the Nazis.

14. The title of this programmatic essay is a wonderful example of a calculated attempt to evoke an all-German pattern resonance. The first part of the title mirrors Kant's well-known late collection of essays, "The Conflict of the Faculties," in which he not only answers his censors who had suppressed the first essay in the volume a few years earlier, but where he also makes

a sensation in East Germany, because it not only acknowledged that either system may develop in a positive direction, and that both sides are capable of peace, but also because it argued that the dialogue across the Iron Curtain was contingent on extensive dialogue between "all societal organizations, institutions, forces and persons" at home. And this on the pages of *Neues Deutschland*, not tucked away in some minor news outlet!

Involved party members read this as a serious invitation for dialogue, which they were only too eager to take up. The paper's two East German co-authors received countless invitations from across the country to discuss it. And the Initiative for Peace and Human Rights, whose members had for years demanded dialogue, invited the authors as well. Finally, it seemed, there was a sign of reform-mindedness in the GDR. Yet, the promise was not redeemed by deeds. Just a few weeks later Kurt Hager criticized the paper with an article in *Neues Deutschland*. And soon after, the authors of the paper were forced to cancel public discussions, including the one with the IFM (FES 1997, 14–25). In its reports to the politburo, the Stasi judged the paper as undermining resolve and battle-readiness of the party, as a masterstroke of "political ideological diversion" (Reissig 2004, 1997ff.). The dialogue at home was killed before it had really begun, but not before giving many people a taste of how exciting party life could be if there was only more of it. Given the blockade of the politburo, international dialogue came to an end as well, not least because its West German critics seemed to have been right after all.[15] In East Germany the disappointment was considerable. Rather than counter-vailing multiply validated understandings of growing "contradictions," the whole affair about the SPD-SED essay validated them even further.

The party state also used propagandistic tools to counteract understandings that the GDR economy was failing. The usual success propaganda does not count in this respect because by then it had lost its power to inspire hope in most people; it was one prong of the contradiction, not a force for its mitigation. Much better was the hope for a significant technological break-through that was connected to the GDR's much-touted microelectronics program, especially its 1 megabyte memory chip project that was narrativ-ized widely as a romantic David beats Goliath story (Maier 1997, 73–77;

---

a strong plea for the freedom of research and debate along with a plea for the cultivation of the powers of self-critique. The title of the SED/SPD paper also reflects an interesting effort at mutual authorization of both parties involved through the agreement on the significance of the Enlightenment tradition in German thought.

15. Just as the politburo canceled the dialogue with dissidents and the church because it feared the recognition of anything that was outside of the control of the party, so did the West German critics fear that the dialogue was affording too much recognition to the GDR, thus potentially stabilizing a political order it wished was not there.

Stokes 2000, 189ff.). Yet the program was consistently bogged down in difficulties, and due to understaffing and underfunding never stood a chance of really closing the gap with Western manufacturers. Even though in summer 1989 Honecker could hand over, to much media fanfare, a 1-megabyte chip to Gorbachev, this was far too little, far too late to make any real difference.

The 1980s were not the first period in which Stasi officers experienced contradictions. Especially in chapters 5 and 6 I have shown Stasi officers wrestling with rearmament in the face of an avowed pacifism, with shaming rituals, with sudden jumps in doctrine, with disquieting events. And yet, what happened in each and every one of these events was that they could be either successfully relativized within the networks of authority in which the officers moved, or the events giving rise to troublesome validations gradually lost their epistemic impact since there were no further events with similar validating effects. A number of *relativization strategies* prevailed over the years, because they were deeply ingrained in Marxist-Leninist ideologies and practices as meta-understandings. Even though I have discussed these strategies before, it is worth the while to recount the four most prevalent ones here. First, in cases where officers felt treated unjustly, the socialist theodicy offered two ways out: either the officer could see that he had failed to self-objectify properly, or he could attribute the course of the events to the failings of a single superior, an individual person who did not get it right. Second, the typical line of defense against seemingly irrational orders or policies was building on understandings about the economy of knowledge. According to these rationalizing understandings, each and every person knew only a small slice of the whole. The necessity of secrecy prevented a more liberal sharing of information, and therefore only those higher up could judge situations properly because they had more of an overview. Third, actions or measures that did not live up to ideas of proper communist behavior could be justified as necessitated by the particular historical context, as a tactic a mere compromise necessary now for the greater good of the socialist project in the long run. Finally, fourth, a most important strategy was to admit the failings of socialism, its imperfect state, but then to point out that this imperfect form of socialism was still far superior to capitalism with its contemptuous logic of exploitation. This last move found expression in a frequently evoked trope. The GDR was described as "the best GDR there is" (*die beste DDR, die es gibt*).

The 1980s offered a lot of possibilities to employ most notably the fourth rationalizing strategy, emphasizing the relative goodness of the GDR by pointing to the evil actions of the imperialist class enemy. Both Ronald Reagan and Margaret Thatcher were most useful antagonists in this morality play. They unwittingly supported socialism in their role as perfect anti-authorities not only through their frequent anticommunist rhetoric, but also through their readiness to engage in military interventions abroad and their antilabor actions at home. In spite of these rich opportunities to fuel the rationalizations of contradictions in the GDR, the possibilities for them to take effect decreased during the 1980s. Says Wolfgang Schermerhorn:

> There was on the one side the realization that there is a lot of crap here, to say it bluntly. But then there was also the realization that we are constrained by the currency situation, the [technology] embargo and evil imperialism. . . . Before, one had doubts once in a while; but they were always relativized by political events, by an insight into the overall situation of society. The *seeming* insight! All that relativizing in arguments with others all of a sudden gave way to the obvious. All of a sudden everything became crystal clear. It was all of a sudden obvious that we needed a drastic cut. There was no other way out, in my opinion, and this is how most others saw it as well. And I say in all clarity, this is one of the reasons that this upheaval, this revolt happened with so little opposition, and without violence.

I think what Schermerhorn is describing here is a process by which a large number of negative resonances, contradictions writ small, experienced in shortages, traffic delays, and problems at work, burst upon the mind as a contradiction writ large. In terms of Marxian dialectics one could say that gradual changes in quantity suddenly made way for a dramatic change in quality. The everyday contradictions as negative resonances began to crystallize in an understanding that there was a Marxian contradiction at work, a self-destructive flaw in the system. Rationalization began to fail because it hinged ultimately on a logic of exception. One can blame individuals only so often before one has to realize that there is more than personal failure at work; pointing to the necessity of secrecy only carries so far in the force of incomprehensible policies, and so on. The sheer frequency of negative resonances, their appearance across the board in different domains of social life, gave them a different quality, mentally posing the otherwise unsayable: if not the systems question then certainly the attestation of a profound crisis in leadership. Doing this put matters all of a sudden in perspective, the various experiences of contradiction resonated across the board. This is what Schermerhorn means, I surmise, with the "sudden" clarity or obviousness he refers to four times in this short passage. No doubt this understanding was quite rudimentary, not well differentiated and articulated. So far, it was more of a placeholder. The officers express it frequently with the words "we realized something had to change." This is of course not what they said in party meetings. However, they said it to their friends at work and at home, and as an understanding it became recognized and therefore actualized in a network of authority. And yet, as Horst Haferkamp says:

I have to say that it is not the case the among each other we did not have conversations about such things [deteriorating economic situation in the GDR]. I mean people who were close to each other, people who got close through work, who trusted each other. This went all the way to pointed conclusions that something needed to be done. I don't say this here to fashion myself retrospectively into a resistance fighter—I have no intention to do that. Such considerations all ended with the thought that we had no illusions about a third way, an illusion that was harbored by many in the fall and winter of 1989/90. . . . For us it was always clear, and the historical development after '89 has proven that there is only "red" or "white," or maybe I should better say "black-brown." Anything in between won't work. This much was clear to us. Changing the power as it was installed in the GDR, warped and contorted as it was in parts, would inevitably mean that they [the black-brown, i.e., clerico-fascist class enemy] would come to power. And we were so happy that they had not been in power since 1945 and we certainly did not want them ever again. And thus all thinking in alternatives came to an end.

But this is to say that the impatience with rationalizing strategies of the first, second, and third kind found its end in the fourth one! What remained was a profound sense of ambivalence. Strong loyalties to socialism as an idea and to the GDR as a country were matched with vague notions that the system needed reform and a mounting distrust in the party leadership. This included a growing skepticism about what party officials said. Increasingly, even functionaries felt that they were not only misinformed, but that they were lied to. The chasm torn open between irreconcilable validations, between the recognitions dispensed in propaganda and the corroborations experienced in everyday life, made language lose its meaning. This was not, as Yurchak (2006) has argued for the post-Stalin years in the Soviet Union, a shift in the mix of meaning dimensions from the descriptive (or in Austin's terms "constative") to the potentially institution forming (or in Austin's terms "performative") dimension of utterances. Instead, language increasingly lost its performative capacity because it could no longer persuade (in Austin's terms it no longer produced uptake). And persuade it did no more because people saw it, at an accelerating pace, as false, that is, as misrepresenting the world they knew.[16] And since institution formation takes invitation and uptake, action and reaction, and that many times over, institutions

---

16. This is to say that in a number of speech situations the performative is dependent on the constative. Austin called the conditions under which a performative utterance produces uptake to create a social effect in alignment with the intentions, the felicity conditions of the performative. He contrasted them with the "truth conditions" of a constative. What the official language

became weakened. More, as propagators of questionable descriptions of the world, the party leadership began to lose authority because, as I argued in chapter 4, understanding and authority are negotiated together. Following the five-year rhythm, the next party congress was scheduled for 1990. The officers and with them many other SED functionaries placed great hope in this event, for that placeholder "something has to change" had to be filled with content rather fast, given the precarious situation of the country. They no longer believed that the current leadership could effect the changes so they hoped for a "biological solution," for a younger generation to take over.

For many dedicated communists, especially of an older generation, the CPSU of the Soviet Union bore the glory of the ultimate arbiter in all matters socialist. Party functionaries who had lived for longer periods of time in the Soviet Union often maintained strong emotional bonds to the country of the October Revolution (e.g., Eberlein 2000; Wolf 1998). If matters went wrong in the GDR, the "country of Lenin" could be relied upon to set things straight. In their imagination the Soviet Union was a big brother after all. These emotional, often romanticized ties with the Soviet Union are in part the reason why the SED's measures against cultural products from the glasnost and perestroika Soviet Union were answered with disbelief, even outrage. In a crisis like this one, where the GDR leadership had lost its authority, many eyes and ears were trained upon Moscow. And yet, Moscow remained largely silent on the internal affairs of the GDR. Gorbachev saw it as part and parcel of his reform measures that the brother countries take care of their own affairs. The Brezhnev doctrine was no longer the compass directing Soviet foreign policy.

Frustrated Change Efforts, Big and Small

Acutely perceiving that the development of the country headed in the wrong direction, some courageous and concerned party officials tried to correct matters to the degree they thought they could. Typically, they did not get very far; and frequently their moves posed serious threats to their careers. At the very top, this is true, for example, for Gerhard Schürer, the head of the state planning commission. According to his own account, he tried to get through a price reform that would limit the subsidies for rents and basic foodstuffs in the GDR in 1979. His proposals were dismissed out of hand as endangering the "unity of economic and social policy" (Honecker's policy platform) and thus basic principles of the current party line (Schürer 1999). Almost a decade later he made an effort to get the general secretary and the

---

of the party-state in late socialism shows, however, is that the felicity conditions may indeed include a number of truth conditions.

politburo to pay attention to the debt trap into which he saw the country sliding. For this purpose he had worked out a thirteen-page brief that he forwarded past his immediate boss, Günter Mittag, directly to Honecker. He also requested a personal meeting. According to Schürer (1996, 155–56), this is what happened next. Honecker forwarded his brief to Mittag with the request for a comment, which ended up being twice as long s Schürer's brief. That comment condemned the brief, stating that the country's indebtedness was under control. Mittag's comment was then submitted to the politburo, carrying Schürer's piece as an attachment. According to Schürer, Honecker opened the discussion in the politburo meeting stating that he fully agreed with Mittag's assessment. He further explained that Schürer's analysis and proposal violated major decisions of the previous two party congresses and hence was unacceptable. That maneuver heralded the end of the reform attempt. Nobody else had questions or comments; the meeting simply moved on to the next item on the agenda. Only after Honecker was deposed did Schürer get a real hearing in the politburo with a devastating report on the state of the GDR's finances that anticipated the country's failure to service its debt obligations for the near future. The People's Chamber learned for the first time about this situation in the meeting of November 13, 1989. The members of the People's Chamber met this news with utter disbelief and anger. And it was this discussion that immediately preceded Mielke's speech.

Schürer's case is symptomatic for party officials' efforts to force more critical discussions about the situation of the country. Lower-ranking functionaries were treated with disciplinary measure for raising critical questions. I have already spoken of Karl Maier's guarded attempts at critique, his efforts to nominate a candidate for party elections from below (see chapter 3, pp. 199–200), and later his mere questioning of ZK resolutions with regard to the party's media policies that almost got him fired (chapter 6, pp. 331–32). He concludes his narrative of change efforts:

One could see that this was a development in the direction of the negative, that above all the distance to the FRG, which was the yardstick for us, became ever bigger, that the people became ever more discontented. Yet, even then one did not have many possibilities to exert influence. One just tried to do one's work well, and one hoped that they up there will understand what's up and that they will initiate new policies. There was de facto no possibility to start such [new] policy or even to offer a fundamental critique of the general line [of the party]. And wherever this was tried, this was blocked instantaneously. . . . *So we learned not to try.* The party discipline was always enforced. Yet the idea [of socialism] as such was not touched by all of this. This was no reason to doubt one's worldview. Instead one saw its imperfect realization, including the problems in affecting corrections.

If I had seen a possibility to intervene more forcefully, I would have used it. But I was blocked frequently and at the end my wings were clipped. (My emphasis)

The situation was absurd. On the one hand the state of the country was such that it had become impossible "to do one's work well," as Maier put it. This was as true for managers in industry, who could not obtain the supplies they needed at the right time in the right amount and in the appropriate quality, as it was for the car repair man who wrestled with exactly the same problem. But it was also no longer possible for party secretaries and for Stasi officers to do their work well either. At the same time, however, people were held responsible for doing their jobs well. They were blamed for failures that in the end they could not be held responsible for because the problem was institutional. Therefore, what was needed was politics, an effort to change the institutional fabric in however small way one could from a given perspective. And yet, in a country where everything was seen from a political angle, where the political seemed to be everywhere, it proved to be entirely impossible for party members to engage in any politics except that prescribed by the leadership. In effect, politics had brought about the death of politics.

A Self-Fetishized Political Order

The only level at which changes in politics could be decided in this situation was the politburo. And even that statement has to be qualified. Given the working habits that had prevailed since Ulbricht rid himself twice in three years of inner-party critics, change could only come from the figure of the general secretary himself.[17] So the whole party looked upward to see what would happen at the top to attend to the crisis of the country. A turn of phrase that surfaced often in my interviews was the expectation of a "redeeming word" (erlösendes Wort) from the leadership about what to do now. Here are two descriptions of the attentive waiting that apparently characterized the whole party in the late summer and fall of 1989. First, Walter Schuster:

> In Berlin there was always a conference in September organized by the Berlin party organization in the Palace of the Republic. It was the conference of best workers and I said I want to go there, because I felt totally out of the loop. At first Mr. Schabowski was speaking, he greeted comrade Honecker, but he said nothing about the problems that really moved the

---

17. This does not mean that the general secretary was a supreme dictator who could have done as he pleased. He was still constrained by the ideology of Marxism-Leninism, the traditions of the party, and until quite recently by Moscow's approval.

people. And I had taken a big [note]book along, to write something down, so that I could tell my people something. Then comrade Mittag came, the same thing. I couldn't even write down a single line. And then this was supposed to be analyzed [he refers here to the "analysis" (*Auswertung*) of propaganda events and their documents]. But there was nothing. Nobody had said anything [of interest]. And this in spite of the fact that there was so much information available [provided by the Stasi]. . . . Yet, everything that was in the slightest bit disagreeable could not be reported. And there were no real discussions anywhere.

And now, much in the same spirit, Klaus Haferkamp, who worked at the time as an OiBE, an officer in special employment in a ministry:

Every Thursday—because Thursday morning the cabinet met—the under-secretary collected his guys from the whole ministry and said, the cabinet has discussed this today and decided that, he informed us, and gave us orientations, we should perhaps pay more attention to this or that. In late summer, early fall '89 he came into the room and was stared at expectantly by those assembled, and then said every time about the same thing: "I know what you are waiting for, just like me, that the leadership will say something about the situation in the country. But unfortunately I have to tell you that this week it did not do it either, neither Monday, nor on Tuesday during the politburo meeting, nor this morning during the cabinet meeting." And then everybody dropped their lower jaw, but not as far anymore [as before], because one stopped expecting that they would ever do it.

Even though the "no tears" comment on October 1, 1989 about the refugees leaving the country (attributed by most officers directly to Honecker) did not bode well (see introduction, p. 3), everybody kept waiting apprehensively. There was nothing else one could do as a party member and functionary. The fortieth anniversary celebrations of the GDR were around the corner, Gorbachev would come to visit. All of this was hoped to be a setting for the "redeeming word" to finally come forth. It was not to be. Instead, totally misjudging the mood in the country, Honecker bored everybody with the usual accolades on the GDR's marvelous achievements. To top everything off, his ditty "socialism in its course can neither be stopped by donkey or horse" sounded eerily out of place. And as such it was experienced as an acute embarrassment. This disappointment was available quite viscerally. Emil Tischler attended the celebration and he reports that for the first time in his long career he could not get into the mood of the celebrations. The feeling of electrification, which had never failed him before in socialist mass events, eluded him this time. "I drove home depressed," he says. And Walter

Schuster concludes: "Nobody got answers for anything; something was celebrated that could no longer be celebrated."

As if adding insult to injury, for the first time in the GDR's history the anniversary events were accompanied by countrywide protests. In Berlin they led to violent clashes, not least because the Stasi was caught cold about who the demonstrators were and what they were up to. Had they known who and what, they would have used their usual tactics to prevent them from reaching their destination. Protest obviously had not only reached a new scale, but also, yet again, new strata of people, as the swelling Monday demonstrations in Leipzig proved week after week. Seen in light of the clashes and the associated mass arrests, Honecker's words sounded worse on the day after the celebrations were over than when they first crossed his lips.

Honecker did not fail to come up with a "redeeming word" during the country's anniversary celebrations (or before or after) because he was senile or dim-witted. The much simpler and more devastating truth is that neither he nor the party in general had anything to say. Nobody had an analysis of the situation and nobody had made plans, either for reforms in some larger sense, or for immediate action attending to the most urgent problems. The party was speechless because it was clueless.[18] Clueless it was because it had institutionally disabled itself from producing adequate understandings of itself in a wider social environment, that is, understandings that would have appeared plausible enough to orient and direct, coordinate and legitimate, successful politics and self-politics. And that, finally, was the consequence of incessantly valuing mobilization ("purity, unity, and unanimity") over controversial, potentially distracting or muddling dispute ("no discussion of mistakes"); the party desired agreement, affirming corroboration, and positive resonance while abhorring disagreement, contradicting corroboration, and negative resonance. It had made the development of useful self-understandings impossible by linking belonging to explicit agreement, thus killing the very intimacy that is the precondition for processes of working through, thinking through, and practicing. The actual development over the course of the next two months bears this analysis out. Krenz, who took over from Honecker, could not invent on the fly what had not been done for decades. The party's institutions, its culture of discourse, its interactional habits, could not be shed overnight. Everybody in the leadership of the party was a product of this culture; their style of interaction had become part of

---

18. Again, it would be a mistake to think that this cluelessness only characterized the politburo. It affected all branches of government. A more detailed analysis of the crisis management in the security organs, if anything mirroring the situation at the party's head, is provided by Walter Süß (1999). Reports from other branches of government as well as the extensive memoir literature provide a similar picture.

their selves; self-objectification was the mode in which they reflected upon the world; and self-objectification was the criterion used to judge the ethical merit of anybody around. The party's political epistemics allowed the dissemination of innovative departures only from its very center. Since challenging ideas could not be brought to the center, they would have to be developed in the center; but by the time one got there, one had unlearned to produce challenging ideas. The party's sclerosis became ever more apparent through the various pronouncements and hectic measures of the next weeks. The various aporias of politics had become one overarching and complete aporia. The party that had done everything to remain in control by creating a mass-mobilizing monolithic intentionality lost everything because of it.

This is not, however, how things appeared to Honecker and most other politburo members until October 7. By and large they felt they knew themselves, their party, their country, the world well enough to keep on going. Their view of the world had been validated in seemingly uninterrupted succession. The leaderships' understandings were virtually drenched in recognition. The institutional fabric was such that in acting they recognized these understandings for one another, the party members recognized them for the leadership, and so did the masses in the many orchestrated rituals of affirmation. All participants did so because the recognition of the party line was the very condition for authority, for active participation in the first place. The validation of official socialist understandings was circular, that is, automated—written into the institutional fabric of GDR society. No doubt, people had inklings that there was a problematic connection between recognition and the reproduction of authority. Occasionally these flared up, for example when leaders began to distrust the reports they received, because they knew at some level they were palliating. One reason why even the party was so fixated on Western interpretations of GDR life was their seeming informational value that could not be produced from within. And yet it was hard for actors in the GDR to make good sense of what was said in the West about the GDR. The promise of hidden insight notwithstanding, it was the class enemy speaking, whose malicious intentions were all too apparent. The secret police appeared like a way out of the difficulties of obtaining reliable information. But then, who knew that they were, perhaps with a few more degrees of freedom, ultimately operating within the same institutional constraints that kept everyone else from saying what needed to be said? In the end, the officials' questions about the capability of party and state to form useful understandings could not be pursued. Everybody continued to act as if these reports produced by the apparat were the real thing. Systematically questioning them would have unsettled too many of the fundamentals. And so the negative resonances leading to the experience of what locals called contradictions were treated with rationalizations amply available in this mirror hall of institutions called actually existing socialism. By the time people became weary even of the standard rationalizing procedures it was too late. The party as an institutional fabric could no longer think of persuasive ways of running the country. In the middle of an existential crisis the party could only act as it had always done: by affirming itself. After all, mobilization was, as Ken Jowitt has argued (1991), the defining characteristic of what he calls "Leninist regimes." The point was to make people see the truth of Marxism-Leninism and to induce them to act accordingly to progress on the path to communism. Everything else was taken to be a potentially costly distraction.

Once positive direct corroborations of Marxist-Leninist doctrines were not forthcoming in the form of demonstrable economic superiority of socialist over capitalist economies, the failed predictions were not allowed to raise serious questions among party members. Less than satisfying economic results were taken to have everything to do with circumstances (geopolitical position, historically better starting positions) or the evil machinations of the enemy (e.g., embargo politics). The meta-understandings exalting Marxism-Leninism did not allow current performances of any kind to have a negative corroborating effect on any central tenet of Marxism-Leninism. If the world did not look as ideology said it did, the problem was not seen in ideology, but in the way one looked at the world. Propagandistically, the void created by the absence of palpable direct corroborations was filled with indirect corroborations and recognitions looking on the surface like direct corroborations. Election results were really seen as approval (even if they were instituted in such a way that disapproval was hard to register in the end even when they were falsified), the declarations of loyalty during mass events such as May Day parades or countrywide youth meetings were taken at face value (even if these events were tightly choreographed). In response to the crisis of credibility, the propaganda machine was just cranked up a notch higher. Sports became a vital arena to prove socialism's valor (even though doping was rampant), and the more so the less direct corroboration through economic performance was available. Even if one knew about such self-deceptions, one could not complain. After all, the party was riding the train of historical laws that had been scientifically developed, and then corroborated by history time and again, for which the success of Red October and more recently the Soviet victory in World War II were the ultimate living proofs. For that reason, there was also no need for attempts to let new understandings radically unsettle old ones. As was incessantly repeated, Leninism was still taken to be the Marxism of the present. The party therefore never saw a reason to subject its guiding theory to fundamental revision. In the meantime, the world changed much faster than socialism's understandings of it. And the reason for that was not some abstract deficit of modernity, some lack of internal institutional differentiation as some Durkheim-Parsons-inspired sociologists maintain (e.g., Meuschel 1992, 10ff.) but a very concrete lack of institutionalized type 3 situations (drawing consequences about the adequacy of understandings from negative validations) and the space to think, work through, and practice novel understandings practiced by them. By effectively fetishizing the understandings of itself ("the party line") it fetishized itself institutionally and thus became incapable of effectively engaging in politics, self-politics included.

A Bloodless Revolution

During the interviews, several officers argued that the revolution of 1989 was bloodless because the party was clueless. I think they are right. Violent repression would have immediately raised the question, "what next?" to which there was no answer. There was no real sense for *what* the blood was supposed to be shed if bloodshed was the way to go. One could have answered with the standard phrase "to preserve the fruits of the revolution," yet just to be immediately thrown back onto the so-urgent question, "yes, but *how* would you preserve its fruits?" And the answer would have been for many: certainly not by killing other people (Süß 1999). This amounts to saying the party could only abdicate. That is what it did while losing 95 percent of its members.

Nevertheless, situations where understanding is lacking, depriving actors of their ability to engage in meaningful action, do not only end in stalemate, they can also descend into violence. The dark secret is that organized violence *can* be generative of archaic understandings by (re-)establishing a friend-foe pattern, which becomes at the same time emotively and kinesthetically enacted, thus creating resonances across different modes of understanding that can be experienced, much like a ritual, as reestablishing order out of chaos. All that is needed is a relatively clear prior understanding differentiating an us vs. them, friend and foe, for *un*systematic violence has none of these effects because no participant knows what others might do next. The party, including the Stasi, operated with a deeply institutionalized friend-foe distinction that might have been mobilized in the conflict. If there had been a new leader with authority, let us say a charismatic Soviet leader (not that there were many of those; self-objectification kills charisma so that Gorbachev was already the last straw) who in January of 1989 would have toppled Mikhail Gorbachev to reinstitute the status quo ante, the GDR leadership could and would have acted differently. In this scenario, there would probably have not been much bloodshed either because orders would have been given to squash demonstrations early on, which in all likelihood would have led the opposition to retract, and ordinary people not previously active in the dissident scene would never have ventured to air their frustration in the streets.

Had such a putsch happened later in the year, let us say in the second half of November, it would have been already too late in the GDR. By then, dissidents and citizens would have had a hard time to withdraw, and resistance could very likely have continued in the streets—in whatever form. However, by that time Stasi officers and other party functionaries were so disenchanted with their party leadership old and new, by then they had talked so much and discussed the situation, had seen so much happening, that they were well on the way to acquire different sets of understandings. Younger and lower-ranking officers had begun to speak up more freely against their own superiors. There had even been a demonstration in the hallowed halls of the secret police headquarters (Eichner 2002). In other words, the old understanding that the party's monopoly of power had to be defended by *all* means, because this is what socialism hinged on, had become significantly de-actualized. Under these conditions it is not unlikely that a significant number of officers would have resisted orders to shoot. And what would have happened if that charismatic leader had appeared sometime between January and November, let's say, at the end of summer? There is no way to tell. The likely outcome would have depended very much on the actual course of events, the contingencies on the way.

Socialism was not brought down by anyone, or any group in particular. Protest could become a mass phenomenon only because it came to be understood as possible through the earlier example of dissidents, and through the performed despair of the latest wave of refugees fed-up enough to leave their entire social existence behind when they fled en masse via Hungary and via West German embassies. The dissidents pioneered protest in increasingly open and more encompassing forms because the party state had time and again shown its utter unwillingness to deal with them in a meaningful, dialogic manner. The refugees were fed up for the same reasons, but also because socialism did not keep its promise of economic development. At the same time the capitalist alternative, dangled tantalizingly in front of their eyes, made ever more palpable by televised images and visitors' stories. The party state was at a discursively fully articulated level ignorant about causes, kind and magnitude of this massive discontent. It was unprepared for it, even shocked by its extent. More, party state officials themselves were willing to let go of socialism because they did not know what to do when suddenly faced with the open expression of dissatisfaction which began to resonate with and articulate their own experiences. They had neither the ideas to develop nor the people to realize reforms once it became clear that reforms were inevitable. And reforms did not happen earlier because the very same political epistemics, which had left the party state devoid of proper understandings about its situation, had failed to impress the urgency of reform on the leadership previously. At the time of awakening during the fortieth anniversary celebrations which through their very ossified form performed in front of everybody's eyes the inability of the party to deal with the crisis of the country, the violent repression of protest was no longer an option because relevant strata of the leadership were not willing to defend the system at the possible cost of significant bloodshed. In other words what brought down socialism in the GDR is the particular conjuncture of the development of understandings among a variety of different actors. The party state failed for its political epistemics.

AN OBITUARY TO ACTUALLY EXISTING SOCIALISM

The discussions about socialism after 1989 have often been conducted in an avuncular tone, mixing moral triumphalism with hindsight certainty. For this reason I feel compelled to begin this section with a trivial remark. Socialism was not the brainchild of a neurotic, psychotic, or perverse imagination; it was neither a dream nor an illusion, its fantastical elements notwithstanding.[19] Socialism had deep experiential roots in the exploitation of human beings by other human beings. Class warfare was a reality in the sense that the riches of some hinged on the impoverishment of others. It must not be forgotten that it was the emancipatory politics fired up by socialist ideals and socialist theorizing (admittedly assisted by nationalism) that brought about the institutional reconfiguration of bourgeois capitalism that we came to know, appreciate, and take for grated in the industrialized world (with some caveats for the United States) as the welfare state. The economic condition of the possibility for the welfare state to emerge were the enormous productivity gains realized in the nineteenth and twentieth centuries that turned a zero-sum competition over a static income pie into the sharing (even if unequal) of seemingly ever-increasing gains. Within the industrialized national welfare state almost everybody could become better off at least economically not only in the course of a single life but also across successive generations. Once the worst excesses of exploitation were thus checked, there nevertheless remained a staggering amount of class prejudice and discrimination. Socialist (or increasingly social-democratic) politics helped to attenuate the physical and psychological injuries inflicted

---

19. See on this issue also the debate in France triggered by Francois Furet's celebrated *The Passing of an Illusion* (1999), which, although raising many important questions about the self-mythologization of communism, failed to appreciate its real basis. For an impassioned critique see, especially, Claude Lefort 2007.

by unjust institutional arrangements without, however, coming ever near the realization of a functioning meritocracy, the idea of which was always used to legitimate the prevailing social order.

In the capitalist, highly industrialized world socialism did a lot of good, then, as a critical ideology mobilizing and orienting a mass movement of workers. As a contender of liberalism it helped to tame capitalism, lending it a more humane face. But this positive effect may have been, as we begin to realize now, more a feature of a dynamic social constellation involving competing social orders rather than the characteristic of any particular order analyzed in isolation. This stunning success of socialism as a critical theory and as a social movement was in part possible because socialists in liberal, capitalist democracies shed some of their core understandings, which had endowed socialist ideology in the nineteenth century, with some of its considerable force. Most notable among these is socialism's metaphysical core, its philosophy of history as a lawlike, preordained development toward an inevitably just human society, that is, communism as a secular paradise. For many labor activists operating within a capitalist order this eschatology served as a wellspring of courage to enter what seemed at first as a very unequal and thus hopeless contest. Mobilizationally effective beliefs (even where false) can lead people to move the proverbial mountains, at least initially, a feat that retrospectively may endow these beliefs with credibility. In socialist countries this is what happened to Marx's philosophy of history, too. As I have shown in chapters 1 and 2, the success of the October Revolution and the victory of the Soviet Union against Nazi Germany in World War II were understood as corroborations of socialism's metaphysical core.

In capitalist countries, however, many socialists became increasingly uncomfortable with socialism's metaphysics. Scientism, secularism, and humanistic liberalism nourished a profound skepticism toward Marx's philosophy of history, which also proved to become a political handicap by making the formation of broader, more inclusive alliances more difficult. Shedding the metaphysics of Marxism was, therefore, experienced as both a doctrinal and a political act of liberation, facilitating socialists' active participation in government, which in turn allowed for the realization of farther-reaching reform projects. The palpable success of the welfare state seemed to make the old Marxism increasingly irrelevant. The consequence was a theoretical dissipation that led the reformist left to believe that it could do without a powerful critical ideology, while driving more radically inclined people into a variety of orthodox and sectarian fringe positions. In capitalist countries, socialism thus ceased to play the critical role it once did, and as a political force it vanished in the form of the Clinton/Blair/Schröder new-left-center soap bubble on the horizon of history. The hallmark of this new left was the weakening of the very welfare state that socialists had always taken pride to have brought on its way. "New left" was basically another term for neoliberal.

In spite of its own best hopes, socialism as an uncontested state ideology fared considerably worse than socialism as a critical and motivational force in capitalist societies. Much of this is due to what I have called socialism's metaphysical core, its philosophy of history, as well as to its self-understanding as the only possible true science of the social world. One could say that in the end, socialism stumbled over its social ontology and its scientific pretensions. And this is so in spite of the fact that Karl Marx was one of the most fruitful thinkers about the ways in which complex institutional arrangements emerge, stabilize, and fall apart. As a critic of the young Hegelians he had developed an exquisite sense for the fallacies of intentionality, exhibited in his analysis of false consciousness, alienation, and commodity fetishism. Yet, child of the Enlightenment that he was, he also believed fervently that there was a way out of the hell of capitalist society, in which good will could become evil, where knowledge could become an instrument of deception, where freedom was in fact slavery. He sincerely thought that he had discovered the conditions for the possibility to exit from this capitalist inferno. The fundamental mistake of the socialisms of Eastern Europe was to assume that after the October Revolution these exit conditions were fulfilled to such a degree that now good intentions and knowledge were freed from their unpredictable institutional entanglements. Under the new historical circumstances, and within the orientations provided by the science of Marxism-Leninism and the party as its legitimate interpreter, wanting the good was seen as identical with the good. In its own estimation the political knowledge necessary for the great transformation was all there. All that was needed was good will, and an iron one at that. The aspect of socialism that was taken to matter was mobilization, the rallying of all behind the goal of the party.

A slightly different way to put this is that the existing socialisms of the Soviet type tried to overcome the unpredictability of reactions to actions, and thus the open-endedness of action itself and the experience of society as an alien other that follows from it, by creating a master-institution, the party, that could predictably link reactions to actions, thus submitting wild, uncontrolled institution formation to the power of planning and will, seemingly healing the rift between subjective intentions and objective outcomes. The subjectivity that mattered in this context was the will of a collectivity, of a party that could be reconciled with the objective precisely because it accommodated itself to the objective in the guise of a law of historical development. For the party to have a will, however, its members had to objectify themselves; they had to give themselves to the party. At first, at least, the members did not experience this as alienation, but rather as a sacrifice that at the same time brought them the gifts of superior meaning. And thus the party came to be fetishized as the sole vehicle capable of leading to salvation. Endowed with a pharisaically good consciousness/conscience it became smug, intolerant, and ultimately, not only unbearable but ignorant—in spite of its good, honorable intentions it created the alienation it believed to have overcome. Lacking humility about its own limitations, a politics of liberation became its own nemesis.

LEARNING FROM SOCIALISM . . .

At this point one might feel tempted to add a new one-phrase designator summarizing what the GDR was "au fond." Konrad Jarausch (1999) has not only provided a critical reflection on the rather long list of previous attempts to produce such synthesizing concepts, but he has argued that such an exercise can stimulate fruitful discussions, once the old ideological battle terms are discarded. And so he offers his own "welfare dictatorship" as a critique of the various takes on "totalitarianism," while providing an alternative to Linz and Stepan's "post-totalitarianism" (1996, 42ff.), or Kocka's "modern dictatorship" (1999), to name only two of the more prominent attempts to synthesize the nature of Eastern European socialisms in a crisp concept. More recently Mary Fulbrook (2005, 12) has added her "participatory dictatorship" with much the same interest. However, I neither want to take sides with any of these contenders, nor do I want to offer such a term on my own. The reasons for my hesitation are these: Even though such a concept may be provocative and thus generative of potentially clarifying scholarly discourse, it must inevitably run afoul of the complexities of lived life. Worse, analysis in such summarizing terms almost inevitably gets us back into the totalizing comparative systems framework, which has, as I have argued in the preface, numbing consequences for the potential of self-critique in the mirror of the other. As an epistemic practice, the totalizing juxtaposition of systems is ironically not dissimilar to those that have bedeviled the party state in the GDR. As an alternative to a juxtaposing comparison of totalized social forms, I have focused on particular process dynamics produced by sets of interlocking institutions which hold lessons for other complex institutional arrangements. The process dynamics I have paid particular attention to are those leading to political aporias, that is, political stalemates owing themselves to the circular formation of interlocking sets of political understandings leading to institutional fetishism and thus the death of politics.

In this spirit I would like to point at the end of this book to two opportunities to learn from socialism.

Politics as an intentional effort to form institutions while mobilizing expertise for this purpose is a ubiquitous phenomenon. Indeed, large-scale political projects are an integral feature to what the social imaginary James Scott (1998) has called "high modernity," and the failures of it are, as he shows, by no means limited to socialism. I have discussed related issues in chapters 1 and 2 as aporias of socialist politics. There I also emphasized that such aporias are specific to particular institutional arrangements, including particular sets of understandings and meta-understandings. It would be easy, however, to point to particular kinds of aporias in liberal democracies. To be sure, these appear to be more local; they have not led to a total collapse of the entire thicket of political institutions—at least not yet. This said, there seem to be a couple of common features to high modernist institutional collapse, as Scott and others before him have pointed out.[20] There are institutional arrangements that fail to make room for contingencies. Politicians often disregard the fact that institutions are always built in collaboration with many human beings at the same time, that is, with people who have their own understandings and intentions. Moreover, high modernist institutional arrangements often do not endeavor to make systematic use of the local knowledge that people produce in building and working within these institutions. To the contrary, local knowledge is often merely overruled from the center, creating forms of local resistance. The flipside of the last two points is that high modernist institutional arrangements typically overvalue a particular form of knowledge that enjoys currency at the center, at the very top of social, political, and economic hierarchies. From these insights many authors have drawn the conclusion that politics within highly complex institutional arrangements has to be more oriented toward a strategy of small steps enabling a process of learning by doing.

The process of a more experimental self-reflexive politics is in need of further illumination, however. I have argued in this book that it is important to study local political epistemics to understand how situations become aporetic. In this context I have pointed to the dynamics that certify understandings as reliable knowledge. I have argued that validating processes across all three forms are susceptible to potentially dangerous self-

---

20. There is quite a tradition in the social sciences that has consistently warned against efforts at large-scale top-down social transformation. It is perhaps a less visible tradition because its proponents, even though united by an attention to local specificities, consideration of contingencies, experimentation, and reversibility, cannot be sorted into a simple left-right scheme. Vico and Herder belong here as much as Owen and Kropotkin, Popper and Berlin, E. F. Schumacher, Cornelius Castoriadis, or Roberto Unger. At times Hayek and Friedman are counted among this group as well. And yet, even though it is true that they speak up consistently for the importance of local initiative and the enablement of adjustments with the benefit of local knowledge, both of these authors have also contributed significantly to market fundamentalism, and thus to the totalization of a single set of governing principles. That this had devastating consequences of the kind the above-mentioned critics have always warned against is evident.

amplifying dynamics. Under the conditions that I have elaborated in chapter 4, the open dialectics of validation can become short-circuited. In situations of social change the results of such circularities are understandings that at the same time feel like certain knowledge while they become ever more inadequate to orient successful political action in a particular situation. The end result may be the catastrophic collapse of institutions, which might have been prevented with better understandings. The question to ask therefore is what kind of arrangements could possibly prevent institutional arrangements from falling into circular knowledge validation? In search for an answer to this question it is useful to remember that in each and every single case circularity is enabled by particular kinds of meta-understandings. In the conclusions to chapter 4, I have, after an investigation of the dialectics of validation, distinguished five basic constellations leading to circular knowledge formation: sectarianism, self-deceptive contingency control, selective event interpretation, provincialism, and selective memory cultivation.

1. Sectarianism, resulting from the tight coupling of agreement and authority attribution, may not only be seen as warranted, but in situations of intense conflict even as necessary. This is often the case where particular kinds of beliefs or practices are seen as constitutive of an organization. The communist parties of Eastern Europe belong here as much as other forms of organized religion.[21] More, there is scarcely an organization that would not isolate members if they questioned certain articles of faith. Danger looms for the organization whenever such dogmas loose their orienting power in the real world. 2. Self-deceptive contingency control occurs when an outcome completely determined by one's own action is mistaken for a contingent outcome with corroborating value. To engage in such practices is by no means the prerogative of communist secret services so obsessed with security that they minutely choreographed events taken to corroborate some understanding of the party. Misreading the hyped-up demand for goods or services as a sign of their quality, mistaking popularity for achievement, are intrinsic characteristics of valuation processes in our time. 3. In cases of selective event interpretation, some evidence is more or less consciously overlooked lest the indirect corroborating power of other more favorable evidence be diminished. Judging what matters and what does not is always subject to some criterion of relevance. This criterion may, however, be made subservient to a favored theory. And again, not only ruling communist parties apply self-serving criteria. 4. Provincialism is a disposition to dismiss out of hand understandings that create negative resonances with existing understand-

---

21. The similarities between the internal organization of the Catholic Church and socialist parties is especially striking given their mutual emphasis on absolute finality, democratic centralism, and obedient self-objectification.

ings. Often enough, such dispositions are hailed as the good sense of tradition, as the superior sense of common sense. 5. Selective memory cultivation, including censorship—a politics of memory—is often welcomed as a contribution to civic duty in many different kinds of contexts. The idea here is to shelter people from the supposedly spoiling (wasteful, demoralizing, corrupting, etc.) influence of particular kinds of understandings.

Considering this list of epistemic vices (socially anchored all!), the solution to the problem of circular validation appears to be a set of well-institutionalized meta-understandings favoring a thick, substantively rich pluralism, undercutting the meta-understandings that sustain these circular dynamics. What would social arrangements look like in which we savored a disagreeing authority (rather than dreading it); where we would appreciate understandings that do not resonate with what we already know (rather than repressing them); where we would acquire a taste for the possibly noncorroborating contingency of events rather than fearing them? In other words, we would need institutional arrangements that help us to live with epistemic tension, arrangements that do not take recourse to de-authorize disagreeing authority (as unsocialist, unpatriotic, etc.), delegitimize negatively corroborating events (as spurious, exceptional, etc.), discredit novel understandings just because they resonate negatively with old ones (as crazy, unjustifiable, merely newfangled, etc.), arrangements that resist convenient forgetting (for the greater glory of nations, religions, firms . . .).

These are the good old principles of open-mindedness in an open society. Although they are well taken, they are easier spelled out than actually institutionalized. Any of the type 3 situations (as I have developed them in the section on the dialectics of validation in chapter 4), any negative validation taken seriously can produce considerable doubt and is therefore prone to undermine agency. Such doubts do not make for efficiency in action, at least in the short run. They may be a severe impediment to any project of mobilization. However, all of us, but especially leaders in business and in politics, revolutionaries and reformers, like clarity because we need or want to act. The question is always: *What is to be done?* Indeed, the greater open-mindedness of a Marx vis-à-vis a Lenin that I have pointed to repeatedly engages in a rather problematic comparison. After all, Lenin ran a party, a revolution, and then a country torn apart by wars civil and foreign. He was a politician whereas Marx only dabbled in politics. At the same time, there is a reason why all of Lenin's more seminal writings predate the revolution. What we have to conclude from this is that the tension between intellectual vigor and political action is one of the real dilemmas of the human condition. Put differently, the different, potentially contradictory aspects of understandings, which can mobilize people into action while orienting them in the world, needs artful balancing.

Yet, doubts are important because our understandings are but selective translations of the world into a symbolic domain. By design they are limited in the kind of guidance they can provide for us, as they inevitably bear the marks of their production, of a particular time and place, of the situation in which they have taken shape. However, the world changes, not least through our relentless use of these symbolizations, which therefore outlive themselves because the world changes in ways our understandings about it cannot foresee; history is an open-ended process. Socialism's rise and decline is a case in point. Thus, understandings need to be renewed, readjusted, redefined, and replaced if they are supposed to provide reasonably good guidance. The driving forces behind this work are the dynamic constellations I have described in the dialectics of validation. These dynamic constellations emerge on relatively firm social grids that prevent them from being changed at mere whim. If the social is arranged well, it produces the nonsocial in the form of individual input to save it from regressive self-constitution. Constitutional politics at its very best is the high art of keeping our institutional arrangements afloat between the permanent Scylla of smug certainties and the Charybdis of self-consuming doubt, so that we can continue to act with some notion of responsibility.

References

PUBLISHED MATERIAL

A note on citation: All texts are referenced by the publication date of the version used for the preparation of this manuscript. In brackets the year of the first publication in the original language is indicated where it is different from the publication date of the text consulted. If we know that the date of first publication also significantly deviates from the time the text was originally written, the year in which the manuscript was completed is provided within the same brackets after a backslash behind the year of first publication in the original language.

Abbott, Andrew. 1988. *The System of Professions*. Chicago: University of Chicago Press.

———. 2001a. *The Chaos of Disciplines*. Chicago: University of Chicago Press.

———. 2001b. *Time Matters: On Theory and Method*. Chicago: University of Chicago Press.

———. 2004. *Methods of Discovery: Heuristics for the Social Sciences*. New York: Norton.

Alexander, Jeffrey. 2006. *The Civil Sphere*. Oxford: Oxford University Press.

Althusser, Louis. 1971 [1968–69]. *Lenin and Philosophy and Other Essays*. New York: Monthly Review Press.

Andert, Reinhold, and Wolfgang Herzberg. 1990. *Der Sturz: Erich Honecker im Kreuzverhör*. Berlin: Aufbau-Verlag.

Apel, Erich, and Günter Mittag, eds. 1964. *Ökonomische Gesetzte des Sozialismus und neues System der ökonomischen Planung und Lenkung der Volkswirtschaft*. Berlin: Dietz.

Arato, Andrew. 1993. *From Neo-Marxism to Democratic Theory: Essays on the Critical Theory of Soviet-Type Societies*. Armonk, NY: M. E. Sharpe.

Arendt, Hannah. 1968 [1950]. *The Origins of Totalitarianism*. San Diego: Harcourt.

———. 1978 [1971]. *The Life of the Mind*. One volume edition. San Diego: Harcourt.

———. 1994 [1965]. *Eichmann in Jerusalem: A Report on the Banality of Evil*. Revised and enlarged edition. Harmondsworth, Middlesex, UK: Penguin.

———. 1998 [1958]. *The Human Condition*. 2nd ed. Chicago: University of Chicago Press.

Aristotle. 1970. *Poetics*. Translated and with an introduction by Gerald F. Else. Ann Arbor: University of Michigan Press.

Ash, Timothy Garton. 1994. *In Europe's Name: Germany and the Divided Continent*. New York: Vintage.

Auerbach, Erich. 1964 [1946]. *Mimesis: Dargestellte Wirklichkeit in der abendländischen Literatur*. 3rd ed. Bern: Francke.

Auerbach, Thomas, Braun Matthias, Eisenfeld Bernd, Gesine von Prittwitz, and Clemens Vollnhals. 2008. *Hauptabteilung XX: Staatsapparat, Blockparteien, Kirchen, Kultur, "politischer Untergrund."* Anatomie der Staatssicherheit: Geschichte, Struktur und Methoden— MfS Handbuch. Berlin: BStU.

Austin, John L. 1962. *How to Do Things with Words.* Cambridge, MA: Harvard University Press.

Axen, Hermann. 1996. *Ich war ein Deiner der Partei: Autobiographische Gespräche mit Harald Neubert.* Berlin: Edition Ost.

Bachelard, Gaston. 1994 [1958]. *The Poetics of Space.* Boston: Beacon Press.

Bahne, Siegfried. 1993. "Die Verfolgung deutscher Kommunisten im sowjetischen Exil." In *Kommunisten verfolgen Kommunisten: Stalinistischer Terror und "Säuberungen" in den kommunistischen Parteien Europas seit den dreißiger Jahren,* ed. Hermann Weber and Dietrich Staritz. Berlin: Akademie Verlag.

Bahro, Rudolf. 1977. *Die Alternative: Zur Kritik des real existierenden Sozialismus.* Cologne: Europäische Verlagsanstalt.

Baker, G. P., and P. M. S. Hacker. 1984. "On Misunderstanding Wittgenstein: Kripke's Private Language Argument." *Synthese* 58 (3):407–50.

Bakhtin, Mikhail. 1981. *The Dialogic Imagination: Four Essays.* Austin: University of Texas Press.

———. 1984 [1929]. *Problems of Dostoevsky's Poetics.* Minneapolis: University of Minnesota Press.

———. 1986 [1953]. *Speech Genres and Other Late Essays.* Austin: University of Texas Press.

Barth, Bernd-Rainer, and Werner Schweizer, eds. 2004. *Der Fall Noel Fiel: Schlüsselfigur der Schauprozesse in Osteuropa—Verhöre und Selbstzeugnisse.* Berlin: Basis Druck.

Baumann, Richard. 1975. "Verbal Art as Performance." *American Anthropologist* 77 (2):290–311.

Bearman, Peter. 1993. *Relations into Rhetorics: Local Elite Social Structure in Norfolk, England, 1540–1640.* Rose Monograph. New Brunswick, NJ: Rutgers University Press.

Bearman, Peter, James Moody, and Jim Faris. 1999. "Blocking the Future: New Solutions for Old Problems in Historical Social Science." *Social Science History* 23 (4):501–33.

Beauvoir, Simone de, 1989 [1949]. *The Second Sex.* New York: Vintage.

Behnke, Klaus, and Jürgen Fuchs, eds. 1995. *Zersetzung der Seele: Psychologie und Psychiatrie im Dienste der Stasi.* Hamburg: Rotbuch Verlag.

Bender, Gerd, and Ulrich Falk. 1999. *Recht im Sozialismus: Analysen Zur Normdurchsetzung in osteuropäischen Nachkriegsgesellschaften, 1944/45–1989.* 3 vols. Frankfurt: Vittorio Klostermann.

Benford, Robert D., and David A. Snow. 2000. "Framing Processes and Social Movements: An Overview and Assessment." *Annual Review of Sociology* 26:611–39.

Benjamin, Walter. 1983. *Das Passagen Werk.* 2 vols. Frankfurt: Suhrkamp.

Benser, Günter, and Gerhard Naumann, eds. 1986. *Dokumente zur Geschichte der SED III: 1971–1986.* Berlin: Dietz.

Berbig, Roland, Arne Born, Jörg Judersleben, Holger Jens Karlson, Dorit Krusche, Christoph Martinkat, and Peter Wruck, eds. 1994. *In Sachen Biermann: Protokolle, Berichte und Briefe zu den Folgen einer Ausbürgerung.* Berlin: Ch. Links.

Berdahl, Daphne. 1999. *Where the World Ended: Re-Unification and Identity in the German Borderland.* Berkeley: University of California Press.

Berger, Peter, and Thomas Luckmann. 1966. *The Social Construction of Reality.* New York: Anchor Books.

Besier, Gerhard. 1995. *Der SED-Staat und die Kirche 1969–1990: Die Vision vom Dritten Weg.* Berlin: Propyläen.

Bhaskar, Roy. 1989. *The Possibility of Naturalism.* New York: Harvester Wheatsheaf.

Bieri, Peter. 2001. *Das Handwerk der Freiheit: Über die Entdeckung des eigenen Willens.* Munich: Carl Hanser.

Biermann, Wolf. 1965. *Die Drahtharfe: Balladen, Gedichte, Lieder.* Berlin: Klaus Wagenbach.

———. 1972. *Deutschland: Ein Wintermärchen.* Berlin: Klaus Wagenbach.

———. 1991. *Alle Lieder.* Cologne: Kiepenheuer and Witsch.

Biggs, Michael. 2003. "When Costs Are Beneficial: Protest as Communicative Suffering." Paper presented at the Comparative Politics Workshop at the University of Chicago.

———. 2005. "Dying without Killing: Self-Immolations, 1963–2002." In *Making Sense of Suicide Missions,* ed. Diego Gambetta, 173–208. Oxford: Oxford University Press.

Billig, Michael. 1996. *Arguing and Thinking: A Rhetorical Approach to Social Psychology.* Cambridge: Cambridge University Press.

BL (Bezirksleitung) Karl-Marx-Stadt der SED, Abteilung für Agitation und Propaganda. 1976 [1961]. "Die Überlegenheit des sozialistischen Weltsystems." In the series Arbeitsmaterial für Propagandisten und Agitatoren.

BL (Bezirksleitung) Suhl der SED, Abteilung für Agitation und Propaganda. 1976. "Zur Herausbildung kommunistischer Überzeugungen und Verhaltensweisen." In the series Arbeitsmaterial für Propagandisten und Agitatoren.

Bloor, David. 1983. *Wittgenstein: A Social Theory of Knowledge.* New York: Columbia University Press.

———. 1991 [1976]. *Knowledge and Social Imagery.* 2nd ed. Chicago: University of Chicago Press.

———. 2002 [1997]. *Wittgenstein, Rules, and Institutions.* London: Routledge.

Bohley, Bärbel. 2005. "Wir wollten sein wie die Schlangen." In *Mut: Frauen in der DDR,* ed. Bärbel Bohley, Gerald Praschel, and Rüdiger Rosenthal. Munich: Herbig.

Boltanski, Luc, and Laurent Thévenot. 2006 [1991/88]. *On Justification: Economies of Worth.* Princeton, NJ: Princeton University Press.

Bonnell, Victoria. 1999. *Iconography of Power: Soviet Political Posters under Lenin and Stalin.* Berkeley: University of California Press.

Borneman, John. 1992. *Living in Two Berlins: Kin, State, Nation.* Cambridge: Cambridge University Press.

Böröcz, József. 2006. "Goodness Is Elsewhere." *Comparative Studies in Society and History* 48 (1):110–38.

Boswell, James. 1945 [1791]. *The Life of Samuel Johnson.* Garden City, NY: Doubleday.

Böttger, Martin. 1995. "Zwiegespräch mit Kurt Zeiseweis." *Zwie-Gespräch* 31:36–38.

Bourdieu, Pierre. 1977 [1972]. *Outline of a Theory of Practice.* Cambridge: Cambridge University Press.

———. 1979. "Public Opinion Does Not Exist." In *Communication and Class Struggle,* ed. A. Mattelart and S. Siegelaub. New York: International General.

———. 1984 [1979]. *Distinction: A Social Critique of the Judgement of Taste.* Cambridge, MA: Harvard University Press.

———. 1990 [1980]. *The Logic of Practice.* Stanford, CA: Stanford University Press.

———. 2000 [1997]. *Pascalian Meditations.* Stanford. CA: Stanford University Press.

Bourke-White, Margaret. 1946. *Dear Fatherland Rest Quietly: A Report on the Collapse of Hitler's "Thousand Years."* New York: Simon and Schuster.

Boyer, Dominic. 2003. "Censorship as a Vocation: The Institutions, Practices, and Cultural Logic of Media Control in the German Democratic Republic." *Comparative Studies in Society and History* 43(3):511–45.

———. 2005. *Spirit and System: Media, Intellectuals, and Dialectic in Modern German Culture.* Chicago: University of Chicago Press.

Boyer, Dominic and Alexei Yurchak. 2010. "American Stiob: Or What Late Socialist Aesthetics of Parody Reveal About Contemporary Political Culture in the West." *Cultural Antropology* 25(2):179–263.

Breyman, Steve. 2001. *Why Movements Matter: The West German Peace Movement and U.S. Arms Control Policy.* Albany: State University of New York Press.

Brie, Michael. 2004. *Die witzige Dienstklasse: Der politische Witz im späten Staatssozialismus.* Berlin: Dietz.

Brovkin, Vladimir. 1988. *The Mensheviks after October: Socialist Opposition and the Rise of Bolshevik Dictatorship.* Ithaca, NY: Cornell University Press.

Brubaker, Roger. 2004. *Ethnicity without Groups.* Cambridge. MA: Harvard University Press.

Brus, Włodzimierz. 2003 (1965–) *Economics and Politics of Socialism: Collected Essays.* London: Routledge.

Bruyn, Günter de. 1996. *Vierzig Jahre: Ein Lebensbericht.* Frankfurt: Fischer.

BStU. 1995–. MfS Handbuch—Anatomie der Staatssicherheit: Geschichte, Struktur, Methoden. Berlin: BStU.

Buber, Martin. 1995 [1923]. *Ich und Du.* Stuttgart: Phillip Reclam jun.

Bunge, Mario. 2004. "How Does It Work: The Search for Explanatory Mechanisms." *Philosophy of the Social Sciences* 34(2):182–210.

Burke, Kenneth. 1969. *A Rhetoric of Motives.* Berkeley: University of California Press.

Burawoy, Michael, and János Lukács. 1992. *The Radiant Past: Ideology and Reality in Hungary's Road to Capitalism.* Chicago: University of Chicago Press.

Burt, Ronald. 1995. *Structural Holes: The Social Structure of Competition.* Cambridge, MA: Harvard University Press.

Carroll, Patrick. 2006. *Science, Culture, and Modern State Formation.* Berkeley: University of California Press.

Cassirer, Ernst. 1997 [1923¹, 1953²]. *Philosophie der symbolischen Formen: Teil 1—Die Sprache.* Reprint of the 2nd ed. Wiesbaden: Primus Verlag.

Castoriadis, Cornelius. 1987 [1975]. *The Imaginary Institution of Society.* Cambridge: MIT Press.

Chandler, Alfred D., and Herman Daems. 1980. *Managerial Hierarchies: Comparative Perspectives on the Rise of the Modern Industrial Enterprise.* Cambridge, MA: Harvard University Press.

Childs, David, and Richard Popplewell. 1996. *The Stasi: The East German Intelligence and Security Service.* New York: New York University Press.

Chirot, Daniel, ed. 1991. *The Crisis of Leninism and the Decline of the Left: The Revolutions of 1989.* Seattle: University of Washington Press.

Chodorow, Nancy. 1999. *The Power of Feelings.* New Haven, CT: Yale University Press.

Choi, Chung-Wan. 1999. *Von der Dissidenz zur Opposition: Die politisch alternativen Gruppen in der DDR von 1978 bis 1989.* Cologne: Verlag Wissenschaft und Politik.

Coase, Ronald H. 1937. "The Nature of the Firm." *Economica* 4:386–405.

Cohen, Jean L., and Andrew Arato. *Civil Society and Political Theory.* Cambridge: MIT Press.

Collins, Harry. 1992 [1985]. *Changing Order: Replication and Induction in Scientific Practice.* Chicago: University of Chicago Press.

Collins, Harry, and Robert Evans. 2007. *Rethinking Expertise*. Chicago: University of Chicago Press.

Collins, Harry, and Trevor Pinch. 1993. *The Golem: What Everybody Should Know about Science*. Cambridge: Cambridge University Press.

———. 1998. *The Golem at Large: What You Should Know about Technology*. Cambridge: Cambridge University Press.

Collins, Randall. 2004. *Interaction Ritual Chains*. Princeton, NJ: Princeton University Press.

Comaroff, Jean, and John Comaroff. 1992. *Ethnography and Historical Imagination*. Boulder, CO: Westview Press.

Connerton, Paul. 1989. *How Societies Remember*. Cambridge: Cambridge University Press.

Conquest, Robert, 1967. *The Politics of Ideas in the USSR*. New York: Praeger.

Conrad, Joseph. 1996. *Lord Jim*. Ed. Thomas C. Moser. New York: Norton.

Crapanzano, Vincent. 1992. *Hermes' Dilemma and Hamlet's Desire: On the Epistemology of Interpretation*. Cambridge, MA: Harvard University Press.

Creed, Gerald. 1998. *Domesticating Revolution: From Socialist Reform to Ambivalent Transition in a Bulgarian Village*. University Park: Pennsylvania State University Press.

Dahn, Daniela. 2001 [1987]. *Prenzlauer Berg-Tour*. Berlin: Rowohlt.

Damasio, Antonio. 1994. *Descartes' Error: Emotion, Reason, and the Human Brain*. New York: Putnam.

———. 1999. *The Feeling of What Happens: Body and Emotion in the Making of Consciousness*. San Diego: Harcourt.

De Grazia, Victoria. 2005. *Irresistible Empire: America's Advance through Twentieth-Century Europe*. Cambridge, MA: Harvard University Press.

Deutscher Bundestag, ed. 1995. *Möglichkeiten und Formen abweichenden und widerständigen Verhaltens und oppositionellen Handelns, die friedliche Revolution im Herbst 1989, die Wiedervereinigung Deutschlands und das Fortwirken von Strukturen und Mechanismen der Diktatur*. In *Materialien der Enquete-Kommission "Aufarbeitung von Geschichte und Folgen der SED-Diktatur in Deutschland,"* Vols. VII.1 and 2. Baden Baden: Nomos.

Dewey, John. 1925. *Experience and Nature*. Chicago: Open Court.

———. 1997 [1910]. *How We Think*. Mineola, NY: Dover.

Diamond, Jared. 2005. *Collapse: How Societies Choose to Fail and Succeed*. New York: Viking.

Diemer, Gebhard, and Eberhard Kuhrt. 1994. *Kurze Chronik der deutschen Frage*. Munich: Olzog.

Dilcher, Gerhard. 1994. "Politische Ideologie und Rechtstheorie, Rechtspolitik und Rechtswissenschaft." In *Sozialgeschichte der DDR*, ed. Hartmut Kaelble, Jürgen Kocka, and Hartmut Zwahr. Stuttgart: Klett-Cotta.

Dilthey, Wilhelm. 1970 [1910]. *Der Aufbau der geschichtlichen Welt in den Geisteswissenschaften*. Frankfurt: Suhrkamp.

DiMaggio, Paul, and Walter Powell. 1983. "The Iron Cage Revisited: Institutional Isomorphism and Collective Rationality in Organizational Fields." *American Sociological Review* 48:147–60.

Djilas, Milovan. 1983 [1955]. *The New Class: An Analysis of the Communist System*. San Diego: Harcourt.

Douglas, Mary. 1982. *Natural Symbols: Explorations in Cosmology*. New York: Pantheon.

Durkheim, Émile. 1982 [1885]. *The Rules of the Sociological Method*. New York: Free Press.

———. 1995 [1912]. *The Elementary Forms of Religious Life*. Trans. Karen Fields. New York: Free Press.

———. 1997 [1893]. *The Division of Labor in Society*. New York: Free Press.

Eberlein, Werner. 2000. *Geboren am 9. November: Erinnerungen*. Berlin: Das Neue Berlin.

Eggertsson, Thráinn. 1990. *Economic Behavior and Institutions*. Cambridge: Cambridge University Press.

Eichner, Klaus. 2002. "Aufstand am Monarchenhügel: Der Aufbruch 1989 im MfS—Ängste und Hoffnungen." In *Unabhängige Autorengemeinschaft "So habe ich das erlebt,"* ed. *Spurensicherung Band IV—Der Niedergang der DDR—Ehrlich gekämpft und verloren*, 187ff. Schkeuditz: GNN Verlag.

Eichner, Klaus, and Andreas Dobbert. 1997. *Headquarters Germany—Die USA Geheimdienste in Deutschland*. Berlin: Edition Ost.

Eisenfeld, Bernd. 1999. "Wehrdienstverweigerung als Opposition." In *Widerstand und Opposition in der DDR*, ed. Klaus-Dietmar Henke, Peter Steinbach, and Johannes Tuchel, 241–56. Cologne: Böhlau.

Ekman, Paul. 1972. *Emotion in the Human Face: Guide-Lines for Research and an Integration of Findings*. Oxford: Pergamon.

Ekman, Paul, and Richard J. Davidson, eds. 1994. *The Nature of Emotion: Fundamental Questions*. Oxford: Oxford University Press.

Elias, Norbert. 1976 [1935]. *Der Prozeß der Zivilisation: Wandlungen des Verhaltens in den weltlichen Oberschichten des Abendlandes*. Frankfurt: Suhrkamp.

———. 1992. *Studien ueber die Deutschen: Machtkämpfe und Habitusentwicklung im 19. und 20. Jahrhundert*. Frankfurt: Suhrkamp.

Eliasoph, Nina. 1998. *Avoiding Politics: How Americans Produce Apathy in Everyday Life*. Cambridge: Cambridge University Press.

Elster, Jon. 1989. *The Cement of Society: A Study of Social Order*. Cambridge: Cambridge University Press.

Engelmann, Roger, and Frank Joestel, eds. 2004. *Grundsatzdokumente des MfS*. Part of *Anatomie der Staatssicherheit: Geschichte, Struktur und Methoden*. Berlin: BStU.

Engelmann, Roger, and Silke Schumann. 1995. "Der Ausbau des Überwachungsstaates: Der Konflikt Ulbricht-Wollweber und die Neuausrichtung des Staatssicherheitsdienstes der DDR 1957." *Vierteljahreshefte für Zeitgeschichte* 43 (1):341–78.

Engels, Friedrich. 1962 [1877]. *Herrn Eugen Dühring's Umwälzung der Wissenschaft* ("Anti-Dühring"), in *MEW*, vol. 20.

Engler, Wolfgang. 1999. *Die Ostdeutschen: Kunde von einem verlorenen Land*. Berlin: Aufbau Verlag.

Eppelmann, Rainer. 1993. *Fremd im eigenen Haus: Mein Leben im anderen Deutschland*. Cologne: Kiepenheuer and Witsch.

Epstein, A. L., ed. 1967. *The Craft of Anthropology*. London: Tavistock.

Epstein, Catherine. 2003. *The Last Revolutionaries: German Communists and Their Century*. Cambridge, MA: Harvard University Press.

Evans-Pritchard, E. E., 1937. *Magic, Witchcraft, and Oracles among the Azande*. Oxford: Clarendon Press.

Eyal, Gil. 2003. *The Origins of Postcommunist Elites: From the Prague Spring to the Breakup of the Soviet Union*. Minneapolis: University of Minnesota Press.

Fabian, Johannes. 1983. *Time and the Other: How Anthropology Makes Its Object*. New York: Columbia University Press.

Fanon, Frantz. 1991 [1952]. *Black Skin, White Masks*. New York: Grove Weidenfeld.

FDJ (Freie Deutsche Jugend). 1986. "Studienjahr der FDJ 1986/87: Zirkel "Partei-

Wissenschaft-Student" zum Studium von Grundfragen der Politik der SED bei der weiteren Gestaltung der entwickelten sozialistischen Gesellschaft." In the series *Propagandistenmaterial.*

Feher, Ferenc, and Agnes Heller. 1986. "Eastern Europe under the Shadow of a New Rapallo." *New German Critique* 35:7–57.

Feix, Lothar. 1999. "Die DDR existierte eigentlich nicht mehr (Der Prenzlauer Berg, & was hat Kultur mit Politik zu tun?)." In . . . *das war doch nicht unsere Alternative: DDR-Oppositionelle zehn Jahre nach der Wende*, ed. Bernd Gehrke, and Wolfgang Rüddenklau. Münster: Westfälisches Dampfboot.

Felsmann, Barbara, and Annett Gröschner, eds. 1999. *Durchgangszimmer Prenzlauer Berg: Eine Berliner Künstlersozialgeschichte in Selbstauskünften.* Berlin: Lukas Verlag.

Ferree, Myra Marx. 1993. "The Rise and Fall of 'Mommy Politics': Feminism and Unification in (East) Germany." *Feminist Studies* 19 (1):89–115.

———. 1994. "The Time of Chaos Was the Best: Feminist Mobilization and Demobilization in East Germany." *Gender and Society* 8 (4):597–623.

FES (Friedrich Ebert Stiftung). 1997. *Das Verfemte Dokument: Zum 10. Jahrestag des SPD/SED Papiers "Der Streit der Ideologien und die gemeinsame Sicherheit."* Berlin: FES, Büro Berlin.

———. 2003. *Tschernobyl und die DDR: Fakten und Verschleierungen—Auswirkungen bis heute?* Magdeburg: FES, Büro Magdeburg.

Festinger, Leon. 1957. *A Theory of Cognitive Dissonance.* Evanston, IL: Row, Peterson.

Figes, Orlando. 1998. *A People's Tragedy: The Russian Revolution, 1891–1924.* London: Penguin.

Fischer, Thea. 1994. "Wofür habe ich mich aufgeräufelt." In *Noch Fragen Genossen!* ed. Brigitte Zimmermann and Hans-Dieter Schütt. Berlin: Neues Leben.

Fish, Stanley. 1980. *Is There a Text in This Class: The Authority of Interpretive Communities.* Cambridge, MA: Harvard University Press.

Fitzpatrick, Sheila. 1993. *The Russian Revolution.* Oxford: Oxford University Press.

———. 1999. *Everyday Stalinism: Ordinary Life in Extraordinary Times: Soviet Russia in the 1930s.* Oxford: Oxford University Press.

Flierl, Bruno. 1998. *Gebaute DDR.* Berlin: Verlag Bauwesen.

Förster, Günter, ed. 1998. *Bibliographie der Diplomarbeiten und Abschlußarbeiten an der Hochschule des MfS.* Berlin: BStU Dokumente, Reihe A.

Foucault. Michel. 1972a [1969]. "The Archeology of Knowledge." In *The Archaeology of Knowledge and the Discourse on Language.* New York: Pantheon.

———. 1972b [1971]. "The Discourse on Language." In *The Archaeology of Knowledge and the Discourse on Language.* New York: Pantheon.

———. 1978 [1976]. *The History of Sexuality: An Introduction.* New York: Vintage.

———. 1980. *Power/Knowledge: Selected Interviews and Other Writings, 1972–1977.* New York: Pantheon.

———. 1991 [1978]. "Governmentality." In *The Foucault Effect: Studies in Governmentality*, ed. Graham Burchell, Colin Gordon, and Peter Miller. Chicago: University of Chicago Press.

———. 1995 [1975]. *Discipline and Punish.* New York: Vintage.

Frank, Mario. 2001. *Walter Ulbricht: Eine deutsche Biographie.* Munich: Siedler.

Frankfurt, Harry. 1988 [1971]. "Freedom of the Will and the Concept of a Person." In *The Importance of What We Care About: Philosophical Essays*, 11–25. Cambridge: Cambridge University Press.

Freud, Sigmund. 2000a [1914]. "Erinnern, Wiederholen, Durcharbeiten." In *Studienausgabe*, suppl. vol., 206–15.

———. 2000b [1923]. "Das Ich und das Es." In *Studienausgabe*, vol. 3, 273–330.

———. 2000c [1920]. "Jenseits des Lustprinzips." In *Studienausgabe*, vol. 3, 213–72.

———. 2000d [1933]. *Neue Folge der Vorlesungen zur Einführung in die Psychoanalyse. Studienausgabe* 1:448–608.

———. 2000e. *Studienausgabe.* Ten plus one supplementary volumes. Frankfurt: Fischer.

———. 2000f [1916/17]. *Vorlesungen zur Einführung in die Psychoanalyse.* In *Studienausgabe*, vol. 1, 33–445.

Fricke, Wilhelm, and Roger Engelmann. 1998. *Konzentrierte Schläge: Staatssicherheitsaktionen und politische Prozesse in der DDR, 1953–1956.* Berlin: Ch. Links.

Friedrich, Carl Joachim. 1956. *Totalitarian Dictatorship and Autocracy.* Cambridge, MA: Harvard University Press.

Frijda, Nico, Antony Manstead, and Sacha Bern, eds. 2000. *Emotions and Belief: How Feelings Influence Thought.* Cambridge: Cambridge University Press.

Frye, Northrop. 1957. *Anatomy of Criticism: Four Essays.* Princeton, NJ: Princeton University Press.

Fulbrook, Mary. 1995. *Anatomy of a Dictatorship: Inside the GDR, 1949–1989.* Oxford: Oxford University Press.

———. 2005. *The People's State: East German Society from Hitler to Honecker.* New Haven, CT: Yale University Press.

Fuller, Steve. 2002 [1988]. *Social Epistemology.* 2nd ed. Bloomington: Indiana University Press.

Furet, François. 1999 [1995]. *The Passing of an Illusion: The Idea of Communism in the Twentieth Century.* Chicago: University of Chicago Press.

Gal, Susan. 1979. *Language Shift: Social Determinants of Linguistic Change in Bilingual Austria.* New York: Academic Press.

———. 1991. "Bartok's Funeral." *American Ethnologist* 18 (3):440–58.

———. 1993. "Diversity and Contestation in Linguistic Ideologies: German Speakers in Hungary." *Language in Society* 22:337–59.

Gal, Susan, and Judith T. Irvine. 2000. "Language Ideology and Linguistic Differentiation." In *Regimes of Language: Ideologies, Polities, and Identities*, ed. Paul V. Kroskrity. Santa Fe, NM: School of American Research Press.

Gal, Susan, and Kligman, Gail. 2000. *Politics of Gender after Socialism.* Princeton, NJ: Princeton University Press.

Gamson, William A. 1992. *Talking Politics.* Cambridge: Cambridge University Press.

———. 1996. *Talking Politics.* Cambridge: Cambridge University Press.

Garfinkel, Harold. 1967. *Studies in Ethnomethodology.* Englewood Cliffs, NJ: Prentice Hall.

Gaus, Günter. 1983. *Wo Deutschland liegt.* Munich: Droemer Knaur.

Gebauer, Gunter, and Christoph Wulf. 1992. *Mimesis: Kultur—Kunst—Gesellschaft.* Reinbek bei Hamburg: Rowohlt.

Geertz, Clifford. 1974. *The Interpretation of Cultures.* New York: Basic Books.

———. 1980. *Negara: The Theater State in Nineteenth-Century Bali.* Princeton, NJ: Princeton University Press.

Gehlen, Arnold. 1997 [1940]. *Der Mensch: Seine Natur und seine Stellung in der Welt.* Wiesbaden: Quelle und Meyer.

Gehrke, Bernd, and Wolfgang Rüddenklau, eds. 1999. *. . . das war doch nicht unsere Alternative: DDR-Oppositionelle zehn Jahre nach der Wende.* Münster: Westfälisches Dampfboot.

Getzler, Israel. 1983. *Kronstadt 1917–1921: The Fate of a Soviet Democracy.* Cambridge: Cambridge University Press.

Giddens, Anthony. 1984. *The Constitution of Society: Outline of a Theory of Structuration.* Berkeley: University of California Press.

Gieseke, Jens. 2000. *Die Haumptamtlichen Mitarbeiter der Staatssicherheit: Personalstruktur und Lebenswelt.* Berlin: Ch. Links.

Gigerenzer, Gerd. 2000. *Adaptive Thinking: Rationality in the Real World.* Oxford: Oxford University Press.

Gill, David, and Ulrich Schröter. 1991. *Das Ministerium für Staatssicherheit: Anatomie des Mielke-Imperiums.* Berlin: Rowohlt.

Glaeser, Andreas. 2000. *Divided in Unity: Identity, Germany, and the Berlin Police.* Chicago: University of Chicago Press.

———. 2003. "Power/Knowledge Failure: Epistemic Practices and Ideologies of the Secret Police in Former East Germany." *Social Analysis* 47 (1):10–26.

———. 2004. "Collective Intentionality, Belonging and the Production of State Paranoia: Stasi in the Late GDR." In *Off Stage/On Display: Intimacies and Ethnographies in the Age of Public Culture,* ed. Andrew Shryock, 244–76. Stanford, CA: Stanford University Press.

———. 2005. "An Ontology for the Ethnographic Analysis of Social Processes: Extending the Extended Case Method." *Social Analysis* 49 (3):18–47.

———. n.d. "From Mechanisms to Process Dynamics."

Glenn, John K. 2001. *Framing Democracy: Civil Society and Civic Movements in Eastern Europe.* Stanford, CA: Stanford University Press.

Gluckman, Max. 1967. "Introduction." In *The Craft of Anthropology,* ed. A. L. Epstein, xi–xx. London: Tavistock.

Goffman, Erving. 1955. "On Face-Work: An Analysis of Ritual Elements in Social Interaction." *Psychiatry* 18 (3):213–31.

———. 1959. *The Presentation of Self in Everyday Life.* New York: Anchor Books.

———. 1986 [1974]. *Frame Analysis: An Essay on the Organization of Experience.* Boston: Northeastern University Press.

Goodwin, Jeff, James Jasper, and Jaswinder Khattar. 1999. "Caught in a Winding, Snarling Vine: The Structural Bias of Political Process Theory." *Sociological Forum* 14 (1):27–54.

Goodwin, Jeff, James M. Jasper, and Francesca Polletta, eds. 2001. *Passionate Politics: Emotions and Social Movements.* Chicago: University of Chicago Press.

Gorbachev, Mikhail. 1987. *Perestroika: New Thinking for Our Country and the World.* London: Collins.

Gordon, Colin. 1991. "Governmental Rationality: An Introduction." In *The Foucault Effect: Studies in Governmentality,* ed. Graham Burchell, Colin Gordon, and Peter Miller. Chicago: University of Chicago Press.

Gould, Deborah. 2009. *Moving Politics: Emotions and Act UP's Fight against AIDS.* Chicago: University of Chicago Press.

Gramsci, Antonio. 1971 [1929–35]. *Selections from the Prison Notebooks.* Ed. and trans. Quentin Hoare and Geoffrey Nowell Smith. New York: International Publishers.

Granovetter, Mark. 1973. "The Strength of Weak Ties." *American Journal of Sociology* 78 (6): 1360–80.

———. 1985. "Economic Action and Social Structure: The Problem of Embeddedness." *American Journal of Sociology* 91 (3):481–510.

Greif, Avner. 2006. *Institutions and the Path to the Modern Economy: Lessons from Medieval Trade.* Cambridge: Cambridge University Press.

Gries, Rainer, and Silke Satjukow. 2002. "Der 'Alltag' und das 'Außeralltägliche' der 'sozialistischen Helden.'" *Aus Politik und Zeitgeschichte*, B 17.

Griffith, Paul E. 1997. *What Emotions Really Are: The Problem of Psychological Categories*. Chicago: University of Chicago Press.

Grimmer, Reinhard, Werner Irmler, Gerhard Neiber, and Wolfgang Schwanitz. 2002a. "Sicherheitspolitik der SED, staatliche Sicherheit der DDR und Abwehrarbeit des MfS." In *Die Sicherheit: Zur Abwehrarbeit des MfS*, ed. Reinhard Grimmer et al. Berlin: Edition Ost.

Grimmer, Reinhard, Werner Irmler, Willi Opitz, and Wolfgang Schwanitz, eds. 2002b. *Die Sicherheit: Zur Abwehrarbeit des MfS*. 2 vols. Berlin: Edition Ost.

Großmann, Werner. 2001. *Bonn im Blick: Die DDR-Aufklärung aus der Sicht ihres letzten Chefs*. Berlin: Das Neue Berlin.

Hacking, Ian. 1995. *Rewriting the Soul: Multiple Personality Disorder and the Sciences of Memory*. Princeton, NJ: Princeton University Press.

Hager, Kurt. 1996. *Erinnerungen*. Leipzig: Faber and Faber.

Häger, Monika. 1990. "Versuch einer Analyse." In *Geschützte Quelle: Gespräche mit Monika H., alias Karin Lenz*, ed. Irena Kukutz and Katja Havemann, 17–28.

Hahn, Alois. 2000. *Konstruktionen des Selbst, der Welt und der Geschichte: Gesammelte Aufsätze zur Kultursoziologie*. Frankfurt: Suhrkamp.

Halbwachs, Maurice. 1992 [1925]. *On Collective Memory*. Chicago: University of Chicago Presss.

Halfin, Igal. 1999. *From Darkness to Light: Class, Consciousness, and Salvation in Revolutionary Russia*. Pittsburgh: University of Pittsburgh Press.

Hallyn, Fernand. 1993. *The Poetic Structure of the World: Copernicus and Kepler*. New York: Zone Books.

Harich, Wolfgang. 1993. *Keine Schwierigkeiten mit der Wahrheit: Zur nationalkommunistischen Opposition 1956 in der DDR*. Berlin: Dietz.

———. 1999. *Ahnenpass: Versuch einer Autobiographie*. Ed. Thomas Grimm. Berlin: Schwarzkopf and Schwarzkopf.

Hartmann, Wolfgang. 2002. "Kaleidoskop: Vorzeichen für ein Scheitern der DDR." In *Unabhängige Autorengemeinschaft "So habe ich das erlebt,"* ed. *Spurensicherung Band IV—Der Niedergang der DDR*, 178ff. Schkeuditz: GNN-Verlag.

Haufe, Gerda, and Karl Bruckmeier, eds. 1993. *Die Bürgerbewegungen in der DDR und in den ostdeutschen Bundesländern*. Opladen: Westdeutscher Verlag.

Havel, Václav. 1990a. *Living in Truth: 22 Essays*. New York: Faber and Faber.

———. 1990b. *The Power of the Powerless: Citizens against the State in Central Eastern Europe*. Armonk, NY: M. E. Sharpe.

Havemann, Katja, and Joachim Widmann. 2003. *Robert Havemann—oder wie die DDR sich erledigte*. Munich: Ullstein.

Havemann, Robert. 1964. *Dialektik ohne Dogma? Naturwissenschaft und Weltanschaung*. Reinbek bei Hamburg: Rowohlt.

Hayek, Friedrich August von. 1988. *The Fatal Conceit: The Errors of Socialism*. Chicago: University of Chicago Press.

Hedström, Peter. 2005. *Dissecting the Social: On the Principles of Analytical Sociology*. Cambridge: Cambridge University Press.

Hedström, Peter, and Richard Swedberg, eds. 1998. *Social Mechanisms: An Analytical Approach to Social Theory*. Cambridge: Cambridge University Press.

Hegel, Georg Wilhelm Friedrich. 1986 [1806]. *Phänomenologie des Geistes*. Works in 20 vols., vol. 3. Frankfurt: Suhrkamp.

Heidemeyer, Helge. 1994. *Flucht und Zuwanderung aus der SBZ/DDR 1945/1949–1961. Die Flüchtlingspolitik der Bundesrepublik Deutschland bis zum Bau der Berliner Mauer.* Düsseldorf: Droste.

Heider, Fritz. 1958. *The Psychology of Interpersonal Relations.* New York: Wiley.

Hellbeck, Jochen. 2006. *Revolution on My Mind: Writing a Diary under Stalin.* Cambridge, MA: Harvard University Press.

Henke, Klaus-Dietmar, Peter Steinbach, and Johannes Tuchel. 1999. *Widerstand und Opposition in der DDR.* Cologne: Böhlau.

Henrich, Rolf. 1989. *Der vormundschaftliche Staat.* Reinbek: Rowohlt.

Herber, Richard, and Herbert Jung. 1968. *Kaderarbeit im System sozialistischer Führungstätigkeit.* Berlin: Staatsverlag der Deutschen Demokratischen Republik.

Herbst, Andreas, Winfried Ranke, and Jürgen Winkler. 1994. *So funktionierte die DDR: Lexikon der Organisationen und Institutionen.* 2 vols. Reinbek bei Hamburg: Rowohlt.

Herder, Johann Gottfried. 1953 [1772/1770]. *Abhandlung über den Ursprung der Sprache.* In *Werke*, vol. 1, 733–830. Munich: Hanser.

———. 2002 [1784–88]. *Ideen zur Philosophie der Geschichte der Menschheit.* In *Werke*, vol. 3.1. Munich: Hanser.

Herzfeld, Michael. 1985. *The Poetics of Manhood: Contest and Identity in a Cretan Mountain Village.* Princeton, NJ: Princeton University Press.

———. 2003. *The Body Impolitic: Artisans and Artifice in a Global Hierarchy of Values.* Chicago: University of Chicago Press.

Heym, Stefan. 2005 [1988]. *Nachruf.* Munich: Bertelsmann.

Hirsch, Ralf, and Lew Kopelew, eds. 1989. *Initiative für Frieden und Menschenrechte: Grenzfall. Vollständiger Nachdruck der in der DDR erschienenen Ausgaben (1986/87).* Berlin: Editors' edition.

Hirschman, Albert, O. 1970. *Exit, Voice, and Loyalty: Responses to Decline in Firms, Organizations, and States.* Cambridge, MA: Harvard University Press.

———. 1993. "Exit, Voice, and the Fate of the German Democratic Republic." *World Politics* 45 (2):173–202.

Hobbes, Thomas. 1994 [1651]. *Leviathan.* Indianapolis: Hackett.

Hochschild, Arlie. 1989. *The Second Shift.* New York: Viking.

Hoeck, Joachim. 2003. *Verwaltung, Verwaltungsrecht und Verwaltungsrechtsschutz in der Deutschen Demokratischen Republik.* Berlin: Duncker and Humblot.

Hollander, Paul. 2006. *The End of Commitment: Intellectuals, Revolutionaries, and Political Morality.* Chicago: Ivan R. Dee.

Honecker, Erich. 1981. *From My Life.* Oxford: Pergamon.

Honneth, Axel. 1992. *Kampf um Anderkennung: Zur moralischen Grammatik sozialer Konflikte.* Frankfurt: Suhrkamp.

Horkheimer, Max, and Theodor W. Adorno. 1971 [1944]. *Dialektik der Aufklärung.* Frankfurt: Fischer.

Hughes, Everett C. 1936. "The Ecological Aspect of Institutions." *American Sociological Review* 1 (2):180–89.

Hull, Matthew S. 2003. "The File: Agency, Authority, and Autography in an Islamabad Bureaucracy." *Language and Communication* 23:287–314.

Izard, Carroll. 1971. *The Face of Emotion.* New York: Appleton-Century-Crofts.

Jäckel, H., ed. 1971. *Rückantworten and die Hauptverwaltung "Ewige Wahrheiten."* Munich: Piper.

Jakobs, Karl-Heinz. 1983. *Das endlose Jahr: Begegnungen mit Mäd.* Düsseldorf: Claassen.

Jakobson, Roman. 1960. "Closing Statement: Linguistics and Poetics." In *Style in Language*, ed. Thomas Sebeok. Cambridge: MIT Press.

James, William. 1956 [1896]. *The Will to Believe (and Other Essays in Popular Philosophy).* New York: Dover.

———. 1975 [1907]. *Pragmatism* and *The Meaning of Truth.* Cambridge, MA: Harvard University Press.

Janka, Walter. 1989. *Schwierigkeiten mit der Wahrheit.* Reinbek bei Hamburg: Rowohlt.

Jarausch, Konrad. 1994. *The Rush to German Unity.* Oxford: Oxford University Press.

———. 1999a. "Care and Coercion: The GDR as Welfare Dictatorship." In Jarausch 1999b, 47–72.

———. ed. 1999b. *Dictatorship as Experience: Towards a Socio-Cultural History of the GDR.* New York: Berghahn.

Jensen, Jody, and Ferenc Miszlivetz. 2006. "The Second Renaissance of Civil Society in East Central Europe—and in the European Union." In *The Languages of Civil Society*, ed. Peter Wagner. New York: Berghahn Books.

Jesse, Eckhard, ed. 2000. *Eine Revolution und ihre Folgen: 14 Bürgerrechtler ziehen Bilanz.* Berlin: Ch. Links.

Joas, Hans. 1992. *Die Kreativität des Handelns.* Frankfurt: Suhrkamp.

———. 1997. *Die Entstehung der Werte.* Frankfurt: Suhrkamp.

Johns, Adrian. 1998. *The Nature of the Book: Print and Knowledge in the Making.* Chicago: University of Chicago Press.

Joppke, Christian. 1995. *East German Dissidents and the Revolution of 1989: Social Movement in a Leninist Regime.* New York: New York University Press.

Joravsky, David. 1970. *The Lysenko Affair.* Cambridge, MA: Harvard University Press.

Jordan, Carlo. 1995. "Akteure und Aktionen der Arche." In *Arche Nova: Opposition in der DDR—Das "grün-ökologische Netzwerk Arche," 1988–90*, ed. Carlo Jordan and Hans Michael Kloth, 37–70. Berlin: Basis Druck.

Jordan, Carlo, and Hans Michael Kloth. 1995. *Arche Nova: Opposition in der DDR—Das "grün-ökologische Netzwerk Arche," 1988–90.* Berlin: Basis Druck.

Jowitt, Kenneth. 1991. "The Leninist Extinction." In *The Crisis of Leninism and the Decline of the Left: The Revolutions of 1989*, ed. Daniel Chirot. Seattle: University of Washington Press.

Kaelble, Hartmut, Jürgen Kocka, and Hartmut Zwahr. 1994. *Sozialgeschichte der DDR.* Stuttgart: Klett-Cotta.

Kahneman, Daniel, and Amos Tversky. 1982 [1974]. "Judgement under Uncertainty: Heuristics and Biases." In *Judgement under Uncertainty: Heuristics and Biases*, ed. Daniel Kahneman, Paul Slovic, and Amos Tversky, 3–20. Cambridge: Cambridge University Press.

Kappelt, Olaf. 1981. *Braunbuch DDR: Nazis in der DDR.* Berlin: Reichmann.

Katz, Jack. 1999. *How Emotions Work.* Chicago: University of Chicago Press.

Keane, Webb. 2003. "Semiotics and the Social Analysis of Things." *Language and Communication* 23:409–25.

Kenawi, Samirah. 1995. *Frauengruppen in der DDR der 80er Jahre: Eine Dokumentation.* Berlin: GrauZone.

Kharkhordin, Oleg. 1999. *The Collective and the Individual in Russia: A Study in Practices.* Berkeley: University of California Press.

Khrushchev, Nikita Sergeyevich. 1956. "Special Report to the XXth Congress of the Communist Party of the Soviet Union," at www.trussel.com/hf/stalin.htm. In "The Crimes of the Stalin Era." *The New Leader*, annotated especially for this edition by Boris I. Nikolaevsky. 1956.

Klein, Thomas. 1995. "Widerspruch und abweichendes Verhalten in der SED." In *Möglichkeiten und Formen*, ed. Deutscher Bundestag, vol. VII.2, 1031–79.

Klein Thomas, Wilfriede Otto, and Peter Grieder. 1997. *Visionen: Repression und Opposition in der SED*. Frankfurt/Oder: Frankfurt Oder Editionen.

Kleßmann, Christoph. 1986. *Die doppelte Staatsgründung: Deutsche Geschichte, 1945–1955*. 4th ed. Bonn: Bundeszentrale für politische Bildung.

———. 1995. "Die Opposition in der DDR vom Beginn der Ära Honecker bis zur polnischen Revolution 1980/81." In *Möglichkeiten und Formen*, ed. Deutscher Bundestag, vol. VII.2, 1081–109.

Klier, Freya. 1989 [1988]. *Abreiß-Kalender: Ein deutsch-deutsches Tagebuch*. Munich: Knaur.

Kligman, Gail. 1988. *The Wedding of the Dead: Ritual, Poetics, and Popular Culture in Transylvania*. Berkeley: University of California Press.

———. 1998. *The Politics of Duplicity: Controlling Reproduction in Ceausescu's Romania*. Berkeley: University of California Press.

Knabe, Hubertus. 1999. *Die West-Arbeit des MfS: Das Zusammenspiel zwischen Abwehr und Aufklärung*. Berlin: Ch. Links.

Knabe, Wilhelm. 1995. "Westparteien und DDR-Opposition: Der Einfluß der westdeutschen Parteien in den achtziger Jahren auf unabhängige politische Bestrrebungen in der ehemaligen DDR." In *Möglichkeiten und Formen*, ed. Deutscher Bundestag, vol. VII.2, 1110–202.

Knight, Amy. 1990 [1988]. *The KGB: Police and Politics in the Soviet Union*. Rev. ed. Boston: Unwin Hyman.

———. 1993. *Beria: Stalin's First Lieutnant*. Princeton, NJ: Princeton University Press.

Knorr-Cetina, Karin. 1999. *Epistemic Cultures: How the Sciences Make Knowledge*. Cambridge, MA: Harvard University Press.

Kocka, Jürgen. 1999. "The GDR: A Special Kind of Modern Dictatorship." In Jarausch 1999b, 17–26.

Koehler, John. 2002. *Stasi: The Untold Story of the East German Secret Police*. New York: Basic Books.

Koestler, Arthur. 1968 [1940]. *Darkness at Noon*. New York: Bantam Books.

Kohli, Martin. 1994. "Die DDR als Arbeitsgesellschaft? Arbeit, Lebenslauf und soziale Differenzierung." In Kaelble, Kocka, and Zwahr.

Kołakowski, Leszek. 1971 [1968]. "Hope and Hopelessness." *Survey: A Journal of East and West Studies* 17 (3):37–52.

———. 2008. [1976–78/1968–76]. *Main Currents of Marxism: The Founders—The Golden Age—The Breakdown*. New York: Norton.

Konrád, Györgi, and Ivan Szelenyi. 1979. *The Intellectuals on the Road to Class Power*. New York: Harcourt, Brace, Jovanovich.

Kornai, János. 1980. *Economics of Shortage*. 2 vols. Amsterdam: North-Holland.

Kornai, János. 1992. *The Socialist System: The Political Economy of Communism*. Princeton, NJ: Princeton University Press.

Kotkin, Stephen. 1995. *Magnetic Mountain: Stalinism as a Civilization*. Berkeley: University of California Press.

———. 2001. *Armaggedon Averted*. Oxford: Oxford University Press.

Kowalczuk, Ilko-Sascha, ed. 2002a. *Freiheit und Öffentlichkeit: Politischer Samizdat in der DDR, 1985–1989*. Berlin: Schriftenreihe des Robert Havemann Archivs, 7.

———. 2002b. "Von 'aktuell' bis 'Zwischenruf': Politischer Samisdat in der DDR." In *Freiheit und Öffentlichkeit*, ed. Ilko-Sascha Kowalczuk, 21–104. Berlin: Schriftenreihe des Robert Havemann Archivs, 7.

Krenz, Egon. 1999. *Herbst 1989*. Berlin: Verlag Neues Leben.

Kripke, Saul. 1982. *Wittgenstein on Rules and Private Language: An Elementary Exposition.* Cambridge, MA: Harvard University Press.

Kuczynski, Jürgen. 1994. *Ein linientreuer Dissident: Memoiren, 1945–1989*. Berlin: Aufbauverlag.

Kuhn, Thomas S. 1962. *The Structure of Scientific Revolutions.* Chicago: University of Chicago Press.

Kukutz, Irena, and Havemann Katja. 1990. *Geschützte Quelle: Gespräche mit Monika H. alias Karin Lenz*. Berlin: Basis Druck.

———. 1995. "Die Bewegung 'Frauen für den Frieden' als Teil der unabhängigen Friedensbewegung der DDR." In Deutscher Bundestag, *Enquete-Kommission "Aufarbeitung von Geschichte und Folgen der SED-Diktatur in Deutschland."* Vol. VII.2, 1285–408. Baden-Baden: Nomos.

Kumar, Krishan. 1991. *1989: Revolutionary Ideas and Ideals.* Minneapolis: University of Minnesota Press.

Kumar, Krishan. 2001 [1989]. *Revolutionary Ideas and Ideals.* St. Paul: University of Minnesota Press.

Kunert, Günter. 1999 [1997]. *Erwachsenenspiele: Erinnerungen.* Munich: Deutscher Taschenbuch Verlag.

Kunze, Reiner. 1976. *Die Wunderbaren Jahre: Prosa.* Frankfurt: S. Fischer.

Kuusinen, Otto Wille, et al. 1960. *Grundlagen des Marxismus-Leninismus: Lehrbuch.* Berlin: Dietz.

Ladd, Brian. 1997. *The Ghosts of Berlin: Confronting German History in the Urban Landscape.* Chicago: University of Chicago Press.

Lahann, Birgit. 1992. *Genosse Judas: Die zwei Leben des Ibrahim Böhme.* Berlin: Rohwolt.

Lakoff, George. 1993. "The Contemporary Theory of Metaphor." In *Metaphor and Thought*, 2nd ed., ed. Andrew Ortony, 202–51. Cambridge: Cambridge University Press.

Lampland, Martha. 1995. *The Object of Labor: Commodification in Socialist Hungary.* Chicago: University of Chicago Press.

Latour, Bruno. 1988. *The Pasteurization of France.* Cambridge, MA: Harvard University Press.

———. 1999. *Pandora's Hope: Essays on the Reality of Science Studies.* Cambridge, MA: Harvard University Press.

———. 2005. *Reassembling the Social: An Introduction to Actor-Network-Theory.* Oxford: Oxford University Press.

Law, John, 1999. "After Actor Network Theory: Complexity, Naming, and Topology." In *Actor Network Theory and After*, ed. John Law and John Hassard. Oxford: Blackwell.

Ledoux, Joseph. 1996. *The Emotional Life: The Mysterious Underpinnings of Emotional Life.* New York: Simon and Schuster.

Lefort, Claude. 1986 [1978]. "Outline of the Genesis of Ideology in Modern Societies." In *The Political Forms of Modern Society: Bureaucracy, Democracy, Totalitarianism.* Cambridge, MA: MIT Press.

———. 2007 [1999]. *Complications: Communism and the Dilemmas of Democracy.* New York: Columbia University Press.

Lengsfeld (previously Wollenberger), Vera. 1992. *Virus der Heuchler: Innenansichten aus Stasi-Akten.* Berlin: Elefanten Press.

———. 2002. *Von nun an ging's bergauf: Mein Weg in die Freiheit*. Munich: Langen-Müller.

Lenin, Vladimir Ilyich. 1960–63. *Collected Works* (cited as CW). 45 vols. Moscow: Foreign Languages Publishing House.

———. 1967a. *Selected Works in Three Volumes* (cited as SW). New York: International Publishers.

———. 1967b [1919]. "A Great Beginning: Heroism of the Workers in the Rear; 'Communist Subbotniks.'" In SW, vol. III, 201–25.

———. 1967c [1917]. "Imperialism, the Highest Stage of Capitalism: A Popular Outline." In SW, vol. I, 673–77.

———. 1967d [1920]. "'Left-Wing' Communism—An Infantile Disorder." In SW, vol. III, 333–420.

———. 1967e [1917]. "The State and Revolution: The Marxist Theory of the State and the Tasks of the Proletariat in the Revolution." In SW, vol. II, 263–361.

———. 1967f [1917]. "The Tasks of the Proletariat in our Revolution: Draft Platform for the Proletarian Party." In SW, vol. II, 21–53.

———. 1967g [1920]. "Eighth All-Russia Congress of Soviets: December 22–29, 1920." In SW, vol. III, 487–515.

———. 1967h [1902]. "What Is to Be Done? Burning Questions of our Movement." In SW, vol. I, 97–256.

———. 1967i [1915]. "Karl Marx: A Brief Biographical Sketch with an Exposition of Marxism." In SW, vol. I, 1–32.

———. 1967k [1918]. "'Left-Wing' Childishness and the Petty-Bourgeois Mentality." In SW, vol. II, 685–709.

Leonhardt, Wolfgang. 1955. *Die Revolution entläßt ihre Kinder*. Cologne: Kiepenheuer and Witsch.

Lévi-Strauss, Claude. 1966. *The Savage Mind*. Chicago: University of Chicago Press.

Lifton, Robert J. 1961. *Thought Reform and the Psychology of Totalism: A Study of Brainwashing in China*. New York: Norton.

Linde, Charlotte. 1993. *Life Stories: The Creation of Coherence*. Oxford: Oxford University Press.

Linz, Juan and Alfred Stepan 1996. *Problems of Democratic Transition and Consolidation: Southern Europe, South America, and Post-Communist Europe*. Baltimore, MD: Johns Hopkins University Press.

Loest, Erich. 1999 [1981]. *Durch die Erde Ein Riß: Ein Lebenslauf*. Munich: Deutscher Taschenbuch Verlag.

Loewenstein, George. 1994. "The Psychology of Curiosity: A Review and Reinterpretation." *Psychological Bulletin* 116 (1):75–98.

Luhmann, Niklas. 1995. *Soziale Systeme*. Frankfurt: Suhrkamp.

Lukács, Georg. 1968 [1923]. *Geschichte und Klassenbewußtsein: Studien über marxistische Dialektik*. Berlin: Malik Verlag.

Lukes, Steven. 1974. *Power: A Radical View*. London: Macmillan.

Luria, Alexander. 1976. *Cognitive Development—Its Cultural and Social Foundations*. Cambridge, MA: Harvard University Press.

Lutz, Catherine. 1988. *Unnatural Emotions: Everyday Sentiments on a Micronesian Atoll and Their Challenge to Western Theory*. Chicago: University of Chicago Press.

Lynch, Michael. 1992. "Extending Wittgenstein: The Pivotal Move from Epistemology to the

Sociology of Science." In *Science as Practice and Culture*, ed. Andrew Pickering, 215–65. Chicago: University of Chicago Press.

———. 1997. *Scientific Practice and Ordinary Action: Ethnomethodology and the Social Scientific Study of Science*. Cambridge: Cambridge University Press.

MacIntyre, Alasdair. 1984 [1981]. *After Virtue: A Study in Moral Theory*. Notre Dame, IN: University of Notre Dame Press.

MacKenzie, Donald, 2006. *An Engine Not a Camera: How Financial Models Shape Markets*. Cambridge, MA: MIT Press.

MacKenzie, Donald, and Judy Wajcman, eds. 1999. *The Social Shaping of Technology*. 2nd ed. Philadelphia: Open University Press.

MacKenzie, Donald, Fabian Muniesa, and Lucia Siu, eds. 2008. *Do Economists Make Markets? On the Performativity of Economics*. Princeton, NJ: Princeton University Press.

Maier, Charles. 1997. *Dissolution: The Crisis of Communism and the End of East Germany*. Princeton, NJ: Princeton University Press.

Mampel, Siegfried. 1996. *Das Ministerium für Staatssicherheit der ehemaligen DDR als Ideologiepolizei: Zur Bedeutung einer Heilslehre als Mittel zum Griff auf das Bewußtsein für das Totalitarismusmodell*. Berlin: Duncker and Humblot.

Mann, Michael. 1984. "The Autonomous Power of the State: Its Origins, Mechanisms, and Results." *European Journal of Sociology* 25:185–213.

Mannheim, Karl. 1951 [1940]. *Man and Society in the Age of Reconstruction*. New York: Harcourt, Brace and Company.

———. 1964 [1928]. "Das Problem der Generationen." In *Wissenssoziologie: Auswahl aus dem Werk*, ed. and with an introduction by Kurt H. Wolff, 509–65. Neuwied: Luchterhand.

———. 1984 [1926]. *Konservatismus: Ein Beitrag zur Soziologie des Wissens*. Ed David Kettler, Volker Meja, and Nico Stehr. Frankfurt: Suhrkamp.

———. 1995 [1929]. *Ideologie und Utopie*. 8th ed. Frankfurt: Vittorio Klostermann.

March, James G., and Johan P. Olsen. 1989. *Rediscovering Institutions: The Organizational Basis of Politics*. New York: Free Press.

Markell, Patchen. 2003. *Bound by Recognition*. Princeton, NJ: Princeton University Press.

Markovits, Andrei, and Philip Gorski. 1993. *The German Left: Red, Green and Beyond*. Cambridge: Polity Press.

Markovits, Inga. 1995. *Imperfect Justice: An East-West German Diary*. Oxford: Oxford University Press.

———. 2005. *Gerechtigkeit in Lüritz: Eine ostdeutsche Rechtsgeschichte*. Munich: C. H. Beck.

Martin, John Levi. 2003. "What is Field Theory?" *American Journal of Sociology*, 109:1–49.

Marx, Karl. 1958a [1932/1845–46]. *Die deutsche Ideologie*. In *MEW*, volume 3, pp. 9–438.

———. 1958b [1888/1845]. "Thesen über Feuerbach." In *MEW*, vol. 3, pp. 5–7.

———. 1960 [1852]. "Der Achtzehnte Brumaire des Louis Bonaparte." In *MEW*, vol. 8, 111–207.

———. 1961 [1859]. *Zur Kritik der Politischen Ökonomie*. In *MEW*, vol. 13, 3–160.

———. 1962a [1871]. "Der Bürgerkrieg in Frankreich." In *MEW*, vol. 17, 313–65.

———. 1962b [1867–93]. *Das Kapital: Kritik der politischen Ökonomie*. 3 vols. In *MEW*, vols. 22–24.

———. 1962c [1891/1875]. "Kritik des Gothaer Programms." In *MEW*, vol. 19, 11–32.

———. 1983 [1903/1857]. "Einleitung zu den Grundrissen der Kritik der politischen Ökonomie." In *MEW*, vol. 42.

Marx, Karl, and Friedrich Engels. 1957–83. *Karl Marx-Friedrich Engels-Werke*. Ed. the Insititut für Marxismus-Leninismus beim ZK der SED. 44 vols. (cited as *MEW*). Berlin: Dietz.

———. 1959 [1848]. "Manifest der kommunistischen Partei." In *MEW*, vol. 4, 459–93.

———. 1978. *The Marx-Engels Reader.* 2nd ed., ed. Robert Tucker. New York: Norton.

Mastnak, Tomaž. 2005. "The Reinvention of Civil Society: Through the Looking Glass of Democracy." *Archive of European Sociology* 46 (2):323–55.

McAdam, Doug. 1982. *Political Process and the Development of Black Insurgency, 1930–1970.* Chicago: University of Chicago Press.

———. "[Political Opportunities: Conceptual Origins, Current Problems, Future Directions.]" In McAdam, McCarthy and Zald 1996, 23–40.

McAdam, Douglas, John D. McCarthy, and Mayer N. Zald. 1996. *Comparative Perspectives on Social Movements: Political Opportunities, Mobilizing Structures, and Cultural Frames.* Cambridge: Cambridge University Press.

McAdam, Douglas, Charles Tilly, and Sidney Tarrow. 2001. *Dynamics of Contention.* Cambridge: Cambridge University Press.

McCarthy, John D., and Mayer N. Zald. 1977. "Resource Mobilization and Social Movements: A Partial Theory." *American Journal of Sociology* 82:1212–41.

McGaugh, James L. 2003. *Memory and Emotion: The Making of Lasting Memories.* New York: Columbia University Press.

Mead, George Herbert. 1934. *Mind, Self, and Society.* Chicago: University of Chicago Press.

Meja, Volker, and Nico Stehr. 1982 [1928]. *Der Streit um die Wissenschaftssoziologie.* 2 vols. Frankfurt: Suhrkamp.

Melucci, Alberto. 1996a. *Challenging Codes: Collective Action in the Information Age.* Cambridge: Cambridge University Press.

———. 1996b. *The Playing Self: Person and Meaning in the Planetary Society.* Cambridge: Cambridge University Press.

Menzel, Rebecca. 2004. *Jeans in der DDR: Vom tiefen Sinn einer Freizeithose.* Berlin: Ch. Links.

Merkel, Ina. 1999. *Utopie und Bedürfnis: Die Geschichte der Konsumkultur in der DDR.* Cologne: Böhlau.

Merton, Robert. 1968. *Social Theory and Social Structure.* New York: Free Press.

———. 1979. *The Sociology of Science: Theoretical and Empirical Investigations.* Chicago: University of Chicago Press.

Meuschel, Sigrid. 1992. *Legitimation und Parteiherrschaft in der DDR.* Frankfurt: Suhrkamp.

Meyer, John W., and Brian Rowan. 1977. "Institutionalized Organizations: Formal Structure as Myth and Ceremony." *American Journal of Sociology* 83:340–63.

Michnik, Adam. 1985. *Letters from Prison and Other Essays.* Berkeley: University of California Press.

Miethe, Ingrid. 1999. *Frauen in der DDR-Opposition: Lebens- und kollektivgeschichtliche Verläufe in einer Frauenfriedensgruppe.* Opladen: Leske und Budrich.

Mill, John Stuart. 1992 [1859]. "On Liberty." In *On Liberty and Utilitarianism.* Introduction by Isaiah Berlin. London: Everyman's Library.

Miłosz, Czesław. 1990 [1953]. *The Captive Mind.* New York: Vintage.

Mittag, Günter. 1963. *Fragen des neuen ökonomischen Systems der Planung und Leitung der Volkswirtschaft.* Berlin: Dietz.

Mittag, Günter, et al. 1969. *Politische Ökonomie des Sozialismus und ihre Anwendung in der DDR.* Berlin: Dietz.

Mitter, Armin, and Stefan Wolle. 1990. *Ich liebe Euch doch Alle! Befehle und Lageberichte des MfS Januar-November 1989.* Berlin: Basis Druck.

Modrow, Hans, ed. 1995 [1994]. *Das Große Haus: Insider berichten aus dem ZK der SED.* 2nd. ed. Berlin: Edition Ost.

———. 1996. *Das Große Haus von außen: Erfahrungen im Umgang mit der Machtzentrale der DDR.* Berlin: Edition Ost.

Mollnau, Karl. 1999. "Sozialistische Gesetzlichkeit in der DDR: Theoretische Grundlagen und Praxis." In Gerd Bender and Ulrich Falk, *Recht im Sozialismus: Analysen Zur Normdurchsetzung in osteuropäischen Nachkriegsgesellschaften, 1944/45–1989.* Vol. 2, 59–196. Frankfurt: Vittorio Klostermann.

Moore, Sally F. 1978. *Law as Process.* London: Routledge.

———. 1986. Social Facts and Fabrications: "Customary" Law on Mount Kilimanjaro, 1880–1980. Cambridge: Cambridge University Press.

Müller-Enbergs, Helmut. 1995. "Warum wird einer IM." In *Zersetzung der Seele: Psychologie und Psychatrie im Dienste der Stasi,* ed. Klaus Behnke and Jürgen Fuchs. Hamburg: Rotbuch Verlag.

———. 1996. *Richtlinien und Durchführungsbestimmungen.* Vol. 1 of *Inoffizielle Mitarbeiter des Ministeriums für Staatssicherheit.* Berlin: Ch. Links.

Müller-Enbergs, Helmut, Marianne Schulz, and Jan Wieglohs. eds. 1991. *Von der Illegalität ins Parlament: Werdegang und Konzept der neuen Bürgerbewegungen.* Berlin: LinksDruck Verlag.

Nathanson, Donald L. 1992. *Shame and Pride.* New York: Norton.

Nehamas, Alexander. 1985. *Nietzsche: Life as Literature.* Cambridge, MA: Harvard University Press.

Nelson, Richard R., and Sidney G. Winter, 1982. *An Evolutionary Theory of Economic Change.* Cambridge, MA: Harvard University Press.

Neubert, Erhart. 1998. *Geschichte der Opposition in der DDR, 1949–1989.* Berlin: Ch. Links.

Neubert, Erhart, and Bernd Eisenfeld. 2001. *Macht, Ohnmacht, Gegenmacht: Grundfragen zur politischen Gegnerschaft in der DDR.* Bremen: Edition Temmen.

Niemann, Heinz, ed. 1993. *Meinungsforschung in der DDR: Die geheimen Berichte des Institutes für Meinungsforschung an das Politbüro der SED.* Cologne: Bund.

Nietzsche, Friedrich. 1976. "Vom Nutzen und Nachteil der Historie für das Leben." In *Unzeitgemäße Betrachtungen.* Stuttgart: Kröner.

Noelle-Neumann, Elisabeth, 1980. *Die Schweigespirale: Öffentliche Meinung unsere soziale Haut.* Munich: Piper.

North, Douglas. 1990. *Institutions, Institutional Change, and Economic Performance.* Cambridge: Cambridge University Press.

———. 2005. *Understanding the Process of Economic Change.* Princeton, NJ: Princeton University Press.

Novalis (Hardenberg, Friedrich von). 1993. *Das Allgemeine Brouillon: Materialien zur Enzyklopädistik.* Hamburg: Meiner.

Olick, Jeffrey. 2007. *The Politics of Regret: On Collective Memory and Historical Responsibility.* London: Routledge.

———. forthcoming. *The Sins of the Fathers: Governing Memory in the Federal Republic of Germany, 1949–1995.* Chicago: University of Chicago Press.

Olick, Jeffrey, and Joyce Robbins. 1998. "Social Memory Practices: From 'Collective Memory' to the Historical Sociology of Mnemonic Practices." *Annual Review of Sociology* 24:105–40.

Olivo, Christiane. 2001. *Creating a Democratic Civil Society in Eastern Germany: The Case of the Citizen Movements and Alliance 90.* New York: Palgrave.

Osa, Maryjane. 2003. *Solidarity and Contention: Networks of Polish Opposition.* Minneapolis: University of Minnesota Press.

Otto, Wilfriede. 2000. *Erich Mielke—Biographie: Aufstieg und Fall eines Tschekisten.* Berlin: Dietz.

———, ed. 1990. "Ernst Wollweber". *Beiträge zur Geschichte der Arbeiterbewegung* 32:655–72.

Parsons, Talcott. 1951. *The Social System.* Glencoe, IL: Free Press.

Pascal, Blaise. 1931. *Pensées.* Definitive edition of the complete works. Ed F. Strowski. Paris: Librairie Ollendorff.

Peirce, Charles Sanders. 1992 [1867–1893]. *The Essential Peirce: Selected Philosophical Writings,* ed. Nathan Houser and Christian Kloesel. Vol. 1.

Perelman, Chaïm, and L. Olbrechts-Tyteca. 1969 [1958]. *The New Rhetoric: A Treatise on Argumentation.* Notre Dame, IN: Notre Dame Press.

Petty, Richard E., and John T. Cacioppo. 1996 [1981]. *Attitudes and Persuasion: Classic and Contemporary Approaches.* Boulder, CO: Westview Press.

Pfaff, Steven. 2006. *Exit-Voice Dynamics and the Collapse of East Germany: The Crisis of Leninism and the Revolution of 1989.* Durham, NC: Duke University Press.

Pflugbeil, Sebastian. 2003. "Tschernobyl und die DDR: Zwischen staatlicher Leugnung und Bürgerbewegung." FES, 24–35.

Pickering, Andrew, ed. 1992. *Science as Practice and Culture.* Chicago: University of Chicago Press.

Pierson, Paul. 2004. *Politics in Time: History, Institutions, and Social Analysis.* Princeton, NJ: Princeton University Press.

Pingel-Schliemann, Sandra. 2002. *Zersetzen: Strategie einer Diktatur.* Berlin: Robert Havemann Archiv.

Plato. 1989 [~378 BCE] *SYMPOSIUM.* Translated by Alexander Nehamas and Paul Woodruff. Indianapolis: Hackett.

Pleitgen, Fritz. ed. 2001. *Die Ausbürgerung: Anfang vom Ende der DDR.* Berlin: Ullstein.

Poletta, Francesca. 2002. *Freedom Is an Endless Meeting: Democracy in American Social Movements.* Chicago: University of Chicago Press.

Pollack, Detlef, and Jan Wieglohs, eds. 2004. *Dissent and Opposition in Communist Eastern Europe: Origins of Civil Society and Democratic Transition.* Aldershot, UK: Ashgate.

Ponomarjow, Boris N., et al. 1984. *Geschichte der Kommunistischen Partei der Sowjetunion.* 6th, rev. ed. Berlin: Dietz

Poppe, Ulrike, Rainer Eckert, and Ilko-Sascha Kowalczuk, eds. 1995. *Zwischen Selbstbehauptung und Anpassung: Formen des Widerstandes und der Opposition in der DDR.* Berlin: Ch. Links.

Popper, Karl. 1966. *The Open Society and Its Enemies.* 2 vols. Princeton, NJ: Princeton University Press.

———. 1971 [1935]. *Logik der Forschung: Zur Erkenntnistheorie der modernen Naturwissenschaft.* 4th ed. Tübingen: J. C. B. Mohr (Paul Siebeck).

———. 1984 [1934]. *Logik der Forschung.* 8th ed. Tübingen: J. C. B. Mohr (Paul Siebeck).

Postone, Moishe. 1996 [1993]. *Time, Labor, and Social Domination: A Reinterpretation of Marx's Critical Theory.* Cambridge: Cambridge University Press.

Pötzl, Norbert. 2002. *Erich Honecker: Eine deutsche Biographie.* Stuttgart: Deutsche Verlags-Anstalt.

———. 2004. "Das Verhältnis Mielke/Honecker und der Rote Koffer." Talk given at BSTU on the occasion of the return of the "red briefcase."

Powell, Walter, and Paul DiMaggio, eds. 1991. *The New Institutionalism in Organizational Analysis*. Chicago: University of Chicago Press.

Przybylski, Peter. 1991. *Tatort Politbüro: Die Akte Honecker*. 2 vols. Berlin: Rowohlt.

Putnam, Hilary. 1975. "The Meaning of 'Meaning.'" In *Mind, Language, and Reality*. Cambridge, MA: Cambridge University Press.

———. 1988. *Representation and Reality*. Cambridge, MA: MIT Press.

Quine, Willard Van Orman. 1951. "Two Dogmas of Empiricism." *Philosophical Review* 60 (1):20–43.

———. 1992. *Pursuit of Truth*. Rev. ed. Cambridge, MA: Harvard University Press.

Rataizik, Siegfried. 2002. "Der Untersuchungshaftvollzug im MfS (Abt. XIV im MfS und in den BV)." In *Die Sicherheit: Zur Abwehrarbeit des MfS*, ed. Reinhard Grimmer et al., 2:495–519.

Rauh, Hans-Christoph, ed. 1991. *Gefesselter Widerspruch: Die Affäre um Peter Ruben*. Berlin: Dietz.

Reddy, Michael. 1993. "The Conduit Metaphor: A Case of Frame Conflict in Our Language about Language." In *Metaphor and Thought*, 2nd ed., ed. Andrew Ortony, 164–201. Cambridge: Cambridge University Press.

Reddy, William M. 2001. *The Navigation of Feeling: A Framework for the History of Emotions*. Cambridge: Cambridge University Press.

Reich, Jens. 1992. *Abschied von den Lebenslügen: Die Intelligenz und die Macht*. Berlin: Rowohlt Berlin.

Reichenbach, Hans. 1951. *The Rise of Scientific Philosophy*. Berkeley: University of California Press.

Reissig, Rolf. 2002. *Der Dialog durch die Mauer: Die umstrittene Annäherung von SED und SPD*. Frankfurt: Campus.

Ricoeur, Paul. 1970. *Freud and Philosophy: An Essay on Interpretation*. New Haven, CT: Yale University Press.

———. 1984 [1983]. *Time and Narrative*. Vol. 1. Chicago: University of Chicago Press.

Riesebrodt, Martin. 1993. *Pious Passion: The Emergence of Modern Fundamentalism in the United States and Iran*. Berkeley: University of California Press.

———. 2007. *Cultus und Heilsversprechen*. Munich: C. H. Beck.

Rorty, Richard. 1989. *Contingency, Irony, and Solidarity*. Cambridge: Cambridge University Press.

Rosaldo, Michelle. 1980. *Knowledge and Passion: Ilongot Notions of Self and Social Life*. Cambridge: Cambridge University Press.

Rose, Nikolas. 2007. *The Politics of Life Itself: Biomedicine, Power, and Subjectivity in the Twenty-First Century*. Priineton, NJ: Princeton Universty Press.

Rosellini, Jay. 1992. *Wolf Biermann*. Munich: C. H. Beck.

Rosenberg, William, ed. 1984. *Bolshevik Visions: First Phase of the Cultural Revolution in Soviet Russia*. Ann Arbor, MI: Ardis.

Ruben, Peter. 1991. *Gefesselter Widerspruch: Die Affäre um Peter Ruben—Basisartikel, Gegenartikel, Gutachten, Stellungnahmen, enthüllendes Aktenmaterial*. Berlin: Dietz.

Ruben, Peter, and Hans Wagner. 1980. "Sozialistische Wertform und dialektischer Widerspruch." In *Gefesselter Widerspruch: Die Affäre um Peter Ruben*, ed. Hans-Christoph Rauh, 53–68. Berlin: Dietz.

Rüddenklau, Wolfgang. 1992. *Störenfried: DDR-Opposition 1986–1989 mit Texten aud den Umweltblättern*. 2nd improved ed. Amsterdam: Basis Druck.

Sahlins, Marshall. 1981. *Historical Metaphors and Mythical Realities: Structure in the Early History of the Sandwich Island Kingdom*. Ann Arbor: University of Michigan Press.

———. 1987. *Islands of History*. Chicago: University of Chicago Press.

Said, Edward. 1978. *Orientalism*. New York: Vintage.

Schabowski, Günter. 1991a. *Der Absturz*. Reinbek bei Hamburg: Rowohlt.

———. 1991b. *Das Politbüro: Ende eines Mythos—eine Befragung*. Ed. Frank Sieren and Ludwig Koehne. Reinbek bei Hamburg: Rowohlt.

Schäffle, A. 1897. "Über den wissenschaftlichen Begriff der Politik." *Zeitschrift für die gesamte Staatswissenschaft* 53.

Schalck-Golodkowski, Alexander. 2000. *Deutsch-deutsche Erinnerungen*. Reinbek bei Hamburg: Rowohlt.

Scheff, Thomas. 1990. *Microsociology: Discourse, Emotion, and Social Structure*. Chicago: University of Chicago Press.

Scheff, Thomas, and Suzanne Retzinger. 1991. *Emotions and Violence: Shame and Rage in Destructive Conflict*. Lexington, MA: Lexington Books.

Scherzer, Landolf. 1989. *Der Erste: Eine Reportage aus der DDR*. Cologne: Kiepenheuer and Witsch.

Schöne, Jens. 2005. *Frühling auf dem Lande? Die Kollektivierung der DDR-Landwirtschaft*. Berlin: Ch. Links.

Schroeder, Klaus, 1998. *Der SED Staat: Geschichte und Strukturen der DDR*. Munich: Bayerische Landeszentrale für poltitische Bildungsarbeit.

Schroeder, Klaus, and Jochen Staadt. 1997. *Das Parlament* (*Supplement: "Aus Politik und Zeitgeschehen"*), 20 June.

Schubbe, Elimar, ed. 1972. *Dokumente zur Kunst-, Literatur-, und Kulturpolitik der SED*. Stuttgart: Seewald.

Schumann, Silke. 2003. "Die Parteiorganisation der SED im MfS." In *Anatomie der Staatssicherheit: Geschichte, Struktur und Methoden—MfS-Handbuch*, 3rd ed., ed. Sucket et al. Berlin: BStU.

Schürer, Gerhard. 1996. *Gewagt und Verloren: Eine deutsche Biographie*. Frankfurt/Oder: Oder Editionen.

———. 1999. "Die gescheiterte Preisreform 1979 in der DDR: Protokoll einer Diskussion." In *Preise sind gefährlicher als Ideen—Das Scheitern der Preisreform 1979 in der DDR: Protokoll einer Tagung*, ed. Rainer Weinert. Berlin: Arbeitshefte der Forschungsstelle Diktatur und Demokratie am Fachbereich Politische Wissenschaft der Freien Universität Berlin, No. 10.

Schütz, Alfred, and Thomas Luckmann. 1981 [1932]. *Der sinnhafte Aufbau der sozialen Welt: Eine Einleitung in die verstehende Soziologie*. Frankfurt: Suhrkamp.

———. 1984. *Strukturen der Lebenswelt*. 2 vols. Frankfurt: Suhrkamp.

Schütz, Gertrud, et al., eds. 1978. *Kleines Politisches Wörterbuch*. Berlin: Dietz.

Scott, James. 1985. *Weapons of the Weak*. New Haven, CT: Yale University Press.

———. 1990. *Domination and the Arts of Resistance: Hidden Transcripts*. New Haven, CT: Yale University Press.

———. 1998. *Seeing Like a State: How Certain Schemes to Improve the World Have Failed*. New Haven, CT: Yale University Press.

Scott, Joan. 2005. *Parité: Sexual Equality and the Crisis of French Universalism*. Chicago: University of Chicago Press.

Searle, John. 1969. *Speech Acts: An Essay in the Philosophy of Language.* Cambridge: Cambridge University Press.

———. 1992. *The Construction of Social Reality.* New York: Free Press.

Sengespeick-Roos, Christa. 1997. *Das ganz Normale tun: Widerstandsräume in der DDR-Kirche.* Berlin: Hentrich.

———. 2006 "Stärkende Rituale: Die Politischen Nachtgebete der Frauen für den Frieden." *Horch und Guck (historisch-literarische Zeitschrift des "Bürgerkomitees 15. Januar")* 56:39–42.

Sennett, Richard. 1996. *Flesh and Stone: The Body and the City in Western Civilization.* New York: Norton.

Service, Robert. 1979. *The Bolshevik Party in Revolution: A Study in Organizational Change, 1917–1923.* London: Macmillan.

———. 2002. *Lenin: A Biography.* Cambridge, MA: Harvard Univesity Press.

———. 2005. *Stalin: A Biography.* Cambridge, MA: Belknap Press of Harvard University Press.

Sewell, William, Jr. 2005. *Logics of History: Social Theory and Social Transformations.* Chicago: University of Chicago Press.

Shapin, Stephen. 1994. *The Social History of Truth: Civility and Science in Seventeenth-Century England.* Chicago: University of Chicago Press.

Silverstein, Michael. 1979. "Language Structure and Linguistic Ideology." In *The Elements: A Parasession on Linguistic Units and Levels,* ed. P. R. Clyne, W. Hanks, and C. Hofbauer, 193–247. Chicago: Chicago Linguistic Society.

———. 1993. "Metapragmatic Discourse and Metapragmatic Function." In *Reflexive Language: Reported Speech and Metapragmatics,* ed. John Lucy, 33–88. Cambridge: Cambridge University Press.

———. 2003. *Talking Politics: The Substance of Style from Abe to "W."* Chicago: Prickly Paradigm Press.

———. 2004. " 'Cultural' Concepts and the Language-Culture Nexus." *Current Anthropology* 45:621–52.

Simmel, Georg. 1989 [1900]. *Philosophie des Geldes.* Frankfurt: Suhrkamp.

———. 1992 [1908]. *Soziologie: Untersuchungen über die Formen der Vergesellschaftung.* Frankfurt: Suhrkamp.

Skilling, H. Gordon. 1989. *Samizdat and an Independent Society in Central and Eastern Europe.* Columbus: Ohio State University Press.

Smelser, Neil. 1962. *Theory of Collective Behavior.* New York: Free Press.

Snow, David A., E. Burke Rochford Jr., Steven K. Worden, and Robert D. Benford. 1986. "Frame Alignment Processes, Micromobilization, and Movement Participation." *American Sociological Review* 51:464–81.

Sohn-Rethel, Alfred. 1970. *Geistige und körperliche Arbeit: Zur Theorie der gesellschaftlichen Synthesis.* Frankfurt: Suhrkamp.

Sölle, Dorothee. 1995. *Gegenwind: Erinnerungen.* Hamburg: Hoffmann and Campe.

Somers, Margret. 1994. "The Narrative Construction of Identity: A Relational and Network Approach." *Theory and Society* 23:605–49.

Sorel, Georges. 1999. *Reflections on Violence.* Cambridge: Cambridge University Press.

Soyfer, Verlery. 1994. *Lysenko and the Tragedy of Soviet Science.* New Brunswick, NJ: Rutgers University Press.

Stalin, Joseph. 1950–. *Werke.* Berlin: Dietz.

———. 1952a [1924]. "Über die Grundlagen des Leninismus." In *Werke,* vol. 6.

———. 1952b [1926]. "Zu den Fragen des Leninismus." In *Werke,* vol. 8.

Staritz, Dietrich. 1996. *Geschichte der DDR*. Erweiterte Neuausgabe. Frankfurt: Suhrkamp.

Stehr, Nico. 2003. *Wissenspolitik: Die Überwachung des Wissens*. Frankfurt: Suhrkamp.

Steiner, André. 1999. *Die DDR Wirtschaftsreform der Sechziger Jahre: Konflikt zwischen Effizienz und Machtkalkül*. Berlin: Akademie Verlag.

——. 2004. *Von Plan zu Plan: Eine Wirtschaftsgeschichte der DDR*. Munich: Deutsche Verlagsanstalt.

Steinmetz, George. 1993. *Regulating the Social: The Welfare State and Local Politics in Imperial Germany*. Princeton, NJ: Princeton University Press.

——. 2002a. "Introduction: Culture and the State." In *State/Culture: State-Formation after the Cultural Turn*, ed. George Steinmetz, 1–49.

——, ed. 2002b. *State/Culture: State-Formation after the Cultural Turn*. Ithaca, NY: Cornell University Press.

——. 2007. *The Devil's Handwriting: Precoloniality and the German Colonial State in Qingdao, Samoa, and Southwest Africa*. Chicago: University of Chicago Press.

Steinmo, Sven, Kathleen Thelen, and Frank Longstreth, eds. 1992. *Structuring Politics: Historical Institutionalism in Comparative Analysis*. Cambridge: Cambridge University Press.

Stern, Daniel. 1985. *The Interpersonal World of the Infant: A View from Psychoanalysis and Developmental Psychology*. New York: Basic Books.

Sternberg, Robert J., ed. 1988. *The Nature of Creativity: Contemporary Psychological Perspectives*. Cambridge: Cambridge University Press.

Stites, Richard. 1989. *Revolutionary Dreams: Utopian Vision and Experimental Life in the Russian Revolution*. Oxford: Oxford University Press.

Stokes, Raymond G. 2000. *Constructing Socialism: Technology and Change in East Germany, 1945–1990*. Baltimore: Johns Hopkins University Press.

Suckut, Siegfried, ed. 1996. *Das Wörterbuch der Staatssicherheit: Definitionen zur politisch-operativen Arbeit*. Berlin: Ch. Links.

Suckut, Siegfried, Ehrhart Neubert, Walter Süß, Roger Engelmann, Bernd Eisenfeld, and Jens Gieseke, eds. 1993–. *Anatomie der Staatssicherheit: Geschichte, Struktur und Methoden—MfS-Handbuch*. Berlin: BStU.

Sudnow, David. 2001. *Ways of the Hand: A Rewritten Account*. Cambridge, MA: MIT Press.

Süß, Walter. 1999. *Staatssicherheit am Ende: Warum es den Mächtigen nicht gelang, 1989 eine Revolution zu verhindern*. Berlin: Ch. Links.

Swidler, Ann. 2001. *Talk of Love: How Culture Matters*. Chicago: University of Chicago Press.

Szelenyi, Ivan. 1988. *Socialist Entrepreneurs: Embourgeoisement in Rural Hungary*. Madison: University of Wisconsin Press.

SZS (Staatliche Zentralverwaltung für Statistik). 1956. *Statistisches Jahrbuch der Deutschen Demokratischen Republik*. Berlin: VEB Deutscher Zentralverlag.

——. 1957. *Statistisches Jahrbuch der Deutschen Demokratischen Republik*. Berlin: VEB Deutscher Zentralverlag.

——. 1961. *Statistisches Jahrbuch der Deutschen Demokratischen Republik 1960/61*. Berlin: VEB Deutscher Zentralverlag.

——. 1970. *Statistisches Jahrbuch der Deutschen Demokratischen Republik 1970*. Berlin: Staatsverlag der Deutschen Demokratischen Republik.

——.1980. *Statistisches Jahrbuch der Deutschen Demokratischen Republik 1980*. Berlin: Staatsverlag der Deutschen Demokratischen Republik.

——. 1990. *Statistisches Jahrbuch der Deutschen Demokratischen Republik '90*. Berlin: Rudolf Haufe Verlag.

Taussig, Michael. 1993. *Mimesis and Alterity: A Particular History of the Senses*. London: Routledge.

Taylor, Charles. 1989. *Sources of the Self: The Making of Modern Identity*. Cambridge, MA: Harvard University Press.

———. 1994. "The Politics of Recognition." In *Multiculturalism: Examining the Politics of Recognition*, ed. Amy Gutmann. Princeton, NJ: Princeton University Press.

———. 2004. *Modern Social Imaginaries*. Durham, NC: Duke University Press.

Thelen, Kathleen. 2004. *How Institutions Evolve*. Cambridge: Cambridge University Press.

Thomas, W. I. 1928. *The Child in America: Behavior Problems and Programs*. New York: Alfred Knopf.

Tilly, Charles. 1977. "Major Forms of Collective Action in Western Europe, 1500–1975." *Theory and Society* 3 (3):365–75.

Timmer, Karsten. 2000. *Vom Aufbruch zum Umbruch: Die Bürgerbewegungen in der DDR 1989*. Göttingen: Vandenhoeck and Ruprecht.

Todorov, Tzvetan. 1992 [1982]. *The Conquest of America: The Question of the Other*. New York: Harper.

Tomkins, Silvan. 1962. *The Positive Affects*. Vol. 1 of *Affect, Imagery, Consciousness*. New York: Springer.

———. 1963. *The Negative Affects*. Vol. 2 of *Affect, Imagery, Consciousness*. New York: Springer.

Torpey, John. 1995. *Intellectuals, Socialism, and Dissent: The East German Opposition and Its Legacy*. Minneapolis: University of Minnesota Press.

Turner, Victor. 1974. *Dramas, Fields, and Metaphors: Symbolic Action in Human Society*. Ithaca, NY: Cornell University Press.

Unger, Roberto Mangabeira. 2004 [1987]. *False Necessity: Anti-Necessitarian Social Theory in the Service of Radical Democracy*. 2nd ed. London: Verso.

Unverhau, Dagmar. 1999. *Das 'NS-Archiv' des Ministeriums für Staatssicherheit: Stationen einer Entwicklung*. Münster: Lit.

Urban, Greg. 2001. *Metaculture: How Culture Moves through the World*. Minneapolis: University of Minnesota Press.

Uschner, Manfred. 1993. *Die zeite Etage: Funktionsweisen eines Machtapparates*. Berlin: Dietz.

Vaughan, Diane. 1999. "The Dark Side of Organizations: Mistake, Misconduct, Disaster." *American Review of Sociology* 25:271–305.

Verdery, Katherine. 1983. *Transylvanian Villagers: Three Centuries of Political, Economic, and Ethnic Change*. Berkeley: University of California Press.

———. 1991. *National Ideology under Socialism: Identity and Cultural Politics in Ceauşescu's Romania*. Berkeley: University of California Press.

———. 1996. *What Was Socialism, and What Comes Next?* Princeton, NJ: Princeton University Press.

———. 2003. *The Vanishing Hectare: Property and Value in Postsocialist Transylvania*. Ithaca, NY: Cornell University Press.

Vico, Giambattista. 1968 [1744]. *The New Science*. Trans. Thomas Goddard Bergin and Max Harold Fisch. Ithaca, NY: Cornell University Press.

———. 1988 [1710]. *On the Most Ancient Wisdom of the Italians Unearthed from the Origins of the Latin Language*. Trans. L. M. Palmer. Ithaca, NY: Cornell University Press.

Volosinov, V. N. 1973 [1929]. *Marxism and the Philosophy of Language*. Cambridge, MA: Harvard University Press.

Voslensky, Michael. 1984 [1991/1970]. *Nomenklatura: The Soviet Ruling Class*. Garden City, NY: Doubleday.

Vygotsky, Lev S. 1978 [1934]. *Mind in Society: The Development of Higher Psychological Processes*. Cambridge, MA: Harvard University Press.

——. 1986 [1975]. *Thought and Language*. Rev. ed. Cambridge, MA: MIT Press.

Wacquant, Loïc. 2004. *Body and Soul: Notebooks of an Apprentice Boxer*. Oxford: Oxford University Press.

Wagner, Peter. 2000. "An Entirely New Object of Consciousness, of Volition, of Thought." In *Biographies of Scientific Objects*, ed. Lorraine Daston. Chicago: University of Chicago Press.

Walter, Friedrich, Peter Förster, and Kurt Starke, eds. 1999. *Das Zentralinstitut für Jugendforschung Leipzig: Geschichte, Methoden, Erkenntnisse*. Berlin: Edition Ost.

Walther, Joachim. 1999 [1996]. *Sicherungsbereich Literatur: Schriftsteller und Staatssicherheit in der Deutschen Demokratischen Republik*. Berlin: Ullstein.

Warner, Michael. 2002. *Publics and Counterpublics*. New York: Zone.

Weber, Herrmann, ed. 1986. *DDR: Dokumente zur Geschichte der DDR 1945–1985*. Munich: Deutscher Taschenbuch Verlag.

Weber, Max. 1980. *Wirtschaft und Gesellschaft*. Tübingen: J. C. B. Mohr (Paul Siebeck).

——. 1988a [1922]. "Einleitung in die Wirtschaftsethik der Weltreligionen." In *Gesammelte Aufsätze zur Religionssoziologie*. Vol. 1. Tübingen: J. C. B. Mohr (Paul Siebeck).

——. 1988b [1922]. "Die 'Objektivität' sozialwissenschaftlicher and sozialpolitischer Erkenntnis." In *Gesammelte Aufsätze zur Wissenschaftslehre*. Tübingen: J. C. B. Mohr (Paul Siebeck).

——. 1988c [1922]. "Zwischenbetrachtung." In *Gesammelte Aufsätze zur Religionssoziologie*. Vol. 1. Tübingen: J. C. B. Mohr (Paul Siebeck).

Wedeen, Lisa. 1999. *Ambiguities of Domination: Politics, Rhetoric, and Symbols in Contemporary Syria*. Chicago: University of Chicago Press.

Wehler, Ulrich. 2007 [1995]. *Deutsche Gesellschaftsgeschichte Band 3: Von der 'deutschen Doppelrevolution' bis zum Beginn des ersten Weltkrieges, 1849–1914*. Munich: C. H. Beck.

Weißhuhn, Reinhard. 1995. "Der Einfluß der bundesdeutschen Parteien auf die Entwicklung widerständigen Verhaltens in der DDR der achtziger Jahre: Parteien in der Bundesrepublik aus der Sicht der Opposition der DDR." In Deutscher Bundestag, *Enquete-Kommission "Aufarbeitung von Geschichte und Folgen der SED-Diktatur in Deutschland."* Vol. VII.2, 1853–949. Baden-Baden: Nomos.

White, Harrison. 2003. *Markets from Networks: Socioeconomic Models of Production*. Princeton, NJ: Princeton University Press.

White, Hayden. 1973. *Metahistory: The Historical Imagination in Nineteenth-Century Europe*. Baltimore: Johns Hopkins University Press.

Whyte, William. 1956. *The Organization Man*. New York: Simon & Schuster.

Whorf, Benjamin Lee. 1956. *Language, Thought, and Reality: Selected Writings*. Cambridge: Technology Press of Massachusetts Institute of Technology.

Wiedmann, Roland. 1995. *Die Organisationsstruktur des Ministeriums für Staatssicherheit 1989*. In Suckut et al. 1993–.

Williams, Raymond. 1977. *Marxism and Literature*. Oxford: Oxford University Press.

Williamson, Oliver. 1985. *The Economic Institutions of Capitalism*. New York: Free Press.

Winnicott, D. W. 1989 [1971]. *Playing and Reality*. London: Routledge.

Wischnjakow, A. S., et al. 1974. *Methodik der politischen Bildung*. Berlin: Dietz.

Wittgenstein, Ludwig. 1984a [1956/1937–44]. *Bemerkungen über die Grundlagen der Mathematik*. In *Collected Works*, vol. VI. Frankfurt: Suhrkamp.

———. 1984b [1952]. *Philosophische Untersuchungen*. In *Collected Works*, vol. I, 225–620. Frankfurt: Suhrkamp.

———. 1984c [1969]. *Über Gewißheit*. In *Collected Works*, vol. VIII, 115–256. Frankfurt: Suhrkamp.

Wolf, Markus. 1998. *Spionagechef im geheimen Krieg: Erinnerungen*. Bielefeld: Econ.

Wolle, Stefan. 1998. *Die heile Welt der Diktatur*. Berlin: Ch. Links.

Wollenberger, Vera: see Lengsfeld, Vera.

Wurmser, Leon. 1998. *Die Maske der Scham. Die Psychoanalyse von Schameffekten und Schamkonflikten*. 3rd ed. Heidelberg: Springer.

Yates, Frances. 1966. *The Art of Memory*. Chicago: University of Chicago Press.

Yurchak, Alexei. 2006. *Everything Was Forever, Until It Was No More: The Last Soviet Generation*. Princeton, NJ: Princeton University Press.

Zerubavel, Eviatar. 2006. *The Elephant in the Room: Silence and Denial in Everyday Life*. Oxford: Oxford University Press.

Ziemke, Earl F. 1990. *The Army in the Occupation of Germany*. Washington, DC: U.S. Army Center for Military History.

Zimmermann, Brigitte, and Hans-Dieter Schütt. 1994. *Noch Fragen Genossen!* Berlin: Neues Leben.

ZK (Zentralkomitee der Sozialistischen Einheitspartei Deutschlands). 1959. *Protokoll der Verhandlungen des V. Parteitages der Sozialistischen Einheitspartei Deutschlands*. Vol. 1. Berlin: Dietz.

———. 1971. *Protokoll der Verhandlungen des VII. Parteitages der Sozialistischen Einheitspartei Deutschlands*. Vol. 1. Berlin: Dietz.

———. 1972. *Die Aufgaben der Agitation und Propaganda bei der weiteren Verwirklichung der Beschlüsse des VIII Parteitages der SED*. Berlin: Dietz.

———. 1978. *Geschichte der Sozialistischen Einheitspartei Deutschlands: Abriß*. Berlin: Dietz.

Žižek, Slavoj. 1989. *The Sublime Object of Ideology*. London: Verso.

UNPUBLISHED MATERIAL

Fortunately, I was able to obtain most of the Stasi documents on which this study relies from sources other than the federal Stasi document center (BStU), which due to its legal framework operates very slowly. For that reason the Stasi documents cited in this book only occasionally use the call numbers of the Stasi document center, and for the most part uses Stasi's system of titles, date, office, and where available, the signature code of the drafting officer. Other source archives are indicated according to the key below. Where possible I have used published documents as an alternative.

Archival Key:

BStU: Archive of Bundesbeauftragte für die Unterlagen der Staatssicherheit der ehemaligen Deutschen Demokratischen Republik (Stasi Document Center), Berlin.

SAPMO BArch: "Stiftung-Archiv Parteien und Massenorganisationen in der DDR" at the Bundesarchiv (German Federal Archives), Berlin branch.

MDA: "Matthias Dommaschk Archiv" in the Robert-Havemann-Gesellschaft, Berlin.

Index

This index lists authors only if they are either directly discussed in the text or referenced repeatedly.